# Territorial and Social Inequalities in Europe

Martin Heidenreich

# Territorial and Social Inequalities in Europe

Challenges of European Integration

 Springer

Martin Heidenreich
Department of Social Sciences,
School of Education and Social Sciences
Carl von Ossietzky University of
Oldenburg
Oldenburg, Germany

ISBN 978-3-031-12632-1        ISBN 978-3-031-12630-7   (eBook)
https://doi.org/10.1007/978-3-031-12630-7

This Springer imprint is published by the registered company Springer Nature Switzerland AG
The registered company address is: Gewerbestrasse 11, 6330 Cham, Switzerland

# Preface

This book sets out to examine social inequalities in Europe, focusing in particular on those caused by economic factors. The starting point is a paradox of European inequality. On the one hand, total income inequality in Europe is significantly lower than in the USA, China, India, Russia, and other parts of the world. This is often seen as a key achievement of the European social model, characterised by egalitarian social structures and a high degree of solidarity within and between states. On the other hand, Europe is also characterised by profound inequalities that have become deeply embedded over time. These inequalities go hand in hand with the exclusion of marginalised groups from the labour market and with considerable and sometimes increasing differences between central and peripheral regions. Furthermore, they are associated with pronounced wealth and labour market inequalities as well as significant rates of persistent poverty, deprivation, educational poverty, low wages, and unemployment. These social and territorial inequalities form the basis for marked social divides between Northern and Southern Europe, East and West, qualified and unqualified employees, younger and older people, men and women, and migrants and non-migrants. As these inequalities are increasingly generated, perceived, and regulated in a European context, this co-existence of egalitarian structures and profound territorial and social inequalities is a fundamental challenge for social cohesion in Europe and European integration. Such a Europeanisation of social inequalities invariably leads us to ask who are the winners and losers of the social transformation processes that have occurred following the introduction of the euro as the common currency, the Eastern enlargement of the EU, and the financial and eurozone crises. Over the course of this volume, this question is explored in relation to the labour market, wages, income inequalities, educational inequalities, wealth and housing, poverty, and exclusion.

The findings presented in this book are based on a comprehensive analysis of a European-wide microdata set on income and living conditions (EU-SILC). They are the result of detailed empirical analyses of social divisions and Europeanisation processes in 30 European countries. Drawing on these analyses, it is possible to chart the transformation of the previously dominant national spaces into a European social space characterised by increasingly open social borders and emerging transnational patterns of divisions, conflicts, and cooperation. This book is the extended, revised, and updated version of a previously published German version (Heidenreich, M. (2022). *Die doppelte Spaltung Europas: Territoriale und soziale Ungleichheiten als zentrale Herausforderungen der europäischen Integration*. Springer. https://doi.org/10.1007/978-3-658-35395-7) .

This volume originated from sub-project 7 of the "Horizontal Europeanisation" research group funded by the German Research Foundation (DFG) from 2012 to 2020 (FOR 1539) and coordinated by the University of Oldenburg. I am very grateful to the DFG for this funding. I would also like to thank my colleagues from the research group for their many years of cooperation and their support in developing a sociological perspective on transnational integration processes in Europe. Special thanks also go to my colleagues Sven Broschinski, Jenny Preunkert, and Matthias Pohlig in Oldenburg who have read and thoroughly commented on countless versions of the following text. I have benefited greatly from their suggestions and support in dealing with the idiosyncrasies of STATA and EU-SILC. I would like to thank Isolde Heyen and Kerstin Zemke for their extraordinary commitment to coordinating the research group and to the writing of this book and Katherine Bird and Nathalie Chandler for the revision of the translation.

Oldenburg, Germany                                             Martin Heidenreich
May 2022

# Contents

# Abbreviations

| | |
|---|---|
| AIC | Akaike information criterion (estimator of prediction error and thereby relative quality of a statistical model) |
| CEE | Central and Eastern European countries |
| Country codes | Southern Europe (CY= Cyprus, EL = Greece, ES = Spain, IT = Italy, MT = Malta, PT = Portugal); British Isles (IE = Ireland, UK = United Kingdom); Central and Eastern Europe (BG = Bulgaria, CZ = Czech Republic, EE = Estonia, HU = Hungary, LT = Lithuania, LV = Latvia, PL = Poland, SK = Slovakia, SI = Slovenia, RO = Romania; RS = Serbia); Continental Europe (AT = Austria, BE = Belgium, CH = Switzerland, DE = Germany, FR = France, LU = Luxembourg, NL = Netherlands); Scandinavia (DK = Denmark, FI = Finland, IS = Iceland, NO = Norway; SE = Sweden). |
| D1, D5, D9 | bottom, middle, and top decile |
| EC | European Communities |
| ECB | European Central Bank |
| ECSC | European Coal and Steel Community |
| EEC | European Economic Community |
| EFTA | European Free Trade Association |
| EPO | European Patent Office |
| EU | European Union |
| EU-15 | 15 EU member states 1995–2004 (AT, BE, DE, DK, EL, ES, FI, FR, IE, IT, LU, NL, PT, SE, UK) |
| EU-27 | 27 EU member states 2007–2013 (EU-28 without Croatia). |
| EU-28 | 28 EU member states 2013–2020 (after the Eastern enlargements 2004, 2007, and 2013 and before Brexit: AT, BE, BG, CY, CZ, DE, DK, EE, EL, ES, FI, FR, HR, HU, IE, IT, LT, LU, LV, MT, NL, PL, PT, RO, SE, SI, SK, UK) |
| EU-SILC UDB | European Union Statistics on Income and Living Conditions User Database |

| GDP  | Gross domestic product |
|------|------------------------|
| ICC  | Intraclass correlation |
| MLD  | Mean logarithmic deviation |
| MNC  | Multinational company |
| OECD | Organisation for Economic Co-operation and Development |
| PPP  | Purchasing power parity (indicators of price level differences across countries; exchange rate of the PPS against the euro). |
| PPS  | Purchasing power standards (fictitious currency unit to compensate for distortions caused by different price levels in different countries). |
| R&D  | Research and development |
| SES  | European Structure of Earnings Survey |
| TFEU | Treaty on the Functioning of the European Union |

# List of Figures

# List of Tables

# Chapter 1
# Introduction

**Abstract** This introductory chapter outlines how social conflicts in Europe are not only determined by inequalities between different social classes, occupations and income and education strata, but also by economic, social and labour market differences between the member states of the EU. Since these territorial and social cleavages play a decisive role in shaping patterns of social cohesion in Europe, they are becoming a huge challenge for the European integration process, particularly since social inequalities are increasingly generated, perceived and regulated at the European level.

One of the most surprising developments during the 2020/22 Covid-19 pandemic was the decision taken in June 2020 to procure vaccines and other medical equipment through the European Union (EU), rather than going it alone at the national level (Brooks & Geyer, 2020). This decision was perplexing because the EU had little power in the health sector, a comparatively small budget and no agency comparable to the US BARDA. Nevertheless, in the middle of the crisis, the 27 member states decided to delegate responsibility to the EU for a matter on which not only the resulting economic costs of the pandemic and the speed of the return to normality depended but also the lives and health of their citizens. After the launch of the vaccination campaign in December 2020, the chosen procurement strategy was initially criticised for being too short-sighted, too slow, too bureaucratic and too cost-conscious. However, the fundamental decision to delegate this decision to the EU has never been seriously questioned. This is all the more surprising given that the United Kingdom, which left the EU in February 2020, and the United States, which prioritised vaccinating its population and initially prevented the export of vaccines, clearly demonstrated the advantages of a national solution. One of the main reasons for the Europeanisation of the vaccination campaign was that a national approach would have left most countries worse off and an uneven supply of vaccines to the European population would have torn the EU apart. This is especially true because the health and economic costs of the pandemic were unevenly distributed in Europe due to the fact that Southern European countries were hit harder during the first phase of the pandemic than Northern countries.

M. Heidenreich, *Territorial and Social Inequalities in Europe*,
https://doi.org/10.1007/978-3-031-12630-7_1

This example shows that in Europe, social cohesion is not only threatened by within-nation inequalities but also by between-nation inequalities. This is a remarkable phenomenon for sociologists because inequalities require common standards of equality (Blau, 1977). In general, these standards do not exist in an international space. In a world of sovereign and independent nation-states, the perceptions of inequalities are usually limited to the national context. This shift to a transnational social space structured by social inequalities[1] is also the result of increasing economic, political and social integration in Europe, as demonstrated by various crises, most recently by the pandemic, and since 2008 by the migration and sovereign debt crises. These crises have affected EU member states very differently and have thus put the numerous territorial and social cleavages that run through the EU onto the political agenda. As a result, transnational cleavages, nationalist tendencies and populist and Eurosceptic movements have gained enormous importance (Lahusen, 2021). These tensions are not only reflected in numerous conflicts between Northern and Southern, Eastern and Western Europe, but also in considerable divides between younger and older people, people with and without a migration background, men and women, the low-skilled and the highly skilled, and temporary and permanent employees. These divisions can be described as double dualisation (Heidenreich, 2016b; Palier et al., 2018), because inequalities in Europe have a social and a territorial dimension. Both the divides between the winners and losers of modernisation and Europeanisation processes and between central and peripheral countries and regions represent a severe threat to European cohesion. This became evident after the financial market and euro crises when trust in the EU reached its lowest point since the beginning of the survey and Europeans' mistrust in the EU strongly increased—in particular among older and low-skilled persons, manual workers, the unemployed, lower social classes and people with financial difficulties (European Commission, DG for Communication, 2020, pp. 134 & 139). In 2016, one of the largest member states, the United Kingdom, also decided to leave the EU.

At the same time, however, the conditions for overcoming the challenges associated with social inequalities are very good. Europe has been undergoing a process of economic and social convergence for decades, as a result of which income inequalities are already considerably lower than in the USA and China.[2] Economic and income inequalities have also continued to decline over the last decade, despite the aforementioned crises. The willingness of European citizens to show cross border solidarity is extraordinarily high (Gerhards et al., 2020). Furthermore, the EU is making huge efforts to improve living conditions in Europe and to further

---

[1] Cf. Faist (2014). We speak of social inequalities "when the possibilities of access to generally available and desirable social goods and/or to social positions endowed with different possibilities of power and/or interaction are permanently restricted, thereby impairing or favouring the life chances of the individuals, groups and societies concerned" (Kreckel, 2004, p. 17; own translation).

[2] With a Gini coefficient of 0.33 (2017; my calculations based on EU-SILC; cf. chap. 7), intra- *and* between-country income inequalities in the EU-28 are significantly lower than national inequalities in the USA (2018: 0.38; see LIS (2020)), China (2010: 0.53-0.55; cf. Xie and Zhou (2014)) or India (2011: 0.38 according to the World Bank or 0.48 according to LIS (2020)).

reduce inequalities despite these crises—for example with the recovery package "Next Generation EU" adopted in July 2020 during the pandemic and the new multi-annual financial framework for the EU budget 2021–2027. In doing so, it is drawing a lesson from centuries of experience in state-building processes (Ferrera, 2003; Rokkan & Flora, 1999): lower inequalities are no guarantee of cohesive political communities, but very high inequalities permanently undermine social cohesion and make societies vulnerable to separatism, protectionism, nationalism and xenophobia, "which led some to propose principles of identity and homogeneity as answers to 'the social question'." (Rosanvallon, 2013, p. 9) This is a lesson the EU has learned from the departure of the UK, the social consequences of the eurozone crisis and the strengthening of populist movements all over Europe (Dijkstra et al., 2020).

This large-scale support for Southern and Eastern European countries can certainly also be explained by the shock at the initial reactions of certain countries to the Covid-19 pandemic. While thousands of people died in Italy during the first wave, Germany and other EU states banned the export of masks and other medical equipment to Italy in March 2020. In this situation, the then Italian Prime Minister noted that Italy was alone at the beginning of the pandemic, or at most received help from China or Russia, but not from the EU. He explained Italy's growing annoyance with the EU by saying that "we feel abandoned by countries that profited enormously from the Union." (Meiler, 2020, p. 2; my translation). He thus adopts a basic idea of compensation theories—economic advantages through transnational interdependencies should also be used to compensate the losers of transnational integration in order to reduce resistance to such opening processes (Rodrik, 2018). The strong exposure of Southern European countries to the latest European crises and the risk of populist mobilisation against the EU were key reasons why France and Germany proposed a European Recovery Fund in May 2020. While economic output in the EU as a whole shrank by 6.1% in 2020, in Spain it fell by 10.8%, in Italy by 8.9% and in Greece by 8.2% (European Commission, 2021).

These countries had already been hit hard by the previous financial market and eurozone crises. These crises were accompanied by enormous social costs in the wake of the pandemic, especially for Italy and the five EU countries (Spain, Ireland, Portugal, Cyprus and Greece) that had to accept a bailout from European and international donors from 2010 onwards. It was only in August 2018 that the third aid programme for Greece was terminated after 8 years of support, as were the strict conditions associated with that programme (Pavolini et al., 2016; Varoufakis, 2017). In Greece, the sovereign debt or eurozone crisis was accompanied by a collapse in economic output that was unprecedented in peacetime, mass unemployment over 25%, youth unemployment rates over 50% and impoverishment of the middle class. The relative poverty rate has only been largely stable because the reference point—the average disposable household income—has fallen by more than a third. More than a third of the population cannot afford key goods and services considered desirable and necessary for an adequate lifestyle. A German journalist reports:

> I know a waiter in Paros who works ten to twelve hours a day, six days a week, and gets 35 euros a day. And on the seventh day, when he is supposed to be off, the boss tells him to clean the restaurant. The working conditions are catastrophic, and the situation is similar in

the public sector. The health sector has suffered greatly, and everyday life in Greece has become very hard indeed. (Kadritzke, 2018; my translation)

A doctor reports:

Often we lack medicines. It happens that we have to work with old surgical instruments that don't work well, or important chemicals are missing in the laboratory and we can't do all the necessary examinations. The patients don't notice all this and we don't want to increase their stress, but we often reach the limits of our possibilities as doctors. (Seralidou, 2018; my translation).

The causes of this crisis can be found at both the national and the European level. On the one hand, the internal causes of the Greek crisis—clientelism, corruption, a dysfunctional public administration, failure to implement reforms—have been pointed out by Featherstone (2015) and Trantidis (2016). On the other hand, the high level of Greek public debt, eurozone membership and the architecture of the euro (Preunkert, 2015) were additional causes of the crisis. While EU membership strongly reduced the costs for public debts, especially for member states with traditionally higher interest rates, economically these debts functioned similarly to debts in foreign currencies, since Greece, like all other eurozone countries, could no longer pursue an independent monetary policy and instruct its central bank to increase the money supply as a basis for an expansionary fiscal policy. From this perspective, the euro thus contributed to exacerbating the crisis and limiting national options for action. Particularly in response to the austerity requirements of the European and international bailout funds, responsibility for poverty and exclusion has been attributed to the EU (Krugman, 2012; Pavolini et al., 2016; Varoufakis, 2017). This diagnosis is essentially shared by Jeroen Dijsselbloem, a former Eurogroup president: "The programme was very long, very hard, with many failures." (Embling, 2018; own translation). An evaluation of the European bailout programmes also stresses "insufficient attention to the underlying social needs of the Greek population."[3]

Without weighing up the relative merits of these endogenous and exogenous explanations of the Greek crisis, this example shows that poverty and exclusion can be explained not only by national factors but also by European factors. This idea will be generalised in this book. *It will be shown that the generation as well as the perception and regulation of social inequalities no longer take place exclusively in the national context.* The more deeply the European integration process intervenes in the lives of Europeans, the more it also influences their life chances and thus patterns and perceptions of social inequality.

This development was also recognised by one of the most prominent Eurosceptics, the journalist and later Foreign Secretary and then Prime Minister of

---

[3] In an assessment of the aid programmes, former EU Commissioner J. Almunia states in retrospect: "Greece and its citizens suffered the consequences of 8 years of economic adjustment, Greece made the world's headlines with the largest debt restructuring in history, an unprecedented fiscal consolidation, and the resulting loss of output and social consequences (...) The composition of fiscal consolidation was not conducive to inclusive growth" (Almunia, 2020, pp. 3&6).

the United Kingdom, Boris Johnson. Emphasising the dramatic social consequences of European bailout policies, he believed that such policies led to Greece becoming a kind of economic colony of the EU, even after the expiry of the bailout programmes—a fate from which he claimed he wanted to save Britain by pursuing a hard Brexit (The Telegraph, 26/08/2018). Boris Johnson rightly pointed to the fact that the EU has become an increasingly important frame of reference for social inequalities. However, instead of strengthening European-wide social security, he proposed to strengthen national social and health services. The famous red bus of the Vote Leave campaign was labelled: "We send the EU £350 million a week, let's fund our NHS instead." This slogan linked national health policy with European issues, implying a trade-off between European and national policies. His argument resonated with the British public because many Brexit supporters lived in economically depressed regions with fewer social services and expected that their decision would improve their situation (Fetzer, 2018). Hence, even for the seemingly most unlikely case, the Brexit campaign, a European dimension of social inequalities can be identified: National policies seemed to be preferable to European ones as the reference to the Greek situation showed.

The pandemic, the eurozone crisis and Brexit thus point to the role of the European context with regard to people's income and life chances. The social effects of economic, monetary, political and social integration processes in Europe on the generation, regulation and perception of social inequalities can be interpreted as a *Europeanisation of social inequalities* (cf. Sect. 2.2 and Heidenreich, 2006).

This indicates a profound change compared to the situation in the post-World War II period when social inequalities were largely generated, perceived and regulated in the national context. Inequalities were produced in relatively closed national economies by national education systems and production and labour market structures, regulated by national systems of industrial relations and by national welfare states. Claims were articulated in national arenas and interests were negotiated between the state and national employers' associations and unions. The "methodological nationalism" criticised by Beck and Grande (2007)[4] could be defended with very good reasons during the period of post-war prosperity, as the socio-cultural, economic and political-institutional context of social inequalities largely coincided within the nation-state (Weiß, 2017). This can be explained firstly by the territorial basis on which an imagined community of equals is based. Since the beginning of the twentieth century, this has been the nation-state (Anderson, 2006; Renan, 1996). Rosanvallon (2013, p. 9) describes the construction of the national welfare state as a reaction to the crisis of equality in the nineteenth century.

---

[4]Beck (2002, p. 51) defines the concept of methodological nationalism as follows: "it equates societies with nation-state societies, and sees states and their governments as the cornerstones of a social science analysis. It assumes that humanity is naturally divided into a limited number of nations, which, on the inside, organize themselves as nation-states and, on the outside, set boundaries to distinguish themselves from other nation-states. It goes even further: this outer delimitation, as well as the competition between nation-states, represents the most fundamental category of political organization."

Secondly, methodological nationalism also refers to the range of economic policies. After the failure of the nineteenth century wave of globalisation, the central arena for economic policies in the post-war period was the national economies (Hirst et al., 2015). Thirdly, the nation-state was the central arena for co-determination and political participation. Democratic participation, negotiations between employers' and workers' associations, political power, administrative rules and the articulation and regulation of conflicts took place largely within the framework of national institutions.

In Europe, the transnationalisation of the social space in which inequalities were generated, perceived and regulated was mainly driven by the creation, deepening and enlargement of the European (Economic) Community, which became the European Union (EU) in 1993. European integration widened the frame of reference for social inequalities in the three dimensions mentioned above. *In economic terms,* the opening of national spaces was driven by the enlargement of the EU from initially 6 to now 27 member states (since 1/2/2020), the customs union which came into force in 1968, the abolition of border controls in 1985 for currently 26 European countries, the single market completed in 1993, and since 1999 the creation of a common currency for now 19 Eurozone member states. *In political-institutional terms,* the EU is a new supranational centre of power (Bach, 2015; Georgakakis, 2017; Georgakakis & Rowell, 2013). This centre is increasingly shaping the lives of Europeans. More and more rights are linked to European citizenship, such as political participation rights in another EU member state and the right to free movement of people, goods, services and capital. The common currency—which replaced an economic adjustment mechanism, exchange rates, with political decisions (Sect. 5.3.1)—has a significant impact on the living conditions of Europeans (Heidenreich, 2014). Therefore, the EU as an institution must increasingly legitimise its decisions (Habermas, 2003). In addition, the frame of reference for assessing one's own social situation will become larger (Delhey & Kohler, 2006). *In socio-cultural terms,* international lifestyles and cross-border practices are becoming more widespread (Delhey et al., 2014; Favell, 2008; Recchi et al., 2019). In addition to classic national and regional solidarities, cross-border solidarities are thus also gaining in importance (Ciornei & Recchi, 2017; Gerhards et al., 2020; Kuhn, 2015).

All these facets of European integration processes influence the life chances of Europeans. On the one hand, they have been the basis for sustained economic growth for many years, from which less wealthy member states in particular have benefited disproportionately. This has significantly reduced economic disparities in the EU (Heidenreich & Wunder, 2008). For decades, these non-controversial effects of European integration have formed the basis for tacit popular support for the European integration process, which Hooghe and Marks (2009) have termed *permissive consensus.* On the other hand, there have always been anxieties that the creation of the customs union and the internal market, the eastward enlargement of the EU, the free movement of people and the liberalisation of services markets (e.g. through the Services and Posting of Workers Directives) would have negative effects on labour market opportunities, wage levels and levels of social protection.

These concerns are not unjustified. Even in the international context, there is growing awareness that different socio-economic groups do not benefit equally from the advantages of increasing economic interdependencies (Rodrik, 2018). Just as there may be winners and losers of globalisation, there may also be winners and losers of Europeanisation (Fligstein, 2008) because every transnational integration process is accompanied by (at least relative) winners and losers. It is generally assumed that younger, well-educated workers are among the winners of Europeanisation—or more broadly modernisation—while low-skilled older workers are more likely to be confronted with the negative consequences of cross-border integration processes. However, it is not quite that simple. For example, most Southern European young people are by no means on the winning side, while older, even low-skilled labour market insiders in highly industrialised countries are by no means among the losers. Identifying the winners and losers of the European integration process thus requires an examination of the various mechanisms and dimensions that affect socio-demographic groups, regions and countries in different ways. In order to reconstruct the cleavages in the EU, it is therefore necessary to analyse group- and country-specific patterns in various dimensions of social inequality.

This book therefore discusses the thesis that the causes, perceptions and regulation of social inequalities are increasingly shaped by the process of European integration. It can be expected that economic, political and socio-cultural integration in Europe is contributing to a Europeanisation of social inequalities. This thesis suggests that EU policies and other transnational factors are becoming more important for explaining social inequalities, that the frames of reference for the perception of social inequalities are no longer limited to the nation-state and that new transnational cleavages and conflict regulation mechanisms might become more important. While the nation-state has emerged as the central arena for the production, perception and regulation of social inequalities in the twentieth century, these national spaces have been cracked open and transformed into a transnational and in particular European space in which inequalities are generated, perceived and regulated at a broader scale, which is also due to various Europeanisation and globalisation processes. The aim of this book is to describe the within- and between-country patterns of social inequalities in Europe, to identify the countries and social groups that are on the winning and losing sides, and to understand the mechanisms by which the Europeanisation of the social space within which inequalities are generated, perceived and regulated takes place.

These cleavages can foster Eurosceptic attitudes and thus undermine support for the European integration process. One indication of this is the split between cosmopolitan and nationally-oriented groups (Kriesi et al., 2006). This division, which has been seized upon by Eurosceptic and populist positions and parties (Kriesi & Pappas, 2015), is closely linked to the division between Europeanisation winners and losers. The relationship between this cosmopolitan-nationalist cleavage and the socio-economic cleavages that are the subject of this book is not discussed here—even though the author is convinced that the social and territorial cleavages of

Europe identified in this book represent a threat to the processes of European integration.

In addition to the cleavages between cosmopolitan and nationally-oriented groups, the cleavages between centre and periphery play a crucial role in the EU. Since its foundation, territorial differences have determined the policies of the European Communities. At the time when the EEC was established, the per capita value added in Italy was about one third less than the level in the Netherlands. Hence, the economic convergence of the member states has always been a central goal of the EU and its predecessors—a goal that was primarily pursued through the opening of borders for goods, services, capital and people, but also through inter-governmental transfers. The economic integration of Europe provided the central basis for unprecedented growth in economic performance and a reduction in eco-nomic differences, initially between Southern, Northern and Continental Europe, and since 1989 between Eastern and Western Europe. This economic convergence was flanked by intergovernmental transfers within the framework of agricultural, structural and regional policies. Both high growth rates and convergence between central and peripheral countries formed the basis for the largely unquestioned support for the EU, as this not only narrowed the differences between wealthier and other EU countries, but also allowed lower social classes to benefit from the economic dynamics. This has changed in recent years. Since the financial and eurozone crises, economic performance and real income have hardly grown at all in the Southern European countries. For some groups, disposable income has even declined (Chap. 7). Economic differences between Southern and Continental Europe not only increased during the eurozone crisis but also during the pandemic. People living in the post-socialist states of Central and Eastern Europe, who had to endure unimaginable hardships and deprivation during the transition from centrally planned economies to liberal market economies, are also no longer prepared to accept the rudimentary forms of social protection and considerable social and territorial inequalities in these countries. The most successful election promises of the Polish PiS party were the introduction of child benefit of 500 Złoty per month in 2016 (initially for the second and any subsequent children) and a higher minimum wage. Both cushioned the hardships of the neoliberal transformation processes which were also attributed to EU membership. It is therefore not surprising that the previously unquestioning support for European integration has come under scrutiny since the various crises of the last decade.

The social and territorial cleavages in Europe, which I previously termed 'double dualization' (Heidenreich, 2016a), form the focus of the following chapters. The aim is to provide an empirically-based analysis of social inequalities in a transnational space. First, the theoretical challenges associated with analysing inequalities in a national-supranational-transnational social space are addressed (Chap. 2). Following a brief explanation of the data and methods (Chap. 3), the economic differences in the EU (Chap. 4) and the social inequalities in the 27 EU member states, the United Kingdom, Norway and Switzerland are described, since Europeanisation processes are not limited to the EU (Olsen, 2002). Social inequalities are a multidimensional phenomenon. Therborn (2013), for instance, distinguishes three dimensions:

*material or resource inequality*, which is classically subdivided into inequality of opportunity and inequality of outcome, *vital inequality* (i.e. life expectancy and health situation; cf. Case & Deaton, 2020) and *existential inequality* (recognition, ability to act, respect; cf. Sen, 1993). The following analyses focus on the first dimension—resource inequality—with inequalities in disposable income at their core (Chap. 7). Income inequality is largely neglected in sociology (DiPrete, 2007; Schwinn, 2021). To begin with, three key determinants of disposable income are therefore examined: First, economic differences in the EU and their evolution (Chap. 4). Although these differences are not social inequalities themselves, they are their central determinants because they are decisive in determining the level of total disposable income and therefore also have a significant influence on within- and between-country inequalities. A central component of disposable household income—in addition to welfare state and inter-family transfers—is wages (Chap. 6). Both the wage levels and the level of labour force participation (Chap. 5) are crucial determinants of disposable income, as the level of disposable household income is largely determined by household members' earned income (or lack thereof). Chapters 5 and 6 therefore discuss the labour market opportunities of the working-age population and wage inequalities. But the role of employment and earnings opportunities goes beyond this economic dimension, since individual well-being, life satisfaction and social prestige depend to a considerable extent on the pursuit of a paid activity, the nature of this activity and its remuneration. Next, within- and between-country patterns of income inequality in Europe are analysed (Chap. 7). The subjective dimensions of economic stress are also taken into account in order to demonstrate the Europeanisation of the frames of reference used by individuals to evaluate their economic and living conditions. Chapter 8 then analyses the main dimensions of disadvantage, poverty and exclusion in Europe. The multidimensionality of disadvantage is analysed on the basis of two composite indicators which are based on the living conditions (Voges, 2006) and capability approaches (Sen, 1993). As in the previous chapter, the subjective dimension is also considered. The extent of equal opportunities in a society depends to a considerable degree on the qualifications and educational background of its workforce. Inequalities in education and occupational skills are therefore considered in more detail in Chap. 9. Chapter 10 discusses wealth and housing inequalities in Europe. Since owner-occupied property accounts for about half of European wealth, the different living and housing conditions of homeowners and tenants in Europe are discussed. Finally, the evolution of social inequality in Europe between convergence, peripheralisation and social exclusion is discussed, together with the four facets of the Europeanisation of social inequalities and the challenges for cohesion in the EU (Chap. 11).

# References

Almunia, J. (2020). *Lessons from financial assistance to Greece: Independent evaluation report.* Luxembourg. Retrieved from European Stability Mechanism, website: https://www.esm. europa.eu/publications/lessons-financial-assistance-greece,https://doi.org/10.2852/082453.

Anderson, B. (2006). *Imagined communities: Reflections on the origin and spread of nationalism* (Revised ed.). Verso.

Bach, M. (2015). *Europa ohne Gesellschaft: Politische Soziologie der Europäischen Integration (2nd, revised edition). Neue Bibliothek der Sozialwissenschaften.* Springer. Retrieved from. https://doi.org/10.1007/978-3-531-93430-3

Beck, U. (2002). The terrorist threat: World risk society revisited. *Theory, Culture & Society, 19*(4), 39–55. https://doi.org/10.1177/0263276402019004003

Beck, U., & Grande, E. (2007). *Cosmopolitan Europe.* Polity.

Blau, P. M. (1977). *Inequality and heterogeneity: A primitive theory of social structure.* Free Press.

Brooks, E., & Geyer, R. (2020). The development of EU health policy and the Covid-19 pandemic: Trends and implications. *Journal of European Integration, 42*(8), 1057–1076. https://doi.org/ 10.1080/07036337.2020.1853718

Case, A., & Deaton, A. (2020). *Deaths of despair and the future of capitalism.* Princeton University Press.

Ciornei, I., & Recchi, E. (2017). At the source of European solidarity: Assessing the effects of crossborder practices and political attitudes. *Journal of Common Market Studies, 55*(3), 468–485. https://doi.org/10.1111/jcms.12507

Delhey, J., Deutschmann, E., Graf, T., & Richter, K. (2014). Measuring the Europeanization of everyday life: Three new indices and an empirical application. *European Societies, 16*(3), 355–377.

Delhey, J., & Kohler, U. (2006). From nationally bounded to pan-European inequalities? On the importance of foreign countries as reference groups. *European Sociological Review, 22*(2), 125–140.

Dijkstra, L., Poelman, H., & Rodríguez-Pose, A. (2020). The geography of EU discontent. *Regional Studies, 54*(6), 737–753. https://doi.org/10.1080/00343404.2019.1654603

DiPrete, T. A. (2007). What has sociology to contribute to the study of inequality trends? A historical and comparative perspective. *American Behavioral Scientist, 50*(5), 603–618. https://doi.org/10.1177/0002764206295009

Embling, D. (2018, September 27). Dijsselbloem: "Griechenland-Hilfsprogramme waren fehlerhaft". Retrieved from https://de.euronews.com/my-europe/2018/09/27/dijsselbloem-griechenland-hilfsprogramme-warenfehlerhaft

European Commission. (2021). *European Economic Forecast: Spring 2021* (Institutional Paper No. 149). Luxembourg. Retrieved from Publications Office of the European Union website: https://ec.europa.eu/info/sites/default/files/economy-finance/ip149_en.pdf

European Commission, DG for Communication (2020). *Public opinion in the European Union: Standard Eurobarometer 92. Autumn 2019.* Brussels. Retrieved from European Commission website: https://ec.europa.eu/commfrontoffice/publicopinion

Faist, T. (2014). On the transnational social question: How social inequalities are reproduced in Europe. *Journal of European Social Policy, 24*(3), 207–222.

Favell, A. (2008). *Eurostars and Eurocities: Free movement and mobility in an integrating Europe.* Blackwell; Wiley.

Featherstone, K. (2015). External conditionality and the debt crisis: The 'troika' and public administration reform in Greece. *Journal of European Public Policy, 22*(3), 295–314. https:// doi.org/10.1080/13501763.2014.955123

Ferrera, M. (2003). European integration and national social citizenship: Changing boundaries, new structuring? *Comparative Political Studies, 36*(6), 611–652.

Fetzer, T. (2018). *Did austerity cause Brexit?* (Warwick economics research papers series No. 1170). Coventry. Retrieved from University of Warwick website: http://wrap.warwick.ac.uk/106313/

Fligstein, N. (2008). *Euroclash: The EU, European identity, and the future of Europe*. Oxford University Press.

Georgakakis, D. (2017). *European civil service in (times of) crisis: A political sociology of the changing power of eurocrats*. Palgrave Macmillan.

Georgakakis, D., & Rowell, J. (2013). *The field of eurocracy: Mapping EU actors and professionals*. Palgrave Macmillan.

Gerhards, J., Lengfeld, H., Ignácz, Z., Kley, F. K., & Pfriem, M. (2020). *European solidarity in times of crisis: Insights from a thirteen-country survey. Routledge advances in sociology*. Routledge.

Habermas, J. (2003). Toward a cosmopolitan Europe. *Journal of Democracy, 14*(4), 86–100.

Heidenreich, M. (2006). Die Europäisierung sozialer Ungleichheiten zwischen nationaler Solidarität, europäischer Koordinierung und globalem Wettbewerb. In M. Heidenreich (Ed.), *Die Europäisierung sozialer Ungleichheit: Zur transnationalen Klassen- und Sozialstrukturanalyse* (pp. 17–64). Campus Verlag.

Heidenreich, M. (2014). Eurokrisen und Vergesellschaftung: Die krisenhafte Europäisierung nationaler Fiskalpolitiken. In M. Heidenreich (Ed.), *Krise der europäischen Vergesellschaftung? Soziologische Perspektiven* (pp. 1–30). Springer.

Heidenreich, M. (2016a). The double dualization of inequality in Europe: Introduction. In M. Heidenreich (Ed.), *Exploring inequality in Europe* (pp. 1–21). Edward Elgar.

Heidenreich, M. (Ed.). (2016b). *Exploring inequality in Europe*. Edward Elgar.

Heidenreich, M., & Wunder, C. (2008). Patterns of regional inequality in the enlarged Europe. *European Sociological Review, 24*(1), 19–36.

Hirst, P., Thompson, G., & Bromley, S. (2015). *Globalization in question* (3rd ed.). Wiley.

Hooghe, L., & Marks, G. (2009). A postfunctionalist theory of European integration: From permissive consensus to constraining dissensus. *British Journal of Political Science, 39*(01), 1–23.

Kadritzke, N. (2018, August 20). „Hier gibt es wirklich Massenarmut": Journalist über Griechenland. Retrieved from Deutschlandfunk Kultur website: https://www.deutschlandfunkkultur.de/journalist-uebergriechenland-hier-gibt-es-wirklich-100.html

Kreckel, R. (2004). *Politische Soziologie der sozialen Ungleichheit* (3rd, revised and expanded edition). In *Theorie und Gesellschaft: Band 25*. Campus.

Kriesi, H., Grande, E., Lachat, R., Dolezal, M., Bornschier, S., & Frey, T. (2006). Globalization and the transformation of the national political space: Six European countries compared. *European Journal of Political Research, 45*(6), 921–956.

Kriesi, H., Pappas, T. S., & Takis, S. (2015). Populism in Europe during crisis: An introduction. In H. Kriesi & T. S. Pappas (Eds.), *European populism in the shadow of the great recession* (pp. 1–19). ECPR Press.

Krugman, P. (2012, January 29). *The austerity debacle*. Retrieved from https://nyti.ms/2kSmBCe

Kuhn, T. (2015). *Experiencing European integration: Transnational lives and European identity*. Oxford University Press.

Lahusen, C. (2021). *The political attitudes of divided European citizens: Public opinion and social inequalities in comparative and relational perspective*. Routledge. https://doi.org/10.4324/9781003046653

LIS. (2020). *LIS inequality and poverty key figures*. Retrieved from http://www.lisdatacenter.org

Meiler, O. (2020, April 20). "Es ist unbestritten: Italien war allein": Interview mit Giuseppe Conte. Retrieved from Süddeutsche Zeitung website: https://www.sueddeutsche.de/politik/conte-italien-coronavirus-1.4881435?reduced=true

Olsen, J. P. (2002). The many faces of Europeanization. *Journal of Common Market Studies, 40*(5), 921–952.

Palier, B., Rovny, A. E., & Rovny, J. (2018). European disunion? Social and economic divergence in Europe, and their political consequences. In P. Manow, B. Palier, & H. Schwander (Eds.), *Welfare democracies and party politics: Explaining electoral dynamics in times of changing welfare capitalism* (pp. 281–297). Oxford University Press.

Pavolini, E., León, M., Guillén, A. M., & Ascoli, U. (2016). From austerity to permanent strain? The European Union and welfare state reform in Italy and Spain. In C. de La Porte & E. Heins (Eds.), *The sovereign debt crisis, the EU and welfare state reform* (pp. 131–157). Palgrave Macmillan. https://doi.org/10.1057/978-1-137-58179-2_6

Preunkert, J. (2015). The hidden side of the crisis. In L. V. Baptista, J. Preunkert, & G. Vobruba (Eds.), *Aftermath: Political and urban consequences of the euro crisis* (pp. 185–2002). Edições Colibri.

Recchi, E., Favell, A., Apaydin, F., Barbulescu, R., Braun, M., Ciornei, I., et al. (2019). *Everyday Europe: Social transnationalism in an unsettled continent*. Policy Press. https://doi.org/10.1332/policypress/9781447334200.001.0001

Renan, E. (1996). What is a nation? In G. Eley & R. G. Suny (Eds.), *Becoming national: A reader* (pp. 41–55). Oxford University Press.

Rodrik, D. (2018). Populism and the economics of globalization. *Journal of International Business Policy, 1*(1-2), 12–33. https://doi.org/10.1057/s42214-018-0001-4

Rokkan, S., & Flora, P. (Eds.). (1999). *Comparative European politics. State formation, nation-building, and mass politics in Europe: The theory of stein rokkan; based on his collected works (1. Publ)*. Oxford University Press.

Rosanvallon, P. (2013). *The society of equals*. Harvard University Press. Retrieved from http://search.ebscohost.com/login.aspx?direct=true&scope=site&db=nlebk&db=nlabk&AN=660037

Seralidou, R. (2018, August 16). „Ein schwer kranker Patient wird mit Aspirin nicht gesund": Griechenland und die Krise. Retrieved from Deutschlandfunk website: https://www.deutschlandfunk.de/griechenland-und-die-krise-4-5-ein-schwer-krankerpatient-100.html

Schwinn, T. (2021). Social inequalities: Theoretical focus. In B. Hollstein, R. Greshoff, U. Schimank, & A. Weiß (Eds.), *Soziologie–sociology in the German-speaking world: Special issue Soziologische revue 2020* (pp. 381–398). De Gruyter. https://doi.org/10.1515/9783110627275-026

Sen, A. (1993). Capabilities and Well-being. In M. C. Nussbaum & A. Sen (Eds.), *Studies in development economics/WIDER. The quality of life* (pp. 30–53). Oxford University Press.

Therborn, G. (2013). *The killing fields of inequality*. Polity.

Trantidis, A. (2016). *Clientelism and economic policy: Greece and the crisis. Routledge advances in European politics* (Vol. 126). Routledge.

Varoufakis, Y. (2017). *Adults in the room: My battle with Europe's deep establishment*. Random House.

Voges, W. (2006). Indikatoren im Lebenslagenansatz: das Konzept der Lebenslage in der Wirkungsforschung. *ZeS Report, 11*(1), 1–6.

Weiß, A. (2017). *Soziologie globaler Ungleichheiten. Suhrkamp Taschenbuch Wissenschaft: Vol. 2220*. Suhrkamp.

Xie, Y., & Zhou, X. (2014). Income inequality in todays China. *Proceedings of the National Academy of Sciences of the United States of America, 111*(19), 6928–6933. https://doi.org/10.1073/pnas.1403158111

# Chapter 2
# Social Inequalities at the National and European Level

**Abstract** This theoretical chapter shows how the consolidation of nation-states was accompanied by the development of domestic forms of civic, political and social rights. Previously, social inequalities could be addressed only within the national framework, which explains the methodological nationalism of inequality research. This is changing as the level of political, economic and social integration intensifies in Europe. A Europeanisation of the determinants and perceptions of social inequalities in Europe can be expected, since disadvantages and advantages can be increasingly attributed to European decisions. This chapter outlines the four ways in which the Europeanisation of social inequalities is taking place: (a) international comparisons of national living conditions; (b) effects of EU policies on people's living conditions; (c) evaluation of personal living conditions in a European and international context; (d) cross-border practices in Europeanised fields of action. It provides the foundation for the following chapters, which explore patterns and developments of social inequalities in Europe and pinpoint which groups and countries are among the winners and losers of Europeanisation.

The European nation-states are the starting point for European integration. These states have emerged over centuries, stabilising their territorial borders through military and diplomatic means and developing their own forms of judicature, administration, taxation, education, political systems and collective identities. This military-administrative, economic, legal-legislative and cultural consolidation of modern territorial states is comprehensively analysed in the works of Rokkan and Flora (1999), Ferrera (2003) and Bartolini (2005). These states were built on processes of drawing and consolidating national boundaries as well as the legal, democratic and social integration of the population (Sect. 2.1).

As a result of the globalisation and Europeanisation of the economy and politics, this dynamic of boundary building and internal structuring and regulation of national space is being reversed (Flora, 2000). Ferrera (2003, p. 646) calls this the "unfreezing" of frozen, nationally regulated cleavages. Transnational factors, regulations and interdependencies are increasingly shaping everyday life. This is illustrated by the considerable difficulties experienced by the United Kingdom after leaving the EU. For example, chilled sausages from England—determined to leave the single

M. Heidenreich, *Territorial and Social Inequalities in Europe*,
https://doi.org/10.1007/978-3-031-12630-7_2

market—can in principle no longer be sent to Northern Ireland, which is still part of the single market. However, national regulatory structures will not be replaced by European rules, European patterns of social inequalities and Europe-wide forms of redistribution. The "methodological nationalism" of inequality research cannot simply be replaced by methodological Europeanism. The European Union is not an entity that ensures the social integration of its citizens in a similar way to national societies (Bach, 2015, Chap. 2). However, this does not mean that Europe is a social space "without society". Europe is more than the single market, the euro or a bureaucratic centre of power, but it is also in many respects less than a nation-state. Despite the increasingly powerful European Parliament, it has not developed a democratic order comparable to a nation-state, since the competences of its decision-making bodies and the loyalties of its constituency are always constrained by national competences and loyalties. It cannot develop redistributive policies comparable to Western or Northern European welfare states because the nation-states have reserved these competences for themselves. It is not an arena in which (mostly national) employers' and workers' associations can represent their interests and negotiate compromises (Streeck, 1997). Therefore, the EU is often described as undemocratic, antisocial or neoliberal. However, it may be more accurate to say that the EU has developed a form of social integration that in many aspects more resembles the economically, politically and socio-culturally more heterogeneous USA than the strongly integrated European nation-states of the post-war period (Münch, 2014). Adopting approaches from organisational sociology and field theory, it will be argued in what follows that these transnational "societalisation" processes can be analysed on the basis of the concepts of social fields and social space (Heidenreich, 2019a)—also because the concept of society should be reserved for the world society (Luhmann, 1982) (Sect. 2.2). The Europeanisation of social inequalities, which will be analysed in the following chapters, thus focuses on a central dimension of European societalisation processes and thus explicitly contradicts the diagnosis of a Europe without society.

## 2.1  Boundary Building and Internal Structuring at National and European Level

Boundary building and structuring are the two essential concepts used by Stein Rokkan to analyse state-building processes in Europe. The starting point of these state-building processes was Europe's ethno-cultural heterogeneity, which was channelled and divided into smaller territorial and political units with the emergence of nation-states. As a result, ethnically largely homogeneous nation-states emerged in Europe (Flora, 2000). Rokkan and Flora (1999) analyse this segmentary differentiation of the vast European space, which had been shaped for centuries by the Roman Empire and later by the Catholic Church, in economic, military-administrative and cultural terms: Instead of Roman settlements and cities integrated into continent-wide trade and communication networks, a self-sufficient, agrarian-feudal mode of production developed; instead of imperial centres, sovereign states that were no longer centrally controlled emerged; instead of the universally oriented Catholic Church, separate vernacular languages, literatures, schools and state churches developed.

The gradual formation and consolidation of state boundaries and thus the consolidation of a closed state territory no longer threatened by exit strategies was the prerequisite for internal structuring processes: the development of internal forms of territorial control, reconciliation of interests and social integration thus became possible (Marshall, 1950). Ferrera (2003) describes this interdependency of boundary building and political, cultural and socio-political structuring processes as "bounded structuring", i.e. as structuring within state borders. The consolidation of state borders and the evolution of nations integrated by the rule of law, democracy and social policy are two sides of the same coin, since external boundaries enable and require internal articulation, regulation and "crystallisation" of conflicts. The emergence of nationally regulated and demarcated forms of society explains why nation-states became the prototypical sociological models of society—models which have been so impressive that some sociologists ignore transnational or European forms of societalisation.

When analysing social inequalities, this dynamic of boundary building and national structuring, social closure and national institution building has two implications. Firstly, in a world structured by nation-states, it is strictly speaking not possible to speak of inequalities between members of different states, since this presupposes a common frame of reference and a common conception of equality and inequality (Blau, 1977). To provide a historical illustration, it would have never occurred to a medieval king or free citizen in Athens to compare his living conditions with those of a peasant, slave or wife. In premodern societies, there was no common standard of comparison for kings and peasants, free citizens and slaves or men and women. The assumption of basic equality among all human beings only emerged with the Enlightenment. The question of what are "the origin and basis of inequality among men" raised by the philosopher Jean-Jacques Rousseau (1755) is often seen as the first question raised by the emerging science of sociology. Rousseau believed that all men were originally (born) equal and tried to explain the emergence of inequality as a result of private property. However, this principle of basic equality among men postulated by Rousseau and his successors was limited in subsequent centuries to only fellow (male) citizens. In previous works, I proposed interpreting this "as an incomplete 'Rousseauean transformation' of premodern understandings of inequalities" (Heidenreich, 2003, p. 316) because the related equality norms were limited to a nation-state. In a "Westphalian world" of separate and sovereign nation-states, citizens of different states live in different socially non-integrated worlds without common standards of equality. As long as there are no generally recognised transnational norms of equality and inequality, the different living conditions between countries are only *disparities*, but not inequalities (Blau, 1977, p. 5; Heidenreich, 2003, p. 316). *Inequalities* presuppose a common social context and overarching norms of equality. Even after the Enlightenment, such transnational norms did not exist in a world of sovereign nation-states.

The nation-state thus became the central frame of reference for social inequalities. In 1882, the French intellectual Ernest Renan (1996) described the nation as "a great solidarity constituted by the feeling of sacrifices made and those that one is still disposed to make." Marshall (1950) analysed the development and institutionalisation of civil, political and social norms of equality—which he termed rights. The social integration of a nation-state thus is based on the guarantee of legal rights for every citizen, by democratic forms of co-determination and by welfare state forms of redistribution (Ferrera, 2003). In addition, it is based on an identification with an "imagined political community" and solidarity with its members, "because, regardless of the actual inequality and exploitation that may prevail in each, the nation is always conceived as a deep, horizontal comradeship." (Anderson, 2006, p. 7) A nation thus is also characterised by common identification and norms of solidarity.

This national pattern of social integration and equality reached its peak in the egalitarian capitalism of the post-war period (Kenworthy, 2004). It was also the golden age of autonomously designed national social orders and inequality policies. In the years following the Second World War, the social integration of the labour force was ensured in most Western European countries by social benefits, strong trade unions, collective agreements, efficient training systems, interregional redistribution and demand-side economic policies. This policy mix caused a significant reduction in within-country income inequalities. This experience has inspired the so-called Kuznets curve, an inverted U-curve proposed by Kuznets (1955) which describes the increase in income inequality with the onset of industrialisation and its decrease with the further advancement of industrialisation and the transition from a classical industrial economy to a wealthy, service-centred society (Moran, 2005). Since the 1970s, however, income inequalities have been increasing again in many developed countries. Instead of decreasing inequalities, a "great U-turn" has been observed and explained by the shift to a service society (Milanović, 2016), by technological change and the globalisation of the economy—in particular by the increasing importance of trade between developed and less developed countries and increasing foreign direct investment (Alderson & Nielsen, 2002). This points to the limits of national models of social integration, which were based on a considerable degree of territorial, economic and social closure.

Most emerging problems could no longer be addressed within the national framework. With the increasing openness of national spaces, the incongruence between political regulatory opportunities and societal regulatory requirements is increasing. In view of the limits of national regulations (for example, in the areas of internal and external security, climate change, social inequality and social security, technological change, data protection, tax evasion, combating a pandemic, terrorism), EU-wide regulations are often used alongside and in place of national regulations.

At the same time, within a theoretical framework inspired by Rokkan and Flora (1999), the EU cannot be expected to develop an external boundary that is as strong as that of nation-states. Such an external boundary would have to prevent the exit of member states, which in turn would increase the pressure to develop intra-European forms of conflict regulation. Bartolini (2005, Chap. 7) doubts that the EU can develop such a hard external border. He explains this by the openness of the single market, the particularities of EU law, which is not limited to a specific territory, the technical orientation of the European monetary policy and the frequent enlargement processes, which make territorial consolidation difficult. Given the interaction between boundary building and internal structuring which is central to Rokkan's approach, the lack of stable external boundaries would also limit the possibilities for developing European forms of social cohesion. The EU facilitates transnational patterns of transactions, communication, cooperation and regulation. But it is not a closed space comparable to a nation-state that limits the exit options of its citizens and members and thus facilitates internal structuring and system building. The EU is a transnational space, characterised by dense communication, a high degree of economic integration and uniform legal frameworks. Bartolini assumes that the open boundaries of the EU impede the evolution of social cohesion comparable to nation-states. It remains to be seen, however, how far this ideal-typical juxtaposition of closed national spaces and open transnational spaces holds up. This argument will have to be addressed empirically, since the openness of the European space is by no means unlimited. Turkey, Russia or Israel, for example, will hardly join the EU. At the same time, nation-states are no longer largely closed economic and social spaces as in the Golden Age of national sovereignty, i.e. in the 1950s and 1960s. Even at that time, national sovereignty was embedded in an international order characterised, according to Rosanvallon (2016), by market-based forms of societalisation, by the recognition of transnational human rights, by the hegemony of the USA and the international monetary order created at Bretton Woods in 1944.

Just as during the post-war period there were no completely sovereign nation-states that could autonomously shape their internal social orders and patterns of inequality, there were arguably no open, transnational spaces in which norms of equality and solidarity played no role at all. Between these two extremes, a pattern of primarily national inequalities, norms of equality and forms of social integration and of to some extent transnational inequalities and solidarities is emerging in Europe. Such a National-European pattern of social inequality will be analysed in the following section.

## 2.2   The Europeanisation of Social Inequalities

With the economic, political and social opening of national spaces, the national structuring of inequalities just described comes under scrutiny. The previous separation between national spaces characterised by civil, political and social norms of equality and international spaces structured by power asymmetries, war, diplomacy and the mutual recognition of sovereign states is being mitigated by European integration. Economic integration and the political deepening of the Union could thus transform disparities—which were not perceived as a violation of supranational norms of equality due to the absence of social integration—into social inequalities (Heidenreich, 2003). This may lead to a Europeanisation of social inequalities—a concept which has been defined as "transnational processes caused by the European integration, which shape the distribution of scarce and desired goods and positions thus shaping the life chances, the social identities, the interests, and values of individuals and social groups." (Heidenreich & Wunder, 2008, p. 33). This transforms the EU into a "transnational frame of reference and allocation for social inequality and its regulation" (Bach, 2015, p. 141; own translation).

The Europeanisation of social inequalities is a result of the closer transnational integration of national societies, which has been termed horizontal Europeanisation (Heidenreich, 2019b). Mau and Verwiebe (2010, p. 303) define this as "contacts, interactions and social relationships between different European countries, as well as various forms of pan-European mobility (exchanges and interaction between Member States)." Examples include the Europeanisation of everyday life (Delhey et al., 2014; Kuhn, 2015; Mau & Mewes, 2012) and also the willingness to show solidarity (Gerhards et al., 2019) and the Europeanisation of collective identifications (Checkel & Katzenstein, 2009; Delanty, 2005; Fligstein et al., 2012; Risse, 2014). While Mau and Verwiebe's (2010) definition refers to the microlevel, it makes sense to also include the transformation of social fields (mesolevel) and social spaces (macrolevel): "Thus, by 'horizontal' (or societal) Europeanisation, we refer to the increasing role of transnational practices, social relationships, interactions, attitudes and inequalities, and an increasing transnationalisation of social fields in Europe as a result of growing cross-border interdependencies and cross-border strategies of (sometimes EU-related) organisations and individuals." (Heidenreich, 2019a, p. 10) Horizontal Europeanisation is often the result of EU policies and the related opportunities and rules. The Europeanisation of social inequalities differs from field-specific Europeanisation processes, for example in administration (Büttner et al., 2019; Georgakakis, 2017; Georgakakis & Rowell, 2013), wage policy (Pernicka et al., 2019), academia (Gengnagel et al., 2019), as it affects the entire social space and not only relatively independent social subfields—which Wacquant and Bourdieu (1993), Fligstein and Stone Sweet (2002) and Kauppi (2018) refer to as fields.

The Europeanisation of social inequalities is a result of the economic, political and socio-cultural integration of Europe. Firstly, the *Europeanisation and globalisation of the economy*—as already mentioned in Sect. 2.1—facilitated the "unfreezing" of national, hitherto institutionally congealed cleavages. Economic integration, which in Europe is primarily being driven by the EU's internal market project (König & Ohr, 2013), creates new opportunities and risks. This refers both to the dynamics and the inequalities within and between countries. An example of inequalities within nations is the divide between higher-skilled, younger and internationally oriented groups of employees and knowledge-based technology and service regions (cf. Chap. 4), which may benefit from such opening processes, while older, lower-skilled employees (Chap. 9) as well as rural and old-industrialised regions and Southern European countries (Chap. 4) could be on the losing side. In the wake of economic opening processes, both previous centre-periphery structures and national patterns of conflict regulation and compromise between different social groups and classes are therefore challenged. This is why Streeck (2014, p. xviii) criticises the EU as a "liberalization machine". The previous corporatist market economy is being replaced by a social and industrial order that is more strongly oriented towards market opportunities and efficiency and in which public economic activities are being replaced by private companies (Scharpf, 1999). This "unfreezing" of national inequality structures can be the result of weaker collective forms of interest representation or lower levels of social expenditures (cf. Chap. 7). At the same time, however, Europe's increased economic and political integration can transform previously accepted disparities between countries into inequalities or even perceived injustices (Varoufakis, 2017). For decades, this Europeanisation of social inequalities was not an issue in Europe because high growth rates contributed to better living conditions in all countries and economic disparities between countries declined (Chap. 4). However, with declining growth rates and a partial reversal of the decades-long convergence process, between-country inequalities became politicised and demands for between-country solidarity increased.

Secondly, *political, legal and administrative integration* in Europe also contributes to this Europeanisation. On the one hand, the EU redistributes resources especially through its agricultural, structural and regional policies; on the other hand, it contributes to a modernisation of European labour market structures and social protection policies through the legal harmonisation of social protection (Leibfried, 2015; Leibfried & Pierson, 1995). Forms of soft governance such as the Open Method of Coordination also promote the harmonisation of national social and employment regulations (Heidenreich & Zeitlin, 2009). Furthermore, the EU member states are strongly integrated in legal terms. This is documented in the *acquis communautaire* and its currently 26,000 legal acts (source: https://eur-lex. europa.eu/browse/directories/legislation.html; accessed 22/2/2022). Europe is a common legal area. This is an important prerequisite for cross-border investment. The most important instrument of political integration, however, which has been often neglected by social scientists, is the monetary union, as this goes hand in hand with considerable demands on the transnational coordination of wage and economic policy (cf. Broschinski, 2020; Pernicka et al., 2019 and Chap. 6).

Third, the increasing importance of *cross-border interactions, practices and perceptions* also contributes to transnational societalisation (cf. Max Weber, 1978, pp. 40–41) for the concept of '*Vergesellschaftung*'). Examples include stays abroad, cross-border communication and interaction, and foreign language skills (Delhey et al., 2014; Gerhards et al., 2017; Kuhn, 2015). The increasing cross-border interactions and linkages are favoured by the free movement of goods, services, capital and people and the creation of a common currency. Transaction theory therefore expects European integration to facilitate transnational transactions, transnational social integration and transnational social cohesion (Delhey, 2004). Deutsch (1953, p. 173), the founder of this theory, predicted that supranational integration processes would make transnational power resources more important, that transnational elites would emerge and that national power relations and class structures would be transformed due to the increasing importance of transnational relations. Recent studies have shown that the process of European integration is changing Europeans' daily practices as well as their attitudes and perceptions. They highlight the transnational activities, attitudes and identifications of citizens, which can also transcend the European borders (Mau & Mewes, 2012; Mau et al., 2008; Roose, 2013). Sect. 7.5 contributes to this debate by demonstrating the importance of a European frame of reference for assessing one's own financial situation.

However, the influence of transnational activities and contacts for a positive attitude towards Europe should not be overestimated. Empirical evidence suggests that the assumption that more transactions mean stronger social cohesion is too optimistic. Kuhn (2011) observes the rise of Eurosceptic attitudes despite increasing transnational interactions and transactions. This apparent contradiction can be explained by the fact that transnational interactions are concentrated in the upper social strata, while the majority of the population has hardly any cross-border contacts and experiences the project of European integration mainly as a threat to the previous securities guaranteed by national institutions. While transnational lifestyles in the upper social strata are accompanied by Europhilic attitudes, lower social strata are often characterised by higher levels of Eurosceptic attitudes and a less cosmopolitan lifestyle. In addition, intensive cross-border activities are only weakly or not at all related to cross-border solidarity (Ciornei & Recchi, 2017, p. 476). European-wide contacts and activities thus are not necessarily accompanied by higher levels of European solidarity. Ciornei and Recchi (2017, p. 476) even suggest the opposite: "the 'easy faces of cosmopolitanism' such as food, tourism, music, literature and clothes, can be a robust individualizing experience but are not straightforward foundations of solidarity across borders".

In a perspective inspired by Rokkan and Flora (1999), the increasing economic, political and social interdependencies in Europe are leading to the "unfreezing" of previous frozen, domestically regulated conflicts. Examples of these new, often cross-border conflicts that directly affect people's living conditions are, for example, the intra-European disputes about the level of transfer payments, about how to deal with migration, the liberalisation of European markets or about a European climate and energy policy. These cleavages, which are dealt with in national and European bureaucracies, in the European Council or the Council of the EU, in the European Parliament, or in the European Central Bank (ECB) might contribute to an institutionalisation of conflict regulation procedures at the EU level. This institutionalisation of such procedures and rules is nothing other than "societalisation" (*Vergesellschaftung*), which might strengthen social cohesion in Europe. However, European societalisation processes are not only based on similarity, solidarity, perceived connectedness, consensus and convergence. Following Georg Simmel (1950), Coser (1965) has emphasised the role of conflict for social integration. Social integration thus may be the outcome of institutionalised forms of conflict regulation. This is precisely the essential function of the institutional network of the EU, in which tens of thousands of employees in national and European agencies, in economic associations and in civil society organisations are negotiating compromises and rules on a daily basis (Joerges & Neyer, 1997). This everyday regulation of conflicts takes place, for example, in the negotiations on the validity of democratic norms, the size of the EU budget, the scope of transfer payments, a European energy or climate policy or the reaction to foreign policy challenges such as Russia's invasion of Ukraine. Furthermore, through the liberalisation of European markets, citizens of one country are directly confronted with the social situation in other countries. Citizens can work in other EU countries as self-employed or employees. In this way, European migrants become directly acquainted with the living and working conditions in their host country and they confront their new colleagues with the conditions in their country of origin—if only because they accept working conditions and wages in slaughterhouses, shipyards or cleaning firms that are unimaginable for their native colleagues. Already the gradual realisation of the internal market since the 1980s and even more so since the enlargements of the EU from 2004 onwards, citizens have been confronted with the working, income and living conditions in other, often considerably poorer EU member states. This also implies a subjective Europeanisation of income inequality (Sect. 7.5). As a result, national class structures and domestic forms of conflict regulation and compromise might increasingly be shaped by European challenges and rules. This applies also to trade unions and industrial relations which have to consider the increasing competition in the eurozone as well as social security systems which can no longer limit the provision of benefits to nationals (Ferrera et al., 2000).

However, the EU has not developed forms of social protection comparable to national systems which are based on the redistribution of benefits to individuals based on their needs or contributions. The EU's redistributive policies, especially in the area of structural and cohesion policy, but also in agricultural policy, are not oriented towards individual need criteria. This has been shown by the debate on a "Social Europe" (Leibfried & Pierson, 1995). Ideological conflicts, conflicts of interest and institutional conflicts block the development of European forms of social protection (Scharpf, 1999). European social policy is characterised less by redistribution than by regulation (Majone, 1996). The focus is on facilitating transnational mobility by the recognition of social rights acquired in a foreign country. In addition, the EU is organising mutual learning processes in the domains of employment and social policy (Heidenreich & Bischoff, 2008; Leibfried, 2015). European integration therefore has created a transnational social space in which the regulation and reduction of social inequality plays only a minor role. The EU tries to reduce social inequalities mostly by better educating the population, improving employability of the labour force and increasing the inclusiveness of employment regimes (cf. Chap. 5), but not by social benefits. Nevertheless, the intensification of intra-European cooperation and competition has not yet led to a "race to the bottom" (Alber & Standing, 2000), i.e. to an erosion of national welfare states and national systems of industrial relations. National structures and policies are still essential for wage and income structures and inequalities (Chaps. 6, 7 and 8).

As a result of overlapping structures of national and European forms of market regulation and social policy, social divides between Europeanisation winners and losers can be expected (Hooghe & Marks, 2018). Fligstein (2008) argues that social groups and classes are affected very differently by European integration. With the increased openness of national borders, transnational elites (politicians, managers, entrepreneurs, skilled employees ...) have more options and can even evade some national rules. The cleavage between nationally embedded groups that rely on the nation-state and its security systems and transnationally-oriented and mobile groups may threaten social cohesion. Vobruba (2008) for example expects a split between transnational elites, who are in favour of European integration and benefit from it, and national elites and the "people", who would rather stick to national forms of regulation and social security. In a similar vein, Recchi et al. (2019), who have analysed the cross-border practices of nearly 6000 Europeans, distinguish between locally anchored populations, returnees, tourists, visitors, virtual transnationals and transnationals. Transnationally mobile groups are on average more highly educated and belong to higher social classes, while locally anchored residents, especially in Southern Europe, are often older, female and less educated. This shows that some groups benefit from transnational opening and integration processes more than other groups. However, a permanent, consistent and stable societal division between Europeanisation winners and losers has not yet have emerged. The thesis of the Europeanisation of social inequalities does not imply such a "crystallisation" of social opportunities and risks along a dividing line of young, mobile, well-educated professionals on one side and older, less skilled and less mobile groups on the other. Such an assumption, which would imply a Europe-wide hierarchy of European elites, national elites and the "people" analogous to the national patterns of stratification, might even impede the analysis of new, EU-related factors and dynamics of social inequality. The emergence of a European-wide class structure is unlikely, because the different dimensions of social inequality do not coalesce. Winners in one dimension—for example young, highly mobile students—can be losers in other dimensions—for example Italian graduates seeking a first job. Therefore, it is more useful to analyse the social and territorial divisions in Europe along various dimensions (income, wages, labour market opportunities, education, wealth), to understand the various forms of Europeanisation and to work out the respective winners and losers (Sect. 11.1).

The Europeanisation of social inequalities will be reconstructed in the following chapters as the result of four different transnational societalisation processes in Europe:

1. A *comparative international perspective*: Europeanisation in this perspective means that comprehensive information about the conditions in other, predominantly European countries are used as the basis for the evaluation and classification of the domestic situation. The determinants of social inequalities and their perception are still largely situated in the national arena, but "Europe" becomes an important comparative framework.

2. A *supranational perspective*: It is assumed that EU policies have a direct impact on the income, living and working conditions of people and nation-state societies.

3. A *transnational frame of reference*: Based on knowledge of living conditions in other European countries, people evaluate their own living conditions in a broader, transnational frame of reference.

4. A *transnational behavioural perspective*: European and transnational social spaces and fields are the basis of cross-border careers, strategies and everyday practices.

First, Europe can be understood as an ensemble of national social spaces. This is the classic approach in international comparative studies (Kohn, 1987). A European influence on nation-states or the living conditions of Europeans is also ignored for methodological reasons (Ebbinghaus, 1998), because this would undermine the independence of the observed entities. Therefore, nation-states are assumed to be independent of each other. The empirical analysis of these units of observation allows statements to be made on the development of regional and national income structures and living conditions in Europe (Beckfield, 2006, 2009, 2013). Whelan and Maître (2009, p. 118) designate the underlying Europeanisation concept as weak, since the framework for perceiving and regulating social inequalities remains national, even if the conditions in other countries are known. Europeanisation in this case means above all a cognitive opening, but also a firm insistence on the overarching importance of national contexts. Societalisation takes place within the national context. A good example is the study by Bach (2015), which is firmly grounded in classical sociological theory and conceptualises societies according to the model of Western national society.

Secondly, the Europeanisation thesis can also highlight the *effects of* European policies and institutions on the social situation of Europeans. In this case, the EU is understood as a supranational institution which shapes the European space. Political decisions and rules, the opening of national markets for capital, services, labour and goods or the introduction of a common currency are examples of the influence of European decisions on living conditions in Europe (Beckfield, 2009). Possible indicators for such a supranational Europeanisation could be the length of EU membership, the timing of the introduction of the common currency, the number of preliminary rulings under §267 TFEU (Beckfield, 2009) and also austerity, bailout, regional, agricultural and activation policies. The question is whether the political integration process has influenced the patterns and evolution of social inequalities in Europe.

Third, the Europeanisation of social inequalities can be understood as a transnationalisation of the frames of references for the evaluation of the social situation. An example of this is the debate on whether the perception of social inequalities takes place in a European context (Fahey, 2007; Goedemé & Rottiers, 2011; Kangas & Ritakallio, 2007; Kley, 2021; Lahusen & Kiess, 2018; Whelan & Maître, 2009). Such a Europeanisation assumes the existence of cross-border frames of reference:

> citizens frame of reference would have to extend their horizons well beyond the national realm, perceiving themselves, or their countries, as part of a larger European or even international stratification system. Furthermore, the perception, whether false or correct, of being advantaged or disadvantaged within this system would have to play an important role in individuals' evaluation of their own life circumstances. Thus the reference groups to which people relate themselves are the litmus test for the appropriateness of EU-wide approaches. (Delhey & Kohler, 2006, p. 126)

In contrast to the first perspective, people do not evaluate their social situation only in comparison with their compatriots (even if they are aware of the European and global context), but compare their own social situation with the living conditions of other Europeans (often in wealthier countries). Empirically, this raises the question of whether and to what extent international and European frames of reference shape the assessment of one's own social situation (Sect. 7.5).

Fourthly, Europe can be the relevant social space for some social fields and activities. In contrast to the third concept, this is not about the Europeanisation of attitudes and perceptions, but about the Europeanisation of social practices. According to Delhey et al. (2014), the Europeanisation of social practices is more relevant than the Europeanisation of attitudes. Sometimes, previously nationally regulated and limited fields of action have been Europeanised. Fligstein and Stone Sweet (2002) have analysed the Europeanisation processes in the fields of trade, organised interests, policy-making, legislation and jurisdiction. My colleagues have examined the Europeanisation of social fields using the examples of migration administration (Lahusen & Wacker, 2019), science policy (Gengnagel et al., 2019), wage policy (Pernicka et al., 2019) and EU professionals (Büttner et al., 2019). They described how administrative actions, universities' third-party funding strategies, collective bargaining and the knowledge of consultants have been opened up to EU-related competences, rules and reputational hierarchies for European specifications, opportunities, and strategies. Such transnational social fields can also have an impact on people's life situations. Examples include intra-European migrants, but also the international careers of European elites in administration, politics, science or business (Favell, 2008).

In the first case, Europe is conceived as an international space consisting of sovereign nation-states. In the second case, Europe is understood as a supranationally regulated space of the member states, thus limiting national sovereignty. In the third case, Europe is understood as a transnational social space that is central to Europeans' perceptions and attitudes. In the fourth case, the focus is on citizens' transnational practices, contacts and interactions, and on organisations' transnational strategies.

In summary: First, the foundations and limits of "methodological nationalism" in inequality research have been discussed. It has been argued that the emergence and consolidation of nation-states was accompanied by the development of domestic forms of redistribution and conflict regulation. After the collapse of the highly integrated world economy of the nineteenth century, the blockades to economic growth could only be overcome within a strengthened national framework. The synchronisation of growing productivity and growing demand could only be achieved through the welfare state, a national economic policy and national systems of collective bargaining. This national regulation of the global economy allowed the deepening and institutionalisation of national norms of solidarity and equality. Social inequalities could practically only be addressed within the national framework. This changed after the deepening and enlargement of the EU since the 1990s. In a single market with a common currency, the economy can no longer be regulated only at the national level. The Europeanisation and globalisation of the economy therefore confront national systems of social security and national patterns of social inequalities with new challenges. Even if the nation-state is still the most important point of reference for assessing one's own social situation, people are increasingly comparing their social situation across borders (Delhey & Kohler, 2006; Lahusen & Kiess, 2018). Thus, a Europeanisation of the determinants and perceptions of social inequalities in Europe can be expected when the causes of disadvantages and privileges are also attributed to European decisions.

In conclusion, four perspectives of such a Europeanisation have been distinguished: (a) international comparisons of living conditions in other countries; (b) effects of EU policies on people's living conditions; (c) evaluation of one's own living conditions in a European and international context; (d) cross-border practices in Europeanised fields of action. These four perspectives on the Europeanisation of social inequalities are taken up in the following chapters in order to discuss the question of how European integration influences the population's living conditions and thus the social and territorial divisions in Europe. Because these influences are not limited to the EU member states, two countries which are closely linked to the EU—Norway and Switzerland—and the United Kingdom, which was a member state of the EU until 2020, are also included in the empirical analysis. Firstly, essential facets of the objective living conditions in Europe are analysed in a comparative perspective in order to describe the convergence or divergence of these living conditions in Europe. Secondly, the potential influence of European policies on individual and household patterns of social inequality will be discussed. Third, the impact of cross-border social interactions and perceptions on social inequalities will be analysed. The fourth facet can be addressed only in a very limited way by the data used in this study.

# References

Alber, J., & Standing, G. (2000). Social dumping, catch-up or convergence? Europe in a comparative global context. *Journal of European Social Policy, 10*(2), 99–119.

Alderson, A. S., & Nielsen, F. (2002). Globalization and the great U-turn. Income inequality trends in 16 OECD countries. *American Journal of Sociology, 107*(5), 1244–1299.

Anderson, B. (2006). *Imagined communities: Reflections on the origin and spread of nationalism* (Revised ed.). Verso.

Bach, M. (2015). *Europa ohne Gesellschaft: Politische Soziologie der Europäischen Integration (2nd, revised edition). Neue Bibliothek der Sozialwissenschaften*. Springer. Retrieved from. https://doi.org/10.1007/978-3-531-93430-3

Bartolini, S. (2005). *Restructuring Europe: Centre formation, system building and political structuring between the nation-state and the European Union*. Oxford University Press.

Beckfield, J. (2006). European integration and income inequality. *American Sociological Review, 71*(6), 964–985. https://doi.org/10.1177/000312240607100605

Beckfield, J. (2009). Remapping inequality in Europe. *International Journal of Comparative Sociology, 50*(5–6), 486–509. https://doi.org/10.1177/0020715209339282

Beckfield, J. (2013). The end of equality in Europe? *Current History, 112*(752), 94–99.

Blau, P. M. (1977). *Inequality and heterogeneity: A primitive theory of social structure*. Free Press.

Broschinski, S. (2020). *Dynamiken von Lohnungleichheiten in Europa: Betriebliche und arbeitsmarktpolitische Anpassungen während der Eurokrise*. VS. Retrieved from https://www.springer.com/de/book/9783658318932

Büttner, S. M., Mau, S., Leopold, L., & Zimmermann, K. (2019). Europeanisation at home? Features and obstacles of domestic EU professionalism. In M. Heidenreich (Ed.), *Horizontal Europeanisation: The transnationalisation of daily life and social fields in Europe* (pp. 175–197). Routledge.

Checkel, J. T., & Katzenstein, P. J. (Eds.). (2009). *European identity*. Cambridge University Press.

Ciornei, I., & Recchi, E. (2017). At the source of European solidarity: Assessing the effects of crossborder practices and political attitudes. *Journal of Common Market Studies, 55*(3), 468–485. https://doi.org/10.1111/jcms.12507

Coser, L. A. (1965). The sociology of poverty: To the memory of Georg Simmel. *Social Problems, 13*, 140–148.

Delanty, G. (2005). The idea of a cosmopolitan Europe: On the cultural significance of Europeanization. *International Review of Sociology, 15*(3), 405–421.

Delhey, J. (2004). *European social integration: From convergence of countries to transnational relations between peoples* (WZB Discussion Paper No. SP I 2004–201). Berlin.

Delhey, J., Deutschmann, E., Graf, T., & Richter, K. (2014). Measuring the Europeanization of everyday life: Three new indices and an empirical application. *European Societies, 16*(3), 355–377.

Delhey, J., & Kohler, U. (2006). From nationally bounded to pan-European inequalities? On the importance of foreign countries as reference groups. *European Sociological Review, 22*(2), 125–140.

Deutsch, K. W. (1953). The growth of nations: Some recurrent patterns of political and social integration. *World Politics, 5*(2), 168–195.

Ebbinghaus, B. (1998). Europe through the looking-glass: Comparative and multi-level perspectives. *Acta Sociologica, 41*(4), 301–313. https://doi.org/10.1177/000169939804100401

Fahey, T. (2007). The case for an EU-wide measure of poverty. *European Sociological Review, 23*(1), 35–47.

Favell, A. (2008). *Eurostars and Eurocities: Free movement and mobility in an integrating Europe*. Blackwell; Wiley.

Ferrera, M. (2003). European integration and national social citizenship: Changing boundaries, new structuring? *Comparative Political Studies, 36*(6), 611–652.

Ferrera, M., Hemerijck, A., & Rhodes, M. (2000). *The future of social Europe: Recasting work and welfare in the new economy*. Celta Editora Oeiras. Retrieved from http://88.255.97.25/reserve/resspring06/INTL%20532%20Z.Onis/The%20Global%20Third%20Way%20Debate%20ch-7.pdf

Fligstein, N. (2008). *Euroclash: The EU, European identity, and the future of Europe*. Oxford University Press.

Fligstein, N., Polyakova, A., & Sandholtz, W. (2012). European integration, nationalism and European identity. *Journal of Common Market Studies, 50*(s1), 106–122.

Fligstein, N., & Stone Sweet, A. (2002). Constructing polities and markets: An institutionalist account of European integration. *American Journal of Sociology, 107*(5), 1206–1243.

Flora, P. (2000). Externe Grenzbildung und interne Strukturierung: Europa und seine Nationen. *Berliner Journal für Soziologie, 10*(2), 151–165. https://doi.org/10.1007/BF03204348

Gengnagel, V., Beyer, S., Baier, C., & Münch, R. (2019). Europeanisation and global academic capitalism: The case of the European Research Council. In M. Heidenreich (Ed.), *Horizontal Europeanisation: The transnationalisation of daily life and social fields in Europe* (pp. 129–151). Routledge.

Georgakakis, D. (2017). *European civil service in (times of) crisis: A political sociology of the changing power of eurocrats*. Palgrave Macmillan.

Georgakakis, D., & Rowell, J. (2013). *The field of eurocracy: Mapping EU actors and professionals*. Palgrave Macmillan.

Gerhards, J., Hans, S., & Carlson, S. (2017). *Social class and transnational human capital: How middle and upper class parents prepare their children for globalization.* Routledge.

Gerhards, J., Ignácz, Z. S., Kley, F. K., Lengfeld, H., & Priem, M. (2019). How strong is European welfare solidarity? Results from a comparative survey conducted in 13 EU member states. In M. Heidenreich (Ed.), *Horizontal Europeanisation: The transnationalisation of daily life and social fields in Europe* (pp. 39–62). Routledge.

Goedemé, T., & Rottiers, S. (2011). Poverty in the enlarged European Union. A discussion about definitions and reference groups. *Sociology Compass, 5*(1), 77–91.

Heidenreich, M. (2003). Regional inequalities in the enlarged Europe. *Journal of European Social Policy, 13*(4), 313–333. https://doi.org/10.1177/09589287030134001

Heidenreich, M. (2019a). The Europeanisation of social fields and the social space: A theoretical framework. In M. Heidenreich (Ed.), *Horizontal Europeanisation: The transnationalisation of daily life and social fields in Europe.* Routledge.

Heidenreich, M. (Ed.). (2019b). *Horizontal Europeanisation: The transnationalisation of daily life and social fields in Europe.* Routledge.

Heidenreich, M., & Bischoff, G. (2008). The open method of coordination: A way to the Europeanization of social and employment policies? *Journal of Common Market Studies, 46*(3), 497–532.

Heidenreich, M., & Wunder, C. (2008). Patterns of regional inequality in the enlarged Europe. *European Sociological Review, 24*(1), 19–36.

Heidenreich, M., & Zeitlin, J. (Eds.). (2009). *Changing European employment and welfare regimes: The influence of the open method of coordination on national reforms.* Routledge.

Hooghe, L., & Marks, G. (2018). Cleavage theory meets Europe's crises: Lipset, Rokkan, and the transnational cleavage. *Journal of European Public Policy, 25*(1), 109–135.

Joerges, C., & Neyer, J. (1997). From intergovernmental bargaining to deliberative political processes: The constitutionalisation of comitology. *European Law Journal, 3*(3), 273–299.

Kangas, O. E., & Ritakallio, V.-M. (2007). Relative to what? Cross-national picture of European poverty measured by regional, national and European standards. *European Societies, 9*(2), 119–145.

Kauppi, N. (2018). Transnational social fields. In T. Medvetz & J. J. Sallaz (Eds.), *The Oxford handbook of Pierre Bourdieu* (Vol. 1). Oxford University Press. https://doi.org/10.1093/oxfordhb/9780199357192.013.8

Kenworthy, L. (2004). *Egalitarian capitalism: Jobs, incomes, and growth in affluent countries.* Russell Sage Foundation.

Kley, S. (2021). How material deprivation impacted economic stress across European countries during the great recession. A lesson on social comparisons. *Acta Sociologica, 000169932110011.* https://doi.org/10.1177/00016993211001121

Kohn, M. L. (1987). Cross-national research as an analytic strategy. *American Sociological Review, 52*(6), 713–731.

König, J., & Ohr, R. (2013). Different efforts in European economic integration: Implications of the EU index. *Journal of Common Market Studies, 51*(6), 1074–1090.

Kuhn, T. (2011). Individual transnationalism, globalisation and euroscepticism: An empirical test of Deutsch's transactionalist theory. *European Journal of Political Research, 50*(6), 811–837.

Kuhn, T. (2015). *Experiencing European integration: Transnational lives and European identity.* Oxford University Press.

Kuznets, S. (1955). Economic growth and income inequality. *American Economic Review, 45*(1), 1–28. Retrieved from https://www.jstor.org/stable/i304619

Lahusen, C., & Kiess, J. (2018). 'Subjective Europeanization': Do inner-European comparisons affect life satisfaction? *European Societies, 21*(2), 214–236. https://doi.org/10.1080/14616696.2018.1438638

Lahusen, C., & Wacker, M. (2019). A European field of public administration? Administrative cooperation of asylum agencies in the Dublin system. In M. Heidenreich (Ed.), *Horizontal*

*Europeanisation: The transnationalisation of daily life and social fields in Europe* (pp. 153–174). Routledge.

Leibfried, S. (2015). Social policy: Left to the judges and the markets. In H. Wallace, M. A. Pollack, & A. R. Young (Eds.), *The new European Union series. Policy-making in the European Union (7th ed., pp. 263–292).* Oxford University Press.

Leibfried, S., & Pierson, P. (Eds.). (1995). *European social policy: Between fragmentation and integration.* Brookings Institution.

Luhmann, N. (1982). The world society as a social system. *International Journal of General Systems, 8*(3), 131–138. https://doi.org/10.1080/03081078208547442

Majone, G. (Ed.). (1996). *Regulating Europe.* Routledge. https://doi.org/10.4324/9780203439197

Marshall, T. H. (1950). *Citizenship and social class* (Vol. 11). Cambridge University Press.

Mau, S., & Mewes, J. (2012). Horizontal Europeanisation in contextual perspective: What drives cross-border activities within the European Union? *European Societies, 14*(1), 7–34.

Mau, S., Mewes, J., & Zimmermann, A. (2008). Cosmopolitan attitudes through transnational social practices? *Global Networks, 8*(1), 1–24.

Mau, S., & Verwiebe, R. (2010). *European societies: Mapping structure and change.* Policy Press.

Milanović, B. (2016). *Global inequality: A new approach for the age of globalization.* The Belknap Press of Harvard University Press.

Moran, T. P. (2005). Kuznets's inverted U-curve hypothesis: The rise, demise, and continued relevance of a socioeconomic law. *Sociological Forum, 20*(2), 209–244. https://doi.org/10.1007/s11206-005-4098-y

Münch, R. (2014). Das europäische Integrationsprojekt in der Krise: Zeichen eines tiefgreifenden Systemwandels? In M. Heidenreich (Ed.), *Krise der europäischen Vergesellschaftung? Soziologische Perspektiven* (pp. 53–86). Springer.

Pernicka, S., Glassner, V., Dittmar, N., & Neundlinger, K. (2019). The contested Europeanisation of collective bargaining fields. In M. Heidenreich (Ed.), *Horizontal Europeanisation: The transnationalisation of daily life and social fields in Europe* (pp. 109–128). Routledge.

Recchi, E., Favell, A., Apaydin, F., Barbulescu, R., Braun, M., Ciornei, I., et al. (2019). *Everyday Europe: Social transnationalism in an unsettled continent.* Policy Press. https://doi.org/10.1332/policypress/9781447334200.001.0001

Renan, E. (1996). What is a nation? In G. Eley & R. G. Suny (Eds.), *Becoming national: A reader* (pp. 41–55). Oxford University Press.

Risse, T. (2014). No demos? Identities and public spheres in the euro crisis. *Journal of Common Market Studies, 52*(6), 1207–1215.

Rokkan, S., & Flora, P. (Eds.). (1999). *Comparative European politics. State formation, nation-building, and mass politics in Europe: The theory of stein rokkan; based on his collected works (1. Publ).* Oxford University Press.

Roose, J. (2013). How European is European identification? Comparing continental identification in Europe and beyond. *Journal of Common Market Studies, 51*(2), 281–297.

Rosanvallon, P. (2016). How to create a society of equals: Overcoming today's crisis of inequality. *Foreign Affairs, 95*(1), 16–22.

Rousseau, J.-J. (1755). *Discours Sur L'Origine et les Fondements de L'Inégalité parmi les Hommes.* Marc Michel Rey.

Scharpf, F. W. (1999). *Governing in Europe: Effective and democratic?* Oxford University Press.

Simmel, G. (1950). *The sociology of Georg Simmel: Translated, edited and with an introduction by Kur H. Wolff. A free press paperback: Vol. 92892.* The Free Press.

Streeck, W. (1997). Neither European nor works councils: A reply to Paul Knutsen. *Economic and Industrial Democracy, 18*(2), 325–337. https://doi.org/10.1177/0143831X97182007

Streeck, W. (2014). *Buying time: The delayed crisis of democratic capitalism.* Verso.

Varoufakis, Y. (2017). *Adults in the room: My battle with Europe's deep establishment.* Random House.

Vobruba, G. (2008). Die Entwicklung der Europasoziologie aus der Differenz national/europäisch. *Berliner Journal für Soziologie, 18*(1), 32–51.

Wacquant, L. J. D., & Bourdieu, P. (1993). From ruling class to field of power: An interview with Pierre Bourdieu on La noblesse d'Etat. *Theory, Culture & Society, 10*(3), 19–44.

Weber, M. (1978). In G. Roth & C. Wittich (Eds.), *Economy and society: An outline of interpretive sociology*. University of California Press.

Whelan, C. T., & Maître, B. (2009). Europeanization of inequality and European reference groups. *Journal of European Social Policy, 19*(2), 117–130.

# Chapter 3
# Data and Methods

**Abstract** This methodological chapter introduces the data and methods used in the following chapters. The educational, wage, income and labour market inequalities within and between 30 European countries are analysed on the basis of a Europe-wide survey on income and living conditions (EU-SILC). EU-SILC is an EU-wide survey on income, poverty and living conditions in Europe, which has been conducted every year since 2004.

In the following chapters, the territorial and social divisions of education, earnings, income, labour market opportunities and wealth in Europe are examined primarily on the basis of the European Union Statistics on Income and Living Conditions (EU-SILC). EU-SILC is a survey that has been carried out since 2004, initially in 15 and now in 35 European countries. Eurostat provides data for 32 countries (in addition to the data for the 28 states that belonged to the EU from 2013–2020, also for Switzerland, Norway, Serbia and Iceland). Uniform definitions and minimum methodological standards apply to the statistics in all participating countries. The survey consists of a household questionnaire and a personal questionnaire for household members aged 16 and over. Data are available at the individual level for approximately 600,000 persons for each year (Eurostat, 2021). This amounts to 8000–57,000 persons per country (and 9.4 million individual data records for the period from 2004 to 2019). EU-SILC aims to standardise and harmonise the instruments and methods used. The income and material living conditions of private households in Europe are recorded in great detail. The EU-SILC survey is designed as a rotating panel: Every year, a quarter of the sample is replaced. Both the sampling and the collection of the SILC data are still fraught with considerable problems. In Germany, for example, Hauser (2007) points to considerable sampling problems due to the underrepresentation of poorly integrated foreigners (especially Turks), younger children and less qualified residents. This is also a result of non-representative samples (Frick & Krell, 2010; Lohmann, 2011; Verma & Betti, 2010). Despite these methodological problems in terms of representativeness, accuracy, comparability and coherence (Wolff et al., 2010), the EU-SILC data are the only available up-to-date data source for international comparative and supranational analyses of income and living conditions in Europe (Guio et al., 2021). The following analyses are based mostly on the cross-sectional data of EU-SILC, since the possibilities for using the longitudinal EU-SILC data are very limited (cf. however Pohlig, 2019). The variables used are described in Appendix 1.

As a rule, the 28 countries that belonged to the EU until the beginning of 2020 are included, i.e. also the United Kingdom. In addition, Switzerland and Norway are included in most cases, as they are very closely linked to the European Union through bilateral treaties or their participation in the European Economic Area and the Schengen area. Switzerland and Norway can be considered de facto members of the European Customs Union and the Single Market due to their close ties with the EU and their extensive adoption of Single Market rules (Erne et al., 2015). They are included because Europeanisation processes are not limited to the EU. A statistical argument for the inclusion of 30 countries is also that for some multilevel analyses at least 30 countries should be included in order to determine the influence of contextual factors (Bryan & Jenkins, 2016).

Since data for Malta, Romania and Bulgaria are only available since 2007 (and for Croatia since 2010 and the UK until 2018), the EU-SILC data for the years from 2007 to 2019 will primarily be used. This period includes the boom years 2007 to 2008, the years 2009 to around 2013 determined by the financial market and euro crises and the subsequent upswing, which ended abruptly with the pandemic in 2020. Since the wage and income data in EU-SILC always refer to the previous year—the income and wage data collected in 2019 thus depict the situation in 2018—this shifts the observed period to the years 2006 to 2018.

The data on the national and regional context are largely taken from Eurostat databases available on the internet (see the list of variables in Appendix 1). Due to frequent reclassifications, especially of regionally differentiated data, the available time series are limited. For example, regional value added per inhabitant (Fig. 4.2) is only available from 2000–2017 as data for the UK were subsequently no longer reported and some countries completely reclassified their regions.

When analysing the European countries, a widespread typology inspired by Gallie (2007) is often employed. This typology distinguishes five country groups—Scandinavian, Continental, Southern, Central and Eastern European countries and the two countries on the British Isles.[1] This typology is an attempt to reduce

---

[1] These five country groups are composed as follows: Southern Europe (CY = Cyprus, EL = Greece, ES = Spain, IT = Italy, MT = Malta, PT = Portugal); British Isles (IE = Ireland, UK = United Kingdom); Central and Eastern Europe (BG = Bulgaria, CZ = Czech Republic, EE = Estonia, HU = Hungary, LT = Lithuania, LV = Latvia, PL = Poland, SK = Slovakia, SI = Slovenia, RO = Romania); Continental Europe (AT = Austria, BE = Belgium, DE = Germany, FR = France, LU = Luxembourg, NL = Netherlands, CH = Switzerland); Scandinavia (DK = Denmark, FI = Finland, SE = Sweden, NO = Norway). The abbreviations largely correspond to the international standard ISO 3166-1 alpha-2. The only exception is the abbreviation EL for Greece, which is common in the EU, instead of GR. The United Kingdom and Ireland are grouped together as the British Isles or liberal countries, since the usual designation as Anglo-Saxon countries focuses too much on the ethnicity of the two countries and ignores the Romano-Celtic, African-Asian and other imprints of the population. Liberal countries include other countries besides Ireland and the UK (USA, Australia, New Zealand, Canada), which are not relevant for a study of inequalities in

the complexity of European countries and to facilitate their presentation. In addition to the three "worlds of welfare"—liberal, social democratic and conservative-corporatist countries (Esping-Andersen, 1990)—this typology also embraces the residual, familialist countries of Southern Europe (Ferrera, 1996) and the post-socialist countries in Central and Eastern Europe (Deacon, 2000). In addition, it shifts the focus from social policies to employment regimes.

The aim of this book is the description of social inequalities in a multidimensional perspective. The most common indicator for measuring and comparing these inequalities is the *Gini index* which varies between 0 and 1. Taking the example of income inequality, 0 means that every household has the same disposable income, while 1 or 100% means that only one household receives all the income. Each inequality measure is based on normative assumptions because it focuses on some—and not on other—parts of the income distribution. For example, the Gini index assumes that any deviation from an equal distribution is equally important. There-fore, the Gini coefficient is particularly sensitive to deviations in the middle of a distribution (and not to extreme poverty or high incomes). The Gini index of income inequality thus is considered to be middle-class biased. The *mean log deviation* (MLD), on the other hand, is particularly sensitive to inequalities at the bottom of the distribution, while the *Theil index* is especially sensitive to inequalities at the top. The normative assumptions are even clearer in the case of decile ratios, which focus only on two points of the distribution. The *decile ratio D9/D1* is the quotient between the highest income of the lowest decile and the lowest income of the highest decile. Like any other inequality measure, this measure relies on normative assump-tions. In this case, the normative assumption is that high and low incomes—and not average incomes—merit most attention. Accordingly, the *decile ratios D9/D5 and D5/D1* focus on the difference between the median (D5) and the upper or lower decile of the distribution. In a similar vein, *poverty indicators* are also based on normative assumptions, as they focus on a particular section of the income curve (such as the usual at-risk-of-poverty ratio, which focuses on households whose disposable household income is lower than 60% of the median income). This ratio ignores changes in the middle of the distribution and focuses on the share of the population below this specific point on the income curve.

A general feature of an analysis of social inequalities in a transnational space is the necessity to distinguish between overall, within- and between-country inequal-ities. Measurements of *within-country inequalities* are the most common. For exam-ple, income inequality in Germany has been estimated by Eurostat (Table ilc_di12) as 0.30 (2018). Its level can be explained by different policies, economic structures and institutions at the regional, national, or European level, but also at the individual and household level, because various groups have a higher or lower income according to their socio-demographic characteristics (gender, migration background, age, education, activity and occupational groups, private lifestyle, health status).

---

Europe. The even more neutral designation as Western European islands is not used, as it also applies to numerous other islands.

*Total inequality* in a transnational space, for example European space, means that income inequality (or wage, educational, skill, or labour market inequality) is calculated for all Europeans irrespective of their nationality. Polish university teachers, Greek farmers and Dutch kings are placed on the same income curve (Fig. 7.1). *Between-country inequalities* are the result of different income levels in various countries. In a comparative perspective, between-country differences are not even considered as inequalities but as disparities (Chap. 2). While these differences are ignored in the calculation of EU-wide inequality indices by Eurostat (Sect. 7.1), they are essential in a transnational perspective, because declining between-country inequalities are interpreted as convergence and increasing inequalities as divergence. In the case of the mean logarithmic deviation (MLD), within- and between-country inequalities add up to total inequality. Therefore, this indicator will often be used when analysing the ratio of within- and between-country inequality. In contrast to the MLD, the Gini coefficient cannot be additively decomposed in within- and between-country inequality. Before comparing monetary data, for example on the wage and income situation, they must be converted into a common unit, either in a common currency or into purchasing power standards (PPS)—an artificial currency unit which takes into account the different purchasing power in different European countries.

# References

Bryan, M. L., & Jenkins, S. P. (2016). Multilevel modelling of country effects: A cautionary tale. *European Sociological Review, 32*(1), 3–22.

Deacon, B. (2000). Eastern European welfare states: The impact of the politics of globalization. *Journal of European Social Policy, 10*(2), 146–161. https://doi.org/10.1177/a012487

Erne, R., Imboden, N., Erne, R., & Imboden, N. (2015). Equal pay by gender and by nationality: A comparative analysis of Switzerland's unequal equal pay policy regimes across time. *Cambridge Journal of Economics, 39*(2), 655–674. https://doi.org/10.1093/cje/bev003

Esping-Andersen, G. (1990). *The three worlds of welfare capitalism.* Princeton University Press.

Eurostat (2021). *EU statistics on income and living conditions: Microdata 2004–2019, release 1 in 2021.* Retrieved from https://ec.europa.eu/eurostat/web/income-and-living-conditions

Ferrera, M. (1996). The `southern model´ of welfare in social Europe. *Journal of European Social Policy, 6*(1), 17–37.

Frick, J. R., & Krell, K. (2010). Measuring income in household panel surveys for Germany: A comparison of EU-SILC and SOEP. *SOEP papers.*

Gallie, D. (Ed.). (2007). *Employment regimes and the quality of work.* Oxford University Press.

Guio, A.-C., Marlier, E., & Nolan, B. (Eds.). (2021). *Improving the understanding of poverty and social exclusion.* Publications Office of the European Union. https://doi.org/10.2785/70596

Hauser, R. (2007). *Probleme des deutschen Beitrags zu EU-SILC aus der Sicht der Wissenschaft: Ein Vergleich von EU-SILC* (p. 69). SOEPpapers.

Lohmann, H. (2011). Comparability of EU-SILC survey and register data: The relationship among employment, earnings and poverty. *Journal of European Social Policy, 21*(1), 37–54. https://doi.org/10.1177/0958928710385734

Pohlig, M. (2019). Unemployment sequences and the risk of poverty: From counting duration to contextualizing sequences. *Socio-Economic Review.* Advance online publication. https://doi.org/10.1093/ser/mwz004.

Verma, V., & Betti, G. (2010). Data accuracy in EU-SILC. In A. B. Atkinson & E. Marlier (Eds.), *Eurostat theme collection. Income and living conditions in Europe* (pp. 57–77). Publication Office of the EU.

Wolff, P., Montaigne, F., & Rojas González, G. (2010). Investing in statistics: EU-SILC. In A. B. Atkinson & E. Marlier (Eds.), *Eurostat theme collection. Income and living conditions in Europe* (pp. 37–55). Publication Office of the EU.

# Chapter 4
# Between Convergence and Agglomeration. Economic and Technological Disparities in the EU

**Abstract** This chapter discusses how economic convergence is coming to an end, at least in Western Europe. Increasing economic disparities, especially between the 15 oldest EU member states, are leading to a territorial concentration of scientific, technological and organisational capabilities. In contrast to the first decades of European integration, when convergence in Europe was achieved mainly through greater integration of markets, poorer households, regions and countries can no longer count on an almost automatic convergence of their living and income conditions through economic integration. Rather, in technological, scientific and economic terms, clear differences can be observed between knowledge-based service regions and cities, and less developed agricultural, industrial and tourist regions. The divide between Northern and Continental European technology and service regions and peripheral, predominantly Southern and Central European regions is considerable. In Central and Eastern Europe, these disparities are partly cushioned by a successful strategy of peripheral industrialisation. The Southern European countries, however, have been hit harder by intensified global competition and by the financial, euro and Covid-19 crises. More integrated markets as well as economic and technological agglomeration are thus giving rise to new differences between a European core area and peripheral regions. This indicates a Europeanisation of economic disparities.

Economic integration is at the centre of the European integration process. It started with the European Coal and Steel Community (ECSC) established in 1951 and the creation of the European Economic Community (EEC; 1957), which was part of the European Communities and in 1993 became the European Union (EU). This political integration was the basis for close economic cooperation, initially within the European Free Trade Association (EFTA) then the European Union Customs Union (1968), the European Single Market (1993) and the European Monetary Union (1999) (Fligstein & Stone Sweet, 2002). A second dimension of economic integration was the enlargement of the EU or its predecessors from initially 6 to now

This chapter is based on Heidenreich (2019).

© The Author(s), under exclusive license to Springer Nature Switzerland AG 2022
M. Heidenreich, *Territorial and Social Inequalities in Europe*,
https://doi.org/10.1007/978-3-031-12630-7_4

37

27 member states (since the exit of the United Kingdom on 1/2/2020). Step by step, the barriers to the cross-border exchange of goods and services, to the movement of capital and to the mobility of people in an area with a current population of 448 million have been abolished or reduced.

For decades, this was accompanied by a convergence of economic and income conditions in the European Union and its predecessors (Barro & Sala-i-Martin, 1991, 1992)—especially before the establishment of European structural and cohesion policies (Boldrin & Canova, 2001). From a neoclassical perspective, the faster catching-up of less developed regions can be explained by the effect of exogenous technological progress and by diminishing marginal returns to factors of production in more developed regions. Since the financial and euro crises, however, an end to convergence and a renewed increase in European inequalities have been observed (Beckfield, 2019). Looking at disadvantaged European regions, Iammarino, Rodriguez-Pose, and Storper (2019, p. 273) diagnose: "Market processes and policies that are supposed to spread prosperity and opportunity are no longer sufficiently effective." This has recently been termed the "revenge of the places that don't matter" (Rodríguez-Pose, 2018). It is a cause of growing dissatisfaction with the EU. Shocked by the increasing support for populist parties and the regional concentration of populist voters in de-industrialised regions and disconnected smaller cities, a "geography of EU discontent" (Dijkstra et al., 2020) has been observed. However, Eurosceptic attitudes are by no means observed solely or exclusively in deprived regions. Even and especially the fastest growing European regions in Central and Eastern Europe are to a considerable extent susceptible to populist currents (Rodríguez-Pose, 2018). Hobolt and de Vries (2016) argue that attitudes towards the European integration process are not only shaped by economic stress and interests, but also by the role of cosmopolitan, national or even ethnic identifications and by the image of the European Union conveyed by the media. However, there is little doubt that attitudes towards European integration are also determined by one's own economic situation and that inhabitants of depressed regions are particularly susceptible to populist attitudes.

Given this background, it is useful to recall the decades-long convergence of regional economic and technological performance in Europe. At the same time, however, the limits of this quasi-automatic convergence have to be studied and their potential impact for social cohesion in Europe discussed. In particular, this chapter will show that, on the one hand, economic differences in Europe are increasing again after many years of convergence (Sect. 4.1). On the other hand, this points to the regional concentration of technological knowledge, but also to the varying degrees to which inclusive labour market structures have been implemented (Sect. 4.2). Thirdly, the different industrial trajectories in the Southern and Eastern European periphery and their underlying reasons will be shown (Sect. 4.3). This chapter concludes with a brief summary (Sect. 4.4). The following analyses are essentially based on aggregated data, mostly regional averages. Individual living and working conditions will be analysed in the subsequent chapters.

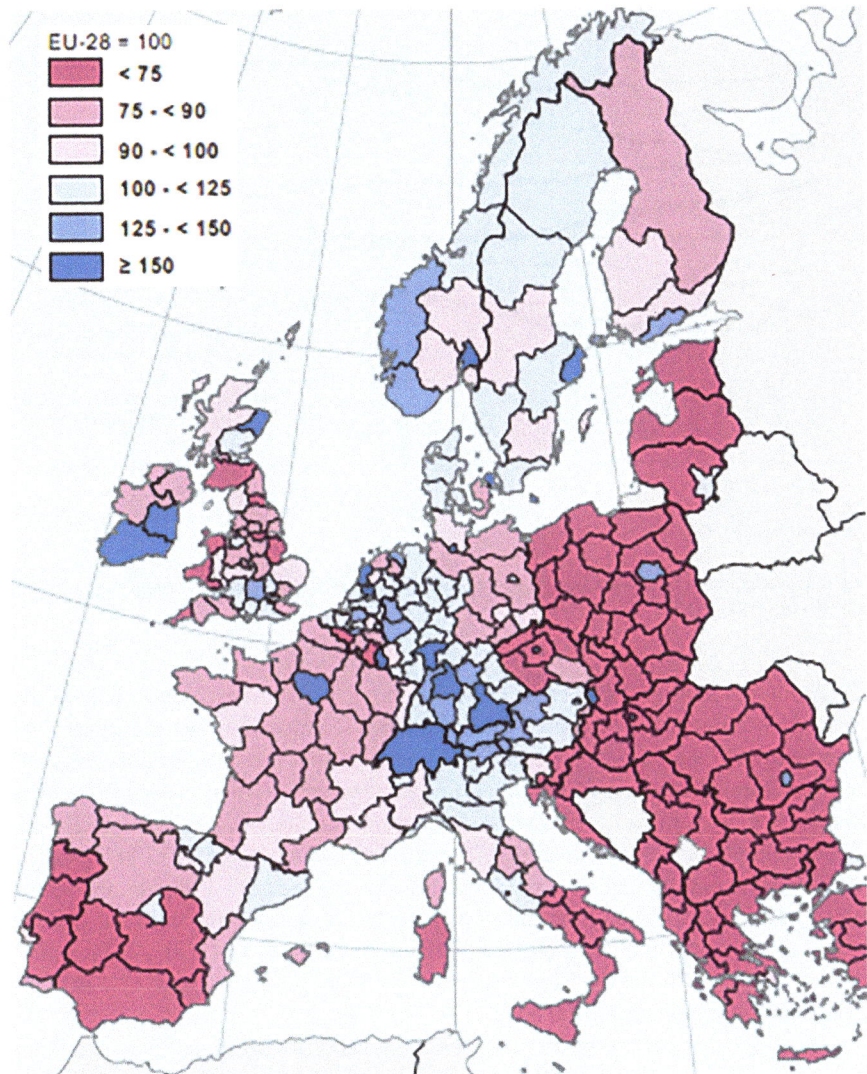

Source: Eurostat, 2019a: Regional Yearbook, p.90

**Fig. 4.1** Regional gross domestic product (adjusted for purchasing power) (in % of EU-28 average; 2017). EU-28 excluding Overseas Territories and Cyprus

## 4.1  Convergence through Economic Integration?

The European Union (EU) is characterised by significant regional differences in economic performance (Fig. 4.1). These are often illustrated by the differences between the economically strongest and weakest European region: Per capita income

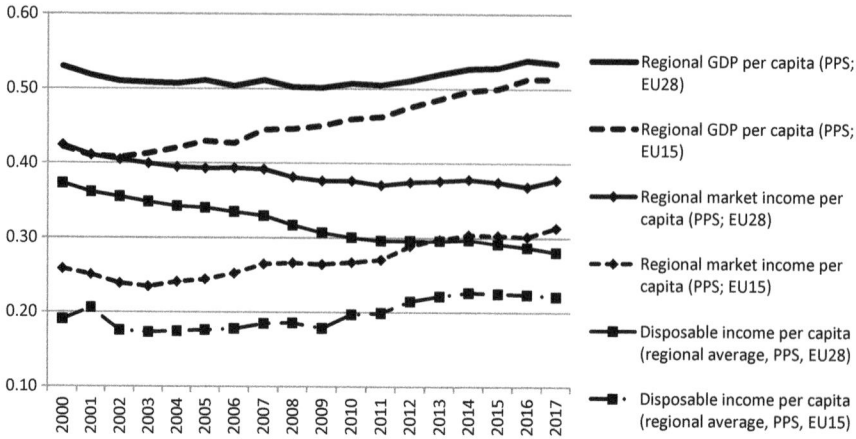

The coefficients of variation (i.e. the standard deviation divided by the mean) of population-weighted average regional gross domestic product (GDP), market income and disposable income per capita (in purchasing power standards) are shown for the 215 and 273 NUTS2 regions of the EU-15 and EU-28 respectively. Sources: Eurostat, tables [nama_10r_2gdp] and [nama_10r_2hhinc].

**Fig. 4.2** Variation in economic performance, market income and disposable income in the EU-28 and EU-15 (2000–2017)

adjusted for purchasing power in central London is 21 times higher than in the northwestern Bulgarian region of Severozapaden—which also has the lowest life expectancy and the highest proportion of young people not in education, employment or training (Eurostat, 2019a). Another measure of dispersion is the ratio between the economically weakest and strongest regions, each home to one-tenth of the population. This so-called decile ratio has fallen from 4.04 (2000) to 2.77 (2017). This means that—adjusted for purchasing power—London and other wealthy regions generated four and three times as much GDP per capita as poorer, mostly Eastern and Southern European regions. A third measure is the coefficient of variation[1] which fell for the European gross domestic product from 0.53 (2000) to 0.50 (2008) and rose again to 0.53 (2017) (Fig. 4.2).

This temporary decline in the coefficient of variation illustrates that economic opening and integration processes between economically very different countries are usually accompanied by significant growth and welfare gains in the less developed countries in particular. In the first decades after the creation of the European Communities, the economic performance of European countries converged rapidly as the less prosperous countries and regions developed more rapidly, thereby reducing economic disparities between European countries and regions (Barro &

---

[1]The coefficient of variation is the standard deviation divided by the mean. The advantage of this measure is that it takes into account the entire distribution of economic performance and not only selected extreme values. Also, the coefficient of variation for a year or a group of countries is independent of the respective mean value and can therefore be compared with other values.

**Table 4.1** Economic convergence of European regions (2000–2017)

|                  | EU-28(1) | EU-15(2) |
|------------------|----------|----------|
| Country dummies  | No       | No       |
| NUTS2 regions    | 273      | 215      |
| $R^2$            | 0.58     | 0.02     |
| Convergence rate | 0.034    | −0.003   |
| Half-life (years)| 21       | −201     |

Regional convergence (absolute beta convergence of purchasing power-adjusted regional gross value added per inhabitant in the NUTS2 regions (2000–2017). For calculation see Barro and Sala-i-Martin (1992, p. 230) and Heidenreich and Wunder (2008)

Sala-i-Martin, 1991).[2] Indeed, a convergence of average regional growth rates of about 2% per year could be observed in Europe for decades (Barro & Sala-i-Martin, 1991, p. 148; Heidenreich & Wunder, 2008, p. 26). Accordingly, the dispersion of regional and national economic performance in the EU decreased significantly until the noughties.

Currently, however, the picture is quite different (Table 4.1): while there is strong convergence (over 3%; column 1) in the EU-28, adjusted for purchasing power, due to the rapid development of the Central and Eastern European regions, economic performance in the 15 old EU member states is no longer converging (column 2). *For the 15 "old" EU member states it can therefore be stated that the decades-long economic convergence process has come to a standstill.*

A more nuanced picture emerges by taking a closer look at the coefficients of variation just mentioned (Fig. 4.2). The differences in the economic performance of the European regions decline until 2008 and then increase again—especially in the 15 "older" member states of the EU. Despite rapid development in the Central and Eastern European regions, the disparities in the EU-28 increase again as many Southern European regions fall behind the Central and Eastern European regions. Thus, the overall dispersion of the regional gross domestic product per capita increases again. *Since the beginning of the new millennium, there has thus been a renewed increase in economic disparities in the EU.* In the case of average regional market income and disposable household income, the opposing developments are even more noticeable: Due to the rapid catching-up processes, especially in Central and Eastern Europe, the differences in the EU-28 are decreasing, while they have been increasing again in the EU-15 since the beginning of the noughties, only to stabilise after the end of the sovereign debt (or euro) crisis (2010–2013).

If this trend stabilises, this could indicate the need for a changing social foundation for European integration. In the first decades of European integration, European

---

[2] Two forms of convergence, known as beta and sigma convergence have to be distinguished: While beta convergence measures the different growth rates of poorer and richer regions and the corresponding speed of adjustment over time, sigma convergence measures the variance or standard deviation of regional or national per capita economic performances at a given point in time. To calculate these coefficients, the corresponding national and regional indicators are expressed in purchasing power standards and weighted by the number of inhabitants.

citizens could assume that their living standard would in general improve, especially in the less developed regions. The EU promised welfare and rapid economic growth—mainly due to the customs union and the single market. This explains the extraordinary attractiveness of the EU for neighbouring, less developed countries, which wanted to join the EC or the EU after the collapse of the Eastern bloc. The picture changed at the latest with the financial and eurozone crises from 2008 onwards: Some countries (Greece, Cyprus) and regions are still below pre-crisis levels in 2017—especially in Italy (Valle d'Aosta, Molise, Isole, Umbria, Lazio), Spain (Ceuta, Melilla, Canarias) and the UK (East Yorkshire and Northern Lincolnshire, Outer London, South and North Eastern Scotland), while in the EU as a whole purchasing power-adjusted economic performance per capita has increased by 15% (Eurostat, [nama_10r_2gdp]. The decade since the financial market and euro crises has thus been a lost decade for many countries and regions, especially in Southern Europe. The economic trajectories have been diverging in particular between Southern, and Central and Eastern Europe not only since the financial and euro crises. As a result, the catching-up process, particularly between the 15 older EU member states, is losing momentum even if the economic differences are significantly smaller compared to previous decades.

In sum: economic development in the European regions, especially during the financial and euro crises since 2008, has been characterised by two opposing trends: while the Central and Eastern European regions grew strongly and moved closer to the European average, Greece, Cyprus and many Italian, Spanish and UK regions declined in relation to the European average. This raises the question of whether this indicates an "end of convergence" (Beckfield, 2019) or whether it will be possible to find other growth models than the dismantling of trade barriers between EU member states. In the first case, the EU will have to develop other forms of social cohesion beyond the promises of economic growth and convergence due to market integration. The EU would have to cope with lasting lines of division between core and peripheral regions and probably also with increasing within-country disparities between more and less developed regions and countries. A starting point for the second scenario would be the recognition of the fact that economic development in the EU is no longer determined—as assumed in neoclassical growth theory—by quasi-automatic convergence as a result of economic integration. Thus, innovation policies focusing in particular on less developed EU regions become more important. This would require a Europeanisation of research and development policies (Borrás, 2004; Kaiser & Prange, 2005). However, such a European-wide innovation strategy might entail other cleavages due to the concentration of innovative capacities. Whether a Europe-wide diffusion of technical knowledge or a territorial concentration and agglomeration of technological knowledge and skills in the EU can be observed will be discussed now.

## 4.2   Between Agglomeration and Diffusion of Technological and Economic Capabilities

With the diminishing importance of almost automatic, "neoclassical" convergence processes, other politically induced dynamics and economic processes may gain in importance—in particular the evolution and diffusion of technological capabilities. This may either favour convergence or lead to increasing economic differences. The agglomeration of economic capabilities would result in the second alternative. The EU is now already characterised by an extraordinary concentration of economic and entrepreneurial capabilities (Heidenreich & Baur, 2015; Midelfart-Knarvik et al., 2002).

Such a regional concentration of high economic performance can be explained by self-reinforcing processes. Analyses in the new economic geography term them dynamic processes of cumulative causation (Krugman, 1991). Successful companies can strengthen a regional economy and thus increase its attractiveness for other companies, which further strengthens the region. The settlement of a company creates location advantages for other companies as well and can thus lead to the emergence of local clusters that favour the further development of scientific, technological and economic strengths and the creation of suitable institutional framework conditions. Such a mutual reinforcement of entrepreneurial competences and national and regional institutions is also at the heart of theories of regional, national, technological and sectoral innovation systems (Asheim & Isaksen, 2002; Cooke et al., 2011). These dynamics are the basis of the regional agglomeration effects that are threatening economic convergence.

In Europe, two different types of regions benefit from such agglomeration effects (Heidenreich, 1998). While many urban service regions can position themselves as central hubs for global information, communication, trade and financial flows, industrial core regions are key to providing high-quality, knowledge-based industrial products. These two types of regions are concentrated in Europe in a central conurbation that stretches from Southern England through the Benelux countries and Germany to Northern Italy and can be traced back to the European city belt that emerged along the former Roman trade routes (Rokkan & Flora, 1999). Recently, this area has been called the Pentagon, as it is bounded by the five cities of Milan, Paris, London, Hamburg and Munich. The largest and most research-intensive European companies are found there (Heidenreich & Baur, 2015). In such a perspective, which focuses on agglomeration and the path-dependent evolution of technological and industrial competences and networks, the development of the Southern European peripheral regions is hindered on the one hand by the fact that they are relatively far away from the core regions of Western Europe and, on the other hand, because they are often not directly integrated into the value chains of focal West European companies. At the same time, the Central and Eastern European regions may have an advantage in this respect, as they were able to integrate themselves more easily into the production and supply chains of Western European companies (for example in the automotive industry) after the collapse of

**EU Countries**

**PATENTS_PER_CAPITA**

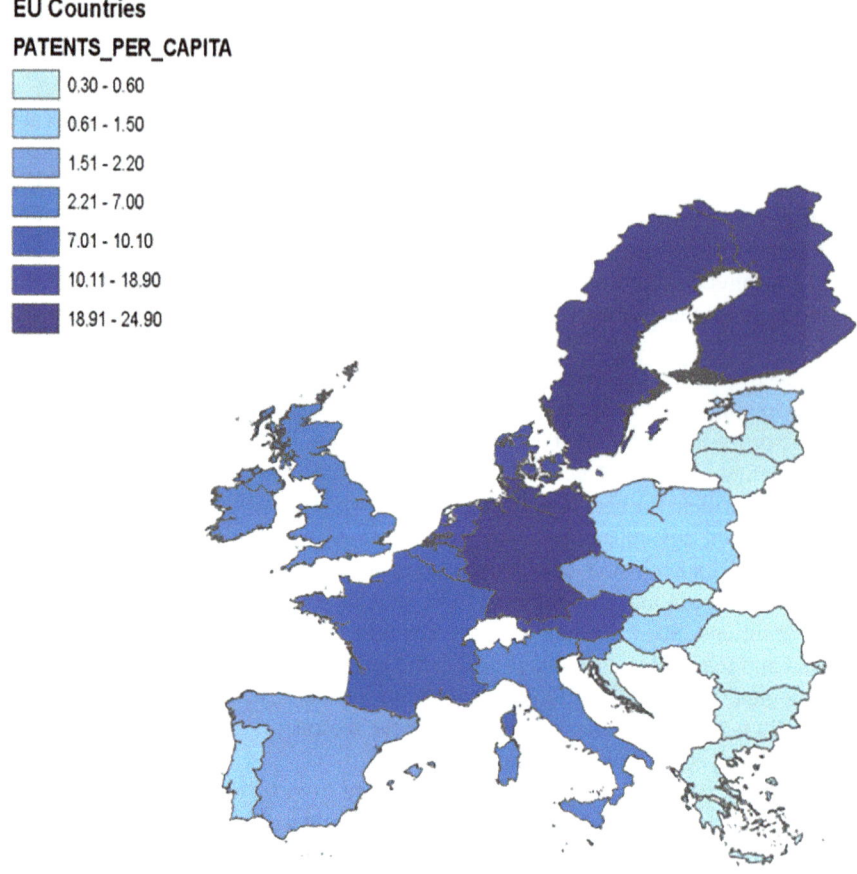

- 0.30 - 0.60
- 0.61 - 1.50
- 1.51 - 2.20
- 2.21 - 7.00
- 7.01 - 10.10
- 10.11 - 18.90
- 18.91 - 24.90

Source: Vezzani, Gkotsis, Hernández, and Moncada-Paternò-Castello (2019, p. 1).

**Fig. 4.3** Patents per 100,000 inhabitants from the business sector (2013–2015)

the socialist regimes. In this perspective, the differential performance of European regions, and thus the different and diverging income levels, are also determined by the path-dependent accumulation of technological capabilities, skills and networks (Iammarino et al., 2019). Thus, considerable differences can to be expected both in the national and in the European context—for example between advanced industrial and service regions and national capitals on the one hand and disconnected old industrial regions, agricultural regions and regions focused on personal services on the other hand. It can be expected that the European economic and social geography is characterised by increasingly deep divisions between core and peripheral regions.

Such a regional concentration of economic capabilities can also be explained by the spatial concentration of technological knowledge or, more specifically, of research and development (R&D). R&D investments and their outcomes, for example patents, are extremely unevenly distributed in the EU (cf. Fig. 4.3). While, for example, in the Braunschweig region 8.5% (2017) of the gross domestic product is invested in research and development, in the Romanian Sud-Vest Oltenia it is only 0.09% (Eurostat, table [rd_e_gerdreg]). The first figure reflects the concentration of Volkswagen's R&D expenditures at Wolfsburg. This can be generalised: Technological capabilities and entrepreneurial decisions are concentrated in a few Western European regions and cities. In 1995, research intensity in the decile of European regions with the highest research performance was almost thirteen times higher than R&D expenditure in the regions with the lowest expenditure. In 2017, the differences between the top and bottom deciles were still 5.1: 1. The most research-intensive decile of European regions invested more than 3.9% of their economic output in R&D in 2017, while the least research-intensive decile only invested a maximum of 0.8%. The 15 most research-intensive regions in the EU-28 are located in Germany (7), the UK (2), Sweden (1), Austria (1), Belgium (2), Denmark (1) and France (1). These 15 regions account for one fifth of total European R&D expenditure. The differences between the number of patent applications from the best-performing and the weakest decile were as high as 38: 1 (2012; Eurostat, table [pat_ep_rtot]).

These differences reflect the concentration of research-intensive, mostly multinational companies—such as Volkswagen in Wolfsburg. The headquarters of 605 of the 1000 most research-intensive European companies are concentrated in only three countries, namely the UK, Germany and France (Vezzani et al., 2019). Such companies are mainly located in national capitals and in the Pentagon, the core European region mentioned above (Heidenreich & Baur, 2015). While MNCs' regional R&D expenditures may also benefit their other locations around the world, very often MNCs' R&D expenditures are concentrated close to the company's headquarters, or at least in the company's home country (Patel & Pavitt, 1991). This concentration of scientific and technological competences leads to increasing economic disparities between central and peripheral European regions (Eurostat, 2019a, Chap. 8).

However, in addition to the accumulation of technological knowledge and entrepreneurial skills, two other factors determine the economic performance of European cities and regions—the skills of the workforce and the inclusiveness of the labour market (Sect. 5.1). An inclusive labour market is characterised by the participation of previously marginalised groups in the labour force—especially women and older people, but also migrants and people with health conditions. The key indicator for more inclusive employment structures is a higher employment rate, i.e. a higher number of employed persons in relation to the total population in the corresponding age group.

With the exception of the last indicator, which is examined in more detail in Chap. 5, the country group-specific developments of these explanatory variables are shown in Fig. 4.4. The split between Northern and Continental European countries on the one hand and Southern and Eastern European countries on the other is clearly visible: Scandinavia and Continental Europe have the highest R&D expenditure, the most patent applications and the highest share of cutting-edge technologies, knowledge-intensive services and academics, while Southern and Eastern

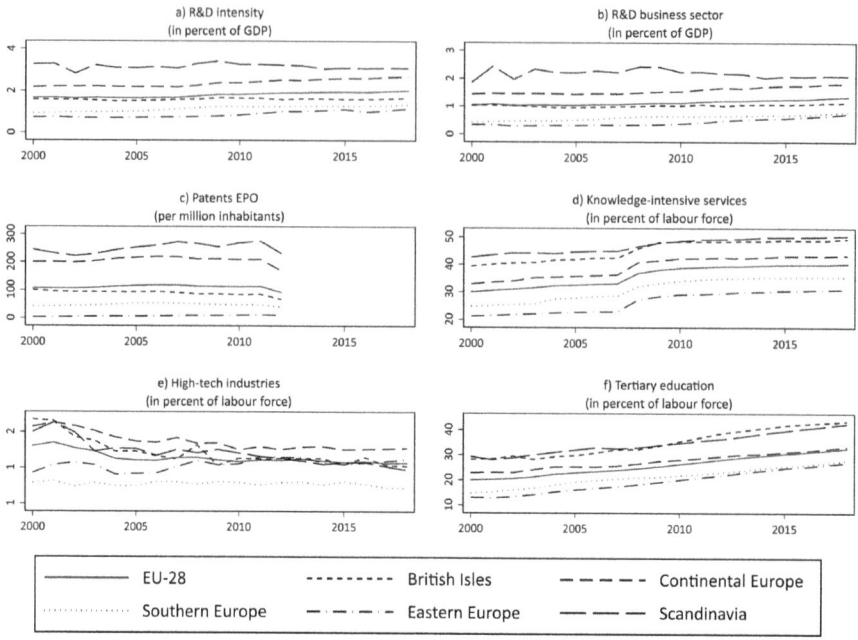

Source: Eurostat; see Appendix 1.

**Fig. 4.4** National determinants of innovativeness (EU-28, Switzerland, Norway; 2000–2018)

European countries have the lowest shares. The United Kingdom and Ireland are mostly between these groups of countries and close to the European mean on these indicators—with the exception of knowledge-intensive services, where the two countries have top scores.

This raises the question of which factors are particularly important for the economic success of regions and thus also contribute to the economic division of Europe into centre and periphery. Is it research and development expenditure and patents, as is often assumed in the debate on innovation and the knowledge society? Or is it the accumulated competencies materialised in industrial structures or knowledge-based services? Or is it the availability and level of education of the labour force and the inclusiveness of the labour market? The question of the relative weight of research and development, knowledge-based economic structures and labour market structures will be discussed below based on panel regressions using European regional data for the period 2000–2018. The dependent variable is the economic performance of the European regions.

The two indicators for the knowledge intensity of the respective regional economies, namely research and development intensity and patent applications to the European Patent Office (EPO), have the expected, significantly positive influence on regional economic performance (Table 4.2, columns 1 and 2). The levels of regional R&D expenditure and patents are thus important causes of the divergent

**Table 4.2** Innovativeness, knowledge-based structures and skills as sources of economic performance (EU-28; 2000–2018)

| GDP (PPS) | (1) | (2) | (3) | (4) | (5) | (6) |
|---|---|---|---|---|---|---|
| Research expenditure (in % of GDP) | 2629.8*** (225.7) | | | | | −72.6 (189.4) |
| Patent applications EPO (per million inhabitants) | | 26.5*** (1.557) | | | | |
| Knowledge-based services (in % labour force) | | | 1037.6*** (36.43) | | | 292.0*** (45.87) |
| High technologies (in % labour force) | | | | 1106.5*** (327.1) | | 247.6 (256.8) |
| Employed persons (15–64 years) (in % population) | | | | | 200.2*** (35.80) | 264.9*** (37.95) |
| High level of education (in % labour force) | | | | | 1168.7*** (29.83) | 972.7*** (43.23) |
| Observations | 2380 | 1500 | 2380 | 2380 | 2380 | 2380 |
| Intraclass correlation | 0.55 | 0.81 | 0.43 | 0.58 | 0.68 | 0.64 |
| $R^2$ | 0.036 | 0.058 | 0.014 | 0.033 | 0.066 | 0.066 |

Source: Own calculations (multilevel regressions) based on Eurostat regional data (NUTS2); dependent variable: regional gross value added (GDP) per inhabitant (adjusted for purchasing power); sources of explanatory variables: Eurostat, tables rd_e_gerdreg, pat_ep_rtot, htec_emp_reg, lfst_r_lfe2en2, lfst_r_lfe2eedu. Regional patent data only available until 2012, therefore not included in the overall model. Constant and dummies for the years included in the model but not shown in table; standard errors in brackets. $^{*}p < 0.05$, ** $p < 0.01$, *** $p < 0.001$

development of the European regions. Furthermore, economic performance also depends on the sectoral structure of the European regions. Both the share of knowledge-intensive services and the employment share of high-tech industries (columns 3 and 4) are correlated with regional economic performance. A high employment rate and a high level of education also have a clear positive influence (column 5). In addition to entrepreneurial and regional innovation strategies, high skill levels and a comprehensive inclusion of employable persons in the labour force are important prerequisites for a high regional economic performance. In the summary model (column 6), the latter two variables and the share of knowledge-based services have a significant impact on economic strength.

In sum: The end of economic convergence in the European Union, and especially in the 15 older member states, might be the result of a spatial concentration of research, development and patenting efforts, of knowledge-intensive services and industries, of highly skilled labour and inclusive labour market structures in the Northern and Continental European regions of the EU. The Southern and Eastern European periphery, on the other hand, is characterised by low R&D expenditure, fewer patents, a less skilled workforce, lower employment rates and more traditional economic structures. However, the two European periphery regions also differ significantly from each other. This will be elaborated in the following section.

## 4.3  Peripheral Trajectories in Southern and Eastern Europe

Initially, it was mentioned that Europe has been characterised by a centre-periphery structure for centuries. The Continental and Northwestern European city belt in the centre of Europe, which has emerged along the old Roman trade routes, has traditionally been characterised by more intensive communication and trade relations, by greater prosperity and by more innovations (Rokkan & Flora, 1999). Complementary to these central regions, peripheral regions have emerged—mainly in Southern and in Central and Eastern Europe. A more detailed insight into the centre-periphery structures in Europe is provided by the economic performance of the European regions—for example, by the question of which regions are above or below the threshold of 75% or 90% of average European economic performance—a threshold that is decisive for access to European Structural Funds. Not all economically weaker European regions (such as Cornwall, parts of Wales, Northern England, Scotland, Northern Ireland, Eastern Germany, Northern and Southern France) are located in Southern, Central and Eastern Europe. Similarly, not all Southern, Eastern and Central European regions can be categorised as peripheral regions. This is especially true for the capital regions in Central, Eastern and Southern Europe, such as Prague, Warsaw, Athens, Bratislava, Rome, Madrid or Lisbon, but also for Northern and Central Italy and Northern Spain. Despite these exceptions, it can be maintained that mostly Southern, Central and Eastern European regions can be considered as peripheral regions due to their lower economic performance. This raises questions about the causes of this peripheral position and the specific potentials for better economic development.

A first observation is that the historical trajectories of Eastern and Southern European countries are similar. After their accession to the European Communities (in Southern Europe mostly in the 1980s, with the exception of founding member Italy, in Central and Eastern Europe since 2004), the countries underwent a rapid process of political and economic modernisation and benefited greatly from membership in the EU and its predecessor organisations. In Sect. 4.1, it has been argued that the dismantling of tariff and non-tariff trade barriers led to rapid economic convergence. Both groups of countries initially converged rapidly in economic terms to the level of the founding states of the EEC—Italy, the Benelux countries, Germany and France. In view of the initially rapid convergence processes, further convergence was also expected in the future. Therefore, before the Great Recession and the eurozone crisis, it would have been inappropriate to describe Italy and Spain, for example, as "peripheral".

Since the collapse of the Eastern Bloc and European reunification, the Central and Eastern European countries on the one hand and the Southern European countries on the other have taken very different trajectories. While a new division of labour emerged between Eastern and Western Europe, the Southern European countries have followed a different path: "emerging industrial regions in Eastern EU sharply differ from the relatively disconnected corporatist peripheries of Southern Europe." (Iammarino et al., 2019, p. 292) While Southern European economies have barely grown in the decade since the beginning of the eurozone crisis in 2010 and have been characterised by very high unemployment and youth unemployment rates, Central and Eastern European countries have grown much faster than other EU countries. Their economic performance has almost reached the Italian and Spanish levels. For example, Czech economic output in 2017 was already higher per capita than in Portugal and Greece.

The reasons for this divergence will be analysed in the following sections. First, three explanations for the different developments in Southern, Central and Eastern Europe are presented (Sect. 4.3.1). These are then reviewed on the basis of European regional data. In particular, regional economic growth and unemployment rates will be used as indicators for the different trajectories (Sect. 4.3.2). The section concludes with a summary (Sect. 4.3.3).

### 4.3.1   Barriers to Modernisation, the Euro and Growth Models. Three Explanations

The different economic and labour market structures and dynamics in Southern and Eastern Europe raise questions about the specificities of the Southern and Eastern European economic trajectories. It is certainly not sufficient to characterise these countries only by their marginal economic position or their lower economic performance (Fig. 4.5a), as the economic, industrial and societal trajectories in Southern and Eastern Europe differ significantly. The different economic and social structures have enabled the respective countries to occupy a special place in the new pan-European division of labour that has emerged since the collapse of the Eastern bloc. This repositioning has continued during the euro and financial market crises since 2007. In the following, three explanations for these different trajectories will be discussed. Five hypotheses are derived from these explanations which focus on the respective financial situation of the countries, their economic and labour market structures, their institutional frameworks and the Europeanisation of the economy.

One explanation for the barriers to development, especially in Southern Europe, incorporates clientelism, corruption and other facets of a "premodern feudal legacy" (Streeck, 2014, p. 150). Streeck (2014) explains "the seemingly ineradicable economic backwardness of the Italian South" (p. 135) by the fact that "Italian government aid was absorbed by local power structures and used to bolster traditional local relations of clientelistic domination." (p. 137) In a similar vein, Featherstone (2011) describes Greece as a pandemonium of state failure: clientelistic policies and corruption, insufficient coordination and efficiency of the administration, low skills,

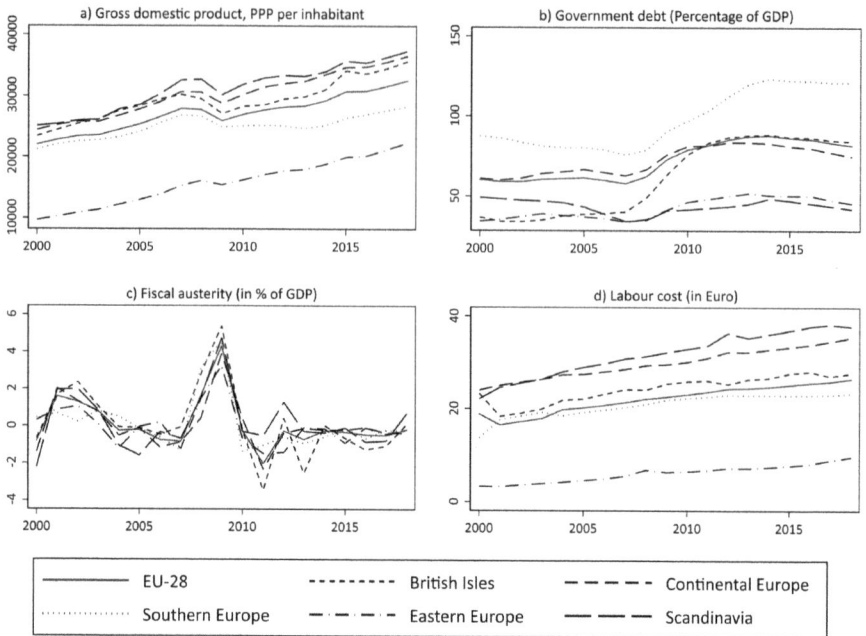

Sources: See Appendix 1, weighted averages.

**Fig. 4.5** Economic performance, debt and labour costs in five European country groups (2000–2018)

legalistic-bureaucratic operation, strong trade union influence in the public sector, lack of transparency and tax evasion, which make structural reforms virtually impossible in the face of "endemic problems of low competitiveness, trade and investment imbalances, and fiscal mismanagement" (Featherstone, 2011, p. 193). Like Streeck, he outlines the EU's limited resources and possibilities for intervention and control. Streeck (2014, p. 145) concludes "that the promise of social and political convergence by means of economic growth, contained in the programme of simultaneous widening and deepening of the European Union, was beyond the bounds of the possible."

However, such an explanation, which ultimately points to administrative and societal barriers to modernisation, is insufficient for comparing Southern and Eastern Europe. Why should the Southern European countries be more clientelistic or traditional than the Central and Eastern European countries, whose economies were dominated for decades by political power, informal relations and networks? In fact, reports on post-socialist oligarchs and the misuse of European agricultural funds do not read very differently from analogous reports on Greece (Gebrekidan et al., 2019). If the chances of rapid economic and social development in Southern Europe are viewed sceptically with reference to clientelistic structures, then the rapid development of the Central and Eastern European countries raises considerable questions, since the conditions for the transition to a market economy in these countries were considerably worse after the collapse of the socialist order (Stark & Bruszt, 2001). The barriers to modernisation in the post-socialist countries were at least as high as in Southern Europe. In view of the rapid economic development even during the euro crisis, however, the initially expected modernisation and development barriers in post-socialist countries largely receded into the background. This explanation will therefore not be pursued further in what follows.

Another explanation for the different economic and labour market structures in Southern and Eastern Europe emphasises the *effects of the financial and euro crises*, the financial situation of the highly indebted Southern European economies (Pérez, 2019) and the associated austerity policies (Blyth, 2013; Moreira et al., 2015; Pavolini et al., 2016). In contrast to the Central and Eastern European countries, most Southern European countries adopted the euro (almost) immediately after the creation of a common European currency zone. One explanation for the disappointing growth of Southern European countries could therefore be the euro and the resulting change in debtor-creditor relations (Pérez, 2019). By joining the European Monetary Union whose third and definitive stage started in 1999, eurozone members relinquished the possibility to devalue their currency. This particularly affected the Southern European countries, as previously they had systematically used currency devaluations rather than institutional control of wage increases as a means of restoring their competitiveness (Iversen et al., 2016). In the first decade after the introduction of the euro, Southern European countries benefited from the abolition of devaluation risks, as this was accompanied by lower interest rates and lower inflation. This led to significant capital inflows into the Southern European countries and thus contributed to the formation of bubbles in the property sector (Spain, but also Ireland), to an increase in public spending (Greece) or to the stabilisation of high government debt (Italy).

These effects of monetary union on financial flows and demand were amplified by the fact that wages and labour costs rose faster in Southern Europe than in Continental and Northern Europe in the first decade after the introduction of the euro (Pérez, 2019, p. 19). This bubble burst with the financial and euro crises. At the same time, the Europeanisation of monetary policy was not accompanied by a Europeanisation of fiscal policy, since the members of the eurozone are not legally obliged to support each other financially (see the non-bailout clause in Article 125 TFEU). This means that the members of the monetary union have to react to asymmetric economic shocks by adjusting their labour costs in real terms, i.e. by lowering employment and wage levels. This can be observed in the Southern European countries, where unit labour costs have fallen significantly since 2010 compared to the EU average (Eurostat, 2020). This has been accompanied by lower economic, employment and income growth (Moreira et al., 2015; Pavolini et al., 2016). Also, five mostly Southern European countries (Greece, Portugal, Cyprus, Spain and Ireland) had to be supported by European and international donors. In return, the countries had to accept strict conditions, especially for the level of public spending, i.e. pursue austerity policies. It *can therefore be assumed that higher public debt and austerity policies go hand in hand with lower growth and a higher unemployment rate (H1)*.

However, after a decade-long phase of slow growth, especially in Italy and Greece, it has become clear that the disappointing development of the Southern European countries cannot be explained only by the euro and its particular architecture (Featherstone, 2011; IMF, 2017; Trantidis, 2016). This is also highlighted by the fact that the accession of Slovakia and the Baltic states to the eurozone did not seem to have slowed down their economic dynamics. The different development paths and labour market situations of Southern European and Central and Eastern European countries must therefore be explained differently.

More decisive, therefore, may have been the specific economic structure and the institutional context that enabled the two groups of countries to pursue different growth paths. The starting point for the analysis of these conditions is the largely successful integration of the Central and Eastern European countries into the European division of labour since the beginning of the 1990s. Accession to the EU (2004, 2007 and 2013) was preceded by the transfer of European regulatory structures, the so-called *acquis communautaire,* to the Central and Eastern European countries (CEE). This made it much easier to recreate economic, political and territorial structures, which had become necessary after the collapse of the socialist economy, and created legal certainty for investors, customers and suppliers. This, and the subsequent accession to the EU, was a central prerequisite for integration into the common market and the customs union. It was only in this context that the lower labour costs in Central and Eastern Europe (Fig. 4.5d) were able to contribute to a reindustrialisation of the CEE countries, even though labour costs have risen considerably after their accession to the EU. On the other hand—and this explains the differences to the Southern European trajectory—the special economic and institutional structures of the Central and Eastern European countries have also proved to be a prerequisite for successful integration into the European division of labour. This enabled them to compete successfully in the European value-added chains and to occupy a place which was then no longer available to Southern European companies and regions.

In the search for the causes of the different economic and social trajectories and labour market structures in Eastern and Southern Europe, analyses of different European growth models can be used as a starting point. In comparative political economy in recent years, distinguishing between different growth models in Europe has been suggested (Hall, 2014, 2018; Iversen et al., 2016). A distinction has been made between the export-oriented growth models of Continental and Northern European countries and the demand-oriented growth models of Southern European countries. In what follows, this approach will be used to explain the different trajectories in Southern and Eastern Europe. The corresponding operationalisation is based on the different economic structures, institutions and labour market structures in the two country groups.

While most studies taking a growth model approach focus on Southern Europe, Hall (2018) also addresses the specific characteristics of the CEE countries and characterises them as export-oriented liberal market economies. He expects the CEE countries to outperform Southern Europe due to their lower production costs. But the group of CEE countries is not homogeneous. Bohle (2018, p. 239) distinguishes between "a dependent export-driven [model] in the Visegrád countries and a dependent debt-driven [model] in the Baltic States". The Visegrád countries have successfully integrated themselves into Western European value chains and thus taken on tasks that would otherwise have been performed in Southern Europe or in non-European low-wage countries (Hall, 2018, p. 18). Four different growth models in Europe *can therefore be expected: while the central Continental European core regions focus on knowledge-based manufacturing and development processes and the urban, especially capital city regions in Europe concentrate on advanced, knowledge-based services, the Central and Eastern European countries specialise on industrial activities, while the central importance of internal demand in the Southern European countries is accompanied by a higher importance of personal services (H2a). Thus, in Central and Eastern Europe strong economic growth and declining unemployment rates can be expected, in contrast to a less positive economic and employment performance in Southern Europe (H2b).*

Furthermore, the different *educational structure of the population* might have played a role in the industrial specialisation of the Central and Eastern European countries, as the share of the population with a low level of education is significantly lower in the Central and Eastern European countries than in the Southern European countries (Fig. 4.6c). It is *to be expected that lower skill levels of workers are associated with lower economic growth and higher unemployment (H3).*

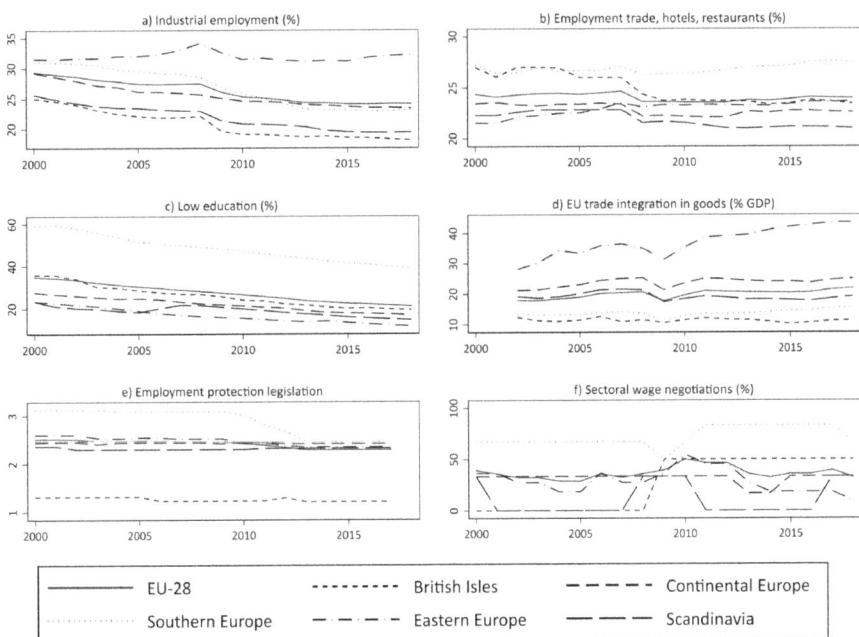

Sources: See Appendix 1, weighted averages. Industrial and service employment (as % of total employment; Eurostat lfsa_egan2); low education (as % of population aged 25-64; Eurostat edat_lfse_04); trade integration: Exports from and imports to other EU-28 countries divided by 2 and GDP; Eurostat [ext_lt_intratrd]; strictness of employment protection (in % of all countries on a scale of 0-6): OECD Employment Protection Database; industry-wide wage bargaining (partly combined with company bargaining; in % of all countries), i.e. categories 2 and 3 of Visser (2019, variable Coord).

**Fig. 4.6** Economic structure and institutions in five European country groups (2000–2018)

The institutional contexts of the respective labour markets also differ (Voßemer et al., 2018). In particular, employment protection legislation and the coordination of collective bargaining vary. The importance of strict employment protection rules was regarded as the core of the European employment situation in the debate on so-called Eurosclerosis (Siebert, 1997, p. 49). The so-called unified theory described the stricter employment protection rules in Europe in comparison with the USA as the cause of the higher unemployment rate, also compared with the USA (Blau & Kahn, 2002), since such rules make not only dismissals but also hiring more difficult. These rules protect above all male breadwinners at the expense of young people and women. Empirically, this is associated with greater segmentation of labour markets, but not with higher unemployment (Nickell, 1997).

Another pillar of Eurosclerotic labour markets was supposed to be the coordination of collective bargaining. Calmfors and Driffill (1988) argue that coordination at the company and national level in particular leads to wages increases in line with productivity increases, thus avoiding a rise in unemployment. While in the export-oriented countries of Northern and Continental Europe nominal wage increases usually take productivity increases into account and thus do not jeopardise the competitiveness of the export-oriented industrial branches, in Southern Europe such a coordination of wage increases was not a priority (Höpner & Lutter, 2018) due to the primacy of domestic demand and the possibility of currency devaluation prior to the introduction of the euro. In view of the conflictual industrial relations, such a coordination was also only possible to a limited extent. It can therefore be expected that stricter employment protection legislation and wage coordination especially at the sectoral level will be accompanied by higher unemployment rates. *This pattern is most likely to occur in Southern Europe, whereas in Central and Eastern Europe, coordination of wage increases at the company level will be more important (H4).* Effects on economic growth cannot be predicted.

Finally, it will be examined whether the core areas of the European integration process—the internal market and monetary union—have an influence on economic performance and the level of unemployment. It can be assumed that *higher economic integration (measured by the share of imports and exports from other EU countries in total value added) and monetary union have a positive impact on economic growth and the labour market (H5).*

### 4.3.2  Debt, Labour Market and Economic Structures and Institutions. Determinants of Peripheral Trajectories in Europe

These five hypotheses are tested below on the basis of data provided by Eurostat and the OECD. These data refer to nations and regions and are thus aggregated and not microdata. They generally refer to the period 2000–2018 and thus cover the boom phase until 2007, the financial market and euro crises and the subsequent years in which the economies of Northern, Eastern and Continental Europe performed well and the liberal and Mediterranean countries gradually overcame the previous crises. Where possible, all data for the 28 countries that were part of the EU until Brexit will be used. Not all the required data for Norway and Switzerland are available. The aim is to work out the specific features of the Central and Eastern European and Southern European countries, also in contrast to other countries with different growth models, economic structures and institutions, and thus to be able to test the previously developed hypotheses.

Figure 4.5 shows the economic and financial contexts for the five European country groups mentioned above. In Southern Europe, not only the purchasing power-adjusted economic output per inhabitant (Fig. 4.5a), but also government debt is significantly higher than in the Central and Eastern European countries (Fig. 4.5b). However, given the higher deficit levels in Southern European countries compared to other groups of countries, no particularly severe austerity policies could be observed in Southern Europe (Fig. 4.5c)—in contrast to the expectations of Moreira et al. (2015) and Pavolini et al. (2016). The high unemployment rate in Southern Europe (Fig. 4.5b) cannot therefore be explained by austerity policies.

In Fig. 4.5d, the very low labour costs in the Central and Eastern European countries also stand out in comparison to Southern Europe (2017: €9 compared to €23 per hour). This explains the particular vulnerability of Southern European countries to asymmetric shocks, but also the impossibility of pursuing a path of economic specialisation based on low labour costs.

Figure 4.6 shows the economic structural and institutional contexts for the five country groups considered. The share of employees in *industry* (which is essentially complementary to the share of service employment) is significantly higher in Central and Eastern Europe than in all other European country groups. It has been consistently above 30% of all employees, while in Southern Europe it has fallen from 31% (2000) to 23% (2018) (Fig. 4.6a). This indicates the rapid deindustrialisation in Southern Europe during the financial and euro crises.

In Southern Europe, on the other hand, the share of *employees in the wholesale and retail trade, hotels and restaurants*, i.e. in the tourism-relevant sectors, remains largely stable. The share of these industries at the end of the period under consideration is far higher in Southern Europe than in all other country groups (Fig. 4.6b). Although Germany and the UK (measured by absolute employment figures; cf. Eurostat, 2019b) are still the largest providers of tourism services, this points to a division of labour between Eastern and Southern Europe: while many Central European locations have been integrated into European-wide and global industrial value chains, many Southern European regions specialise in tourism, especially in Greece, Cyprus, Malta and Spain. H2a can thus be seen as confirmed.

The share of *low-skilled persons* (Fig. 4.6c) measures the share of the population aged 25–64 with pre-primary, primary and secondary education. In Southern Europe this share is above the European average and in Central and Eastern Europe below the European average. In Southern Europe this can be explained by the high importance of agriculture and simple personal services, while the low share in Central and Eastern Europe can perhaps be interpreted as the legacy of socialist educational efforts and industrial specialisation. The share of medium education in Southern Europe is also much lower than in Central and Eastern Europe. Southern European countries provide more academic training for young people—without, however, having corresponding skill-intensive economic structures (with the exception of the public sector). If it can be confirmed that higher regional educational levels are associated with lower unemployment rates, then the different educational structures in Southern and Eastern Europe just reported would explain the regime-specific differences in unemployment rates thus supporting H3.

The high trade integration of the Central and Eastern European countries into the EU-28 is remarkable (Fig. 4.6d). The high share of intra-EU imports and exports suggests that these countries have benefited greatly from economic integration into the single European market.

With regard to *employment protection* (Fig. 4.6e), there are no (longer) significant differences between the European country groups—with the exception of the more liberal British and Irish regulations. While *collective bargaining* in Greece, Italy, Spain and Portugal was initially coordinated at the national level—sometimes in conjunction with sector-wide coordination (Visser, 2019)—it has since been coordinated mainly at the sectoral level (Fig. 4.6f). In Central and Eastern Europe, on the other hand, the company level plays a central or important role complementary to the sectoral level in most countries—with the exception of Slovenia and Slovakia (Visser, 2019). If it can be shown that a correlation exists between the degree of coordination of collective bargaining and the regional unemployment rate, this could be taken as a confirmation of H4.

On the basis of the previously discussed explanatory approaches, various multivariate panel regressions are now used to examine if the financial, economic structural, educational and institutional contexts just presented can explain regional growth (Table 4.3) and regional unemployment (Table 4.4) in the EU-28. The first column of each table shows that *higher government debt*—as predicted by classical economics due to the crowding out of private investment by government debt—is associated with lower growth and higher unemployment. *Austerity policies* reduce economic growth (Table 4.3, columns 1 and 5). When interpreting this, it should be borne in mind that a positive value of the austerity indicator means a more generous fiscal policy, i.e. public deficits minus interest payments are higher. One explanation for this could be that cuts in public spending reduce economic performance by almost the same amount (Górnicka et al., 2018). However, austerity policies have no significant impact on regional unemployment (Table 4.4, columns 1 and 6). This result could indicate that the high unemployment rates in Southern Europe are not the result of pronounced austerity policies. An austerity-induced curbing of public deficits in Southern Europe cannot be discerned. However, even the higher level of public debt during the euro and financial crises was not enough to avoid the decline in economic growth and the rise in unemployment in Southern Europe. In Central and Eastern Europe, on the other hand, low debt favours higher growth and falling unemployment rates. H1 can thus only be partially confirmed: Higher government debt, but not the austerity policies actually pursued, are associated with lower growth and higher unemployment rates.

**Table 4.3** Determinants of regional economic growth in the EU-28 (2003–2018)

| | Public budget (1) | Economic structure (2) | Labour market (3) | Europeanisation (4) | Total (5) |
|---|---|---|---|---|---|
| Public debt (in % of GDP) | −0.023*** (0.0034) | | | | −0.017*** (0.0038) |
| Austerity (in % of GDP) | 0.089** (0.029) | | | | 0.10*** (0.028) |
| Industry & construction (in % of all employees) | | 0.029*** (0.0080) | | | 0.020* (0.0080) |
| Employees in trade, restaurants, hotels (in % of all employees) | | 0.072*** (0.014) | | | 0.075*** (0.013) |
| Low-skilled (as % of population 25–64 years) | | | −0.050*** (0.0073) | | −0.047*** (0.0074) |
| Trade integration with EU countries (% of GDP) | | | | 0.053*** (0.0095) | 0.036** (0.011) |
| Member eurozone | | | | −1.17*** (0.29) | −0.72* (0.34) |
| Observations | 3326 | 3326 | 3326 | 3326 | 3326 |
| Intraclass correlation | 0.088 | 0.18 | 0.14 | 0.096 | 0.15 |
| Pseudo-$R^2$ | 0.041 | 0.029 | 0.031 | 0.029 | 0.045 |

Dependent variable: real growth in regional value added (Eurostat, table [nama_10r_2gvagr]); for explanatory variables see Appendix 1 and Fig. 4.6. Trade integration and austerity policy indicators are lagged by 1 year. Constant and year dummies included in the models but not shown. The variables in the second and third columns refer to the regional level and the variables in the first and fourth columns refer to the national level. Hierarchical linear models for 274 regions in 28 countries. Constants and year dummies included in the model but not shown here. Standard errors in parentheses. * $p < 0.05$, ** $p < 0.01$, *** $p < 0.001$

The different economic structures are also major determinants of the different growth and unemployment rates (column 2): Higher shares of *employees in industry* and *trade, restaurants and hotels* are associated with higher economic growth and—in the case of industrial employees—with lower regional unemployment rates. As the share of industrial employees is significantly higher in Central and Eastern European countries than in Southern Europe, hypothesis H2b predicts higher growth and lower unemployment in Central and Eastern Europe. The higher share of industrial employees reflects the successful integration of the Central and Eastern European economies into European-wide and global value chains (Bohle, 2018). According to Hall (2018), this was made possible by lower labour costs, weaker trade unions, low corporate taxes, low social spending and flexible labour markets.

**Table 4.4** Determinants of regional unemployment in the EU (2003–2018)

| | Debt | Economic structure | Labour market | Institutions | Europeanisation | Total |
|---|---|---|---|---|---|---|
| | (1) | (2) | (3) | (4) | (5) | (6) |
| Public debt (in % of GDP) | 0.18*** (0.0063) | | | | | 0.13*** (0.0074) |
| Austerity (in % of GDP) | 0.032 (0.040) | | | | | 0.063 (0.036) |
| Industry & construction (in % of all employees) | | −0.22*** (0.013) | | | | −0.18*** (0.011) |
| Employees in trade, restaurants, hotels (in % of all employees) | | −0.041 (0.022) | | | | −0.035 (0.018) |
| Low-skilled (as % of population 25–64 years) | | | 0.10*** (0.013) | | | 0.20*** (0.012) |
| Strictness employment protection legislation | | | | −8.16*** (0.51) | | −4.82*** (0.55) |
| Intermediary coordination of wage bargaining | | | | 3.52*** (0.34) | | 1.96*** (0.31) |
| Trade integration with EU countries (in % of GDP) | | | | | −0.24*** (0.025) | −0.17*** (0.024) |
| Member eurozone | | | | | −1.55* (0.77) | −1.91** (0.69) |
| Observations | 3179 | 3179 | 3179 | 3179 | 3179 | 3179 |
| Intraclass correlation | 0.70 | 0.47 | 0.37 | 0.67 | 0.55 | 0.86 |
| Pseudo-$R^2$ | 0.59 | 0.53 | 0.49 | 0.55 | 0.50 | 0.67 |

Dependent variable: Regional unemployment: (Eurostat, table [lfst_r_lfu3rt]; explanatory variables see Appendix 1 and Fig. 4.6. Constant and year dummies included in the models but not shown. The variables in the second and third columns refer to the regional level and the variables in the first and fourth columns refer to the national level. Hierarchical linear models for 272 regions in 26 countries, since the strictness of employment protection in Malta and Cyprus could not be determined. Standard errors in parentheses. * $p < 0.05$, ** $p < 0.01$, *** $p < 0.001$

The lower share of industry in Southern Europe is partly compensated by a more important role of hotels, restaurants and wholesale and retail trade. This reflects the specialisation of many Southern European regions on tourism. However, the increasing attractiveness of non-European destinations, the effects of climate change and the pandemic since 2020 also highlight the risks of this strategy.

A higher share of *low-skilled people* is associated with lower economic performance and higher unemployment (Tables 4.3 and 4.4, column 3). This confirms H3 which expected a positive relationship between lower educational levels, lower value added and higher unemployment. The higher share of low-skilled persons in Southern Europe (2017: 40% compared to 12% in Central and Eastern Europe and 22% in the EU-28) thus is linked to higher unemployment rates. In Central and Eastern Europe, on the other hand, the share of employable persons with a medium education is significantly higher than in Southern Europe and the EU as a whole (2018: 61% compared to 34% and 46% respectively). This again reflects the industrial specialisation of these countries. A higher share of low-skilled persons is related to higher regional unemployment rates.

In contrast to other analyses of European labour markets (Boeri & Garibaldi, 2009; Siebert, 1997), *stricter employment protection* is not associated with higher but with lower unemployment (Table 4.4, column 4). One reason for this strong negative correlation is that some of the countries that have particularly strict employment protection (in addition to Portugal and Italy, also the Czech Republic, Germany, Latvia, Slovenia and Sweden) have also grown rapidly during the financial and eurozone crises. The labour markets in these countries are characterised by low unemployment rates.

The positive correlation between regional unemployment and an *intermediary coordination of wage bargaining* confirms Calmfors and Driffill's (1988) thesis: a high degree of coordination at the industry level (partly in conjunction with the company level) is associated with higher unemployment, as less consideration is given to the economic consequences of high wages in industry-wide wage negotiations than in negotiations at the company or national level (Table 4.4, column 4). The lower fragmentation of collective bargaining systems in Southern Europe compared to Central and Eastern European countries may thus also have contributed to higher unemployment. As expected by H4, wage bargaining at the sectoral level thus is associated with higher unemployment, especially in Southern Europe.

In the next step (Table 4.3, column 4), the influence of economic and monetary Europeanisation was examined. It turns out that closer economic integration is associated with higher economic growth, while monetary integration had a negative effect during the euro crisis. This effect is also found in the summary model (Table 4.3, column 5). Consistent with H5, closer economic integration is associated with lower unemployment (Table 4.4, column 5). Eurozone membership is also associated with lower unemployment. However, this effect is only significant at the 5%-level in the summary model (Table 4.4, column 6).

The two full models (Tables 4.3, column 5; 4.4, column 6) demonstrate that the previously significant factors retain their influence even after the inclusion of all the other variables. The direction and even the magnitude of the influence remain largely the same. Only the negative influence of strict employment protection becomes significantly smaller.

What does this mean for the Central, Eastern and Southern European countries and regions? It has been established that a lower share of industrial employees and a higher share of low-skilled person have a decisive impact on explaining lower growth and higher unemployment rates in Southern Europe, while the Central and Eastern European labour markets benefit from lower indebtedness, a stronger industrial sector and a more decentralised collective bargaining system. Furthermore, it has been shown that the economic and monetary integration of Europe has led to a Europeanisation of the determinants of economic growth and unemployment.

### 4.3.3  Two Trajectories

The aim of this section is to explain the different economic and labour market developments in Southern, Central and Eastern Europe and to review which effects economic and monetary Europeanisation have on economic growth and unemployment. Several explanations for the different economic and employment patterns have been discussed: Higher levels of debt and deficit in Southern Europe and the EU-wide debt and deficit rules might have given rise to austerity policy which have hit the Mediterranean labour markets particularly hard; barriers to modernisation and a higher rigidity of Southern European labour markets, or the existence of different growth models in Southern and Western Europe, in particular the differences between more demand-oriented economies in Southern Europe and more export-oriented market economies in Western and Eastern Europe.

It can be concluded that austerity policies are associated with lower economic growth. However, a clear increase in unemployment as a result of more restrictive government spending cannot be ascertained. In view of the higher deficits in Southern Europe, it is hardly possible to speak of austerity. High government debt, on the other hand, clearly has negative effects on the labour market and economic growth. Furthermore, it has been shown that a smaller industrial sector, a lower educational level and collective bargaining at the sectoral level are associated with lower growth rates and higher regional unemployment. This mainly reflects the situation in Southern Europe. The higher Southern European share of employees in wholesale and retail trade, restaurants and hotels and thus in the tourism industry is associated with higher growth, but not with lower unemployment. A classical explanation for higher regional unemployment could not be confirmed: stronger employment protection is even associated with lower unemployment—a surprising result which merits further analysis. These results can be interpreted as evidence of the limits of the Southern European growth model and the failure of an employment regime that is associated with a strong exclusion of women, migrants, the unskilled and young people from the labour market. In contrast, after the long and painful post-socialist transformation processes, the population in Central and Eastern European countries is increasingly benefiting from integration into the European market and into European and global industrial value chains. A higher share of skilled labour, but also weaker trade unions, lower wage costs and more decentralised collective bargaining systems in many countries have favoured rising economic performance and falling unemployment rates even during the financial market and euro crises. In the overall context of this book, it is also important to note that economic and monetary Europeanisation has a significant impact on economic growth and unemployment.

Overall, the analyses presented here point to two different economic and social trajectories in the Eastern and Southern European periphery. In Central and Eastern Europe, weak trade unions, high and rising shares of industrial workers, a high proportion of medium-skilled workers, relatively low wage costs (also as a result of low social expenditure), weak trade unions and considerable inflows of foreign direct investment and EU funds (Bohle, 2018) facilitated a peripheral industrialisation. Declining unemployment and the lower share of unemployed marginal groups in the labour market indicate the successful implementation of a strategy of dependent industrial development. In contrast, such a path was not open to most Southern European countries and regions. Higher wages and labour costs, stronger trade unions, more strongly regulated labour markets and a high proportion of a low-skilled working-age population have tended to hamper industrial development paths in Southern Europe. The economic structures and the high technological skills of enterprises in Catalonia, the Basque Country, Piedmont or Lombardy are not the norm, as a low educational level and low R&D spending make it difficult to concentrate on knowledge-based industries. As a result, many Southern European regions have opted for a different approach based more on services and a dualisation of the economy and labour markets. Prototypically, this can be illustrated on the one hand by the protected working conditions and relatively high wage and unit labour costs, especially in the public sector (Broschinski et al., 2018), and on the other hand by the atypical and partly seasonal activities in tourism, the retail trade or other personal services. Unemployment and the persistent segmentation of Mediterranean labour markets (Barbieri & Cutuli, 2016) thus reflect not only the eurozone area's deficient institutionalisation, traditional barriers to modernisation or the legacy of rigid labour protection legislation, but also the difficulties in finding a new role in a European and global division of labour given low skills and low R&D expenditure. Decades of stagnating labour productivity in Italy (Calligaris et al., 2016) and high unemployment rates in Spain and Greece in particular point to the limits of the Mediterranean growth model. It can be assumed that the Southern European barriers to development can only be overcome through higher research and development expenditure, better vocational qualifications and better technology transfer. Rising labour costs might also confront Eastern European countries with similar challenges in the near future.

## 4.4   Summary and Outlook

It has been shown that the almost automatic convergence of economic performance in the EU has reached its limits. The economic differences between European regions are no longer as huge as they were in the 1980s, when many poorer Southern European countries joined the European Communities, or in the 2000s, when ten Central and Eastern European countries joined the EU (Poland, Hungary, the Czech Republic, Slovakia, Slovenia, Estonia, Latvia, Lithuania, Romania, Bulgaria, followed by Croatia in 2013). Unlike in the past, less developed regions can no longer count on an almost automatic alignment with Western high-income countries. On the contrary. The territorial agglomeration of scientific, technological and organisational competences in the EU is causing economic disparities to increase again, especially between the 15 "old" EU member states. This also has considerable consequences for the social cohesion of the EU: unlike in the first decades of European integration, in which convergence in Europe was sought primarily through market integration as a result of the dismantling of trade barriers, poorer households and regions cannot count on an automatic improvement in their living and income conditions through economic integration. The economic benefits of cross-border trade are no longer sufficient to counter the concentration of technological knowledge, established businesses, skilled labour, efficient infrastructure and inclusive labour markets in the core Continental and Northern European regions of the EU. The hope of counteracting this concentration of technological and economic competences through European agricultural, regional and structural policies (Bachtler et al., 2016) has always been limited (Boldrin & Canova, 2001; Puga, 2002). A *double dualisation* can therefore be observed in Europe, not only in the labour market, but also in terms of economic performance and innovativeness. In technological, scientific and economic terms, there is not only a split between knowledge-based, inclusive service metropolises and less developed agricultural, industrial or tourist regions, but also a Europe-wide split between central Northern and Continental European technology and service regions and peripheral, predominantly Southern and Central European regions. This is also indicated by the higher unemployment rates in Southern, Central and Eastern Europe. However, the strategy of *peripheral industrialisation* chosen in Central and Eastern Europe has until now been very successful and since the noughties has led to a rapid reduction in the high unemployment rates that accompanied the post-socialist transformation processes. Southern Europe, on the other hand, was disproportionately affected by intensified global competition, especially following China's accession to the World Trade Organization (2001), by the euro crisis and more recently by the Covid-19 pandemic. The causes of these crises were different in each case—a specialisation in simpler, design-intensive industrial goods as the basis for flexible specialisation (Piore & Sabel, 1984), high government debt and property bubbles, and a specialisation in personal services, especially in tourism (Eurostat, 2019b). The consequences, however, were always similar: Above-average slumps in economic output, high unemployment rates and the elimination of simpler, either industrial or tertiary activities.

The economic dynamics described so far offer only a limited basis for assessing individual income and living conditions, since regional averages cannot be used to draw conclusions about individual living conditions. Therefore, in the following, the inequality of labour market opportunities, wages and incomes within and between the EU countries are examined on the basis of microdata.

# References

Asheim, B., & Isaksen, A. (2002). Regional innovation systems: The integration of local 'sticky'and global 'ubiquitous' knowledge. *Journal of Technology Transfer, 27*(1), 77–86.

Bachtler, J., Mendez, C., & Wishlade, F. (2016). *EU cohesion policy and European integration: The dynamics of EU budget and regional policy reform*. Taylor & Francis.

Barbieri, P., & Cutuli, G. (2016). Employment protection legislation, labour market dualism, and inequality in Europe. *European Sociological Review, 32*(4), 501–516. https://doi.org/10.1093/esr/jcv058

Barro, R. J., & Sala-i-Martin, X. (1991). Convergence across states and regions. *Brookings Papers on Economic Activity, 1*, 107–182.

Barro, R. J., & Sala-i-Martin, X. (1992). Convergence. *Journal of Political Economy, 100*(2), 223–251.

Beckfield, J. (2019). *Unequal Europe: Regional integration and the rise of European inequality*. Oxford University Press.

Blau, F. D., & Kahn, L. M. (2002). *At home and abroad: U.S. labor-market performance in international perspective*. Russell Sage Foundation.

Blyth, M. (2013). *Austerity: The history of a dangerous idea*. Oxford University Press.

Boeri, T., & Garibaldi, P. (2009). Beyond eurosclerosis. *Economic Policy, 24*(59), 409–461. https://doi.org/10.1111/j.1468-0327.2009.00225.x

Bohle, D. (2018). European integration, capitalist diversity and crises trajectories on Europe's eastern periphery. *New Political Economy, 23*(2), 239–253. https://doi.org/10.1080/13563467.2017.1370448

Boldrin, M., & Canova, F. (2001). Inequality and convergence in Europe's regions: Reconsidering European regional policies. *Economic Policy, 16*(32), 206–253.

Borrás, S. (2004). System of innovation theory and the European Union. *Science and Public Policy, 31*(6), 425–433.

Broschinski, S., Preunkert, J., & Heidenreich, M. (2018). Lohnentwicklungen im öffentlichen Sektor. *Österreichische Zeitschrift Für Soziologie, 43*(S1), 117–145. https://doi.org/10.1007/s11614-018-0300-3

Calligaris, S., Del Gatto, M., Hassan, F., Ottaviano, G. I. P., & Schivardi, F. (2016). *Italy's productivity conundrum: A study on resource misallocation in Italy* (European economy–discussion papers no. 030).

Calmfors, L., & Driffill, J. (1988). Bargaining structure, corporatism and macroeconomic performance. *Economic Policy, 3*(6), 13–61.

Cooke, P., Asheim, B., Boschma, R., Martin, R., Schwartz, D., & Tödtling, F. (Eds.). (2011). *Handbook of regional innovation and growth*. Edward Elgar. https://doi.org/10.4337/9780857931504

Dijkstra, L., Poelman, H., & Rodríguez-Pose, A. (2020). The geography of EU discontent. *Regional Studies, 54*(6), 737–753. https://doi.org/10.1080/00343404.2019.1654603

Eurostat. (2019a). *Eurostat regional yearbook: 2019 edition (2019 edition). Statistical books: Vol. 2019*. Publication Office of the EU. Retrieved from https://ec.europa.eu/eurostat/de/publications/statistical-books/regional-yearbook

Eurostat. (2019b). *Tourism industries–employment*. Retrieved from https://ec.europa.eu/eurostat/statistics-explained

Eurostat. (2020). *Labour cost levels by NACE Rev. 2 activity (lc_lci_lev): [lc_lci_lev]*. Retrieved from https://appsso.eurostat.ec.europa.eu/nui/show.do?dataset=lc_lci_lev

Featherstone, K. (2011). The Greek sovereign debt crisis and EMU: A failing state in a skewed regime. *Journal of Common Market Studies, 49*(2), 193–217. https://doi.org/10.1111/j.1468-5965.2010.02139.x

Fligstein, N., & Stone Sweet, A. (2002). Constructing polities and markets: An institutionalist account of European integration. *American Journal of Sociology, 107*(5), 1206–1243.

Gebrekidan, S., Apuzzo, M., & Novak, B. (2019, November 4). The money farmers: How oligarchs and populists milk the E.U. for millions. *New York Times*, www.nytimes.com/2019/11/03/world/europe/eu-farm-subsidy-hungary.html.

Górnicka, L., Kamps, C., Koester, G., & Leiner-Killinger, N. (2018). *Learning about fiscal multipliers during the European sovereign debt crisis: Evidence from a quasi-natural experiment. Working paper series/European Central Bank: No 2154 (may 2018)*. European Central Bank. https://doi.org/10.2866/957767

Hall, P. A. (2014). Varieties of capitalism and the euro crisis. *West European Politics, 37*(6), 1223–1243.

Hall, P. A. (2018). Varieties of capitalism in light of the euro crisis. *Journal of European Public Policy, 25*(1), 7–30. https://doi.org/10.1080/13501763.2017.1310278

Heidenreich, M. (1998). The changing system of European cities and regions. *European Planning Studies, 6*(3), 315–332. https://doi.org/10.1080/09654319808720464

Heidenreich, M. (2019). Wirtschaftliche und soziale Disparitäten in der EU: Zwischen Konvergenz und Agglomeration. *Informationen Zur Raumentwicklung., 3*, 80–89.

Heidenreich, M., & Baur, N. (2015). Locations of corporate headquarters in Europe. Between inertia and co-evolution. In S. M. Lundan (Ed.), *Transnational corporations and transnational governance (Vol. 38, pp. 177–208)*. Palgrave Macmillan. https://doi.org/10.1057/9781137467690_7

Heidenreich, M., & Wunder, C. (2008). Patterns of regional inequality in the enlarged Europe. *European Sociological Review, 24*(1), 19–36.

Hobolt, S. B., & de Vries, C. (2016). Turning against the union? The impact of the crisis on the Eurosceptic vote in the 2014 European Parliament elections. *Electoral Studies, 44*, 504–514. https://doi.org/10.1016/j.electstud.2016.05.006

Höpner, M., & Lutter, M. (2018). The diversity of wage regimes: Why the Eurozone is too heterogeneous for the euro. *European Political Science Review, 10*(01), 71–96. https://doi.org/10.1017/S1755773916000217

Iammarino, S., Rodriguez-Pose, A., & Storper, M. (2019). Regional inequality in Europe: Evidence, theory and policy implications. *Journal of Economic Geography, 19*(2), 273–298. https://doi.org/10.1093/jeg/lby021

IMF. (2017). *Greece: Ex-post evaluation of exceptional access under the 2012 extended arrangement-press release; staff report; and statement by the executive director for Greece. IMF staff country reports*. International Monetary Fund.

Iversen, T., Soskice, D., & Hope, D. (2016). The Eurozone and political economic institutions. *Annual Review of Political Science, 19*, 163–185.

Kaiser, R., & Prange, H. (2005). Missing the Lisbon target? Multi-level innovation and EU policy coordination. *Journal of Public Policy, 25*(2), 241–263.

Krugman, P. (1991). *Geography and trade. Gaston Eyskens lecture series*. MIT Press.

Midelfart-Knarvik, K. H., Overman, H. G., Redding, S., & Venables, A. J. (2002). Integration and industrial specialisation in the European Union. *Revue Économique, 53*(3), 469–481. https://doi.org/10.2307/3502978

Moreira, A., Alonso Dominguez, Á., Antunes, C., Karamessini, M., Raitano, M., & Glatzer, M. (2015). Austerity-driven labour market reforms in southern Europe: Eroding the security of labour market insiders. *European Journal of Social Security, 17*, 202–225.

Nickell, S. (1997). Unemployment and labor market rigidities: Europe versus North America. *Journal of Economic Perspectives, 11*(3), 55–74. https://doi.org/10.1257/jep.11.3.55

Patel, P., & Pavitt, K. (1991). Large firms in the production of the world's technology: An important case of "non-globalisation". *Journal of International Business Studies, 22*(1), 1–21.

Pavolini, E., León, M., Guillén, A. M., & Ascoli, U. (2016). From austerity to permanent strain? The European Union and welfare state reform in Italy and Spain. In C. de La Porte & E. Heins (Eds.), *The sovereign debt crisis, the EU and welfare state reform* (pp. 131–157). Palgrave Macmillan. https://doi.org/10.1057/978-1-137-58179-2_6

Pérez, S. A. (2019). A Europe of creditor and debtor states: Explaining the north/south divide in the Eurozone. *West European Politics, 15*(1), 1–26. https://doi.org/10.1080/01402382.2019.1573403

Piore, M. J., & Sabel, C. F. (1984). *The second industrial divide: Possibilities for prosperity*. Basic Books.

Puga, D. (2002). European regional policies in light of recent location theories. *Journal of Economic Geography, 2*(4), 373–406. https://doi.org/10.1093/jeg/2.4.373

Rodríguez-Pose, A. (2018). The revenge of the places that don't matter (and what to do about it). *Cambridge Journal of Regions, Economy and Society, 11*(1), 189–209. https://doi.org/10.1093/cjres/rsx024

Rokkan, S., & Flora, P. (Eds.). (1999). *Comparative European politics. State formation, nation-building, and mass politics in Europe: The theory of stein rokkan; based on his collected works (1. Publ)*. Oxford University Press.

Siebert, H. (1997). Labor market rigidities: At the root of unemployment in Europe. *Journal of Economic Perspectives, 11*(3), 37–54. https://doi.org/10.2307/2138183

Stark, D., & Bruszt, L. (2001). *Postsocialist pathways: Transforming politics and property in east Central Europe (Repr). Cambridge studies in comparative politics*. Cambridge University Press.

Streeck, W. (2014). *Buying time: The delayed crisis of democratic capitalism*. Verso.

Trantidis, A. (2016). *Clientelism and economic policy: Greece and the crisis. Routledge advances in European politics* (Vol. 126). Routledge.

Vezzani, A., Gkotsis, P., Hernández, H., & Moncada-Paternò-Castello, P. (2019). *Technological innovation activities in the EU: A new perspective* (INDUSTRIAL R&I–JRC Policy Insights No. JRC116219). Sevilla. Retrieved from European Commission, JRC-Seville website: www.ec.europa.eu/jrc/en/publications

Visser, J. (2019). *ICTWSS data base. version 6.1*. Amsterdam. Retrieved from Amsterdam Institute for Advanced Labour Studies AIAS website: http://uva-aias.net/en/ictwss

Voßemer, J., Gebel, M., Täht, K., Unt, M., Högberg, B., & Strandh, M. (2018). The effects of unemployment and insecure jobs on Well-being and health: The moderating role of labor market policies. *Social Indicators Research, 138*(3), 1229–1257.

# Chapter 5
# European Labour Markets between Segmentation and Activation

**Abstract** This chapter analyses the double dualisation of European labour markets. They are characterised by divisions between labour market insiders and outsiders on the one hand and between more inclusive and more exclusive employment regimes on the other hand. Scandinavia and the United Kingdom are characterised by higher activity and employment rates and thus by more inclusive employment regimes, while the employment regimes in Southern, Central and Continental Europe are more exclusive. The activity and employment rates of women, low-skilled, younger and older employees and migrants are lower. The between-country inequalities on the labour markets have been reinforced in recent decades by education, activation and childcare policies. On the one hand, these policies have led to a significant increase in employment rates, especially in countries with already inclusive employment regimes. On the other hand, the employment opportunities of low-skilled, health-impaired and young workers have declined and unemployment among the low-skilled, migrants and young people has risen in Southern Europe in the wake of the financial market and euro crises. The financial and euro crises thus contributed to the stabilisation and reinforcement of inequalities between central and peripheral countries and between labour market insiders and outsiders. The introduction of the euro might have contributed to the deepening of these gaps, because the architecture of the common currency excludes devaluations and transfers. Therefore, unemployment is one of the remaining instruments for reacting to asymmetric shocks.

Labour markets in Europe are characterised by numerous divisions. These divisions also shape the European economic and social model because the exclusion of some groups from the labour force, precarious forms of employment and divisions between centre and peripheries threaten social cohesion in Europe (Lahusen, 2021). In the following sections, the territorial and social divisions of the European labour markets between centre and periphery and between labour market insiders and outsiders will be described and analysed. First, however, six ideal-typical characteristics of European labour markets will be elaborated.

A first feature of the labour markets in Europe is their still largely *national regulation*. Institutions that shape them—such as labour law, social security, trade union representation, training systems, and social norms that shape the labour supply of, for example, women, young people or migrants—are largely national. It has also been established in European treaties that the EU member states regulate labour markets largely on their own, even if the EU can facilitate the free movement of workers by harmonising social rights (Leibfried, 2015). Also, opportunities for mutual learning have been made permanent through the so-called Open Method of Coordination since 1999 (Heidenreich & Zeitlin, 2009; Zeitlin & Vanhercke, 2018). Workers' rights, social dialogue, employability or the prohibition of discrimination, for example in wages or recruitment, continue to be among the EU's core competences in labour policy, even if most facets of labour markets are regulated at national level. The EU's general principle of equal treatment and non-discrimination (Sect. 6.2) and the free movement of people indicate the limitations to this national regulation.

In addition to the central position of national labour market regulations, the de facto closure of national labour markets must also be taken into account. Even if the free movement of people is a central pillar of the Single Market, the intra-European mobility of workers is still significantly lower than the mobility between non-European and EU countries. Before the financial market and euro crises began, the share of the labour force born in another EU country was 2.4% (2007). Ten years later, this share has doubled (2017: 4.7%), but the share of the labour force from non-EU countries has increased almost as much (from 5% to 8.4%). Thus, the share of EU citizens in the foreign-born labour force was still about one third.

A second feature of European labour markets is their *strong institutional embeddedness*. National institutions influence both the extent of labour force participation, the level of unemployment and the share of long-term unemployed. In Sect. 5.1, the ensemble of family, social, educational, labour, fiscal and economic policy institutions that support or hinder greater labour market inclusion are referred to as *employment regimes*. Based on Gallie (2007b), five different European employment regimes can be distinguished (Chap. 3). On this basis, it is possible to discuss whether the European Employment Strategy pursued since 1999 has contributed to a higher inclusiveness of European labour markets.

A third feature of European labour markets is their *lower degree of inclusion*.[1] Whereas in the early 1970s, 63.6% of the working-age population in the EU-15 was still in the labour force, by the mid-1990s this figure had fallen to 60.3%. Over the same period, the US employment rate increased from 63.6% to 73.5%. Even though this difference has now narrowed to about two percentage points, the employment rate in some, mostly Southern and Eastern European countries is significantly lower than in Scandinavia or the USA. A lower level of inclusion cannot be explained as solely the result of collective bargaining arrangements and welfare state regulations that make work more expensive or lead to low incentives to take up gainful

---

[1] Labour market inclusion can be measured by the employment rate, which is defined as the ratio of the employed population to the working-age population, i.e. the population aged 15 to under 65 years (more recently: 20–64 years). The activity or participation rate is defined as the ratio of the total labour force (unemployed and employed) to the working-age population.

employment. Considerable importance is also attached to the reconciliation of family and employment. A detailed analysis in Sect. 5.2. shows which institutions facilitate more inclusive employment regimes and which people are systematically less integrated into the labour market and thus also more affected by poverty and exclusion.

A fourth feature of European labour markets is the deep and durable *segmentation between labour market insiders and outsiders*. This is the result of a closure of privileged jobs for mostly domestic, qualified men in the prime age of 25 to 54 years. Based on analyses conducted jointly with Sven Broschinski and Matthias Pohlig (Broschinski et al., 2020), an outsider index based on five labour market-related risks is proposed in Sect. 5.3 On this basis, it is possible to determine which socio-demographic groups are primarily affected by the risk of being excluded from the labour force, being low-paid or being employed on a temporary basis. Next, which countries are particularly affected by these risks and how these risks evolved before, during and after the financial market and eurozone crisis will be described.

A fifth feature of European labour markets is *high and persistent unemployment* compared to the US and Japan. One indicator of the persistence of unemployment is the share of long-term unemployed who have been out of work for a year or more. Their share of all unemployed is around four-tenths in the EU-28 (2018: 37.7%) and rises significantly during cyclical upswings (2014: 43.8%; Eurostat, table lfsa_upgacob). This raises the question of which groups are particularly affected by the risks of unemployment and long-term unemployment and to what extent these risks also depend on the institutional environment. It can be assumed that the risks of exclusion are particularly high among women, young people, older people, migrants, the low-skilled and the disabled (Sect. 5.4).

This points to another feature of European labour markets: their centre-periphery divide. While the EU achieved considerable success in converging economic performance and income conditions, at least until the onset of the financial and euro crises from 2008 onwards, the unemployment rates in Greece and Germany differed by 22 percentage points at the height of this crisis (2013: 27.5% and 5.2% respectively). Such a range is not unusual for Europe: already in 1994, the difference between the country with the lowest (Luxembourg) and the highest unemployment rate (Spain) in the then European Community was 19 percentage points. The centre-periphery structures of European labour markets were reinforced by the weaknesses of the Southern European economies (Chap. 4) and the institutional consequences and deficits of European monetary union. The euro abolished a key mechanism that had previously helped to reduce economic differences: flexible exchange rates. The abolition of this buffer mechanism led to an increasing division between the more inclusive labour markets in Northern and Continental Europe and the more exclusive labour markets in particular in Southern Europe. In addition, European treaties explicitly exclude international transfers, even if asymmetric shocks might require them in a currency union (Mundell, 1961).

In Sect. 5.5, the results of the within- and between-country divides in European labour markets are summarised.

## 5.1   Inclusive and Exclusive Employment Regimes in Europe

Labour markets are the "arenas in which workers exchange their labor power in return for wages, status, and other job rewards."(Kalleberg & Sørensen, 1979, p. 351) Neoclassical approaches assume that supply and demand in labour markets, as in all other markets, are determined by the price, i.e. by wages and labour costs. The employment level results from the balance of supply and demand; unemployment is analysed in this perspective as a voluntary decision for more leisure time. If the deliberately simplifying assumptions of such models—such as the assumptions of a homogeneously skilled and motivated labour force, fully informed, utility-maximising actors, free and readily available information and information-processing capacities, and market transparency—are gradually modified, more realistic approaches emerge. Unemployment can then be explained as the result of wages above the equilibrium level. Such higher wages can be the result of minimum wages, or collectively agreed wages. The employers may also decide to pay wages above the equilibrium, so-called efficiency wages, in order to increase their employees' commitment. In all three cases, the supply of labour will exceed the demand, which in the neoclassical perspective leads to unemployment.

In contrast to such simplified model assumptions, institutionalist and segmentation theories point to the social embeddedness of labour markets. They focus on non-market forms of coordination and allocation, in particular by power relations and institutions. Some groups tend to monopolise access to privileged positions and exclude women, foreigners, or young people from these positions (Sørensen, 1983). These processes of social closure highlight the importance of power relations in labour markets. Often, processes of social closure are even engrained in institutions which, for example, protect the jobs of insiders with a higher seniority in contrast to younger labour market entrants, or link internal careers to full-time jobs and longer, uninterrupted work experience. From a neoclassical perspective, such institutions are only seen as "market imperfections", as "politics against markets" (Esping-Andersen, 1985) or even as the outcome of a "taste for discrimination" (Becker, 1993). Examples for these labour-market regulating institutions are the education system, labour law, labour relations, the welfare state and also the norms regarding families and private lifestyles. These institutions are not independent from each other, but they are often characterised by similar logics. Therefore, it is useful to focus on interdependent sets of institutions which are usually described as employment regimes (Bosch, 2018; Schmid, 2008). Such employment regimes can be defined as the *totality of institutions that regulate the scope and nature of (potential) labour supply and demand and thus shape the exchange relations in the labour market.*

These institutional regimes shape the actions and thinking of the actors precisely because they are taken for granted. They are characterised by *institutional complementarities*, i.e. by interactions and structural similarities between different institutional spheres. For example, while a traditional gender regime supports the employment of male main breadwinners, strong industrial trade unions dominated by skilled workers fight for permanent full-time jobs secured by collective agreements, especially for men. At the same time, a tax system could favour part-time employment of women, while social policy focuses on financial support through child benefits rather than benefits in kind such as day-care centres for smaller children, which would allow higher female employment rates. Contrary to what this ideal-typical description of the post-war German employment regime suggests, employment regimes are by no means uniform, coherent, consensually shared regulatory structures. Rather, they are latently conflict-prone, as they only provisionally regulate the differences in interests and perceptions between the groups of actors. Employment regimes are thus the ensemble of rules of the game that regulate the disputes about participation in working life and about the validity of family, company, collective agreement and social security rules.

This institutional embeddedness of European employment regimes has been the focus of comparative economic studies for decades. Following the Eurosclerosis theses of the early 1980s (Olson, 1982), the institutional determinants of unemployment were analysed and the rigidity of European labour markets was identified as the central cause of higher unemployment rates compared to the USA (Siebert, 1997). Specifically, a high degree of unionisation and collective bargaining coverage were identified as central causes of high unemployment rates. The degree of centralisation of collective bargaining is also considered an important factor influencing the level of employment: In contrast to company and national bargaining, regional and industry-wide bargaining is said to have a negative influence on employment levels (Calmfors & Driffill, 1988). Strict employment protection legislation is also considered to be at the core of the European employment problem, as are low wage inequalities and compressed wages due to collective agreements, statutory minimum wages, high unemployment benefits or high minimum income levels. Blau and Kahn (2002, p. 256) summarise these analyses as follows:

> the U.S. experience of declining unemployment, falling steady real wages, and rapidly rising wage inequality and the EU experience of rising unemployment, rising real wages, and comparatively stable relative-wage levels are two sides of the same coin. The United States permitted real and relative wages to adjust, while many countries in Europe (. . .) chose to let employment take the brunt of the shocks.

From a socio-historical perspective, it can be added that the institutional peculiarities of European labour markets reflect the institutional legacy of industrial society, which has shaped Europe longer and more strongly than other parts of the world (Therborn, 1995). The highly standardised and industrialised employment regime of post-war Europe was characterised by mutual reinforcements between a standard industrial employment relationship, male-dominated marriages and industrial mass production. At the centre of this employment regime was the so-called normal employment relationship, i.e. "employment relationships that are ideally permanent and continuous, which take place in a (preferably large-scale) company on a full-time basis and which require skilled workers" (Mückenberger, 1985, p. 429; own translation).

Such a (stylised) industrial employment regime resolves the trilemma of social cohesion, successful participation in a globalised, innovation-centred economy and broad inclusion of the working-age population in the labour force in favour of the first two objectives: First, *social cohesion* is based on the legal protection of jobs and financial redistribution in an employment-centred welfare state. Secondly, this employment regime also proved successful in economic terms in the post-war period of prosperity, since the stronger regulation of labour relations by collective agreements, labour law and trade unions, dual vocational training and social security systems allowed the specialisation on *high-quality industrial products* (Streeck, 1991). However, a third goal—the *inclusion* of the working-age population in the labour force—was not achieved, as the employment rates of women, young people, older people, migrants and disabled people were lower than those of domestic, qualified men.

However, such a stylised description ignores the variety of European employment regimes (Gallie, 2007a), first of all the difference between exclusive and inclusive labour markets: The Southern, Central and Continental European countries come closest to the ideal type of rigid labour markets and exclusive employment systems described above, while the employment systems on the *British Isles* and in *Scandinavia* are clearly more inclusive. These differences could be explained on the one hand by different economic structures: While the Southern and Continental European countries are characterised by industrial employment relationships, the Scandinavian and liberal countries rely more strongly on personal or social services. Secondly, institutional differences matter: The *liberal countries*, represented in Europe by the United Kingdom and to some extent by Ireland, are characterised by lower social contributions and transfer payments. Family-related services and transfer payments are low. These institutional characteristics are associated with high employment rates and lower unemployment rates. Women, youth, older people and the unemployed are strongly involved in the labour market. The *Mediterranean countries*, on the other hand, are in many respects the opposite model to the liberal employment regimes: Education levels and spending on education are significantly lower, while the share of social contributions in taxes and duties is higher, employment protection is stronger and wage spread in the lower income range is lower. These countries are characterised by low employment rates and high unemployment rates. *Continental European countries* occupy an intermediate position between the liberal and the highly regulated Mediterranean labour markets. Employment protection is as high as in the Southern European countries. However, the welfare state is more developed and employment rates are very high. The *Scandinavian countries* are characterised by a high wage spread (with household income distributed in an egalitarian way), high spending on education, high education levels and strong trade unions. Employment rates are well above the average of other country groups. The *Central and Eastern European countries* share the experience of a socialist order and the post-socialist transformation processes, characterised by the collapse of the previous economic and industrial structures, temporarily high unemployment rates, low, but increasing social protection expenditures, a departure from the egalitarian wage structures of socialist countries, a high proportion of industrial workers and a rapid decline in union density. It was not until the end of the noughties that employment rates gradually increased again and more inclusive employment relationships with greater welfare state protection gradually emerged (compare, however for the heterogeneity of the Central and Eastern European countries Bohle, 2018).

To sum up: Traditionally, European labour markets are characterised by a high level of labour segmentation. They are divided into insider or primary markets for native, skilled men with permanent contracts and outsider or secondary markets for women, young people, migrants, disabled or unskilled people. This division is also the result of a stronger regulation of labour markets through employment protection laws, strong trade unions, effective collective agreements and welfare state protection against social risks. While primary labour markets were characterised by egalitarian wage structures for skilled, unionised workers, other groups of people were either relegated to roles outside of the labour market (care and child-rearing activities for women, early retirement for older people, apprenticeships for young people, deportation for migrants . . .), to atypical jobs (such as temporary or part-time jobs) (Eichhorst & Marx, 2015) or they were unemployed. The paradox of European labour markets thus consisted in the simultaneity of egalitarian wage structures, strong trade unions, comprehensive systems of social security and low labour force participation and employment rates, high unemployment and long-term unemployment rates and the exclusion of marginal groups from the labour market or at least from protected job opportunities.

This ideal-typical model of egalitarian, but also segmented labour markets, however, applies mostly to the Southern and Continental European countries and less to the more inclusive labour markets in the Scandinavian countries and the British Isles. While the *liberal countries* in the British Isles are characterised by individualised wage bargaining systems, limited social security and active education policies, in *Scandinavia* the state and trade unions play a central role in regulating employment relations, providing social benefits and supporting individualised private living forms. In the *Southern European countries,* traditional patterns of workplace regulation and family-centred living forms are more important. Indicators are the lower importance of formal education, strong employment protection legislation and a crucial role of traditional family patterns (indicated for example by high expenditures for pensions and the absence or rudimentary state of minimum income schemes which would allow more individualised lifestyles). The level of social security in *Continental European countries* is higher, while *Central and Eastern European countries* are currently still characterised by low employment and participation rates, a high share of medium education and low social protection rates. These institutional contexts are an important determinant of the high inclusiveness of the liberal and Scandinavian employment regimes and the exclusive regimes in Southern, Central and Eastern Europe.

However, such a description of European employment regimes has some weaknesses and limitations. Firstly, the central task of comparative research is to replace country or regime names ("Southern Europe") with explanatory variables (Kohn, 1987). Different patterns of labour force participation cannot be explained by the ultimately unsatisfactory reference to, for example, Southern European peculiarities, mentalities or work cultures, but should be explained, for example, by the different composition of the working-age population and by different national institutional contexts. This is the task of the next section.

Secondly, the analysis of European employment regimes presented here is static. Path dependencies, inertia and locking effects of institutionally embedded labour markets are highlighted. The shift from "segmented-egalitarian" to more inclusive, but in some dimensions also more unequal labour market structures is underestimated. The segmented labour market structures, especially in Continental and Southern Europe, are transformed on the one hand through the stronger inclusion of previously marginalised groups in the labour market: the activity and employment rates, especially of women and older people, are rising, just as the number of migrants is increasing in most European countries. On the other hand, atypical forms of employment are also increasing. Temporary, part-time and low wage jobs, temporary work, mini-jobs or self-employment are becoming more important (Eichhorst & Marx, 2015). This pluralisation of work is the result of more flexible forms of production (Broschinski, 2020, pp. 48–58), a tertiarisation and globalisation of the economy and the dualisation of labour market institutions (Emmenegger et al., 2012). This shift will be discussed in the following two sections.

## 5.2   Determinants of Labour Force Participation

Over the past three decades, the European employment regimes described above have undergone significant changes as a result of an internationally concerted shift towards more inclusive forms of employment. Activity and employment rates have increased significantly (Fig. 5.1a and c). This raises the question of which factors and policies have enabled this shift towards greater inclusion of the working-age population in the labour force and which countries and groups have particularly benefited from this.

A classic explanation for higher activity (or labour force participation) rates in Europe is the internationally coordinated shift to activation policies. Activation can be understood as "the removal of options for labour market exit and unconditional benefit receipt by members of the working-age population. Through the conceptual and practical combination of demanding and enabling elements, activating labour market policies aim at overcoming individual barriers to employment such as lack of employability due to long-term unemployment, poor skills and personal problems." (Eichhorst et al., 2008, p. 5) This implies a restructuring of European welfare states (Hemerijck, 2013): unconditional benefit receipt, which had been legitimised as a social civil right, is replaced by the introduction of contract-like obligations such as reintegration agreements, with which the unemployed assume certain obligations (further training, job applications ...) in return for financial support (Serrano Pascual, 2007). This shift is a reaction to the high unemployment rates in Europe, to the persistence of unemployment and to low activity rates. Since the Jobs Study of

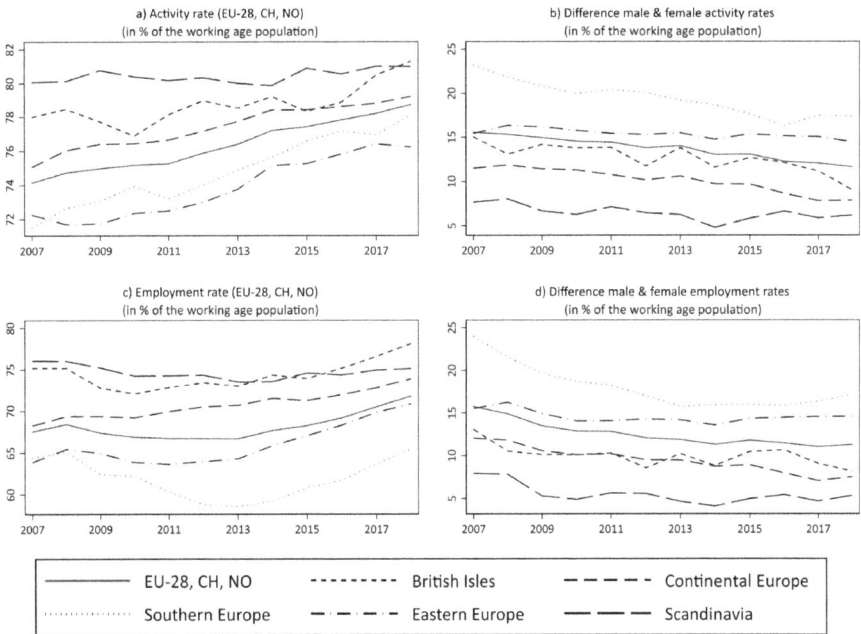

**Fig. 5.1**  Labour force participation and employment in Europe (2007–2018). (**a**) Activity rate (EU-28, CH, NO). (**b**) Difference male and female activity rates. (**c**) Employment rate (EU-28, CH, NO). (**d**) Difference male and female employment rates

the OECD (1994), the low inclusiveness of the Continental and Southern European labour markets has received particular attention at the political level as well. Countries with higher social security, strong trade unions and employment protection legislation have increasingly focused on activating the unemployed, women, older people, migrants, or the disabled. These groups are no longer relegated to alternative roles outside the labour market in unemployment insurance, in the household, in early retirement, abroad or in nursing homes, but they are increasingly included into the labour force either by sanctions and restrictions ("demanding policies") or by enabling measures such as a better childcare, further training or better job placement.

These enabling facets of activation policies go far beyond classical labour market policy. This has been captured by the social investment concept (Morel et al., 2012a, b). This concept refers to the importance of "policies that both invest in human capital development (early childhood education and care, education and lifelong learning) and that help to make efficient use of human capital (through policies supporting women's and lone parents' employment, through active labour market policies . . ." (Morel et al., 2012a, p. 5) These policies have also shaped the "European Pillar of Social Rights" (de La Porte, 2019; Vandenbroucke, 2018). Against such a background, Boeri and Garibaldi (2009) postulated the end of

"Eurosclerosis", i.e. rigid labour markets characterised by low labour mobility, low incentives for the unemployed to return to work, extensive employment protection for core workforces and a tendency to exclude women, young people, older people and migrants from privileged labour market positions. This assertion reflects the hope that the modernisation of European employment regulations which began with the "Jobs Study of the OECD" (1994) and which continued with the European Employment Strategy from 1997 onwards can create more inclusive labour markets (Weishaupt, 2011).

Crucial indicators for higher inclusion are higher employment and activity rates, which became—in addition to lower unemployment rates—central indicators for successful labour market policies. It was possible to increase the employment rates in the EU-28 from 69.8% (2007) to 73.2% (2018) and activity rates from 74.9% to 78.4% (Eurostat, table lfsi_emp_a). Figure 5.1 shows the regime- and gender-specific developments in the European activity and employment rates. The activity rate has increased in all country groups (Fig. 5.1a). *This indicates a fundamental societal and political change, which reflects not only the activation of the unemployed, but also a stronger involvement of women and older people in the labour market (also due to increased training activities, better childcare and the end of early retirement programmes).* The highest increases can be observed in Central, Eastern and Southern Europe, i.e. in the country groups with the lowest activity rates, while they rose much more slowly in Northern and Northwestern Europe. This points to an equalisation of activity rates that can also be observed at the national level. The corresponding coefficient of variation in the 30 states considered has decreased from 0.08 (2000) to 0.06 (2018) (Eurostat, table lfsa_argan). The increasing activity rates were mainly achieved through a higher involvement of women in the labour market. As a result, the differences between male and female activity rates decreased (Fig. 5.1b). This decrease was strongest in the Southern European countries—even though the gender gaps in activity rates are still highest in Southern Europe. In Scandinavia, and since the beginning of the 2010s also in Continental Europe, these gaps are now smaller than ten percentage points.

The level of unemployment determines the difference between activity and employment rates (Fig. 5.1c). The figure shows a steep rise in the United Kingdom and Ireland from 2015 onwards and largely stable employment rates in Scandinavia. It is hardly surprising that the employment rate in Southern Europe—which was still somewhat higher than in Central and Eastern Europe at the beginning of the period under consideration—is significantly lower than in the other country groups. The deep slump from 2008 onwards had a long-lasting effect. It was only a decade later that the Southern European countries had overcome the plunge in employment rates. Despite the labour market slump, the gender gaps between activity and employment rates in Southern Europe have narrowed (Fig. 5.1d)—an indication of the decline of predominantly male industrial jobs and the erosion of the traditional gender division of labour in Southern Europe, which was based on the male breadwinner model. Women are therefore no longer disproportionately affected by economic downturns. In Continental Europe, too, the gap between the employment rates of women and men is decreasing, albeit at a somewhat slower pace than in Southern Europe. Given

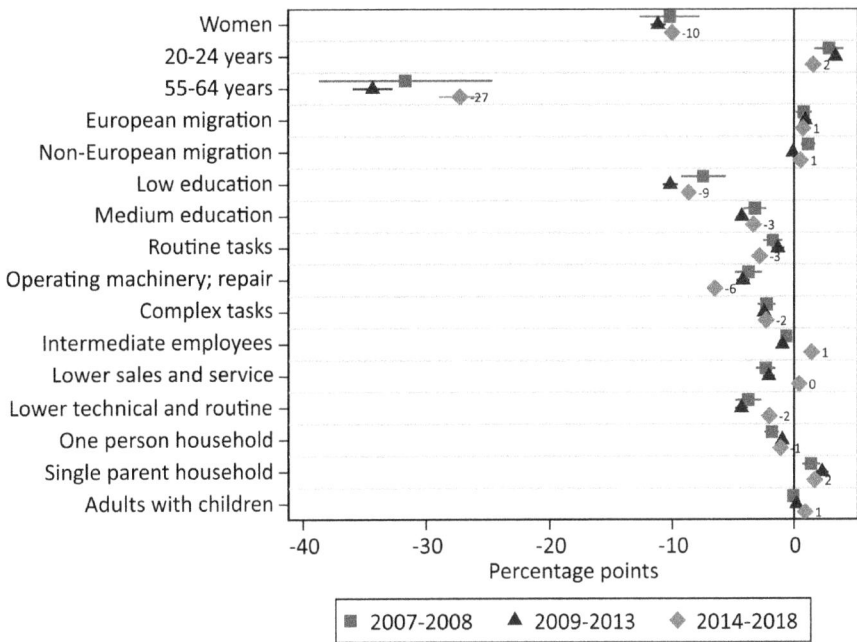

Source: EU SILC UDB, logistic regressions based on cross-sectional data. Shown are average marginal effects (Mood, 2010) of group-specific odds of being employed or unemployed - for all persons aged 20-64 from 2007-2018 for 28 EU countries, Switzerland and Norway (Croatia from 2010). The reference groups are averagely qualified, native men aged 25-54 from the upper service class with very demanding tasks ("problem solving, decision making, creativity"). The value of -27 (2014-2018) for older people thus means that - with an average activity rate of 77 % - they have a activity rate 27 percentage points (pp) lower than people aged 25-54 - taking all other factors into account.

**Fig. 5.2**  Group-specific differences in activity rates in Europe (2007–2018)

the socialist experience of very high female labour force participation, the stable and high gender gaps in Central and Eastern Europe are surprising. The difference of about 15 percentage points between the gender-specific activity and employment rates suggests that the post-socialist transformation processes were accompanied by a *retraditionalisation of the gender-specific division of labour.*

In sum: the activity and employment rates in Southern Europe are clearly below the EU average, while the rates in Northern and Northwestern Europe clearly exceed the European average.

However, this does not yet answer the question of which factors influence the labour force participation of the population. A first step towards an answer is the analysis of the group-specific differences. Figure 5.2 shows that the likelihood that people of working age are part of the labour force depends mainly on three factors: age, gender and education. Occupations, social class and household situation also play a significant, albeit rather small role. Taking all other factors into account, the activity rates of university graduates, men and people in the core age group of 25–55 years are above average. The labour force participation of women, older people and people with low education and executive jobs is lower. The declining labour force participation of older people during the crisis is clearly visible; they are an important buffer for the labour market. In a crisis, older people can be excluded from the labour market, since (early) retirement provides a socially recognised and financially sustainable alternative to employment. The jobs of manual workers, such as machine operators, and the less qualified are also disproportionately at risk. The situation is different for women. Their labour force participation declines only slightly during the crisis. But the thesis that women are the relative winners of the financial market and euro crises (Heidenreich, 2016b) cannot be upheld when all socio-demographic variables included here are taken into account. However, their activity rate declines by only one percentage point. And this decline is already made up for as of 2014. The trend towards greater inclusion of women, which could already be seen on the basis of the unadjusted data (Fig. 5.1b), thus continued after the euro crisis even when other characteristics (the so-called composition effects) were taken into account. People with a low level of education are increasingly pushed into inactivity. Their participation in the labour market is significantly lower than that of people with a medium and high level of education. This gap continues to widen. In addition to the four groups mentioned above, there are other groups that may become unemployed, but not inactive: Young people, single parents and migrants. Their activity rate remains above average even in the financial and euro crises. These crises thus have affected groups differently: while older people in particular and, to a much lesser extent, the low-skilled and women are pushed out of the labour force, young people, single parents and migrants remain in the labour force but suffer from higher unemployment risks.

The previously described differences between the activity rates of the five employment regimes are no longer significant when the individual characteristics just described are taken into account—with the exception of the Scandinavian countries where the employment rate is still significantly higher than in the Continental European countries. The first step in the above-mentioned replacement of names thus was successful: Regime names can be replaced by individual characteristics. The next step is now to explain the different activity rates for women, older people and the other groups shown in Fig. 5.2, thus replacing names by institutional contexts, because the different patterns of labour force participation are also determined by national institutions. Firstly, in view of technological changes and the accompanying polarisation of skills (Acemoglu & Autor, 2011; Goos & Manning, 2007; Goos et al., 2009), it can be expected that countries with a better developed education system and more qualified employees have a structural advantage in the creation of new jobs, since better educated persons tend to work longer—especially if this is flanked by training offers for older people (Blossfeld, 2011). In the following, the impact of educational efforts—indexed by the level of *public educational expenditure*—is considered (in addition to individual educational attainment). Secondly, *public childcare and other social services* will play an important role. When the state takes over childcare and care work, such services can make it easier for women in particular to take up gainful employment. Social services can also contribute to the reintegration of unemployed and inactive persons into the labour market in the context of *activation policies*. Thirdly, *financial benefits for children and families* ("child allowance") may have a negative impact on women's labour force participation as it reduces financial incentives to take up work. Fourth, a European influence could also be observed if *austerity policies* during the euro crisis from 2010 onwards lead to lower labour force participation.

The dependent variable in the following models is a binary variable taking the values of 0 or 1: Either a person in working age is part of the labour force (i.e. employed or unemployed) or he/she is inactive. Therefore, binary logistic multilevel regressions are used (with countries and years as additional levels). Bryan and Jenkins (2016) recommend including at least 30 countries in such models. Therefore, in addition to the 28 countries that belonged to the EU from 2013–2020, Norway and Switzerland are also included, as they are closely intertwined with the EU. The coefficients in the corresponding tables are (as in Fig. 5.2) average marginal effects expressing the average effect of the respective expression of the independent variable compared to a reference group (Mood, 2010). A one percentage point increase in education expenditure (as a percentage of GDP) reduces the probability of participating in the labour force by 2.2 percentage points.

This means that higher *public spending on education* is associated with significantly lower labour force participation (Table 5.1, M1). This is a completely surprising result. Figure 5.3a sheds some light on this finding: It shows that low-skilled workers are significantly less involved in the labour force than medium and high-skilled workers. The increasing share of skilled persons due to educational expansion thus has favoured a higher labour force participation. At the same time, ceteris paribus, labour force participation decreases as education expenditure increases. This possibly points to the declining marginal benefit of education efforts in terms of labour market policy: In countries with high education spending, labour force participation is also significantly higher due to the higher level of education, but the increase is not proportional as it declines somewhat as education spending increases.

*Adult participation in continuing education* is associated with a significantly positive but very small increase in labour force participation (Table 5.1, M2).

Family-related benefits, which amount to about 2.2% (2017) of gross domestic product (GDP) across Europe, are divided into cash benefits and benefits in kind. Higher *spending on family-related services* (such as childcare) encourages higher labour force participation (Table 5.1, M3). In contrast, higher financial benefits for families are associated with lower labour force participation. This effect might be negative because child benefits may act as a wage replacement and reduce incentives to take up work (Table 5.1, M4). The two effects of material and financial child benefits are about equally strong, but operate in different directions.

Higher expenditure on *active labour market policies* (in % of GDP; weighted by the number of unemployed) is associated with higher labour force participation (Table 5.1, M5). Activation policies thus support the unemployed in finding work and also reduce the proportion of discouraged people who withdraw from the labour market. This effect is very strong and significant. Especially the low-skilled benefit

**Table 5.1** National contexts of individual labour force participation (2007–2018; EU-28, Switzerland, Norway)

| | M1 | M2 | M3 | M4 | M5 | M6 |
|---|---|---|---|---|---|---|
| Expenditure on education (% of GDP) | $-0.022^{***}$ (0.0060) | | | | | |
| Further education (% of population 25–64 years) | | $0.0024^{***}$ (0.00069) | | | | |
| Family-related benefits in kind (% of GDP) | | | $0.028^{*}$ (0.011) | | | |
| Child benefits (in % of GDP) | | | | $-0.034^{***}$ (0.0081) | | |
| Activation policies (% of GDP) | | | | | $0.12^{***}$ (0.020) | |
| Austerity (% of GDP) | | | | | | $-0.00085$ (0.00086) |
| Observations | 1,676,211 | 1,676,211 | 1,676,211 | 1,676,211 | 1,676,211 | 1,676,211 |
| Countries | 30 | 30 | 30 | 30 | 30 | 30 |
| ICC (year/country) | 0.080 | 0.061 | 0.061 | 0.064 | 0.066 | 0.069 |
| AIC | 1303849.9 | 1303852.4 | 1303858.5 | 1303846.8 | 1303828.6 | 1303862.7 |

Source: Own calculations based on a 50% sample of EU-SILC 2007–2018. See Appendix 1 for the explanatory variables. The table reports the average marginal effects for the chances of employable persons aged 20–64 being employed or unemployed in contrast to being inactive. The coefficients are the result of 6 binary logistic multilevel regressions based on EU-SILC cross-sectional data. The models control for the effects of the survey years and the socio-demographic characteristics mentioned in Fig. 5.2 even though they are not listed here. ICC: Intraclass correlation. $*$ p < 0.05, $**$ p < 0.01, $***$ p < 0.001

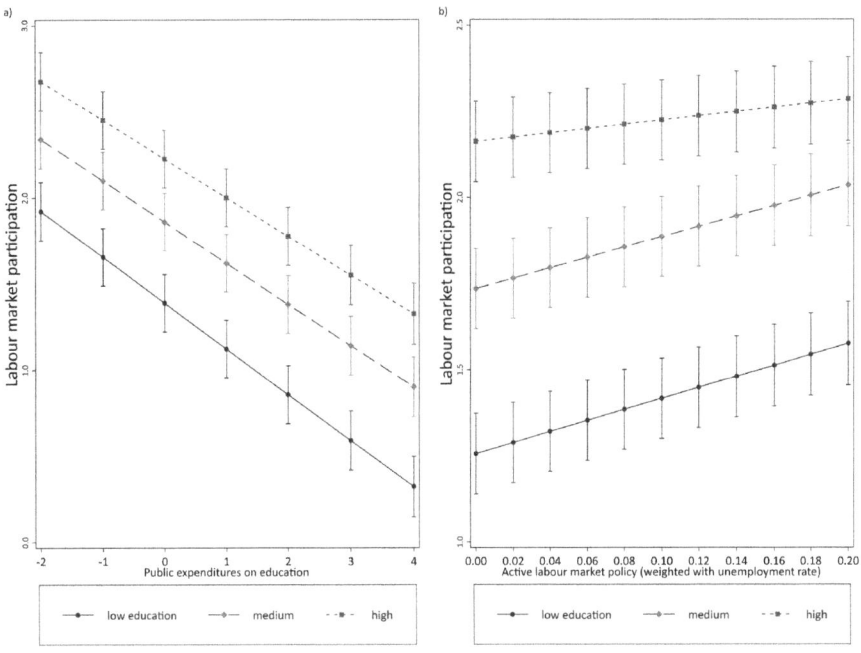

Source: See Table 5.1. Predicted marginal effects (95% confidence interval).

**Fig. 5.3** National and individual determinants of labour force participation in the EU-28, Switzerland and Norway (2007–2018)

from activation measures (Figure 5.3b). This significantly reduces the differences between high- and low-skilled workers.

Despite relevant reports on the negative impact of *austerity policies* on political attitudes (Fetzer, 2018), labour market reforms (Moreira et al., 2015), female labour force participation (Karamessini & Rubery, 2014) and on living conditions especially in Greece (Almunia, 2020), no significant impact of austerity policies on labour force participation can be observed (Table 5.1, M6). This confirms the finding reported in Chap. 4 that austerity policies have no significant impact on average regional unemployment (Table 4.4). This can also be explained by the fact that public austerity policies were only pursued for a short period of time and mainly in the (mostly) Southern European crisis countries where they were also cushioned by the European Central Bank and the European rescue funds.

In sum: the differences between the five employment regimes can largely be explained by a different composition of the working-age population: The labour force participation of older, less healthy and low-skilled persons entrusted with simpler tasks is generally lower than that of younger, healthy, male and higher-skilled persons engaged in more demanding tasks. The composition of the labour force is influenced by different national contexts. The public education and training system not only contributes to the provision and long-term maintenance of skills, but also to higher labour force participation because higher-skilled employees and better trained older employees generally work longer. The significantly lower public expenditure on education in Southern Europe (on average 4% in 2018, compared to 4.8% in Continental and 6.4% in Northern Europe) as well as the lower partici- pation of adults in further education (on average 8.8% in 2018, compared to 13.4% in Continental and 28% in Northern Europe) will thus contribute to lower educa- tional attainment and thus lower labour force participation in Southern Europe and, on the other hand, explain the significantly higher activity rates in Northern, Con- tinental and Northwestern Europe. The higher female employment rates in Northern, Continental and Northwestern Europe, on the other hand, point to the greater importance of family-related services. These are significantly better funded in Northern and Continental Europe than in Southern and Eastern Europe (2018: 1.8% and 1% of GDP, respectively, compared to 0.4% and 0.5%). These services are a central pillar of more inclusive employment systems because they relieve families and women in particular of childcare and care responsibilities. This also applies to active labour market policies, which are mainly pursued in Northern Europe (1% of GDP). Even though Southern and Continental European countries spend on average 0.4% of GDP (2018) on active labour market policies, their importance is much higher in Continental Europe due to lower unemployment rates. They contribute to the reintegration of the unemployed into employment. Austerity policies do not seem to have a systematic influence on the level of labour force participation.

## 5.3   The Segmentation of Labour Markets in the Euro Crisis[2]

In the previous section, the question of who is part of the labour force was discussed. In this section, the question will be whether people who are part of the labour force are employed or unemployed and whether they have a good or a bad job. This question addresses the segmentation of European labour markets. According to Kalleberg (2011, pp. 9–10), good jobs are characterised by good pay, additional company benefits, scope for decision-making in terms of time and content, social and job security. In contrast, bad jobs are poorly paid, precarious, insecure and with little autonomy of action. In dual labour market theory, the segmentation of the labour market into good and bad jobs is analysed as a division into primary and secondary labour markets. Primary labour markets consist mainly of the internal labour markets of the civil service and large companies, which require either academic qualifications or company-specific experience and competences. They can be accessed by specific ports of entry. Internal advancement on internal career ladders promotes the accumulation of company-specific competences (Doeringer & Piore, 1971). From a sociological perspective, labour market segmentation is the

---

[2]This section draws on Broschinski et al. (2020).

expression of social relations of domination (Reich et al., 1973), processes of social closure (Kalleberg & Sørensen, 1979; Sørensen, 1983) and discrimination. From an economic point of view, different labour market segments are characterised by higher or lower labour turnover costs. These are the costs for hiring, qualifying and, if necessary, dismissing workers. Insiders are more difficult to replace than outsiders—for example, young people, the unqualified or the unemployed whose previous qualifications have been devalued by a long period of unemployment (Lindbeck & Snower, 1988). Accordingly, companies treat insiders with care—by offering them higher "efficiency wages", implicit contracts and lower unemployment risks, while the laws of supply and demand, lower equilibrium wages and higher unemployment risks are reserved for labour market outsiders.

The following section analyses how the patterns of labour market segmentation within and between EU states (Heidenreich, 2016a; Palier et al., 2018) have evolved during and after the financial and euro crises since 2008. After a theoretical and methodological introduction (Sect. 5.3.1), the section describes which socio-demographic groups are particularly affected by unemployment, low-wage and job insecurity risks and which institutions shape these risks (Sect. 5.3.2). The section concludes with an overview of the group- and country-specific distribution of labour market risks in the euro crisis. These patterns are interpreted as the result of power relations between creditor and debtor countries and between labour market insiders and outsiders, especially in the countries most affected by the euro crisis.

### 5.3.1 Monetary Union and Labour Markets

As already mentioned in Chap. 4, the European Monetary Union (EMU) is characterised on the one hand by the abolition of exchange rates between eurozone member states, on the other hand by limits to national debts and thirdly by a no-bailout rule. The first feature implies that national economies lose an important buffer against external shocks: the possibility to devalue their currency (De Grauwe, 2016, p. 206; Mundell, 1961). Second, the debt rules limited the possibilities of the already heavily indebted Southern European countries to incur further debts during the financial and euro crises since 2008. Third, the no-bailout clause in the European Treaties (Article 125 TFEU) impedes an anti-cyclical European reaction to the crises because stimulus programmes and labour market policies were considered to be the responsibility of the nation-states. The creation of the European Monetary Union thus has limited the monetary and also budgetary sovereignty of states and has not created alternative buffer mechanisms, for example a coordinated fiscal policy or cross-border transfers (with the limited exception of the European rescue funds).

Thus, the labour market became the most important buffer in the eurozone crisis. States that are hit harder by an economic crisis can no longer reduce their unit labour costs through devaluations, but must lower them through productivity increases, layoffs or wage cuts. Other states can reduce the adjustment burdens of the countries in crisis through stronger wage increases, an expansionary budgetary policy or transfer

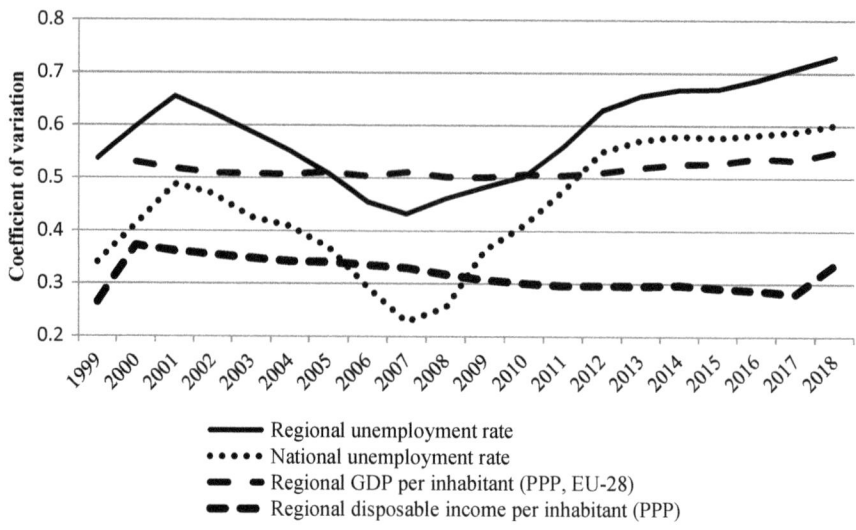

**Fig. 5.4** Variation in regional and national unemployment and economic performance (EU-28; 1999–2018)

payments. As early as the 1960s, Mundell (1961, p. 659) emphasised that the extent of adjustments in deficit countries is also dictated by the behaviour of creditor countries: "In a currency area comprising different countries with national currencies the pace of employment in deficit countries is set by the willingness of surplus countries to inflate." This raises the question of how the burden of adjustment is distributed between states. If creditor countries rely on low wage increases and restrictive budgetary policies, the margins for deficit countries are reduced. They have to reduce their employment levels or their wages and labour costs even more. This is often referred to as real devaluation (compared to the devaluation of currencies under flexible exchange rates). Thus, in times of crisis, the euro could contribute firstly to higher unemployment and greater divergences between the labour markets of the 19 eurozone member states, since the monetary buffers between them have been abolished. Secondly, a crisis always raises the question of how the adjustment burdens are distributed between labour market insiders and outsiders. It can be expected that outsiders are particularly affected by a deterioration in their employment and wage situation, thus deepening the segmentation of European labour markets.

Classical analyses of European labour markets have highlighted the central importance of unemployment as an adjustment mechanism, while the US labour market tends to rely on wage inequalities (Blau & Kahn, 2002). Empirically, this assumption can only be partially confirmed. As predicted, the coefficients of variation of national and regional unemployment rates increase significantly in the financial and eurozone crises since 2008—and much more than the fluctuations in average regional value added and disposable income (Fig. 5.4). It is noteworthy, however, that the variation in unemployment rates does not decrease again after the end of the euro crisis in 2013—as was previously observed in the boom phase until

2007. The variations in the unemployment rates continue to rise and thus, together with the still high level of unemployment in Southern Europe (Fig. 5.5b), point to a durable split in the European labour markets, especially along the North-South axis—a split that cannot only be attributed to the monetary union.

In Sect. 5.1, it has already been argued that European labour markets are classically characterised by egalitarian wage structures and lower activity and employment rates of marginalised groups. In the subsequent debate, it was pointed out that this analysis neglects alternatives to unemployment such as greater flexibility through fixed-term contracts (DiPrete, 2007, p. 612; Maurin & Postel-Vinay, 2005). Fixed-term contracts and other atypical forms of employment (Eichhorst & Marx, 2015) are an equivalent way of responding to economic challenges, in addition to unemployment and lower wages. The advantage of flexible employment contracts is that they are associated with lower political costs in contrast to unemployment. Therefore, fixed-term contracts, but also part-time work, temporary work or solo self-employment could be an attractive alternative to reduce labour costs. According to Maurin and Postel-Vinay (2005, p. 249), job security is a key parameter for adjustment to macroeconomic shocks in Europe. The OECD (2015, p. 29) reports that in 26 predominantly European member states, more than half of the new jobs created between 1995 and 2007 were atypical jobs. These are often characterised by lower wages, less training, poorer working conditions and limited opportunities for more stable employment. This also points to a *change from egalitarian-exclusive employment arrangements to more inclusive but more segmented labour market structures.* This change has also been highlighted by the thesis of marginal flexibilisation. It emphasises that the flexibilisation of the labour market leads to a further weakening of employment protection for labour market outsiders and to a further deregulation of the already flexible employment conditions for temporary workers. This contributes to a further erosion of stable employment relationships (Barbieri & Cutuli, 2016). The effects of European integration, and in particular monetary union, on the labour markets are therefore not limited to their impact on unemployment, as assumed by the theory of the optimum currency area (Mundell, 1961).

The extent to which national labour markets in Europe are segmented will now be discussed. Not only the unemployed, but also temporary workers, low-wage workers, involuntary part-time workers and the self-employed without employees are considered as outsiders (Schwander & Häusermann, 2013, p. 252). Other labour market outsiders—temporary workers, contract workers or those not subject to social security contributions—cannot be identified with the EU-SILC data and thus cannot be included in the following analysis. But it can be assumed that these risks overlap with the five risks considered here. Therefore, the labour market outsider index presented in the next section (Fig. 5.5a) can be interpreted as a conservative estimate of the share of labour market outsiders and thus the level of segmentation between insiders and outsiders.

A second question is which groups are affected by these labour market risks. It can be expected that these risks are concentrated among women, young people, low-skilled persons and people with a migration background. In contrast to a general *segmentation of* the labour market, which at least theoretically will affect all groups equally, the social concentration of segmentation risks can be termed *marginalisation* (Heidenreich, 2015; Kalleberg, 2011).

The following section will analyse the extent to which unemployment, low-wage jobs, temporary employment, solo self-employment and involuntary part-time work have increased during the financial market and euro crises since 2008, which countries and groups are particularly affected by these labour market risks and whether European and transnational policies have influenced national patterns of labour segmentation. These questions are discussed below for the years before, during and after the financial market and eurozone crises.

## 5.3.2  Labour Market Risks in Europe

The following analysis considers the level, the country-group-specific and the social distribution of the previously described labour market risks for the years from 2007 to 2018 on the basis of the EU-SILC data. Five country groups and four disadvantaged groups (women, young people, low-skilled people and people with a migration

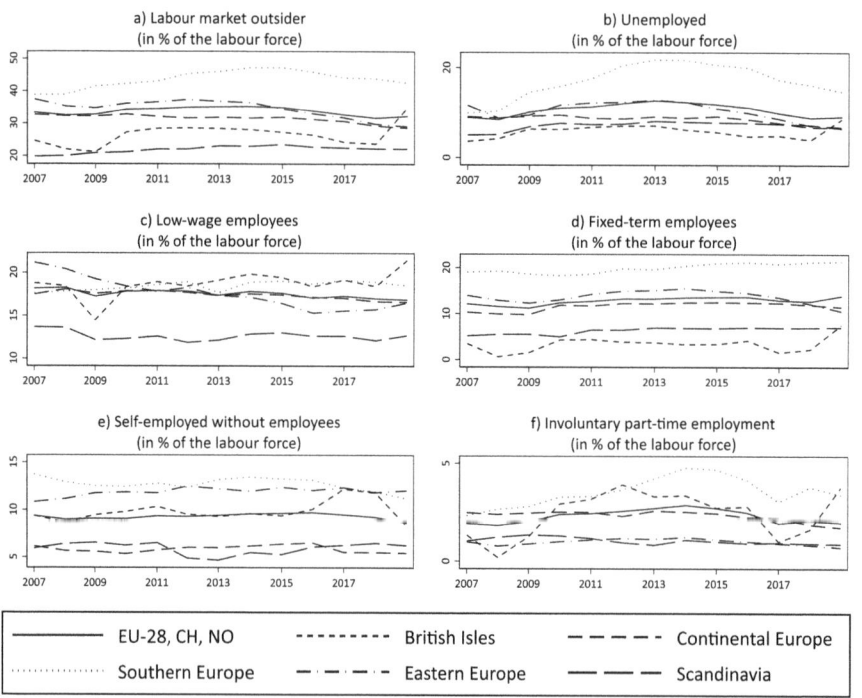

Source: EU SILC UDB, own calculations. Share of unemployed, low-paid (i.e. less than two-thirds of the median gross hourly wage), involuntary part-time or temporary employed and self-employed without employees as % of labour force aged 20-64, 2007-2018 (EU-28, until 2010 excluding Croatia).

**Fig. 5.5** Labour market outsiders in Europe. Five employment risks (2007–2018). (**a**) Labour market outsider. (**b**) Unemployed. (**c**) Low-wage employees. (**d**) Fixed-term employees. (**e**) Self-employed without employees. (**f**) Involuntary part-time employment

background) are considered. Figure 5.5 describes the share of labour market outsiders in the total labour force in 28 EU countries (until 2010 without Croatia) and in
Norway and Switzerland from 2007–2018.

Figure 5.5a shows that the outsider risk is much higher than the unemployment
rate (Fig. 5.5b). This is already evident from the construction of the outsider index,
since people who are employed on a temporary or involuntary part-time basis, who
receive a low wage or who are self-employed without employees are taken into
account in addition to the unemployed. As previously expected, the outsider index
shows a clear difference between the highly segmented, more exclusive labour
markets in Southern Europe and the inclusive labour markets in Scandinavia and
also on the British Isles. The Mediterranean countries are characterised by the
highest unemployment rates, a high proportion of low-wage earners and self-
employed without employees and the highest proportion of temporary and involuntary part-time workers. In the wake of the financial and euro crises, this share
increased in Southern Europe from 38.9% (2008) to 47.2% (2014), before declining
slightly (2018: 43.9%). This was a result of increasing unemployment. Economic
shocks in the monetary union were thus mainly buffered by unemployment. The
outsider risk is particularly high in Spain, Greece, Poland, Croatia, Cyprus, Ireland
and Portugal. In these countries, more than 40% of the labour force aged 20–64 is
affected by at least one of the five risks mentioned—compared to an EU average of
36%. At the other end of the spectrum are the Scandinavian countries, where on
average 22–25% of the labour force is counted among the outsiders—mainly due to
the egalitarian wage structure and thus the lower share of low-wage earners
(Fig. 5.5c). Besides Denmark, Norway and Sweden, the share of labour market
outsiders is also lower in Romania, Switzerland and the UK (Fig. 5.6). The increase
especially in Greece, Spain, but also in Portugal and Cyprus is due to the rise in
unemployment during the euro crisis. A small contribution was also made by the
increasing share of involuntary part-timers in Cyprus, Spain and Italy. The other
labour market risks hardly react to the financial market and euro crises: the shares of
temporary employees, solo self-employed and low-wage earners remain largely
stable before and after the eurozone crisis. However, the Southern European countries take a top position in these three risks. In Central and Eastern Europe, the shares
of low-wage workers decline significantly (especially in Poland, Hungary, Latvia,
Romania and Bulgaria). In the wake of rapid economic development, unemployment
in Central and Eastern Europe is also declining significantly (Fig. 5.5b), so that the
share of labour market outsiders has fallen from 37.5% (2007) to 29.8% (2018),
reaching the level of Continental European countries. During the financial and euro
crises and in the following years, the differences between highly segmented labour
markets in Southern Europe and the more inclusive labour markets in the rest of
Europe have thus widened considerably. And this divide has hardly narrowed after
these crises. Therefore, the pandemic in 2020/22 once again violently hit the
segmented and fragile labour markets in Southern Europe. In addition to this
deepening split between Southern Europe and the other countries, another remarkable realignment of national labour market policies can be noted, especially in
Continental Europe: The share of labour market outsiders has declined from

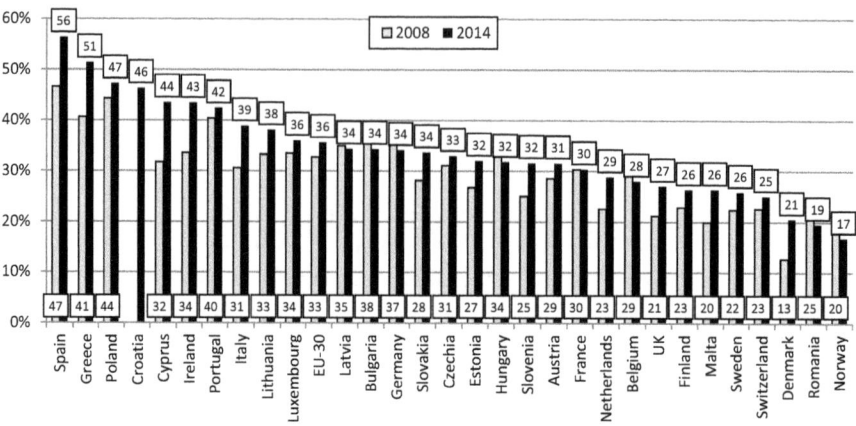

Source: EU SILC 2014 und 2018, own calculations. Share of unemployed, low-paid or temporarily employed labour force, involuntarily part-time employed or self-employed without employees as a percentage of total labour force aged 20-64.

**Fig. 5.6** Labour market outsiders (2008 and 2014; in % of the labour force)

33.1% (2007) to 29.5% (2018) (especially in Germany and Belgium, but also in France). Instead of the previous dichotomous structure (inclusive employment regimes in Scandinavia and the British Isles, exclusive regimes in the rest of Europe), a tripartite division of European labour markets is emerging, as the outsider shares in Continental, Central and Eastern Europe are now significantly below the Southern European level. However, they do not yet reach the low levels of the Northern and Northwestern European countries. The outsider shares are still significantly and permanently higher than in Scandinavia. And in comparison to liberal countries, the shares of temporary employees and the unemployed are higher, since temporary employment is hardly necessary from a company's point of view, given the weak protection against dismissal in the liberal countries (Fig. 5.6).

Women, young people, migrants, unskilled persons with health issues and those with routine tasks in lower sales and service occupations are affected more than other groups by the five outsider risks considered. This raises the question of how large this difference is in comparison to the respective reference groups (men in the core age group, persons with a high education, natives with lower technical and routine jobs living in households with adults and children). When considering the group-specific risks of being an outsider, it does not make sense to look at the effects of the individual socio-demographic characteristics separately, because the outsider risks of migrants, for example, are massively overestimated if their different educational levels are not taken into account. In Fig. 5.7, the risks of being an outsider in contrast to the reference group are shown for three different periods dominated by the financial crisis, the eurozone crisis and the upswing after these crises. For example, young people aged up to 25 years in 2014–2018 have an outsider risk which is 264% higher than the risk of the core age group of 25 to 54 years when all the other variables are included. The risk of employees with routine tasks is 93% higher than

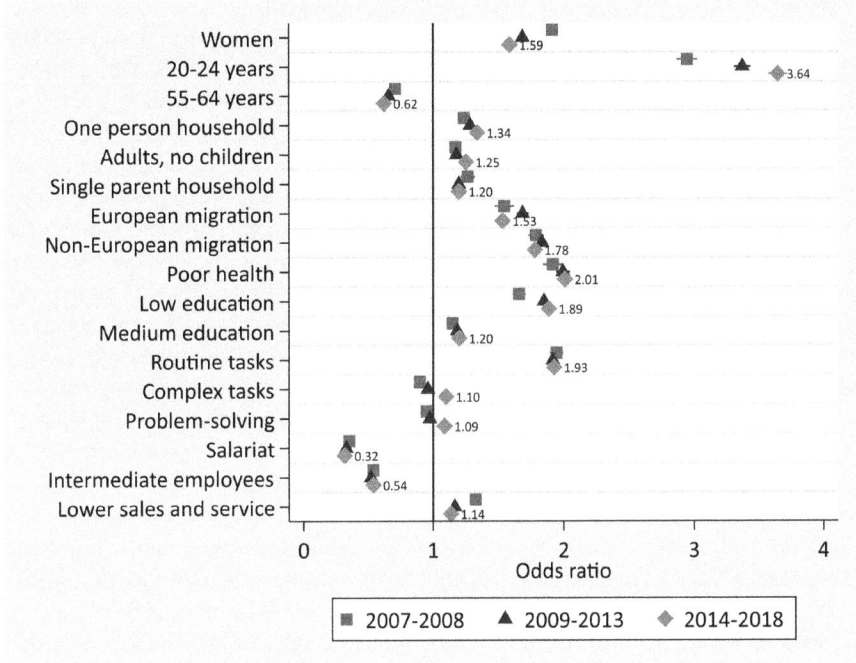

Source: EU SILC 2007-2018, logistic multilevel regressions. Shown are the odds ratios for the group-specific risks of being unemployed, low-paid, temporarily employed, involuntarily part-time employed or self-employed without employees (in % of the labour force aged 20-64 years) from 2007-2018 for 30 European countries (EU-28, Switzerland, Norway). As reference groups, native men with high education aged 25-54 in good health with lower technical and routine jobs ("Operating machinery and electronic equipment; driving vehicles; maintenance and repair") living in households with adults and children were chosen. All the active and inactive persons where all the socio-demographic variables are available (also the occupational class and the required skills of the job) are included.

**Fig. 5.7** Individual determinants of outsider risks in 30 European countries (2007–2018)

the outsider risks of persons with operating, driving, maintenance and repair tasks; the outsider risk of people with poor health is twice as high as the risk of healthy people. Women (+ 59%), European and non-European migrants (53% and 78% higher respectively), unskilled workers (+ 89%) and singles and single parents also have a significantly higher outsider risk, while older employees, and higher and intermediate service classes have a lower risk. The outsider risks of young people, the health-impaired and the unskilled have risen continuously since 2007–2008, while the risks of women and older people have fallen. In particular, women are relative winners in this dimension of the transformation from an industrial to a knowledge-based service society, because their outsider risk is still much higher than that of men—but the outsider gap is declining.

The next step analyses which facets of the national context influence the outsider risks of the labour force. The effects of five different factors on the segmentation of European labour markets will be discussed. (1) First, the influence of economic and employment structures. It can be assumed that a high *share of industrial employees* lowers this risk, since industry is the classic domain of the normal employment relationship. In addition, trade unions are particularly strong in manufacturing industries. Therefore, the degree of unionisation and its interaction with the share of industrial employment will be included in a multilevel regression (Table 5.2). (2) A *high employment rate* as an indicator of an inclusive labour market could also reduce outsider risks, as jobseekers from more vulnerable groups will find a job more easily. This could be seen as an indirect outcome of the European Employment Strategy, as this strategy has focused attention on increasing employment rates overall and especially for women and older people (Heidenreich & Zeitlin, 2009). Therefore, an interaction with gender will also be included, as women in particular are expected to benefit from more inclusive labour markets. (3) Furthermore, social investments might contribute to a lower segmentation of labour markets into insiders and outsiders. This is the assumption made by the social investment approach, which sees social policy as a productive factor (Morel et al., 2012a). Two institutions which are crucial for such an approach will be considered. First, it will be examined whether a *stronger activation of the unemployed*—indexed by a higher spending on active labour market policies—is correlated with a lower share of outsiders. This would be a clear indication of the effectiveness of the European Employment Strategy whose core consists of activation policies. (4) Furthermore, the importance of public *spending on education* will also be included, as higher investments in education might be associated with more inclusive labour markets. In both cases, the interaction with the educational level of the labour force will also be included, as it can be expected that especially lower-skilled workers benefit from social investments. (5) Last but not least, it will be directly examined whether the financial and euro crises and the accompanying *austerity policies* have an impact on the outsider risks of the labour force.

The results of the corresponding models are shown in Table 5.2 (without the individual variables). The first model M1 confirms that a high *share of industrial employment* is correlated with lower labour market segmentation because the industrial sector is more strongly characterised by normal employment relationships regulated by trade unions. This is especially true—according to the corresponding interaction effect—if the share of unionised employees in a country is also high. Even if the share of industrial workers declines in the course of an increasing service orientation, strong trade unions can nevertheless prevent a high share of outsiders (cf. Fig. 5.8a).

A high *employment rate* (Table 5.2, M2) is associated with lower risks of precarious contracts und unemployment. Given the high employment rates in Scandinavian and Continental European labour markets (Bosch et al., 2009), this points to the impact of these countries' more inclusive employment regimes on labour market segmentation. The positive interaction effect with gender shows that women's already high risk of being an outsider (due to fixed-term contracts, involuntary part-time work and low wages) increases even further in inclusive labour markets. Women have a higher risk of being an outsider than men. And this risk increases by another 0.5% for every percentage point that the employment rate rises—an even darker picture than the one drawn on the basis of Fig. 5.7.

**Table 5.2** National and individual determinants of outsider risks (30 European countries; 2007–2018)

| | M1 (Industry) | M2 (Employment) | M3 (Activation) | M4a (Education) | M4b (Education * Expenditure) | M5 (Austerity) |
|---|---|---|---|---|---|---|
| Industrial employees | −0.021** (0.001) | | | | | |
| Union density | −0.005 (0.004) | | | | | |
| Industry * unions | −0.00048** (0.000) | | | | | |
| Employment level | | −0.050** (0.001) | | | | |
| Employment level # women | | 0.007** (0.001) | | | | |
| Activation | | | −5.803** (0.393) | | | |
| Activation # low education | | | −3.452** (0.318) | | | |
| Activation # medium education | | | −3.369** (0.258) | | | |
| Public expenditure on education | | | | −0.040+ (0.022) | 0.058* (0.023) | |
| Education expenditure # low education | | | | | −0.182** (0.014) | |
| Education expenditure # medium education | | | | | −0.105** (0.011) | |
| Austerity | | | | | | −0.007+ (0.004) |
| Constant | −2.181** (0.078) | −2.130** (0.062) | −2.158** (0.072) | −2.153** (0.072) | −2.164** (0.072) | −2.159** (0.076) |
| Respondents | 227,235 | 218,946 | 231,009 | 234,013 | 234,013 | 234,013 |
| Wald Chi$^2$ | 23,462 | 23,230 | 24,335 | 24,222 | 24,315 | 24,222 |
| Intraclass correlation | 0.056 | 0.038 | 0.051 | 0.050 | 0.050 | 0.054 |
| McFadden pseudo-R$^2$ | 0.131 | 0.148 | 0.141 | 0.133 | 0.134 | 0.130 |
| AIC | 2.51e+05 | 2.41e+05 | 2.55e+05 | 2.60e+05 | 2.59e+05 | 2.60e+05 |

Source: EU-SILC 2007–2018 (10% sample). Binary logistic multilevel regression (individuals, countries *years, countries). Standard errors of regression coefficients in parentheses. + $p < 0.05$, * $p < 0.01$, ** $p < 0.001$. 28 EU countries, Switzerland and Norway. Individual characteristics (household composition, health) were taken into account as control variables in the above models, but are not shown. Context variables are explained in Appendix 1

The significant effects of *active labour market policies* (Table 5.2, M3) confirm the results of evaluation studies that find more positive than negative effects of activation policies on the labour market (Kluve, 2010; Taru, 2016): Higher expenditure on active labour market policies (weighted by the unemployment rate) is associated with a lower risk of being an outsider. The likewise negative interaction effects with education show that it is mainly the part of the labour force that has low and medium qualifications that benefits from this. This is also shown in Figure 5.8c: The risk of exclusion for all qualification groups decreases when the importance of activation policies increases. However, the low-skilled benefit more than the high-skilled. The effectiveness of activation policies also differs between *genders*. It could be assumed that women in particular benefit from them, as their participation in the labour force is lower. However, this is not the case: men benefit more than women from active labour market policies (Figure 5.8d). A possible explanation for the further increase in the already high risks of women could be that activation measures are more effective in industrial jobs than in personal services. Figure 5.8e shows the changing impact of activation policies during the economic cycle. Activation policies seem to be particularly effective during the crisis, shielding the labour force somewhat from unemployment, earnings and precariousness risks. However, the differences are only significant in an extreme scenario (deep crisis, strong activation) compared to moderate growth.

Model 4a in Table 5.2 indicates that higher *public spending on education* is associated with lower labour market risks. However, model 4b in Table 5.2 shows that this is only true for the low and medium skilled, while the low outsider risks of the higher skilled (the reference group) increase to some extent. The decreasing outsider risk for low-educated can also be shown graphically (Figure 5.8f): In a knowledge-based society with a high share of high-skilled and high investment in education, the relative privileges of academically qualified workers decline to some extent.

Model 5 in Table 5.2 examines the effects of austerity policies in the wake of the financial and euro crises and thus the effects of national, European and international crisis management. Since a positive value of the austerity indicator implies a laxer fiscal policy (minus interest payments), the negative coefficient indicates that more austerity is associated with higher labour market risks. However, this effect is only significant at the 5% level and must therefore be interpreted very cautiously in the context of the results presented above, which have not shown a systematic relationship between austerity policies, unemployment and labour market participation.

In sum: more than one third, and in some, especially Southern European countries more than half of the European labour force must be considered as labour market outsiders because they are affected by at least one of the five labour market risks considered. The exclusion of young people, the health-impaired and workers in routine jobs is particularly strong. These patterns of exclusion are also the result of national policies and institutions. The share of labour market outsiders and thus the level of labour market segmentation is determined on the one hand by national economic and labour market structures (especially the employment share of the industrial sector, the inclusiveness of the labour market and the educational level)

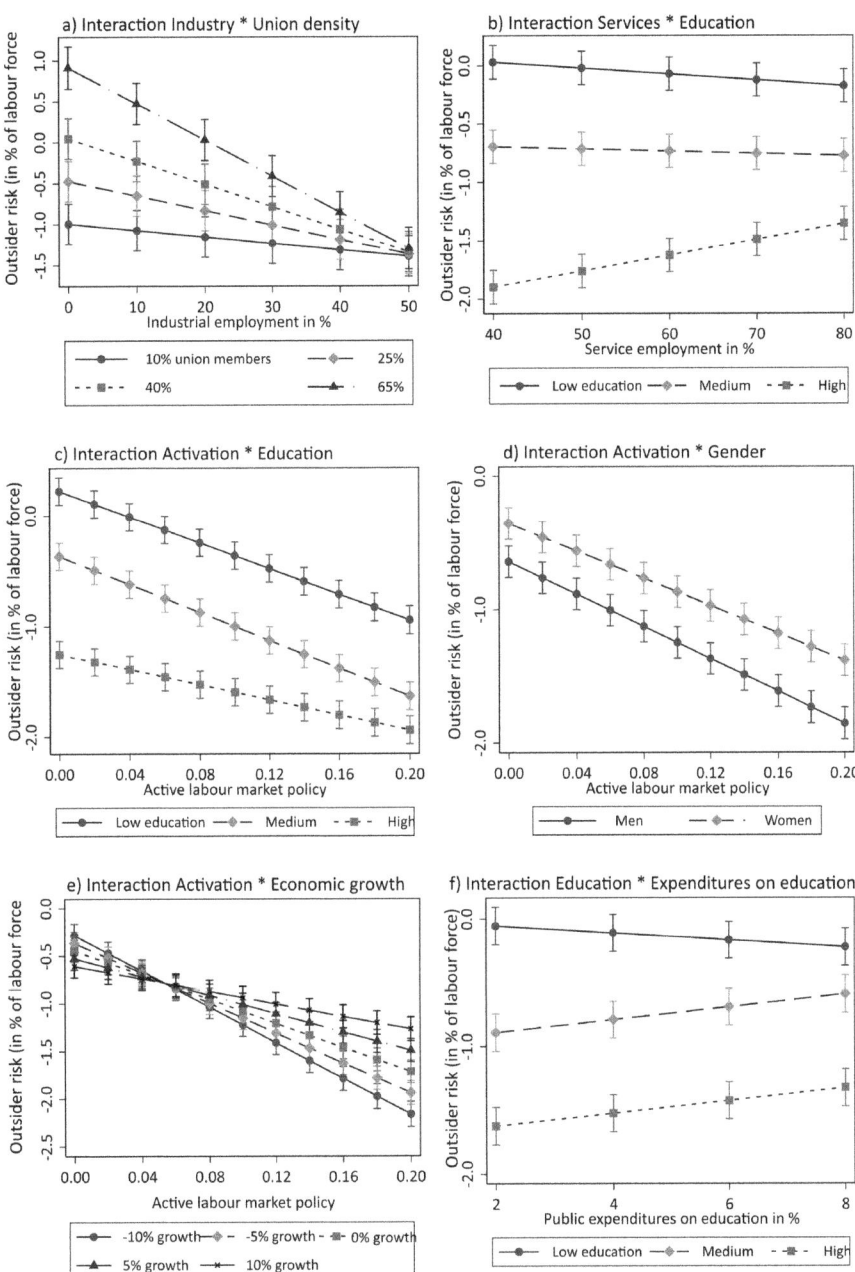

Source: Own calculations on the basis of EU-SILC 2007-2018.

**Fig. 5.8** National and individual determinants of outsider risks in the EU-28, in Switzerland and Norway (2007–2018). Predicted marginal effect (95% CI). **a**) Interaction industry * union density. (**b**) Interaction services * education. (**c**) Interaction activation * education. (**d**) Interaction activation * gender. (**e**) Interaction activation * economic growth. (**f**) Interaction education * expenditures on education

and depends on the other hand also on labour market regulating institutions (trade unions, education systems) and the corresponding policies (education policies, active labour market policies, austerity policies). Since the European Employment Strategy focuses on higher employment rates and higher qualifications and an activation of the labour force, an influence of EU policies on the segmentation of the labour markets can also be assumed: While the European Employment Strategy aims at a higher inclusiveness of labour markets, the European and international bailout programmes and the related austerity policies may have contributed to increasing labour market risks, a stronger segmentation of the labour markets and an exclusion of young people, the low-skilled, women and migrants.

## 5.4  Long-Term Unemployment. The Achilles' Heel of the European Social Model

The previously mentioned debate on the "unified theory" (Blau & Kahn, 2002) has shown that unemployment, and especially long-term unemployment, is the Achilles' heel of the European social model. Since the 1970s, unemployment rates in Europe have increased by a few percentage points with each economic downturn (1974: 3.1%; 1994: 11.1% in the EU-15), while at the same time unemployment rates in the US have remained stable at around 6%. This was accompanied in Europe by an entrenchment of unemployment—documented by a high share of long-term unemployed (1 year and longer), which in the EU-28 stood at 42.9% of all unemployed in 2018. In this regard, the country groups described above differ significantly (cf. Figure 5.9d): while the more inclusive employment regimes in Scandinavia and the British Isles rarely exceed long-term unemployment rates of 30% of all unemployed, the rates in the more exclusive Central, Continental and Southern European employment regimes are mostly above 40%. However, when interpreting these figures, the counter-cyclical dynamics of long-term unemployment must be taken into account. For example, the share of long-term unemployed among all unemployed fell very sharply in 2009, as a large number of employed people became unemployed, increasing the relative weight of the short-term unemployed (Fig. 5.9a). Subsequently, the rate increased again, as the short-term unemployed are hired first and the unemployment rate declines. Thus, on the one hand, the long-term unemployment rate of 70.3% (2018) in Greece points to the encouraging recovery of the Greek economy after the sovereign debt crisis from 2010 onwards. On the other hand, unemployment has become more entrenched in Southern Europe after the crisis: Not only as a share of all unemployed (Fig. 5.9d), but also in relation to the total labour force (Fig. 5.9b), the share of long-term unemployed is rising considerably, while the share of short-term unemployed has declined since 2013. Women, the unskilled, migrants and young people are more affected in Southern Europe than in any other European country group (Fig. 5.9c).

The persistence of unemployment is extremely problematic both economically and socially. The long-term unemployed are much more difficult to reintegrate into

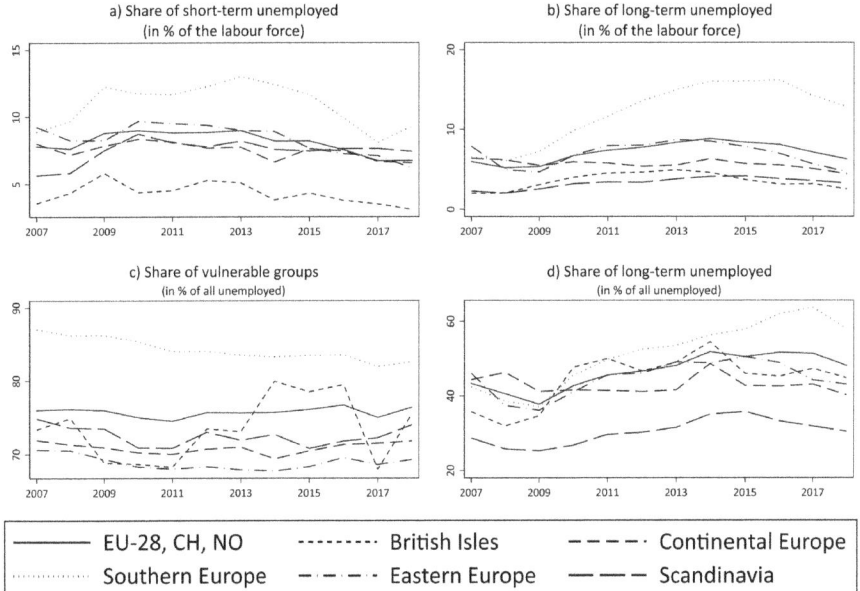

Source: Own calculations on the basis of EU-SILC 2007-2018, vulnerable groups are women, unskilled, young people and migrants. Long-term unemployed are unemployed for one year and longer.

**Fig. 5.9** Short-term and long-term unemployment in the EU-28, Switzerland and Norway (2007–2018). (**a**) Share of short-term unemployed. (**b**) Share of long-term unemployed. (**c**) Share of vulnerable groups. (**d**) Share of long-term unemployed

the labour market than the short-term unemployed. The chances of reintegrating them into the labour market decrease strongly with increasing duration of the unemployment spell. Long-term unemployment implies considerable psychological stress, loss of self-esteem and the destruction of workers' skills and motivations. Economists refer to this as hysteresis effects (Blanchard, 2006): after a longer period of unemployment, workers' skills, motivation to work and their chances of getting a new job decrease significantly. In any case, a period of unemployment leaves scars that are seen even many years later in lower earnings (Gangl, 2006). Even a short crisis can thus have long-term, structural consequences for the labour market.

The Eurosclerosis thesis analyses the comparatively high European long-term unemployment levels as a result of labour market institutions in Europe, for example social benefits, wage replacement benefits, minimum wages, trade unions, collective agreements and lower wage differentials between high and low-skilled workers (Blanchard, 2006; Nickell, 1997). However, shortly before the start of the euro crisis, some authors diagnosed the end of Eurosclerosis (Boeri & Garibaldi, 2009). A key indicator was the decline in long-term unemployment (Fig. 5.9) which has been interpreted as the "disappearance of European structural unemployment" (Boeri & Garibaldi, 2009, p. 412). The subsequent increase in unemployment and also in the share of long-term unemployed in the labour force (2009: 2.9%; 2013:

5.1%) shows that the previous decrease can also be explained by the preceding boom phase. Another evolution might be more important for overcoming Eurosclerosis—a transformation of the institutional setting that shapes European labour markets. The aforementioned labour and social policy institutions might have a declining influence on the risk of becoming long-term unemployed (Heidenreich, 2015), while other institutions are moving into the focus of attention, some of which are also shaped by EU policies:

- *Active labour market policies* are considered to be the most important instrument to prevent the consolidation of unemployment and thus long-term unemployment. As already argued, activation policies focus on stronger incentives for the unemployed to look for a new job ("demanding"). Furthermore, they also aim at improving the conditions for taking up gainful employment ("enabling"). Such activation policies are also inspired by the European Employment Strategy and the Open Method of Coordination (Heidenreich & Zeitlin, 2009; Zeitlin & Vanhercke, 2018).
- In addition, the social investment approach (Morel et al., 2012a) highlights the role of childcare, education and the health system for improving the availability, time, qualification and health conditions for a higher labour force participation of single parents, less qualified and health-impaired employees. Thus, it can be expected that a good *public education system* could also reduce the risk of long-term unemployment by raising the skill level of the workforce.
- In the course of the introduction of the euro since 1999 and the euro crisis, the euro countries have committed themselves to observing debt limits. This applies in particular to the five mostly Southern European crisis countries, which were bailed out with European and international aid from 2010 onwards and in exchange had to accept fiscal restraint. This raises the question of whether *austerity policies* contribute to the consolidation of unemployment.
- Last but not least, an *inclusive labour market*, i.e. a higher employment rate, also means a lower risk of becoming an outsider or long-term unemployed.

Formulated as a hypothesis: *The risk of becoming long-term unemployed can be expected to be lower in countries with inclusive labour markets, comprehensive activation policies, a well-developed education system and a lower emphasis on austerity policies (III).*

In addition to institutional contexts, the risk of long-term unemployment is also determined by the segmentation of the labour force. In a sociological perspective (Parkin, 1974), segmentation processes and the associated unemployment risks can also be explained by processes of social closure between different organisational, occupational and skill groups. According to Lindbeck and Snower (1988), the exclusion of some groups from attractive employment opportunities is caused by high costs of recruitment, on-the-job training and also dismissal, and higher costs due to absenteeism and to health impairments, which make it less attractive to recruit vulnerable groups despite lower wages. These costs act as entry barriers for outsiders and protect internal jobs for insiders whose privileged position is also based on their tacit knowledge. In addition, long-term unemployment can also contribute to the erosion of qualifications and work attitudes, and to poor health. *It can therefore be expected, secondly, that less qualified workers with poorer health in less demanding occupations are disproportionately affected by long-term unemployment (H2).*

Thirdly, social groups are affected differently. This can be interpreted as a *marginalisation* of vulnerable groups (Heidenreich, 2015). Already Doeringer and Piore (1971) expect that women, young people and ethnic minorities have worse chances to access internal labour markets. Older workers, men (who are disproportionately represented in the manufacturing sector) and migrants might also be disproportionately affected. In addition to work- and performance-related determinants, ascriptive characteristics such as migration status, age and gender may also have an impact on the re-employment chances of the unemployed. *It can be expected that older people, women and people with a migration background will be more affected by long-term unemployment than others (H3).*

These three hypotheses target the individual and institutional determinants of the risk of being long-term unemployed. They focus on the polarisation and dualisation of European labour markets and on the marginalisation of vulnerable groups (Heidenreich, 2015). They will be tested on the basis of binary logistic multilevel regressions. The dependent variable is the probability of unemployed persons being unemployed for 1 year and longer—once again a dichotomous variable. The explanatory variables are, at the individual level, gender, age, education and occupational skills (ILO, 2012) and, at the national level, the employment level, public expenditure on education, the extent of active labour market policies (in relation to the level of unemployment) and austerity policies indicated by the primary budget balance.

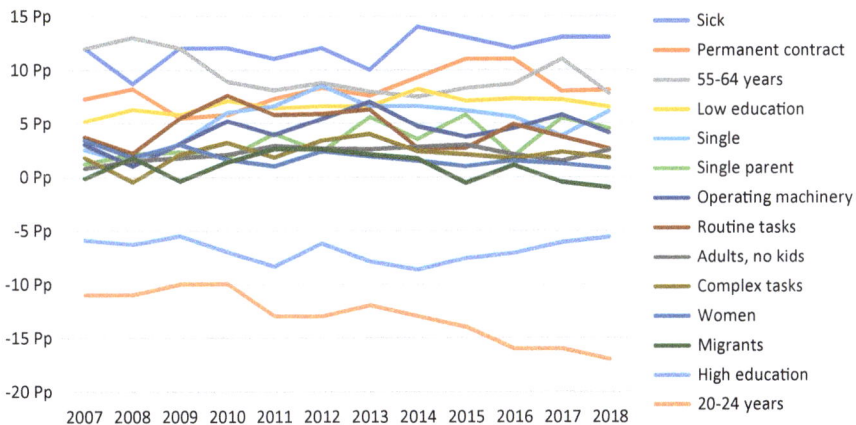

Source: EU SILC 2007-2018, logistic multilevel regressions based on cross-sectional data. Shown are the average marginal effects of the group-specific odds of becoming long-term unemployed - for the unemployed aged 20-64 from 2007-2018 for 28 EU countries, Switzerland and Norway. These effects can be interpreted as percentage points (pp). Highly qualified native men aged 25-54 with high education, good health, very demanding tasks ("problem solving, decision making, creativity") and permanent contracts living in households with children were chosen as reference groups.

**Fig. 5.10**   Relative long-term unemployment risk of different groups (2007–2018)

First, the effects of the socio-demographic characteristics of the unemployed on the risk of becoming long-term unemployed are analysed (Fig. 5.10). Unemployed people with health problems, for example, have a 13 percentage points higher risk than unemployed people with a good or satisfactory state of health. Overall, the risks of becoming long-term unemployed are higher for female, health-impaired, low-skilled unemployed who were previously engaged in simpler tasks than for healthy, skilled men who were engaged in more demanding tasks before becoming unemployed. Poor health, low education and a less demanding job are thus key determinants of the risk of becoming long-term unemployed. In 2018, the long-term unemployment risk of *older workers* is 8 percentage points higher and the risk of *young people* is 17 percentage points lower than the risk of the core 25–54 age group. Young people are more likely to be inactive or unemployed, but less likely to become long-term unemployed because comparatively they have more many alternatives: They can withdraw from the labour market, for example by returning to their family of origin, starting their own family, studying or migrating. The risk of unemployed *single parents* becoming long-term unemployed is 4.5 percentage points higher than in classic nuclear families (households with adults and children). Unemployed persons with a *migration background* had a higher risk of becoming long-term unemployed during the crisis (2010–2014). In other years, they even have a lower risk than natives. This can be explained by the fact that migrants either accept any job in order not to be unemployed or they leave the country. Previously permanently employed people have a higher risk of becoming long-term unemployed than those who were temporarily employed, which may indicate that they are more selective in accepting a new job in order to preserve their previous competences. In sum: Hypothesis 2 can be fully confirmed. In particular, the health-impaired and unskilled unemployed who previously performed simpler jobs have high chances of becoming and remaining long-term unemployed. Hypothesis 3 can be confirmed above all for older people, but also for women. Migrants have somewhat higher chances of becoming long-term unemployed, especially in times of crisis. This may refer to the fact that migrants, but not more women, can be more easily redirected to alternative roles outside the labour market, i.e. sent to their country of origin. Women's risks are on average two percentage points higher than men's.

Testing the first hypothesis requires looking at the national labour market structures and institutions that might shape group-specific long-term unemployment risks (Table 5.3). The first indicator, the employment level, is operationalised by the *employment rate*. It refers to the inclusiveness of an employment regime and reflects the central goal of European employment policy (Weishaupt, 2010). The first two models in Table 5.3 point to the fact that a stronger inclusion of employed people effectively prevents unemployment from becoming permanent. The interaction effect with the respondent's educational level in the first model shows that especially the less skilled unemployed are among the relative losers. Their relative risk of long-term unemployment increases with the employment level. This confirms the thesis of skill-biased technological change (Autor et al., 2003). The interaction effect

**Table 5.3** National and individual determinants of the long-term unemployment risk of the unemployed (30 European countries; 2007–2018)

| | M1 | M2 | M3 | M4 | M5 | M6 | M7 | M8 |
|---|---|---|---|---|---|---|---|---|
| Employment level | −0.032** (0.002) | −0.018** (0.001) | | | | | | |
| Employment level # low education | 0.020** (0.002) | | | | | | | |
| Employment level # medium education | 0.000 (0.002) | | | | | | | |
| Employment level # women | | −0.008** (0.001) | | | | | | |
| Activation | | | −5.943** (0.455) | −6.002** (0.387) | | | | |
| Activation # low education | | | 0.640+ (0.368) | | | | | |
| Activation # medium education | | | −1.577** (0.342) | | | | | |
| Activation # women | | | | −0.874** (0.248) | | | | |
| Austerity | | | | | −0.023** (0.008) | −0.030** (0.007) | | |
| Austerity # low education | | | | | −0.006 (0.004) | | | |
| Austerity # medium education | | | | | −0.004 (0.004) | | | |
| Austerity # women | | | | | | 0.006+ (0.003) | | |
| Public expenditure on education | | | | | | | −0.202** (0.038) | −0.167** (0.037) |

(continued)

**Table 5.3** (continued)

|  | M1 | M2 | M3 | M4 | M5 | M6 | M7 | M8 |
|---|---|---|---|---|---|---|---|---|
| Education expenditure # low education |  |  |  |  |  |  | 0.066** (0.014) |  |
| Education expenditure # medium education |  |  |  |  |  |  | -0.044** (0.013) |  |
| Education expenditure # women |  |  |  |  |  |  |  | -0.069** (0.010) |
| Constant | -1.153** (0.085) | -1.164** (0.087) | -1.165** (0.084) | -1.164** (0.084) | -1.234** (0.099) | -1.235** (0.100) | -1.185** (0.089) | -1.180** (0.090) |
| Cases | 203,961 | 203,961 | 215,240 | 215,240 | 218,525 | 218,525 | 218,525 | 218,525 |
| Wald Chi$^2$ | 8204 | 8029 | 8628 | 8578 | 8486 | 8488 | 8591 | 8541 |
| Intraclass correlation | 0.087 | 0.088 | 0.085 | 0.086 | 0.107 | 0.107 | 0.091 | 0.092 |
| McFadden pseudo-R$^2$ | 0.064 | 0.062 | 0.063 | 0.062 | 0.047 | 0.047 | 0.061 | 0.061 |
| AIC | 2.53e+05 | 2.53e+05 | 2.67e+05 | 2.67e+05 | 2.71e+05 | 2.71e+05 | 2.71e+05 | 2.71e+05 |

Source: Own calculations on the basis of EU-SILC 2007–2018 (50% sample). Multilevel logistic regressions based on cross-sectional data. The group-specific odds of becoming long-term unemployed for unemployed persons aged 20–64 (regression coefficients are shown—from 2007–2018 for 28 EU countries, Switzerland and Norway. Individual factors (gender, age, migration status, education, activity group) were taken into account in the models, but not shown here. The reference groups of the above interaction effects are men, persons aged 25–54 and academics, respectively. Employment level: National employment rate at age of 15–64 years. * p < 0.05, ** p < 0.01, *** p < 0.001

with gender in the second model shows that higher employment rates reduce the risk of unemployed women becoming long-term unemployed.

Models 3 and 4 in Table 5.3 examine the impact of national *activation policies* (in relation to the unemployment rate). These policies are also a central pillar of the European Employment Strategy (Bonoli, 2010; Hemerijck, 2013; Zeitlin, 2009). They are associated with a lower risk of becoming long-term unemployed. However, average and highly skilled workers benefit more than the unskilled. Women, on the other hand, are among the relative winners; their risk of becoming long-term unemployed is significantly reduced by activation policies.

Third, it can be expected that *austerity policies,* especially in the euro area, lead to persistent unemployment (Blyth, 2013; Karamessini & Rubery, 2014; Moreira et al., 2015). This hypothesis is supported by models 5 and 6 (Table 5.3) if the coding is taken into consideration: The higher the government deficit (net of interest payments), the lower the risk of becoming long-term unemployed. This is true for all skill groups. However, the negative effect of austerity policies on the employment situation of women assumed by Karamessini and Rubery (2014) is not supported by the interaction effect with gender. On the contrary, the risk of becoming long-term unemployed is even significantly lower for women than for men with a high level of austerity (but only at the 10% level).

The last two models in Table 5.3 examine the impact of spending on public education on the risk of becoming long-term unemployed. As expected, this risk clearly and strongly decreases—especially for women (model 8). This could refer to the increased employment opportunities for women in service sectors (Heidenreich, 2016b). Above all, middle and upper skill groups benefit from public education efforts (model 7). In countries with higher education spending, their long-term unemployment risk is above average. H1 can thus be confirmed for all contextual factors considered, i.e. for employment levels, activation policies, austerity policies and education levels.

In sum: The risk of becoming long-term unemployed is determined by both individual and national factors. At the individual level, gender, age, household type, health situation, educational level and (previous) occupational position have a strong influence on the risk that the unemployed become or remain long-term unemployed. Higher educational qualifications, a higher occupational position and a permanent contract decisively reduce the risk of becoming long-term unemployed. Single parents, older people, health-impaired people and women, and to some extent also people with a migration background, have a significantly higher risk of becoming long-term unemployed than qualified, younger, male and native unemployed. The increasing risks of low-skilled and health-impaired unemployed people indicate that increased unemployment can lead to a permanent erosion of skills, motivations and ties to the labour market. This risk also differs markedly between European countries. Before the crisis, it was particularly low in the Nordic countries and the British Isles and significantly higher in the Continental, Southern and Eastern European countries. These regime-specific differences have largely reappeared after the crisis, even though Southern European countries are now in the lead and Central and Eastern European labour markets have become somewhat more inclusive. This threatens the social integration and long-term growth potential of Southern European countries and contributes to an increasing division of the EU. In particular, the serious and permanent exclusion of the low-skilled and unskilled should be a cause for serious concern.

Higher employment levels, higher spending on education, active labour market policies and less pronounced austerity policies are associated with a lower risk of becoming long-term unemployed. In particular, women benefit from more inclusive employment, education and activation policies, while the unskilled are on the losing side. The unskilled, but also the health-impaired and older unemployed people benefit less from inclusive labour market, activation and education policies than other groups. The differences between the groups even increase. This can also be shown graphically: Active labour market policies (Fig. 5.11a), higher public spending on education (Fig. 5.11b) and more inclusive labour markets (Fig. 5.11c) reduce

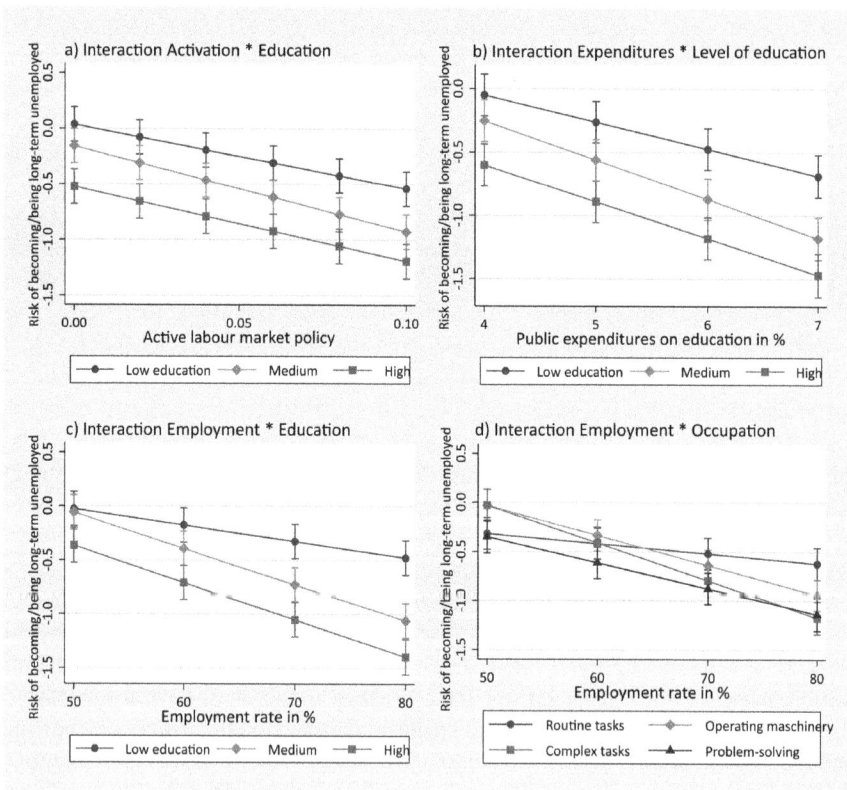

Source: Own calculations on the basis of EU-SILC 2007-2018 (50% sample); 95% confidence intervals; indicated is the risk of unemployed people becoming long-term unemployed. EU-28, Switzerland and Norway.

**Fig. 5.11** National and individual determinants of long-term unemployment risk in Europe (2007–2018). (**a**) Interaction activation * education. (**b**) Interaction expenditures * level of education. (**c**) Interaction employment * education. (**d**) Interaction employment * occupation

the chances of the unskilled unemployed becoming long-term unemployed. But at the same time, the better qualified unemployed benefit significantly more from these policies. This points to the *paradox of more inclusive labour market policies and social investment strategies:* Even if they significantly improve the situation of unskilled and routine workers (Fig. 5.11d), they also widen the gap between them and higher-skilled people with more demanding jobs. The downside of meritocratically legitimised forms of inequality, which are intensively discussed in the US (Markovits, 2019; Sandel, 2020), also affects the destiny of lower social classes. And the bitter fates of the unskilled, the long-term unemployed and other excluded groups are further exacerbated by the fact that they now also have to blame themselves for their failures (Eribon, 2013): In the context of more inclusive policies, these groups could now be encouraged and challenged, they could go on to further education, they could look for better and more demanding jobs, since all paths are open to them thanks to inclusive labour markets and socially investing labour market policies. Markovits (2019, p. 14) writes: "Meritocratic exclusion reaches opportunities as well as outcomes, and meritocratic values add a moral insult to these material injuries." In addition to material disadvantages and exclusion (Cantillon, 2011; Vandenbroucke & Vleminckx, 2011), inclusive policies thus add shame to the "basket of deplorables" (as H. Clinton called them) who did not make it.

## 5.5   Summary: Labour Market Inequalities within and Between European Countries

In the introduction to this chapter, six central features of European labour markets were described: The still largely national regulation of European labour markets, their strong institutional embeddedness, their lower degree of inclusion, the considerable disparities between European core regions and peripheries, the split between labour market insiders and outsiders and high levels of persistent unemployment. Accordingly, labour market inequalities in Europe are characterised by significant disparities between centre and periphery and between core and marginal groups in the labour market. These differences are institutionally stabilised. This has been diagnosed both by the Eurosclerosis and rigidity theses (Siebert, 1997), the "unified theory" of European and American labour markets (Blau & Kahn, 2002) and the diagnosis of an egalitarian European capitalism (Kenworthy, 2004). These theories focused on the institutionally strongly embedded European labour markets, which are stabilised by a close coupling with neighbouring institutional spheres such as social security, family structures, industrial relations or education systems. These institutions are at the core of employment regimes (Gallie, 2007a; Schmid, 2005, 2008).

The inclusiveness of labour markets differs significantly between the five employment regimes identified in Europe. While a greater proportion of the working-age population is included in the labour force in Northern Europe and on the British Isles, the employment regimes in Southern, Central and Continental Europe are more exclusive. Still in the noughties, the latter were characterised by comparatively high unemployment and long-term unemployment rates and by significantly higher (long-term) unemployment risks of health-impaired, less qualified, female or younger employees. The individual and institutional characteristics that can explain the respective patterns of labour force participation (Sect. 5.2), outsider status (Sect. 5.3) and long-term unemployment (Sect. 5.4) were identified.

In the next step, the impact of labour market and education policies on the transformation of the European employment regimes has been analysed. Between an activation turn and the financial and euro crises, higher inclusion of the working-age population in the labour force was achieved. The increased inclusion of women and older people in the labour force has been facilitated by investments in education, family-related benefits in kind and activation policies. Higher employment levels and higher spending on active labour market policies are also associated with a lower risk of the unemployed becoming long-term unemployed. Activation policies thus have met their expectations, even if the shift to a stricter conditionality has been sharply criticised (Serrano Pascual, 2007). Also, the declining unemployment rates and the lower number of long-term unemployed and the increasing employment rates in the EU-15 (20–64 years; 1997: 65%; 2017: 72%), for women (54%; 67%) and for older people (55–64 years; 36%; 59%) support this positive evaluation of activation policies.

Complementary to the activation turn, however, the financial and euro crises from 2008 onwards have also had a strong and negative impact on European labour markets. In these crises, the labour market became the most important buffer for economic shocks (property bubbles, bad loans by banks, high national debt, risk of sovereign debt default . . .) due to the abolition of flexible exchange rates. This led to an exorbitant rise in unemployment rates from 2009 onwards and to increasing differences between the European unemployment rates. Especially in Southern Europe, not only the overall unemployment rates but also the unemployment rates of the low-skilled, migrants and young people increased significantly. Austerity policies increase the chances of becoming (long-term) unemployed. The crises slowed down the trend towards more inclusive and flexible employment arrangements, especially in Southern Europe. They contributed to a stabilisation and partial reinforcement of insider-outsider differences.

In conclusion, the lines of division in European labour markets are still considerable—especially between Southern and Northern and Continental Europe and between more and less skilled employees. However, there are some indications of a transformation of the previously exclusive employment regimes. First, the labour market situation in Central and Eastern Europe has clearly improved with the gradual end of the post-socialist transformation processes and accession to the EU. After a period of high mass unemployment, employment rates have risen again and unemployment rates have fallen, even during the financial and euro crises. In particular, the already high employment rates in the Baltic countries and the Czech Republic reached peaks of over 75% of all 20–64-year-olds, while Italy reached just 62%.

Also in economic terms, seven Central and Eastern European countries had a higher purchasing power-adjusted per capita income than Greece and Portugal in 2017 (Czech Republic, Slovenia, Estonia, Lithuania, Slovakia, Poland and Hungary). This highlights the reorganisation of the European periphery, i.e. the catching up of the Central and Eastern European countries and their shift to inclusive employment regimes, while the still highly exclusive employment regimes in Southern Europe are falling behind. Even in the crisis-ridden decade from 2008 onwards, the trend towards rising employment rates continued despite temporary slumps. Before the pandemic, these rates were higher for almost all countries than in 2008, the peak of the previous cycle.

Secondly, the social foundations of segmentation processes have changed. While classical institutions such as the level of unemployment benefits, social protection or employment protection seem to have a declining explanatory power in many models (not shown here), other institutions such as educational institutions, activation policies or childcare facilities turn out to be important factors influencing the level of labour force participation, the risk of being an outsider or the risk of becoming long-term unemployed. Furthermore, socio-demographic characteristics, whose influence on labour force participation or unemployment rates can only be understood as the result of discrimination, are losing importance: the relative chances of women or migrants being employed, outsiders and long-term unemployed hardly differ now from those of men and native persons when controlling for age and educational level. Instead, the employment opportunities for low-skilled, health-impaired and younger workers with routine jobs have deteriorated considerably. Compared to ascriptive forms of discrimination between core and vulnerable labour market groups, meritocratic fractures of the labour force are becoming more important.

Thirdly, the increasing importance of transnational, especially European, processes, structures and decisions indicates a Europeanisation of labour market inequalities. This is especially true for the important role of activation and social investment policies. Since 1997, the EU has contributed with the European Employment Strategy to broader inclusion of vulnerable groups into the labour market, thus transforming the exclusive employment regimes in Continental Europe. The success of these policies is documented in particular in the increasing employment and activity rates of women and older people. Starting from a lower employment level, the Central and Eastern European and to some extent even the Southern European countries have also followed this path. This paradigmatic shift is made possible by institutions such as better childcare or better education and training opportunities for older workers as well. However, the architecture of the eurozone has contributed to a backlash in particular in Southern Europe, because it implied that most of the burden of the euro crisis has had to be shouldered by the Southern European labour markets.

# References

Acemoglu, D., & Autor, D. (2011). Skills, tasks and technologies: Implications for employment and earnings. In D. E. Card & O. Ashenfelter (Eds.), *Handbooks in economics: Vol. 5. Handbook of labor economics: Volume 4B (1st ed., Vol. 4, pp. 1043–1171)*. North-Holland. https://doi.org/10.1016/S0169-7218(11)02410-5

Almunia, J. (2020). *Lessons from financial assistance to Greece: Independent evaluation report.* Retrieved from European Stability Mechanism, website: https://www.esm.europa.eu/publications/lessons-financial-assistance-greece https://doi.org/10.2852/082453.

Autor, D. H., Levy, F., & Murnane, R. J. (2003). The skill content of recent technological change: An empirical exploration. *Quarterly Journal of Economics, 118*(4), 1279–1333.

Barbieri, P., & Cutuli, G. (2016). Employment protection legislation, labour market dualism, and inequality in Europe. *European Sociological Review, 32*(4), 501–516. https://doi.org/10.1093/esr/jcv058

Becker, G. S. (1993). *Human capital: A theoretical and empirical analysis, with special reference to education.* University of Chicago Press.

Blanchard, O. (2006). European unemployment: The evolution of facts and ideas. *Economic Policy, 21*(45), 6–59. https://doi.org/10.1111/j.1468-0327.2006.00153.x

Blau, F. D., & Kahn, L. M. (2002). *At home and abroad: U.S. labor-market performance in international perspective.* Russell Sage Foundation.

Blossfeld, H.-P. (Ed.). (2011). *Aging populations, globalization and the labor market: Comparing late working life and retirement in modern societies.* Edward Elgar.

Blyth, M. (2013). *Austerity: The history of a dangerous idea.* Oxford University Press.

Boeri, T., & Garibaldi, P. (2009). Beyond eurosclerosis. *Economic Policy, 24*(59), 409–461. https://doi.org/10.1111/j.1468-0327.2009.00225.x

Bohle, D. (2018). European integration, capitalist diversity and crises trajectories on Europe's eastern periphery. *New Political Economy, 23*(2), 239–253. https://doi.org/10.1080/13563467.2017.1370448

Bonoli, G. (2010). The political economy of active labor-market policy. *Politics and Society, 38*(4), 435–457.

Bosch, G. (2018). Strukturen und Dynamik von Arbeitsmärkten. In F. Böhle, G. G. Voß, & G. Wachtler (Eds.), *Handbuch Arbeitssoziologie: Band 2: Akteure und Institutionen* (Vol. 42, pp. 325–359). Springer. https://doi.org/10.1007/978-3-658-21704-4_11

Bosch, G., Lehndorff, S., & Rubery, J. (Eds.). (2009). *European employment models in flux: A comparison of institutional change in nine European countries (1. Publ).* Palgrave Macmillan UK. https://doi.org/10.1057/9780230237001

Broschinski, S. (2020). *Dynamiken von Lohnungleichheiten in Europa: Betriebliche und arbeitsmarktpolitische Anpassungen während der Eurokrise.* VS. Retrieved from https://www.springer.com/de/book/9783658318932

Broschinski, S., Heidenreich, M., & Pohlig, M. (2020). *Polarization and marginalization during the Eurozone crisis: The persistence of Eurosclerosis* (Oldenburger Studien zur Europäisierung und zur transnationalen Regulierung No. 26). Retrieved from https://uol.de/cetro/publikationen/oldenburger-studien

Bryan, M. L., & Jenkins, S. P. (2016). Multilevel modelling of country effects: A cautionary tale. *European Sociological Review, 32*(1), 3–22.

Calmfors, L., & Driffill, J. (1988). Bargaining structure, corporatism and macroeconomic performance. *Economic Policy, 3*(6), 13–61.

Cantillon, B. (2011). The paradox of the social investment state: Growth, employment and poverty in the Lisbon era. *Journal of European Social Policy, 21*(5), 432–449.

De Grauwe, P. (2016). *Economics of monetary union* (Eleventh ed.). Oxford University Press.

DiPrete, T. A. (2007). What has sociology to contribute to the study of inequality trends? A historical and comparative perspective. *American Behavioral Scientist, 50*(5), 603–618. https://doi.org/10.1177/0002764206295009

Doeringer, P. B., & Piore, M. J. (1971). *Internal labor markets and manpower analysis*. Heath Lexington Books; Sharpe. Retrieved from https://books.google.de/books?id=jgpNnQEACAAJ

Eichhorst, W., Kaufmann, O., & Konle-Seidl, R. (2008). *Bringing the jobless into work? Experiences with activation schemes in Europe and the US*. Springer.

Eichhorst, W., & Marx, P. (2015). Non-standard employment in post-industrial labour markets. In W. Eichhorst & P. Marx (Eds.), *Non-standard employment in post-industrial labour markets: An occupational perspective* (pp. 1–25). Edward Elgar. https://doi.org/10.4337/9781781001721

Emmenegger, P., Häusermann, S., Palier, B., & Seeleib-Kaiser, M. (2012). How we grow unequal. In P. Emmenegger, S. Häusermann, B. Palier, & M. Seeleib-Kaiser (Eds.), *International policy exchange series. The age of dualization: The changing face of inequality in deindustrializing societies* (pp. 3–26). Oxford University Press.

Eribon, D. (2013). *Returning to Reims. Introduction by George Chauncey; translated by Michael Lucey*. MIT Press.

Esping-Andersen, G. (1985). *Politics against markets*. Princeton University Press.

Fetzer, T. (2018). *Did austerity cause Brexit?* (Warwick economics research papers series No. 1170). Coventry. Retrieved from University of Warwick website: http://wrap.warwick.ac.uk/106313/

Gallie, D. (Ed.). (2007a). *Employment regimes and the quality of work*. Oxford University Press.

Gallie, D. (2007b). Employment regimes and the quality of work. In D. Gallie (Ed.), *Employment regimes and the quality of work* (pp. 1–33). Oxford University Press. https://doi.org/10.1093/acprof:oso/9780199230105.001.0001

Gangl, M. (2006). Scar effects of unemployment: An assessment of institutional complementarities. *American Sociological Review, 71*(6), 986–1013.

Goos, M., & Manning, A. (2007). Lousy and lovely jobs: The rising polarization of work in Britain. *The Review of Economics and Statistics, 89*(1), 118–133.

Goos, M., Manning, A., & Salomons, A. (2009). Job polarization in Europe. *American Economic Review, 99*(2), 58–63. https://doi.org/10.1257/aer.99.2.58

Heidenreich, M. (2015). The end of the honeymoon: The increasing differentiation of (long-term) unemployment risks in Europe. *Journal of European Social Policy, 25*(4), 393–413. https://doi.org/10.1177/0958928715594544

Heidenreich, M. (2016a). The double dualization of inequality in Europe: Introduction. In M. Heidenreich (Ed.), *Exploring inequality in Europe* (pp. 1–21). Edward Elgar.

Heidenreich, M. (2016b). Women as the relative winners of the eurozone crisis? Female employment opportunities between austerity, inclusion and dualization. In M. Heidenreich (Ed.), *Exploring inequality in Europe* (pp. 107–138). Edward Elgar.

Heidenreich, M., & Zeitlin, J. (Eds.). (2009). *Changing European employment and welfare regimes: The influence of the open method of coordination on national reforms*. Routledge.

Hemerijck, A. (2013). *Changing welfare states*. Oxford University Press.

ILO. (2012). *International standard classification of occupations // structure, group definitions and correspondence tables: Structure, group definitions and correspondence tables. ISCO-08: Volume I // v. 1*. ILO. Retrieved from https://www.ilo.org/public/english/bureau/stat/isco/index.htm

Kalleberg, A. L. (2011). *Good jobs, bad jobs: The rise of polarized and precarious employment systems in the United States, 1970s to 2000s. American Sociological Association's rose series in sociology*. Russell Sage Foundation.

Kalleberg, A. L., & Sørensen, A. B. (1979). The sociology of labor markets. *Annual Review of Sociology, 5*(1), 351–379.

Karamessini, M., & Rubery, J. (2014). The challenge of austerity for equality. *Revue De L'OFCE, 133*(2), 15. https://doi.org/10.3917/reof.133.0015

Kenworthy, L. (2004). *Egalitarian capitalism: Jobs, incomes, and growth in affluent countries*. Russell Sage Foundation.

Kluve, J. (2010). The effectiveness of European active labor market programs. *Labour Economics, 17*(6), 904–918. https://doi.org/10.1016/j.labeco.2010.02.004

Kohn, M. L. (1987). Cross-national research as an analytic strategy. *American Sociological Review,* *52*(6), 713–731.

de La Porte, C. (2019). *The European pillar of social rights meets the nordic model.* Retrieved from Swedish Institute for European Policy Studies website: http://www.sieps.se/en/publications/201 9/the-european-pillar-of-social-rights-meets-the-nordic-model2/

Lahusen, C. (2021). *The political attitudes of divided European citizens: Public opinion and social inequalities in comparative and relational perspective.* Routledge. https://doi.org/10.4324/ 9781003046653

Leibfried, S. (2015). Social policy: Left to the judges and the markets. In H. Wallace, M. A. Pollack, & A. R. Young (Eds.), *The new European Union series. Policy-making in the European Union (7th ed., pp. 263–292).* Oxford University Press.

Lindbeck, A., & Snower, D. (1988). *The insider-outsider theory of employment and unemployment.* MIT Press.

Markovits, D. (2019). *The meritocracy trap: How America's foundational myth feeds inequality, dismantles the middle class, and devours the elite.* Penguin Press.

Maurin, E., & Postel-Vinay, F. (2005). The European job security gap. *Work and Occupations,* *32*(2), 229–252.

Mood, C. (2010). Logistic regression: Why we cannot do what we think we can do, and what we can do about it. *European Sociological Review, 26*(1), 67–82.

Moreira, A., Alonso Dominguez, Á., Antunes, C., Karamessini, M., Raitano, M., & Glatzer, M. (2015). Austerity-driven labour market reforms in southern Europe: Eroding the security of labour market insiders. *European Journal of Social Security, 17,* 202–225.

Morel, N., Palier, B., & Palme, J. (2012a). Beyond the welfare state as we knew it? In N. Morel, B. Palier, & J. Palme (Eds.), *Towards a social investment welfare state? Ideas, policies and challenges* (pp. 1–30). Policy Press.

Morel, N., Palier, B., & Palme, J. (Eds.). (2012b). *Towards a social investment welfare state? Ideas, policies and challenges.* Policy Press.

Mückenberger, U. (1985). Die Krise des Normalarbeitsverhältnisses: Hat das Arbeitsrecht noch Zukunft? *Zeitschrift Für Sozialreform, 31*(7), 415–434.

Mundell, R. A. (1961). A theory of optimum currency areas. *American Economic Review, 51*(4), 657–665.

Nickell, S. (1997). Unemployment and labor market rigidities: Europe versus North America. *Journal of Economic Perspectives, 11*(3), 55–74. https://doi.org/10.1257/jep.11.3.55

OECD. (1994). *The OECD jobs study: Facts, analysis, strategies. Unemploymenmt in the OECD area* (pp. 1950–1995). OECD.

OECD. (2015). *In it together: Why less inequality benefits all.* OECD.

Olson, M. (1982). *The rise and decline of nations: Economic growth, stagflation, and social rigidities.* Yale University Press. Retrieved from http://www.jstor.org/stable/10.2307/j.ctt1 nprdd. https://doi.org/10.2307/j.ctt1nprdd

Palier, B., Rovny, A. E., & Rovny, J. (2018). European disunion? Social and economic divergence in Europe, and their political consequences. In P. Manow, B. Palier, & H. Schwander (Eds.), *Welfare democracies and party politics: Explaining electoral dynamics in times of changing welfare capitalism* (pp. 281–297). Oxford University Press.

Parkin, F. (1974). Strategies of social closure in class formation. In F. Parkin (Ed.), *The social analysis of class structure* (pp. 1–18). Tavistock Publications.

Reich, M., Gordon, D. M., & Edwards, R. C. (1973). A theory of labor market segmentation. *American Economic Review, 63*(2), 359–365.

Sandel, M. J. (2020). *The tyranny of merit: What's become of the common good?* Farrar Strauss & Giroux.

Schmid, G. (2005). Social risk management through transitional labour markets. *Socio-Economic Review, 4*(1), 1–33.

Schmid, G. (2008). *Full employment in Europe: Managing labour market transitions and risks.* Edward Elgar.

Schwander, H., & Häusermann, S. (2013). Who is in and who is out? A risk-based conceptualization of insiders and outsiders. *Journal of European Social Policy, 23*(3), 248–269.

Serrano Pascual, A. (2007). Reshaping welfare states: Activation regimes in Europe. In A. Serrano Pascual & L. Magnusson (Eds.), *Reshaping welfare states and activation regimes in Europe* (pp. 11–34). Peter Lang.

Siebert, H. (1997). Labor market rigidities: At the root of unemployment in Europe. *Journal of Economic Perspectives, 11*(3), 37–54. https://doi.org/10.2307/2138183

Sørensen, A. B. (1983). Processes of allocation to open and closed positions in social structure. *Zeitschrift für Soziologie, 12*(3), 203–224.

Streeck, W. (1991). On the institutional conditions of diversified quality production. In E. Matzner & W. Streeck (Eds.), *Beyond Keynesianism: The socio-economics of production and full employment* (pp. 21–61).

Taru, M. (2016, May). *Overview of meta-analysis of active labour market programs. EXCEPT Working Papers: No. 5*. Tallinn University. Retrieved from http://www.except-project.eu/working-papers

Therborn, G. (1995). *European modernity and beyond: The trajectory of European societies, 1945–2000*. Sage.

Vandenbroucke, F. (2018). *The European pillar of social rights: From promise to delivery: An introduction to the ESU debate*. Retrieved from www.euvisions.eu/europea-social-union-public-forum-debate-vandenbroucke/

Vandenbroucke, F., & Vleminckx, K. (2011). Disappointing poverty trends: Is the social investment state to blame? *Journal of European Social Policy, 21*(5), 450–471. https://doi.org/10.1177/0958928711418857

Weishaupt, J. T. (2010). A silent revolution? New management ideas and the reinvention of European public employment services. *Socio-Economic Review, 8*(3), 461–486.

Weishaupt, J. T. (2011). *From the manpower revolution to the activation paradigm: Explaining institutional continuity and change in an integrating Europe. Changing welfare states*. Amsterdam University Press.

Zeitlin, J. (2009). The open method of coordination and reform of national social and employment policies: Influences, mechanisms, effects. In M. Heidenreich & J. Zeitlin (Eds.), *Changing European employment and welfare regimes: The influence of the open method of coordination on national reforms* (pp. 214–245). Routledge.

Zeitlin, J., & Vanhercke, B. (2018). Socializing the European semester: EU social and economic policy co-ordination in crisis and beyond. *Journal of European Public Policy, 25*(2), 149–174. https://doi.org/10.1080/13501763.2017.1363269

# Chapter 6
# Wage Inequalities in the EU

**Abstract** This chapter discusses between- und within-country wage inequality, which is a major determinant of income inequality. Wage inequalities in Europe are shaped by national institutions and wage policies, in particular the respective share of industrial employment, union strength, minimum wages and spending on social protection. Significant wage inequalities are accompanied by a high proportion of low-paid jobs and low wages for women, young people, migrants and the unskilled. Europeanisation can also be observed in the wage dimension. Economic integration in Europe is accompanied by significant reductions in between-country wage differences. Mainly due to the 'catching-up' of Central and Eastern European countries, total and between-country wage inequalities are decreasing significantly. For a long time, this has reduced the fears of wage dumping which can be the reverse side of the European single market. Secondly, not only the single market but also the common currency points to the European dimension of wage policy. Wages become a central buffer for economic shocks. Therefore, wage cuts due to austerity policies have been expected. However, this assumption cannot be supported. European bailouts during the euro crisis may even have helped cushion wage losses. Third, also in the subjective dimension, a transnationalisation of wage inequalities can be observed: Particularly in wealthier and more unequal countries, low wages are accompanied by increasing economic stress.

This chapter examines the unequal distribution and evolution of wages in the EU.[1] Wages are a key dimension of labour market inequality, alongside the employment inequalities considered previously, because the market income of most households is determined by the number of employed members and the wages they earn. Households with low wages or few wage earners are more vulnerable to poverty and exclusion than other households. Classically, wage structures in Europe are described as egalitarian compared to the US (DiPrete, 2007). The gaps between insiders and outsiders described in the previous chapter can also be expected in terms

---

[1] In the following, all income from paid employment—i.e. wages for blue-collar workers and salaries for white-collar workers and civil servants—is referred to as wages or earnings.

of wages. A first aim of this chapter therefore is to analyse the contradictory combination of relatively egalitarian and at the same time segmented wage structures within the European countries. Secondly, wage structures also have a European dimension, even if wage policies are largely formulated and regulated nationally (Höpner & Lutter, 2018). Market opening processes such as that in Europe are a challenge to national wage and collective bargaining structures, which could lead to an increase in within-country and a decrease in between-country wage inequalities (Beckfield, 2006, 2009). In addition, among the members of the European monetary union, the euro crisis might also have contributed to an increase in between-country inequalities, since the adjustment of wages, the so-called real devaluation, has been an important feature of national and European reactions to the eurozone crisis since 2010. The second aim of this chapter is thus to highlight this European dimension.

Following a brief overview of the academic discussion on wage formation (Sect. 6.1), the next section discusses the relationship between the still largely national structuring of wage setting and its central importance for the economic, monetary and social integration of Europe (Sect. 6.2). Subsequently, the development of between- and within-country wage inequalities is analysed in order to answer the question of whether wages in the EU are converging (Sect. 6.3). In the next section, the structure and development of national wage inequalities in the EU during and after the financial market and euro crises are described and the determinants of European inequality patterns are elaborated (Sect. 6.4). The subsequent section takes a closer look at low-wage earners and examines the impact of low wages on the risk of poverty and life satisfaction (Sect. 6.5). The chapter concludes with a brief summary (Sect. 6.6).

## 6.1   Wages as Essential Dimension of Social Inequality

A central yardstick for assessing people's economic situation are their financial resources, in general measured by the level of their disposable income (Chap. 7). This income can be obtained in three ways: By transfer payments from the state (for example unemployment benefits or pensions), from other family members or as remuneration from self-employment or employment. For most people and households, wages are the most important income source. Therefore, wage levels and wage inequalities are essential for assessing the social situation in a country or in Europe. There are five reasons for this: First, increasing wage inequalities are a central cause of increasing market inequalities. All other things being equal—in particular a comparable employment intensity of households and a comparable redistribution through taxes and social contributions—higher wage inequalities also mean higher income inequalities.

Secondly, independently of the level of income inequalities, wage inequalities can also be perceived as unfair and contribute to divisions in society. This is documented, for example, in the discussion about the level of managerial earnings or top earners' share of total earnings (Piketty & Saez, 2014; Piketty et al., 2018).

The explosive nature of this perceived injustice—many people find it inappropriate for managers to earn a hundred times more than their employees—can be illustrated with a thought experiment: The economy of a small country is characterised, on the one hand, by large corporations oriented towards the global market and, on the other hand, by a high proportion of personal services, often provided by the state (health, childcare, nursing, education, employment services . . .). While the global companies can pay very high wages to their globally active managers, wages for personal services (and thus in many cases also wages for women) are significantly lower. Despite considerable wage differences between global and domestic companies, income inequalities in this thought experiment may be very small due to comprehensive welfare state and tax redistributions or to marriages between persons in the two sectors. This country would thus combine high wage inequalities with low income inequalities. However, the economic dualisation would be accompanied by further divisions, such as territorial, sectoral, age-, skill- and gender-specific divisions. Thus, unequal wages could threaten the cohesion of society despite egalitarian income structures, because wage levels are always also an expression of how society values the respective activity. Not only work and income, but also the level of wages and the related social recognition are an important basis for social integration.

This is also expressed in the debate on in-work poverty (Lohmann & Marx, 2018): If people cannot secure their livelihood despite having a full-time job, this is usually seen as deeply unfair—even if they receive enough money from private or public transfers, for example a guaranteed minimum income. This previous thought experiment illustrates that decoupling notions of fair wages and sufficient income provision only works to a limited extent. A significant gap between low and top earners can undermine the belief in the legitimacy of the economic order. The threat this poses to the cohesion of society has been described by Dahrendorf (1996, p. 239) in an impressive way: "However, poverty and unemployment threaten their very fabric. Civil society requires opportunities of participation which in the OECD societies (if not universally) are provided by work and a decent minimum standard of living. Once these are lost by a growing number, civil society goes with them." For Dahrendorf, the rise of populist authoritarian regimes is an indicator of such a disintegration. Because of their impact on income inequality and social cohesion, wage inequalities are thus a central facet of social inequalities. This is true, first of all, in the national context. But if the level and evolution of wages in a country are permanently lower than the European average and its inhabitants no longer see the possibility of achieving a decent standard of living through their earnings, this will also undermine social cohesion in the EU.

Thirdly, technological change can lead to increasing wage inequalities. This can be expected on the basis of the thesis of skill-biased technological change (Autor et al., 2003). This thesis assumes that technological change will increase the demand for highly skilled labour. A consequence would be increasing wage inequality between highly and low-skilled workers. While this thesis expects a relative decrease in low-skilled jobs, the polarisation thesis predicts a decreasing importance of routine jobs. Since these jobs, which are both blue- and white-collar jobs, often require a medium qualification, the polarisation thesis expects increasing levels of high- und low-skilled activities and decreasing levels of intermediary tasks (Chap. 9). Examples of low-skilled but non-routinised activities are cleaning, delivery, warehousing, sales, care and logistics activities. This then leads to a polarisation between high- and low-skilled, between "lovely and lousy jobs" (Goos & Manning, 2007). Both the skill-biased technology change and the polarisation theses thus expect an increase in highly skilled, problem-solving activities and also an increase in wage inequalities. The American example in particular has been used to vividly describe the social consequences of this increase (Case & Deaton, 2020).

Fourth, wages and wage structures are also shaped by national institutions. They are not just technologically or economically determined. This is emphasised by both economic and sociological approaches. In the economic discussion, wage levels are analysed as the result of supply and demand on the labour market. However, this basic neoclassical model is a simplified model that has been further developed in various directions by making more realistic assumptions. In particular, the importance of economic, technological and institutional contexts has been elaborated in various approaches ranging from human capital theory to efficiency wage, contract theories, search and matching theories to segmentation theories (Ashenfelter & Card, 1999; Card & Ashenfelter, 2011). National institutions such as minimum wages, social security, trade unions, collective bargaining systems or labour law, and in particular employment protection legislation (Gonalons-Pons & Gangl, 2021) thus become the focus of attention (Blanchard, 2006; Blau & Kahn, 2002). In contrast, sociological approaches start from the dual role of labour markets as markets and as arenas structured by power relations, social closure and inequality and highlight the dual function of wages as the central source of income for most people and as expenditures and essential determinants of company competitiveness (Braverman, 1998; Kalleberg & Sørensen, 1979). A labour market is always a contested terrain characterised by conflicts about the control of the labour process (Reich et al., 1973). These conflicts shape organisational structures, the use of technology and personnel and human resource management. They also contribute to the segmentation of labour markets into primary and secondary markets, into internal and external markets, into good and bad jobs (Kalleberg, 2011). Wage structures are shaped to a considerable extent by social and legal norms. Societal institutions such as health and safety at work, collective bargaining and collective agreements, labour law, minimum wages, unemployment benefits and other forms of social protection are therefore crucial in shaping national wage structures.

In sum: wages are central components of income, wage levels are decisive for subjective perceptions of justice and for social cohesion, wage structures are shaped by technological dynamics and embedded in national institutions. Fifthly, wages play a crucial role in European monetary union and are a crucial challenge to cross-border economic integration. The last point will be elaborated in the next step.

## 6.2 Wages in the European Integration Process

A central economic and institutional context for national wage policies is the EU. At first sight, this is surprising, as the EU has no original competences in the area of wage policy. Many of the previously mentioned studies therefore refer to individual European countries (Blau & Kahn, 2002; DiPrete, 2007). The role of the EU is rarely addressed (cf. however Broschinski, 2020; Fernández-Macías & Vacas, 2015; Pereira & Galego, 2019; Pernicka et al., 2019). Nevertheless, wages and wage inequalities have been an important reference point for European policies since the beginning of the European integration process. This stems firstly from their importance for maintaining living standards in a transnational economic space characterised by intensified cross-border competition, and secondly from their role for the common currency.

First, at the heart of European integration is the creation of a common economic area as a basis for cross-border trade and economic integration. Workers can emigrate or commute to other member states because of higher wages and they can offer their services abroad. At the same time, this can exert pressure on wages and working conditions in high-wage countries. European integration was thus always a challenge to national wage structures. Therefore, increased wage competition and the risk of wage dumping have been important reference points for European integration, even if they are rarely articulated openly. The founding treaties of the European Economic Community (1957) already enshrined the principle that men and women should be paid equally for equal work (Pollack & Hafner-Burton, 2000). This was not intended to prevent wage dumping between member states, but to make it fair. The principle of fairness, which also governs international trade agreements (Rodrik, 2018), was therefore institutionalised in the EU and its predecessor organisations as the principles of equal treatment and non-discrimination. The principle that men and women should be treated equally in wage matters which has now become Article 157 of the Treaty on the Functioning of the European Union (TFEU)was taken up and generalised by the European Court of Justice and is now enshrined as a general principle in the Treaty of the European Union (Article 2), in the Charter of Fundamental Rights and in numerous directives derived from it. It prohibits not only unequal pay between men and women for equal work or work of equal value, but also other forms of discrimination (TFEU, Art. 18, 19) based on age, ethnic and national origins, religion or beliefs, sexual orientations and disabilities. This general principle of equal treatment could have been the starting point for a policy against cross-border forms of wage dumping. However, the comparison with Switzerland in particular—where wage dumping was prevented by so-called accompanying or flanking measures (Erne et al., 2015)—makes it clear that the protection of national wage structures was not sought in the EU. A major reason for this is that the setting of wages and the way they are set were and are exclusive competences of the nation-states or the national social partners (Streeck, 1998). Nevertheless, the EU has indeed anchored the principle of "equal pay for equal work in the same place" in the Posting of Workers Directive adopted in 1996 and revised in 2016, thus attempting to put a stop to cross-border wage dumping. However, it was hardly possible to enforce this principle through individual complaints. And the European Court of Justice put a stop to collective actions through a series of rulings (Viking, Laval, Rüffert; cf. Blanke, 2008), as they must be proportionate and must not restrict the right of European companies to free movement in the internal market. Collective forms of interest representation and the binding nature of collective bargaining rules have thus been weakened by cross-border liberalisation and deregulation processes in the EU (Bengtsson, 2016; Joerges & Rödl, 2009; N. Reich, 2008). The access of companies from other EU member states to the domestic market takes precedence over the protection of national wage structures. As a result, attempts to protect domestic wage structures occasionally took the form of a fight against immigration (e.g. during the refugee crisis in 2015, the Brexit vote in 2016 or the Swiss mass immigration initiative in 2014). A social question was reframed as an ethnic-nationalist question.

Second, a European-wide wage coordination mechanism does not exist—even though it might be necessary in the context of a European monetary union in order to avoid exorbitantly high divergences in unemployment rates or corresponding transfer payments (Höpner & Lutter, 2018; Pernicka et al., 2019). Both the primacy of national industrial relations, differences between national wage-setting institutions and the primacy of the internal market imply that neither the forms nor the outcomes of wage setting are effectively regulated at the European or eurozone level. Only during the euro crisis did the EU and the IMF temporarily partially assume a coordinating function with the so-called *memoranda of understanding* which accompanied the European-international bailout programmes (Broschinski, 2020, p. 100).

In view of the weaknesses of transnational forms of wage coordination, the EU has recently turned to minimum wages. In an important social policy initiative by the Juncker Commission, an appropriate minimum wage was requested in 2017 in the European Pillar of Social Rights:

> Workers have the right to fair wages that provide for a decent standard of living. Adequate minimum wages shall be ensured, in a way that provides for the satisfaction of the needs of the worker and his/her family in the light of national economic and social conditions, whilst safeguarding access to employment and incentives to seek work. In-work poverty shall be prevented. All wages shall be set in a transparent and predictable way according to national practices and respecting the autonomy of the social partners. (European Parliament, Council of the European Union & European Commission, 2017, 6th principle)

This is the EU's response to the weakening of trade unions across Europe, the increase in in-work poverty (Lohmann & Marx, 2018) and a presumed increase in wage inequality. It remains an open question whether the European Pillar of Social Rights will contribute to stronger social cohesion at the European level. In any case, Sect. 6.4 will confirm the impact of existing national minimum wages on the level of wage inequalities, especially in the lower part of the wage distribution.

While minimum wages aim to reduce domestic wage inequalities, they do not affect cross-border inequalities and do not facilitate wage coordination beyond national borders. This however is a crucial point for the Economic and Monetary

Union. The institutionalisation of a common European currency for initially 11 and now 19 countries implied the abolition of flexible exchange rates which were the most important buffer for asymmetric economic shocks (Sect. 5.3.1). As the optimum currency area theory has emphasised since the 1960s (Friedman, 1997; Mundell, 1961), the abolition of flexible exchange rates requires alternative buffers against asymmetric shocks. This buffer function can be assumed by intergovernmental transfers, by cross-border mobility, by flexible wages or flexible working times. Since the European monetary union is characterised by the institutional separation of a Europeanised monetary policy from national fiscal policies and a non-bailout clause (Preunkert, 2015), intergovernmental transfers are only possible to a limited extent—even if the corresponding rule in Article 125 of the Treaty on the Functioning of the EU was considerably stretched during the euro crisis. The between-country mobility of the European labour force remains low. The lack of other means of reacting to asymmetric shocks explains the crucial role of wage adjustment strategies (in addition to the previously discussed labour market adjustment strategies).

This raises the question of how wages and within- and between-country wage inequalities have evolved in the EU during and after the financial market and euro crises. Firstly, it can be expected that intensified economic exchange due to the liberalisation and integration of markets leads to a gradual reduction in wage differentials between EU member states—a convergence process which will not be stopped by the financial market and euro crises. *This effect will be greater the larger the wage gaps between the countries are (H1). Second, the primacy of economic liberalisation and deregulation, the low importance of rules to prevent wage dumping and the lack of transnational buffers for asymmetric economic shocks could lead to increasing within-country wage inequalties (H2). Third, these factors could also lead to increasing shares of low-wage workers (i.e. workers earning less than two-thirds of the median hourly wage) (H3).* These hypotheses specify the second and fourth Europeanisation concepts initially mentioned, raising the questions about the significance of EU policies on people's earnings situation and about the transnational structuring of the field of wage policy—even in the absence of institutionalised European wage coordination (Höpner & Lutter, 2018; Pernicka et al., 2019).

These three hypotheses, which relate to pan-European and within- and between-country wage inequalities, will be discussed on the basis of analyses of Europe-wide and between-country wage inequalities (Sect. 6.3) and national wage inequalities in the EU (Sect. 6.4). Subsequently, the distribution and evolution of low wages in Europe is analysed as a specific facet of national wage inequalities (Sect. 6.5). Finally, the results are summarised (Sect. 6.6).

## 6.3   The Evolution of Wage Inequalities across Europe

Chapter 4 showed that economic liberalisation in the EU can contribute to cross-border convergence of economic performance. In particular, the integration of less developed countries and regions into cross-border value chains could therefore lead to the cross-border equalisation of wage levels. This has been observed in recent years especially in Central and Eastern Europe. It can therefore be expected that economic integration in Europe will be accompanied by a decreasing EU-wide wage differential.

Europe-wide wage inequalities can be calculated in two ways—either as wage inequalities between all dependent employees in the EU, or as a (weighted) average of national wage inequalities. In the first case, between-country inequalities are also included. This can be justified by the fact that wage developments and national collective bargaining can only be adequately framed in the context of a common economic and monetary area. In the second case, between-country wage inequalities are omitted, because wage policy is seen as a primarily national policy field emphasising the ineffectiveness of transnational wage coordination (Höpner & Lutter, 2018). In line with the former perspective, the development of wage inequalities in the EU-28 (excluding Croatia, which only joined the EU in 2013, but still including the UK) will be examined first. Based on Fernández-Macías and Vacas (2015), an increase in these inequalities can be expected. This study notes a decrease in wage inequalities between 2004 and 2008, followed by an increase: "The main driver behind the increase in wage inequality after 2008, nevertheless, was within-country inequality, which until that point had remained more or less stable. But such increase was to a large extent driven by developments in the UK, without which the overall EU within-country component of inequality remained more or less stable as a result of rather diverse developments at the country level." (Fernández-Macías & Vacas, 2015, p. 61).

In contrast to this study, the results presented below are in line with the recent study by Broschinski (2020, p. 143). This study observes a continuous decrease (and not an increase!) in wage inequality within the EU-28 (excluding Croatia) between 2006 and 2016 (measured both by the Theil and Gini coefficients and by the decile ratios D9/D1 and D5/D1). Broschinski (2020, p. 144) explains the difference to the study by Fernández-Macías and Vacas (2015) as follows: "First, the authors use gross monthly earnings in full-time equivalents instead of gross hourly wages. Second, their sample includes 24 member states instead of the 27 used here, thus excluding Bulgaria and Romania in the distribution."

Figure 6.1 shows six common indicators for gross hourly wage inequality for the EU-28 (excluding Croatia), Norway and Switzerland and the 15 EU Member States that were already part of the EU before 2004 (EU-15). These and the following figures refer to the gross hourly wages of all employees aged 15–64 (excluding apprentices). To calculate average working hours, gender- and country-specific working hours are calculated for full-time and part-time employees (cf. in detail on the calculation of gross hourly wages adjusted for purchasing power Broschinski,

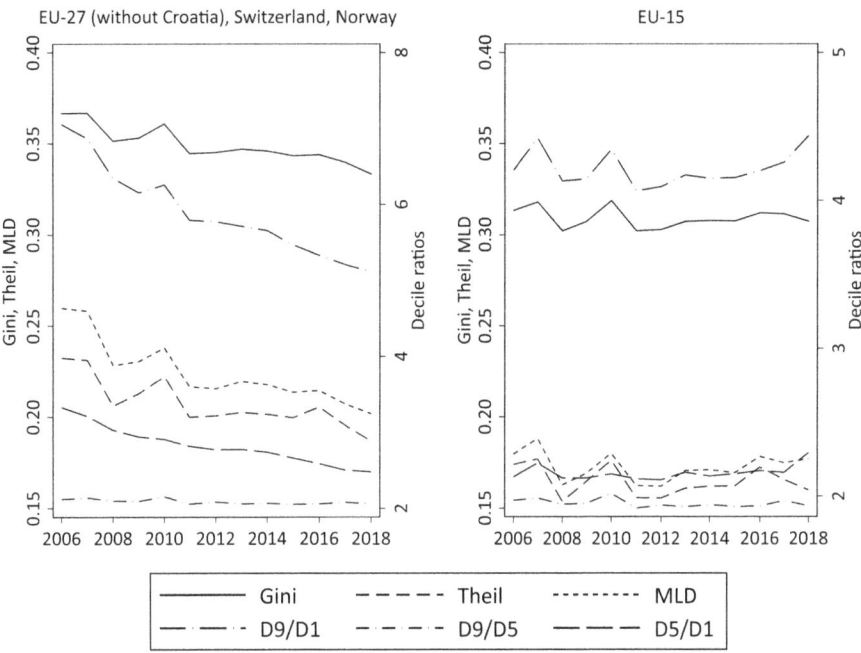

Source: Own calculations based on price-adjusted gross hourly earnings based on EU-SILC UDB 2007-2019 (2018 excluding the UK). The first three indicators are shown on the left-hand scale and the decile ratios on the right-hand scale.

**Fig. 6.1** Inequalities in gross hourly wages in Europe (2006–2018; PPS)

2020, pp. 119–120). The six inequality indices used primarily differ in terms of their sensitivity to inequalities in different regions of the wage distribution (see Chap. 3).

For the EU-27, Switzerland and Norway, Fig. 6.1 shows clearly decreasing wage inequalities, with the exception of 2009/10. The Gini coefficient decreases from 0.37 (2006) to 0.33 (2018). This value is significantly lower than in the US; Fernández-Macías and Vacas (2015, p. 1) estimate the corresponding value at 0.40. It is also lower than in Bulgaria (2017: 0.38), Lithuania (0.35), Latvia (0.35) and is as high as the wage inequalities in Cyprus, Estonia and the UK. The wage inequality between the upper and the lower decile (D9/D1) declines even more significantly, from 7.1 to 5.2. What is remarkable, however, is a broad stability in the upper half of the wage distribution: the decile ratio D9/D5 stagnates at 2.1. This indicates that the rapid wage convergence in the enlarged EU was mainly due to the catching-up of the Central and Eastern European countries—which were at the bottom of the wage hierarchy at the beginning of the period under consideration. This is also indicated by the fact that the MLD has fallen much faster than the Theil index.

The situation in the 15 oldest EU member states, on the other hand, is quite different (Fig. 6.1). In the EU-15 (excluding the Central and Eastern European countries, Malta and Cyprus that joined since 2004), wage inequalities are, firstly,

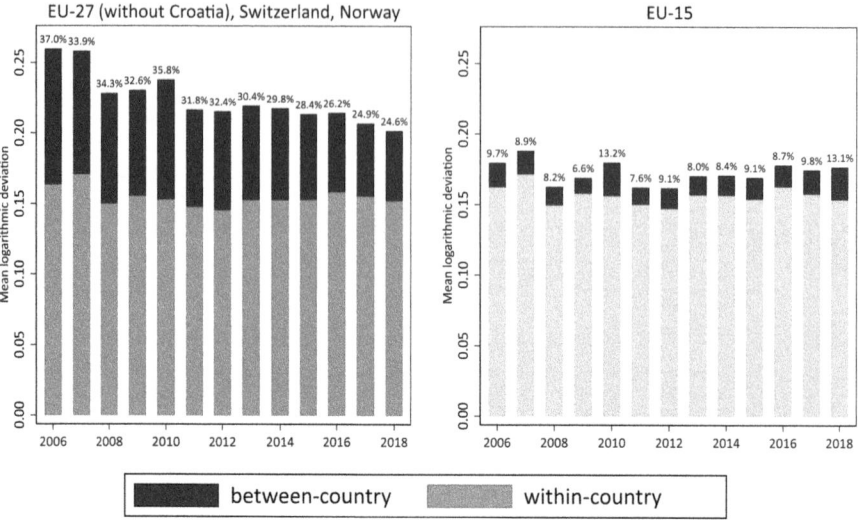

Source: Own calculations based on price-adjusted gross hourly wage based on EU-SILC UDB 2007-2019.

**Fig. 6.2** Evolution of within- and between-country wage inequalities in Europe (MLD, 2006–2018)

significantly lower than in the EU-27. The Gini coefficient was already at 0.31 in 2006, but then remained at this level until 2017 with some fluctuations. This also applies to the three decile ratios, the Theil index and the MLD. When also considering the findings presented in the previous chapter, this can be interpreted as the (at least temporary) end of convergence through economic integration between wealthier and other developed countries (Barro & Sala-i-Martin, 1991): A reduction of Europe-wide wage differentials through relocation of production, wage increases in low-wage areas (such as on the Iberian Peninsula since the 1980s or in Central and Eastern Europe immediately after the fall of communism) and a concomitant decrease in between-country inequalities can no longer be expected from 2006–2017 in the 15 oldest EU member states. To test this assumption, Fig. 6.2 decomposes Europe-wide wage inequalities into within- and between-country inequalities.

Figure 6.2 shows the level and development of between- and within-country wage inequalities in the EU-27 (without Croatia), Norway, Switzerland and the EU-15. Analogous to Fig. 7.2, the mean logarithmic deviation (MLD) is chosen as an indicator, because it is particularly sensitive to changes in the lower range. On the one hand, it can be seen that the inequalities between the "old" EU member states in particular are significantly lower than in the enlarged EU (plus Norway and Switzerland) from 2006 onwards. Secondly, the within-country inequalities in the two groups of countries do not differ systematically from each other, i.e. the countries that joined the EU recently are on average not characterised by significantly higher or lower inequalities. Third, the left-hand panel shows a rapid convergence of

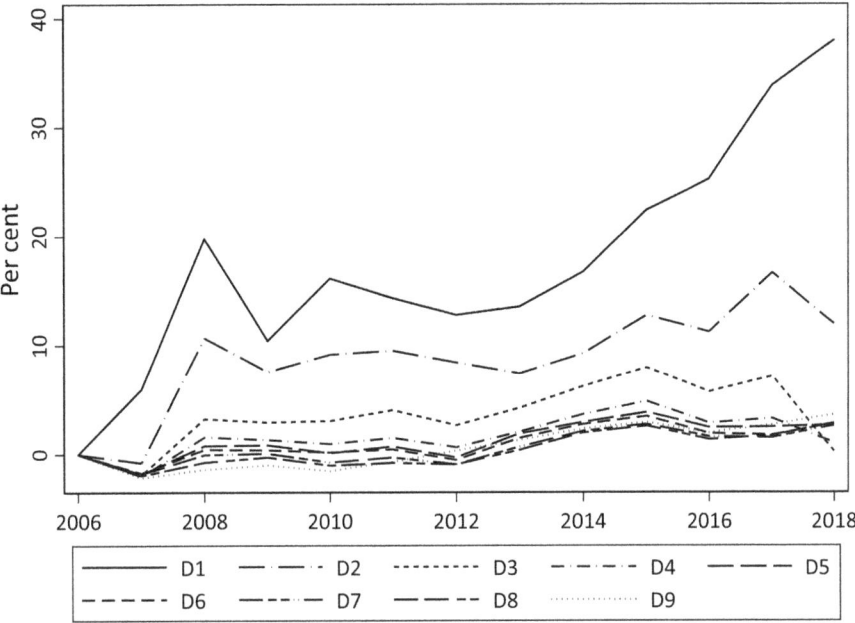

Source: Own calculations based on EU-SILC 2007-2019.

**Fig. 6.3** Evolution of real wages in Europe in various deciles (EU-27 without Croatia, Switzerland, Norway; 2006 = 100%)

European wage structures, i.e. gross hourly wages in the 27 countries of the enlarged EU, Norway and Switzerland are converging rapidly, with between-country wage inequality and the share of between-country wage inequality in total wage inequality falling from 37% (2006) to 24.6% (2018). This points to rapid convergence in the enlarged EU: Central and Eastern Europe have caught up quickly through production relocations, for example in the automotive industry, and through the Europeanisation of markets, and have been able to integrate successfully into European and global value chains.

In the 15 old member states, on the other hand, the between-country share of wage inequalities is around 9%. If a trend can be discerned at all, it is that of a decrease until the beginning of the euro crisis in 2009 and a subsequent increase. In the case of the Southern European countries, convergence thus seems to have reached its limits. Here, the effects of the demand-led growth models of the Southern European countries (Iversen et al., 2016; Hall, 2014) and the accompanying asymmetric effects of the euro crisis are particularly worthy of consideration (Heidenreich, 2015). These have also slowed down economic growth in the Southern European countries (Chap. 4) and thus limited the wage increases to be redistributed.

Looking at the development of real wages for the nine different deciles, Fig. 6.3 shows that especially lower wages have increased, while wages in the upper seven deciles have stagnated across Europe. The increase in the lower three deciles reflects once again the rapid development of the Central and Eastern European countries.

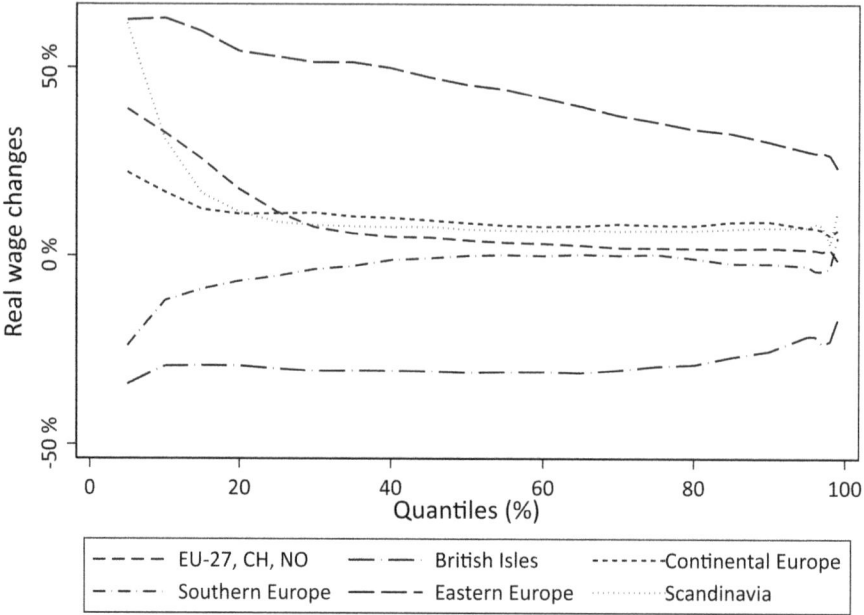

**Fig. 6.4** Real wage changes in different earnings hierarchies. Five European country groups; 2006–2018

Source: Own calculations based on EU-SILC 2007-2019.

This assumption can be confirmed and refined by looking at the evolution in real wages in five European country groups. In Fig. 6.4, wage development in the EU-28 (excluding Croatia), Switzerland and Norway and in five country groups from 2006–2018 is plotted at various wage levels from the bottom to the top 5% of the wage hierarchy. With the exception of Central and Eastern European countries, the period under consideration was a lost decade for average earners. Wages are also stagnating in the top half even a decade after the onset of the financial and euro crises. Only in the bottom quarter are there significant wage increases of 10% or more in three of the five country groups. In Central and Eastern Europe, gross hourly wages have risen the most across Europe—and especially in the lower wage groups. While the lower wage groups earned 50% more in real terms, this growth has already halved in the eighth decile. The Eastern European growth rates are only surpassed by the extraordinary growth in the very lowest wage group in Scandinavia. However, these increases in the very lowest range—the bottom 5% earn 62% more—are so high that they may be due to survey errors. This is also to be suspected because no other information is available on such exorbitant increases. At the other end of the spectrum are the Southern European countries and the British Isles. On the one hand, wage changes in these two groups of countries are below the European average. Secondly, wage losses can be observed in all wage groups. Thirdly, in Southern Europe these losses are concentrated in the lowest wage groups. The lowest decile has suffered losses 12 percentage points greater than the median wage earner. On the

**Table 6.1** Decomposition of wage inequalities in the EU-28, Switzerland and Norway (excluding Croatia; 2006–2018)

|  | Gini | D9/D1 | D9/D5 | D5/D1 |
|---|---|---|---|---|
| 2018 | 0.334 | 5.000 | 2.081 | 2.403 |
| 2006 | 0.365 | 6.751 | 2.142 | 3.151 |
| Change | −0.030 | −1.751 | −0.062 | −0.748 |
| Composition | 0.001 | 0.113 | 0.009 | 0.044 |
| Structural effect | −0.032 | −1.864 | −0.071 | −0.792 |
| Composition |  |  |  |  |
| Gender | 0.000 | −0.001 | −0.001 | 0.001 |
| Age | −0.002 | −0.040 | −0.007 | −0.011 |
| Migration | 0.001 | 0.011 | 0.007 | −0.003 |
| Education | 0.001 | 0.021 | 0.011 | −0.002 |
| Social class | 0.002 | 0.082 | 0.015 | 0.022 |
| Economic sector | 0.001 | 0.023 | −0.005 | 0.017 |
| Occupation | 0.000 | −0.006 | 0.003 | −0.006 |
| Part-time | 0.000 | 0.003 | 0.003 | −0.002 |
| Country | −0.002 | 0.020 | −0.016 | 0.028 |
| Structural effect |  |  |  |  |
| Gender | 0.001 | −0.350 | −0.032 | −0.151 |
| Age | 0.001 | −0.009 | −0.010 | 0.033 |
| Migration | −0.001 | 0.027 | −0.006 | 0.027 |
| Education | 0.001 | 0.151 | 0.005 | 0.098 |
| Social class | −0.010 | 0.419 | −0.042 | 0.164 |
| Economic sector | −0.007 | −0.630 | 0.001 | −0.330 |
| Occupation | −0.005 | −0.068 | −0.038 | −0.013 |
| Part-time | 0.000 | 0.086 | −0.003 | 0.059 |
| Country | 0.034 | −0.598 | 0.324 | −0.676 |

Source: EU-SILC 2007 and 2019 (UK: 2018), own calculations. Decomposition of the real gross hourly wage adjusted for purchasing power based on RIF regressions. For method and procedure see Firpo et al. (2018) and Broschinski (2020)

British Isles, wage losses in the lowest decile were almost as high as for median earners, but they were an almost unimaginable 29% lower. This suggests that Brexit can be explained not only by the traditional Euroscepticism of the British, but also by the effects of the financial market and property crises.

The described developments in wages might have been distorted by composition effects, for example due to increasing unemployment (Broschinski, 2020; Vacas-Soriano, 2018). If mainly low-wage earners have lost their jobs (or were not hired), then the "real" wage losses would be even higher than previously described, because the average educational level and thus the previously expected remuneration of the remaining employees have increased. Therefore, in Table 6.1 wage inequalities are decomposed into compositional and structural effects (cf. Broschinski, 2020, p. 202, also for more detailed, also country-specific analyses). The explanatory characteristics are gender, age, migration background, educational level, social class, economic sector, occupational skills, part-time or full-time employment and the country. The third row shows that wage inequality decreases for all four inequality indicators listed in the table. This decline can hardly be explained by a change in the composition (row 4 relative to row 3) of the labour force. However, education and social class each show clearly positive composition effects: Employees' higher occupational skills mainly have an effect in the upper income range (D9/D5), while class effects are associated with higher inequalities especially in the lower range. This could be explained by the lower importance of simple jobs and the higher employment level in Central and Eastern European countries. However, the decisive factor for the decrease in inequalities, especially in the lower half of the distribution (D5/D1), is the negative structural effects of gender, economic sectors and countries. The relative increase in women's pay can be explained by their higher educational levels and employment opportunities in the expanding service sector. The sectoral and country effects could refer to the wage increases in the booming Central and Eastern European industrial sector. These developments are partly counteracted by positive structural effects of education and social class—an indication of the better pay of higher-skilled and service classes. Overall, the negative structural effects are by far stronger and counteract the effects of improved pay for higher-skilled and upper service classes, thus contributing to declining wage inequalities despite the structural shift to higher skills and a service economy.

In sum: Increasing wage inequalities cannot be observed in Europe and in the EU (Fernández-Macías & Vacas, 2015). On the contrary, wage inequalities in the EU-28 (excluding Croatia), Switzerland and Norway have decreased significantly from 2006–2018. The decline of wage inequalities in the 29 countries observed is entirely due to the decreasing between-country inequalities—a result of the rapid economic development of the Central and Eastern European countries and the related wage increases. It is mainly employees in the lower half of the wage hierarchy who have benefited from this. Their wages—in contrast to the lower wages in Southern Europe and the British Isles—have increased more than in all other European areas. In the 15 older member states, on the other hand, the convergence of wages has come to a standstill since the financial market and euro crises. For these countries, an end of convergence (Beckfield, 2019) can be observed, because on the one hand the previous drivers of convergence—the economic differences between Northern and Southern Europe—are becoming less important. While the Eastern European advancement is driven by considerable economic and wage differences and an integration of previously largely closed markets, these factors no longer play a decisive role for Southern Europe. On the other hand, the close monetary coupling between very differently regulated countries—which Hall (2014) contrasts as supply- and demand-driven growth regimes—has had a negative impact on Southern Europe during the euro crisis due to their higher debts. However, the highest real wage losses of all five country groups considered have been recorded by the British Isles, although the UK—the largest of the two countries—has not adopted the euro. Low earners there are still experiencing real wage losses ten years after the start of the financial market crisis. Finally, the structural causes of the decreasing wage inequalities were examined with the help of a decomposition analysis. This showed that structural effects in particular explain the wage evolutions previously analysed—above all the improved earnings opportunities of women and the rapid development of Central and Eastern European countries and their industries. These factors have so far still succeeded in counteracting "inequality-increasing" composition effects such as increased use and improved pay of higher-skilled and upper service classes. The considerable wage losses in Southern Europe and the British Isles as well as the stable wage inequalities in the upper income segment (D9/D5) are clear effects of the financial market and euro crises.

The following section analyses the national wage structures and their evolution before, during and after the financial market and euro crises of 2008–2013. In addition, the institutions and decisions which shape patterns of wage inequality are considered.

## 6.4   National Wage Inequalities in Europe

Different national wage levels are a key source of economic and social inequalities in Europe (Fig. 6.5). In 2018, gross hourly wages for all full-time and part-time dependent employees aged 15–64 averaged €2.53 in Bulgaria, €31.58 in Switzerland

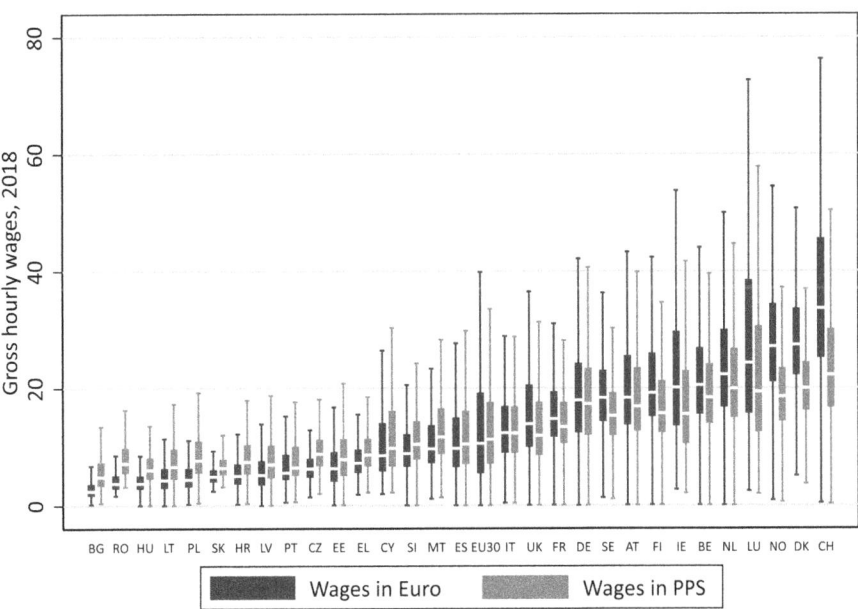

Box: median line, upper & lower quartile (IQR); whiskers: maximum 1.5 times the IQR; Source: EU-SILC 2019.

**Fig. 6.5** Gross hourly wages in the EU-28, Norway and Switzerland (in euros and purchasing power standards, 2018)

and €13 in all 30 countries considered. These wage differences are accompanied by considerable differences in disposable income. Here, however, the different purchasing power in the various EU countries must be considered, since employees can afford significantly more with one euro in Bulgaria than in Denmark. If this correction factor, the so-called purchasing power standards (PPS), is applied, the gross hourly wage in Bulgaria is 5 PPS, in Switzerland 21 PPS and in total 12.48 PPS. While the wages of Swiss workers in euros are twelve times higher than those of Bulgarian workers, their purchasing power is "only" four times higher. Different wage levels are thus an important cause of intra-European income differences. However, due to public and intra-family redistributions, income differences are usually much smaller than wage differences. The median disposable income of Swiss households, for example, is "only" three times higher than that of Bulgarian households.

Complementary to these between-country differences, wages also vary within a country. This is also indicated in Fig. 6.5 by the size of the boxes containing the middle half of the data and the so-called whiskers, which are 1.5 times the interquartile range (IQR), i.e. the length of the boxes. A good three-quarters of all wage inequalities in the EU are due to within-country differences. Wage inequalities (measured by the Gini) are higher in some countries than in the EU as a whole. This is the case, for example, in Bulgaria (a Gini-coefficient 0.39 in 2018), Cyprus (0.35), Latvia (0.34) and Spain (0.35). In contrast, very egalitarian wage structures can be observed in Slovakia (0.19), Denmark (0.23), Greece (0.23) and Sweden (0.24). The weighted average of the 30 European countries considered is a Gini coefficient of 0.284 (2018). This value is lower than the Europe-wide Gini coefficient of wage inequality (2018: 0.334), as the latter value also takes into account between-country wage inequalities.

Figure 6.6 shows the evolution of wage inequality since 2006. An initial result is the largely stable national patterns in many countries. However, in ten countries the Gini changes by a tenth or more. This can be expected during a turbulent period, marked for instance by the ongoing transformation processes in Central and Eastern Europe, by a global financial market crisis and the euro crisis. While wage inequality declined in 14 EU countries, it increased in 14 countries—notably Bulgaria (+40%), Malta (+29%), Spain (+24.5%) and Italy (+17.2%). The largest decreases could be observed in Slovakia (−27.9%), Romania (−24.9%), Greece (−16.8%), Poland (−15.8%), Sweden (−14.7%) and Slovenia (−14%). Measured by the D9/D1 ratio, increases (+10% and more) were highest in Spain, Bulgaria, Italy and Malta, while inequalities fell most in Romania, Poland, Sweden, Slovakia, Greece, Lithuania, Slovenia, Portugal and Croatia. This decline can be attributed, on the one hand, to rapid growth and the reversal of the previously egalitarian wage patterns in Central and Eastern Europe and, on the other hand, to the drastic wage reductions in some Southern European countries, in particular in Portugal and Greece. Broschinski (2020) convincingly elaborates the downside of more egalitarian wage structures in the crisis: on the one hand, the dismissal or non-employment of young people, low-skilled workers and workers with simple jobs and, on the other hand, lower earnings of higher-skilled workers, managers and public sector workers. In

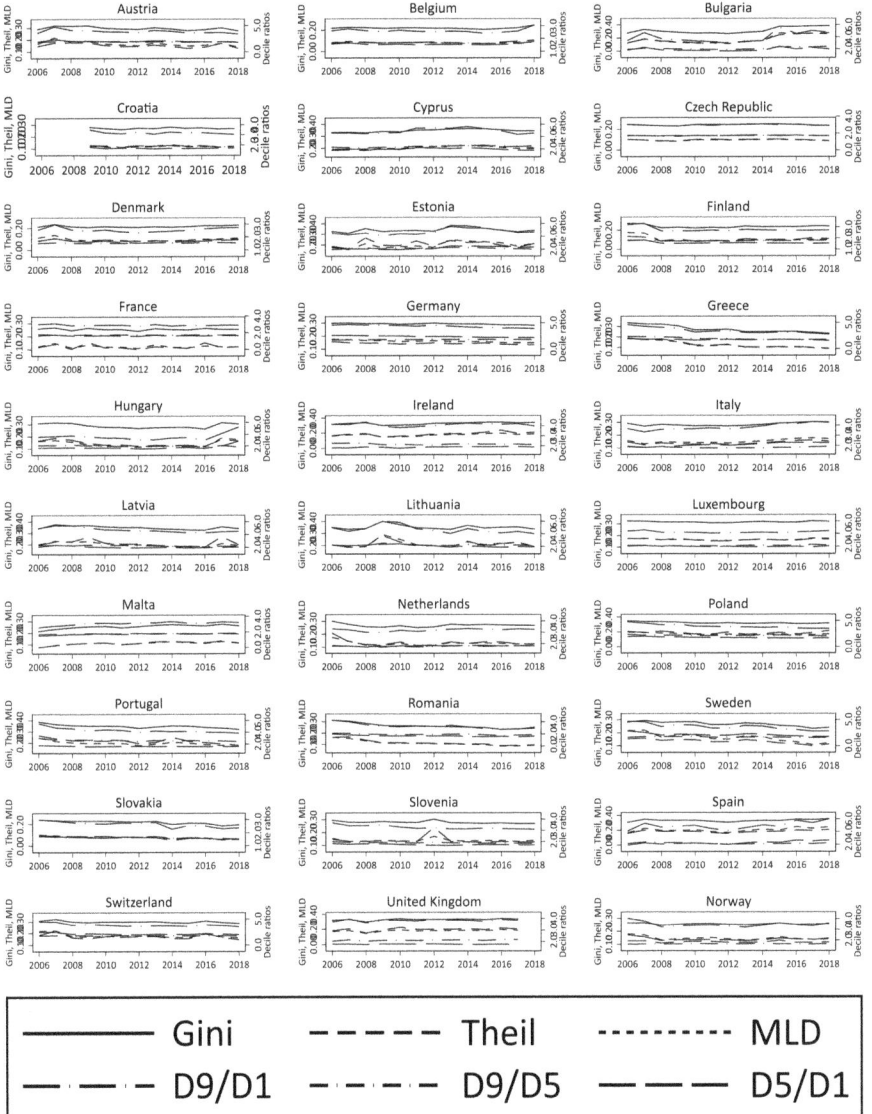

**Fig. 6.6** Inequalities in gross hourly wages in the 28 EU Member States, Switzerland and Norway (2006–2018; PPS)

other Southern and Central European countries, however, inequalities increased significantly (especially in Spain, Bulgaria and Italy). The fact that both higher and lower wage inequalities can be observed in the two regimes where most changes are observed highlights the essential role of national institutions and policies.

The two sub-indices relating to the upper (D9/D5) and the lower half of the wage distribution (D5/D1) have evolved somewhat differently from the comprehensive inequality indices. In the upper part, a significant increase of more than 10% can be observed in Bulgaria and Germany, while decreasing higher wages can be observed in 15 countries (especially in Lithuania, Poland, Romania, Slovakia and Greece). The clear increases in Southern Europe are mainly due to higher wages in Spain (+9%) and Italy (+5.7%). In the lower half, wage inequalities decreased in 16 countries, especially (i.e. by more than 10%) in Sweden, Romania, Poland, Finland, Greece and Slovenia, while they increase by more than 10% in Malta, Bulgaria, Italy and Spain.

On the basis of similar data, Broschinski (2020, pp. 186–188) identifies four different patterns. He terms stable patterns of wage inequality a *parallel shift* and assigns Belgium, France, the United Kingdom and partly Austria and Hungary to this pattern. In the case of a significant decline in the level of earnings, this would mean that the lower and upper wages would decline in parallel. This can be observed in the United Kingdom. In this case, declining wages there are only partially prevented by minimum wages, collective agreements, unemployment benefits or a minimum income. Such an institutional protection of lower wages hardly exist in the United Kingdom (Gangl, 2006, p. 999).

In Germany, Sweden or Finland, the situation is quite different. Even though real wages in these countries are largely stagnating, wages in the bottom decile are rising relatively. This points to binding collective agreements, strong trade unions or effective minimum wages. Broschinski (2020, p. 188) terms this pattern *compression from below* and assigns Latvia, Lithuania, Slovenia, Poland, Slovakia and partly Denmark to it. Another pattern—*compression from above*—is characterised by a relative decline in inequalities overall and especially in the top half (Greece, Portugal, Romania and partly Luxembourg). In these and in other countries, higher wage earners (D9) are not among the winners of the crisis. Exceptions are top wage earners in booming countries such as Bulgaria or Latvia.

At the other end of the spectrum are countries where median wages remain largely stable, but lower wages decline above-averagely (Italy and Spain). The result is increasing inequalities. This outcome can be explained by weak trade unions, a low level of collective bargaining and low levels of social protection for lower wage groups, as both countries lack effective minimum income protection (Natili, 2018, 2019). Broschinski (2020, p. 188) terms this pattern *polarisation* and also assigns Cyprus, Malta, Bulgaria, Estonia and partly the Netherlands, Czech Republic and Ireland to it.

These patterns can partly be assigned to individual employment regimes. Figure 6.7 shows the regime-specific differences of four national wage inequality coefficients and their developments in order to reduce the complexity of the patterns shown in Fig. 6.6. Since the differences between the regimes are significant,[2] such an

---

[2] In analyses of variance, F-tests were used to compare the differences within and between the groups.

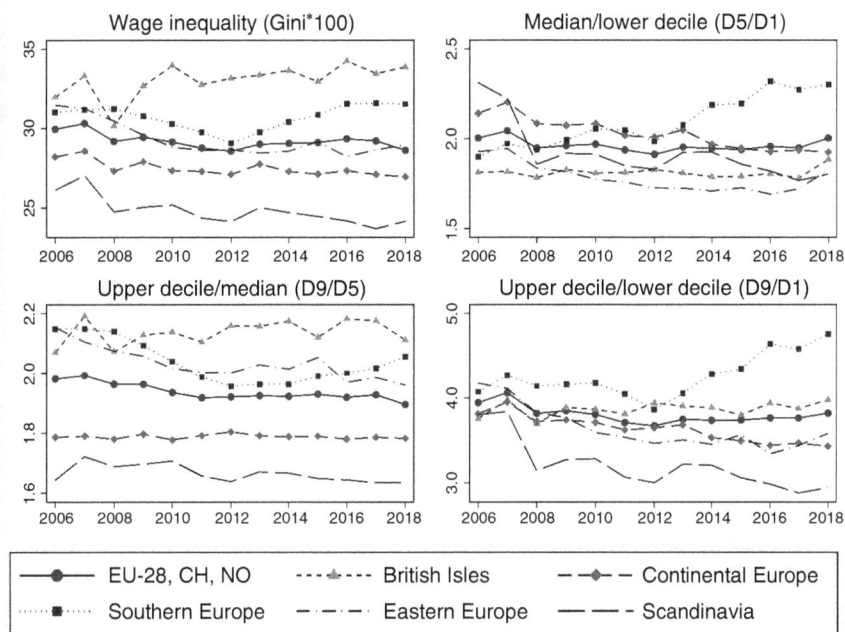

Source: Own calculations based on EU-SILC 2007-2019. The graphs show four indicators for wage inequality weighted by the number of employed people in employment.

**Fig. 6.7** Regime-specific wage inequalities in the EU-28, Norway and Switzerland (excluding Croatia; 2006–2018)

aggregation can be justified, even if the differences between, for example, an egalitarian Romania and a very unequal Bulgaria or between Greece and Cyprus are considerable. This summary shows that the UK and Ireland are characterised by high and largely stable wage inequalities and Scandinavia by comparatively low and decreasing wage inequalities. Wage inequalities in Central and Eastern Europe are declining significantly from initially very high levels, while Continental Europe keeps a stable intermediary position. The low level of wage inequalities in the upper half of the wage hierarchy in Continental Europe is striking (D9/D5). In Southern Europe, inequalities in the lower half of the wage hierarchy (D5/D1) are increasing very strongly. This points to the erosion of collective bargaining, also in the wake of the euro crisis (Broschinski, 2020). On the British Isles, inequalities in the lower half of the wage hierarchy are surprisingly low—an indication of the effectiveness of wage floors such as the minimum wage. The overall stability of weighted national inequalities in Europe is thus the result of very different national and regime-specific developments.

The four patterns proposed by Broschinski (2020) and reported above partly overlap with the previously described regime-specific patterns. Southern European countries in particular are characterised by a *polarisation* of wage structures at the bottom and a *compression from the top*. Scandinavia is characterised by a *compression from below*, while in Central and Eastern Europe, with accents that vary from country to country, both *compression from above and from below* can be observed. The largely stable situation in Continental Europe and on the British Isles can be interpreted as a *parallel shift*. In general, even at the national level wage inequalities are not increasing. Exceptions to this rule are Bulgaria and Malta.

In view of the very different economic development in the respective countries, it makes sense to include not only wage inequalities but also changing wage levels, since the decline in wage inequalities in booming Slovakia has to be interpreted differently than in the shrinking Greek economy. This will be discussed now.

Figure 6.8 shows the development of price-adjusted real wages from 2006–2018 for the middle (D5), the lowest (D1) and the highest decile (D9). The respective wages were normalised to 100 in 2006 (or 2009 for Croatia). Looking first at the median wage (D5), the enormous increase in Bulgaria is striking—an increase of 109%. Somewhat lower are the increases in Romania (+97), Latvia (+85), Slovakia (+82) or Estonia (+82), but still significantly higher compared to Germany (+9). The situation is depressing in Italy (−4%), Greece (−16%), Cyprus (−14%) and especially in the UK, which has seen a 27% fall in inflation-adjusted real wages from 2006–2017. Brexit can thus not only be explained by traditional British Euroscepticism, but points to a collapse in economic performance unprecedented in peacetime, and the accompanying social and political consequences (Alabrese et al., 2019; Fetzer, 2018). Other countries also suffered real wage losses for several years compared to pre-crisis times, but were able to overcome them by 2017/8 (for example Germany, Romania, Hungary or Portugal). Especially in the Central and Eastern European countries, the lowest wage groups (D1) have benefited significantly more than the median earners. This is especially true for Romania, Poland, Slovakia, Latvia and Lithuania, but also for Germany, Finland, Greece and Norway. Bulgaria is one of the few countries (together with Cyprus and Malta) where the wages of higher earners (D9) have developed significantly better than those of average and low earners. These results point to clear differences in national wage developments.

The national contextual factors that explain these different wage developments are examined in more detail below. The level and structure of wages reflect, on the one hand, different national specialisations and productivity levels (Chap. 4) and, on the other hand, different national collective bargaining systems. Decisions on wage policy are made mostly at the national level. Therefore, determinants of national wage structures can be found mostly at this level (Broschinski, 2020). Höpner and Lutter (2018, p. 76) list some of the relevant dimensions: "membership levels in trade unions and employers' associations, organizational degrees of fragmentation along political and profession lines, the presence of central collective agreements, vertical centralization and horizontal signaling, state intervention in wage bargaining, minimum wages, and inflation indexation".

Table 6.2 examines the influence of some of these determinants on wage developments for 28 EU countries, Switzerland and Norway for the period 2006–2017 on the basis of panel regressions. The dependent variables are the previously discussed indicators for wage inequalities, i.e. the D9/D1, the D5/D1 and the D9/D5 ratios and the Gini coefficient.

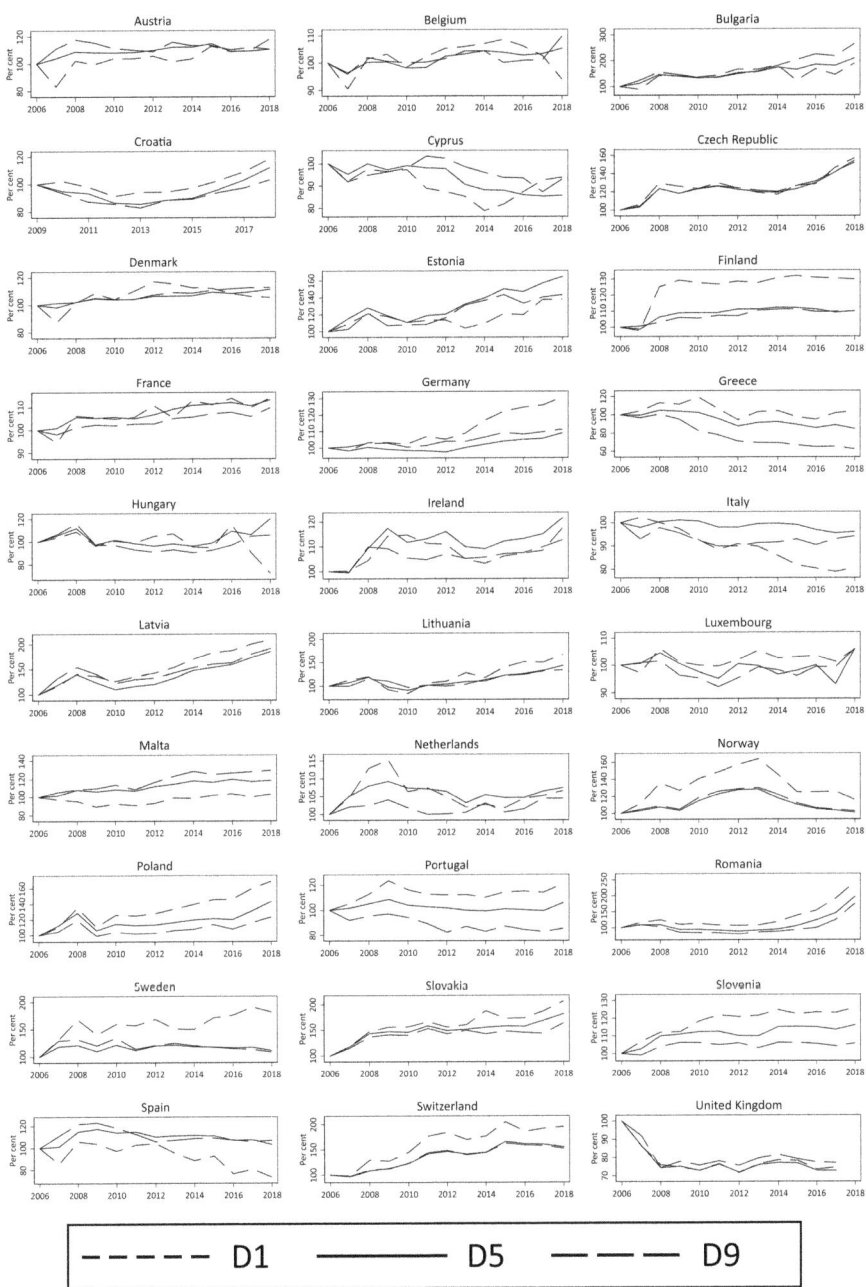

Source: Own calculations based on EU-SILC 2007-2019. Gross hourly wages adjusted for inflation.

**Fig. 6.8**  Real wage development in 27 EU member states (2006–2018; 2006 = 100%)

**Table 6.2** Institutional determinants of national wage inequality in Europe (2006–2018)

|  | D9/D1 | D5/D1 | D9/D5 | Gini |
|---|---|---|---|---|
| Change in GDP | −0.029* | −0.004 | −0.007* | −0.001 |
|  | (0.013) | (0.005) | (0.003) | (0.001) |
| Industrial employees (%) | −0.065*** | −0.018*** | −0.013** | −0.004*** |
|  | (0.015) | (0.005) | (0.004) | (0.001) |
| Union density (%) | −0.025*** | −0.004 | −0.009*** | −0.001*** |
|  | (0.006) | (0.002) | (0.002) | (0.000) |
| Intermediary wage coordination | −0.219** | −0.058* | −0.065*** | −0.014*** |
|  | (0.072) | (0.026) | (0.018) | (0.003) |
| Bargaining coverage | 0.005 | 0.001 | 0.003*** | 0.0005*** |
|  | (0.003) | (0.001) | (0.001) | (0.000) |
| Bargaining coverage * change GDP | 0.0005* | 0.000 | 0.0001* | 0.000 |
|  | (0.000) | (0.000) | (0.000) | (0.000) |
| Minimum wage (% monthly wage) | −1.340*** | −0.655*** | 0.015 | −0.023 |
|  | (0.390) | (0.144) | (0.108) | (0.019) |
| Social protection expenditure (as % of GDP) | −0.037* | −0.006 | −0.007 | −0.002** |
|  | (0.016) | (0.006) | (0.004) | (0.001) |
| Austerity (%) | 0.003 | 0.001 | −0.001 | −0.000 |
|  | (0.009) | (0.003) | (0.002) | (0.000) |
| Observations | 335 | 335 | 335 | 335 |
| $R^2$ (between countries) | 0.3755 | 0.3325 | 0.1261 | 0.1888 |
| Hausman test ($Chi^2$) | 49.6 | 18.5 | 0.35 | 19.99 |

Source: Own calculations on the basis of EU-SILC 2007–2019 and other Eurostat databases (see Appendix 1) for 27 EU member states (without Croatia), Switzerland and Norway. * $p < 0.05$, ** $p < 0.01$, *** $p < 0.001$. Panel regressions (random effects). Dependent variable: four indicators for wage inequality. Time dummies and constants included in the model but not shown. Standard errors in parentheses

A high *share of industrial workers* (as a % of total employment) is associated with lower wage inequalities. Industry has been the backbone of egalitarian wage structures (Kenworthy, 2004). In particular, the lower half of the wage distribution is compressed, for example by more demanding skilled jobs and a higher effectiveness of collective bargaining and workplace codetermination compared to services. The shift to a service economy thus might create low-paid jobs on the one hand and well-paid jobs on the other (Nollmann, 2006).

*Higher union density* is also associated with more egalitarian wage structures. Strong unions are not only correlated with lower wage inequalities in the lower half of the wage distribution, but are even associated with a lower spread in the upper part. This points to the positive influence of union bargaining policies on the median (DiNardo et al., 1996, p. 1026): the wage spread is lower not because upper wages are lower, but because median wages are higher.

*Wage coordination* at an intermediate level (i.e. either at the regional or the industry level) also has a significant negative effect on wage inequality compared to national or company coordination of wage bargaining. This can be interpreted along the lines of Calmfors and Driffill (1988). These authors argue that intermediary coordination of wage policy at the regional or industry level is associated with higher unemployment, since at this intermediary level the moderating influence on wage developments is smallest. Unlike centralised or decentralised wage coordination, trade unions at an intermediate level do not have to care as much about the macroeconomic consequences of their wage policies. This avoids wage dumping, but it also implies the bankruptcy of companies that might have been viable with lower wages. This reduces wage inequalities in the lower part of the distribution. Empirical evidence shows that intermediary wage coordination not only reduces wage inequalities in the lower half of the distribution, but also in the upper half.

It is to be expected that a high *degree of collective bargaining coverage,* i.e. a high proportion of employees whose pay is regulated by collective agreements, is associated with lower wage inequalities in the lower half of the wage hierarchy. Empirically however, higher wage inequalities especially in the upper half of the distribution are observed when controlling for the other contextual factors. This surprising result can be explained when the positive interaction effect between bargaining coverage and the change in GDP is taken into account. While wage inequalities in the upper part of the distribution decrease significantly, especially in the crisis countries (Broschinski, 2020), these wage inequalities remain largely constant in the countries with a higher growth rate. The positive correlation between wage inequality and wage bargaining thus points to the stabilising effects of high bargaining coverage during an inequality-reducing shock (Broschinski, 2020, p. 227)—and also to the fact that such a protection against declining wages is significantly lower in the case of a shrinking gross domestic product.

Statutory *minimum wages*, as well as strong trade unions and a high degree of collective bargaining coverage, prevent a large gap between middle and lower wages (Dingeldey et al., 2017; Grimshaw et al., 2013). This is also the reason why a national minimum wage was introduced in Germany in 2015. In view of weaker trade unions and declining collective bargaining coverage, especially in eastern Germany, no other way was seen to prevent low wages (Burauel et al., 2018). The correlation between minimum wages and wage inequality is also statistically evident: the level of the minimum wage (in % of the median wage) is negatively correlated with the overall wage spread (D9/D1) and the wage spread at the bottom (D5/D1). This corresponds to the results of other studies (Broschinski, 2020, p. 67).

A higher level of *social protection* implies in general a higher reservation wage (Gerstung, 2019; Grimshaw, 2011). A reservation wage is the wage that employees must earn so that they are not financially better off with unemployment benefits or a minimum income. Therefore, it can be expected that a developed welfare state is associated with lower wage inequalities. This expectation can be confirmed for the D9/D1 ratio and the Gini coefficient (Table 6.2).

Finally, in Table 6.2 an attempt was made to identify a European influence on patterns of national wage inequality. Given the Troika's *austerity* measures during the euro crisis (Preunkert, 2015), such an influence could be measured via national austerity policies, i.e. a change in public spending (excluding interest payments). However, the corresponding indicator is not significant. Following Broschinski

(2020, p. 241), this can be explained by the fact that austerity policies have led to wage adjustments especially in the upper echelons of the public sector:

> This can be interpreted as an expression of collective and coordinated action to safeguard employment by exchanging wages for employment guarantees (. . .) In highly coordinated systems with strong trade unions, it is easier to find common strategies for dealing with sharp declines in public spending, which not only increases job security for all groups of employees, but accordingly also contributes to the maintenance of public services. (Broschinski, 2020, 250–251; own translation)

In sum: central institutions of egalitarian capitalism (Kenworthy, 2004)—strong trade unions, high minimum wages, a welfare state, collective bargaining at the regional or sectoral level and a larger industrial sector—are associated with lower wage inequalities. A significant influence of austerity policies on wage inequality cannot be observed.

In the next step, the impact of the previously described egalitarian national institutions on wage levels (and not on wage inequalities, as in the previous table) will be analysed (Table 6.3). It turns out that wages are higher in countries with a high share of industrial employment (model 1) and high minimum wages (model 5). They are lower with strong trade unions (model 2), an intermediary coordination of wage bargaining (model 3), high collective bargaining coverage (model 4) and good social protection (model 6). In the summary model (10), all these variables—with the exception of high bargaining coverage—remain significant. This might indicate that some national institutions contribute to a more egalitarian wage distribution, but also to lower wages.

In order to test the European influence, we further check if the level of public debt, public austerity policies and membership in the eurozone have an effect on individual gross hourly wages (and not only on wage inequality). Model 7 shows that higher public debt is correlated with lower wages—a reflection of the higher debt ratios especially in the Southern European countries. Austerity policies are positively correlated with the level of gross wages (model 8). Since positive values of the austerity indicator point to higher public spending in interest-adjusted terms, this means that higher deficits are associated with higher wages. This could mean that wage losses are partly cushioned by more generous fiscal policies. This effect is also significant in the summary model (10). Model 9 includes eurozone membership and the interaction with austerity policies. The effect of austerity policies remains significant. The negative interaction effect points to differences between euro and non-euro countries: The positive effect of higher government spending on wage levels is significantly weakened in the euro countries—possibly an indication of the special architecture of the eurozone, which imposes limits on fiscal policies.

It sum: Wage gaps and wage inequalities in the EU-28 differ clearly between the member states. Adjusted for purchasing power, the wages of Danish employees are four times higher than those of Bulgarian workers, while the Gini coefficients of national wage inequalities range from 0.19 (Slovakia) to 0.39 (Bulgaria). Also the development of real wages from 2006–2018 differs clearly between the European countries: while median wages in Bulgaria have increased by 109%, they have decreased by 27% in the UK. Employees in Italy, Greece and Cyprus also suffered significant declines. Wage inequality (measured by the Gini) decreased in

**Table 6.3** Individual and national determinants of gross hourly wages in the crisis years (2006–2018; EU-28, Switzerland, Norway)

| | (1) | (2) | (3) | (4) | (5) | (6) | (7) | (8) | (9) | (10) |
|---|---|---|---|---|---|---|---|---|---|---|
| Industrial employment | 0.002** (0.000) | | | | | | | | | 0.001** (0.000) |
| Union density | | −0.006** (0.000) | | | | | | | | −0.006** (0.000) |
| Wage coordination (intermediary level) | | | −0.078** (0.002) | | | | | | | −0.054** (0.002) |
| Bargaining coverage | | | | −0.001** (0.000) | | | | | | −0.000 (0.000) |
| Minimum wage | | | | | 0.274** (0.010) | | | | | 0.177** (0.011) |
| Social protection expenditure (% GDP) | | | | | | −0.002** (0.000) | | | | 0.009** (0.001) |
| Public debt (%) | | | | | | | −0.002** (0.000) | | | −0.002** (0.000) |
| Austerity | | | | | | | | 0.001** (0.000) | 0.003** (0.001) | 0.002** (0.001) |
| Eurozone (19) | | | | | | | | | 0.310 (0.196) | 0.323 (0.224) |
| Eurozone * austerity | | | | | | | | | −0.002** (0.001) | −0.004** (0.001) |
| Observations | 743,017 | 743,017 | 743,017 | 743,017 | 743,017 | 743,017 | 743,017 | 743,017 | 743,017 | 743,017 |
| ICC | 0.569 | 0.626 | 0.562 | 0.565 | 0.583 | 0.569 | 0.585 | 0.560 | 0.547 | 0.613 |
| McFadden pseudo-$R^2$ | 0.623 | 0.623 | 0.623 | 0.623 | 0.623 | 0.623 | 0.624 | 0.623 | 0.623 | 0.624 |
| AIC | 943,778 | 943,489 | 942,596 | 943,957 | 943,276 | 943,946 | 942,491 | 943,935 | 943,939 | 941,039 |

+ $p < 0.10$, * $p < 0.05$, ** $p < 0.01$. Multivariate multilevel regression with log real gross hourly wage as dependent variable based on EU-SILC 2006–2018 (50% sample). Standard errors in parentheses. Individual control variables, year dummies and constants included in the models but not shown

approximately half of the European countries considered, while it increased in the other half. Inequalities increased by more than 10% in Bulgaria, Malta, Spain and Italy. The largest decreases can be registered in Slovakia, Romania, Greece, Poland, Sweden and Slovenia. Overall, there is a tendency for average wage inequalities to increase in Southern Europe and the British Isles and to decrease in Scandinavia and Eastern Europe. However, the differences between Greece and Spain, for example, illustrate that the homogeneity of regime-specific development patterns—although statistically significant—should not be overestimated. The often assumed rigidity of European institutions and wage structures (Blau & Kahn, 2002; Nickell, 1997; Siebert, 1997), which was already vehemently criticised by (DiPrete, 2007), can be rejected in view of the dynamics observed.

National economic structures and institutions are crucial for the level and development of national inequality. It has been shown that egalitarian wage structures are the result of a strong industrial sector, strong trade unions, regional and sector-wide wage negotiations, high minimum wages and an advanced welfare state. This institutional setting of egalitarian capitalism can be found above all in Continental, Northern and to some extent in Central and Eastern Europe. Higher service shares, weaker trade unions, a lower or absent minimum wage and lower welfare benefits, on the other hand, are associated with greater wage inequalities—an indication of the more service-centred trajectories in Southern Europe and the British Isles. Surprisingly, this is also true for higher levels of collective bargaining coverage—possibly a statistical artefact reflecting the high collective bargaining coverage in many Southern European countries (Visser, 2019).

The effects of the financial market and euro crises are mediated through these national institutions. As a result, wage inequalities have increased overall and in particular in the lower half of the wage distribution, especially in Italy and Spain, while they have decreased in Greece and Portugal. This could reflect the relatively high minimum wages in Greece (2017: 48% of the median wage) and Portugal (60%), while Italy has no national minimum wage and Spain (40%) only a relatively low minimum wage. Collective forms of interest representation have been weakened in Southern Europe by rapid deindustrialisation, which is an important factor in understanding increasing wage inequalities. This also has implications for the pursuit of high- and low-road strategies: While lower wage inequalities and the corresponding "beneficial constraints" (Streeck, 1997) favour specialisation in higher-skilled and better-paid employees and in sophisticated, innovative products, higher wage inequalities allow lower labour and wage costs and specialisation in products with a lower value added (Gerstung, 2019, p. 89).

Austerity policies have no significant impact on wage inequalities. However, higher government debt is associated with lower wages, while higher government spending, i.e. less austerity, is associated with higher wages. This could indicate that monetary and fiscal measures have prevented even more significant wage losses for the mainly Southern European crisis countries. Given the public consensus on the negative effects of the crisis policy (Almunia, 2020), which was largely driven by the European Commission, the International Monetary Fund and the European Central Bank, this is a surprising result. However, this effect disappears in the summary model.

## 6.5   Group-Specific Wage Differences and Low Wages in Europe

After having analysed Europe-wide and national wage inequalities, inequalities within countries, the wage levels of different socio-economic groups and the distribution of low-paid jobs will be discussed. The aim is to analyse the paradoxical structure of national wage inequalities: On the one hand, in most European countries wage inequalities are significantly lower than in the USA, but on the other hand, the differences between the various social groups are considerable. It is to be expected that the combination of egalitarian and at the same time strongly segmented structures already described in Chap. 5 also shape European wage structures.

The group-specific differences are analysed in Fig. 6.9 (analogous to the models in Table 6.3) on the basis of microdata for three periods—for the years (mostly) before the financial and euro crises (2006–2008), for the euro crisis (2009–2013) and the years after the euro crisis (2014–2018). Since the dependent variable of the model is the logarithmised real gross hourly wage adjusted for purchasing power, the values can be interpreted as percentage changes (Broschinski, 2020, p. 150). First,

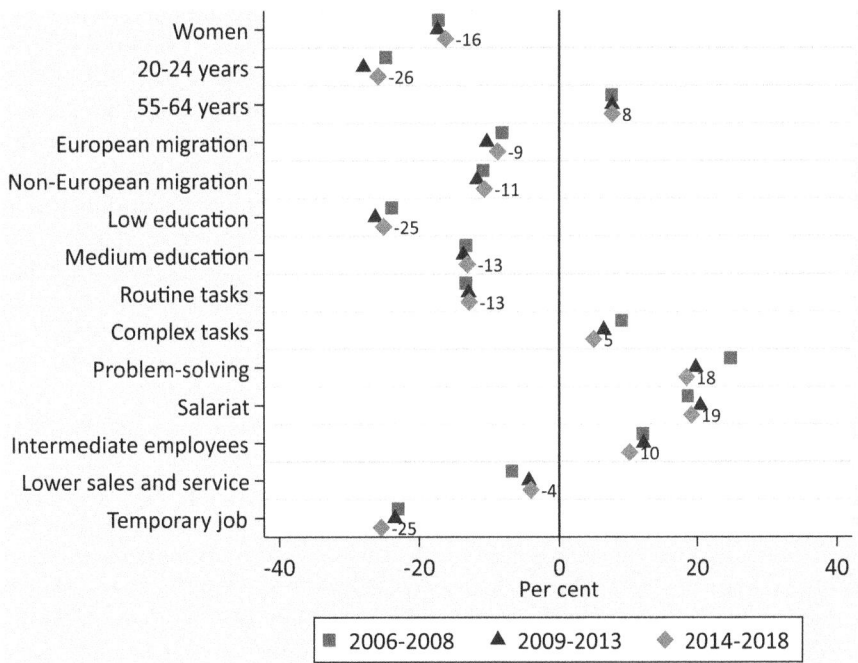

Source: Own calculations on the basis of EU-SILC 2007-2019 (for UK: 2018). The group-specific wage differences are calculated in comparison to the reference group, i.e. men, persons aged 25-54, academics, manual workers (machine operators, repair) with permanent contracts.

**Fig. 6.9** Group-specific differences in gross hourly wage (EU-28; Switzerland, Norway; 2006–2018)

we look at the four groups where labour market risks are particularly concentrated: Women, young people, migrants and the low-skilled. Taking all other socio-professional characteristics into account, women earn 16–18% less than men—a high adjusted gender pay gap, but one that tends to decrease. Young people earn about 26% less and older people 8% more than the core age group of 25–54 years. This points to an exceptionally strong segmentation of European labour markets along the age dimension, as younger workers are often labour market outsiders or new entrants who have not yet reached positions in internal labour markets. Migrants earn 11% less than natives, holding all other factors constant. In addition to age-, gender- and origin-specific segmentation, European labour markets are also divided along the educational and occupational dimensions: Employees with basic school education earn 24–26% less than graduates and 13–14% less than employees with a medium education. Unskilled and semi-skilled workers with routine tasks earn 14% less than skilled workers and machine operators, who in turn earn 19% less than workers with problem-solving tasks and decision-making competences. This corresponds to the difference between upper service classes (defined on the basis of Harrison & Rose, 2006) and simple technical and routine jobs. The significantly lower pay of fixed-term employees (−23 to −25%) again points to a deep division between good and bad jobs (Kalleberg, 2011). European labour markets are thus split along gender-, age-, origin-, skill- and contract-specific lines into insider and outsider markets. Most coefficients in Fig. 6.9 are largely stable for the three periods considered. However, the relative deterioration of fixed-term and low-skilled workers (−2 percentage points each) is striking. This contrasts with better pay for simple services (+ 3 percentage points). While the latter observation can easily be explained by the upgrading of simple, non-routine tasks (Goos & Manning, 2007), the wages of low-skilled and fixed-term employees have significantly deteriorated in comparison to those of other employees—and the gaps are even widening.

Another way to look at national wage inequalities is to focus on a particular point on the wage curve, such as top earners (Atkinson et al., 2011) or low-wage earners who are paid less than two-thirds of the median gross hourly wage. A low wage is usually seen as an indication of a bad or precarious job (Kalleberg, 2011). The distribution of low-wage risks thus might be seen as another indicator of labour market segmentation, in addition to the activity, employment and unemployment rates previously discussed. This reflects the situation in the more institutionally embedded Continental and Northern European employment regimes, where low wages are often regarded as a violation of the principle of fair wages, because everyone should be able to live from his or her own work. This norm is enforced through minimum wages, high union density, collective bargaining systems, above-average increases for lower wages or the public recognition of collective agreements as obligatory (Kalina & Weinkopf, 2018). This norm still shapes national wage structures in the EU, as shown in the previous section.

However, there is also another way of conceiving the relationship between low wages and labour market segmentation. In the institutionally weaker regulated employment systems of liberal countries, low wages are seen as an expression of high flexibility and a prerequisite for inclusive labour markets. In this perspective, low wages enable low-skilled workers to participate in the labour force instead of being unemployed or inactive (Blau & Kahn, 2002). Therefore, low wages might also be seen as a prerequisite for a low level of labour market segmentation. Work instead of poverty is the motto, whose historical roots can be traced back to early industrialisation (Himmelfarb, 1984). In a similar vein, activation policies have also contributed to a cultural re-evaluation of low-paid jobs. The credo of an activating welfare state is that work is better than unemployment (Bonoli, 2010). Low wages are seen as legitimate if they facilitate access to the labour market. On the one hand, a higher share of low wages is thus seen as an indicator of labour market segmentation; on the other hand, low wages are seen as a means of avoiding the need for assistance and as a bridge into the labour market and thus as a way of creating inclusive labour markets and reducing labour market segmentation. The following analysis focuses on how the level and distribution of low-wage risks reflect this ideological juxtaposition.

Reflecting the inclusive employment regimes of the Scandinavian countries, the share of low-wage workers (excluding apprentices; 15–64 years) in total employment is lowest in these countries (Fig. 6.10), namely 17%. In the Southern European countries, the share of low-wage workers is higher (20%), as these countries do not rely on activation policies or flexible labour markets (with the exception of marginal flexibilisation of already precariously employed workers; cf. Barbieri, 2009). These countries thus rely both on exclusion from employment and on exclusion from well-

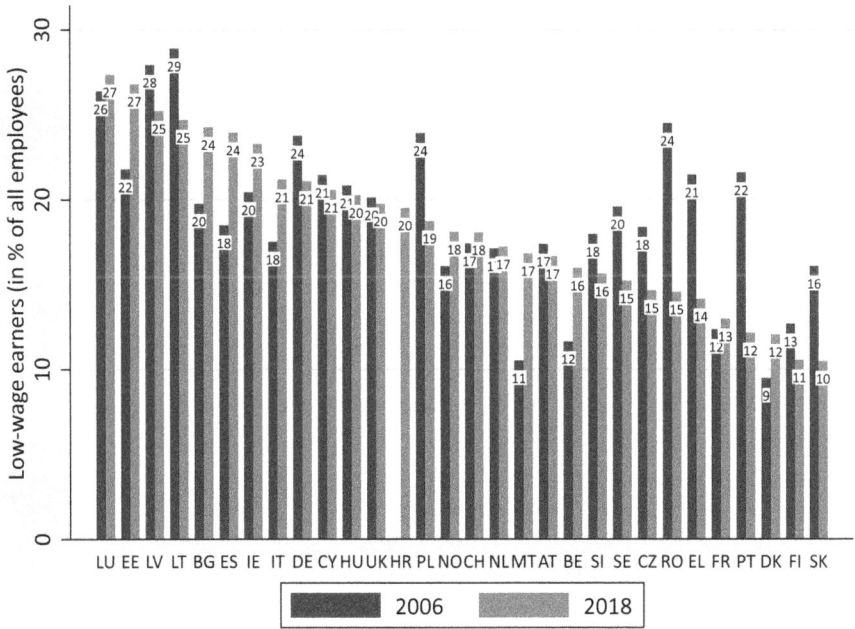

Source: Own calculations on the basis of EU-SILC 2007 & 2019

**Fig. 6.10**  Low-wage employment in Europe (EU-28, Switzerland, Norway; 2006, 2018)

paid jobs. Presumably, the high share of low-wage jobs reflects the peripheral tertiarisation strategy described in Chap. 4 which relies on low-cost services and low labour costs. Increasing low-wage shares, especially in Spain and Italy, are a result of the increasing wage inequalities already reported. In the course of the extraordinarily deep economic slump in Southern Europe and corresponding austerity programmes, a reduction in labour costs was achieved on the one hand by lowering higher wages (for example in Portugal and Greece) and on the other hand by reducing wages at the bottom of the wage hierarchy. In Central and Eastern Europe, on the other hand, a slight decrease in the share of low-wage earners from 21% to 19% can be observed, as the share of low-wage earners decreases significantly, especially in Poland, the Czech Republic, Romania and Slovakia. This points to a pendulum movement of the post-socialist countries. While wage structures were very egalitarian under socialism, inequalities and the share of the low-wage sector as well as unemployment increased rapidly in the course of the post-socialist transformation. Unemployment and wage inequalities receded after accession to the EU and the integration into European-wide value chains.

The low-wage shares in the Anglo-Saxon and Southern European countries hardly differ. Only in Continental Europe is their share slightly higher and in Central and Eastern Europe and Scandinavia their shares are significantly lower.

**Excursus: Low-Wage Employment in the Structure of Earnings Survey and in EU-SILC**

Very often statistics on low-wage employment in Europe are based on the Structure of Earnings Survey (SES), which is conducted every 4 years (cf. for example Kalina & Weinkopf, 2018, p. 13). Therefore, I will briefly discuss the discrepancies between this dataset and the EU-SILC data used here. The databases of these two surveys differ fundamentally: while the EU-SILC data are based on data collected from private households—household members aged 16 and over are surveyed—the SES is a sample survey of enterprises. Enterprises with at least 10 employees from all sectors except public administration are covered. Data on public and small enterprises are provided by some countries on a voluntary basis. This leads to an underestimation, because low-wages are mainly paid by very small companies. In Germany, for example, two million out of 7.4 million low-wage workers were employed in enterprises with fewer than 10 employees in 2015 (Bruttel et al., 2017, p. 476). Nevertheless, the shares of low-wage workers reported by both surveys are almost identical for many countries. For 2014, for example, the SES calculated a share of 22.46% for Germany and a share of 23.1% based on EU-SILC. Larger deviations are found for Belgium (2014: 7 percentage points higher in EU-SILC), Cyprus (+5.2 pp), Finland (+5.6 pp), Croatia (−7.3 pp), Italy (+10.4 pp), Luxembourg (+16.2 pp), Romania (−11.2 pp), Sweden (+15.7 pp) and Slovakia (−11.4 pp). Higher values in EU-SILC can probably be explained by the exclusion of smaller enterprises in the Structure of Earnings Survey SES and possibly also by an underestimation by enterprises of the actual hours worked (on the latter point, see also Kalina & Weinkopf, 2017, p. 9 and Burauel et al., 2018). Nevertheless, it is not plausible that, according to the SES, only 2.6% of employees in Sweden are paid low wages. It is possible that some groups of workers, especially foreign workers, systematically do not appear in official company statistics because their earnings do not comply with collective agreements. In two countries, Romania and Slovakia, the share of low-paid workers in EU-SILC is lower than in the Structure of Earnings Survey. Since the results in 2006 (when the shares of low-paid workers were much higher in both countries) were largely the same, these discrepancies could be explained by the transmission of older company data. Overall, there is much to suggest that the share of low-paid workers is captured more comprehensively and reliably in EU-SILC than in SES.

Table 6.4 shows the social distribution and development of low-paid jobs. In particular, women, young people, migrants from third countries, unskilled workers, workers with simple commercial and service tasks, workers in trade, hotels and restaurants and artistic professions, and temporary and part-time workers are low paid. These figures point to a clear gender, age, skill, activity and contractual divide and therefore also to a permanent segmentation of European labour markets.

Figure 6.11 shows the odds ratios of different socio-economic groups having a low-paid job in relation to the respective reference group (controlling for the effects of the other variables). The odds ratio of 1.99 for low-skilled employees means, for example, that their chances of having a low-wage job between 2014 and 2018 are twice as high as those of high-skilled employees (more precisely: 99% higher). Young people have an almost 2.5 times higher chance than workers in the core age group of 25–54, while migrants from other European and non-European countries have 60% and 59% higher chances respectively. Women have a 73% higher chance of being low paid than men, and employees in routine jobs are 69% more likely to be low paid than workers with more skilled manual jobs (operating machinery, driving, maintaining, repairing). The type of employment is also important: part-time workers have a 23% higher chance and fixed-term employees have a 192% higher chance of being low paid. Low-wage jobs are concentrated in the retail sector, restaurants and hotels. Ascribed characteristics (gender, age, migration status) therefore still have a stronger influence than achieved characteristics (low education, having a routine job, working in a low-wage industry). The segmentation of European labour markets thus still takes place to a considerable extent on the basis of ascribed characteristics, i.e. as marginalisation (Heidenreich, 2015),

Since 2009, the level of the minimum wage has a significant and negative influence on the probability of taking up a low-wage job. This is due not only to the direct effects of minimum wages, but also to the so-called *ripple effect* (Grimshaw, 2011): Even if minimum wages are usually significantly below the low-wage threshold, this effect means that the wages just above the minimum wage are also raised, "pushing up" all the wages in the lower part of the wage distribution.

At the beginning of this chapter, I raised the question of whether low wages are a social problem at all or should not be welcomed as an opportunity for marginalised workers to enter the labour market. An indicator for such a positive evaluation of low-paid jobs would be a high mobility of low-wage workers into better-paid jobs

**Table 6.4**  Low-wage risks in Europe (2006 and 2018)

|  | 2006 | 2018 |
|---|---|---|
|  | Total | Total |
| Men | 14.9 | 15.0 |
| Women | 24.1 | 22.3 |
| 15–24 years | 40.9 | 42.2 |
| 25–54 years | 17.4 | 17.4 |
| 55–64 years | 16.1 | 15.3 |
| Local | 18.5 | 17.1 |
| Other EU countries | 20.1 | 26.9 |
| Third countries | 28.3 | 28.8 |
| Low education | 28.0 | 31.9 |
| Medium education | 21.9 | 22.1 |
| High education | 9.1 | 9.2 |
| Routine activities | 39.8 | 41.3 |
| Machine operation | 23.8 | 24.4 |
| Complex tasks | 10.5 | 10.9 |
| Problem-solving | 5.8 | 6.4 |
| Service class | 6.9 | 7.2 |
| Qualified employees | 15.9 | 15.5 |
| Small self-employed |  | 34.8 |
| Sales; simple services | 38.9 | 30.4 |
| Routine workers | 28.9 | 29.3 |
| Agriculture | 39.6 | 41.7 |
| Manufacturing | 16.4 | 13.7 |
| Construction | 21.1 | 18.0 |
| Trade | 29.2 | 25.7 |
| Transport | 16.9 | 17.0 |
| Hotels, restaurants | 41.0 | 41.3 |
| IT, communication |  | 9.5 |
| Financial services | 5.9 | 6.0 |
| Business services | 19.2 | 20.3 |
| Public administration | 7.6 | 7.6 |
| Education, social work | 12.1 | 13.4 |
| Health | 17.5 | 20.1 |
| Art, entertainment | 31.7 | 34.7 |
| Full-time | 17.0 | 16.1 |
| Part-time | 31.2 | 30.6 |
| Permanent | 16.9 | 15.7 |
| Temporary | 37.3 | 39.5 |
| Total (29 countries) | 19.2 | 18.6 |

Source: Own calculations based on EU-SILC UDB 2007 and 2019 for EU-28 (excluding Croatia), Switzerland, Norway. UK: 2017 instead of 2018. In % of all dependent employees; 15–64 years, without apprentices

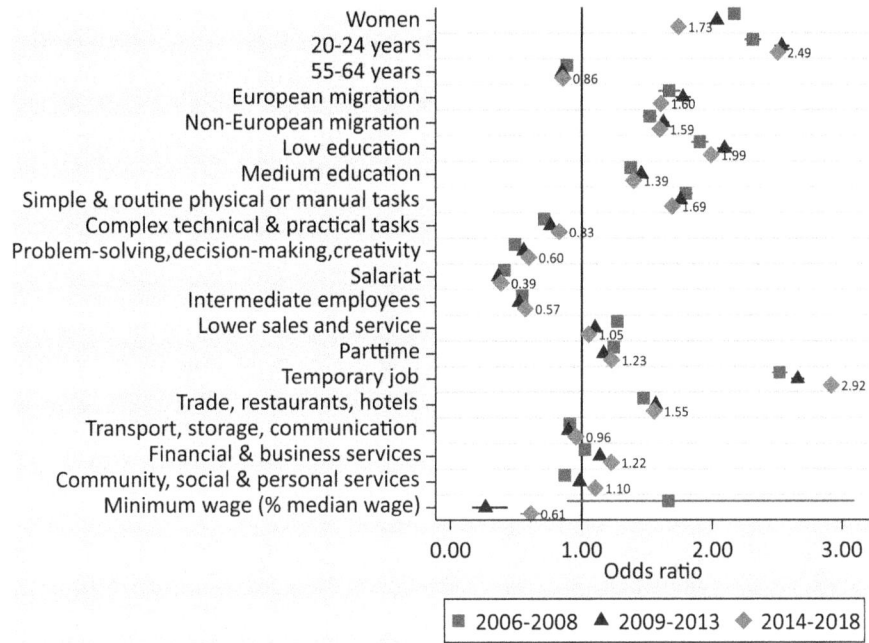

Source: Own calculations on the basis of EU-SILC 2007-2019. Binary logistic multilevel regression with the probability of working in a low-wage job as dependent variable. The reference group is explained in Figure 6.9.

**Fig. 6.11** Individual determinants of low-wage jobs (2007–2018; EU-28, Switzerland, Norway)

(Grabka & Göbler, 2020). Such a mobility analysis is hardly possible on the basis of EU-SILC data. However, the risks of poverty and dissatisfaction associated with low-wage jobs can be calculated. First, in order to determine the poverty risks of low-wage jobs, the household context has to be taken into account. According to EU-SILC (2007–2018), only about one fifth of European low-wage earners live in poor households (20.2%) and only about one fifth of the poor are low-wage earners (19.2%). Poverty and low pay are thus largely separate worlds. These worlds overlap only when low-wage earners are the only wage earners, which is the case in only 5.5% of all households. In general, low-wage earners are thus mostly additional earners. 81% of low-wage earners live in households with at least two persons in employment. Low-wage earners are therefore mostly living in households with medium to high work intensity. These are households whose members engage in gainful employment for at least half of the possible working hours. Therefore, while the poverty rate is higher for low-wage earners than for others in the EU-28 from 2007–2018 (20.8% versus 16.4%), the risk of poverty is higher for fixed-term employees (25.8%), persons with simple, manual and routine jobs (26.3%), small entrepreneurs and the self-employed (23.2%), the unskilled (24.2%), those with a non-European migrant background (26.7%) or young people (15–24 years; 22.4%). Both due to the fact that low-wage earners have a job at all and due to their inclusion in a household in which usually at least one other person is employed, the poverty risk of low-wage earners is comparatively low. The same is true for material deprivation, which affects 22.1% of low-paid workers compared to 17% of other respondents, or for subjectively perceived economic stress ("making ends meet"), reported by 28.1% of low-paid workers and 24.9% of other respondents. Low-paid work is therefore associated with higher risks of poverty and deprivation on the one hand, but on the other hand it also means that these risks are significantly lower than for other labour market outsiders such as young people, the low-skilled and non-European migrants. *Low wages cannot be equated with poverty or exclusion.* But they are nevertheless an indicator for a bad job and a segmented labour market.

This ambivalent evaluation also shapes subjective perceptions. In 2013, the life satisfaction of low-wage earners was 7.0 on an eleven-point scale (0: completely dissatisfied; 10: completely satisfied) and was thus just as high as that of other respondents. Satisfaction with their financial situation, on the other hand, was significantly lower among low-wage earners (5.5) than among other respondents (6.0). The influence of low wages on life and financial satisfaction is explored in Table 6.5 for a selected year at the peak of the euro crisis.

In addition to socio-demographic control variables and the fact of being low-paid or not, the median national household income was included as a context variable, which, as in all similar studies (Clark et al., 2008; Diener, 2000; OECD, 2013), has a significant influence on financial and life satisfaction. Whether someone has a low-wage job or not has a significant impact on life satisfaction (model 1) and on financial satisfaction (model 3), as shown by the negative coefficients. The national pattern of wage inequality measured by the Gini coefficient however has no impact on life or financial satisfaction. When an interaction with median household income and—following the recommendations made by Heisig and Schaeffer (2019)—random slopes are included, this effect become even stronger (models 2 and 4). The relationship between low pay and life and financial satisfaction also differs significantly across countries, as shown by the positive coefficient of the median national income. In richer countries, life and financial satisfaction is higher than in poor countries. The positive interaction of national income with low pay suggests that in richer countries, life and financial satisfaction are disproportionately higher among low-wage workers (models 2 and 4). Employees in low-wage jobs are more satisfied with their financial situation in wealthier countries than in poorer countries. This interaction effect (model 4) can thus be interpreted as an indication of a *Europeanisation of the frame of reference for* evaluating one's own wage situation, since low wages are perceived as less painful in rich countries than in poorer countries.

**Table 6.5**  Financial and life satisfaction in Europe (2013; 30 countries)

| | Life satisfaction | | | | Financial satisfaction | | | |
|---|---|---|---|---|---|---|---|---|
| | (1) | | (2) | | (3) | | (4) | |
| | b | se | b | se | b | se | b | se |
| Low wage | −0.24*** | (0.01) | −0.52*** | (0.10) | −0.49*** | (0.02) | −0.73*** | (0.14) |
| Wage inequality (Gini) | 0.86 | (0.98) | 0.84 | (0.97) | 0.84 | (1.34) | 0.82 | (1.35) |
| Median national income | 0.07*** | (0.01) | 0.06*** | (0.01) | 0.11*** | (0.02) | 0.10*** | (0.02) |
| Low wage*income | | | 0.02** | (0.01) | | | 0.02* | (0.01) |
| Constant | 5.97*** | (0.64) | 6.03*** | (0.63) | 4.44*** | (0.87) | 4.49*** | (0.87) |
| Cases | 110,829 | | 110,829 | | 111,061 | | 111,061 | |
| Intraclass correlation | 0.062 | | 0.060 | | 0.083 | | 0.083 | |
| McFadden pseudo-R2 | 0.136 | | 0.138 | | 0.213 | | 0.216 | |
| AIC | 431,809 | | 431,627 | | 467,187 | | 466,895 | |

Source: Own calculations on the basis of EU-SILC 2012. * $p < 0.05$, ** $p < 0.01$, *** $p < 0.001$. Multilevel regression with life satisfaction and financial satisfaction (11 expressions from 0: completely dissatisfied to 10: completely satisfied), as dependent variables. Standard errors (se) in parentheses. Sample: dependent employees; 15–64 years, without apprentices. In the second and fourth model, an interaction effect and random slopes for the risk of having a low-paid job are included. In addition to the 28 EU Member States in 2013, Switzerland and Norway were also included. The control variables included, but not presented here are gender, age, migration status, education, occupational level, social class, type of employment contract (temporary/permanent) and duration of working hours (full-time/part-time)

## 6.6  Conclusion

In this chapter, the patterns and dynamics of wage inequality in Europe during and after the financial and euro crises since 2008 have been discussed. This points to the field of wage policy, which is still largely nationally regulated (Pernicka et al., 2019). However, wage policy also has a European dimension and European implications, as attempts at economic integration in general require the regulation of wage competition ("wage dumping") (Rodrik, 2018). Due to the close integration of trade in the European single market and the dismantling of non-tariff trade barriers, it could even have been expected that a higher priority would have been given to protection against wages perceived as unfair. In fact, rules against wage dumping were already incorporated into the founding treaties of the European Economic Community in 1957. However, in the balancing act between the protection of national wage structures and the liberalisation of markets, the EU has generally given priority to the free movement of labour and services. The principle of "equal pay for equal work in the same place" or the even more radical principle of "equal pay for equal work" have always been only partially enforced. This was possible due to the rapid growth in the first decades of European integration and a high level of social security, which reduced the need for protectionist moves. However, the introduction of a common currency in the 19 member states of the eurozone strengthened the European dimension of wage policies, as the abolition of flexible exchange rates eliminated essential buffers for national economies. Their function has been taken over mostly by employment and wage policy. Particularly in the Southern European crisis countries, real wages fell significantly in the context of the eurozone sovereign debt crises from 2010 onwards. This was also an aim of EU crisis policy, which— for example with the memoranda of understanding (Broschinski, 2020, p. 93)—took over functions of (otherwise weakly developed) European wage coordination. This raises the question of whether these adjustment processes have led to a gradual reduction in wage differentials between EU member states, whether wages have fallen during the financial and euro crises from 2008 onwards, whether domestic wage inequalities and thus also the shares of low-wage employees have increased, which groups were particularly affected by low wages and whether the European institutions have an influence on wages. These questions were examined on the basis of the EU-SILC data, especially for the years 2006–2018.

Firstly, a decrease in total and between-country wage inequalities could be observed in Europe and the EU. This result is in line with the study by Broschinski (2020) and contradicts the observations of Fernández-Macías and Vacas (2015), who analysed fewer countries for a shorter period of time using a different wage concept. This decrease is mainly explained by the catching-up of Central and Eastern European countries. Therefore, mainly the lowest wages across Europe have increased since 2006. As a result, the share of between-country wage inequality has fallen from more than a third to less than a quarter. In the 15 older member states, on the other hand, between-country wage inequalities have stagnated at a considerably lower level (less than one tenth of total inequalities). The wage structures of these countries had already converged in previous decades.

Secondly, the financial and euro crises have led to real wage losses mostly in the upper wage groups across Europe, while low-wage earners were even able to record wage increases in the years from 2006 onwards. However, the differences between the individual country groups are considerable. While wages in the British Isles and Southern Europe have declined significantly, they have risen in Central and Eastern Europe, but also in the lower wage groups in Northern and Continental Europe. This again points to a clear split between Northern and Southern Europe, but also to a significant decline in European wage inequalities as Central and Eastern Europe catches up. However, the rising shares of higher-educated and higher-skilled service classes suggest that wage inequalities may also rise again in Europe when the Central European catch-up process has worn off. For the time being, however, an end to convergence cannot be observed in the EU or in Europe.

Thirdly, the national wage structures in Europe are characterised by considerable group-specific wage differences. Controlling for all other factors, women earn 16% less than men after the crisis years, young people 26% less than people in their prime, migrants 10% less than natives and the unskilled 25% less than academics. Some countries (Bulgaria, Latvia, Lithuania, Spain) have very high and others (Slovakia, Denmark) very low wage inequalities. The UK and Ireland are characterised by high and largely stable wage inequalities and Scandinavia by comparatively low and decreasing wage inequalities. Wage inequalities in Central and Eastern Europe rose very sharply in the first years of the post-socialist transformation processes and are since declining significantly. Continental Europe remains stable in the midfield. The level of wage inequality is still determined by the egalitarian institutions of the European post-war period: A high share of industrial employment, strong trade unions, sector-wide and regional wage negotiations, a high minimum wage and high social protection spending are accompanied by more egalitarian wage structures. However, not only wage inequality, but also wage levels are important for people's living conditions. And these developed very differently in the EU member states. While real wages in Bulgaria increased by 109% from 2006–2018, they stagnated in Italy and declined significantly in Greece, Cyprus and especially in the UK—in the latter case by 27%.

Fourthly, a European influence on wage inequalities can be partially identified. Wage inequalities are still largely determined by national institutions. However, wage levels are negatively correlated with the level of public debt and national austerity policies. This influence is smaller in the eurozone than in other European countries. This points to the fact that European institutions such as the bailout funds or the European Central Bank (ECB) may even have contributed to cushioning wage losses.

Finally, the extent and development of low-paid jobs was analysed, describing their increase especially in some Southern European countries and their decrease in Central and Eastern Europe. The extent of low-paid jobs reflects the already previously described segmentation of European labour markets, as women, young people, migrants and the unskilled in particular receive low wages. However, low pay cannot be equated with poverty or exclusion, as the risks of poverty are significantly higher for those not in employment. Low-paid jobs reduce both life and financial satisfaction, especially in poorer countries where low-paid workers are more dissatisfied with their situation. This might indicate a Europeanisation and transnationalisation of the frames for evaluating one's own pay.

Overall, the profound social and territorial division of the EU into winners and losers, into centre and periphery, into rapidly developing and stagnating countries and regions also shapes the wage structures—even if wage inequalities have actually become smaller during the crisis.

# References

Alabrese, E., Becker, S. O., Fetzer, T., & Novy, D. (2019). Who voted for Brexit? Individual and regional data combined. *European Journal of Political Economy, 56*, 132–150. https://doi.org/10.1016/j.ejpoleco.2018.08.002

Almunia, J. (2020). *Lessons from financial assistance to Greece: Independent evaluation report.* Luxembourg. Retrieved from European Stability Mechanism, website: https://www.esm.europa.eu/publications/lessons-financial-assistance-greece https://doi.org/10.2852/082453.

Ashenfelter, O. C., & Card, D. (Eds.). (1999). *Handbooks in economics: Vol. 5. Handbook of labor economics: Volume 3C.* Elsevier.

Atkinson, A. B., Piketty, T., & Saez, E. (2011). Top incomes in the long run of history. *Journal of Economic Literature, 49*(1), 3–71. https://doi.org/10.1257/jel.49.1.3

Autor, D. H., Levy, F., & Murnane, R. J. (2003). The skill content of recent technological change: An empirical exploration. *Quarterly Journal of Economics, 118*(4), 1279–1333.

Barbieri, P. (2009). Flexible employment and inequality in Europe. *European Sociological Review, 25*(6), 621–628. https://doi.org/10.1093/esr/jcp020

Barro, R. J., & Sala-i-Martin, X. (1991). Convergence across states and regions. *Brookings Papers on Economic Activity., 1*, 107–182.

Beckfield, J. (2006). European integration and income inequality. *American Sociological Review, 71*(6), 964–985. https://doi.org/10.1177/000312240607100605

Beckfield, J. (2009). Remapping inequality in Europe. *International Journal of Comparative Sociology, 50*(5–6), 486–509. https://doi.org/10.1177/0020715209339282

Beckfield, J. (2019). *Unequal Europe: Regional integration and the rise of European inequality.* Oxford University Press.

Bengtsson, E. (2016). Social dumping cases in the Swedish labour court in the wake of Laval, 2004–2010. *Economic and Industrial Democracy, 37*(1), 23–42. https://doi.org/10.1177/0143831X14532855

Blanchard, O. (2006). European unemployment: The evolution of facts and ideas. *Economic Policy, 21*(45), 6–59. https://doi.org/10.1111/j.1468-0327.2006.00153.x

Blanke, T. (2008). *Die Entscheidungen des EuGH in den Fällen Viking, Laval und Rueffert: Domestizierung des Streikrechts und europaweite Nivellierung der industriellen Beziehungen* (Oldenburger Studien zur Europäisierung und zur transnationalen Regulierung No. 8). Retrieved from www.cetro.uni-oldenburg.de/de/download/Nr._18_jm.pdf

Blau, F. D., & Kahn, L. M. (2002). *At home and abroad: U.S. labor-market performance in international perspective.* Russell Sage Foundation.

Bonoli, G. (2010). The political economy of active labor-market policy. *Politics and Society, 38*(4), 435–457.

Braverman, H. (1998). *Labor and monopoly capital: The degradation of work in the twentieth century (25. Anniversary ed.).* Monthly Review Press.

Broschinski, S. (2020). *Dynamiken von Lohnungleichheiten in Europa: Betriebliche und arbeitsmarktpolitische Anpassungen während der Eurokrise.* VS. Retrieved from https://www.springer.com/de/book/9783658318932

Bruttel, O., Baumann, A., & Himmelreicher, R. (2017). Der gesetzliche Mindestlohn in Deutschland: Struktur, Verbreitung und Auswirkungen auf die Beschäftigung. *WSI-Mitteilungen, 70*(7), 473–481. https://doi.org/10.5771/0342-300X-2017-7-473

Burauel, P., Grabka, M. M., Schröder, C., Caliendo, M., Obst, C., & Preuss, M. (2018). *Auswirkungen des gesetzlichen Mindestlohns auf die Lohnstruktur: Studie im Auftrag der Mindestlohnkommission.* Retrieved from. DIW website: https://www.diw.de/sixcms/detail.php?id=diw_01.c.595973.de

Calmfors, L., & Driffill, J. (1988). Bargaining structure, corporatism and macroeconomic performance. *Economic Policy, 3*(6), 13–61.

Card, D. E., & Ashenfelter, O. (2011). *Handbooks in economics: Vol. 5. Handbook of labor economics: Volume 4B (1st ed.).* North-Holland. Retrieved from http://www.sciencedirect.com/science/handbooks/15734463/4/part/PB

Case, A., & Deaton, A. (2020). *Deaths of despair and the future of capitalism.* Princeton University Press.

Clark, A. E., Frijters, P., & Shields, M. A. (2008). Relative income, happiness, and utility: An explanation for the Easterlin paradox and other puzzles. *Journal of Economic Literature, 46*(1), 95–144.

Dahrendorf, R. (1996). Economic opportunity, civil society and political liberty. *Development and Change, 27*(2), 229–249. https://doi.org/10.1111/j.1467-7660.1996.tb00587.x

Diener, E. (2000). Subjective Well-being: The science of happiness and a proposal for a national index. *American Psychologist, 55*(1), 34.

DiNardo, J., Fortin, N. M., & Lemieux, T. (1996). Labor market institutions and the distribution of wages, 1973-1992: A semiparametric approach. *Econometrica, 64*(5), 1001–1044. https://doi.org/10.2307/2171954

Dingeldey, I., Etling, A., Kathmann, T., & de Beer, P. (2017). Niedriglohnentwicklung und Lohnungleichheit im Drei-Länder-Vergleich: Der Einfluss kollektiver Akteure. *WSI-Mitteilungen, 70*(7), 499–506. https://doi.org/10.5771/0342-300X-2017-7-499

DiPrete, T. A. (2007). What has sociology to contribute to the study of inequality trends? A historical and comparative perspective. *American Behavioral Scientist, 50*(5), 603–618. https://doi.org/10.1177/0002764206295009

Erne, R., Imboden, N., Erne, R., & Imboden, N. (2015). Equal pay by gender and by nationality: A comparative analysis of Switzerland's unequal equal pay policy regimes across time. *Cambridge Journal of Economics, 39*(2), 655–674. https://doi.org/10.1093/cje/bev003

European Parliament, Council of the European Union, & European Commission. (2017). *The European pillar of social rights.* Luxembourg. Retrieved from Publications Office of the European Union website: https://ec.europa.eu/info/publications/european-pillar-social-rights-booklet_en doi:10.2792/95934 .

Fernández-Macías, E., & Vacas, C. (2015). *Recent developments in the distribution of wages in Europe.* Publication Office of the EU. Retrieved from https://www.eurofound.europa.eu/publications/report/2015/working-conditions-labour-market/recent-developments-in-the-distribution-of-wages-in-europe

Fetzer, T. (2018). *Did austerity cause Brexit?* (Warwick economics research papers series No. 1170). Coventry. Retrieved from University of Warwick website: http://wrap.warwick.ac.uk/106313/

Firpo, S., Fortin, N., & Lemieux, T. (2018). Decomposing wage distributions using recentered influence function regressions. *Econometrics, 6*(2), 28. https://doi.org/10.3390/econometrics6020028

Friedman, M. (1997, August 28). *The Euro: Monetary unity to political disunity?* Retrieved from Project Syndicate website: https://www.project-syndicate.org/commentary/the-euro%2D%2Dmonetary-unity-to-political-disunity

Gangl, M. (2006). Scar effects of unemployment: An assessment of institutional complementarities. *American Sociological Review, 71*(6), 986–1013.

Gerstung, V. (2019). *Niedriglohnbeschäftigung im Wohlfahrtsstaat: Der Einfluss von Ideen und Institutionen auf den Niedriglohnsektor (1st ed. 2019). Vergleichende Politikwissenschaft.* Springer. https://doi.org/10.1007/978-3-658-27640-9

Gonalons-Pons, P., & Gangl, M. (2021). Regulated earnings security: The relationship between employment protection and unemployment scarring over the Great Recession. *Socio-Economic Review.* Advance online publication. https://doi.org/10.1093/ser/mwaa049.

Goos, M., & Manning, A. (2007). Lousy and lovely jobs: The rising polarization of work in Britain. *The Review of Economics and Statistics, 89*(1), 118–133.

Grabka, M. M., & Göbler, K. (2020). *Der Niedriglohnsektor in Deutschland: Falle oder Sprungbrett für Beschäftigte?* Bertelsmann Stiftung. https://doi.org/10.11586/2020032

Grimshaw, D. (2011). *What do we know about low wage work and low wage workers? Analysing the definitions, patterns, causes and consequences in international perspective.* ILO.

Grimshaw, D., Bosch, G., & Rubery, J. (2013). Minimum wages and egalitarian pay bargaining in comparative perspective. In D. Grimshaw (Ed.), *Routledge research in employment relations. Minimum wages, pay equity, and comparative industrial relations* (pp. 227–259). Taylor and Francis.

Hall, P. A. (2014). Varieties of capitalism and the euro crisis. *West European Politics, 37*(6), 1223–1243.

Harrison, E., & Rose, D. (2006). *The European socio-economic classification (ESeC) user guide.* Colchester.

Heidenreich, M. (2015). The end of the honeymoon: The increasing differentiation of (long-term) unemployment risks in Europe. *Journal of European Social Policy, 25*(4), 393–413. https://doi.org/10.1177/0958928715594544

Heisig, J. P., & Schaeffer, M. (2019). Why you should always include a random slope for the lower-level variable involved in a cross-level interaction. *European Sociological Review, 35*(2), 258–279. https://doi.org/10.1093/esr/jcy053

Himmelfarb, G. (1984). The idea of poverty. *History Today, 34*(4), 22–30.

Höpner, M., & Lutter, M. (2018). The diversity of wage regimes: Why the Eurozone is too heterogeneous for the euro. *European Political Science Review, 10*(01), 71–96. https://doi.org/10.1017/S1755773916000217

Iversen, T., Soskice, D., & Hope, D. (2016). The Eurozone and political economic institutions. *Annual Review of Political Science, 19*, 163–185.

Joerges, C., & Rödl, F. (2009). Informal politics, formalised law and the 'social deficit' of European integration: Reflections after the judgments of the ECJ in Viking and Laval. *European Law Journal, 15*(1), 1–19.

Kalina, T., & Weinkopf, C. (2017). *Niedriglohnbeschäftigung 2015: Bislang kein Rückgang im Zuge der Mindestlohneinführung* (IAQ-Report No. 2017–6). Retrieved from Institut Arbeit und Qualifikation website: https://duepublico2.uni-due.de/go/iaq-report/2017/06

Kalina, T., & Weinkopf, C. (2018). *Niedriglohnbeschäftigung 2016: Beachtliche Lohnzuwächse im unteren Lohnsegment, aber weiterhin hoher Anteil von Beschäftigten mit Niedriglöhnen* (IAQ-Report No. 2018–06). DuEPublico: Duisburg-Essen Publications Online, University of Duisburg-Essen. https://doi.org/10.17185/DUEPUBLICO/47959.

Kalleberg, A. L. (2011). *Good jobs, bad jobs: The rise of polarized and precarious employment systems in the United States, 1970s to 2000s. American Sociological Association's Rose series in sociology.* Russell Sage Foundation.

Kalleberg, A. L., & Sørensen, A. B. (1979). The sociology of labor markets. *Annual Review of Sociology, 5*(1), 351–379.

Kenworthy, L. (2004). *Egalitarian capitalism: Jobs, incomes, and growth in affluent countries.* Russell Sage Foundation.

Lohmann, H., & Marx, I. (Eds.). (2018). *Handbook on in-work poverty.* Edward Elgar. https://doi.org/10.4337/9781784715632

Mundell, R. A. (1961). A theory of optimum currency areas. *American Economic Review, 51*(4), 657–665.

Natili, M. (2018). Explaining different trajectories of minimum income schemes: Groups, parties and political exchange in Italy and Spain. *Journal of European Social Policy, 28*(2), 116–129.

Natili, M. (2019). *The politics of minimum income: Explaining path departure and policy reversal in the age of austerity. Work and welfare in Europe.* Springer. https://doi.org/10.1007/978-3-319-96211-5

Nickell, S. (1997). Unemployment and labor market rigidities: Europe versus North America. *Journal of Economic Perspectives, 11*(3), 55–74. https://doi.org/10.1257/jep.11.3.55

Nollmann, G. (2006). Erhöht Globalisierung die Ungleichheit der Einkommen? *Kölner Zeitschrift Für Soziologie Und Sozialpsychologie, 58*(4), 638–659.

OECD. (2013). *Guidelines on measuring subjective Well-being.* OECD. https://doi.org/10.1787/9789264191655-en

Pereira, J. M. R., & Galego, A. (2019). Diverging trends of wage inequality in Europe. *Oxford Economic Papers, 71*(4), 799–823. https://doi.org/10.1093/oep/gpy072

Pernicka, S., Glassner, V., Dittmar, N., & Neundlinger, K. (2019). The contested Europeanisation of collective bargaining fields. In M. Heidenreich (Ed.), *Horizontal Europeanisation: The transnationalisation of daily life and social fields in Europe* (pp. 109–128). Routledge.

Piketty, T., & Saez, E. (2014). Inequality in the long run. *Science, 344*(6186), 838–843. https://doi.org/10.1126/science.1251936

Piketty, T., Saez, E., & Zucman, G. (2018). Distributional national accounts: Methods and estimates for the United States. *Quarterly Journal of Economics, 133*(2), 553–609.

Pollack, M. A., & Hafner-Burton, E. (2000). Mainstreaming gender in the European Union. *Journal of European Public Policy, 7*(3), 432–456. https://doi.org/10.1080/13501760050086116

Preunkert, J. (2015). The hidden side of the crisis. In L. V. Baptista, J. Preunkert, & G. Vobruba (Eds.), *Aftermath: Political and urban consequences of the euro crisis* (pp. 185–2002). Edições Colibri.

Reich, M., Gordon, D. M., & Edwards, R. C. (1973). A theory of labor market segmentation. *American Economic Review, 63*(2), 359–365.

Reich, N. (2008). Free movement v. social rights in an enlarged union-the Laval and Viking cases before the ECJ. *German Law Journal, 9*(2), 125–161.

Rodrik, D. (2018). Populism and the economics of globalization. *Journal of International Business Policy, 1*(1–2), 12–33. https://doi.org/10.1057/s42214-018-0001-4

Siebert, H. (1997). Labor market rigidities: At the root of unemployment in Europe. *Journal of Economic Perspectives, 11*(3), 37–54. https://doi.org/10.2307/2138183

Streeck, W. (1997). Beneficial constraints: On the economic limits of rational voluntarism. In J. R. Hollingsworth (Ed.), *Cambridge studies in comparative politics. Contemporary capitalism: The embeddedness of institutions* (pp. 197–218). Cambridge University Press.

Streeck, W. (1998). The internationalization of industrial relations in Europe: Prospects and problems. *Politics and Society, 26*(4), 429–459.

Vacas-Soriano, C. (2018). The 'great recession' and low pay in Europe. *European Journal of Industrial Relations, 24*(3), 205–220. https://doi.org/10.1177/0959680117715932

Visser, J. (2019). *ICTWSS data base. version 6.1.* Retrieved from Amsterdam Institute for Advanced Labour Studies AIAS website: http://uva-aias.net/en/ictwss

# Chapter 7
# Europeanisation of Income Inequality Before and During the Eurozone Crisis: Inter-, Supra- and Transnational Perspectives

**Abstract** In this chapter, three facets of the Europeanisation of income inequality are discussed. First, Europe is an international social space in which national patterns of income inequality and their evolution can be compared. It will be shown that the decades-long increase of within-nation income inequality and the decrease of between-nation income inequality, especially in the 15 old EU member states, came to a standstill after the financial and euro crises. Secondly, the EU can be understood as a politically-regulated supranational field which also shapes the income situation of households. In recent decades, the Central and Eastern European countries in particular have benefited most from the economic and monetary integration of the EU. Thirdly, Europe is a transnational social field that also influences perceptions of income inequality and economic stress. An indication of the Europeanisation of frames of reference for the perception of social inequalities is that a lower position in the European income hierarchy is associated with higher economic stress. This shows that individual financial situations are also assessed in a European and transnational context.

Disposable income[1] is the central economic foundation for the livelihood of private households. The development and distribution of this income is at the centre of the public and academic debate on social inequalities (DiPrete, 2007). In contrast to wages paid to individuals, disposable income is the sum of all income available to a household—of course (equivalence-) weighted by the number of household members. Compared to value added or national income, which Alvaredo et al. (2018) use as an inequality indicator, it includes all income received by individual household members, i.e. wages, capital income, income from self-employment and social benefits minus taxes and social contributions. In contrast to wealth (Chap. 10)—a stock variable—disposable income is a flow variable, i.e. income during a certain period of time, usually a year.

---

[1](Disposable) income is the purchasing power-adjusted, equivalence-weighted net household income (less any payments of tax and social insurance contributions and including pensions and other social benefits).

The OECD has presented convincing evidence for the rise in within-country income inequality since the 1980s (OECD, 2011, 2015, 2019). Alderson and Nielsen (2002) have explained this increase by the globalisation of goods, capital and labour markets. Nollmann (2006), on the other hand, points to domestic causes, such as the heterogeneity of the growing service sector. Other factors are the pluralisation of lifestyles, as smaller households and more single-person households imply greater inequalities: When people with different income levels decide to live in different households, a poor and a rich household may emerge from what otherwise would have been an average-earning larger household. Educational homogamy (Blossfeld & Timm, 2003) is also associated with less intra-family redistribution and thus greater national inequality. Technological change has an indirect effect, because it affects the wages of household members.

European inequalities are, similar to global inequalities, composed of within- and between-country inequalities. In the global context, it has been shown that between-country inequality accounts for two-thirds to four-fifths of total inequality (Milanović, 2016, p. 129). Global inequality has declined in recent decades due to rapid economic development (Bourguignon, 2015; Milanovic, 2013, 2016). A similar pattern has been observed for Europe (Heidenreich, 2003, 2016).

Wilkinson and Pickett (2010) have shown that national income inequality is correlated with numerous negative societal trends such as low life expectancy, high infant mortality, poor literacy and numeracy, homicide, obesity, mental illness, drug and alcohol addiction, a high proportion of prisoners and teenage births, and low social mobility. Even Covid-19-related mortality is associated with levels of income inequality—with Italy and Spain having very high scores on both dimensions and Norway, Austria and Denmark having very low scores. Higher levels of equality are thus associated with better health, higher life satisfaction and stronger social cohesion. Particularly in less affluent countries, the negative effects of income inequality can be explained to a considerable extent by status anxiety. However, in line with happiness research (Clark et al., 2008), Delhey and Dragolov (2014) point out that not only income *inequality,* but also *income levels* strongly influence life satisfaction.

Traditionally, income inequality is analysed and compared primarily on a national scale. Due to the increasing political, economic and social interdependencies in Europe, however, the national level is less and less sufficient to understand the determinants, dynamics and also perceptions of inequality. This already became clear during the European sovereign debt, banking and economic crisis since 2008 and even more so in the pandemic from 2020 onwards (Anderson et al., 2020). Through its economic, monetary and political integration, the EU is developing into a social space that has a considerable influence on its population's living conditions. Europe is also becoming an important reference point for the perception of social inequalities. Responsibility for disadvantages and privileges are increasingly attributed to European decisions and processes due to the deepening of the integration process. In the best case, this can lead to stronger cross-border solidarity (Gerhards et al., 2020) and institutionalised forms of such solidarity. Examples of this are the creation of the rescue funds, the ECB's programmes to buy up securities or the EU's

"Next Generation" reconstruction plan during the coronavirus crisis. At the same time, however, cross-border conflicts and resentments may also increase. Examples include significant dissatisfaction with the EU during the euro and coronavirus crises, the rise of populist parties in many countries (Norris & Inglehart, 2019), or massive conflicts between populist governments and the EU.

A Europeanisation of income inequalities can thus manifest itself in different ways (cf. Sect. 2.2): First, domestic patterns of income inequality development can be analysed and compared within the territory of the EU. "Europe" in this case is treated as an *international* social space for the analysis and comparison of national inequalities. Secondly, the Europeanisation of social inequalities can be understood as a result of the *supranational* policies and regulatory patterns of the EU. This has already been elaborated in Chap. 4 using the example of the Single Market and the Customs Union. Another example is the euro, whose architecture was also decisive for the labour market crisis, especially in Southern Europe (Chap. 5). Third, Europe can also be understood as a *transnational* social space determined by cross-border societalisation processes (Heidenreich, 2019; Mau & Mewes, 2012). In this case, Europeans also assess their social situation in a cross-border context. It is thus necessary to extend the national frame of reference to include a transnational and European frame of reference as well, in order to also reconstruct the patterns and dynamics of Europe-wide income inequalities and, if possible, to also describe the effects of cross-border processes, decisions and attitudes on these patterns and their perceptions. Here we focus on the period from 2006 onwards, i.e. before, during and after the European financial market, sovereign debt and economic crisis.

First, the development of Europe-wide income inequality, the relative importance and the evolution of its within- and between-country components will be analysed (Sect. 7.1). Subsequently, the evolution of national income inequalities is examined in an *international* comparative perspective. This also touches upon the question of whether the EU is a neoliberal project of border opening and market integration that has contributed to an increase in income inequality (Beckfield, 2019) (Sect. 7.2). Next, the relative weight of three ways of reducing income inequality—flexible employment forms, redistribution within the family and public redistribution by welfare states—are elaborated. The first two paths prove to be significantly more effective in reducing inequalities than welfare state redistribution (Sect. 7.3). In Sect. 7.4, national and *supranational* factors that shape the income risks of Europeans are elaborated. Subsequently, the impact of between- and within-country income inequalities on the subjective perception of people's own income situation is shown. This enables us to also demonstrate the role of *transnational* perceptions of income inequalities (Sect. 7.5). The chapter concludes with a short summary and outlook (Sect. 7.6).

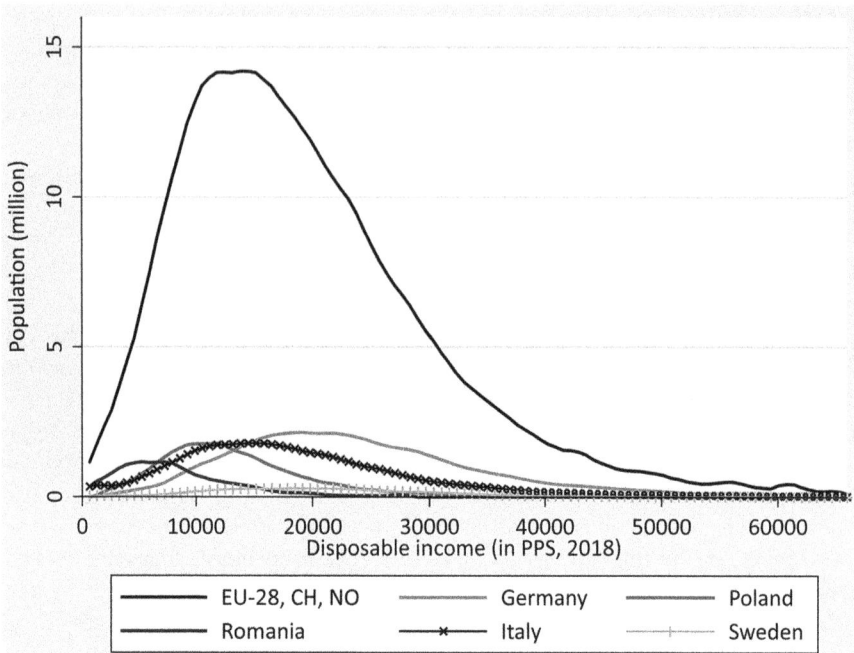

Source: EU-SILC 2019. Values for 30 countries (EU-28, Norway and Switzerland) and five selected countries. The
results of the 2019 survey refer to disposable income in 2018.

**Fig. 7.1**  Income inequality in Europe (2018)

## 7.1   The Evolution of Income Inequality in Europe

Similar to labour market and wage inequalities, income inequality can be divided
into a between- and within-country component. Traditionally, inequality research
focuses on within-country inequality, i.e. inequality of disposable income between
poorer and richer households in the same country. This is somewhat polemically
referred to as methodological nationalism (Beck & Grande, 2007). However, the
nation-state is still the most important arena for the perception and regulation of
income inequality. Nevertheless, the EU and the strong mutual dependencies and
exchange relations in Europe (Kuhn, 2015) are contributing to the transformation of
previous transnational *disparities* into European-wide *inequalities* (Heidenreich,
2003). Before analysing the subjective dimensions of this transformation (7.5), its
objective dimensions—the level and evolution of overall income inequality in
Europe and its within- and between-country components—will be discussed.

Figure 7.1 gives an overview of the level of income inequality in Europe and in
selected nation-states. This graph maps the incomes of the European population in
2018; every resident of the 30 countries considered (28 EU member states, Norway,
and Switzerland) is included regardless of nationality. This graph shows, for example, that Germany has a more egalitarian income structure (0.27) than Romania

**Table 7.1** Income inequality and poverty in the EU, Norway, Switzerland and the USA (2018)

| | EU-15 | Eurozone (19) | EU-25 | EU-28, CH, NO | For comparison: USA |
|---|---|---|---|---|---|
| Gini (weighted national values) | 0.299 | 0.284 | 0.284 | 0.288 | 0.384 |
| Gini (transnational) | 0.303 | 0.302 | 0.310 | 0.322 | |
| Decile ratio (D9/D1) | 4.078 | 4.185 | 4.382 | 4.33 | 5.861 |
| Poverty (60%; national poverty thresholds) | 16.6 | 16.3 | 16.2 | 16.6 | 24.3 |
| Poverty (60%; EU-wide poverty threshold) | 14.2 | 15.5 | 17.2 | 20.2 | |

Source: Own calculations based on EU-SILC 2019 (UK: 2018). The figures for the USA are taken from the LIS Inequality Key Figures (accessed 24/6/2021)

(Gini $= 0.34$). On this basis, the Gini coefficient of pan-European income inequality can be calculated as 0.32 (2018). This points to a significant decline in Europe-wide income inequality, because in 2006 the European-wide Gini coefficient of income inequality was still 0.35. These coefficients are higher than the Gini coefficient given by Eurostat (0.30 and 0.31 respectively according to Eurostat, table ilc_di12). The reason for this discrepancy is that Eurostat calculates the measure of Europe-wide inequality as a weighted average of the national inequalities thus excluding between-country inequalities. Europe-wide inequalities can thus be calculated in two different ways (cf. Table 7.1). The approach used by Eurostat (weighted national averages) is appropriate if the EU is seen as a community of sovereign states, but not as a social space characterised by common standards of equality and solidarity. In contrast to this "international" inequality concept, the second, the "transnational" approach assumes common Europe-wide standards of equality and thus also takes between-country inequality into account. Thus, even though the numerical values of the two types of inequality do not differ greatly, they are based on different understandings of inequality. The figures presented above show that the weighted sum of within-country income inequality in Europe has increased slightly over the last decade, while pan-European inequality has decreased significantly. Only when between-country income inequality and the new EU member states are excluded, does it make sense to talk of an end of convergence (Beckfield, 2013, 2019). Table 7.1 compares these trans- and international inequality concepts for Europe and also shows the corresponding indicators for the USA. Even in a transnational perspective, income inequality across 30 European countries is lower than in the US. This is a perplexing result, as the EU-28, Switzerland and Norway are very heterogeneous countries without a common economic and social policy, whereas the USA is a nation-state with a common identity and common policies. Measured by the weighted sum of national Gini coefficients, inequality in the EU-15 and the 30 European countries is similar. When between-country inequalities are included, the larger the group of countries considered, the greater the inequality. This indicates that the new EU members are not significantly more unequal, but they are still poorer than the older member states. This is also reflected by Europe-wide poverty rates (Table 7.1). The rate is highest when the 30 countries considered below (EU-28,

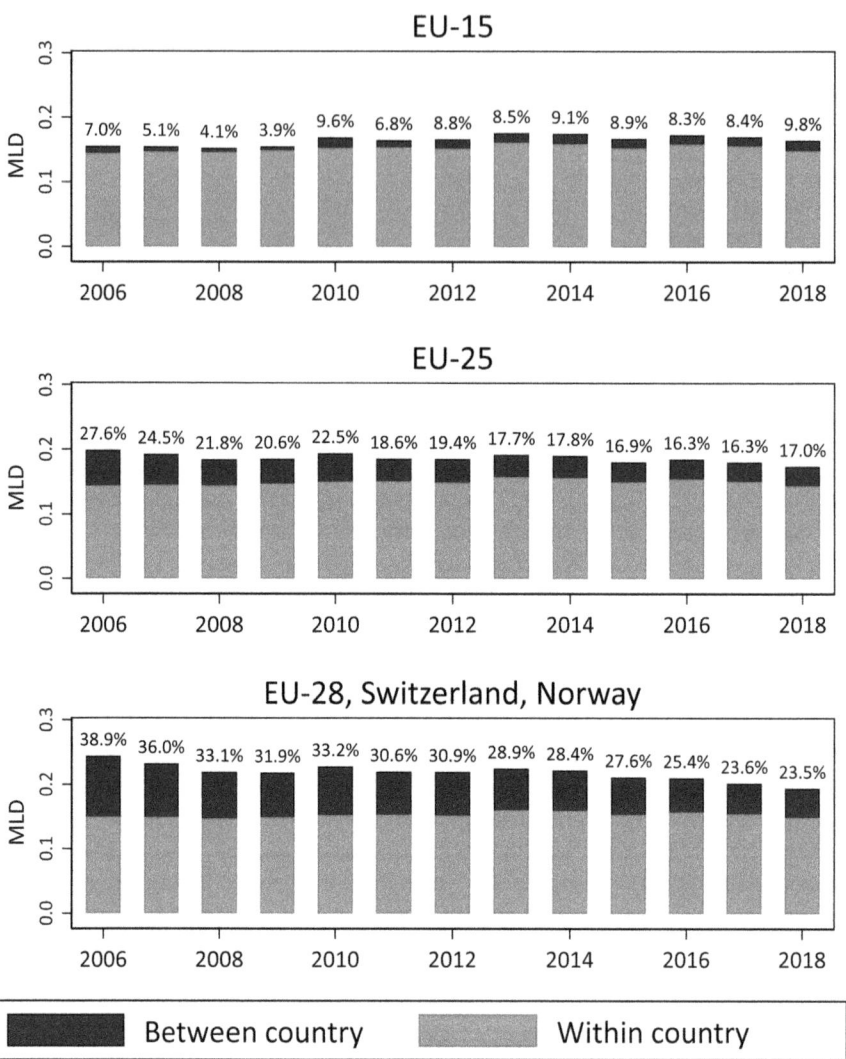

Source: Own calculations based on EU-SILC 2007-2019 for EU-28 countries, Norway and Switzerland. Until 2009 without Croatia, 2018 without the United Kingdom. The incomes of the years indicated were determined in the surveys of the following year. EU-15: The EU member states before the fifth EU enlargement. EU-25: The EU member states as of 1.5.2004. EU-28: The EU member states after the accession of Romania, Bulgaria and Croatia and before the withdrawal of the United Kingdom.

**Fig. 7.2** Development of within- and between-country income inequalities in Europe (2006–2018)

Switzerland and Norway) are included, since the 13 new member states mostly have a lower income.

This raises the question of the extent and development of total income inequality in Europe. In Fig. 7.2, total income inequality between all Europeans is "split" into inequalities between citizens of a state and inequalities between states. The inequality measure used is the mean logarithmic deviation (MLD), which is 0 when income is equally distributed and becomes greater when inequality increases (especially in higher income groups). Unlike the Gini index, the MLD can be additively decomposed into within- and between-country inequalities.

At the beginning of the time series shown in Fig. 7.2 for the EU-25 and the EU-28 (after the accession of Croatia and before Brexit) plus Switzerland and Norway, Europe was still divided to a considerable extent into poor and rich countries. In 2006, more than a quarter of income inequality was due to between-country differences; in the 30 European countries, their share was even almost two-fifths. Since then, there has been a significant levelling of income in the EU-25 and EU-28, with the between-country share of inequalities falling from 27.6% to 17% and from 38.9% to 23.5% respectively (2018). Inequalities between residents of poor and rich countries have narrowed significantly. The EU has once again proved to be a key driver of income convergence in Europe, following the Eastern enlargements of 2004, 2007 and 2013, when 13 mostly Central European countries joined the EU.

However, this convergence process has stalled and is even being reversed since the beginning of the euro crisis in the EU-15. While the convergence between West and East is continuing, the North-South differences are increasing again in the wake of the financial market and euro crises and later the pandemic. An increase in between-country inequalities can be observed. In 1996, these were still 10.7% of the total inequalities of the EU-15 states (Heidenreich & Härpfer, 2010). The already considerable levelling of living conditions at that time continued until 2009 due to the single market, the legal harmonisation of the EU, the introduction of the common currency and the huge capital flows to Southern Europe. By the end of the noughties, the share of between-country inequality in the EU-15 was only about 4%. In the wake of the euro crisis, however, the share of between-country inequality has risen again to 9.8% (2018). Centre-periphery differences are thus increasing again, especially between Northern and Southern Europe.

While the convergence between West and East can be explained by economic integration after the fall of the Berlin Wall and by political integration into the EU, the increasing income inequalities between Southern and Northern Europe point on the one hand to a changing economic context: In particular, the decades-long stagnation of labour productivity in Italy (Calligaris et al., 2016) and the lower export and research performance of Southern European countries (cf. Chap. 4) indicate a declining competitiveness—especially in a new phase of globalisation starting with the accession of China to the World Trade Organization. On the other hand, the common currency may have hit economies with demand-led growth models particularly hard (Iversen et al., 2016): While wages and labour costs in Southern Europe increased more than in Germany in the first decade of the euro, with the financial and euro crises from 2008 onwards, this post-euro introduction bubble burst and the initially observed convergence reported in Fig. 7.2 was reversed. One result of these crises was a relative decline of unit labour costs in all Southern European countries compared to the eurozone since 2010 (see Eurostat, table [nama_10_lp_ulc]). This is the background for the increasing income inequality in the EU-15 states reported in Fig. 7.2.

In sum: While the convergence of the EU-28, Switzerland and Norway continued in the last decades, it has come to a standstill in the old EU member states since the financial and euro crises—after decades of increasing within-country inequalities and decreasing between-country inequalities (Beckfield, 2006; Heidenreich, 2003). This points to different developments in the EU: on the one hand, the catching-up process of the post-socialist countries of Central and Eastern Europe has continued, while the Southern European countries have fallen behind again in the wake of the euro crisis. This was accompanied by high unemployment and falling employment rates. While the catching-up process can be explained by the rapid and successful integration of Central and Eastern European countries into the economic, political and legal structures of the EU, the emerging divergence between Northern and Southern Europe also points to the different growth regimes of export- and demand-oriented countries (Hall, 2014; Iversen et al., 2016).

## 7.2   The Development of National Income Inequalities

Income inequalities in Europe are mostly inequalities between citizens of the same country. In the 30 countries considered, these make up more than three quarters of the total inequalities; in the old member states of the EU even 90% (Fig. 7.2). The inequalities in real household income before, during and after the financial market and euro crises are shown in Fig. 7.3. A first insight is that the average national income levels clearly differ. The highest incomes are achieved in Northern and Continental Europe and the British Isles, the lowest in Southern and Eastern Europe. A second observation is the varying degrees of income inequality: In the Scandinavian countries, incomes are concentrated in the middle of the distribution, while the income curves of the Southern European, Baltic or liberal countries are stretched. Third, for some countries, particularly in Scandinavia and Central and Eastern Europe, increasing income inequality is also clearly visible: Not only has the most recent curve shifted significantly to the right compared to the income curve for 2006—indicating an increase in real incomes—but the more recent curves for 2012 and 2018 are also flatter and more elongated, i.e. the country has become more unequal.

However, such curves and their changes are too complex to be captured at a glance. Therefore, numerous inequality measures have been proposed, which, however, always highlight only specific areas and aspects of the curves just considered and neglect other aspects. This reflects the different normative assumptions of these measures already discussed in Chap. 3.

The Gini index—probably the best-known inequality measure—measures the deviation from an equal distribution. Figure 7.4 shows that by far the highest inequalities are still found in some Southern European (Spain, Greece, Portugal, Italy) and Eastern European countries (the Baltic States, Bulgaria and Romania),

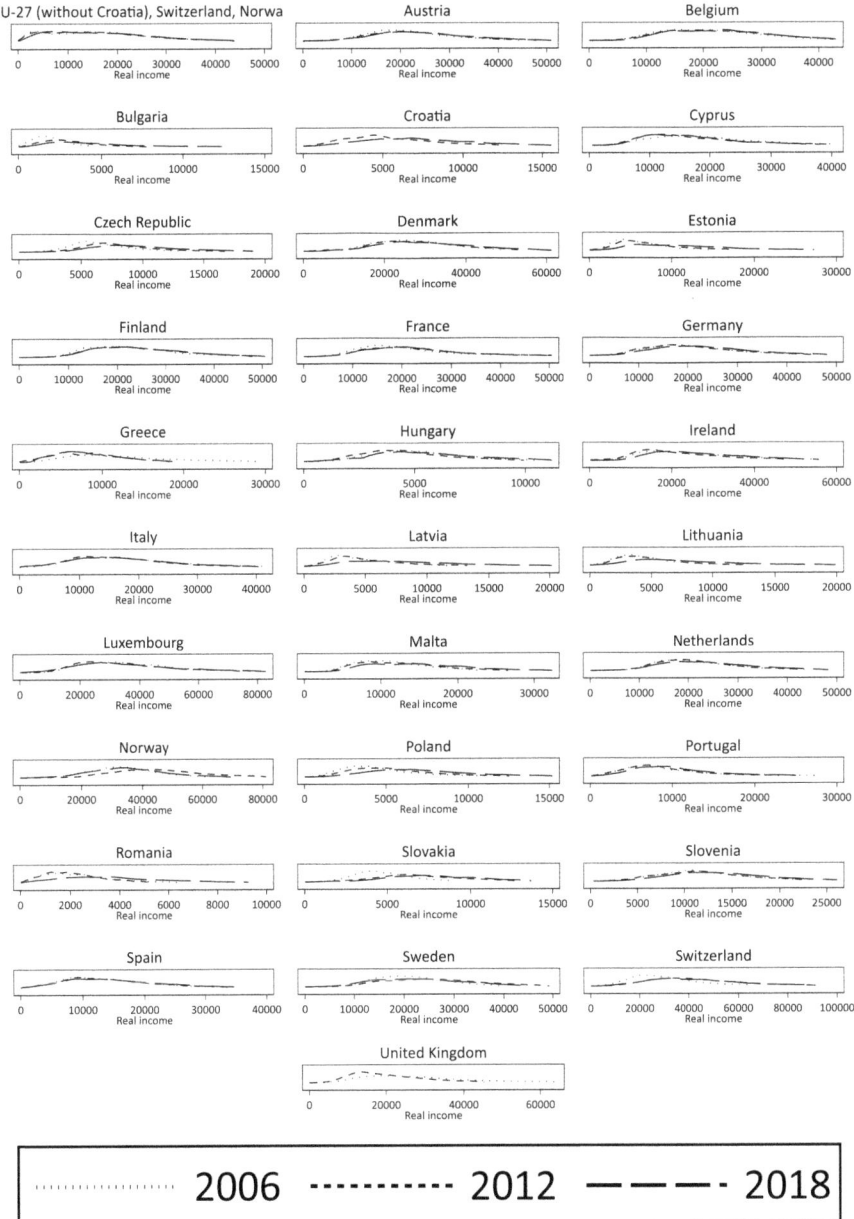

**Fig. 7.3** Trends in national disparities in disposable income in the EU-28, Norway and Switzerland (2006, 2012, 2018). Source: EU-SILC. Top-coding of highest 5 %; UK: 2017 instead of 2018

while the Scandinavian and some Central European countries are still the most egalitarian ones. Inequalities in some formerly very egalitarian Northern and Continental European countries have tended to increase (especially in Denmark, Sweden

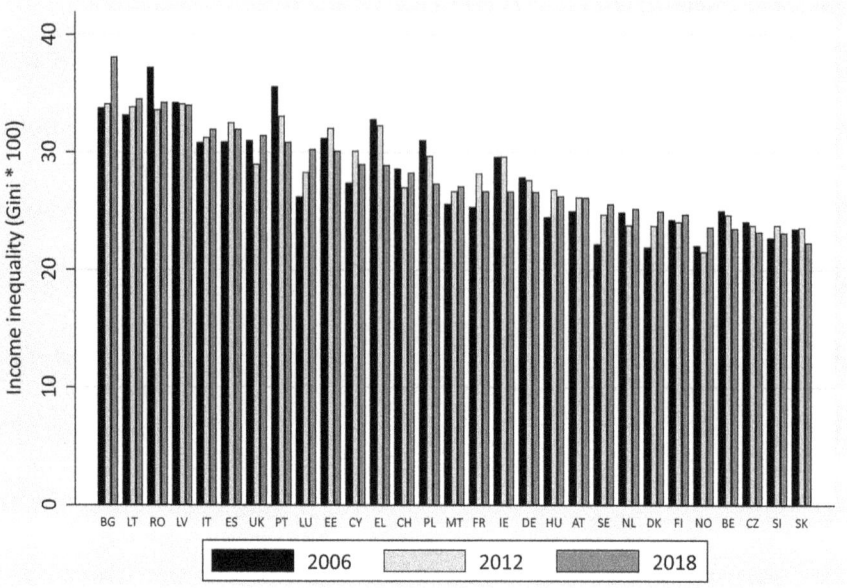

Source: Own calculations on the basis of EU-SILC 2007, 2013 & 2019

**Fig. 7.4** Gini coefficient of disposable income (2006; 2012, 2018; in %; EU-28, Switzerland, Norway)

and Norway), while they have tended to decrease in some Central, Eastern and Southern European countries with previously higher levels of inequalities (especially in Portugal, Poland, Greece and Romania). Overall, income inequalities in the EU countries have converged over the period under consideration. Since 2015, the coefficient of variation of income inequality has been falling. The number of countries in which inequalities increased by more than one percentage point is slightly higher than the number of countries in which they decreased (13 compared to 8). The previously very strong differences between the different "welfare state families" in Europe—for example between the traditionally more unequal liberal and Mediterranean countries on the one hand and the more egalitarian Northern and Continental European countries on the other—are shrinking. At the same time, the weighted mean of national income inequalities for the 30 countries considered remains at 0.29. Thus, these figures show a Europe which is becoming more homogeneous, but not more equal or unequal.

These results—which refer to a period of only 13 years—are at odds with the increasing income inequality observed since the 1980s for developed countries—especially in the US and the UK (Alderson & Nielsen, 2002; OECD, 2011, 2015). This increase in income inequality has been termed the "great U-turn". Instead of the secular decline in inequality predicted by Kuznets (1955), an increase in income inequality was explained, on the one hand, by the globalisation of goods, capital and labour markets (Alderson & Nielsen, 2002) and, on the other hand, by technological change due to a *"skill-biased technological change"* (Autor et al., 2003) or a polarisation of employment opportunities (Goos & Manning, 2007). This will be discussed in detail in Chap. 9. On the basis of these theses, an increasing gap between households with high- and low-skilled employees or between employees with non-routine and routine jobs can be predicted. Public austerity policies might have the same effect (Blyth, 2013, p. 15). Therefore, it can be assumed that income and living conditions in European countries are increasingly diverging (cf. on the political dimensions of these dualisation processes Emmenegger et al., 2012; Rueda, 2014). Mau (2015) therefore diagnoses an erosion of the middle classes in Europe.

Given this background, it comes as a surprise that average national income inequalities in the EU, as measured by the Gini index, have been essentially stable since 2008. Even when focusing on the countries particularly affected by the crisis (i.e. Italy and the five countries that had to be rescued by European-international bailout programmes—Greece, Cyprus, Spain, Portugal and Ireland), the picture does not change. In Italy and Spain, income inequality has increased by one point, while it has decreased in Greece, Ireland and Portugal and remained at the same level in Cyprus. The relative stability of national inequality patterns is in marked contrast to the first 10 years after the introduction of the euro (1999–2008), when the Gini coefficient rose by more than one percentage point in 13 EU countries, while it fell significantly in only five. *The trend towards rising national income inequality was thus halted during the crisis.*

This raises the question of whether this basic stability of European inequality patterns contradicts the thesis of a "great U-turn", i.e. the assumption of increasing income inequalities for developed economies. This requires longer time series of as many of the current EU member states as possible. An important step in this direction is the study by Beckfield (2019, introduction and chap. 4), which has reported increasing national inequalities from 1980–2010 on the basis of the Luxembourg Income Study and the corresponding (apparently unweighted) Gini coefficients of initially five countries at the beginning of the 1980s (France, Great Britain, Spain, Germany, Sweden). However, since inequalities do not necessarily evolve in a linear fashion and European countries differ in size, the chosen method is not convincing. Therefore, in order to produce longer time series for the development of national income inequality in the EU, (a) different data sets have to be used by combining LIS, EU-SILC and World Bank data, (b) the national inequality measures have to be weighted by population size (Milanovic, 2013, p. 199), and (c) in the case of incomplete data, the share of the EU population for which the aggregate ratios were calculated is given. This is done for the period 1980–2018 for the EU-28 in Fig. 7.5. The results in this figure give a very different picture to Beckfield (2019, p. 6): while Beckfield observes an increase in the average within-country income inequalities in the EU from 0.26 to 0.31 (2010), in Fig. 7.5 the Gini of the weighted within-country inequalities varies between 0.29 and 0.31. Incidentally, this result is also supported by Beckfield (2019, p. 197) himself, who in Fig. 4.2 presents weighted data on within-country income inequality in 14 Western European EU member states since the mid-1980s. The corresponding Gini coefficients vary between 0.30 and 0.31, which can hardly be interpreted as an "end of convergence". For total European inequality, the results contradict this thesis even more.

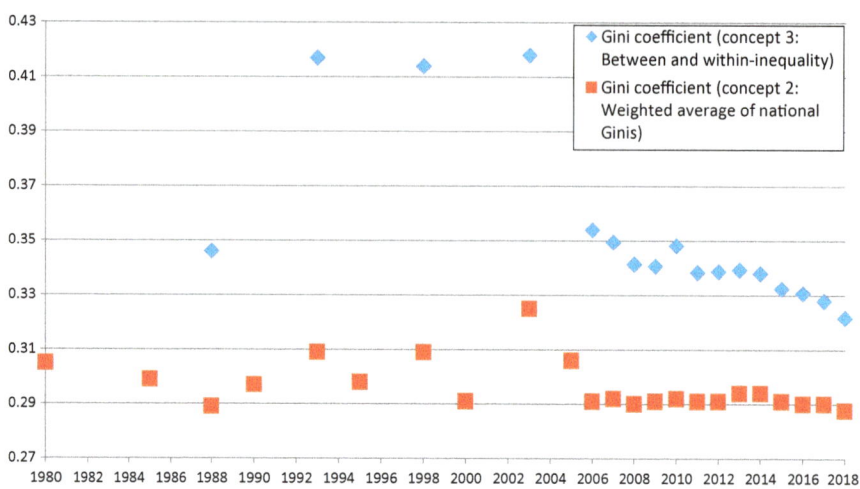

Source: Lakner and Milanovic (2013): 1988 (56 %); 1993 (94 %); 1998 (93 %); 2003 93 %) ; Eurostat, table ilc_di12 based on EU-SILC: from 2005-2019 (99-100 %); Luxembourg income study (2019): 1980 (51 %); 1985 (80 %), 1990 (85 %); 1995 (97 %); 2000 (99 %). The LIS data are organised in waves, which also include survey years that are 2-3 years before or after the years mentioned. The population share of the countries for which the Gini coefficients for income inequality are available in the total population of the 28 countries that were members of the EU in 2019 is shown in brackets.

**Fig. 7.5**  Within- and between-country income inequalities in the EU (1980–2018)

Europe-wide inequalities were higher than 0.40 after the collapse of the Comecon area and then declined to a Gini of 0.32 (EU-28; 2018). In sum: An increase in EU-wide income inequalities cannot be observed, but a basic stability of within-country inequalities and a decline of Europe-wide inequalities since the 1990s.

Before discussing possible reasons for the stabilisation of within-country income inequalities in Europe, a closer look will be taken at the income situation in Europe. First, the aggregate inequality measures for the bloc hides the fact that countries may evolve very differently even given a broad stability at the aggregate level. For example, national income inequality measured by the Gini coefficient increased by 3–4 points in Bulgaria, Luxembourg, Sweden and Denmark from 2006 to 2018, while it decreased by 3–4 points in Portugal, Greece, Poland and Romania (Fig. 7.4). This indicates the crucial importance of national policies, such as the considerable importance of activation policies and the restructuring of universalist welfare states in Scandinavia (Bengtsson, 2014) and the expansion of welfare state protection in Central and Eastern European countries (see Sect. 7.3).

Secondly, the evaluation of income inequalities also depends on the development of absolute income levels. People are not only concerned with inequalities, but also with income levels and income changes, i.e. improvements or deteriorations compared to a previous situation. Here, the national differences in the wake of the financial market and euro crises are considerable: while median price-adjusted household incomes have risen considerably in Central and Eastern Europe in particular from 2006 to 2018—for example, in Bulgaria by 122%, in Estonia by 80%, in Lithuania by 76% and in Latvia and Slovakia by 67%—they have fallen in Greece by 28%, in the UK by 21% from 2006 to 2017, in Cyprus by 11% and in Italy by 4%. The development of price-adjusted household income in Spain (+10%) and Portugal (+15%) was somewhat better. Precisely those countries that were hit hardest by the financial and euro crises have again suffered very high losses as a result of the pandemic in 2020/22, as these countries rely strongly on services and are therefore particularly vulnerable.

Thirdly, the incomes of different groups evolve differently (Fig. 7.6): In some countries, the lower two or three deciles were effectively protected against the crisis by corresponding minimum protections (for example in Belgium, Bulgaria, Germany, Estonia, Finland, Greece, Ireland, Croatia, Malta, Poland, Slovenia, the Czech Republic and Cyprus), in other countries not (Denmark, Italy, Latvia, Lithuania, Luxembourg, the Netherlands, Austria, Romania, Sweden, Slovakia, Spain, Hungary, the United Kingdom and Switzerland). In some countries the middle class bore the brunt of the shock (Bulgaria, France, Malta, the UK and Cyprus), in others the middle class was disproportionately protected. The typical curve for this constellation—an inverted U—can be found above all in Latvia, the Netherlands, Romania, Slovakia and Switzerland. In some countries, the wealthier households fared better than others in the crisis (Bulgaria, Denmark, Finland, France, Lithuania, Malta, Sweden, United Kingdom, Cyprus and Norway)—partly also due to rising property prices and rental income (Piketty, 2014), in other countries they were disproportionately affected by the crisis (Belgium, Germany, Greece, Ireland, Croatia, Poland, Portugal, Romania, Slovakia, the Czech Republic and Switzerland)—possibly also due to low interest rates in the eurozone. In Germany, the second decile shows very nicely the gap between recipients of social benefits and other low-income households that are no longer eligible: The social situation of some members of the lower middle class has deteriorated more than the situation of means-tested social benefits recipients. This once again highlights the crucial role of national employment, tax and welfare policies with corresponding effects on different income groups. This is considered in more detail in the next section.

The above figure illustrates considerable variations even within the five European country groups. In order to condense this information, Fig. 7.7 reports group-specific developments in the lower, middle- and upper-income deciles, in the lower (D1/D5) and upper income range (D9/D5) and across the entire distribution (D9/D1).

Price-adjusted median disposable income (Fig. 7.7a) is significantly higher in Scandinavia (27,000 PPS in 2018) than in Continental Europe (23,000 PPS) and the British Isles (21,000 PPS). Southern European households are still far better off than Central and Eastern European households (14,000 PPS compared to 6000 PPS), even after the crisis and post-socialist catch-up. Nevertheless, the income situation of Central and Eastern European households has improved significantly in the period under consideration.

Income inequalities remain broadly stable in Southern Europe (Gini 201: 0.32), the British Isles (Gini 2017: 0.31), Central and Eastern Europe (0, 29) and Continental Europe (0.26), while they increase somewhat in Scandinavia from a very low level (Gini 2006: 0.23; Gini 2018: 0.25) (Fig. 7.7b). Also on the basis of the mean

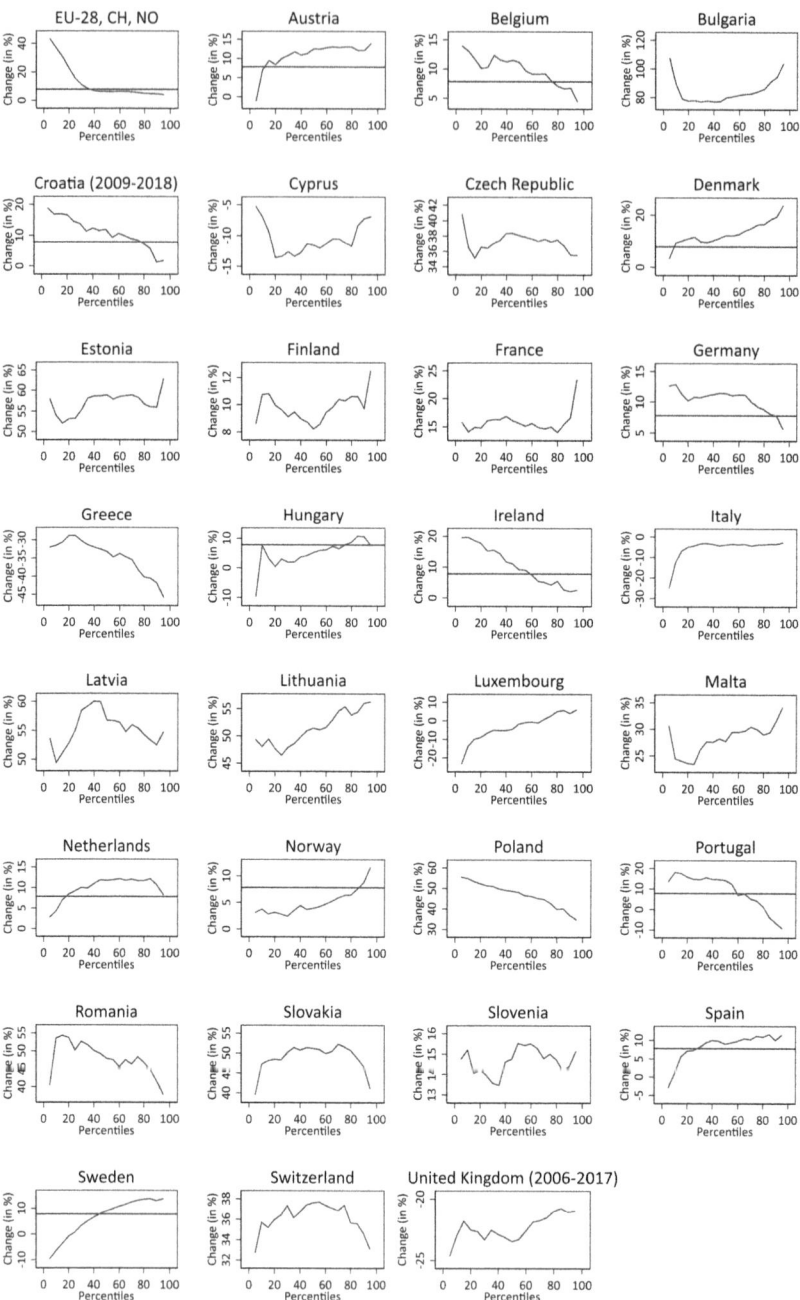

Note: The horizontal line in some sub-graphs of Figure 7.6 indicates that real means-weighted household net income increased by 7.8 % on average in the EU-28, Norway and Switzerland from 2006 to 2018 (UK: 2017, Croatia from 2009). In countries without such a line, real income has either increased significantly more (for example in Estonia) or decreased significantly (Greece, Italy, UK, Cyprus) over this period.

**Fig. 7.6** Development of disposable income in the different income percentiles (28 EU countries, Switzerland, Norway, 2006–2018)

logarithmic deviation (MLD) (Fig. 7.7c), the increase in inequalities in Southern Europe and their decrease in Eastern Europe is clearly visible. In Central and Eastern Europe, income inequality has been declining since the mid-1990s, also due to falling unemployment and rising employment figures, after initially rising sharply during the post-socialist transformation processes.

Figure 7.7d shows that the real incomes of the lowest *income group (D1)* initially collapsed significantly especially in the Anglo-Saxon and Southern European countries and have not yet reached the initial level again in 2017/18. The poorer households in the British Isles had a 12% lower price-adjusted income in 2017 than in 2006, while Southern European households had a 5% lower income. Poorer households in Scandinavian and Continental European countries saw increases (+5% and +16% respectively), although these were dwarfed by the rapid increases in Eastern Europe (+22%). *Median disposable income (D5)* has declined by 19% in price-adjusted terms from 2006 to 2017 on the British Isles, while it has stagnated in Southern Europe and increased by 14% and 10% respectively in Continental Europe and Scandinavia. Central and Eastern European households have 57% higher incomes (Fig. 7.7e). The picture is similar in the upper income range (D9). However, the incomes of the richer households show a below average development in Central and Eastern Europe (+37%) and above average in Scandinavia (+17%).

The last row of Fig. 7.7 reports the decile ratios D5/D1, D9/D5 and D9/D1. The decile ratio in the *lower half of the income distribution* (D5/D1) shows on the one hand that poorer households in Scandinavia and Continental Europe are relatively much better off than poorer Southern and Eastern European households. However, the gaps to the middle income have widened in all country groups in the last decade—especially in Southern and Eastern Europe. In the upper half of the income distribution (D9/D5), the differences between the very egalitarian regimes (Continental Europe and Scandinavia) and the other country groups have remained largely the same. Only in Scandinavia and Central and Eastern Europe can increasing inequalities be observed (Fig. 7.7h). This also applies to the overall income distribution (D9/D1; cf. Fig. 7.7i). These country groups have thus become more unequal, although the spread of incomes at the lower end has narrowed significantly in Eastern Europe (Fig. 7.7d).

In sum: For at least three decades, national income inequalities in Europe have been on average largely stable. The corresponding Gini index for the weighted national inequalities can be estimated at around 0.29–0.30. However, the data for the 1980s largely refer to Western Europe. For this period, a Gini of 0.30 may therefore be somewhat overestimated, as inequalities may have been lower in the then still socialist countries of Eastern Europe. The claim of increasing national income inequalities in Europe (Beckfield, 2019, p. 209) does not correspond to the evidence shown here. The broad overall stability, even in turbulent times

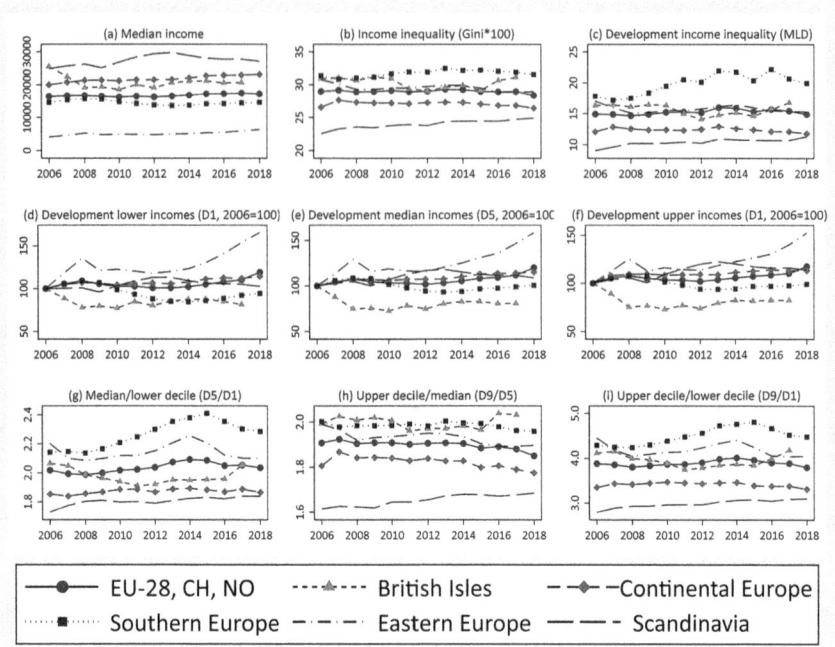

**Fig. 7.7** Development of price-adjusted income and income inequality in the EU-28, Switzerland and Norway (2006–2018). (**a**) Median income. (**b**) Income inequality (Gini*100). (**c**) Development income inequality (MLD). (**d**) Development lower incomes (D1, 2006 = 100). (**e**) Development median incomes (D5, 2006 = 100). (**f**) Development upper incomes (D1, 2006 = 100). (**g**) Median/ lower decile (D5/D1). (**h**) Upper decile/median (D9/D5). (**i**) Upper decile/lower decile (D9/D1)

characterised by the collapse of the socialist economic and social order, the enlargement and deepening of the EU, the globalisation and digitalisation of the economy, the rise of China, the opening of capital and goods markets, and the financial and euro crises, points to the central importance of national institutions and policies that effectively cushioned these far-reaching transformations. In the same period during which disposable income inequality in the USA rose from 0.31 (1979; LIS) to 0.38 (2018; LIS), European countries were able to preserve a central prerequisite for the social cohesion of their imagined political communities, a comparatively low level of inequality. However, Europe-wide stability goes hand in hand with considerable country-specific differences and dynamics. In particular, increasing income levels and decreasing national inequalities in Central and Eastern Europe are striking. However, the long-term stagnation of disposable incomes in Southern Europe and the significant increase in inequalities in the Western EU member states are more dangerous for social cohesion in Europe in the medium term.

## 7.3   National Income Inequalities: The Role of Labour Markets, Families and Social Policy

In the previous section, the crucial roles of national policies and labour market structures for the levels and evolution of national inequality were mentioned. Welfare mix approaches emphasise that not only welfare state benefits are important for ensuring individual welfare, but also market and family structures (Esping-Andersen, 1990, 1999). The income and living situation of households thus is determined by a "welfare triangle" of state, (labour) market and family. Sometimes civil society (in particular non-governmental organisations) and communities are added (Evers & Laville, 2004). In this section, the relative importance of national labour markets, private lifestyles and welfare state protection for the national patterns of income inequality will be examined on the basis of four different forms of inequalities shown in Fig. 7.8.

The first curve in this figure refers to the inequalities in gross hourly earnings of all employed persons, the second to the inequalities in earnings of the full-time

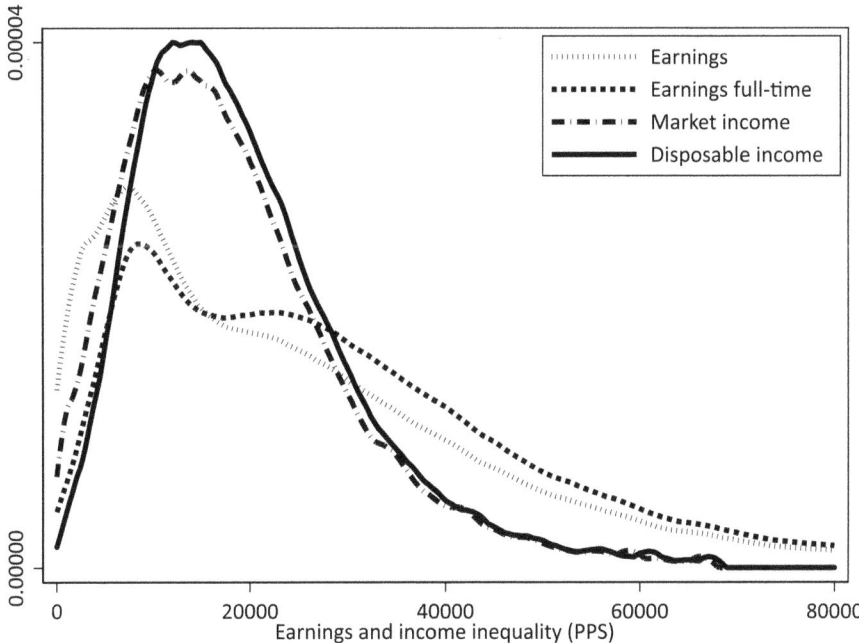

**Fig. 7.8** Earnings and income inequality in the EU-28, Switzerland and Norway (2018)

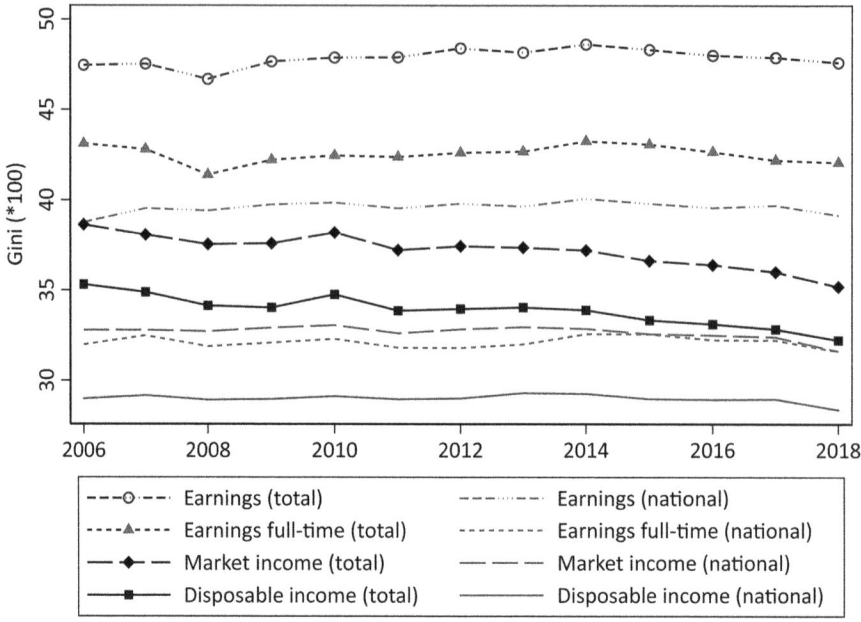

Source: EU-SILC 2007-2019; weighted national and Europe-wide Gini coefficients (in %).

**Fig. 7.9** Earnings and income inequality in the EU-28, Norway and Sweden (2006–2018)

employed in the same age groups, while the third and the fourth curves report the inequalities in market and disposable incomes. While *earnings* inequalities refer to the individual gross annual wages and salaries of individual employed persons aged 15–64 years (without apprentices), disposable and market income are calculated for households. *Market income* is the net household income weighted by household size before taxes, social contributions and benefits, while *disposable income* is the net household income after taxes, social contributions and benefits. It can be seen in Fig. 7.8 that individual wages and salaries are significantly more unequally distributed across all employed persons than across full-time employees. For the 30 countries considered (EU-28, Switzerland, Norway), the corresponding Gini coefficients of the Europe-wide inequalities are 0.47, 0.41, 0.35 and 0.32. The weighted national Gini coefficients of these four distributions are 0.42, 0.33, 0.33 and 0.29 respectively.

These four distributions can now be analysed in terms of two types of differences. First, following the explanations in Sects. 6.3 and 7.1, the differences between the pan-European and the weighted national inequalities can be considered. These differences can be seen in Fig. 7.9, which shows the development of the Europe-wide and national Gini indices for earnings and income inequality. For the four selected indicators, the inequalities for the 30 countries considered (i.e. including the differences between countries; black lines with symbols) and the weighted mean values of the national inequalities (grey lines without symbols) are shown. While

Europe-wide and national earnings inequalities have remained largely stable, disposable and market income inequalities have become significantly lower in the European context. This points to the previously mentioned catching up of the Central and Eastern European countries. In the national context, these inequalities have also remained largely stable. The thesis that income inequalities in Europe are increasing in the wake of the euro crisis and the accompanying austerity policies can thus be rejected (Blyth, 2013; Karamessini & Rubery, 2014; Pavolini et al., 2016).

Equally interesting, however, are the differences between the four types of inequalities, because these differences can be interpreted as indicators for more *flexible labour markets, pluralised lifestyles and welfare state redistributions.*

The *flexibilisation* of the labour market will lead to an increase in earnings inequalities, as more diverse forms of work are accompanied by more employment opportunities, which sometimes are lower paid than "regular" jobs. Therefore, the difference between the earnings inequalities for all and for full-time employees can be interpreted as an indicator of the deregulation and *flexibilisation of employment relationships*. This difference reflects mostly the lower earnings of part-time workers, but also lower hourly wages of irregular contracts, for example, fixed-term jobs and workers who are not subject to social security contributions. It increases when atypical forms of employment become more important. At the same time, labour force participation is increasing due to the flexibilisation of employment relationships, as more people are involved in paid employment. If only the work intensity of already affluent households increases, this may lead to higher income inequalities. However, when poorer households participate to a greater extent in the labour force, a higher work intensity in these households will reduce income inequality (Kenworthy & Pontusson, 2005).

The *pluralisation* of lifestyles will in general lead to higher income inequalities, because smaller households reduce opportunities for sharing incomes between inactive, unemployed, low-paid and high-paid household members. Therefore, one indicator of the *pluralisation of private lifestyles* is the difference between earnings and market income inequalities. In a society consisting only of employed singles, the distributions of earnings and market incomes would be identical. If non-working people are included, the difference between households with predominantly working and non-working members will become very large. Since employed and inactive persons (children, pensioners, unemployed ...) mostly live together in societies dominated by male breadwinners and larger households, the difference between (individual) earnings inequalities and household-related market inequalities will be lower, since the incomes of active and inactive persons in households are divided among all household members. A pluralisation of private lifestyles, however, will lead to greater market inequalities, since well-paid, low-paid, unemployed and inactive household members are now less likely to live in the same household. The difference between earnings and market inequalities increases. A huge difference between earnings and market inequalities may thus refer to smaller households, shorter working lives and traditional employment patterns (Pfau-Effinger, 2004). For the 30 countries considered (EU-28, Switzerland, Norway), the corresponding Gini coefficients are 0.42 and 0.33 when the weighted national Gini coefficients of the two distributions are considered. Family formation processes thus reduce individual earnings inequality by 9 points, while the flexibilisation of forms of work increases earnings inequality across all employees by 9 points compared to the earnings of full-time employees. The effects of family formation processes and the flexibilisation of employment on inequalities therefore work in opposite directions: *A pluralisation of lifestyles and living forms increases income inequalities, while an increasing importance of atypical forms of employment reduces them. It can be stated that a more flexible labour market acts as a buffer for a more pluralised society, because it counters increasing inequalities* (Fig. 7.11).

The difference between inequalities in market income and disposable income points to the importance of the *welfare state*, as redistributive policies reduce income inequalities through taxes and social benefits. On average, income inequality is 3.8 points lower than the inequality of market income. The differences between the curves in Fig. 7.8 illustrate that the reduction of inequalities from 0.42 to 0.33 and then to 0.29 is mainly the result of redistribution within families and only in the second step the result of public redistribution.

Overall, the correlation between a flexibilisation of employment relationships and the extent of intra-family redistribution is very strong. Inequality between households is significantly reduced by household members entering different and differently paid employment relationships. The extent of intra-family redistribution and the contribution of more flexible forms of employment to lower inequalities in the EU-28, Norway and Sweden are more important than welfare state redistribution (7.7 and 7.6 points compared to 3.5 points). Also, the extent of family and labour market redistribution differs considerably more between the different European states than the variation in welfare state redistribution. The coefficients of variation of these three indicators are 0.73, 0.51 and 0.45 indicating a huge diversity in private living forms.

The relative weight of these three inequality-related processes differs in the 30 European countries considered. Figure 7.10 shows the different earnings and income inequalities. On this basis, the three indicators described for the flexibilisation of labour markets, the pluralisation of lifestyles and welfare state redistribution are determined for each country (Fig. 7.11).

The most *flexible employment relationships*—measured by the difference in Gini coefficients for earnings inequality between all employed persons and those in full time employment—are found in Finland (13.8 percentage points) and the Netherlands (13.5). It can be seen that even very egalitarian countries—which are plotted on the right in the figure—may be characterised by high earnings differentials. This applies, for example, to Slovenia, Belgium, Norway or Finland. This is often accompanied by high levels of redistribution within families.

With regard to *redistribution within families* (i.e. the difference between earnings and market income inequality), the Romanian case is the first to catch the eye. Only in this country is family redistribution strongly negative, as a very egalitarian structure of earnings (Gini = 0.25) is accompanied by a significantly higher inequality of market income (Gini = 0.36). This might point to the country's agrarian structure and the associated high share of family workers and the below-average

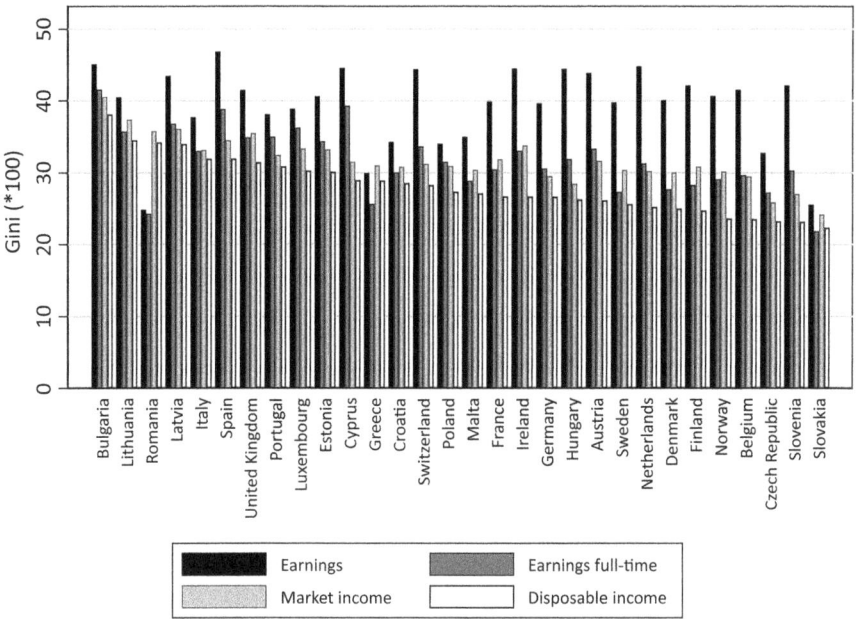

**Fig. 7.10** Earnings and income inequality in Europe (EU-28, Switzerland, Norway, 2018)

share of wage earners. Market income is thus determined to a considerable extent by the incomes of farmers and the self-employed, which will differ strongly according to the size of their lands or companies. In Greece, too, intra-family redistribution is slightly negative. In all other countries, the direct economic function of the family as a business or landowner has become less important.[2] Redistribution within families is most effective in reducing inequality in Hungary (16 percentage points), the Netherlands (14.6) and Slovenia (15.1), but also in Switzerland, Spain, Austria, Finland and Germany—mostly countries with more traditional family structures and policies. But in contrast to the previously formulated expectations, the redistribution within families is surprisingly low in the Southern and also in some Eastern European countries. This highlights a limitation of the chosen indicator, i.e. the difference between the earnings and market income inequalities: When women are completely excluded from the labour market as shown by a low female activity rate, they receive no wages and therefore are not included in the statistics on earnings inequality. This indicator therefore measures mostly the differences between a

---

[2]The French sociologist Pierre Bourdieu has pointed out that modernisation in no way means that the family loses its central importance for the reproduction of social inequalities. However, in a meritocratic society, this reproduction no longer takes place directly through the accumulation and inheritance of economic capital, but through family support in the accumulation of educational titles, relationships and a class-specific habitus (Bourdieu, 1984, 1988).

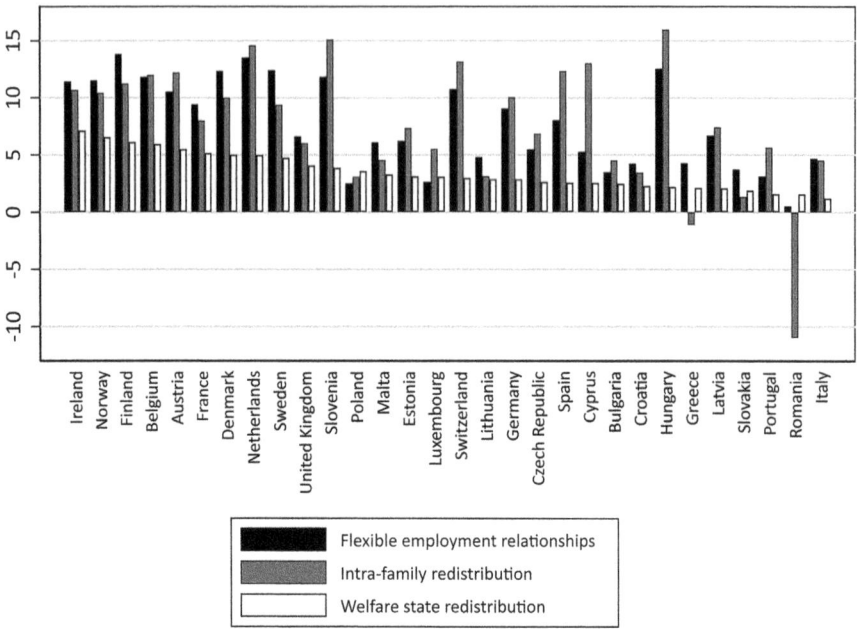

**Fig. 7.11** Families, the welfare state and flexible forms of employment. Three ways to reduce income inequality (EU-28, Switzerland, Norway; 2018)

partial modernisation of lifestyles and the related "one-and-a-half-earner" model and a "dual-earner" model.

The extent of *welfare state redistribution* is measured as the percentage difference between market income inequality and disposable income inequality (Kenworthy & Pontusson, 2005; Fig. 7.11). In 2018, this redistributive intensity is highest in Finland at 7.1 percentage points (followed by Norway, Finland, Belgium and Austria) and lowest in Italy at 1.2 points (followed by Romania, Portugal, Slovakia and Latvia). Not surprisingly, the Scandinavian countries are at the top, while the Central, Eastern and Southern European countries have the lowest redistribution intensity (Fig. 7.11). The effectiveness of welfare state redistribution remains largely constant over time—with the exception of a sharp increase in redistribution in Ireland during the crisis and a decline in welfare state redistribution in Scandinavia before the crisis. Contrary to the European Commission/DG EMPL (2019, p. 87), no increase in the inequality-reducing effects of welfare state and tax measures can be identified compared to 2008 on the basis of the data used here.

At the European level, redistribution within families and by welfare states are positively correlated. However, these two types of redistribution follow different logics. In some countries, a strongly developed welfare state is accompanied by considerable intra-family redistribution (for example in Finland, Ireland, Austria or the Netherlands). In other countries (such as Spain, Cyprus or Slovenia), which rely heavily on intra-family redistribution, the extent of welfare state redistribution is low. This increases the vulnerability to income risks linked to pluralised lifestyles, for example divorce, single parenthood or the decision to live alone, because these risks are not cushioned by the welfare state. The United Kingdom is at the other end of the spectrum because a well-developed welfare state goes hand in hand with individualised lifestyles and a correspondingly lower redistribution within the family. In general, however, there is no trade-off between public and family-based forms of social security.

In sum: national inequalities in disposable income to a considerable extent reflect national earnings inequality and atypical forms of employment, which in general are higher in the Northern and Continental European countries. Private lifestyles also contribute to reducing national inequality in particular in countries characterised by a partial modernisation of lifestyles. Households in these countries are often composed of both full- and part-time earners which implies huge levels of within-family redistribution. The importance of redistribution within households is lower in countries with dual earner households, but also with traditional male breadwinner models. In general, family redistribution is more important than public redistribution through taxes and social contributions. Income inequalities are thus not only reduced by welfare states, but also by a flexibilisation of employment relations and by intra-family redistribution. This points to the central importance of national institutions, which will be considered next.

## 7.4   Institutional and Individual Determinants of National Income Inequalities

Even though Europe-wide inequality patterns have been broadly stable over the last 13 years, the differences between egalitarian and unequal countries—for example between Slovakia and Bulgaria—are considerable. This raises the question of which determinants shape these within-country income inequalities. Two sets of factors can be distinguished. On the one hand, national institutions and economic structures, and on the other, the composition of the population and the labour force. For example, national income inequalities may increase due to the weakening of trade unions or a stronger service orientation of the economy, but also due to a higher share of skilled or female labour. These factors will now be discussed.

An examination of the national determinants of income inequality usually starts with the classic study by Kuznets (1955), which points to the importance of economic structures and institutions. Kuznets (1955) predicts initially increasing and then declining income inequalities in the course of industrialisation. He explains the initial increase in the course of Western modernisation by the increasing employment shares and higher wages in industry compared to low-paid agricultural jobs, which were still dominant at the beginning of the nineteenth century. Inequalities are highest when workers are evenly distributed between low- and high-productivity sectors. When industry and its accompanying institutions (trade unions, welfare state, education systems . . .) prevail, inequalities decrease again. François Nielsen (1994) and Francois Nielsen and Alderson (1997) operationalise the explanatory factor crucial to Kuznets' (1955) explanation as sector dualism. Furthermore, heterogeneity in educational attainment, population growth, economic development, ethnic discrimination and the degree of urbanisation are included as explanatory variables. In addition to these internal factors, Alderson and Nielsen (2002) include the impact of globalisation. The authors conclude that globalisation—measured by foreign direct investments, imports from less developed countries and immigration—leads to an increase in national income inequality. In contrast, Nollmann (2006, p. 638) emphasises the importance of domestic factors, in particular the polarisation between high- and low-skilled jobs within the service sector.

Following this research tradition, the factors that have influenced the extent of national and regional income inequality over the last two decades will be discussed on the basis of Table 7.2. As far as this is possible on the basis of EU-SILC data, regional income inequalities are also considered, as these can also differ significantly within a country. For example, Greater London has a Gini index almost five points higher than that of Wales. In addition to regional and national contextual factors, the impact of supranational and European processes will also be considered.

The first question to be examined is whether the classic institutions of equalitarian capitalism (*welfare state, trade unions, education systems*) have an influence on the level of inequality. At the centre of egalitarian social models is the standard industrial employment relationship (Kenworthy, 2004; Thelen, 2012). As an indicator for this relationship, the share of *industrial employees* is included in the following model (Table 7.2). Second, in the last decades Europe has shifted towards more inclusive employment policies (Sect. 5.1). An indicator for such a policy shift is the *share of women in the labour force*. Furthermore, global and European dynamics are to be included, which can lead to a change in national inequality patterns. It can also be assumed that the *globalisation of the economy*—measured by the integration of goods, services, capital and labour markets—and the policy of budget consolidation ("*austerity*") contribute to higher inequality in the EU (Blyth, 2013).

The corresponding hypotheses on the impact of egalitarian institutions, inclusive policies and European and global dynamics are tested for the period from 2007 to 2018 (column 1), for the years before the financial market and euro crises (2007–2008, column 2), for the years during the crises (2009–2013, column 3) and after the crises (2014–2018, column 4). The models in Table 7.2 show that a higher share of *industrial employment, stronger trade unions* and a higher level of *social protection* during and after the financial and eurozone crises were associated with lower income inequality. Incomes in industrialised countries and regions are more egalitarian than in countries and regions with a stronger service sector. Also, a *higher share of skilled workers* reduces income inequality at least after the crises. A higher *female employment rate* is associated with a more egalitarian income structure in all periods considered, as greater female labour force participation can increase income and the number of labour force members per household even in less affluent

**Table 7.2** Determinants of national and regional income inequality before and during the Great Recession (2007–2018) in the EU-28, Switzerland and Norway

| | 2007–2018 | 2007–2008 | 2009–2013 | 2014–2018 |
|---|---|---|---|---|
| Share of employees in industry (as % of all employed persons) | −0.16** (−2.89) | −0.14 (−1.64) | −0.20** (−5.40) | −0.21** (−5.34) |
| Female employment rate (% of women aged 15–64) | −0.05+ (−1.76) | −0.06 (−1.18) | −0.09** (−3.01) | −0.11** (−5.47) |
| Average level of education (in % of 15–64 year old inhabitants) | −0.04 (−1.51) | −0.08 (−1.62) | −0.05+ (−1.76) | −0.06* (−1.96) |
| Social expenditure (in % of gross domestic product) | −0.08 (−1.20) | −0.38** (−4.47) | −0.18** (−2.74) | −0.19* (−2.18) |
| Union density (% of employees) | −0.06** (−3.67) | −0.06** (−2.82) | −0.07** (−4.00) | −0.07** (−3.43) |
| Austerity (change in primary budget balance excluding interest expenditure) | −0.01 (−0.54) | 0.1 −1.02 | −0.03 (−1.28) | −0.01 (−0.40) |
| Economic globalisation (KOF A) | −0.11** (−3.94) | −0.12* (−2.57) | −0.10** (−2.89) | −0.10** (−3.00) |
| Number of cases (regions/countries x years) | 1238 | 238 | 630 | 370 |
| Log-likelihood | −2440 | −544 | −1287 | −636 |
| Wald chi$^2$ | 48.12 | 230.44 | 220.07 | 246.28 |
| "Interstate" intraclass correlation | 0.44 | 0.32 | 0.33 | 0.72 |
| "Interregional" intraclass correlation | 0.32 | 0.44 | 0.39 | 0.17 |
| Intertemporal intraclass correlation | 0.03 | 0.00 | 0.02 | 0.02 |
| Pseudo-R$^2$ | 0.54 | 0.40 | 0.57 | 0.59 |
| AIC | 4904 | 1112 | 2598 | 1297 |

Notes: $+ p < 0.10$, $* p < 0.05$, $** p < 0.01$; in brackets: $t$-values. Dependent variable: Regional and national Gini indices for disposable income inequality. Source: own calculations based on EU-SILC 2007–2018. Data for Croatia from 2009 onwards. Contextual variables from Eurostat, Visser (2019) and Gygli et al. (2019). The dependent variables are lagged by 1 year (cf. on the procedure Heidenreich, 2010)

households (Kenworthy & Pontusson, 2005). Thus, in addition to the classical egalitarian institutions of industrial society (industry, trade unions, social policy, vocational or technical training at the intermediary level), it can be expected that another set of institutions also contributes to a more egalitarian income distribution—institutions that facilitate the increasing labour force participation and employment rates of women in particular: childcare facilities, training institutions and activation policies.

Contrary to expectations, *austerity policies* have no significant effect on the level of income inequality in Europe, neither during nor after the crises (Blyth, 2013; Pavolini et al., 2016). Surprisingly, increased *economic integration into the European and global economy* is also associated with a significantly negative impact on income inequality. Against the backdrop of the work by Alderson and Nielsen (2002), OECD (2011) and Rodrik (1997, 2018), the opposite, namely increasing income inequality, was expected. A detailed inspection of the data (cf. Figure 7.7) points to opposing trends in Central, Eastern and Southern Europe: while the Gini coefficient of income inequality in Central and Eastern Europe decreases significantly over the period under consideration, it increases in Southern and Northern Europe. At the same time, the KOF index for economic globalisation (Gygli et al., 2019) increased far more in Central and Eastern Europe than in Southern and Northern Europe. The surprising negative correlation between globalisation and inequality in Europe thus points to the fact that the economic globalisation of Central and Eastern Europe was accompanied by the decline of the initially very high levels of income inequality during the post-socialist transition (Aristei & Perugini, 2012).

These results show that the on average stable patterns of national inequality shown in the previous section are very fragile. Lower inequalities are largely the result of a comparatively large industrial sector, advanced welfare states, strong trade unions and vocational and technological training at the middle qualification level. These institutions reflect the egalitarian European social model (Therborn, 1995) which is being challenged by deindustrialisation, tertiarisation, financialisation, globalisation, digitalisation, academicisation and individualisation. The EU and the European nation-states have so far been able to maintain their previous levels of income inequality and adapt their social models, even exporting them to Eastern Europe, while the USA has had to accept a dramatic increase in the face of similar challenges (Atkinson et al., 2011; Case & Deaton, 2020). This was also achieved in Europe by strengthening institutions that enabled the inclusion of a larger proportion of the working-age population in the labour force—especially women, but also older people and the unemployed. Activation and social investment strategies through inclusive employment policies as well as childcare and education policies (Morel et al., 2012) may thus have contributed to the continuation of egalitarian social structures alongside the classical egalitarian institutions of European industrial societies.

How this was possible will now be analysed by taking into account individual and household characteristics of the population. The contribution of socio-demographic changes to higher or lower income inequalities will be examined on the basis of decomposition analyses. These analyses decompose changing patterns of income inequality into mechanisms that have a direct effect on inequality (structural effects) and effects due to a changed composition of the population (composition effects; Firpo et al., 2018). An example of such a composition effect is that a higher proportion of smaller or single-person households is associated with higher inequalities. When a couple divorces, two new households might emerge, often one poorer and one wealthier, because the previous redistribution within the same household has ended. As previously argued, the pluralisation of private lifestyles thus may increase income inequalities and poverty risks (Peichl et al., 2011). A structural effect, on the other hand, would be if these changes were taken as an opportunity to better protect single parents against poverty risks, for example, through higher child benefits or better childcare. This would reduce the poverty risks of single parents even if the composition of the population remained the same. These decomposition analyses, which are mainly used for a better understanding of wage inequalities

**Table 7.3** Decomposition of changing income inequalities in selected EU member states (Gini, income: 2006–2018)

| | Spain | France | Poland | Sweden | UK (2017) | EU-28/HR, CH, NO |
|---|---|---|---|---|---|---|
| Gini 2018 | 0.298 | 0.251 | 0.280 | 0.233 | 0.308 | 0.308 |
| Gini 2006 | 0.293 | 0.240 | 0.322 | 0.206 | 0.349 | 0.349 |
| Change | 0.005 | 0.011 | −0.041 | 0.027 | −0.040 | −0.040 |
| Composition effect | 0.015 | 0.013 | 0.018 | 0.013 | 0.004 | 0.004 |
| Structural effect | −0.009 | −0.001 | −0.059 | 0.013 | −0.044 | −0.044 |
| Composition effect | | | | | | |
| Age | 0.001 | 0.004 | 0.000 | −0.001 | 0.001 | 0.002 |
| Migration | 0.001 | 0.000 | 0.000 | 0.003 | 0.002 | 0.000 |
| Education | 0.004 | 0.004 | 0.007 | 0.001 | 0.008 | 0.003 |
| Social class | 0.005 | 0.003 | 0.007 | 0.009 | 0.006 | 0.001 |
| Sectoral structure | 0.000 | 0.002 | 0.001 | 0.001 | 0.001 | 0.000 |
| Household type | 0.001 | 0.000 | 0.003 | 0.001 | −0.001 | 0.000 |
| Work intensity | 0.002 | −0.002 | 0.000 | 0.000 | −0.007 | −0.002 |
| Structural effect | | | | | | |
| Age | 0.005 | −0.003 | −0.002 | 0.000 | 0.006 | 0.000 |
| Migration | 0.006 | 0.001 | 0.000 | 0.002 | −0.001 | 0.003 |
| Education | 0.009 | −0.002 | −0.009 | 0.006 | −0.006 | 0.014 |
| Social class | −0.022 | −0.002 | 0.009 | −0.017 | 0.006 | −0.003 |
| Sectoral structure | −0.002 | 0.000 | −0.001 | 0.011 | 0.007 | 0.007 |
| Household type | 0.009 | 0.001 | −0.015 | 0.002 | 0.001 | −0.001 |
| Work intensity | 0.045 | −0.093 | 0.029 | −0.115 | −0.053 | 0.068 |

Source: EU-SILC 2006, 2019. EU-28 excluding Croatia plus Norway and Switzerland. The reference groups chosen were 25–54 years old, persons with medium qualifications, natives, persons employed in industry or agriculture, persons with routine jobs, persons living in adult households without children. $^*p < 0.10$, $^{**} p < 0.05$, $^{***} p < 0.01$

(Broschinski, 2020), will be used in the following analysis of changing income distributions. The analysis thus refers to the household level. Individual characteristics of the head of household (such as age, migration background, education, social class or economic sector) are only relevant insofar as they influence household incomes.

In the following analysis, the changes in the Gini coefficient between 2006 and 2018 in five selected countries and in the EU-28 (excluding Croatia), Norway and Switzerland are decomposed into structural and compositional effects. Here, age, migration background, education, social class and sectoral sector, household type and work intensity of households were included (Table 7.3). When comparing the composition and structural effect, it can be seen first that the two effects work in opposite directions, with the exception of Sweden: The composition effect is usually positive, while the structural effect is often smaller or even negative (in 16 of the 29 countries considered). The changing composition of the population is thus usually accompanied by higher inequalities, while the income differences in identical groups becomes smaller.

Among the *composition effects, higher education* plays an important role on the supply side of the labour market. Over the 13-year period analysed here, the share of persons with tertiary education increases by 7 percentage points in the 29 countries considered, while the share of persons with low qualifications decreases by 5 percentage points. The composition effect of higher compared to medium qualifications is positive in the five countries considered as well as in the average of the 29 countries, while on average the corresponding effect for low qualifications is negative: Higher educated persons thus contribute to higher income inequalities. This can be explained not only by higher earnings of higher qualified individuals, but also by the tendency to marry within the same educational strata (Blossfeld & Timm, 2003). The inequality-reducing effects of lower education reflect the impact of egalitarian institutions, because trade unions and social benefits may contribute to the stabilisation of earnings opportunities of low-skilled groups. On the supply side of the labour market, the *increasing share of single-person households* contributes to greater inequalities, as the income situation of single-person households will vary more than that of larger households due to a higher level of within-family redistribution. The composition effect of age also has a positive sign: As the age of respondents increases, and thus demographic aging, inequalities also increase. Only the *work intensity of households*, which measures the extent of gainful employment in relation to the available time budget of the working-age members of the households, shows slightly negative composition effects on average and in 16 countries—but only in one of the countries in Table 7.3, in the UK. This points to a higher work intensity of households and corresponding reductions in income inequality. While the shares of jobless households increase in many cases, the share of work-intense households, in which almost 100% of the available time is spent on gainful employment, increases at the same time. While the first development led to increasing inequalities in Spain, a higher work intensity reduced income inequalities in France and especially in the UK.

On the demand side of the labour market, occupational changes and in particular higher shares of skilled service activities promote increasing inequalities. *Thus, more education, older workers and more workers in skilled and high-level service activities contribute to higher income inequalities, while a higher work intensity of households reduces inequalities.*

These positive, inequality-enhancing composition effects are reduced by opposing *structural effects in* 19 of the countries considered. On the supply side of the labour market, the structural effect of *education* is on average positive in the EU countries. Income differentials between people with lower and medium qualifications increase. Households with a high *work intensity* (50% and more of the available time budget is actually spent in employment) also contribute to increasing inequalities. The differences between less and more work-intensive households increase significantly. In contrast, the structural effect of *single parents* is clearly negative. This may point to targeted social support for these households. The structural effect of social class is slightly negative, while the structural effect of the *sectoral structure* is significantly more positive: skilled and simple service jobs and a job in retail trade, restaurants or transport were associated with higher inequalities in 2018 than in 2006, as their relative position worsened compared to the reference group of middle-skilled and skilled workers in industry.

In sum: The structural change of the economy and society, which is documented in a changing household structure, a changing composition and role of social classes and an expansion of higher education, as well as a polarisation of employment opportunities and work intensity are important drivers of income inequalities. This trend is partly offset by negative structural effects. The negative, i.e. income-reducing structural effects of social classes and household types may point to protective measures in labour law and social policy. However, the positive, i.e. "inequality-increasing" structural effects of greater work intensity and higher education must also be emphasised. The income differences between persons with high and medium education are increasing, as are the differences between different economic sectors and between persons with and without a migration background.

Now the interaction and the partly opposing dynamics of compositional and structural effects will be examined more closely using the example of two countries with increasing inequalities. In *France,* the growth of the service classes and the expansion of upper secondary education are the strongest inequality drivers. This is counteracted by negative structural effects in age and in the composition and work intensity of households. In particular, younger and older people are better off—for example, because of the minimum wage and a generous pension system. Single-person households and households with children are also able to improve their relative income position—presumably due to all-day childcare. The biggest winners are households with an already high propensity to work. This points to a conflictual balance between a structurally-based increase in income inequality and egalitarian institutions such as the minimum wage or minimum income support. In *Sweden,* the strong increase in inequalities points to an increasing share of migrants, a decreasing share of industrial employees and a strong increase in highly skilled professionals in production-related services and IT. Furthermore, the relative income position of migrants is deteriorating. The egalitarian Swedish model is thus challenged by a changing sectoral structure of the economy and greater heterogeneity in the work-force. However, the increasing propensity to work among already highly work-intensive households contributes to lower inequalities, similar to France.

In conclusion: The average level of income inequality in the EU has not increased since the financial and eurozone crises in the EU. This stability of national income inequality in Europe can be largely explained by the egalitarian structures and institutions of the post-war period: A higher share of industrial workers, a high share of skilled blue- and white-collar workers, higher social spending and a stronger position of trade unions are associated with lower income inequalities. However, this apparent hyper-stability masks a very fragile equilibrium that is challenged by changing economic and employment structures and the changing educational level of the population. This becomes particularly clear when the individual and house-hold levels are considered. The example of education is the best way to describe the contested terrain of inequality. Due to the higher education of the population, the distance between the wages and incomes of the highly educated and low and medium skilled persons increases, as shown by positive composition effects. At the same time, family-based forms of social security are becoming less important, as indicated by the decreasing household size and the considerable poverty risks of single parents and single-person households. In some cases, it is possible to cushion this inequality-increasing pressure through better forms of social protection or higher levels of labour market participation, which is documented in the negative, "inequality-reducing" structural effects of jobless households. Overall, however, higher education and more individualised lifestyles push in the direction of higher income inequalities. Complementary to these effects on the supply side of the labour market, the demand for labour is also changing. This is documented in changing occupational and class structures: the middle and upper service classes—managers, professionals, engineers, teachers and senior administrators—and simpler service occupations are becoming more numerous, while the employment shares of skilled administrative, service and trade occupations, skilled workers and semi-skilled workers remain constant or are shrinking. Across Europe, however, the "inequality-enhancing" effects of the changing class structure are smaller than those of increasing education. The "inequality-enhancing" effects of higher education are further strengthened by a positive structural effect of education, i.e. by the higher income of the higher skilled. The structural effect of social classes, on the other hand, is clearly negative: compared to unskilled and semi-skilled routine workers, almost all other social classes can improve their income position. The only exceptions are skilled workers and simpler technical occupations.

The broad stability of income inequalities in Europe is thus the fragile result of countervailing economic and institutional dynamics and individual and household strategies to maintain and improve their social position. This is accompanied by substantial challenges: In the face of considerable economic transformations and corresponding shifts in the class structure, better-off households in particular are increasing their level of education and their volume of work. At the same time, less qualified people, singles and jobless households are falling even further behind. Households thus try to cope with the challenges of individualised lifestyles and economic change by increasing their educational efforts and their labour market participation. This might be interpreted as a meritocratic trap, as it further increases the income gaps between these households and households with a lower skill level and work intensity (Markovits, 2019; Sandel, 2020; Young, 1994). This increase in inequalities can be cushioned by minimum wages, minimum security and more inclusive labour market policies. However, this also means that households are exposed to considerable stress—and not only poorer households, but also average-earning households. Therefore, the determinants of subjectively perceived difficulties in making ends meet ("economic stress") will be discussed below.

## 7.5   The Importance of the National and the European Context for Europeans' Economic Stress

This section discusses how the development of between- and within-country income inequalities in the EU influences people's subjective perception of their own economic situation. The starting point is the assumption that one's own economic situation is also assessed in comparison to the situation of other people and that fellow citizens are a particularly important reference group (Clark et al., 2008; Diener, 2000). This raises the question whether the perceived economic situation is also influenced by transnational and European benchmarks. However, some researchers already doubt the initial assumption that a household's perceived economic situation depends primarily on the relative level of disposable income. They assume that the underlying needs, which can be explained biologically and psychologically, hardly depend on the social context (Veenhoven, 1991, p. 32). This implies that economic stress is higher in poorer countries because people have less money to live on and are therefore also affected by various facets of material deprivation (Townsend, 1979). Sacks et al. (2010, p. 2) succinctly summarise the relevant happiness and life satisfaction research and conclude that life satisfaction depends on disposable income and that relative income levels are only of secondary importance. In a similar vein, Delhey and Dragolov (2014) show that a higher income increases happiness independently of comparisons with national or other reference groups.

However, other authors emphasise that economic and life satisfaction also depend on the respective social context, i.e. on friends and colleagues, the comparison with fellow citizens or other Europeans. One's own standard of living is also judged according to what is considered acceptable in the respective societal context. Such a perspective is fundamental to a sociological understanding of poverty (Chap. 8). As Simmel (1965, p. 138) points out: "The poor, as a sociological category, are not those who suffer specific deficiencies and deprivations, but those who receive assistance or should receive it according to social norms." Poverty, like equality and inequality, is thus socially constructed. Since the nineteenth century, the relevant social framework has been the nation-state, which is considered to be the relevant political community (Anderson, 2006) or the community of solidarity (Renan, 1996). In a nation-state, demands for justice, respect or equality can be articulated, addressed to politicians and legally enforced by welfare institutions. Social security has therefore become a core task of European nation-states. Wilkinson and Pickett (2010) also provide empirical evidence of the importance of relative income position for various facets of social cohesion. Kley (2021) confirms the importance of national frames of reference for the impact of material deprivation on subjective economic stress.

In the course of European integration, however, "Europe" is also increasingly becoming the addressee of social policy expectations and demands. A household in Bulgaria may assess its own situation as bad not only because its income is lower than that of an average Bulgarian household, but also because it is lower than incomes in Germany or the UK, where some relatives and acquaintances work and where a person could easily get a job as a nurse. Also, the causes of one's own economic situation could be attributed to the EU, since it could be argued that the EU has intensified the competition in the labour market through free movement or forced a country into austerity programmes in the wake of the euro crisis. In this case, it makes sense to assume a transnational standard of assessment. Thus, the perceived economic situation might not only be determined by individual, household, regional or national factors, but also by the European and transnational context (Fahey, 2007; Heidenreich & Wunder, 2008). The Europeanisation thesis therefore claims that subjective feelings of deprivation, inequality and poverty also refer to a European frame of reference (cf. Delhey & Kohler, 2006; Goedemé & Rottiers, 2011; Kangas & Ritakallio, 2007; Lahusen & Kiess, 2018; Teney, 2016). Whelan and Maître (2009, p. 118) describe the underlying concept of Europeanisation as strong, as it implies "that people perceive themselves as part of a larger European stratification system. Furthermore, the perception of being advantaged or disadvantaged within this system would have to play an important role in individuals' evaluations of their own life circumstances." According to this strong concept of Europeanisation, explicitly rejected by Whelan and Maître (2009), Europe is understood as a social space that is also relevant for the assessment of social inequalities. Similar to Whelan and Maître (2009), Kley (2021) also finds no evidence for the Europeanisation of frames of reference.

Empirically, the controversy of whether household economic stress is shaped by absolute income levels or by national or even European frames of reference can be discussed by means of a question regularly asked in EU-SILC about the subjective perception of the household's economic situation: "Thinking of your household's total income, is your household able to make ends meet, namely, to pay for its usual necessary expenses?" This question can be answered on a six-point scale from (recoded) "very easily" (1) to "with great difficulty" (6). The answers to this question are taken as an indication of the perceived economic situation or economic stress. This stress will mainly depend on the household's economic situation. A low income will usually translate into greater economic stress than a high one. Accordingly, it can be expected that women, younger and older people, low-skilled people, singles, single parents, migrants and the unemployed are more likely to rate their own situation as poor. This will not be shown here once again (Watson et al., 2018). Instead, it will be discussed whether, in addition to the absolute income level, national and European frames of reference and European decisions and policies also influence perceived economic stress.

The absolute income level explains a significant part of the variation in stress levels between countries (31% at the household level). Figure 7.12 shows the average economic stress for poorer, median and richer households at the peak of the eurozone crisis. Richer households are more able to make ends meet than poorer households and economic stress is significantly higher in poorer countries such as Bulgaria and Greece than in wealthier countries such as Germany or Sweden. Economic stress thus is very strongly correlated with average disposable household income.

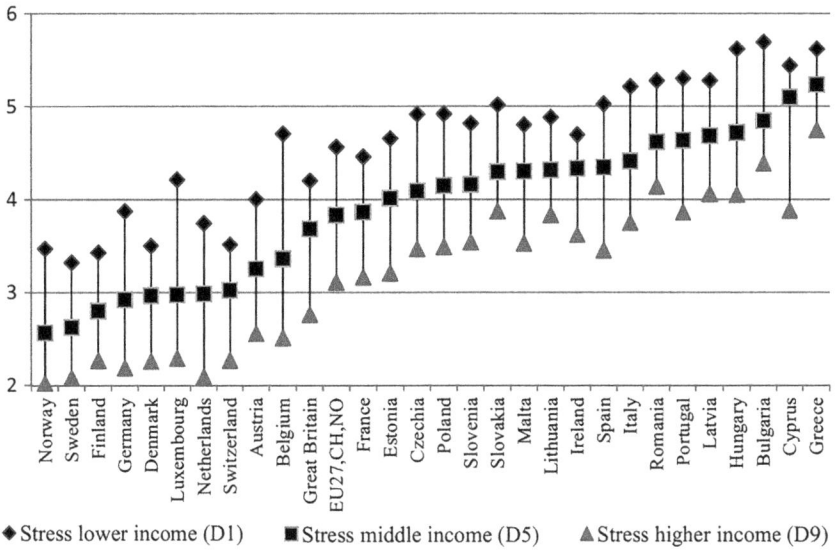

◆ Stress lower income (D1)     ■ Stress middle income (D5)     ▲ Stress higher income (D9)

Source: EU-SILC 2013; economic stress for the middle of the lowest (D1), median (D5) and top (D9) deciles. Question:
"Is your household able to make ends meet? Response alternatives: 6: With great difficulty. 1: Very easily. No.: 551.827).

**Fig. 7.12** Economic stress in 27 EU countries, Norway and Switzerland in the top, middle and
bottom income deciles (2013)

Figure 7.13 gives an overview of the development of economic stress in different
income groups in five different country groups since 2007. It can be seen that the
subjective economic stress of the population in the Southern and Eastern European
countries is significantly higher than in the other country groups. This is true for the
lower, median and upper income groups, which are shown separately in Fig. 7.13a,
c, and e. The subjective economic stress in the Southern and Eastern European
countries is higher than in the other country groups. In the Anglo-Saxon and Western
European countries, the overall stress level is significantly lower. The lowest stress
level in all income groups is in Scandinavia, while the Southern and Eastern
European countries are always at the top. Even high-income households in these
countries have significant problems making ends meet. The average economic stress
in the top decile in Southern and Eastern Europe is 3.6 on a six-point scale—a value
that is about as high as the economic stress in the lowest (!) income decile in
Scandinavia (3.5). This again points to a clear polarisation between peripheral and
core regions in Europe. However, the differences between Eastern and Southern
Europe are also remarkable. In Southern Europe, economic stress is just as high as in
Central and Eastern Europe, even though incomes in Central and Eastern European
countries are still significantly lower on average than in Southern Europe. The
greater impact of the financial and euro crises and the associated deterioration of
the economic situation leads to increasing economic stress in all income and country
groups from 2009 onwards. This increase is particularly strong in Southern Europe

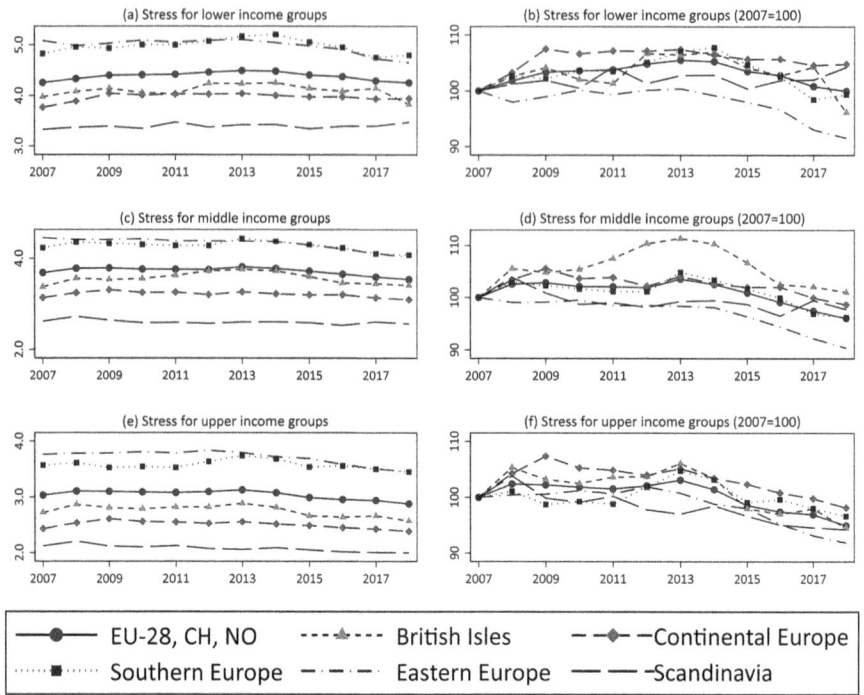

Source: EU-SILC 2007-2018, own calculations. Figure 7.13a, c, e show the absolute levels of subjective economic stress (SES) in 27 EU countries (EU-28 excluding Croatia) on a six-point scale as a function of relative national income position (bottom, middle and top decile). Figure 7,13b, d, f show the developments in economic stress since the base year 2007 = 100.

**Fig. 7.13** Subjective economic stress in five country and three income groups (2007–2018). (**a**) Stress for lower income groups. (**b**) Stress for lower income groups (2007 = 100). (**c**) Stress for middle income groups. (**d**) Stress for middle income groups (2007 = 100). (**e**) Stress for upper income groups. (**f**) Stress for upper income groups (2007 = 100)

from 2012 to 2015 (Fig. 7.13). Stress also increases significantly in the two Anglo-Saxon countries, which were also very strongly affected by the financial and eurozone crises. Increasing economic stress may also have contributed to the fact that the Greek and British populations voted in 2015 and 2016, in effect, to leave the eurozone and the EU respectively. In Northern and Continental Europe, on the other hand, economic stress for all income classes reached the pre-crisis level of 2007 in 2018, while in Eastern Europe it decreased significantly.

However, the data in Fig. 7.12 also indicate that households in countries with a comparable average income—such as Lithuania and Greece—perceive similar incomes in very different ways. Economic stress is almost one point lower in Lithuania on the six-point scale (4.2 instead of 5.1). Despite comparable incomes, the differences between Sweden (2.6) and France (3.7) are even greater. This suggests that in addition to the absolute level of disposable income, people's subjective perception of their own economic situation is also influenced by other factors.

In the following, I will empirically examine the role of national and transnational frames of reference (or evaluation standards) for subjective economic stress in order to investigate whether and in what sense a Europeanisation of these standards can be observed. If such a Europeanisation can be observed, this would also contradict the claims of Whelan and Maître (2009) and Kley (2021) who claim that, at least for material deprivation, there is no such Europeanisation. In order to show such a Europeanisation, it is also necessary to distinguish European standards from effects of the absolute income level. This is difficult since a higher income in general also implies an improvement in the European context. This raises the question of how the impact of absolute income levels and of a European frame of reference can be distinguished. One possibility for distinguishing these effects would be a systematic comparison of EU and non-EU countries. Since the EU-SILC surveys also include Norway, Switzerland, Serbia and Iceland, this would even be possible. However, the very close integration of the countries mentioned with the EU undermines such a strategy (Ebbinghaus, 1998). EU and non-EU countries are not separated societies. Possible commonalities between EU and non-EU countries can also reflect cross-border diffusion.

Since it is also not possible to compare economic stress in Europe with other world regions, I will examine in three different ways in which economic stress evolves in Europe and *to what extent national and European frames of reference and the absolute level of income influence it.* The starting point for these analyses is the consideration that the income situation can develop very differently at the household level and in the national and European context. If the purchasing power-adjusted income of a household has not changed in a certain period, then economic stress should remain the same if it is determined primarily by the *absolute income level.* In this case, a higher income should be accompanied by lower stress, even if the situation of the household may have deteriorated relative to the national or European average. If, on the other hand, the *national frame of reference* determines the stress level, a different evolution can be expected: If the national average income has increased very strongly (as in Poland, for example) or decreased (as in Greece during the euro crisis), it can be expected that subjective economic stress shrinks (or increases) even if income remains constant. After all, compared to the national average, a Polish household would be in a (relatively) worse situation than before, while a Greek household would have improved its relative position. However, if a *European frame of reference* exists, households with a constant income should report a slight increase in economic stress if their financial position has relatively worsened due to an increasing European average income. In this respect, different stress levels can be expected if the absolute income level, the national or a European frame of reference shape people's perception of their own economic situation.

Based on these considerations, the relative weight of the absolute income level and the national frame of reference for perceived economic stress will first be

**Table 7.4** Effects of income and labour market inequalities on subjective economic stress (2013)

|  | (1) | (2) | (3) | (4) |
|---|---|---|---|---|
| Disposable household income | −0.54*** | −0.54*** | −0.54*** | −0.54*** |
|  | (0.04) | (0.04) | (0.04) | (0.04) |
| National average income | −0.81*** | −0.39* | −0.69*** | −0.71*** |
|  | (0.17) | (0.19) | (0.14) | (0.17) |
| Interaction household x national income | −0.03 | −0.03 | −0.03 | −0.03 |
|  | (0.07) | (0.07) | (0.07) | (0.08) |
| Income inequality |  | 0.09*** |  |  |
|  |  | (0.02) |  |  |
| Unemployment |  |  | 0.03*** |  |
|  |  |  | (0.001) |  |
| Outsiders |  |  |  | 0.03*** |
|  |  |  |  | (0.01) |
| Constant | 3.50*** | 3.51*** | 3.51*** | 3.50*** |
|  | (0.08) | (0.08) | (0.07) | (0.08) |
| Cases | 221,958 | 221,958 | 216,997 | 221,958 |
| Wald chi$^2$ | 10,655 | 10,683 | 11,599 | 10,669 |
| Intraclass correlation | 0.159 | 0.151 | 0.116 | 0.137 |
| McFadden pseudo-R$^2$ | 0.438 | 0.438 | 0.442 | 0.438 |
| AIC | 648,868 | 648,865 | 633,808 | 648,871 |

Source: EU-SILC 2013, own calculations. Dependent variable: Question: "Is your household able to make ends meet?" Response alternatives: 1: With great difficulty. 6: Very easily. Two-level models with random slopes for 28 EU countries, Switzerland and Norway. Control variables: Gender, age, education and migration status of household respondents; household and average income logarithmised; income inequality: Gini index of disposable income inequality, unemployment rate: as % of working population aged 15–74; Eurostat, [lfsa_urgan]; outsiders: head of household either unemployed, low-paid, temporarily employed, self-employed without employees or involuntarily part-time employed (national mean; in % of all employees). Standard errors in brackets. * $p < 0.05$, ** $p < 0.01$, *** $p < 0.001$

determined for 1 year at the peak of the euro crisis (Table 7.4). In the next step, the longitudinal data from EU-SILC are analysed at the microlevel with a view to the question of whether economic difficulties are identified more with respect to the national or the European frame of reference (Table 7.5). Here, however, the absolute income level must be ignored. In the next step, the longitudinal character of national data is exploited at the macrolevel to analyse the level of respondents' income and its development in comparison to the national and the European average (Table 7.6). A common result of these three different analyses is that subjective economic stress is influenced by national and transnational, also European frames of reference. The dependent variable is identical in all cases (however, sometimes recoded differently).

In the first step, the extent to which the level of disposable income, but also the labour market situation, determine the perceived economic stress of European households will be discussed. In addition to the usual control variables, disposable household income, national average income and an indicator for the level of national income inequality are included in the four two-level models shown in Table 7.4.

**Table 7.5** Economic stress in Europe during the financial market and euro crises (2008–2013)

| Economic stress | (1) | (2) | (3) | (4) |
|---|---|---|---|---|
| Disposable income relative to the national median (in € 100) | −0.381*** (0.0533) | | 1.280** (0.395) | 1.069* (0.403) |
| Disposable income relative to the European median (in € 100) | | −0.408*** (0.0631) | −1.658*** (0.407) | −1.655*** (0.408) |
| Interaction effect national income (€ 100) * European income (€ 100) | | | | 0.0339*** (0.00543) |
| Constant | 3.873*** (0.0178) | 3.876*** (0.0175) | 3.883*** (0.0172) | 3.887*** (0.0171) |

Notes: Panel regression with fixed effects for households, standard errors (clustered by country) in parentheses. Data: EU-SILC longitudinal data; years 2008–2013; number of cases: 1,224,468 households; dependent variable: "How does your household manage with monthly income?" (scale from 6 = "very poorly" to 1 = "very well"); countries: Austria, Belgium, Bulgaria, Cyprus, Czech Republic, Denmark, Estonia, Finland, France, Greece, Hungary, Iceland, Ireland, Italy, Lithuania, Luxembourg, Malta, Netherlands, Norway, Poland, Portugal, Romania, Slovakia, Slovenia, Spain, Sweden, United Kingdom. Calculations: Matthias Pohlig. * $p < 0.05$, ** $p < 0.01$, *** $p < 0.001$

In the first model in Table 7.4, disposable income and the national average income are taken into account in addition to some socio-demographic control variables. As expected, it can be confirmed that the absolute level of disposable income and the national average income have a strong influence on economic stress. Households with higher incomes and households in richer countries have less difficulty making ends meet. The interaction between national and household income has no additional significant influence. The second model looks at whether the extent of national income inequality has an impact on subjective economic stress. Based on Wilkinson and Pickett (2010), it can be assumed that higher levels of inequality intensify status competition and economic stress. This is indeed the case. Higher income inequality (measured by the Gini coefficient of disposable income) is correlated with higher economic stress, even when income levels are included.

The last two models in Table 7.4 address a different question, namely that of the possible influence of *European policies* on subjective economic stress. Since the impact of the eurozone crisis contributed to higher unemployment and a stronger labour market segmentation (Chap. 5), model 3 analyses whether the national unemployment rate has an impact on the perceived economic situation of individual households. This is the case. This can be interpreted as an indication of an indirect influence of the EU, since during the euro crisis the European monetary union was confronted with considerable pressure on the national labour markets of the 19 euro countries, but also of other European countries—firstly due to the elimination of flexible exchange rates, secondly due to the lack of transfer mechanisms, thirdly due to conditions imposed as part of international rescue policies and fourthly due to a slump in the economy that also put pressure on the labour markets of non-euro countries. In the fourth model, the labour market position of the head of household is taken into account. If he or she is an outsider, i.e. unemployed, temporarily

**Table 7.6** Importance of individual characteristics and the national and European reference level for subjective economic stress (28 EU Member States; 2005–2018)

| | Time dummy (0) | | Individual (1) | | Longitudinal section (2) | | Random slope (3) | |
|---|---|---|---|---|---|---|---|---|
| | OR | se | OR | se | OR | se | OR | se |
| Intersection | 0.326*** | 0.011 | 0.448*** | 0.090 | 0.156*** | 0.102 | 0.193*** | 0.170 |
| Time | 0.999 | 0.003 | 1.036*** | 0.000 | 1.464*** | 0.027 | 1481*** | 0.051 |
| Income (log.) | | | 0.257*** | 0.003 | 0.246*** | 0.003 | 0.214*** | 0.065 |
| National average (stand.) | | | | | 30.067*** | 0.134 | 14.634*** | 0.145 |
| Difference national average (stand.) | | | | | 0.862* | 0.072 | 0.864 | 0.079 |
| Distance EU income | | | | | 0.901*** | 0.005 | 0.919*** | 0.006 |
| Difference EU average | | | | | 1.022*** | 0.006 | 1025*** | 0.007 |
| Interaction national-income*time | | | | | 0.282*** | 0.097 | 0.271*** | 0.213 |
| Interaction EU income*time | | | | | 1.038*** | 0.003 | 1039*** | 0.006 |
| Variances random effects | | | | | | | | |
| σ2 | 3.29 | | 3.29 | | 3.29 | | 3.29 | |
| Countries* Years (τ00) | 0.07 | | 0.07 | | 0.07 | | 0.07 | |
| Countries | 1.05 | | 0.64 | | 0.52 | | 0.50 | |
| Country*Income (τ11) | | | | | | | 0.13 | |
| Covariance Intercept* Slope (ρ01) | | | | | | | −0.09 | |
| AIC | 5,153,609 | | 4,380,915 | | 4,331,589 | | 4,313,687 | |
| Cases, Countries, Year*Country | 4,990,519; 28; 377 | | 4,743,666; 28; 377 | | 4,743,666; 28; 377 | | 4,743,666; 28; 377 | |

Source: EU-SILC 2005–2018, own calculations. Binary logistic two-level region with random slopes for a maximum of 28 EU countries. The dependent variable is the dichotomised response to the question on economic stress (1: considerable difficulties or difficulties in making ends meet; 0: some or no difficulties). In the model the odds ratios (OR) and standard errors (se) are reported. In models 1–3, individual controls (age, migration status and educational and occupational levels) are included, but not shown. The case numbers refer to the persons surveyed, the number of countries and the survey periods multiplied by the number of countries. Income refers to the previous years. * $p < 0.05$, ** $p < 0.01$, *** $p < 0.001$

employed, low-paid, self-employed without employees or involuntarily part-time employed (Chap. 5), then the economic stress on the household is also higher. It can therefore be assumed that not only the income situation but also the labour market situation, which has been significantly exacerbated by the euro crisis, contribute to increased subjective economic stress. Since this crisis was not limited to the euro or EU member states, non-euro and two non-EU countries are also included.

Next, the impact of the relative income level on subjective economic stress is analysed on the basis of longitudinal data (Table 7.5). In these models, the previously analysed impact of the absolute income level on economic stress is disregarded, since only *changes* in disposable household income and economic stress are considered. Comparable income data over time were obtained by adjusting the household incomes for inflation. In this way, the influences of the national and European frames of reference can be determined and compared. Columns 1 and 2 of Table 7.5 first report the relationship between changes in a household's income position relative to the national or European median and changes in economic stress. *Both in the case of an improvement in household income compared to the national average and in the case of an improvement compared to the European average, subjective economic stress decreases.* When comparing the coefficients, the changes relative to the European context ($-0.408$ compared to $-0.381$) turn out to be even stronger than in comparison to the national context. In column 3, both relative income positions are included. This is possible because the income position of a household can develop differently compared to the national and European average incomes. An improvement for example in the Greek context can still mean a deterioration in a European context. In the third column of Table 7.5 it can be seen that the changes in income positions in the European and national context are significant. However, the latter are positive indicating a decreasing marginal benefit of additional income. In the fourth model, the interaction between the changes in national and European income positions is included. This has a significant positive effect on the change in economic stress. This can be interpreted as a saturation effect: The improvement in the income position in the European context leads to lower economic stress. This effect is somewhat reduced by a complementary increase in the national context.

It can be stated that improvements in the relative income position in the European context contribute to lower economic stress, even when the national context is taken into account. The European frame of reference, in addition to the national frame, shapes people's assessment of their own economic situation. Given the convergence of consumer prices and consumption patterns in Europe, this result should not be surprising. However, it also means that European-wide income differences, which are still considerable, may erode social cohesion in particular in the European Union when the expectations about social protection, especially in less wealthy countries, rise faster than the income level. In any case, citizens and voters also assess their economic situation in a European perspective.

In a third step based on the work of Fairbrother (2014), the influence of the European level for the development of economic stress will be examined in a longitudinal perspective distinguishing now the influence of the absolute income level from the impact of income in relation to the national average.[3] The starting point is again the consideration that household income adjusted for purchasing power, the national average income and the national average income in relation to the European average generally develop differently. For example, a 10% increase in national average income may mean a deterioration compared to the European average if the latter has increased by 20%. If the national and European income levels have an influence on subjective economic stress, then an increase of 15% would mean, that in relation to the national average income economic stress would decrease, while stress in relation to a European frame of reference would increase. In order to determine these influences (in addition to the level of absolute income), the national average income and the distance to the EU-28 average are decomposed into four longitudinal and cross-sectional effects. In the case of national average income, the cross-sectional effect corresponds to the country-specific income average for all years and the longitudinal effect corresponds to the distance from this average, which varies from year to year. In the case of the distance from the EU average, the cross-sectional effect corresponds to the average distance of the national average income from the Europe-wide income and the longitudinal effect to the annual distance from this mean income. Thus, the analysis of cross-sectional data at the individual level can be combined with the analysis of longitudinal data at the national and European levels. In the following models, the previously used indicator for subjective economic stress is used again, but this time in a dichotomised form in order to be able to run binary logistic regressions.

Table 7.6 shows that individual factors, the national context and the European level have a significant influence on subjectively perceived economic difficulties. For the calculation of the four models in this table, EU-SILC data for 28 EU countries from 2005 to 2018 were used. At first, models 1–3 show that—even when individual control variables are taken into account (gender, age, migration background, educational and occupational level)—a higher disposable household income is associated with less economic stress. This is documented by an odds ratio of 0.257 shown in Model 1. In model 2, also the four cross-sectional and longitudinal effects described above and the interactions of the cross-sectional effects with time are included. A higher national average income throughout the period under consideration is associated with lower stress. However, an increase in national average disposable income over time is only associated with a slightly significant decrease in economic stress in model 2 (0.862). In the next step, this relationship is no longer significant (model 3). This result can be interpreted as a variant of the Easterlin paradox (Easterlin, 1974, p. 118), which observes that in spite of a positive association between income and happiness at a given time, over time "higher income was not systematically accompanied by greater happiness." The same seems to be true for economic stress.

The importance of the European frame of reference is indicated by the evolution of national income relative to the European level. This indicator has a significant

---

[3]Christian Spörlein pointed out and explained this method to me, and helped me enormously with its implementation. I am extremely indebted to him for this collegial support.

negative influence on economic stress in models 2 and 3, i.e. a high income also in relation to the EU level is associated with lower economic stress (0.901). The European reference level thus reinforces the stress-reducing effect of a high national average income. A higher national average income compared to the EU average is associated with lower economic stress—controlling for the disposable and national income trends. The interaction effects of the national and European cross-sectional effects over time are also statistically significant (0.282 and 1.038) and point in the same direction as the main effects. Overall, European integration thus contributes to providing citizens with a higher degree of economic security. Over time, however, this is not true, as an increase in national income relative to the European average income is associated with higher economic stress. The corresponding odds ratio is slightly greater than 1 (1.022 and 1.025 respectively). This result might reflect the higher stresses, anxieties and status competition that accompany higher growth rates. Despite European systems of social security, the gains and losses of economic opening processes are unevenly distributed (Rodrik, 2018). The associated anxieties could also explain the slight but statistically significant increase in economic stress over time.

Model 4 includes the correlations between increasing incomes and decreasing economic stress, the so-called "random slopes", which differ from country to country. These slopes differ so clearly that the assumption of equal slopes can be rejected.[4] This is once again a clear indication of the central importance of national frames of reference. However, Table 7.6 demonstrates once again the influence of the European level on subjective economic stress. Therefore, in addition to the undeniable role of the absolute, purchasing power-adjusted income level and the national average income, which can be taken as an indicator of the importance of a national frame of reference, the European and in particular the EU level also have a clear impact on economic stress. Both the cross-sectional and longitudinal effects of the European level have a significant impact on subjective economic stress. This result is corroborated by the fact that it is consistent with the previous analyses.

In sum, it can be stated that the subjective perception of income inequality reflects not only individual living and income situations, but also national and European policies and frames of reference. It was shown that subjective economic stress depends on absolute income levels and thus on the availability of adequate financial resources. Secondly, the available means are also assessed in relation to the national average income. Stress is particularly high in countries with a more unequal income distribution. Thirdly, economic stress is also determined by the relative income

---

[4]Whelan and Maître (2009) conclude from this that a Europeanisation of social inequalities does not take place (cf. also Kley, 2021). This is not a compelling interpretation, since different slopes only indicate that the connection between objective inequalities and subjectively perceived stress in Europe are not identical in every country. This may also point to different aspirations when it comes to discussing financial constraints: It is possible, for example, that even with very similar average incomes adjusted for purchasing power, the British are much less willing than the Irish to broach the subject of economic difficulties. Even within the same country, random slopes may differ between different regions.

position in the European context. The European frame of reference thus also influences people's subjective perception of their own financial situation. Last but not least, national policies (as indicated by the national inequality patterns) and European policies, for example the bailout programmes and their impact on the labour market—indicated by national unemployment rates and the extent of labour market segmentation— also play a role in European citizens' perceived economic stress.

## 7.6   Summary and Outlook

The methodological nationalism of inequality research assumes that the social relations and institutional structures which determine the distribution of life and income opportunities can mostly be analysed within the borders of a nation-state. This assumption is being challenged by the Europeanisation and transnationalisation of markets, politics, administration, law, social relations and social practices. A central challenge for the sociology of social inequality is therefore the study of transnational, especially European, spaces and references standards. In this chapter, the Europeanisation of income inequalities has been described on the basis of three of the previously proposed four conceptions of Europeanisation (Sect. 2.2). First, Europe was conceptualised as an international social space in which national patterns of income inequality and the development of differences between nations can be compared. Secondly, the EU was examined as a politically regulated supra-national field that shapes the income situation of households, especially through economic and monetary integration, and thirdly, Europe was analysed as an emerging transnational social field that also influences subjectively perceived economic stress. The fourth concept, which refers to the significance of transnational practices, did not play a role in this chapter.

First, the development of inequality within and between nations was analysed. Two central, decades-long developments (Beckfield, 2006, 2019; Heidenreich, 2003)—increasing within-country income inequality and decreasing between-country income inequality—have come to a halt since 2008. Especially in the 15 "old" EU member states, between-country inequalities are increasing again. This is also a result of the euro crisis, which put an end to the huge capital flows to the Southern European countries after they joined the common currency. Devaluations are no longer possible in a monetary union and countries can no longer decide on their own monetary policy, thus also limiting the scope of their fiscal policies. Even if national patterns of income inequality have on average remained broadly stable, the increasing unemployment rates have had a marked and negative effect on subjective economic stress.

Secondly, the economies of the Central and Eastern European countries grew at an above-average rate even during the crises. This was accompanied by a European-wide convergence of income levels and reduced between-country income inequalities. This is also a result of their accession to the EU. After the collapse of the socialist economies, the post-socialist countries adopted the *acquis communautaire* and integrated themselves in European and global value chains. Both the dramatic economic decline and the exorbitantly high unemployment figures as well as the rapid economic rise of the CEE countries were therefore shaped to a considerable extent by the EU and its legal and institutional framework. They were also the greatest beneficiaries of EU funds.

Third, changes in the European income hierarchy correlate with changes in economic stress. This supports the assumption of a Europeanisation of frames of reference. Income inequality can therefore not only be analysed in a national context. It is increasingly generated and regulated at the European level as well. The standards by which households assess their financial situation are also influenced by the European and transnational context.

# References

Alderson, A. S., & Nielsen, F. [Francois] (2002). Globalization and the great U-turn. Income inequality trends in 16 OECD countries. American Journal of Sociology, 107(5), 1244–1299.

Alvaredo, F., Chancel, L., Piketty, T., Saez, E., & Zucman, G. (2018). *World inequality report 2018*. Belhaven Press. Retrieved from https://wir2018.wid.world/.

Anderson, B. (2006). *Imagined communities: Reflections on the origin and spread of nationalism*. Verso.

Anderson, J., Tagliapietra, S., & Wolff, G. B. (2020). A framework for a European economic recovery after COVID-19. *Intereconomics, 55*(4), 209–215. https://doi.org/10.1007/s10272-020-0904

Aristei, D., & Perugini, C. (2012). Inequality and reforms in transition countries. *Economic Systems, 36*(1), 2–10.

Atkinson, A. B., Piketty, T., & Saez, E. (2011). Top incomes in the long run of history. *Journal of Economic Literature, 49*(1), 3–71. https://doi.org/10.1257/jel.49.1.3

Autor, D. H., Levy, F., & Murnane, R. J. (2003). The skill content of recent technological change: An empirical exploration. *Quarterly Journal of Economics, 118*(4), 1279–1333.

Beck, U., & Grande, E. (2007). *Cosmopolitan Europe*. Polity.

Beckfield, J. (2006). European integration and income inequality. *American Sociological Review, 71*(6), 964–985. https://doi.org/10.1177/000312240607100605

Beckfield, J. (2013). The end of equality in Europe? *Current History, 112*(752), 94–99.

Beckfield, J. (2019). *Unequal Europe: Regional integration and the rise of European inequality*. Oxford University Press.

Bengtsson, M. (2014). Towards standby-ability: Swedish and Danish activation policies in flux. *International Journal of Social Welfare, 23*(1), S54–S70.

Blossfeld, H.-P., & Timm, A. (2003). *Who marries whom? Educational systems as marriage markets in modern societies. European studies of population: Vol. 12*. Kluwer Academic.

Blyth, M. (2013). *Austerity: The history of a dangerous idea*. Oxford University Press.

Bourdieu, P. (1984). *Distinction: A social critique of the judgement of taste*. Harvard University Press.

Bourdieu, P. (1988). *Homo academicus*. Stanford University Press.

Bourguignon, F. (2015). *The globalization of inequality*. Princeton University Press.

Broschinski, S. (2020). *Dynamiken von Lohnungleichheiten in Europa: Betriebliche und arbeitsmarktpolitische Anpassungen während der Eurokrise*. VS. Retrieved from https://www.springer.com/de/book/9783658318932

Calligaris, S., Del Gatto, M., Hassan, F., Ottaviano, G. I. P., & Schivardi, F. (2016). *Italy's productivity conundrum: A study on resource misallocation in Italy* (European Economy - Discussion Papers No. 030). Brussels.

Case, A., & Deaton, A. (2020). *Deaths of despair and the future of capitalism*. Princeton University Press.

Clark, A. E., Frijters, P., & Shields, M. A. (2008). Relative income, happiness, and utility: An explanation for the Easterlin paradox and other puzzles. *Journal of Economic Literature, 46*(1), 95–144.

Delhey, J., & Dragolov, G. (2014). Why inequality makes Europeans less happy: The role of distrust, status anxiety, and perceived conflict. *European Sociological Review, 30*(2), 151–165.

Delhey, J., & Kohler, U. (2006). From nationally bounded to Pan-European inequalities? On the importance of foreign countries as reference groups. *European Sociological Review, 22*(2), 125–140.

Diener, E. (2000). Subjective well-being: The science of happiness and a proposal for a national index. *American Psychologist, 55*(1), 34.

DiPrete, T. A. (2007). What has sociology to contribute to the study of inequality trends? A historical and comparative perspective. *American Behavioral Scientist, 50*(5), 603–618. https://doi.org/10.1177/0002764206295009

Easterlin, R. A. (1974). Does economic growth improve the human lot? Some empirical evidence. In P. A. David & M. W. Reder (Eds.), *Nations and households in economic growth: Essays in honor of Moses Abramovitz* (1st ed., pp. 89–125). Stanford University Press. https://doi.org/10.1016/B978-0-12-205050-3.50008-7

Ebbinghaus, B. (1998). Europe through the looking-glass: Comparative and multi-level perspectives. *Acta Sociologica, 41*(4), 301–313. https://doi.org/10.1177/000169939804100401

Emmenegger, P., Häusermann, S., Palier, B., & Seeleib-Kaiser, M. (2012). How we grow unequal. In P. Emmenegger, S. Häusermann, B. Palier, & M. Seeleib-Kaiser (Eds.), *International policy exchange series. The age of dualization: The changing face of inequality in deindustrializing societies* (pp. 3–26). Oxford University Press.

Esping-Andersen, G. (1990). *The three worlds of welfare capitalism*. Princeton University Press.

Esping-Andersen, G. (1999). *Social foundations of postindustrial economies*. Oxford University Press.

European Commission/DG EMPL. (2019). *Labour market and wage developments in Europe*. Publication Office of the EU. Retrieved from https://ec.europa.eu/social/main.jsp?langId=en&catId=89&furtherNews=yes&newsId=9485 https://doi.org/10.2767/399955

Evers, A., & Laville, J.-L. (Eds.). (2004). *Globalization and welfare. The third sector in Europe*. Edward Elgar.

Fahey, T. (2007). The case for an EU-wide measure of poverty. *European Sociological Review, 23*(1), 35–47.

Fairbrother, M. (2014). Two multilevel modeling techniques for analyzing comparative longitudinal survey datasets. *Political Science Research and Methods, 2*(1), 119–140. https://doi.org/10.1017/psrm.2013.24

Firpo, S., Fortin, N., & Lemieux, T. (2018). Decomposing wage distributions using recentered influence function regressions. *Econometrics, 6*(2), 28. https://doi.org/10.3390/econometrics6020028

Gerhards, J., Lengfeld, H., Ignácz, Z., Kley, F. K., & Pfriem, M. (2020). *European solidarity in times of crisis: Insights from a thirteen-country survey. Routledge advances in sociology*. New York.

Goedemé, T., & Rottiers, S. (2011). Poverty in the enlarged European Union. A discussion about definitions and reference groups. *Sociology Compass, 5*(1), 77–91.

Goos, M., & Manning, A. (2007). Lousy and lovely jobs: The rising polarization of work in Britain. *The Review of Economics and Statistics, 89*(1), 118–133.

Gygli, S., Haelg, F., Potrafke, N., & Sturm, J.-E. (2019). The KOF globalisation index – Revisited. *The Review of International Organizations, 18*(2), 266. https://doi.org/10.1007/s11558-019-09344-2

Hall, P. A. (2014). Varieties of capitalism and the euro crisis. *West European Politics, 37*(6), 1223–1243.

Heidenreich, M. (2003). Regional inequalities in the enlarged Europe. *Journal of European Social Policy, 13*(4), 313–333. https://doi.org/10.1177/09589287030134001

Heidenreich, M. (2010). Einkommensungleichheiten in Europa: Multiple Raumbezüge sozialer Ungleichheiten in einem regional-national-europäischen Mehrebenensystem. *Zeitschrift für Soziologie, 39*(6), 426–446. https://doi.org/10.1515/zfsoz-2010-0601

Heidenreich, M. (2016). The Europeanization of income inequality before and during the eurozone crisis: Inter-, supra- and transnational perspectives. In M. Heidenreich (Ed.), *Exploring inequality in Europe* (pp. 22–47). Edward Elgar.

Heidenreich, M. (Ed.). (2019). *Horizontal Europeanisation: The transnationalisation of daily life and social fields in Europe*. Routledge.

Heidenreich, M., & Härpfer, M. (2010). Einkommensungleichheiten in der Europäischen Union. Ihre inner- und zwischenstaatliche Dynamik und ihre subjektive Bewertung. In M. Eigmüller & S. Mau (Eds.), *Gesellschaftstheorie und Europapolitik: Sozialwissenschaftliche Ansätze zur Europaforschung* (pp. 245–273). VS. https://doi.org/10.1007/978-3-531-92008-5_12

Heidenreich, M., & Wunder, C. (2008). Patterns of regional inequality in the enlarged Europe. *European Sociological Review, 24*(1), 19–36.

Iversen, T., Soskice, D., & Hope, D. (2016). The Eurozone and political economic institutions. *Annual Review of Political Science, 19*, 163–185.

Kangas, O. E., & Ritakallio, V.-M. (2007). Relative to what? Cross-national picture of European poverty measured by regional, national and European standards. *European Societies, 9*(2), 119–145.

Karamessini, M., & Rubery, J. (2014). The challenge of austerity for equality. *Revue De L'OFCE, 133*(2), 15. https://doi.org/10.3917/reof.133.0015

Kenworthy, L. (2004). *Egalitarian capitalism: Jobs, incomes, and growth in affluent countries*. Russell Sage Foundation.

Kenworthy, L., & Pontusson, J. (2005). Rising inequality and the politics of redistribution in affluent countries. *Perspectives on Politics, 3*(03), 449–471.

Kley, S. (2021). How material deprivation impacted economic stress across European countries during the great recession. A lesson on social comparisons. *Acta Sociologica, 000169932110011*. https://doi.org/10.1177/00016993211001121

Kuhn, T. (2015). *Experiencing European integration: Transnational lives and European identity*. Oxford University Press.

Kuznets, S. (1955). Economic growth and income inequality. *American Economic Review, 45*(1), 1–28. Retrieved from https://www.jstor.org/stable/i304619

Lahusen, C., & Kiess, J. (2018). 'Subjective Europeanization': Do inner-European comparisons affect life satisfaction? *European Societies, 21*(2), 214–236. https://doi.org/10.1080/14616696.2018.1438638

Lakner, C., & Milanovic, B. (2013). *World panel income distribution (LM-WPID) database*. Retrieved from https://www.worldbank.org/en/research/brief/World-Panel-Income-Distribution

Markovits, D. (2019). *The meritocracy trap: How America's foundational myth feeds inequality, dismantles the middle class, and devours the elite*. Penguin Press.

Mau, S. (2015). *Inequality, marketization and the majority class: Why did the European middle classes accept neo-liberalism? Palgrave master series*. Palgrave Macmillan.

Mau, S., & Mewes, J. (2012). Horizontal Europeanisation in contextual perspective: What drives cross-border activities within the European Union? *European Societies, 14*(1), 7–34.

Milanovic, B. (2013). Global income inequality in numbers: In history and now. *Global Policy, 4*(2), 198–208.

Milanović, B. (2016). *Global inequality: A new approach for the age of globalization*. The Belknap Press of Harvard University Press.

Morel, N., Palier, B., & Palme, J. (Eds.). (2012). *Towards a social investment welfare state? Ideas, policies and challenges*. Policy Press.

Nielsen, F. [Francois], & Alderson, A. S. (1997). The Kuznets curve and the great U-turn: Income inequality in US counties, 1970 to 1990. *American Sociological Review, 62*(1), 12–33.

Nielsen, F. [François] (1994). Income inequality and industrial development: Dualism revisited. *American Sociological Review, 59*(5), 654–677.

Nollmann, G. (2006). Erhöht Globalisierung die Ungleichheit der Einkommen? *Kölner Zeitschrift Für Soziologie Und Sozialpsychologie, 58*(4), 638–659.

Norris, P., & Inglehart, R. (2019). *Cultural backlash: Trump, Brexit, and authoritarian populism*. Cambridge University Press.

OECD. (2011). *Divided we stand: Why inequality keeps rising*. OECD.

OECD. (2015). *In it together: Why less inequality benefits all*. OECD.

OECD. (2019). *Under pressure: The squeezed middle class*. OECD. https://doi.org/10.1787/689afed1-en

Pavolini, E., León, M., Guillén, A. M., & Ascoli, U. (2016). From austerity to permanent strain? The European Union and welfare state reform in Italy and Spain. In C. de La Porte & E. Heins (Eds.), *The sovereign debt crisis, the EU and welfare state reform* (pp. 131–157). Palgrave Macmillan. https://doi.org/10.1057/978-1-137-58179-2_6

Peichl, A., Pestel, N., & Schneider, H. (2011). Mehr Ungleichheit durch kleinere Haushalte? Der Zusammenhang zwischen Veränderungen der Haushaltsstruktur und der Einkommensverteilung in Deutschland. *Zeitschrift für ArbeitsmarktForschung, 43*(4), 327–338. https://doi.org/10.1007/s12651-011-0068-4

Pfau-Effinger, B. (2004). Socio-historical paths of the male breadwinner model: An explanation of cross-national differences. *British Journal of Sociology, 55*(3), 377–399.

Piketty, T. (2014). *Capital in the twenty-first century*. Harvard University Press.

Renan, E. (1996). What is a nation? In G. Eley & R. G. Suny (Eds.), *Becoming national: A reader* (pp. 41–55). Oxford University Press.

Rodrik, D. (1997). Has globalization gone too far? *California Management Review, 39*(3), 29–53.

Rodrik, D. (2018). Populism and the economics of globalization. *Journal of International Business Policy, 1*(1–2), 12–33. https://doi.org/10.1057/s42214-018-0001-4

Rueda, D. (2014). Dualization, crisis and the welfare state. *Socio-Economic Review, 12*(2), 381–407.

Sacks, D. W., Stevenson, B., & Wolfers, J. (2010). *Subjective well-being, income, economic development and growth* (Working Paper No. 16441). National Bureau of Economic Research. https://doi.org/10.3386/w16441

Sandel, M. J. (2020). *The tyranny of merit: What's become of the common good?* Farrar Strauss & Giroux.

Simmel, G. (1965). The poor (translated by Claire Jacobson). *Social Problems, 13*(2), 118–140.

Teney, C. (2016). Does the EU economic crisis undermine subjective Europeanization? Assessing the dynamics of citizens' EU framing between 2004 and 2013. *European Sociological Review, 32*(5), 619–633. https://doi.org/10.1093/esr/jcw008

Thelen, K. (2012). Varieties of capitalism: Trajectories of liberalization and the new politics of social solidarity. *Annual Review of Political Science, 15*, 137–159.

Therborn, G. (1995). *European modernity and beyond: The trajectory of European societies, 1945–2000*. Sage.

Townsend, P. (1979). *Poverty in the United Kingdom: A survey of household resources and standards of living*. Campus: Vol. 242. University of Chicago Press.

Veenhoven, R. (1991). Is happiness relative? *Social Indicators Research, 24*(1), 1–34.

Visser, J. (2019). *ICTWSS data base. version 6.1*. Amsterdam. Retrieved from Amsterdam Institute for Advanced Labour Studies AIAS website: http://uva-aias.net/en/ictwss

Watson, D., Maitre, B., Grotti, R., & Whelan, C. T. (2018). *Poverty dynamics of social risk groups in the EU: An analysis of the EU Statistics on Income and Living Conditions, 2005 to 2014. Social inclusion report:* no. 7. Department of Employment Affairs and Social Protection. Retrieved from http://www.esri.ie

Whelan, C. T., & Maître, B. (2009). Europeanization of inequality and European reference groups. *Journal of European Social Policy, 19*(2), 117–130.

Wilkinson, R. G., & Pickett, K. (2010). *The spirit level: Why equality is better for everyone. Pinguin sociology*. Penguin.

Young, M. D. (1994). *The rise of the meritocracy: With a new introduction by the author*. Transaction Publishers.

# Chapter 8
# Cumulative Risks of Poverty and Exclusion

**Abstract**  This chapter focuses on the losers of the previously analysed economic, employment, wage, and income inequality patterns. Two multidimensional indicators for the poverty and deprivation risks of the population and the employment and wage risks of the labour force are proposed for the analysis of the territorial and social dualisation of Europe. While multiple poverty and deprivation risks are more pronounced in Central and Eastern Europe, employment risks are very high in Southern Europe. The Northern and Western European countries are privileged in all respects. Both indicators demonstrate the precarious situation of low-skilled workers with simple tasks (especially manual workers) compared to academics, the upper service class and problem-solving jobs. The inequalities are particularly high between different social classes, employment groups and educational levels. Europe is thus characterised by the territorial and social concentration of multiple and persistent forms of inequalities. Winners and losers can be clearly distinguished. The chapter shows that, in spite of the relatively low levels of income inequality, the idea of a cohesive, egalitarian Europe is a myth.

In the discussion on poverty and exclusion, it is often pointed out that monetary poverty in Germany and in Europe has fluctuated for years between 15% and 17%—measured as the share of households whose disposable income is less than 60% of the median income. Neither is there a clear, lasting increase nor is this value alarmingly high, for example in comparison with the USA or China. While "deaths by despair" are discussed in the USA (Case & Deaton, 2015, 2020), Europe is characterised by relatively egalitarian income structures. However, such a diagnosis fails to recognise the accumulation of social disadvantages and their concentration among specific population groups, the spatial concentration of disadvantages and the entrenchment of disadvantageous living and employment situations within and across European nation-states. Europe and its population are divided in many ways (Lahusen, 2021). The term dual or double dualisation (Heidenreich, 2016; Palier et al., 2018) refers to the territorial and social division of Europe, i.e. the division into centre and periphery and into winners and losers. On the loser side, these fractures are accompanied by the accumulation, concentration and consolidation of poverty and exclusion. This chapter will identify which groups and countries in Europe belong to these losers and how they are particularly affected by the concentration of disadvantageous life situations.

In the following sections, the multidimensionality of poverty and thus the limits of a purely monetary poverty concept are discussed (Sect. 8.1). Income poverty in Europe is then analysed as an essential, but by no means comprehensive indicator of social disadvantage (Sect. 8.2). Given its limits, two multidimensional indicators for social and work-related deprivation are proposed (Sects. 8.3 and 8.4). These multiple deprivations are considered for the period 2007–2018 for 30 European countries (EU-28, Switzerland and Norway) in order to be able to describe the territorial and social divisions in Europe. Subsequently, the influences of these poverty, deprivation and employment risks on the life satisfaction and the role of national institutions are examined (Sect. 8.5). In conclusion, the chapter discusses the limits of a meritocratic legitimisation of poverty and exclusion (Sect. 8.6).

## 8.1  Poverty: A Multidimensional Phenomenon

People suffer from various forms of deprivation, exclusion and disadvantage. They may suffer from bad health conditions; they may be angry with their neighbours, children, partners, parents or colleagues; they may be lonely; they may be afraid of crime, terrorism, unemployment and loss of status; or they may be poor, deprived, have little education, few opportunities for political participation, or have bad, too small or too expensive accommodation in problematic residential environments. Many such problems have little to do with a person's income or social position. This is impressively illustrated by the French sociologist Bourdieu, Accardo, and Ferguson (1999), who with 19 co-authors published 60 interviews conducted with people from all levels of society in France. These interviews dealt with the most diverse forms of suffering across the whole spectrum of society. A consistent theme of the interviews is the diversity of reported suffering. However, according to Bourdieu, a common cause for many of the reported experiences of suffering is the state's withdrawal from responsibility for the common good (education, urban development and housing, regulation of the economy, social work, dealing with crime, integration of migrants):

> Producing awareness of these mechanisms that make life painful, even unlivable, does not neutralize them; bringing contradictions to light does not resolve them. But, as skeptical as one may be about the social efficacy of the sociological message, one has to acknowledge the effect it can have in allowing those who suffer to find out that their suffering can be imputed to social causes and thus to feel exonerated; and in making generally known the social origin, collectively hidden, of unhappiness in all its forms, including the most intimate, the most secret. (Bourdieu et al., 1999, p. 629)

This diversity of suffering, of disappointed hopes, of failed life plans and efforts has been described by writers and philosophers far more thoroughly, earlier and more comprehensively than by social scientists—for example by Leo Tolstoy in the first sentence of the novel *Anna Karenina*: "Happy families are all alike; every unhappy family is unhappy in its own way." Social problems therefore cannot be reduced to income poverty. In addition to (absolute or relative) income poverty, social sciences have proposed other concepts to capture suffering, disadvantage and exclusion—such as the multidimensional concept of living situations (Voges, 2006), the concept of inclusion proposed by the European Commission or the capability concept (Sen, 1993), which also inspired the creation of the Human Development Index (UNDP, 2019).

A suitable sociological starting point for recording disadvantage and social exclusion is Simmel's concept of poverty, which deliberately does not define poverty in terms of the lack of resources or financial means, but by the acceptance of support. Simmel used the example of impoverished upper-class persons to argue that poverty is socially constructed through the acceptance of assistance:

> The acceptance of assistance thus excludes the assisted person from the premises of his status and provides visible proof that the poor person is formally déclassé. Until this happens, class prejudice is strong enough to make poverty, so to say, invisible; and until then poverty is individual suffering, without social consequences. All the assumptions on which the life of the upper classes is based determine that a person may be poor in an individual sense, that is, that his resources may be insufficient for the needs of his class, without his having to recur to assistance. For this reason, no one is socially poor until he has been assisted. (Simmel, 1965, p. 138).

Coser (1965, p. 145) emphasises the accompanying disenfranchisement of the poor and the restriction of their decision-making possibilities, thus concretising the declassification of the poor emphasised by Simmel:

> When monies are allocated to them, they do not have free disposition over their use. They must account to the donors for their expenses and the donors decide whether the money is spent 'wisely' or 'foolishly'. That is, the poor are treated in this respect much like children who have to account to parents for the wise use of their pocket money; the poor are infantilized through such procedures.

This understanding of poverty as social declassification points to the social construction of poverty by the state in the nineteenth century. While poverty had been a self-evident and unquestioned aspect of human existence for centuries, English poverty policy was concerned with drawing a symbolic line between morally questionable paupers and the respectable, albeit poor, workers. Himmelfarb (1984) in particular emphasises the moral distinction between the working poor and the unemployed lower classes, which Marx called the *Lumpenproletariat*. Early poverty policies aimed to make the former group "responsible moral agents", to remove them from the pernicious influences of the latter group and also to distinguish them semantically from the poor by terming them working class. The second group, on the other hand, which according to Himmelfarb (1984) included the sick and infirm, the orphans, the decrepit elderly, but also the drunkards, petty criminals and outcasts, stood outside the moral order of early industrial society (Himmelfarb, 1984, p. 26).

The morally charged stigmatisation and exclusion of the poor also shaped the institutional separation between employment and social policies in Germany. In contrast to the working or temporarily unemployed population, "[t]he 'needy' poor population, on the other hand, (…) do not engage in gainful employment: they cannot work, are 'incapacitated for work', or do not want to work, are 'work-shy'" (Leibfried & Tennstedt, 1985, 73; own translation). Such a stigmatisation of some fractions of the poor was only conceptually overcome by the recognition of social rights in the emerging welfare state (Marshall, 1950, p. 47). Due to this recognition, poverty is no longer considered to be a result of individual failure or misbehaviour, but a result of market failure that can be politically corrected. In this case, support for the poor is no longer assistance in the Simmelian sense, which leads to the exclusion and declassification of those in need of help, but an expression of (in principle reciprocal) solidarity between members of society. "Deserving poor", hit by risks to be borne through no fault of their own, and "undeserving poor", characterised by a self-inflicted need for assistance, are thus two opposed normative reference points which frame the debates on poverty and social exclusion.

The distinction between deserving and undeserving poor, which had already characterised social and labour politics at the local level in the nineteenth century (Whiteside, 2007), could be abandoned within the framework of a universalist welfare state. In an ideal case, social assistance becomes an individual, legally enforceable right of every citizen (Serrano Pascual, 2007). However, the realities in European welfare states are still different. The classical distinction between the poor and workers, between social and labour policy still characterises the architecture of the corporatist welfare states of Continental Europe (Esping-Andersen, 1990). The institutional separation between minimum income protection systems, which aim at meeting basic needs, and status-maintaining insurance systems, still reflects the classic distinction between anti-poverty and workers' policy. In the residual welfare states of Southern Europe, the split between poverty and workers' policy, between meeting needs and securing status, is even more pronounced: outside of national unemployment, health insurance and pension systems, minimum income protection hardly exist at the national level. The family and the church are still essential safety nets for those in need (Bahle et al., 2011; Ferrera, 1996). The division between deserving and undeserving poor thus still characterises the structures of many welfare states.

This points to the fact that every understanding of poverty, deprivation or social exclusion has a normative bias. There is no objective, neutral concept for measuring and describing poverty, deprivation and exclusion (Chap. 3). Whether a poverty threshold is set at a dollar a day or at 60% of the national or European median income or if it aims at the encompassing, unconditional satisfaction of human needs—it always reflects assumptions about the causes of precarious living situations and statements about the adequacy of the respective support. This is not an argument against the use of the respective indicators, but a reminder of the necessity of discussing the respective normative and societal implications. These different normative implications also explain the diversity of concepts and indicators. These indicators not only reflect the controversial nature of the corresponding concepts, but also the multidimensionality of poverty and exclusion. This will be elaborated in the following on the basis of selected theoretical approaches (Weziak-Bialowolska, 2016).

Usually, poverty in Europe is measured by the share of households with an equalised disposable household income (after social transfers) below 60% of the equivalised national median income. "Equalised" simply means that the size of the households is taken into consideration. The 60% threshold is an example of a relative poverty concept—in contrast to an absolute concept such as the one dollar a day proposed in the 1980s by the World Bank, according to which people live in extreme poverty if they live in households with an income of (price-adjusted) 1.90 US dollars a day. A relative concept of poverty is less a measure of the insufficient availability of financial resources than a measure of inequality (Darvas, 2019). Poverty in a country remains the same even if each household increases its available resources tenfold. The usual poverty concept focuses on the available financial resources and not on the goods and services that can be procured with them to achieve social participation and an adequate standard of living. The normative basis of the concept are the assumptions on the one hand that poverty and exclusion always have to be determined relatively to the situation of other members of society, and that on the other hand it can be reduced through the provision of financial resources. The disadvantages of such a concept of monetary poverty will be discussed in the next section (Sect. 8.2).

The deprivation concept, on the other hand, does not focus on the available resources, but on the actual supply of material and immaterial goods considered essential. It was proposed by the British social scientist Townsend (1979), further developed by Whelan and Maître (2013) and operationalised by the European Commission. According to Townsend (1979, p. 31),

> Individuals, families and groups in the population can be said to be in poverty when they lack the resources to obtain the types of diet, participate in the activities, and have the living conditions and amenities which are customary, or at least widely encouraged or approved, in the societies to which they belong. Their resources are so seriously below those commanded by the average individual or family that they are, in effect, excluded from ordinary patterns, customs and activities.

The normative basis of this concept is thus the comprehensive, unrestricted participation in the "ordinary patterns, customs and activities" of a society. Given this background, the European Commission has operationalised material deprivation as the inability to pay for at least three of the following nine expenses:

> unexpected expenses, afford a one-week annual holiday away from home, a meal involving meat, chicken or fish every second day, the adequate heating of a dwelling, durable goods like a washing machine, colour television, telephone or car, being confronted with payment arrears (mortgage or rent, utility bills, hire purchase instalments or other loan payments). (https://ec.europa.eu/eurostat/statistics-explained/index.php?title=Glossary:Material_depri vation; retrieved on 5/11/2021)

This operationalisation is more specific than Townsend's proposal (1979), as it focuses on an inability to afford these items. Its normative basis is the idea of a *European-wide minimum standard* in the affordability of these goods and services considered to be necessary to lead an adequate life.

Townsend (1979) is concerned with the opportunities for participation in social life and thus with avoiding social exclusion. The concepts of social inclusion and exclusion go beyond the idea of avoiding an inadequate standard of living. This is shown by the following definition, produced by the European Council, which also refers to participation in social networks, the development of one's own abilities and competences, the importance of political and social participation and the subjective perception of one's own life situation as dimensions of an inclusive society:

> Social exclusion is a process whereby certain individuals are pushed to the edge of society and prevented from participating fully by virtue of their poverty, or lack of basic competencies and lifelong learning opportunities, or as a result of discrimination. This distances them from job, income and education opportunities as well as social and community networks and activities. They have little access to power and decision-making bodies and thus often feeling powerless and unable to take control over the decisions that affect their day to day lives. (Council of the European Union, 2004, p. 8)

This concept differs radically from Simmel's concept of poverty, since it tries to avoid the declassification and social exclusion diagnosed by Simmel as a by-product of social assistance. This also applies to the concept of living situations, which focuses on all aspects important for people's welfare. Voges et al. (2003, p. 44) emphasise the importance of health, housing, education, mobility, participation in the cultural and political sphere, integration in social groups. In addition to the actual provision of these goods and services, the living conditions approach also takes into account people's actual scope for action and their ability to realise opportunities, thus taking up the central concern of the capability approach (Sen, 1993). Therborn (2013) proposes a similarly comprehensive concept of inequality. He distinguishes between *vital inequality* (which is documented in different health statuses and different life expectancies), *existential inequality* (through discrimination and the exclusion of women, for example) and *material or resource inequality,* which includes both inequality of opportunity and inequality of outcome.

These very broad understandings of poverty, social inclusion, living conditions, capabilities and opportunities try to avoid the declassification and exclusion characteristic of social assistance according to Simmel and Coser and to enable comprehensive social participation. The normative basis of multidimensional poverty concepts is thus the idea of avoiding social exclusion in as many areas of society as possible. Empirically, however, it is difficult to measure multidimensional disadvantages.

A first objective of this chapter is therefore to describe the distribution of income poverty in Europe (Sect. 8.2). Secondly, two different concepts for the multidimensional measurement of poverty and exclusion are proposed (Sect. 8.3) and used for the analysis of the social and territorial fractures of the European population (Sect. 8.4). Thirdly, the influence of multiple disadvantages on the subjective well-being of Europeans is analysed (Sect. 8.5). The chapter concludes with a short summary (Sect. 8.6).

## 8.2   Income Poverty: A Central Dimension of Social Exclusion

Basically, two notions of equality can be distinguished: Equality of outcome and equality of opportunity. Equality of outcome refers to the equal distribution of resources or benefits, equality of opportunity refers to the opportunities to acquire these resources. Income poverty is an example that the principle of equality of outcome is violated. The territorial and social distribution of income poverty and the respective winners and losers will be shown.

Usually, poverty in Europe is defined as relative poverty, even if absolute poverty also exists in Europe (Gaisbauer et al., 2019). As previously mentioned, the most common poverty concept is the 60% threshold: Households with an equalised disposable income of less than 60% of the national median income are considered to be at risk of poverty. Thus, income poverty refers only to a specific part of the income curve. Scientists and statistical offices have chosen the 60% cut-off point to operationalise the construct "poverty risk" in a way that is easy to measure and compare. The disadvantages of such an operationalisation are obvious. As discussed in detail in Sect. 7.5, happiness research has shown that absolute rather than relative income levels play a central role in life satisfaction (Clark et al., 2008). A monetary poverty concept also ignores all non-material disadvantages and exclusion processes. In a review of subjectively perceived social problems (health, material deprivation, unemployment, sleeplessness, loneliness, anxiety …) Halleröd and Larsson (2008, p. 23) found that these problems were hardly correlated with income poverty. Voges (2006, 2; own translation) points to two further problems of the resource approach: On the one hand, it "presupposes the rational actor who uses his resources economically, as otherwise considerable scarcity can arise. Secondly, it implicitly assumes that with sufficient financial means (. . .) all essential goods for basic needs can be acquired." Furthermore, a points-based indicator such as a poverty threshold of 60% does not meet any of the criteria that corresponding measures should have (Goebel & Krause, p. 62; UNDP, 2019, p. 136): first, the *focus criterion* is violated. This criterion states that a changed situation of the non-poor should not change the statistically recorded situation of the poor. However, if the median income increases due to an improvement in the income situation in the upper income range, the poverty rate declines, even if the situation of the poor remains unchanged. The *monotonicity criterion* is also violated. This states that the poverty rate should change if the financial situation of the poor improves or worsens significantly. However, a doubling of the standard of living in a country by no means leads to a lower poverty rate. Nor does a general lowering of living standards (as in Greece during the euro crisis) go hand in hand with a higher poverty rate. The compression of the income curve at the lower end can even cause it to fall. Furthermore, the *Pigou Dalton or transfer criterion* (UNDP, 2019, p. 136) is also violated. This criterion states that income transfers from richer to poorer households increase social welfare and that this must be reflected in the corresponding indices. However, income transfers from richer to poorer households do not lead to a reduction in measured poverty as long as the latter still remain below the poverty threshold. In conceptual terms, the 60% threshold is thus not convincing as an indicator of poverty. Despite these limitations, the structure, development and group-specific levels of poverty will be described in the following, as the poverty rate is the best-known and commonly used indicator of poverty, deprivation and exclusion. Below-average household income has become a relevant reference point for national social policies and a socially accepted operationalisation of poverty. The simplicity of the monetary poverty index is the major reason why more comprehensive poverty and exclusion concepts inspired by Simmel (1965) and Bourdieu et al. (1999) could not become established in the public and academic debate.

Countries with an egalitarian income structure (Scandinavia, the Netherlands, but also the Czech Republic, Slovakia or Slovenia) tend to have lower poverty rates, while both inequality and poverty are very high in Eastern and Southern European countries. This correlation is not surprising, as the poverty rate is determined by the lower part of the income curve, while the Gini coefficient depends on the shape of the same curve (Darvas, 2019). This also means that the factors for explaining national inequalities discussed in Sect. 7.4 also largely explain the level of national poverty rates. With the exception of Malta, the Eastern and Southern European countries have a Gini coefficient of 0.32 and above and a poverty rate of 19% and above. In the middle ground between these two groups are most Continental European countries and the British Isles, but also Hungary, Poland and Malta (Table 8.3). Accordingly, poverty rates in Southern Europe are far above and in Scandinavia far below the EU average (in 2013 at around 20% and 13% respectively; see Table 8.3, last row). The central importance of national policies is also reflected in the fact that the correlation between national poverty rates and the level of disposable income is rather low, even if poverty rates tend to be lower in richer countries than in poorer ones. But even at a comparable income level, the poverty rate varies between 9% (Czech Republic) and 23% (Greece). This highlights the crucial role of national social, labour market and wage policies.

It has been shown in Sect. 7.5 that people's subjective assessment of their own economic situation also reflects the European context. Thus, in line with Delhey and Kohler (2006), Fahey (2007) and Lahusen and Kiess (2018) it can be assumed that a European poverty threshold in addition to a national poverty rate is also relevant for perceived deprivation and social exclusion. But what are the effects of a European poverty threshold? This European poverty threshold corresponded to a value of about 9000 purchasing power standards (PPS) in 2013, i.e. 60% of the median income of 15,200 PPS. Measured against this threshold, the European poverty rate in the wealthier, mostly Northern and Western European EU countries is, by construction, lower than the national poverty rates, while it is higher than the national rates in the 15 Southern and Central European countries whose incomes are lower than the EU average (Table 8.3). This also means that national poverty rates measured against a European threshold are strongly correlated with the level of median national income. Measured against a European-wide poverty threshold, 92% of Romanians and 79% of Bulgarians and hardly any Luxembourgers are poor in a European context (see Table 8.3, column 3). However, poverty is not limited to Central and

Eastern Europe: Half of Greeks were poor in 2013—about as many as in Poland and more than twice as many as before the start of the euro crisis (2008: 26%). The weighted average of the national poverty rates, 16.7%, is significantly lower than the Europe-wide poverty rate of 23.1% (Table 7.1). This difference between the two poverty rates points to the still high between-country income disparities in Europe following the last EU enlargements. Besides Malta and Cyprus, 11 poorer Central and Eastern European countries joined the EU from 2004 to 2013.

In terms of the *group-specific impacts, the poverty risks* of younger people, migrants (especially from third countries), the low-skilled and unemployed, the employed with simple tasks, blue-collar workers and smaller self-employed, singles and single parents are far above the European average in 2013 (Table 8.1). These are the groups which are often disadvantaged in technological and economic transformations. When other years are also included and the socio-demographic characteristics of the interviewees are controlled for (Fig. 8.1), these patterns remain stable: The poverty risks of young people are more than three times as high as people in the core age group between 25 and 54 years. The poverty risk of single parents is four times as high as the risk of adults with children (precisely: 4.15 times as high between 2014 and 2018). The poverty risk of people with a European migration background is 50% higher than that of natives—and people with a non-European background have a 79% higher risk. And people living in households with a low work intensity or who are unemployed have a poverty risk which is eight or three times higher, respectively, than the risk of people in a household with a higher work intensity or without unemployed household members.

However, these patterns vary from country to country and from regime to regime (Table 8.1). This allows conclusions to be drawn about *regime- and country-specific social, family and employment policies.* For example, the high poverty rates of *young persons* both in the Scandinavian and Mediterranean countries point to completely different social constellations: While young people in the Scandinavian countries leave their parental homes at an early age in order to live independently, work or complete their education and are supported by a universal welfare state, such broad support does not exist in Southern Europe. Youth unemployment is also extraordinarily high. As a result, many young people often continue to live in their parental home, but without benefiting from the advantages of a dynamic labour market and the comprehensive social protection of their Scandinavian peers. In Southern and Northern Europe, poverty rates for *third-country migrants* are also comparatively high—an indication that inclusion of this group is rather difficult either because of the tight labour market situation in Southern Europe or because of the high language and skill requirements in Scandinavia. Compared to other families with children, the *poverty risk of single parents* in Continental Europe is comparatively high (2013: 31%). Due to the focus of corporatist welfare states on the insurance of employment-related risks, non-working parents are mainly protected by minimum income schemes. In Eastern Europe, the huge differences between the *poverty rates of employed and unemployed people* are striking—an indication of rather low social protection for the unemployed. The high poverty rates of the *unskilled* in many Central and Eastern European countries (37% on average) can be explained by the

**Table 8.1** Regime and group-specific poverty rates (in %; 18–64 years; EU-28, Switzerland, Norway; 2013)

| | British Islands | Continental Europe | Southern Europe | Eastern Europe | Scandinavia | Total |
|---|---|---|---|---|---|---|
| Men | 14.4 | 13.7 | 19.1 | 16.7 | 13.4 | 15.8 |
| Women | 14.8 | 15.2 | 20.1 | 16.3 | 12.6 | 16.5 |
| 15–24 years | 22.3 | 19.7 | 26.5 | 21.3 | 31.9 | 22.5 |
| 25–55 years | 12.8 | 13.1 | 19.5 | 16.2 | 10.6 | 15.3 |
| 55–64 years | 15.0 | 15.3 | 16.2 | 14.2 | 7.4 | 14.8 |
| Without migration background | 13.1 | 13.3 | 17.1 | 16.3 | 11.0 | 14.8 |
| European migration | 14.0 | 14.3 | 31.9 | 13.4 | 16.4 | 19.7 |
| Non-European migration | 22.4 | 26.0 | 35.1 | 22.4 | 30.9 | 28.3 |
| Low education | 23.7 | 25.0 | 28.1 | 37.3 | 18.6 | 28.0 |
| Medium education | 15.8 | 15.0 | 17.2 | 15.0 | 13.4 | 15.5 |
| High education | 8.4 | 8.4 | 7.9 | 4.1 | 8.4 | 7.6 |
| Employed | 7.6 | 8.4 | 11.9 | 11.1 | 6.1 | 9.5 |
| Unemployed | 46.1 | 46.0 | 39.7 | 41.0 | 35.5 | 42.0 |
| Routine task | 23.5 | 26.0 | 33.3 | 31.2 | 20.7 | 28.9 |
| Operating machinery; repair | 15.3 | 16.8 | 18.7 | 17.0 | 13.2 | 17.0 |
| Complex tasks | 8.6 | 7.8 | 8.7 | 5.2 | 7.1 | 7.7 |
| Problem-solving | 5.4 | 6.0 | 5.7 | 3.2 | 5.5 | 5.3 |
| Upper service class | 5.3 | 6.3 | 5.8 | 4.0 | 5.4 | 5.7 |
| Intermediate employees | 10.0 | 11.5 | 10.0 | 7.5 | 9.3 | 10.3 |
| Self-employed (SMEs) | 19.4 | 18.4 | 24.4 | 31.1 | 22.4 | 24.7 |
| Simple services | 16.8 | 20.0 | 18.3 | 13.1 | 15.7 | 17.4 |
| Lower technical & routine tasks | 19.5 | 22.7 | 6.5 | 20.1 | 13.3 | 22.3 |
| Single-person households | 25.5 | 28.4 | 23.2 | 23.2 | 29.3 | 26.6 |
| Adults without children | 9.3 | 9.4 | 14.1 | 11.7 | 7.0 | 11.0 |
| Single parents | 29.1 | 30.8 | 31.5 | 27.7 | 23.8 | 29.8 |
| Adults with children | 15.9 | 10.9 | 23.0 | 18.9 | 7.5 | 16.6 |
| Total | 14.6 | 14.4 | 19.6 | 16.5 | 13.0 | 16.1 |

Source: Own calculations based on EU-SILC UDB 2013

low wages and the large low-wage sector in these countries (Sect. 6.5). The differences between simple and problem-solving jobs in Southern and Eastern Europe are very high: while the poverty risk of problem-solving jobs is equally low in all European regions (about 5%), *almost one third of people with simple jobs are affected by poverty in Eastern and Southern Europe*—significantly more than in

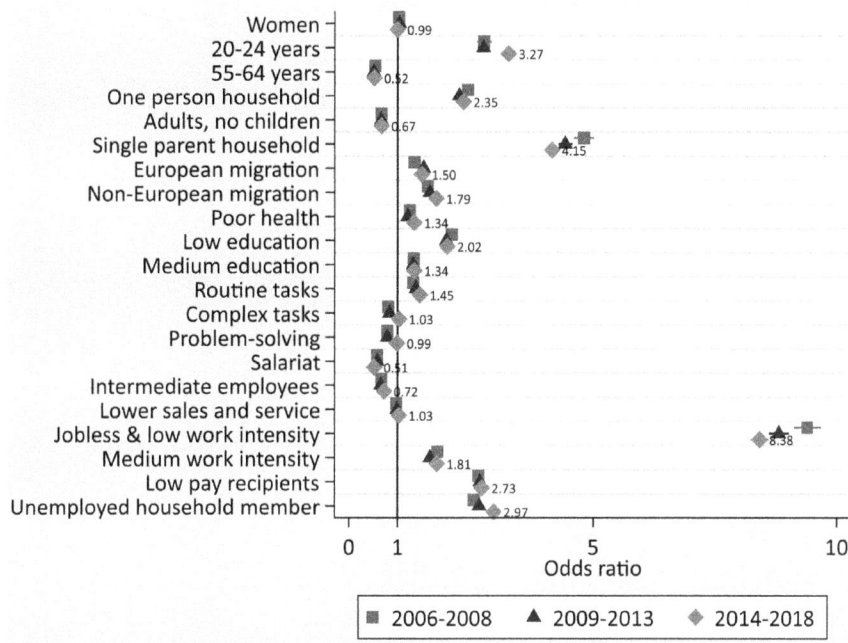

Source: Own calculations on the basis of EU-SILC 2007-2019. Binary logistic multilevel regression with the probability of being poor as dependent variable. The group-specific poverty risks are given in comparison to the reference group, i.e. native, highly educated men aged 25-54, manual workers (machine operators, repair) with a sufficient wage level and living in a household with a medium or high work intensity and without an unemployed person in the household.

**Fig. 8.1** Group-specific poverty rates (18–64 years; EU-28, Switzerland, Norway; 2006–2018)

the rest of the EU, where "only" one quarter of this group is affected by poverty. The exclusion of unskilled people with simple jobs is thus particularly high in the European periphery, even if it could have been expected that the peripheral industrialisation model of the Eastern countries (Sect. 4.3) might also have created jobs for lower-skilled workers.

A final point concerns the persistence of poverty. Many negative consequences of poverty emerge only when a person is poor for a longer time. In particular, a lack of prospects, doubts about one's own ability and one's own worth, up to a loss of a sense of time and the destruction of social ties have been documented many times since the famous study on the long-term unemployed of Marienthal (Jahoda et al., 1933/2002). In economics, the de-skilling, devaluation and demotivation effects related to long-term unemployment are used to explain the inertia, the "hysteresis" of unemployment even in boom phases (Blanchard, 2006). Since long-term unemployment is a central cause of poverty, these results also apply to persistent poverty.

On the basis of the EU-SILC longitudinal data set, Eurostat calculates the persistent poverty risks of Europeans (Table 8.2). About one tenth of Europeans are persistently poor. A comparison with national poverty rates (Table 8.3) suggests

**Table 8.2** Risk of persistent poverty in the EU-28, Norway and Switzerland (% of population; 2007–2018)

| | 2007 | 2008 | 2009 | 2010 | 2011 | 2012 | 2013 | 2014 | 2015 | 2016 | 2017 | 2018 |
|---|---|---|---|---|---|---|---|---|---|---|---|---|
| Belgium | 7.8 | 9.0 | 9.2 | 9.3 | 8.0 | 9.9 | 8.7 | 9.5 | 9.8 | 9.8 | 11.0 | 10.2 |
| Bulgaria | | | 10.7 | 16.4 | 16.9 | 12.9 | 13.4 | 16.5 | 16.2 | 15.3 | 15.9 | 15.9 |
| Czechia | | 3.9 | 3.7 | 5.5 | 4.2 | 4.3 | 4.1 | 3.4 | 4.5 | 4.3 | 4.4 | 6.3 |
| Denmark | 4.7 | 4.9 | 2.7 | 6.3 | 6.4 | 5.7 | 5.1 | 5.3 | 4.3 | 7.2 | 5.5 | 4.7 |
| Germany | | 7.2 | 8.1 | 9.1 | 10.4 | 10.4 | 10.6 | 9.5 | 11.3 | 10.5 | 11.6 | 10.5 |
| Estonia | 11.1 | 13.6 | 12.9 | 9.9 | 10.5 | 12.0 | 9.3 | 11.2 | 13.1 | 13.5 | 16.1 | 15.6 |
| Ireland | 11.6 | | | | 8.8 | 13.2 | 9.1 | 11.6 | 10.8 | 10.8 | 9.3 | 10.5 |
| Greece | 13.1 | 13.0 | 16.1 | 17.6 | 10.5 | 13.8 | 12.4 | 14.5 | 13.3 | 15.2 | 14.0 | 12.5 |
| Spain | 10.2 | 11.0 | 12.5 | 11.6 | 12.7 | 13.3 | 12.1 | 14.3 | 15.8 | 14.8 | 14.7 | 14.0 |
| France | 6.4 | | | | | 7.0 | 8.3 | 7.9 | 8.5 | 8.0 | 7.9 | 7.8 |
| Croatia | | | | | | | 13.2 | | 14.7 | 14.5 | 15.2 | 14.8 |
| Italy | 14.6 | 12.7 | 13.0 | 11.6 | 11.8 | 13.1 | 13.2 | 12.9 | 14.3 | 14.5 | 13.9 | 15.3 |
| Cyprus | | 9.9 | 10.1 | 9.2 | 8.6 | 8.3 | 10.0 | 7.3 | 7.3 | 7.6 | 6.6 | 7.1 |
| Latvia | | 12.6 | 15.6 | 10.5 | 9.3 | 12.6 | 12.1 | 10.8 | 10.1 | 15.2 | 14.9 | 15.5 |
| Lithuania | | 10.9 | 11.4 | 7.4 | 7.7 | 12.3 | 10.2 | 16.0 | 14.3 | 13.5 | 16.1 | 15.6 |
| Luxembourg | 8.9 | 8.4 | 8.8 | 6.0 | 6.5 | 7.1 | 9.2 | 8.7 | 12.0 | 9.5 | 8.6 | 7.6 |
| Hungary | | 7.7 | 8.6 | 5.7 | 8.3 | 7.6 | 7.3 | 8.6 | 7.2 | 7.9 | 5.8 | 5.7 |
| Malta | | 7.7 | 7.7 | 9.1 | 11.4 | 9.7 | 8.4 | 10.7 | 12.7 | 10.7 | 10.8 | 10.9 |
| Netherlands | 5.1 | 6.4 | 4.7 | 8.2 | 7.7 | 5.8 | 6.5 | 7.7 | 7.3 | 7.2 | 5.6 | 8.0 |
| Austria | | 5.6 | 6.2 | 6.5 | 9.8 | 8.7 | 8.9 | 8.5 | 8.8 | 8.1 | 9.1 | 10.2 |
| Poland | | 10.4 | 10.2 | 10.5 | 10.1 | 10.7 | 9.0 | 10.7 | 10.1 | 9.7 | 9.1 | 10.5 |
| Portugal | 14.1 | 13.1 | 9.8 | 13.2 | 13.6 | 11.4 | 11.7 | 12.0 | 13.6 | 11.5 | 14.2 | 12.0 |
| Romania | | | | 18.0 | 17.5 | 18.7 | 17.1 | 19.5 | 19.3 | 20.2 | 19.1 | 19.9 |
| Slovenia | | 7.7 | 7.0 | 6.9 | 7.5 | 6.1 | 7.5 | 9.5 | 8.1 | 8.5 | 8.2 | |
| Slovakia | | 4.5 | 5.4 | 6.0 | 7.8 | 8.6 | 7.1 | 9.8 | 7.4 | 7.7 | | 7.7 |
| Finland | 7.6 | 6.8 | 6.5 | 7.7 | 7.5 | 7.4 | 7.0 | 7.0 | 8.3 | 6.0 | 6.0 | 5.2 |

| Sweden | 2.1 | 2.6 | 3.7 | 4.9 | 4.1 | 7.2 | 7.6 | 6.6 | 7.0 | 6.1 | 7.1 | 5.7 |
|---|---|---|---|---|---|---|---|---|---|---|---|---|
| United Kingdom | | 8.5 | 8.0 | 7.4 | 6.9 | 8.6 | 7.8 | 6.5 | 7.3 | 9.4 | 7.8 | 8.6 |
| EU-28 | | | | 10.0 | 9.8 | 10.3 | 10.0 | 10.3 | 10.9 | 11.0 | 10.8 | 11.0 |
| Norway | 5.9 | 5.6 | 5.7 | 5.5 | 5.2 | 6.6 | 6.2 | 5.5 | 7.4 | 5.0 | 5.2 | 5.3 |
| Switzerland | | | | | | | 7.7 | 6.5 | 6.1 | 7.0 | 5.8 | 8.8 |

Note: The proportion of persistently poor is given as the percentage of the population living in households where the equivalised disposable income was below the at-risk-of-poverty threshold for the current year and at least two out of the preceding 3 years. Source: Eurostat, table [ilc_li21]. Data accessed on 12/2/2021

**Table 8.3** Poverty and deprivation risks of the European population (EU-28, Switzerland, Norway; 2013; 18–64 years; in %)

| | Income (in PPS) (1) | Poverty (nat. threshold) (2) | Poverty (EU threshold) (3) | Deprivation (4) | Low work intensity (5) | Low education (6) | Poor health (7) | Subjective poverty (8) | Disadvantaged 18–64 years (H) | Multiple deprivation index M0 |
|---|---|---|---|---|---|---|---|---|---|---|
| Luxembourg | 28,171 | 15.6 | 1.6 | 5.7 | 14.1 | 31.7 | 6.7 | 13.4 | 20.7 | 7.7 |
| Norway | 26,756 | 10.8 | 2.6 | 4 | 21.2 | 20.2 | 4.3 | 6.6 | 11.8 | 4.5 |
| Switzerland | 26,571 | 14.4 | 2.3 | 3.7 | 19 | 16.2 | 2.7 | 11.8 | 11.6 | 4.1 |
| Austria | 20,976 | 14.4 | 5.9 | 9.9 | 18.2 | 19.8 | 7.6 | 14 | 18.7 | 7.2 |
| Sweden | 20,063 | 15.7 | 6.4 | 5.1 | 24.6 | 17.4 | 2.4 | 7.5 | 15.1 | 5.7 |
| Denmark | 19,839 | 11.3 | 5.3 | 8.8 | 25 | 21.6 | 4.1 | 11.8 | 19.4 | 7.6 |
| Belgium | 19,639 | 15 | 6.6 | 11.8 | 18.7 | 25.4 | 6.9 | 20.9 | 22.6 | 9.7 |
| Germany | 19,460 | 15.8 | 7.3 | 11.5 | 24.3 | 11.4 | 6.8 | 9.1 | 18.4 | 7.6 |
| Netherlands | 19,280 | 10.2 | 4.2 | 8.1 | 21.4 | 23.7 | 2.8 | 15.4 | 19.5 | 7.3 |
| France | 19,210 | 13.7 | 5.5 | 12 | 21.5 | 23.3 | 6.8 | 20.7 | 22.9 | 9.0 |
| Finland | 19,187 | 11.8 | 4.5 | 8.4 | 24 | 21.8 | 3.7 | 6.8 | 15.6 | 5.8 |
| Cyprus | 16,978 | 15.3 | 10.7 | 36 | 12.4 | 25.7 | 5.8 | 59.4 | 45.0 | 17.9 |
| United Kingdom | 16,817 | 15.9 | 11.5 | 11.4 | 19.7 | 15.2 | 5.4 | 21 | 19.2 | 7.4 |
| Ireland | 16,736 | 15.7 | 11.4 | 24.7 | 13.7 | 23.8 | 2.8 | 36.8 | 34.9 | 14.0 |
| Italy | 15,347 | 19.1 | 18.6 | 23.8 | 18.8 | 40.8 | 10.2 | 41.5 | 40.5 | 18.0 |
| Malta | 15,264 | 15.7 | 15.7 | 19.8 | 15 | 53.2 | 3.4 | 37 | 40.6 | 16.9 |
| Spain | 14,189 | 20.2 | 23.1 | 16.9 | 14.3 | 38.9 | 6.9 | 38.8 | 40.3 | 17.8 |
| Slovenia | 14,154 | 14.5 | 17.3 | 17 | 15.3 | 17.4 | 5.2 | 33.1 | 27.9 | 11.4 |
| Czech Republic | 10,733 | 8.6 | 32.3 | 15.9 | 18.1 | 11.9 | 7.5 | 31.8 | 28.0 | 11.5 |
| Portugal | 9916 | 18.7 | 43.6 | 25.6 | 17.2 | 49.6 | 15.6 | 46.9 | 55.3 | 25.8 |
| Slovakia | 9604 | 12.8 | 44.2 | 23.1 | 11.9 | 13.3 | 9.9 | 36.5 | 35.5 | 14.7 |

| | | | | | | | | | | |
|---|---|---|---|---|---|---|---|---|---|---|
| Poland | 9180 | 17.3 | 49.5 | 25.5 | 12.1 | 15.2 | 10.8 | 32.9 | 40.8 | 17.3 |
| Greece | 9121 | 22.5 | 49.8 | 37.3 | 16.4 | 31.3 | 8.7 | 78.3 | 61.9 | 28.5 |
| Estonia | 8908 | 18.4 | 51.1 | 19.4 | 17.5 | 15.3 | 10.8 | 23.4 | 36.6 | 15.6 |
| Croatia | 7359 | 19.5 | 63.5 | 34.7 | 14.2 | 22.4 | 11.7 | 62.5 | 59.2 | 26.4 |
| Lithuania | 7282 | 20.5 | 64.7 | 31.7 | 18.2 | 19.4 | 12.7 | 32.9 | 43.7 | 19.4 |
| Hungary | 7278 | 14.9 | 69.8 | 45.5 | 17.4 | 21 | 13.3 | 54.9 | 60.7 | 28.3 |
| Latvia | 6585 | 19.3 | 68.8 | 40.4 | 16.1 | 19.6 | 13.7 | 54.4 | 58.3 | 26.1 |
| Bulgaria | 5829 | 21 | 78.6 | 58 | 16.1 | 23.5 | 9.8 | 65.2 | 66.4 | 31.5 |
| Romania | 3896 | 22.7 | 92.4 | 47.1 | 15.2 | 29.5 | 8.2 | 51.1 | 68.4 | 31.1 |
| EU-28, CH, NO | 15,573 | 16.5 | 22.5 | 18.6 | 19 | 23.6 | 7.5 | 28.3 | 32.3 | 13.9 |

Source: Own calculations based on EU-SILC 2013. Disposable income and the corresponding values refer to the previous year. *Income* is expressed in purchasing power standards (PPS). Column 1 shows the *median income*. In a low *work intensity* household, adults engage on average in gainful employment for no more than one-fifth of the possible working hours. *Poverty rates* (as a percentage of the national or European threshold) were calculated with reference to 60% of the national or European median income. *Material deprivation* means that people are unable to meet at least three of the following nine expenses: Rent and utilities, heating, meals, holidays, car, washing machine, television, telephone. People aged 25–64 who have completed lower secondary education or less (ISCED 0–2) are considered to have a *low education*. Persons who describe their state of health as poor or very poor are recorded in the penultimate column. *Subjectively poor* are persons who rate the financial situation of their household as poor or very poor. The calculation of the deprivation indices was based on 2 out of 7 deprivations (k = 2) and the 7 deprivations were standardised to the age group of 18–64 years, as otherwise the share of non-working (pensioner) households would have been too large

that about two-thirds of all poor people are persistently poor—a very high share. This is especially true for Eastern and Southern European countries such as Romania, Bulgaria, the Baltic States, Greece, Spain or Italy. Poverty is least entrenched in Scandinavia, but also in the Czech Republic and the Netherlands. The lower poverty and persistent poverty rates in these countries point to more inclusive labour market and—in the case of the Western European countries—to social policies that effectively reduce the extent of persistent financial exclusion.

It can thus be stated that the typical patterns of poverty and exclusion, which primarily affect younger people, migrants, the low-skilled with simple tasks, manual workers and single parents, are reinforced by the particular features of the five economic, employment and welfare state regimes under consideration. This can be observed mainly for low-skilled persons with simple jobs in Southern and Eastern Europe. This points to a social and territorial accumulation of disadvantages that puts an extreme strain on social cohesion in the respective nation-states, but also in Europe as a whole.

In the following, other relevant indicators of disadvantage could be discussed in detail—such as educational poverty (Sect. 9.4), life expectancy and life satisfaction (Kahneman & Deaton, 2010), the share of low-wage employment (Maitre et al., 2012), the working poor (Andreß & Lohmann, 2008), the long-term unemployed (Heidenreich, 2015) and the precariously employed (Dörre, 2014; Kalleberg, 2009, 2011) as well as social participation and the housing and asset situation (Chap. 10). There are convincing arguments for each of these indicators and also for the corresponding subjective indicators (satisfaction with the financial situation, health, housing situation . . .). Instead of a confusing and ultimately opaque accumulation of information on different forms and patterns of disadvantage, a different approach is chosen. Two summary indicators of general and work-related disadvantage will be proposed.

## 8.3  Multiple Poverty and Employment Risks in Europe

In Sect. 8.1, it was argued that poverty and exclusion can only be meaningfully understood as a multidimensional concept. On the basis of Bourdieu et al. (1999), the heterogeneity of disadvantages has been stressed. This raises the question of which facets of disadvantage need to be considered in order to capture poverty and exclusion and how they can be aggregated. The aim is to avoid an arbitrary selection and weighting of indicators. Given the advantages of a simple index like the previously discussed poverty rate, another challenge is to propose an index that is easy to understand and communicate. After all, an index like the poverty rate—however questionable it may be from a theoretical point of view (cf. Sect. 8.2)—has motivated and enabled political efforts to reduce poverty, both at national and at European and global levels. This applies both to national poverty reports (Bundesministerium für Arbeit und Soziales, 2021) and to the European goal of reducing the number of poor and excluded people by 20 million (Darvas, 2019), as well as to the Millennium Development Goals formulated by the UN (Sachs, 2012), whose central aim was to halve extreme poverty. This raises the question of which indicators should meaningfully be included in the calculation of a multidimensional index of poverty and exclusion.

A proposal for such a multidimensional index can be based on other studies and indices. At the global level, in addition to a poverty index the UN also includes indicators for life expectancy and the expected and mean years of schooling in its Human Development Index (UNDP, 2019). Numerous deprivation and exclusion indicators have also been proposed at the European level in the context of the Open Method of Coordination (Atkinson et al., 2004, 2017). Similarly, at the national level, a broad set of indicators aligned with the concept of living situations have been developed, for example in the regular poverty and wealth reports of the German Ministry of Labour and Social Affairs (2021).

Considering this background, two different indices will be proposed for the multiple poverty and deprivation risks of the population and for the employment risks of the labour force. The first indicator focuses on household-related risks and the second on the risks associated with the labour market. The national values for these indicators are presented in Tables 8.3 and 8.4. The aim of these indices is to develop aggregate measures for multiple exposures to social risks based on microdata for the population and the labour force. On this basis, the different social situations between and within the Southern, Central and Eastern European country groups can be analysed. The development of the two indices is first illustrated by using the data for 2013, i.e. for the peak of the euro crisis, which hit the Southern European countries particularly hard. Subsequently, the development of these indices is examined over time.

The index for poverty and social exclusion proposed by the European Commission can be taken as a starting point, as there are theoretically convincing arguments for the three indicators included: The risk of living in a household with very low work intensity, severe material and social deprivation and poverty (see Appendix 1). The share of households with a very low work intensity reflects the adult household members' involvement in the labour force (see Table 8.3). The index for material deprivation refers to more or less sufficient availability of goods and services and can thus be seen as an indicator of the standard of living. The at-risk-of-poverty rate refers to the relative scarcity of financial resources compared to compatriots. Weziak-Bialowolska (2016) proposes another index which also focuses on health, education and living standards, for example indicators for poor health and educational poverty. The inclusion of these indicators in addition to the indicators proposed by the Commission are useful because they highlight deprivation in domains which are also essential for an adequate living situation. Since it was previously shown that the level of disposable income has an influence on financial stress in a European context as well, the previously discussed European-wide poverty index is also included. The poverty and deprivation index presented in Table 8.3 therefore includes indicators for poor health, educational poverty, material deprivation and low work intensity of households, as well as national and European poverty rates and subjective perceptions of financial stress. In comparison with the living situation

**Table 8.4** Income and employment risks of the European labour force (EU-28, Switzerland, Austria; 18–64 years; 2013; in %)

| | Unemployment (1) | Long-term unemployment (2) | Poor unemployed (3) | Working poor (4) | Low wages (5) | Solo self-employed (6) | Fixed-term contracts (7) | Involuntary part-time work (8) | Multiple deprivation (H) | Multiple deprivation index M0 |
|---|---|---|---|---|---|---|---|---|---|---|
| Luxembourg | 6.1 | 2.9 | 40.7 | 11.6 | 26.6 | 4.5 | 8.7 | 2.7 | 15.7 | 4.4 |
| Norway | 3.1 | 1.7 | 32.9 | 5.9 | 13.0 | 5.1 | 5.2 | 1.2 | 6.9 | 1.9 |
| Switzerland | 3.2 | 1.0 | 21.0 | 6.8 | 13.8 | 6.3 | 8.6 | 1.9 | 7.1 | 1.8 |
| Austria | 8.7 | 3.3 | 35.0 | 8.2 | 16.2 | 7.5 | 6.0 | 1.9 | 11.3 | 3.4 |
| Sweden | 7.0 | 3.1 | 40.4 | 7.4 | 14.5 | 5.2 | 8.3 | 1.3 | 12.7 | 3.9 |
| Denmark | 9.0 | 3.8 | 31.3 | 4.8 | 7.4 | 0.2 | 5.1 | 0.3 | 7.3 | 2.5 |
| Belgium | 10.6 | 6.9 | 39.0 | 5.1 | 9.5 | 6.4 | 9.8 | 4.1 | 14.2 | 5.0 |
| Germany | 8.1 | 6.1 | 65.0 | 9.3 | 20.9 | 3.8 | 13.3 | 2.5 | 17.5 | 5.9 |
| Netherlands | 5.4 | 2.4 | 20.5 | 5.2 | 13.7 | 9.5 | 8.6 | 2.8 | 8.6 | 2.4 |
| France | 9.2 | 4.6 | 33.6 | 7.9 | 10.7 | 7.4 | 14.7 | 3.5 | 15.4 | 4.8 |
| Finland | 9.8 | 5.0 | 32.5 | 4.4 | 9.0 | 7.3 | 7.2 | 1.1 | 11.3 | 3.9 |
| Cyprus | 18.4 | 7.0 | 24.2 | 8.7 | 22.2 | 7.6 | 13.5 | 4.5 | 24.0 | 7.3 |
| United Kingdom | 4.7 | 2.9 | 48.1 | 7.7 | 17.8 | 9.2 | 4.2 | 3.3 | 10.7 | 3.3 |
| Ireland | 17.4 | 13.8 | 35.9 | 4.7 | 20.8 | 9.1 | 8.9 | 11.5 | 26.0 | 9.1 |
| Italy | 12.6 | 8.4 | 40.5 | 10.7 | 17.7 | 16.2 | 13.6 | 5.0 | 24.7 | 8.2 |
| Malta | 4.4 | 2.9 | 47.3 | 6.0 | 17.9 | 8.8 | 6.4 | 1.0 | 10.8 | 3.4 |
| Spain | 30.1 | 19.0 | 39.8 | 9.4 | 17.1 | 9.5 | 23.0 | 7.7 | 36.3 | 13.3 |
| Slovenia | 15.0 | 8.0 | 38.5 | 6.6 | 14.4 | 6.7 | 6.4 | 0.8 | 17.6 | 6.4 |
| Czech Republic | 9.7 | 6.0 | 40.0 | 4.4 | 15.9 | 12.9 | 13.3 | 0.6 | 13.8 | 4.7 |
| Portugal | 21.1 | 15.0 | 35.9 | 9.4 | 13.6 | 7.8 | 16.1 | 3.7 | 28.2 | 10.2 |
| Slovakia | 12.1 | 9.5 | 39.3 | 5.7 | 15.0 | 11.6 | 12.1 | 0.8 | 19.2 | 6.8 |

| | | | | | | | | | |
|---|---|---|---|---|---|---|---|---|---|
| Poland | 12.9 | 8.1 | 37.9 | 10.6 | 18.9 | 13.0 | 30.2 | 1.8 | 25.2 | 7.9 |
| Greece | 29.6 | 22.9 | 42.8 | 10.4 | 15.8 | 20.6 | 15.2 | 8.0 | 38.1 | 14.0 |
| Estonia | 9.3 | 4.4 | 45.0 | 7.9 | 20.6 | 4.5 | 1.6 | 1.5 | 12.8 | 4.1 |
| Croatia | 25.7 | 19.0 | 39.7 | 6.1 | 14.2 | 5.3 | 16.8 | 0.6 | 33.0 | 12.8 |
| Lithuania | 12.7 | 8.2 | 55.5 | 9.8 | 24.8 | 5.8 | 3.9 | 1.7 | 18.0 | 6.2 |
| Hungary | 14.3 | 7.4 | 46.2 | 7.6 | 12.1 | 6.4 | 10.5 | 0.5 | 18.1 | 6.4 |
| Latvia | 14.3 | 9.5 | 44.2 | 10.1 | 22.4 | 5.0 | 4.4 | 2.7 | 19.5 | 6.5 |
| Bulgaria | 16.9 | 13.5 | 42.3 | 8.0 | 12.7 | 5.4 | 7.2 | 1.9 | 23.3 | 8.6 |
| Romania | 3.5 | 3.2 | 47.4 | 17.4 | 16.3 | 20.5 | 1.8 | 0.1 | 17.6 | 4.5 |
| EU-28, CH, NO | 11.6 | 7.4 | 42.1 | 8.8 | 16.4 | 9.3 | 12.6 | 3.2 | 19.4 | 6.5 |

Source: Own calculations based on EU-SILC 2013. (Long-term) unemployed, low-wage workers (2/3 of the median wage), temporary workers and involuntary part-time workers are reported as % of the dependent labour force. Working poor are employed persons at risk of poverty. Unemployed poor (as % of unemployed) are their counterpart among the unemployed. The multiple deprivation indices are based on two deprivations each (k = 2). They and the working poor are expressed as a percentage of the 18–64 year old labour force

approach, it must be emphasised that indicators for social capital and networks or people's social and cultural embeddedness (workplace, neighbourhood, religious or ethnic communities; cf. Voges, 2006, p. 3) are not included due to the lack of such data in EU-SILC.

In detail (Table 8.3), the index of poverty and deprivation risks for the population includes, firstly, whether an interviewee is poor on the basis of the national poverty threshold (60% of national median income) (column 2), then an indicator for material deprivation (column 4) and a further indicator for work intensity (column 5). These indicators were proposed by the EU in its Europe 2020 strategy to determine poverty and exclusion. They are measured dichotomously. If an interviewee is either poor or deprived or lives in a household with a low work intensity, then it can be assumed that the respective household is poor and socially excluded. Given the role of a European poverty threshold for subjectively perceived economic stress (Sect. 7.5), an indicator for poverty in a European context has also been included (column 3). The difficulties in making ends meet discussed already in Sect. 7.5 were also considered (column 8). This indicator is more strongly correlated with the European than with the national poverty rate at both the micro- and national macrolevels (Fahey, 2007). Due to the central importance of education, a low level of education is used as an indicator of educational poverty (column 6). Finally, since people's well-being depends to a considerable extent on their health, which is also determined by their social context (Beckfield et al., 2015; Israel, 2016), an indicator for subjective health was included (column 7)—following the suggestion made by Weziak-Bialowolska (2016). These seven variables are positively correlated with each other. A factor analysis distinguishes two subgroups, one referring to financial deprivation (poverty in the national and European context, deprivation, financial stress) and the other to forms of social exclusion (educational poverty, low work intensity and health problems). The high correlations in the first subgroup are not surprising, as material deprivation refers to goods, opportunities and services whose availability depends on financial means—for example, a minimum of 1 week's annual holiday or adequate heating of the home. The seven indicators have been compiled in Table 8.3. This table is sorted by the median national household income, which is not included in the index (column 1).

At the national macrolevel, the picture is remarkably mixed. Even though less prosperous countries are in general characterised by higher poverty and exclusion rates—Bulgaria and Romania are close to the top of the list in almost all dimensions—there are notable exceptions to this rule: Slovakia and the Czech Republic, for example, have low national poverty rates, low work intensity rates and low levels of educational poverty. This shows once again the heterogeneity of national conditions. At the same time, these highly aggregated data point to the necessity of integrating the diversity of indicators in one multidimensional index.

But how can this be done? A first strategy would be to measure the share of people who are disadvantaged in at least one of the dimensions. The result would be that 60% of Europeans are disadvantaged in at least one dimension—a value which is simply too high to take as an indicator of deprivation and social exclusion: If everybody is excluded, nobody is excluded. In addition, it would mask the difference between people disadvantaged in one or in more dimensions. The challenge of measuring poverty and exclusion in a multidimensional perspective has mainly to answer two questions: Who is disadvantaged and how strongly are these people affected by these disadvantages? The corresponding indicators should comply with the previously mentioned transfer criterion: If the situation within the group of the disadvantaged improves, the indicator should decrease. Thus, if a low-income person catches up on his or her secondary school leaving certificate, this rate should decrease. Furthermore, "a change in the situation of the non-poor should not change the measured situation of the poor", just as "a change in the situation of a person classified as poor must also lead to a change in the poverty measure" (Goebel & Krause, 2018, p. 62). These conditions are fulfilled in the cases of the two multidimensional poverty indices H and M0 shown in Table 8.3, calculated on the basis of Alkire and Foster (2011). The lower limit for diagnosing multiple deprivation was set at experiencing two disadvantages. H is then the proportion of the population aged 18–64 that is disadvantaged in at least two of the seven dimensions shown in the table. This is the case for about one third (32.6%) of the European population. The multidimensional deprivation index M0 corresponds to the proportion of the poor population multiplied by the average number of deprivations (relative to the maximum possible number of deprivations) affecting the poor.

A numerical example: Since about one third of the European population is disadvantaged in at least two dimensions, and on average in 3 out of 7 possible dimensions (more precisely: 43.1%), M0 is calculated as the product of 1/3 times 3/7. This roughly corresponds to the actual value of 14%. M0 thus reflects the extent of the disadvantaged group of people as well as the intensity of these disadvantages. It is noteworthy that in the countries with the largest shares of multiply disadvantaged people (Bulgaria, Romania, Greece, Hungary, Croatia …) the intensity of disadvantage is also the highest, while in Switzerland, Norway, Sweden, Finland, Austria and the Netherlands both values are very low. The differences across Europe are very high: in Bulgaria the group of the doubly disadvantaged is almost eight times higher than in Switzerland, while the intensity of their disadvantages is almost six times higher. Subjectively perceived economic stress and the fact of being poor in a European context have the strongest influence on the extent of multiple deprivation, followed by educational poverty and material deprivation.

Similar to Table 8.3, Table 8.4 provides an overview on employment-related risks affecting the labour force. Here, two groups of risks are to be distinguished: First, the risks associated with being unemployed and second, the risks associated with being employed. First, persons in the labour force can become unemployed (column 1) or long-term unemployed, i.e. be unemployed for a year or more (column 2). Furthermore, the unemployed can also be poor, i.e. live in a household with a low disposable income (column 3). Since every long-term unemployed person is also unemployed, being long-term unemployed automatically counts as experiencing multiple disadvantages. This higher weight of long-term unemployment is justified by the discouragement and de-skilling effects of long-lasting unemployment (Blanchard, 2006). Similar to the unemployed, employed people can also be poor (column 4). Another risk is having a low wage (column 5). Low pay is usually defined as a wage that is less than two-thirds of the average hourly wage (Sect. 6.5). In-work poverty does not primarily reflect low pay (Sect. 6.5). Further employment-related risks are atypical or precarious work. In particular, self-employed persons without employees (column 6), fixed-term employment (column 7) and part-time workers will be considered here. Since part-time employment is a normal employment relationship in many countries, especially for women, only part-time jobs are counted where the interviewees state that they would like to work more hours (column 8). About a quarter of all part-time workers are involuntarily part-time employees.

The risks of unemployed and employed people were included with equal weighting in the calculation of an index of multiple deprivation, i.e. the three indices of the first group are weighted with 17% each and the five indices of the second group with 10% each. Then another multidimensional deprivation and precarity index was calculated based on Alkire and Foster (2011), this time with a threshold of 20%. This means that, even without further disadvantages, the long-term unemployed are counted as multiply disadvantaged, while the short-term unemployed are only counted as disadvantaged if they are also poor. Persons with atypical employment are only counted as multiply disadvantaged if they are precariously employed in at least two ways (for example, as fixed-term and involuntary part-time workers) or if they were also poor or low paid. The level of the two index values is largely determined by the level and duration of unemployment and the share of the working poor.

One fifth of the European labour force is multiply disadvantaged (19.4%). The multiple deprivation index M0, which also takes the severity of the disadvantages into account, is 6.5%. National differences in the work-related risks of the labour force are even greater than those previously reported for the European population. The share of the multiply disadvantaged (H) and the deprivation index M0 are respectively eight and 21 times higher in Greece than in Switzerland. The five other crisis countries (Spain, Portugal, Ireland, Italy and Cyprus) are also in the top group, as is Croatia, which only joined the EU in 2013. This points to the extraordinary impact of the euro crisis in particular on the Southern European labour force. Both the high proportion of the labour force affected by multiple deprivation (a quarter to a third) and the extent of this deprivation (8–14%) point to an extraordinary intensity and spread of the euro crisis. In other countries (Denmark, the Netherlands, Malta, the UK, Finland, Austria or Sweden), workers are considerably better protected from the employment and income risks mentioned. Germany, despite its low unemployment rate, only ranks in the middle of the multiple disadvantage indices (behind Romania, Slovenia or the Czech Republic). This points mainly to the large low-wage sector (21% of the labour force) and thus to the dark side of insider-outsider labour markets (Lindbeck & Snower, 1988). This high share is both the result of the divide between East and West Germany and employment relations which are not subject to social insurance contributions (the so-called mini-jobs) and which are very attractive for married women in particular.

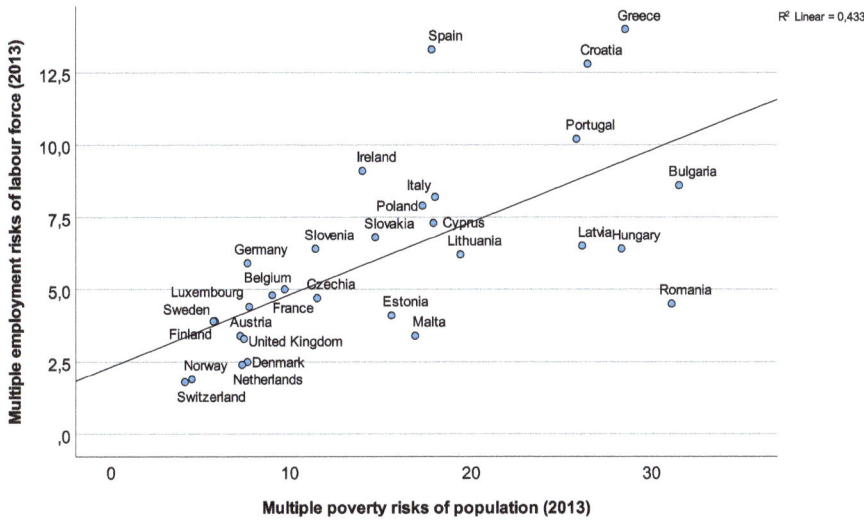

**Fig. 8.2**  Multiple poverty and employment risks (M0) in the EU, Norway and Switzerland (2013; % of population respective labour force aged 18–64)

Figure 8.2 graphically compares the described multiple risks of the population and the labour force for 2013. Three groups of countries can be identified: Firstly, the mostly Continental and Northern European countries where the poverty and employment risks are clearly below the EU average, then the Central and Eastern European countries, where the poverty and deprivation risks of the population have a comparatively higher weight than the employment risks (for example Romania, Bulgaria, Hungary, Latvia or Lithuania) and finally the mostly Southern European countries (especially Greece, Portugal, Spain, and Italy, but also Croatia) with high poverty risks for the population, but even higher employment risks for the labour force. These are the countries above the regression line in Fig. 8.2. *The analysis of multiple disadvantages has thus revealed the complementary strengths and weaknesses of the Southern and Eastern European periphery: While poverty and deprivation risks tend to be concentrated in Central and Eastern Europe, employment risks are relatively more important in Southern Europe.* This graph reflects the social and spatial division of Europe better than purely economic or financial indicators, as it captures the exclusion of significant parts of the population in numerous areas of life (work, education, standard of living, financial resources, health, social security) more comprehensively than, for example, the concentration on value added or disposable income.

It can be assumed that these different risk profiles also shape the type of populism that has emerged in Southern and Eastern Europe (Manow, 2018; Rodrik, 2018). While in Central and Eastern Europe the upgrading of social protection and an ethnic-nationalist legitimised defence against refugees and other foreigners takes precedence, in the South the focus is on left-wing populism that opposes international finance capitalism or the EU as the transmission belt of globalisation in order to close off national markets and employment opportunities. *The European Union must thus secure its cohesion by tackling the tension between poverty and deprivation on the one hand and precarious work and unemployment on the other.* And unlike Ulysses, it cannot tie itself to a mast to listen to the populist chants of the left-wing populist Scylla in the South and the right-wing populist Charybdis in the East and point out that social and employment policies are primarily nation-state tasks, but must actively secure its cohesion by combating both facets of exclusion.

The next step is to describe the development of the two deprivation indices over time. Figure 8.3b, d show the income and employment risks of the European labour force indices over time for the EU-28 plus Norway and Switzerland, the six countries particularly affected by the euro crisis (Italy, Cyprus, Greece, Spain, Portugal and Ireland) and the Central and Eastern European countries. Figure 8.3a, c show the poverty and deprivation risks of the population (especially) in Southern, Central and Eastern Europe over time. When looking at these graphs, the contrast between the 30 countries under consideration (EU-28, Norway, Switzerland), the six crisis countries mentioned and Central and Eastern Europe is striking. While the multiple poverty risks remain largely stable for the 30 countries, the poverty risks of the population in many Central and Eastern European countries at the beginning of the financial market crisis are considerably higher than in the EU (three times higher in Bulgaria and more than twice as high in Romania, 85% higher in Poland and Hungary). In other Central European countries (such as the Czech Republic and Slovenia), the multiple poverty and deprivation rate was already well below the average for all countries in 2007. Only Portugal has such dramatically high values in Southern Europe in 2007, with a multiple poverty rate 10 percentage points higher than the average (13%). The Greek multiple poverty index, at 20%, is 7 percentage points higher than the average. Eleven years later, the picture has changed fundamentally: The multiple poverty rates have decreased significantly, especially in Latvia and Poland, and they are now below the average of the 30 countries in the Czech Republic, Estonia, Slovenia and Poland. However, in the (mainly Southern European) countries strongly impacted by the euro crisis it has increased significantly and in Greece dramatically to 27%. In Portugal it has stabilised at a very high level. Spain and Italy are clearly above average. Only in Ireland is the multiple poverty rate now once again below average after a temporary increase. Thus, a new geography of social inequalities in Europe can be observed: In 2018, the share and intensity of multiple poverty and deprivation in the South (Greece, Portugal, Spain, Cyprus) and in the East of the EU (Bulgaria, Romania, Hungary, Croatia, Lithuania) are still above the European average. Almost all Central and Eastern European countries have succeeded in improving the situation of their population, whereas no Southern European country has managed to do so. The turbulent years of the financial market and euro crises were a lost decade for Southern Europe. This is

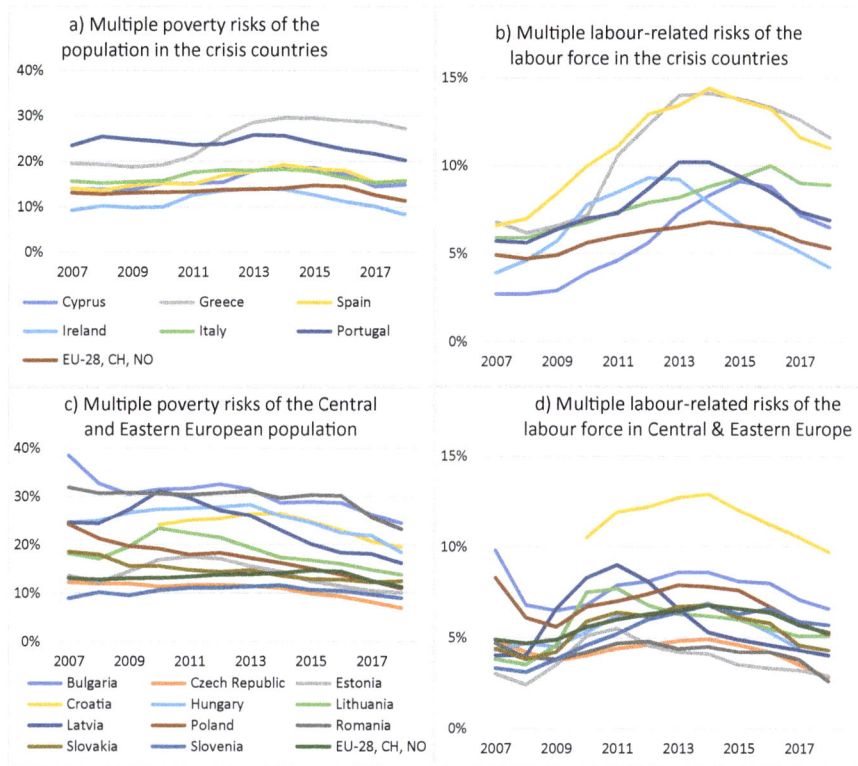

**Fig. 8.3** Multiple poverty and labour-related risks (M0) in the EU-28, Switzerland and Norway (2007–2018; in % of the population or labour force aged 18–64). (**a**) Multiple poverty risks of the population in the crisis countries. (**b**) Multiple labour-related risks of the labour force in the crisis countries. (**c**) Multiple poverty risks of the Central and Eastern European population. (**d**) Multiple labour-related risks of the labour force in Central and Eastern Europe

especially true for Greece, where at the height of the crisis almost 30% of the population was multiply disadvantaged.[1]

The differences are even more pronounced for the multiple labour-related disadvantages (Fig. 8.3c, d). Multiple employment risks increased dramatically in the crisis countries from an already high level. And these risks have not receded after the crisis. In 2018, they were still significantly higher than before the crisis (especially in Cyprus, Greece, Spain and Italy, but also in Portugal). Only in Ireland have

---

[1] This again points to the fact that Greece has been particularly strongly affected by the financial market and euro crises since 2007. The special role of Greece is lost from view if Greece is summarily assigned to the group of demand-driven countries (Iversen et al., 2016). Despite structural similarities with the other Southern European countries, Greece certainly occupies a special position in Southern Europe due to its weak economic structure, its dysfunctional state sector, its patronage-based politics (Featherstone, 2011) and minimal social protection.

employment risks decreased. In all Southern European crisis countries, labour-related risks were far above the European average in 2018. In Greece and Spain, they were even twice as high. These countries are therefore entering the next crisis, the Covid-19 pandemic, in an extraordinarily weakened state. The picture is quite different in Central and Eastern Europe. With the exception of Bulgaria and Poland, employment risks there were already below average in 2007. In 2018, the situation had improved significantly in Poland and Bulgaria due to the decline in unemployment. Only the newly acceded Croatia is still characterised by very high risks. In the rest of Europe, labour market risks quickly receded again; in 2018, they were similar to the levels before the financial market and euro crises.

It can thus be stated that the euro crisis was above all a labour market crisis. This is documented in the considerable increase in labour-related risks in Southern Europe, while these risks decreased in particular in Central and Eastern Europe. With the exception of Greece, however, the crisis was not accompanied by an impoverishment of the population, even if the proportion of the multiply disadvantaged in Italy or Portugal, in Bulgaria, Croatia and Romania is clearly above the EU average. This was already the case before the crisis. The ranking of countries according to the multiple poverty index remains largely stable. At the top, alongside Greece and Portugal, are still the Central and Eastern European countries with a low level of social security (especially Bulgaria, Romania, Hungary and the Baltic states). This points to partly different and complementary challenges of the Central and Southern European countries. *While in Southern Europe the political challenge is primarily to reduce employment-related risks, in particular by a more inclusive labour market policy* (Heidenreich & Rice, 2016)*, many Central and Eastern European countries face the challenge of reducing poverty risks by expanding social security systems.*[2]

## 8.4  Social Fractures in Europe: The Durability and Accumulation of Social Risks and Opportunities

After the analysis of national differences in deprivation, poverty and labour-related risks, this section will focus on the social fractures in Europe. In order to highlight the double dualisation of Europe, the question to be addressed is which groups are particularly affected by poverty and labour-related risks? Are there any groups which are systematically affected positively or negatively by these risks? These groups might be designated as Europeanisation winners and losers (Lahusen, 2021), even if the Europeanisation and globalisation of the economy is only one facet of

---

[2]This does not imply that the lack of national minimum social security systems in many southern European countries (for example in Italy, Greece, Spain . . .; cf. Bahle et al., 2011) is irrelevant. But the relatively high levels of social protection point to the fact that the challenge is primarily the restructuring of social security systems (especially pension systems) rather than their construction.

broader processes of social and economic change (in addition to the increasing importance of the service sector, the expansion of further education and the automation and digitalisation of the economy and society). It can be expected that unemployed, low-skilled people with simple jobs, employees with routine jobs, single parents, young people, and migrants, who are particularly affected by monetary poverty (Sect. 8.2) will have also the highest deprivation and employment risks. On the other hand, employees with demanding jobs, the upper service classes and the highly qualified could also be among the winners in a multidimensional perspective. This section analyses whether these expectations can be confirmed by the data.

The discussion of which groups are particularly affected by poverty, deprivation and employment risks uses the same indicators as in the previous section. Table 8.5 shows, first, that social risks and disadvantages are *not* concentrated mostly among women and migrants from other European countries. The social differences between men and women—with the exception of the lower work intensity of households to which women belong—and between natives and other Europeans—with the exception of the higher poverty rate of EU migrants—are small. Among immigrants from other EU countries, even the share of households with a low work intensity is lower than among natives. This could be interpreted as a result of the free movement of labour in the EU: Unemployed migrants from other European countries can easily return to or remain in their native social context. Measured by the index for multiple disadvantages, M0, for the seven social risks shown in Table 8.5, natives hardly differ from citizens who were born in another European country or have its nationality. However, the differences to people from third countries are extraordinarily high: the risk of poverty is about twice as high. The risk of deprivation, subjective poverty and the proportion of unqualified people are also significantly higher. Migrants are thus not a uniform group. In particular, there are considerable differences between EU citizens and citizens of other countries (Kalter & Granato, 2018). The composition of households also has an influence on social risks. Single parents have the highest risk: they are five times more likely to be economically inactive and 54% more likely to be at risk of poverty, poor health and deprivation than households with more than one adult and at least one child. Young people (15–24 years) have only a slightly higher multiple risk than people in the core age group up to 54 years, even if they have higher risks of living in poor households with low work intensity, because they are healthier.

By far the most important determinant of social opportunities and risks is the level of *education*. The share of households with low work intensity is three times higher among people with low education than in academic households, the risk of poor health is about five times higher, the chance of objective and subjective poverty is five times higher and the risk of deprivation is six times higher. In total, the risk of multiple poverty and deprivation for the *low-skilled* is 11 times higher than for

**Table 8.5** Poverty and deprivation of different social groups in 30 European countries (18–64 years; 2013)

| | Poverty (nat. threshold) (1) | Poverty (EU threshold) (2) | Deprivation (3) | Low work intensity (4) | Low education (5) | Poor health (6) | Subjective poverty (7) | Multiple deprivation index M0 2013 |
|---|---|---|---|---|---|---|---|---|
| Men | 15.8 | 22.2 | 18.8 | 5.2 | 21.0 | 5.4 | 28.3 | 0.135 |
| Women | 16.5 | 22.5 | 19.5 | 8.2 | 20.9 | 6.0 | 29.0 | 0.143 |
| 15–24 years | 22.5 | 28.5 | 22.8 | 5.8 | 20.8 | 1.3 | 31.1 | 0.157 |
| 25–55 years | 15.3 | 21.3 | 18.8 | | 17.9 | 4.5 | 28.8 | 0.124 |
| 55–64 years | 14.8 | 21.9 | 18.1 | 29.2 | 30.7 | 12.4 | 26.6 | 0.177 |
| Without migration background | 14.8 | 21.9 | 18.2 | 7.3 | 20.8 | 6.1 | 27.4 | 0.134 |
| Other European country | 19.7 | 17.6 | 19.3 | 5.9 | 18.2 | 4.4 | 28.4 | 0.132 |
| Third country | 28.3 | 23.5 | 29.1 | 5.1 | 25.5 | 6.2 | 39.3 | 0.193 |
| Low education | 28.0 | 33.5 | 33.5 | 9.3 | 1.0 | 10.1 | 46.7 | 0.328 |
| Medium education | 15.5 | 24.3 | 19.2 | 6.5 | 0.0 | 5.4 | 28.6 | 0.111 |
| High education | 7.6 | 9.9 | 7.4 | 5.5 | 0.0 | 2.6 | 14.4 | 0.043 |
| Employed | 9.5 | 15.8 | 13.3 | 2.5 | 14.8 | 2.5 | 21.8 | 0.084 |
| Unemployed | 42.0 | 46.2 | 44.7 | 2.8 | 35.1 | 7.9 | 58.0 | 0.313 |
| Routine task | 28.9 | 34.6 | 36.9 | 6.9 | 47.0 | 10.0 | 47.3 | 0.273 |
| Operating machinery; repair | 17.0 | 25.8 | 22.0 | 6.8 | 25.0 | 6.7 | 32.6 | 0.159 |
| Complex tasks | 7.7 | 10.2 | 9.4 | 6.5 | 8.6 | 4.2 | 16.9 | 0.06 |
| Problem-solving | 5.3 | 8.1 | 5.3 | 6.5 | 2.6 | 2.5 | 11.4 | 0.035 |
| Upper service class | 5.7 | 8.4 | 6.8 | 6.3 | 4.7 | 3.2 | 13.4 | 0.043 |
| Intermediate employees | 10.3 | 13.3 | 14.3 | 7.3 | 15.5 | 5.5 | 23.6 | 0.093 |
| Self-employed (SMEs) | 24.7 | 35.5 | 20.4 | 3.5 | 29.1 | 3.4 | 32.5 | 0.182 |
| Simple services | 17.4 | 23.3 | 22.6 | 6.5 | 21.5 | 6.0 | 33.0 | 0.151 |
| Lower technical and routine tasks | 22.3 | 33.9 | 30.8 | 6.5 | 38.1 | 9.1 | 41.5 | 0.226 |

| | | | | | | | | |
|---|---|---|---|---|---|---|---|---|
| Single-person household | 26.6 | 24.0 | 24.3 | 19.9 | 18.4 | 10.1 | 27.9 | 0.171 |
| Adults without children | 11.0 | 18.2 | 16.6 | 10.0 | 22.5 | 6.7 | 25.3 | 0.123 |
| Single parents | 29.8 | 25.4 | 32.8 | 2.6 | 20.4 | 6.8 | 41.2 | 0.194 |
| Adults with children | 16.6 | 25.5 | 18.8 | 0.3 | 20.2 | 3.4 | 30.9 | 0.135 |
| EU-28, CH, NO (total) | 16.1 | 22.4 | 19.1 | 6.7 | 20.9 | 5.7 | 28.7 | 0.139 |

Source: Own calculations based on EU-SILC 2013. 30 countries: EU-28, Switzerland and Norway. Seven exclusion indicators explained in Table 8.3 reproduced depending on gender, age group, migration background, educational level (ISCED), employment status, ISCO qualification group (ILO, 2012), socio-professional status (ESEC-5; cf. Rose & Harrison, 2010) and household type

academics—an extremely high value.[3] Regardless of whether this crucial role of education is explained by inherited cultural capital (Bourdieu, 1984), by a lower demand for low qualifications (Autor et al., 2003) or by a declining importance of routine activities (Acemoglu & Autor, 2011; Goos & Manning, 2007), the risks of illness, poverty and deprivation shown in Table 8.5 differ so markedly between the educational strata that it contradicts the assumption of an egalitarian European society. The corresponding differences between occupational groups are equally high: The risk of *people with simple jobs* living in working-poor households are three times higher than that of people in problem-solving jobs, their risk of illness is four times as high and their subjective and objective poverty seven times as high. In total, the risk of people with *simple jobs* being multiply disadvantaged is 10 times higher than those in problem-solving jobs. These two occupational groups seem to work and live in completely different worlds. The differences between *upper and lower social classes,* i.e. between the upper service class and lower technical and routine tasks, are of a similar order of magnitude: the lower group has a threefold higher risk of poor health, a five times higher risk of poverty, a six times higher risk of deprivation and a seven times higher risk of multiple poverty and deprivation. The *unemployed* also have a significantly higher risk of poverty, deprivation, low education and poor health than the employed.

    This reveals two types of factors that are decisive for social opportunities and risks: On the one hand, factors that are independent of professional achievements and that are usually described in sociology as ascriptive characteristics (gender, age, household type, migration background), and on the other hand, factors that reflect educational or occupational achievements (Parsons, 1970). Discrimination based on ascriptive characteristics has also been reduced by legal provisions (for example by the prohibition of most types of discrimination in Article 21 of the Charter of Fundamental Rights of the European Union). The differences between different educational and occupational groups, on the other hand, are extraordinarily high. As is to be expected in a meritocracy, these achieved inequalities play a considerably higher role than inequalities based on ascriptive characteristics. This raises the question of whether the huge inequalities based on different education levels and occupations are still considered legitimate or whether the legitimacy claim of these inequalities has reached its limits (Markovits, 2019; Sandel, 2020; Young, 1994). These limits reflect the inherent cruelty of meritocratic systems which might suggest that the disadvantaged themselves are to blame for their situation because they failed in school or in their job.[4] Therefore, shame about one's own failure might be the most bitter implication of poverty and deprivation. This subjective dimension of deprivation will be discussed in Sect. 8.6.

---

[3] This odds ratio is calculated as the quotient of the respective chances of the two groups. Using the example of the low and high skilled: $10.9 = (0.328/(1–0.328))/(0.043/(1–0.043))$.

[4] Young (1994, p. XVI) rather emphasises the complementary attitudes among the new, meritocratically legitimised elite: "If the rich and powerful were encouraged by the general culture to believe that they fully deserved all they had, how arrogant they could become, and, if they were convinced it was all for the common good, how ruthless in pursuing their own advantage."

The next step is to discuss how the employment-related risks differ between the different socio-economic groups (Table 8.6). *Men and women* face the same level of multiple employment risks, but they differ in the sub-indicators: While low-wage and involuntary part-time work risks are significantly higher for women than for men, women have a lower risk of being working poor, as the mere fact of female employment is often sufficient to lift a household above the poverty line. Age-specific risks are significantly higher for *young people* due to higher unemployment, lower wages and fixed-term contracts. Their multiple employment risks are 30% higher than those of the core age group of 25–54 years. These factors and also the risks of in-work poverty and long-term unemployment explain the significantly higher risks of *third-country nationals* in comparison to native or European citizens. The work-related risks of single parents are significantly higher than those of other households (mainly due to higher risks of involuntary part-time work and in-work poverty). Partly by definition, the social risks of the *unemployed* are also higher. In the past, they have more often been low-paid, employed on a fixed-term basis or involuntarily employed part-time. The differences in employment-related risks between different educational levels, occupational groups and social classes are greater than the differences between different genders, age groups and countries of origin: These risks are five times higher among the *low-skilled* than among the high-skilled (mainly due to the higher unemployment risks), eight times higher among the *employees with routine tasks* than among the problem-solvers, and six times higher among the blue-collar workers than among the upper service class. It is noteworthy that employment-related risks (except the risk of being self-employed without employees) are concentrated among low-skilled employees with simple technical and routine tasks. Their risks are far higher than those of other groups. This demonstrates once again the profound segmentation of the labour force into employees with good and bad jobs (Kalleberg, 2011).

In conclusion, it can be stated that multiple poverty and employment risks are concentrated in particular among unskilled employees with simple and operational tasks. This group is permanently, and not only in times of crisis, strongly affected by the 14 risks discussed in this section. This group is thus consistently disadvantaged both financially and in the employment and education systems. Analytically, two forms of legitimation for the observed inequalities have been distinguished—one based on ascribed characteristics such as gender, age or migration status, and the other based on achieved characteristics such as educational achievement or occupational level. Elsewhere I have suggested contrasting these two forms as marginalisation and dualisation (Heidenreich, 2015). The previously discussed results have shown a clear marginalisation, but an even more pronounced dualisation of living conditions and labour markets in Europe. This issue will be discussed once again in the concluding Sect. 8.6.

The social and territorial division of Europe shapes not only the objective social situation of the population, but also their subjective assessment of their living situation. This subjective dimension will now be examined more closely on the basis of data on life satisfaction.

Table 8.6 Employment-related risks of different social groups (EU-28, Switzerland, Norway; 18–64 years; 2013; in %)

| | Unemployment (1) | Long-term unemployment (2) | Working poor (3) | Low wages (4) | Solo self-employed (5) | Fixed-term contracts (6) | Involuntary part-time work (7) | Multiple deprivation (M0) |
|---|---|---|---|---|---|---|---|---|
| Men | 12.0 | 7.7 | 9.3 | 12.8 | 11.4 | 12.0 | 1.6 | 0.065 |
| Women | 11.2 | 7.2 | 8.2 | 20.2 | 6.9 | 13.3 | 4.9 | 0.065 |
| 15–24 years | 14.2 | 7.5 | 10.2 | 30.2 | 4.0 | 37.6 | 5.9 | 0.114 |
| 25–55 years | 11.0 | 7.0 | 8.5 | 16.0 | 9.3 | 11.2 | 3.0 | 0.060 |
| 55–64 years | 13.7 | 10.1 | 9.8 | 10.8 | 12.8 | 6.7 | 2.8 | 0.065 |
| Without migration background | 11.1 | 7.2 | 8.0 | 15.6 | 9.4 | 12.2 | 2.9 | 0.062 |
| Other European country | 11.6 | 6.5 | 12.4 | 21.7 | 10.3 | 14.7 | 5.0 | 0.071 |
| Third country | 17.3 | 11.1 | 16.4 | 24.2 | 8.0 | 16.4 | 6.5 | 0.107 |
| Low education | 25.9 | 17.9 | 15.6 | 24.9 | 12.2 | 18.7 | 6.6 | 0.136 |
| Medium education | 10.8 | 6.9 | 9.1 | 19.9 | 9.1 | 12.7 | 1.9 | 0.062 |
| High education | 5.9 | 3.1 | 4.4 | 7.9 | 7.9 | 10.3 | 3.2 | 0.031 |
| Employed | 0.2 | 0.9 | 9.2 | 16.4 | 9.8 | 12.6 | 3.2 | 0.230 |
| Unemployed | 100 | 57.8 | 5.9 | 25.3 | 5.8 | 34.7 | 12.7 | 0.348 |
| Routine task | 24.7 | 16.6 | 17.9 | 34.2 | 5.5 | 23.1 | 10.9 | 0.143 |
| Operating machinery; repair | 14.5 | 9.6 | 11.0 | 21.5 | 11.3 | 14.1 | 3.7 | 0.073 |
| Complex tasks | 5.8 | 3.4 | 5.2 | 9.5 | 7.9 | 8.5 | 1.3 | 0.029 |
| Problem-solving | 3.8 | 1.8 | 3.7 | 5.7 | 8.6 | 9.2 | 1.0 | 0.020 |

| | | | | | | | |
|---|---|---|---|---|---|---|---|
| Upper service class | 4.6 | 2.5 | 3.9 | 7.2 | 6.7 | 8.5 | 1.1 | 0.021 |
| Intermediate employees | 10.0 | 6.3 | 6.0 | 15.0 | 0.1 | 11.3 | 2.3 | 0.046 |
| Self-employed (SMEs) | 31.0 | 11.8 | 24.7 | 51.1 | 78.2 | 0.0 | 0.0 | 0.048 |
| Simple services | 14.9 | 9.5 | 10.3 | 28.9 | 0.0 | 16.8 | 7.0 | 0.082 |
| Lower technical and routine tasks | 20.6 | 14.0 | 12.9 | 25.6 | 0.0 | 17.9 | 5.2 | 0.107 |
| Single-person household | 14.7 | 10.0 | 13.2 | 15.0 | 9.1 | 13.3 | 3.4 | 0.088 |
| Adults without children | 12.0 | 7.7 | 5.7 | 17.1 | 9.1 | 13.8 | 3.6 | 0.060 |
| Single parents | 14.4 | 9.6 | 19.0 | 21.2 | 6.5 | 11.4 | 6.3 | 0.101 |
| Adults with children | 10.1 | 6.3 | 9.5 | 15.9 | 9.8 | 11.5 | 2.6 | 0.061 |
| EU-28, CH, NO (total) | 11.6 | 7.5 | 8.8 | 16.4 | 9.3 | 12.6 | 3.2 | 0.065 |

Source: Own calculations based on EU-SILC 2013. Seven of the employment-related risks explained in Table 8.4 for different gender and age groups, educational levels (ISCED), employment status, ISCO occupational groups (ILO, 2012), socio-professional status (ESEC-5; cf. Rose & Harrison, 2010), household types and with different migration backgrounds

## 8.5    The Impact of Social Disadvantages on Life Satisfaction

The question of the social determinants of subjective well-being is at the centre of a broad range of international research on the extent and determinants of happiness, life satisfaction and subjective well-being (Clark et al., 2008; Diener, 2000; Veenhoven, 1991). The importance of the material situation, available financial resources, social relationships and employment, health, education and housing on people's life satisfaction have been convincingly shown (OECD, 2013). This debate will now be briefly summarised, with a particular focus on national determinants. Subsequently, the impact of the previously discussed indicators for social risks on life satisfaction will be examined.

Life satisfaction refers to broader judgments by an individual "about his or her life as a whole, as well as about domains such as marriage and work." (Diener, 2000, p. 34) It is measured with the question "Overall, how satisfied are you with your life nowadays?" on an 11-point scale (0: not at all satisfied; 10: completely satisfied). Life satisfaction also depends on the respective social position, especially income and a socially determined minimum level of goods and resources (Townsend, 1979). It varies depending on age, gender, ethnicity, health, family and employment status, social class and education (OECD, 2013).

From an international perspective, higher disposable income is the most important factor explaining higher life satisfaction. However, economic growth over time does not lead to higher life satisfaction—a phenomenon known as the Easterlin paradox (Sect. 7.5). Clark et al. (2008) explain this paradox by showing that current income is compared less with past income and more with the income of contemporary fellow countrymen. In contrast, in a careful review of previous studies, Sacks et al. (2010) argue that life satisfaction depends primarily on the absolute level of income and not on the income of the respective reference groups (Veenhoven, 1991). Other studies have found that the Gini index of national income inequality also has an influence on life satisfaction (Wilkinson & Pickett, 2010)—even if this influence is probably quite small (Delhey & Dragolov, 2014). Other crucial contextual factors are the level of unemployment, labour market policies (Wulfgramm, 2014), social trust and other cultural dimensions (Diener, 2009).

Based on ad-hoc modules of EU-SILC, life satisfaction in Europe can be determined for the years 2013 and 2018 (Fig. 8.4). Overall, life satisfaction in the EU increased significantly during this period, i.e. after the end of the financial and euro crises (from 7.1 to 7.3 points). The Scandinavian countries show the highest life satisfaction (with a value of 7.8), followed by the liberal and Continental European countries. In Southern Europe (6.6 and 7.1 respectively) and in Central and Eastern Europe (6.8 and 7.1 respectively), life satisfaction is considerably lower; both groups of countries are clearly below the European average. Some results are surprising— such as the high life satisfaction in Ireland (even at the peak of the euro crisis) and in Romania, one of the poorest EU countries. Life satisfaction is highest in affluent countries such as Ireland, Finland, Sweden or Denmark, lowest in Bulgaria, but also in Croatia, Lithuania, Greece or Hungary. In the period under consideration,

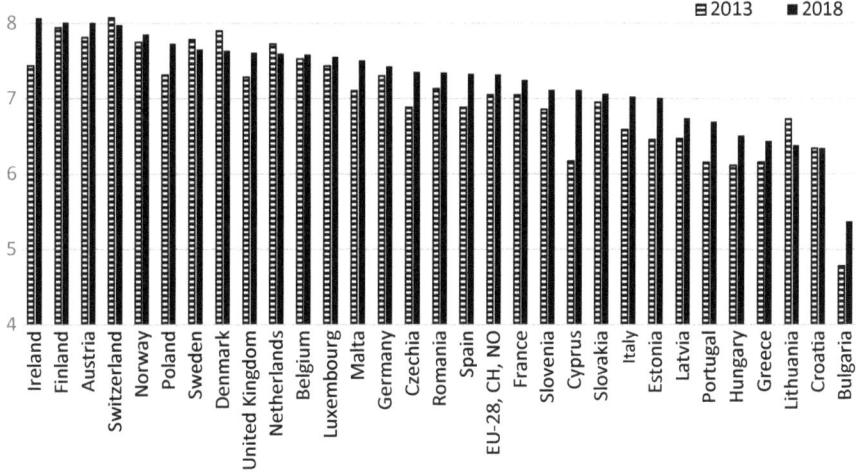

Source: EU-SILC 2013 and 2018. Data for 28 EU Member States, Switzerland and Norway.

**Fig. 8.4** Life satisfaction in 30 European countries (2013 and 2018)

satisfaction increased most in Ireland, Estonia, Cyprus, Portugal and Bulgaria and decreased significantly in Denmark, the Netherlands and Sweden. Life satisfaction has converged across the EU, as shown by a declining coefficient of variation.

Figure 8.5 shows life satisfaction in five different income groups for 2018. The difference in life satisfaction between the top and bottom quintiles is 1.5 points on the 11-point satisfaction scale, much smaller than the gap between the countries with the highest and lowest life satisfaction (Fig. 8.5). Nevertheless, the nation-state is still the arena with the greatest influence on people's life satisfaction. Only a minimal proportion of individual differences (4% according to the MLD) can be explained by differences between nation-states. In this context, European integration cannot be expected to have a strong effect on life satisfaction.

Now the impact of the seven social risks presented in Table 8.3 on the population's life satisfaction will be examined. Since the importance of income for life satisfaction has been confirmed in numerous other studies, it can only be a question of whether these indicators have an additional influence. In the first model in Table 8.7 only the annual dummies were included, the intraclass correlations indicate that 11% of the differences could be explained by the national level, but 60% by common socio-economic characteristics of household members. Different members of the same household are not independent individuals, since they have by definition the same income and also other common characteristics. Therefore, the household level has been included as a separate level in the multilevel models. The positive value for 2018 compared to 2013 indicates that life satisfaction has increased significantly since 2013. The halving of the corresponding coefficient (from 0.29 in model 1 to 0.14 in model 3) shows that the higher life satisfaction was also achieved to a considerable extent by the decreasing levels of poverty and exclusion. In model 2, disposable income is included in addition to some control

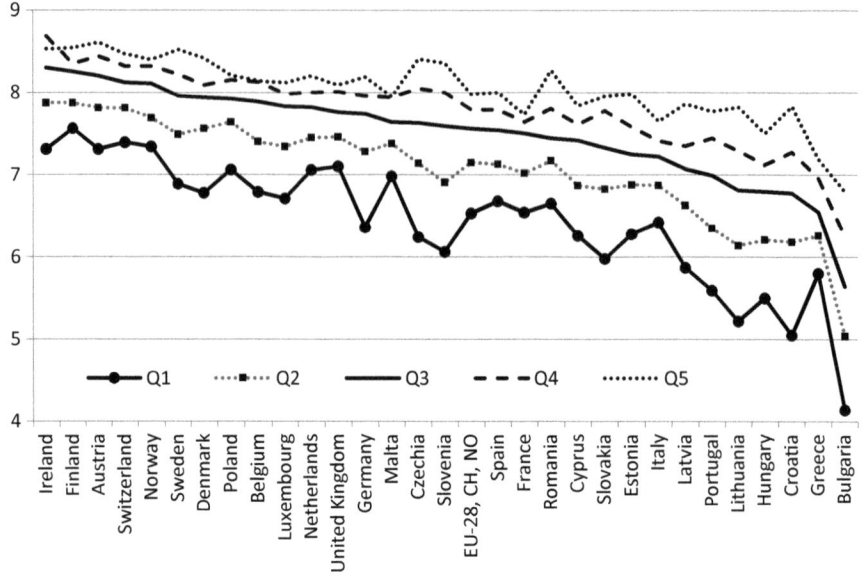

Source: EU-SILC 2018.

**Fig. 8.5**  Life satisfaction in 30 European countries in different income quintiles (2018)

variables (gender, age, migration status, household type). In line with central results of happiness research, the expected positive effect on life satisfaction can be seen. Model 3 includes the poverty and deprivation indicators described earlier. All seven indicators are highly significant and—with the exception of low work intensity— have a negative impact on overall life satisfaction. Therefore, it can be stated that a high risk of poverty, lack of goods and opportunities, a low level of education, financial stress and health constraints are associated with lower life satisfaction, while a low work intensity is associated with higher life satisfaction. The additional free time seems to outweigh the financial disadvantages. Since all seven variables were measured dichotomously, the coefficients can be compared directly: Health status has the strongest influence on individual satisfaction, followed by subjective poverty and experiences of deprivation. Compared to these three dimensions, objective poverty risk and educational poverty have a lower impact on life satisfaction (Table 8.7, column 3). This shows once again that deprivation cannot be reduced to the lack of financial resources. In the context of the Europeanisation debate, it is noteworthy that both poverty on a national and a European scale has a highly significant impact on life satisfaction. The magnitudes of both coefficients are also comparable ($-0.17$ and $-0.13$ respectively)—a further indication of the independent role and the significant impact of the European frame of reference. By including the seven poverty and deprivation indicators, the proportion of explained variance ($R^2$) increases to 24%, i.e. a considerable part of life satisfaction can be explained by different experiences of poverty, deprivation and exclusion.

**Table 8.7**  Impact of poverty and employment risks on life satisfaction in Europe (2013 and 2018)

|  | (1) | (2) | (3) | (4) | (5) |
|---|---|---|---|---|---|
| Survey year 2018 | 0.29*** | 0.22*** | 0.14*** | 0.24*** | 0.13*** |
|  | (0.0064) | (0.0062) | (0.0057) | (0.0061) | (0.0057) |
| Disposable income |  | 0.54*** | 0.16*** | 0.43*** | 0.16*** |
|  |  | (0.0040) | (0.0045) | (0.0043) | (0.0045) |
| European migration background |  |  | −0.053*** | −0.075*** | −0.053*** |
|  |  |  | (0.014) | (0.015) | (0.014) |
| Non-European migration background |  |  | −0.060*** | −0.19*** | −0.059*** |
|  |  |  | (0.010) | (0.011) | (0.010) |
| Low work intensity |  |  | 0.25*** |  | 0.26*** |
|  |  |  | (0.010) |  | (0.010) |
| Poor (national poverty threshold) |  |  | −0.17*** |  | −0.17*** |
|  |  |  | (0.010) |  | (0.010) |
| Poor (European poverty threshold) |  |  | −0.13*** |  | −0.13*** |
|  |  |  | (0.0094) |  | (0.0094) |
| Deprivation |  |  | −0.78*** |  | −0.78*** |
|  |  |  | (0.0087) |  | (0.0087) |
| Educational poverty |  |  | −0.20*** |  | −0.20*** |
|  |  |  | (0.0064) |  | (0.0064) |
| Bad health |  |  | −1.42*** |  | −1.42*** |
|  |  |  | (0.0097) |  | (0.0096) |
| Subjectively poor |  |  | −0.81*** |  | −0.81*** |
|  |  |  | (0.0077) |  | (0.0077) |
| Unemployed |  |  |  | −0.74*** |  |
|  |  |  |  | (0.012) |  |
| Long-term unemployed |  |  |  | −0.21*** |  |
|  |  |  |  | (0.014) |  |
| Working poor |  |  |  | −0.089*** |  |
|  |  |  |  | (0.010) |  |
| Low wage recipient |  |  |  | −0.088*** |  |
|  |  |  |  | (0.0088) |  |
| Solo self-employed |  |  |  | −0.037*** |  |
|  |  |  |  | (0.0088) |  |
| Fixed-term contracts |  |  |  | −0.14*** |  |
|  |  |  |  | (0.0079) |  |
| Involuntary part-time |  |  |  | −0.33*** |  |
|  |  |  |  | (0.018) |  |
| Income inequality (Gini) |  |  |  |  | −5.15*** |
|  |  |  |  |  | (0.30) |
| Observations | 491,997 | 491,997 | 491,997 | 491,997 | 491,997 |
| Interstate intraclass correlation | 0.11 | 0.066 | 0.055 | 0.073 | 0.046 |
| Intraclass correlation (between households) | 0.60 | 0.56 | 0.50 | 0.55 | 0.49 |

(continued)

**Table 8.7** (continued)

|                | (1)       | (2)       | (3)       | (4)       | (5)       |
| -------------- | --------- | --------- | --------- | --------- | --------- |
| $R^2$          | 0.0030    | 0.083     | 0.24      | 0.12      | 0.24      |
| AIC            | 1,982,202 | 1,964,052 | 1,889,020 | 1,943,595 | 1,888,722 |

Dependent variable: Life satisfaction of the population aged 18–64 years (N = 491,997) in 2013 and 2018 in 28 EU member states, Norway and Switzerland. Multilevel regressions with three levels (countries, households, individuals). The explanatory poverty and deprivation indicators at the microlevel are measured dichotomously. In all models, age, gender and household type and a constant were included but not reported in the table. Migration background (citizenship or place of birth in another EU country or a third country) is reported in contrast to natives. $p < 0.05$; ** $p < 0.01$; *** $p < 0.001$

In the next step, the impact of atypical employment and other employment-related risks on life satisfaction is analysed (Table 8.7, column 4). These risks all have a highly significant negative impact on life satisfaction. Unemployment has the strongest impact, followed by in-work poverty, long-term unemployment and involuntary part-time work. The effects of solo self-employment, low-wage employment and fixed-term contracts are comparatively low—which can also be partly explained by a lower weight of these risks (Table 8.4). Overall, these risks (which can only affect people in employment) explain only 12% of life satisfaction—significantly less than the exclusion and poverty risks.

Finally (Table 8.7, column 5), the influence of an egalitarian income distribution (measured by the Gini index) on life satisfaction is examined. This is associated with higher life satisfaction. Wilkinson and Pickett's (2010) assumption that lower inequalities contribute to greater well-being can thus also be confirmed when the previously mentioned exclusion and poverty indicators are taken into account. Higher income inequalities have a significant negative impact on life satisfaction. The decrease in the Akaike information criterion (AIC) in the comparison of the two models 4 and 5 shows that the inclusion of national income inequalities considerably improves the quality of the model.

In sum: life satisfaction varies considerably between Northern and Western Europe on the one hand and Eastern, Central and Southern Europe on the other. At the peak of the euro crisis, life satisfaction in Southern Europe was significantly lower than in Northern and Western Europe. This is also true for Central and Eastern Europe. The selected poverty and exclusion indicators are clearly and highly significantly correlated with lower life satisfaction. Low work intensity of a household, low income, low educational attainment, material deprivation, health impairments and subjective economic stress are associated with lower life satisfaction. The fact that this is also true when disposable income is included indicates that the various facets of poverty and disadvantage have an independent impact that cannot be explained solely by the level of household income.

## 8.6  Summary

This chapter has analysed which countries and which social groups are among the losers of modernisation and cross-border integration processes. Initially, taking the example of income poverty, it was shown that the Southern European countries are particularly disadvantaged, as they have the highest poverty rates—even though income in some Eastern European countries is still significantly lower than in Southern Europe. But some Eastern European countries (Romania, Bulgaria and the Baltic countries) also have above-average poverty rates. Europe and the EU are thus clearly divided into a Northwestern centre and a Southern and Eastern European periphery. The level of poverty risks is mostly determined by national policies. While countries such as the Czech Republic tend to be characterised by egalitarian income structures and low poverty rates, countries such as Greece are characterised by high income inequalities and poverty rates even with similar average income levels. A significant proportion of income poverty (more than 60%) is persistent poverty, i.e. it lasts for several years and thus limits consumption, leisure, and participation opportunities in a permanent way. The high and entrenched poverty in Southern Europe in contrast to Eastern Europe cannot be explained by higher social protection expenditure in Central and Eastern Europe. On the contrary: in 2013, for example, the expenditure on social protection as a share of the GDP in the Czech Republic was 20.2% of GDP and in Greece 26.4%. The egalitarian socialist traditions in the Czech Republic and other Central European countries, which were quickly forgotten in the course of the post-socialist transformation processes (Aristei & Perugini, 2012), are less decisive for the more egalitarian income distribution than the higher educational levels among the workforce as well as different growth models: The Central European countries have successfully integrated themselves into the European value chains and produce industrial products at low cost. This enables them to involve more persons into the labour force (Sect. 4.3). This is documented not only in lower poverty rates, but also in a higher share of industrial workers, and higher activity and employment rates (Sect. 5.2). Income risks are concentrated among younger people, migrants, low-skilled workers with simple tasks, manual workers, the unemployed and single parents.

These spatial and social inequality patterns were examined in more detail in the next step on the basis of indicators for multiple poverty, deprivation and exclusion risks for households and individuals, and multiple employment and wage risks for the labour force. Here again, clear differences between Central and Eastern Europe on the one hand and Southern Europe on the other emerge. While employment risks are very high in Southern Europe, as the euro crisis was primarily a labour market crisis, multiple poverty risks are more pronounced in Eastern Europe. In addition to Greece and Portugal, the Central and Eastern European countries without a developed welfare state (especially Bulgaria, Romania, Hungary and the Baltic states) are still in the lead. Compared to Eastern and Southern Europe, the poverty and employment risks are significantly lower in the Northern and Western European states.

The poverty and employment risks of low-skilled workers with simple tasks are extraordinarily high. Compared to academics and problem-solving jobs, their risks are ten times higher. The multiple disadvantages of women, single parents, migrants or young people, on the other hand, are lower, although public and academic debate focuses mainly on these disadvantages. As expected in a modern society (Parsons, 1970), disadvantages due to acquired characteristics are far more important than disadvantages due to ascribed characteristics. The European welfare states have succeeded in reducing the determinants of social inequalities in many areas that are based on ascription and thus perceived as illegitimate and discriminatory. This has been achieved, on the one hand, by non-discrimination rules (for example, by Article 21 of the Charter of Fundamental Rights of the European Union) and, on the other hand, through intra-familial and welfare state forms of redistribution. The flip side of this meritocratic turn, however, is considerable disparities between different social classes, employment groups and levels of education. The European Union is thus characterised by the territorial and social concentration of multiple, permanent and entrenched forms of disadvantage and patterns of division. Winners and losers can be clearly distinguished.

Social inequalities thus can be legitimised to a considerable extent in meritocratic terms, i.e. as the result of successes or failures in the education and employment system. Meritocratic justifications of inequality are the basis for the legitimacy of modern societies. In some cases, it is even disputed that performance-related forms of inequality are inequalities at all and not just differences:

> Even under competitive conditions, better qualified people earn more, but wage differentials only compensate for additional expenses for training. In this respect, such differences do not actually exist, but only in appearance. Permanent income differentials are only possible if one departs from the model of full competition. (Berger, 2004, 368; own translation)

In comparison to this market-radical position, other sociological approaches concentrate on criticising the ascriptive allocation of opportunities as discrimination—such as the critique of monopoly rents due to processes of social closure (Sørensen, 1983), the role of social origins for educational opportunities (Bourdieu, 1984) or the role of inherited wealth (Piketty, 2014). Meritocratically based forms of inequality thus might implicitly be considered as legitimate in these approaches. However, the acceptance of meritocratically legitimised forms of social inequality reaches its limits in the case of very high inequalities. Rosanvallon (2013, pp. 255–256) distinguishes three reasons for this: Firstly, the idea of equal opportunities delegitimises welfare state redistribution that is based on the principle of equality of outcomes. Second, it often goes hand in hand with the approval of personal enrichment. Thirdly, due to the lack of a definition of a "minimum level of resources society ought to provide[,] [e]quality of opportunity is often linked to compassion but not to social rights." Even if basic social security is accepted for humanitarian reasons, it is no longer understood as a social right of citizens. High inequalities can thus undermine welfare state forms of redistribution and the ethical foundations of meritocracies.

These challenges to meritocratically legitimised inequalities can be most easily illustrated by the American example: According to Hall (2017), resistance to redistribution also reflects a belief in high social mobility that has long since ceased to exist (Corak, 2013; OECD, 2018). Second, in the US, top earners' (the top 0.1%) share of total income has risen from about 3% in the 1970s to over 12% in 2000. It is now higher than at the beginning of the twentieth century (Atkinson et al., 2011, p. 8). Even if these top earnings are often earnings from employment and not from capital, these inequalities have lost their legitimacy even in the USA, as shown by several movies on the financial crisis (Too big to fail, The Big Short, 99 Homes, Margin Call . . .) or by the discussion on "deaths by despair" (Case & Deaton, 2020). The journalist Nicholas Kristof (2020) describes these deaths through drug addiction, suicide and alcoholism in a very touching way, using the example of his former classmates. However, these stories are not only narratives "from the new world". Given the extraordinarily high level of educational, class and occupational inequalities, the meritocratic legitimisation of inequalities might also reach its limits in Europe as indicated by populist and Eurosceptic movements (Manow, 2019).

In sum: social inequalities can only partly be explained by classic, non-economically justified discrimination against migrants, young people, older people and women. Instead of these ascriptive characteristics, educational and occupational achievements and social class play a central role in the distribution of social opportunities and risks. This chapter has highlighted the concentration of risks and disadvantages among unskilled workers. Such an accumulation of risks points to the dark side of a meritocracy, which the British sociologist and politician Michael Young described as early as 1958 (Young, 1994). In this essay, the author satirically described the division of a society into a school-legitimised, achievement-oriented and power-conscious elite and a detached, disenfranchised underclass of losers who failed early in the school system. Social status was no longer legitimised by birth but by educational success. According to Young, educational certificates became the basis of a new ruling class, while people who failed in the school system were permanently disadvantaged in all areas of society and could not even raise their voices in the political system because they had been deprived of their once eloquent and charismatic leaders through individualised advancement and education. The new meritocratically legitimised inequalities feel even more bitter than the old inequalities legitimised by social origins, because the losers in this meritocratic competition will in general attribute their failure to themselves. The territorial and social fractures described in this chapter thus point to the extent of such a meritocratic legitimisation of social inequalities in Europe as well.

# References

Acemoglu, D., & Autor, D. (2011). Skills, tasks and technologies: Implications for employment and earnings. In D. E. Card & O. Ashenfelter (Eds.), *Handbooks in economics: Vol. 5. Handbook of labor economics: Volume 4B* (1st ed., Vol. 4, pp. 1043–1171). North-Holland. https://doi.org/10.1016/S0169-7218(11)02410-5.

Alkire, S., & Foster, J. (2011). Counting and multidimensional poverty measurement. *Journal of Public Economics, 95*(7–8), 476–487. https://doi.org/10.1016/j.jpubeco.2010.11.006

Andreß, H.-J., & Lohmann, H. (Eds.). (2008). *The working poor in Europe: Employment, poverty and globalisation.* Edward Elgar.

Aristei, D., & Perugini, C. (2012). Inequality and reforms in transition countries. *Economic Systems, 36*(1), 2–10.

Atkinson, A. B., Guio, A.-C., & Marlier, É. (Eds.). (2017). *Statistical books / Eurostat. Monitoring social inclusion in Europe* (2017 edition). Publication Office of the EU. Retrieved from https://publications.europa.eu/en/publication-detail/-/publication/42ce7bf1-3f63-11e7-a08e-01aa75ed71a1/language-en https://doi.org/10.2785/60152

Atkinson, A. B., Marlier, E., & Nolan, B. (2004). Indicators and targets for social inclusion in the European Union. *Journal of Common Market Studies, 42*(1), 47–75.

Atkinson, A. B., Piketty, T., & Saez, E. (2011). Top incomes in the long run of history. *Journal of Economic Literature, 49*(1), 3–71. https://doi.org/10.1257/jel.49.1.3

Autor, D. H., Levy, F., & Murnane, R. J. (2003). The skill content of recent technological change: An empirical exploration. *Quarterly Journal of Economics, 118*(4), 1279–1333.

Bahle, T., Hubl, V., & Pfeifer, M. (2011). *The last safety net: A handbook of minimum income protection in Europe.* Policy Press. https://doi.org/10.2307/j.ctt9qgs60

Beckfield, J., Bambra, C., Eikemo, T. A., Huijts, T., McNamara, C., & Wendt, C. (2015). An institutional theory of welfare state effects on the distribution of population health. *Social Theory & Health, 13*(3–4), 227–244.

Berger, J. (2004). Über den Ursprung der Ungleichheit unter den Menschen. *Zeitschrift für Soziologie, 33*(5), 354–374. https://doi.org/10.1515/zfsoz-2004-0501

Blanchard, O. (2006). European unemployment: The evolution of facts and ideas. *Economic Policy, 21*(45), 6–59. https://doi.org/10.1111/j.1468-0327.2006.00153.x

Bourdieu, P. (1984). *Distinction: A social critique of the judgement of taste.* Harvard University Press.

Bourdieu, P., Accardo, A., & Ferguson, P. P. (1999). *The weight of the world: Social suffering in contemporary society* (P. P. Ferguson, Trans.). Stanford University Press.

Bundesministerium für Arbeit und Soziales. (2021). *Lebenslagen in Deutschland: Der sechste Armuts- und Reichtumsbericht der Bundesregierung.* Retrieved from https://www.bmas.de

Case, A., & Deaton, A. (2015). Rising morbidity and mortality in midlife among white non-Hispanic Americans in the 21st century. *Proceedings of the National Academy of Sciences of the United States of America, 112*(49), 15078–15083. https://doi.org/10.1073/pnas.1518393112

Case, A., & Deaton, A. (2020). *Deaths of despair and the future of capitalism.* Princeton University Press.

Clark, A. E., Frijters, P., & Shields, M. A. (2008). Relative income, happiness, and utility: An explanation for the Easterlin paradox and other puzzles. *Journal of Economic Literature, 46*(1), 95–144.

Corak, M. (2013). Income inequality, equality of opportunity, and intergenerational mobility. *Journal of Economic Perspectives, 27*(3), 79–102. https://doi.org/10.1257/jep.27.3.79

Coser, L. A. (1965). The sociology of poverty: To the memory of Georg Simmel. *Social Problems, 13*, 140–148.

Council of the European Union. (2004). *Joint report by the Commission and the Council on social inclusion* (No. 7101/04). Council of the European Union Brussels. Retrieved from https://ec.europa.eu/employment_social/soc-prot/soc-incl/joint_rep_en.htm

Darvas, Z. (2019). Why is it so hard to reach the EU's poverty target? *Social Indicators Research, 141*(3), 1081–1105. https://doi.org/10.1007/s11205-018-1872-9

Delhey, J., & Dragolov, G. (2014). Why inequality makes Europeans less happy: The role of distrust, status anxiety, and perceived conflict. *European Sociological Review, 30*(2), 151–165.

Delhey, J., & Kohler, U. (2006). From nationally bounded to Pan-European inequalities? On the importance of foreign countries as reference groups. *European Sociological Review, 22*(2), 125–140.

Diener, E. (2000). Subjective well-being: The science of happiness and a proposal for a national index. *American Psychologist, 55*(1), 34.

Diener, E. (2009). Subjective well-being. In E. Diener (Ed.), *Social indicators research series: Vol. 37. The science of well-being: The collected works of Ed Diener* (pp. 11–58). Springer.

Dörre, K. (2014). Precarity and Social Disintegration: A Relational Concept. *Journal Für Entwicklungspolitik, 30*(4), 69–89.

Esping-Andersen, G. (1990). *The three worlds of welfare capitalism.* Princeton University Press.

Fahey, T. (2007). The case for an EU-wide measure of poverty. *European Sociological Review, 23*(1), 35–47.

Featherstone, K. (2011). The Greek sovereign debt crisis and EMU: A failing state in a skewed regime. *Journal of Common Market Studies, 49*(2), 193–217. https://doi.org/10.1111/j.1468-5965.2010.02139.x

Ferrera, M. (1996). The 'Southern model' of welfare in social Europe. *Journal of European Social Policy, 6*(1), 17–37.

Gaisbauer, H. P., Schweiger, G., & Sedmak, C. (Eds.). (2019). *Absolute poverty in Europe: Interdisciplinary perspectives on a hidden phenomenon.* Policy Press. https://doi.org/10.2307/j.ctvf3w3zg

Goebel, J., & Krause, P. (2018). Quantitative Messung von Armut. In P. Böhnke, J. Dittmann, & J. Goebel (Eds.), *UTB Sozialwissenschaften: Vol. 4957. Handbuch Armut: Ursachen, Trends, Maßnahmen* (pp. 56–68). Verlag Barbara Budrich.

Goos, M., & Manning, A. (2007). Lousy and lovely jobs: The rising polarization of work in Britain. *The Review of Economics and Statistics, 89*(1), 118–133.

Hall, P. A. (2017). The political sources of social solidarity. In K. G. Banting & W. Kymlicka (Eds.), *The strains of commitment: The political sources of solidarity in diverse societies* (1st ed., pp. 201–232). Oxford University Press.

Halleröd, B., & Larsson, D. (2008). Poverty, welfare problems and social exclusion. *International Journal of Social Welfare, 17*(1), 15–25. https://doi.org/10.1111/j.1468-2397.2007.00503.x

Heidenreich, M. (2015). The end of the honeymoon: The increasing differentiation of (long-term) unemployment risks in Europe. *Journal of European Social Policy, 25*(4), 393–413. https://doi.org/10.1177/0958928715594544

Heidenreich, M. (2016). The double dualization of inequality in Europe: Introduction. In M. Heidenreich (Ed.), *Exploring inequality in Europe* (pp. 1–21). Edward Elgar.

Heidenreich, M., & Rice, D. (2016). Integrating social and employment policies at the local level: Conceptual and empirical challenges. In M. Heidenreich & D. Rice (Eds.), *Integrating social and employment policies in Europe* (pp. 16–50). Edward Elgar.

Himmelfarb, G. (1984). The idea of poverty. *History Today, 34*(4), 22–30.

ILO. (2012). *International standard classification of occupations // Structure, group definitions and correspondence tables: Structure, group definitions and correspondence tables. ISCO-08: Volume 1 // v. 1.* ILO. Retrieved from https://www.ilo.org/public/english/bureau/stat/isco/index.htm

Israel, S. (2016). The Europeanization of social determinants and health in the Great Recession. In M. Heidenreich (Ed.), *Exploring inequality in Europe* (pp. 164–194). Edward Elgar.

Iversen, T., Soskice, D., & Hope, D. (2016). The Eurozone and political economic institutions. *Annual Review of Political Science, 19*, 163–185.

Jahoda, M., Lazarsfeld, P. F., & Zeisel, H. (2002). *Marienthal: The sociography of an unemployed community* (originally published in German in 1933). Transaction (Original work published 1933).

Kahneman, D., & Deaton, A. (2010). High income improves evaluation of life but not emotional well-being. *Proceedings of the National Academy of Sciences, 107*(38), 16489–16493.

Kalleberg, A. L. (2009). Precarious work, insecure workers: Employment relations in transition. *American Sociological Review, 74*(1), 1–22.

Kalleberg, A. L. (2011). *Good jobs, bad jobs: The rise of polarized and precarious employment systems in the United States, 1970s to 2000s.* American Sociological Association's Rose series in sociology. Russell Sage Foundation.

Kalter, F., & Granato, N. (2018). Migration und ethnische Ungleichheit auf dem Arbeitsmarkt. In M. Abraham & T. Hinz (Eds.), *Arbeitsmarktsoziologie: Probleme, Theorien, empirische Befunde* (3rd ed., pp. 355–387). Springer. https://doi.org/10.1007/978-3-658-02256-3_10

Kristof, N. (2020, January 18). Are my friends' deaths their fault or ours? We need to move from pointing fingers to offering helping hands. *New York Times.* Retrieved from https://nyti.ms/3 66iAfZ

Lahusen, C. (2021). *The political attitudes of divided European citizens: Public opinion and social inequalities in comparative and relational perspective.* Routledge. https://doi.org/10.4324/9781003046653

Lahusen, C., & Kiess, J. (2018). 'Subjective Europeanization': Do inner-European comparisons affect life satisfaction? *European Societies, 21*(2), 214–236. https://doi.org/10.1080/14616696.2018.1438638

Leibfried, S., & Tennstedt, F. (1985). Armenpolitik und Arbeiterpolitik: Zur Entwicklung und Krise der traditionellen Sozialpolitik der Verteilungsformen. In S. Leibfried & F. Tennstedt (Eds.), *Politik der Armut und die Spaltung des Sozialstaats.* Suhrkamp.

Lindbeck, A., & Snower, D. (1988). *The insider-outsider theory of employment and unemployment.* MIT Press.

Maitre, B., Nolan, B., & Whelan, C. T. (2012). Low pay, in-work poverty and economic vulnerability: A comparative analysis using EU-SILC. *The Manchester School, 80*(1), 99–116. https://doi.org/10.1111/j.1467-9957.2011.02230.x

Manow, P. (2018). *Die politische Ökonomie des Populismus* (Vol. 2728). Suhrkamp.

Manow, P. (2019). Politischer Populismus als Ausdruck von Identitätspolitik? Über einen ökonomischen Ursachenkomplex. *Aus Politik Und Zeitgeschichte, 69*(9–11), 33–40. Retrieved from http://www.bpb.de/apuz/286510/politischer-populismus-als-ausdruck-von-identitaetspolitik-ueber-einen-oekonomischen-ursachenkomplex?p=all

Markovits, D. (2019). *The meritocracy trap: How America's foundational myth feeds inequality, dismantles the middle class, and devours the elite.* Penguin Press.

Marshall, T. H. (1950). *Citizenship and social class* (Vol. 11). Cambridge University Press.

OECD. (2013). *Guidelines on measuring subjective well-being.* OECD. https://doi.org/10.1787/9789264191655-en

OECD. (2018). *A broken social elevator? How to promote social mobility.* OECD Publishing. https://doi.org/10.1787/9789264301085-en

Palier, B., Rovny, A. E., & Rovny, J. (2018). European disunion? Social and economic divergence in Europe, and their political consequences. In P. Manow, B. Palier, & H. Schwander (Eds.), *Welfare democracies and party politics: Explaining electoral dynamics in times of changing welfare capitalism* (pp. 281–297). Oxford University Press.

Parsons, T. (1970). Equality and inequality in modern society, or social stratification revisited. *Sociological Inquiry, 40*(2), 13–72. https://doi.org/10.1111/j.1475-682X.1970.tb01002.x

Piketty, T. (2014). *Capital in the twenty-first century.* Harvard University Press.

Rodrik, D. (2018). Populism and the economics of globalization. *Journal of International Business Policy, 1*(1–2), 12–33. https://doi.org/10.1057/s42214-018-0001-4

Rosanvallon, P. (2013). *The society of equals.* Harvard University Press. Retrieved from http://search.ebscohost.com/login.aspx?direct=true&scope=site&db=nlebk&db=nlabk&AN=660037

Rose, D., & Harrison, E. (Eds.). (2010). *Social class in Europe: An introduction to the European socio-economic classification* (Vol. 10). Routledge.

Sachs, J. D. (2012). From millennium development goals to sustainable development goals. *The Lancet, 379*(9832), 2206–2211. https://doi.org/10.1016/S0140-6736(12)60685-0

Sacks, D. W., Stevenson, B., & Wolfers, J. (2010). *Subjective well-being, income, economic development and growth* (Working Paper No. 16441). National Bureau of Economic Research. https://doi.org/10.3386/w16441

Sandel, M. J. (2020). *The tyranny of merit: What's become of the common good?* Farrar Strauss & Giroux.

Sen, A. (1993). Capabilities and well-being. In M. C. Nussbaum & A. Sen (Eds.), *Studies in development economics / WIDER. The quality of life* (pp. 30–53). Oxford University Press.

Serrano Pascual, A. (2007). Reshaping welfare states: Activation regimes in Europe. In A. Serrano Pascual & L. Magnusson (Eds.), *Saltsa – joint programme for working life research in Europe: 54 // No. 54. Reshaping welfare states and activation regimes in Europe* (pp. 11–34). Peter Lang.

Simmel, G. (1965). The poor (translated by Claire Jacobson). *Social Problems, 13*(2), 118–140.

Sørensen, A. B. (1983). Processes of allocation to open and closed positions in social structure. *Zeitschrift für Soziologie, 12*(3), 203–224.

Therborn, G. (2013). *The killing fields of inequality.* Polity.

Townsend, P. (1979). *Poverty in the United Kingdom: A survey of household resources and standards of living. Campus: Vol. 242.* University of Chicago Press.

UNDP. (Ed.) (2019). *Human Development Report: Beyond income, beyond averages, beyond today.* Inequalities in human development in the 21st century. LANHAM: Bernan Press.

Veenhoven, R. (1991). Is happiness relative? *Social Indicators Research, 24*(1), 1–34.

Voges, W. (2006). Indikatoren im Lebenslagenansatz: das Konzept der Lebenslage in der Wirkungsforschung. *ZeS Report, 11*(1), 1–6.

Voges, W., Jürgens, O., Mauer, A., & Meyer, E. (2003). *Methoden und Grundlagen des Lebenslagenansatzes: Endbericht.* Bremen.

Weziak-Bialowolska, D. (2016). Spatial variation in EU poverty with respect to health, education and living standards. *Social Indicators Research, 125,* 451–479. https://doi.org/10.1007/s11205-014-0848-7

Whelan, C. T., & Maître, B. (2013). Material deprivation, economic stress, and reference groups in Europe: An analysis of EU-SILC 2009. *European Sociological Review, 29*(6), 1162–1174.

Whiteside, N. (2007). Unemployment revisited in comparative perspective: Labour market policy in Strasbourg and Liverpool, 1890-1914. *International Review of Social History, 52*(1), 35–56. https://doi.org/10.1017/S002085900600277x

Wilkinson, R. G., & Pickett, K. (2010). *The spirit level: Why equality is better for everyone. Pinguin sociology.* Penguin.

Wulfgramm, M. (2014). Life satisfaction effects of unemployment in Europe: The moderating influence of labour market policy. *Journal of European Social Policy, 24*(3), 258–272.

Young, M. D. (1994). *The rise of the meritocracy: With a new introduction by the author.* Transaction Publishers.

# Chapter 9
# Education, Occupational Skills and Social Mobility

**Abstract** In this chapter, educational and occupational inequality within and between European countries is analysed. Europe is divided into countries that rely on an effective education system and employ trained workers for demanding tasks (often in services), and countries with less developed education systems, where lower-skilled workers on average are entrusted with simple and routine tasks. This gap is accompanied by significant social inequalities between different educational strata, occupational groups and social classes. Indicators for these inequalities are different income opportunities and patterns of social mobility. In Europe, children of highly-educated parents are six times more likely to finish high school than other children. This raises the question of how the occupational skills of the workforce evolve in the course of technological and economic change. Three national patterns can be identified. In half of the countries considered, an *upgrading* of skill levels was observed—especially in service-centred Scandinavian and liberal countries and in some Continental European countries. In more industrialised countries, on the other hand, a *polarisation* can be observed. In a third group of countries, those with a higher share of personal services, even an expansion of lower-paid jobs, i.e. a *downgrading* of the occupational structure, can be observed. While skill upgrading is associated with a gap between higher- and lower-skilled workers, specialisation in lower value-added activities is associated with educational poverty and polarised occupational structures.

Education and occupational skills are a crucial foundation for economic growth (Chap. 4), for labour market, earnings and income opportunities (Chaps. 5–7) for life satisfaction, and participation in society. The previous chapter emphasised the central importance of educational degrees for social status. The French sociologist Pierre Bourdieu has also pointed out that the modern school system has fundamentally changed the way social inequalities are reproduced. A family-based reproduction of social inequalities (for example, through birth, inheritance or the use of family contacts) has been transformed into a *family-based reproduction of social inequalities with an educational component*—sometimes termed a school-mediated or scholastic mode of reproduction (Bourdieu, 1984, 1996). The offspring of privileged families still have considerably better chances of attaining a higher

© The Author(s), under exclusive license to Springer Nature Switzerland AG 2022    247
M. Heidenreich, *Territorial and Social Inequalities in Europe*,
https://doi.org/10.1007/978-3-031-12630-7_9

education. These advantages, however, are less the result of the direct inheritance of economic and cultural capital, but they rather reflect the advantages of children from higher social classes in the education system and in the acquisition of diplomas and other educational titles. Unlike property titles, educational titles cannot simply be inherited, but must be acquired. This is also risky for children from well-off families, as they can fail in the school system (Bourdieu, 1996, p. 287). However, due to their better starting conditions and more extensive family support, these risks are considerably lower than for children from simpler backgrounds, who may be disadvantaged in numerous dimensions (housing conditions, local schools, social networks, parental support, self-confidence ...). The overall societal advantage of a school-mediated reproduction of social inequalities is its higher legitimisation, since inequalities can now be justified meritocratically through achievements in the school system. However, this points to the role of the state, since it must certify and guarantee the value of the acquired cultural capital:

> The more the competences measured are recognized by the school system, and the more 'academic' the techniques used to measure them, the stronger is the relation between performance and educational competences. The latter, as a more or less adequate indicator of the number of years of scholastic inculcation, guarantees cultural capital more or less completely, depending on whether it is inherited from the family or acquired at school, and so it is an unequally adequate indicator of this capital. (Bourdieu, 1984, p. 13).

In order to play out its full effectiveness, at least in the labour market, cultural capital increasingly requires confirmation through the education system, that is, its transformation into educational titles. Bourdieu thus understands educational and academic titles as state-institutionalised, legally guaranteed forms of cultural capital. The state is the guarantor of the value of an educational title, in a sense the central bank for symbolic capital (Wacquant & Bourdieu, 1993, p. 39). The education system has become "the sole and supreme guarantor of all professional titles" (Bourdieu, 1991, p. 26).

Thus, education systems are closely linked to national structures and policies. A Europeanisation of education, occupational skills and class structures can only be expected to a limited extent. However, national education systems are also opening up as educational and vocational titles are being compared across Europe and the world (for example through the OECD's PISA studies or through the ISCED and ISCO classifications explained below). Educational and professional skills are also increasingly being recognised across Europe as a prerequisite for cross-border labour mobility. The most advanced field is certainly the Europeanisation of academic education (Maassen & Musselin, 2009). This was made possible by the concerted reform of university courses within the framework of the Bologna Process to create a single European Higher Education Area. The Erasmus programme has also enabled greater mobility of students and teachers. Some European Schools are also driving these Europeanisation processes (Drewski et al., 2018). This is accompanied by a Europeanisation of research through the European Research Framework Programmes and the European Research Council (Gengnagel et al., 2019). Since 2002, the EU has also been trying to harmonise vocational training systems across borders (Powell & Trampusch, 2012). Educational, vocational and academic titles are thus on the one hand the result of national policies and education systems, but on the other hand are increasingly compared, regulated, reformed and used across Europe.

In this chapter, attention is drawn to another factor that shapes skill and class structures at least as much as national or European institutions: economic and technological change, the opportunities to specialise or not in advanced industries and services, and thus the central or peripheral position of the respective country or region in the European space.

This raises the question of the winners and losers in the competition for higher educational titles, occupational skills and professional positions in a cross-border and European context as well: Which countries, regions and social groups are the winners of such a competition? Where are educational poverty,[1] exclusion and the polarisation of occupational skills concentrated? And to what extent are educational inequalities transmitted intergenerationally, thus limiting the chances of intergenerational mobility? And which factors favour higher intergenerational mobility? These questions are discussed below in five steps: First, the national patterns of educational and occupational inequalities are described (Sect. 9.1). Summarising previous results it is then argued that Europeans' income and labour market opportunities are determined to a considerable extent by their educational degrees and occupational skills (Sect. 9.2). In the next step, intergenerational mobility is examined (Sect. 9.3). With the increasing importance of educational attainment, educational poverty becomes a central dimension of social exclusion. In Sect. 9.4, national and regional patterns of educational poverty and their structural determinants are analysed. Then the discussion turns to whether technological change and the Europeanisation and globalisation of the economy lead to an increase or a polarisation of occupational structures (Sect. 9.5). In a final outlook, education policies in Europe are located between the Scylla of meritocratic divisions and the Charybdis of educational poverty and the polarisation and devaluation of skills (Sect. 9.6). An important insight is that education and occupational skills are not only determined by institutions, but also by national and regional economic structures and growth models.

---

[1] Educational poverty is understood as a level of education "that is insufficient in a society for equal participation in the labour market and social life" (Solga, 2017, 447; own translation). Educational poverty can be operationalised by low education (Lohauß et al., 2010), this is the share of the population that has completed at most lower secondary education (ISCED 0–2).

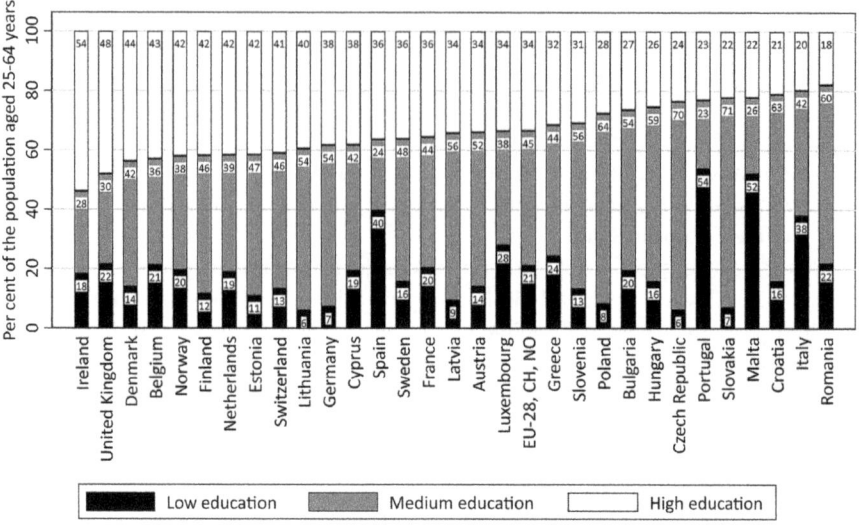

Source: EU-SILC 2018.

**Fig. 9.1** Educational attainment of the 25–64 year-old population in the EU-28, Switzerland and Norway (2018)

## 9.1 National patterns of education, occupations and social classes

The concept of education focuses on the skills and competences of a person that have been systematically acquired within the framework of professional or vocational training or an educational institution. The acquired competences are usually formally certified by a diploma. The recognition of certain skills and competences and their transferability are the subject of social processes of interpretation, definition and negotiation. This social construction of education is highlighted by the sociologist Pierre Bourdieu (1983), who analysed education as cultural capital and educational certificates as institutionalised cultural capital. At the same time, the level of education is the result of individual educational decisions, which also depend on the expected costs and returns. Human capital theory (Becker, 1993) focuses on these calculations. In recent decades, education has become an increasingly important prerequisite for the population's social status, occupational success and social mobility as well as a country's prosperity. This raises the question of the international comparability of educational certificates produced by different national education systems. The most common international scale of educational attainment is the International Standard Classification of Education (ISCED), developed by UNESCO, which distinguishes nine broad categories (ISCED 0–8) and a residual category (9). These are often grouped together as low (ISCED 0–2), medium (ISCED 3–4) and high levels of education (ISCED 5–8; cf. Fig. 9.1).

Educational levels in Europe vary greatly from country to country (Fig. 9.1). While about half of the Irish and British have a high, usually academic education,

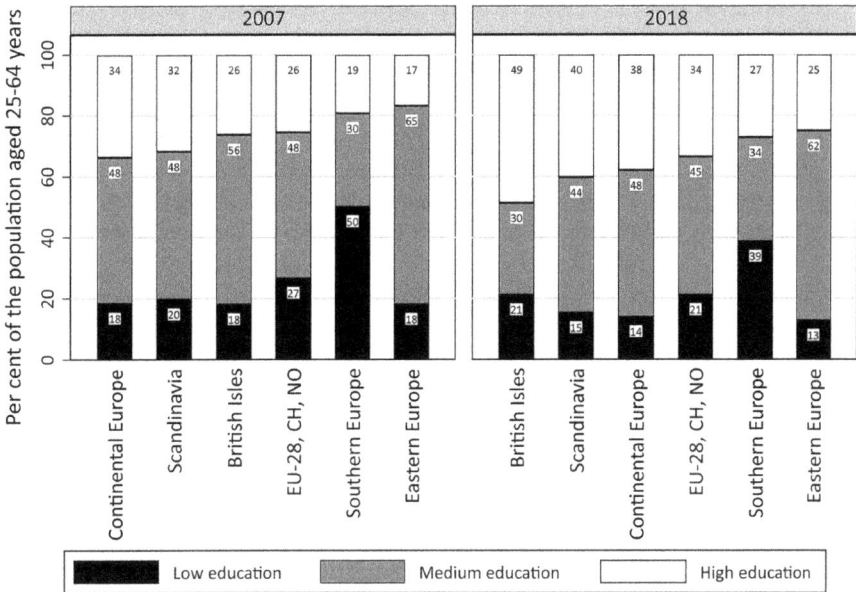

Source: Own calculations on the basis of EU-SILC 2007 and 2018.

**Fig. 9.2** Educational attainment in five European country groups (2007 and 2018)

less than a fifth of Romanians, Italians, Croats, Maltese, Slovaks, Portuguese and Czechs aged 25–64 have attended university. As already mentioned earlier (Chap. 4), over a third of Spaniards, Italians, Portuguese and Maltese have only a low level of education, i.e. primary or lower secondary education (ISCED 0–2).

Formal education levels of 25–64-year-olds are highest in Scandinavia and the British Isles, and lowest in Southern and Eastern Europe (Fig. 9.2). The rapid academicisation of the working-age population on the British Isles and in Scandinavia over the period 2007–2018 is noteworthy. These differences also reflect the respective national economic structures—for example, deindustrialisation and a stronger service orientation (Chap. 4). The share of people with a low level of education has declined most in Southern Europe. At 39%, however, it is still far above the average for other country groups. On the one hand, this points to the lack of a vocational training system at the national level and to the often only local organisation of vocational training in classic industrial districts such as in central Italy or the Basque Country (cf. Piore & Sabel, 1984). The low proportion of low-skilled workers in Central and Eastern Europe is remarkable (2007: 18%: 2018: 13%)—an indication of the high value of formal education in many of the former socialist "workers' and peasants' states" which partly also have a deeply rooted industrial legacy (in particular in Czechia). The largely stable level of intermediate education in Central and Eastern Europe (65% and 62% respectively), but also in Continental Europe (48%), points to the continued importance of industrial and industry-related activities and sectors (Chap. 4).

The differences in educational levels between European countries raise the question whether these differences correspond to factual differences in competences. At the aggregate national level, this is only the case to a limited extent (Fig. 9.3). Measured against the reading literacy of 15-year-olds as determined by the OECD's PISA study (for 2018 or for Spain for 2015), one should expect, for example a very low proportion of low-educated persons in Estonia, because Estonia is the European leader in reading literacy, but also in science and mathematics literacy (with 523, 523 and 530 points respectively). Instead, 21% of Estonian young people have a low education, well above the European average. Reading skills in Spain, Portugal and Italy are also significantly higher than could be expected given the high proportion of young people with a low education. At the other end of the spectrum is Cyprus, where low reading skills (424 points) are accompanied by a very low proportion of educationally poor young people (9% in 2018). The factual competence levels of the younger population in some Southern European countries may thus be better than the level indicated by the formal educational level. The surprisingly weak correlation between competences and educational attainment shows that—as Bourdieu (1984, 1996) has expected—educational titles are the result of national assessment and classification strategies. The "conversion rate" of competencies such as the mathematical, scientific and reading competencies measured by the OECD into formal certificates differs from country to country—or even from region to region, as evidenced by the discussions on the relative significance of a baccalaureate obtained in Bremen or Bavaria. Despite the efforts of international organisations and research projects, educational titles can therefore only be compared internationally to a limited extent. Even alternative indicators such as the number of years spent in the education system (Schneider, 2010) do not solve this problem. However, this does not mean that formal education titles are meaningless. Formal certificates (or their absence) may well lead to people being excluded from privileged positions and situations regardless of actual competences. The famous Thomas theorem ("If people define situations as real, they are real in their consequences") also applies to educational titles.

In contrast to education, an occupation is characterised by the skills and knowledge required to perform the demands associated with a particular task. These include functionally required and extra-functional competences such as loyalty, punctuality, sense of responsibility, diligence, flexibility, perceptiveness, technical intelligence and technical sensitivity, but also key qualifications such as the ability to work autonomously and in teams, intrinsic work motivation, communication skills, and the ability to learn, which is necessary to cope with open and complex situations. International comparability of occupations and the related skill requirements is usually based on the International Standard Classification of Occupations (ISCO) proposed by the International Labour Organization (ILO), which at its most general level distinguishes ten different main occupational groups (ISCO-08: 0–9) (managers, academic occupations, technicians, clerical workers, service occupations, farmers, skilled workers, machine operators, unskilled workers, soldiers). The ILO (2012) has combined these groups into four skill groups (see Appendix 1). These range from simple and routine tasks to problem-solving skills and creativity.

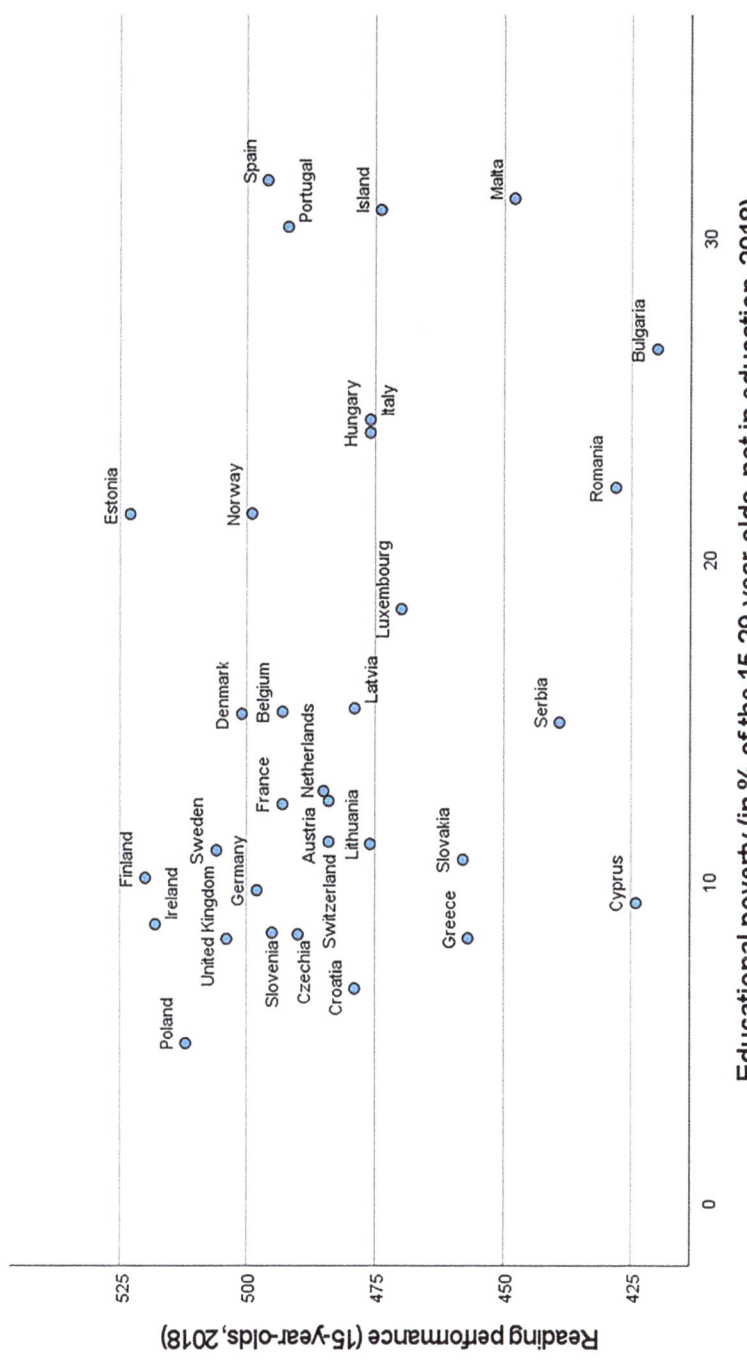

**Fig. 9.3** Relationship between formal national educational and competence levels (2018)

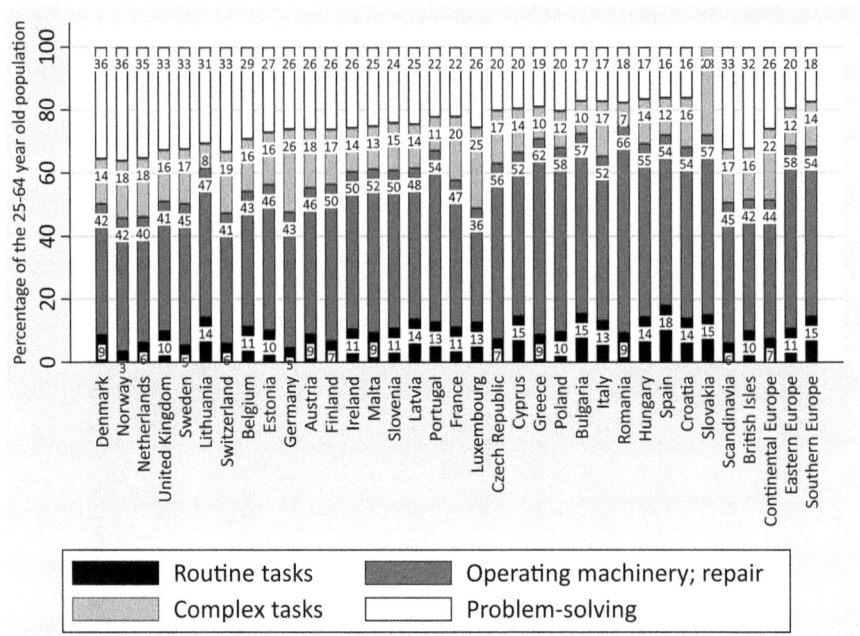

**Fig. 9.4** Occupational and skill levels of the working-age population in the EU-28, Switzerland and Norway (2018). Source: EU-SILC 2018

The occupational structures differ from country to country (Fig. 9.4). While in Denmark, the Netherlands, the United Kingdom or Sweden, Norway, Switzerland, Germany and Luxembourg about half of 25–64-year-olds are engaged in complex and problem-solving activities, this is the case for only one third or less of the working-age population in 12 mostly Central and Eastern European countries, but also in Spain and Portugal. This also points to the different economic structures. While the Scandinavian and Anglo-Saxon countries focus on more demanding service activities, in Southern, Central and Eastern Europe the focus is on simple and routine tasks, especially in industry, but also in agriculture and the service sector. Routine activities in particular are threatened by the automation and digitalisation of the economy (Arntz et al., 2018; Autor et al., 2003; Goos & Manning, 2007) and the related employment and wage risks.

Given the different economic and occupational structures of the European countries, it can be expected that the class structure also differs. This is indeed the case (Fig. 9.5). The class scheme used is the European Socio-Economic Classification (ESEC), which focuses on the distinction between employers, self-employed and employees. Employees are in turn differentiated into (organisationally controllable) labour contracts and service relationships characterised by higher human capital (Müller et al., 2007; Rose & Harrison, 2010). Rose and Harrison (2010, p. 11) sum up the sociological content of this distinction, which is at the heart of the ESEC classification:

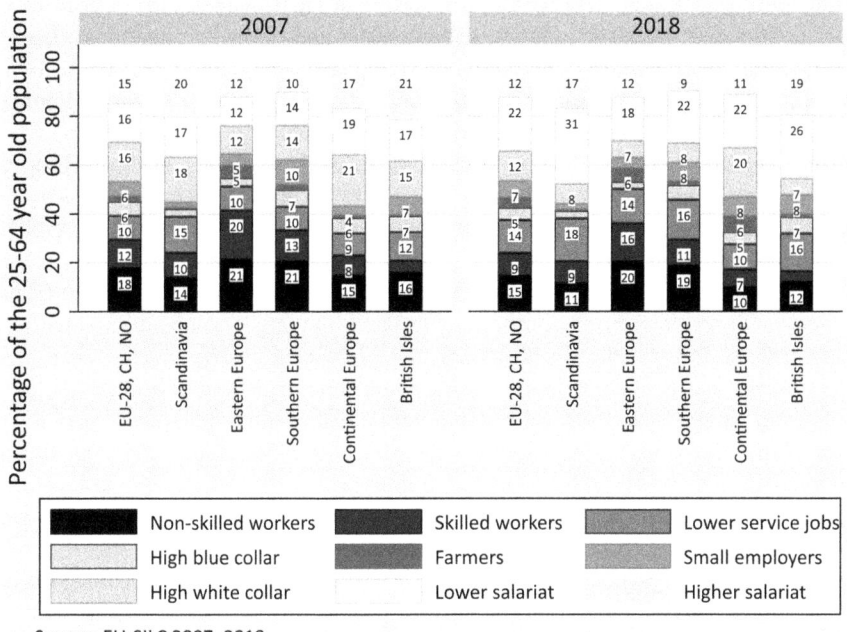

Source: EU-SILC 2007, 2018.

**Fig. 9.5** Social classes in five European country groups (2007 and 2018). Source: EU-SILC 2007, 2018

[D]ifferent modes of regulating employment emerge on account of two contractual hazards faced by employers; those of work monitoring and human asset specificity (...) Monitoring problems are particularly difficult when the amount and quality of work cannot be scrutinized directly or easily (...) Asset specificity concerns the amounts of job- or organization-specific skills, expertise and knowledge (...) and/or the investments by the employer in employees' work competences (...) Work situations with low monitoring problems and low asset specificity can be adequately and efficiently handled by a 'labour contract' (...) for work situations with high monitoring problems and high asset specificity (...), the 'service relationship' is a more adequate and better suited response.

Nine different social classes emerge, at the top the upper service class or "*higher salariat*" comprising higher grade professionals and engineers, administrative and managerial occupations, managers and owners of large enterprises (2007: 15%; 2018: 12% of workforce), and at the bottom routine occupations performed by *nonskilled and semi-skilled workers* (2007: 18%; 2018: 15%). The upper service class comprises 12% of the European workforce. Its share is particularly high in Scandinavia and the British Isles, and particularly low in Southern, Central and Eastern Europe. The *lower salariat*, i.e. lower grade professional, administrative and managerial occupations and higher grade technicians and supervisory occupations is an expanding class. Its share has increased from 16% to 22% from 2007–2018. Unlike the upper service class, this class is not only particularly large in Scandinavia and the British Isles, but also in Continental Europe. It is smallest in the Central and Eastern European countries. The strong expansion of this class also seems to have been partly caused by the upgrading of intermediate services, sales and clerical occupations ("*higher grade white-collar workers*"). Their share has fallen from 16% to 12%. However, the share of lower services, sales and clerical occupations ("*lower grade white-collar workers*") has increased European-wide from 10% (2007) to 14% (2018). As expected, the share of *semi- and unskilled and skilled workers* (routine workers and lower technical occupations) are particularly high in Central and Eastern European countries (2007: 41%; 2018: 36%). Their share is also surprisingly high in Southern Europe (2007: 34%; 2018: 30%). It is higher than in heavily industrialised Continental Europe, where the share of unskilled and skilled workers has fallen from 23% to 17%. The surprisingly high share of semi-, un- and skilled workers in Southern Europe points to artisanal and small- and medium-sized companies. In Continental Europe, on the other hand, the larger companies, which are more oriented towards the world market, have relocated their production and thus also routine tasks to some extent to China and Central and Eastern Europe.

In sum: The educational level of the Southern European population is very low, even if the competences measured by the OECD's PISA studies are sometimes comparable to those of pupils in other countries with a higher educational level. In Continental, Central and Eastern Europe, the middle educational level plays an important role, while the Scandinavian and Anglo-Saxon countries focus on academic education. Low levels of education especially in Southern Europe, but also in Central and Eastern Europe, mean that fewer people have the educational titles that give them access to good employment, earnings and life opportunities. In addition, the demand for academically qualified workers is also lower in Continental, Southern and Eastern Europe than in Scandinavian and Anglo-Saxon countries, as more people are entrusted with manual and routine tasks and thus exposed to higher labour market risks. Class structures in Europe differ considerably between the countries and country groups: On the one hand, there are the service-centred countries in Scandinavia and the British Isles, but also in Continental Europe. These countries are characterised by higher employment shares of the upper and lower service classes and skilled service occupations. On the other hand, there are the Southern, Eastern and Central European countries with a lower service share and a higher share of unskilled and skilled workers. The social divisions which are the result of these class structures will be discussed in the next two sections.

## 9.2   Income and Labour Market Inequalities Between Social Classes

The employment, wage and income inequalities between different educational levels, occupational groups and social classes have already been touched upon in previous chapters. However, in these chapters individual characteristics were mostly treated as control variables. In the following, the results from the previous chapters will first be summarised in order to highlight the diverging income and employment opportunities related to different educational and occupational levels and social classes.

The analysis of European labour markets (Chap. 5) showed that, taking into account other individual control variables, the *labour force participation of* people with a high level of education is almost 10 percentage points higher than that of people with a low level of education (Fig. 5.2). The differences between the various occupational groups are much smaller: machine operators have a four percentage points lower labour force participation and employees with routine tasks even have a higher labour force participation than persons with complex tasks. The risk of being *unemployed, low-paid, temporarily employed, involuntarily part-time employed or self-employed without employees* is 89 per cent higher for persons with low education in 2014–2018 than for persons with academic education (Fig. 5.7). Those employed in routine tasks are 25 points more likely to be unemployed than those with creative or problem-solving jobs. The *risk of long-term unemployment* is about 12 percentage points higher for people with low education than for academics (Fig. 5.10). Machine operators and routine workers have a 3–4 percentage points higher risk than problem-solvers. Occupations and the educational level are also key determinants of wage and income opportunities: The *gross wages* of low-skilled workers are a quarter lower than those of academics (Fig. 6.9). The upper service class earns 26% more per hour than employees with routine tasks. A quarter of the low-skilled and manual workers earn only a low wage (Fig. 6.9). 29.3% of the employees with routine tasks were remunerated with *low wages* in 2018, in contrast to only 6.4% of employees with problem-solving and decision-making functions and 7.2% of the members of the upper service class (Table 6.4). Low-skilled workers have about four times the *poverty risk* of high-skilled workers (2013: 28% vs. 8%; Table 8.1). Employees with simple jobs have a five times higher poverty risk than problem-solvers.

These figures give an impression of the profound social divisions along the dimensions of education, occupation and social class. However, the focus of the previous chapters was mainly on national and European patterns of social inequalities and their institutional determinants. Individual determinants of social situation have been treated mostly as control variables. Therefore, analogous to Table 6.3, the income situation of European households will now be used as an example to reconstruct how the educational, occupational skills and class situation determine the level of disposable income (Fig. 9.6 and Table 9.1) taking into account age, gender, migration status, and household type as control variables. The coefficients of the following models can be interpreted as percentages because the logarithmised values of disposable household income were used (Fig. 9.6). A first result is that the disposable incomes of unskilled people are 31% lower than the incomes of high-skilled people. These income gaps are even larger than the wage gaps between high and low skilled (Table 6.3). This points to the accumulation of social advantages and disadvantages: Highly qualified people choose corresponding partners. Birds of a feather flock together (Blossfeld & Timm, 2003). The income difference between working-class and upper service class households is about 21%. This is as high as the corresponding wage differences (Table 6.3). The income advantage of the upper

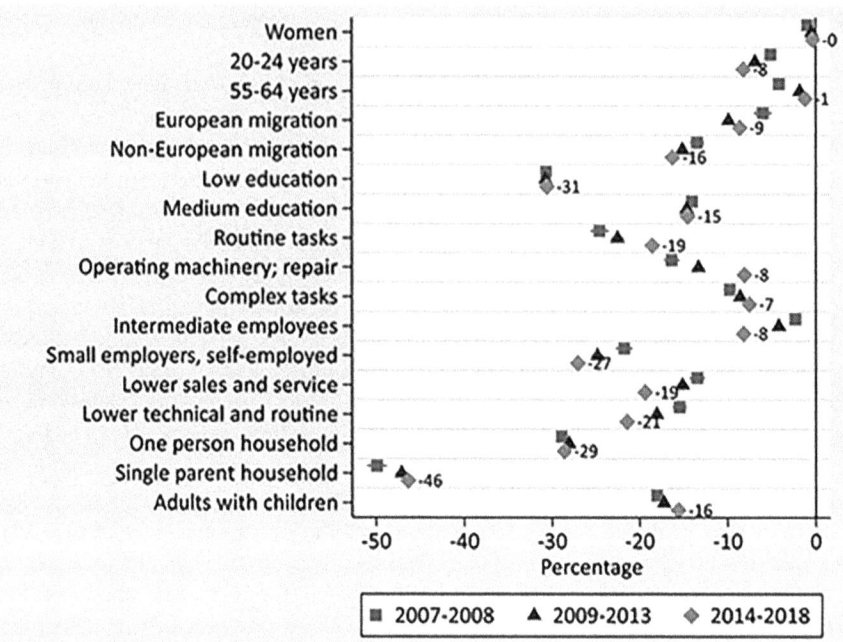

Source: EU SILC 2007-2018. Multivariate multilevel regression with the logarithmised level of real disposable income as dependent variable based on EU-SILC 2007-2018. 50% sample. Income data refer to the previous year. Until 2010 without Croatia. The figure shows percentage differences in disposable income compared to the reference group. The reference groups are academically qualified, native men from the upper service class aged 25-54 with problem-solving jobs who live in households without children.

**Fig. 9.6** Educational, occupational and class-specific determinants of disposable income (EU-28, Switzerland, Norway; 2007–2018)

service class (higher professions and engineers; senior administrative professions, managers and owners of large enterprises) over lower technical employees and skilled workers is thus considerable. It has also increased significantly since the beginning of the financial market and euro crises. The differences between the most demanding activities (problem-solving, decision-making) and routine work, machine and plant operators are becoming smaller. It can thus be stated that the income differences between different educational strata are permanently high, while the income differences between the social classes are even increasing and the income differences between different occupational groups are somewhat decreasing. The latter reinforces DiPrete (2007), who warned against focusing primarily on inequalities between different occupations instead of income inequalities, as differences *within different occupational* groups might increase due to technological and economic changes. A focus on differences between different occupational groups could therefore imply that other causes of increasing inequalities are ignored.

In the next step, these results will be specified for the five country groups which can be distinguished in Europe (Table 9.1). While the disposable income of low-skilled households is overall about one third lower than that of academic

**Table 9.1**  Education, occupational skills and class as determinants of disposable income in five European country groups (2007–2018; EU-28, Switzerland, Norway)

| | British Isles | Continental Europe | Southern Europe | Central and Eastern Europe | Scandinavia |
|---|---|---|---|---|---|
| *Education (Ref. high)* | | | | | |
| Low education (ISCED 0–2) | −0.250*** (0.004) | −0.222*** (0.002) | −0.361*** (0.003) | −0.428*** (0.002) | −0.169*** (0.003) |
| Medium education (ISCED 3–4) | −0.136*** (0.004) | −0.124*** (0.002) | −0.162*** (0.003) | −0.245*** (0.002) | −0.065*** (0.002) |
| *Occupational group (ref. problem- solving)* | | | | | |
| Simple and routine tasks | −0.161*** (0.010) | −0.235*** (0.004) | −0.254*** (0.005) | −0.232*** (0.004) | −0.169*** (0.006) |
| Operating machinery; repair | −0.115*** (0.008) | −0.160*** (0.003) | −0.146*** (0.005) | −0.111*** (0.004) | −0.085*** (0.005) |
| Complex tasks | −0.101*** (0.005) | −0.106*** (0.002) | −0.107*** (0.003) | −0.047*** (0.003) | −0.065*** (0.003) |
| *Social class (Ref. upper service class)* | | | | | |
| Intermediate employees | −0.117*** (0.007) | −0.056*** (0.002) | −0.071*** (0.004) | −0.033*** (0.003) | −0.073*** (0.004) |
| Small employers, self-employed | −0.172*** (0.009) | −0.134*** (0.004) | −0.316*** (0.004) | −0.300*** (0.004) | −0.108*** (0.006) |
| Lower sales and service tasks | −0.228*** (0.008) | −0.168*** (0.003) | −0.204*** (0.004) | −0.126*** (0.004) | −0.163*** (0.005) |
| Lower technical and routine work | −0.245*** (0.008) | −0.195*** (0.003) | −0.256*** (0.004) | −0.124*** (0.003) | −0.152*** (0.005) |
| Observations | 130,469 | 549,485 | 535,751 | 765,760 | 248,622 |
| Countries | 2 | 7 | 6 | 11 | 4 |
| Wald Chi$^2$ | 39,214 | 153,388 | 147,240 | 215,421 | 91,756 |
| Intraclass correlation | 0.042 | 0.247 | 0.205 | 0.435 | 0.260 |
| McFadden pseudo-R$^2$ | 0.244 | 0.340 | 0.359 | 0.474 | 0.393 |
| AIC | 193,087 | 612,940 | 926,198 | 1,110,216 | 194,752 |

Notes: + $p < 0.10$, * $p < 0.05$, ** $p < 0.01$. For calculation see Fig. 9.6. Standard error (se) in brackets. Constant not shown

households, it is 36% lower in Southern Europe and as much as 43% lower in Central and Eastern Europe. In Scandinavia (−17%) and the British Isles (−25%), this gap between different *educational levels* is much smaller. This points to the fact that the relatively low shares of university graduates in Southern and Eastern Europe are accompanied by higher income disparities. The income of households headed by an employee engaged in *routine activities* is almost a quarter lower than that of problem-solvers and decision-makers. These *occupation-specific* income differentials are particularly high in Southern, Continental and Central Europe and particularly low in the service-dominated Scandinavian and Anglo-Saxon countries. These comparatively small income differentials across skill and occupation groups, despite the highly unequal income conditions in the UK, reinforce the warning just recalled by DiPrete (2007). The incomes of *working-class households* are about a fifth lower than those of the upper service class. These differences are particularly high in Southern Europe and the British Isles and particularly low in Scandinavia and Central Europe. These class-specific differences reveal the well-known differences between unequal and egalitarian societies. Income inequalities are particularly high in the Baltic and South-Eastern European countries. Overall, these results suggest that income inequalities between different educational levels and occupational groups are higher in countries with lower levels of academicisation and a lower share of more demanding service activities, i.e. mainly in Southern, Central and Eastern Europe. The income differences between different classes, on the other hand, are rather shaped by political structures and decisions. They are particularly high in Southern Europe and the British Isles. *It can be stated that the household incomes of the low-skilled, of people with routine jobs, of small employers and the self-employed are clearly below the income of the respective reference groups.*

In a meritocratic perspective, the poorer labour market, earnings and income opportunities of the low-skilled could be considered legitimate if they can be attributed to different talents, efforts and performance in school and jobs. However, such a meritocratic legitimisation of inequalities cannot be justified if it can be shown that different educational opportunities can be inherited in a similar way to wealth. The next section examines whether this is the case.

## 9.3   Intergenerational Inheritance of Educational Opportunities

In a meritocratic society, the tensions between egalitarian norms and social inequalities are resolved by the principle of equal opportunities and the claim that existing inequalities are the result of different achievements. This implies that social inequalities not based on merit are "in open contradiction to the promise of equality in modern society" (Berger, 2019, 6; own translation). If every person is the architect of his or her own destiny—regardless of gender, social origin, ethnic or migrant background, place of residence or sexual orientation—then social inequalities can be seen as legitimate. Equality of opportunity is thus the central basis for legitimising social inequalities in a meritocracy. Only inequalities that are not based on the monopolisation of social opportunities (Parkin, 1974), can be considered legitimate. Ensuring equality of opportunity does not require an egalitarian distribution of social resources, but it does require "equality in the endowment of persons with the necessary resources to achieve certain outcomes" (Berger, 2019, 10; own translation).

A significant impact of social origin on educational, occupational and life chances would obviously violate the principle of equal opportunities. Such an influence would also be particularly bitter for historical reasons, since the claimed moral superiority of modern society over feudal society was based precisely on the abolition of class-based and birth-related privileges which were at the heart of pre-modern societies. As already argued in Chaps. 6 and 8, the American sociologist Talcott Parsons analysed them as privileges based on ascriptive characteristics and contrasted them with inequalities based on achievement (Parsons, 1970). In this perspective, social inequality can only be considered legitimate if it is accompanied by equality of social opportunities and rights.

For decades, educational research has demonstrated in an extraordinarily differentiated and convincing manner that such equality of educational opportunities does not exist (Becker & Lauterbach, 2016). This also applies to the expansion of education, which was justified in the 1950s and 1960s by the claim that education is a civil right, but which in fact has even led to an increase in the influence of social origin in most countries (Shavit & Blossfeld, 1993). A clear distinction can be made between primary and secondary effects of social origin, i.e. between origin-dependent differences in school performance and different educational decisions even with the same school performance (Jackson et al., 2007). The parents' class position thus affects the educational opportunities of their children on the one hand through the parents' limited possibilities and resources to promote and support their children. On the other hand, parents from lower social classes often decide against further education even if the school performance of their children is good, thus reducing their children's educational opportunities. A key finding of the PISA studies is that these two effects of social origin are particularly high in Germany. Schleicher (2019, p. 19) reports that the gap between the reading skills of students from the top and bottom tenth of the social structure is more than 170 points on a scale whose average is around 500. This corresponds to a gap of about four school years.

The impact of social origin on the educational level of the interviewees can also be illustrated with EU-SILC data for 2005, 2011 and 2019. Based on a classic mobility table (Table 9.2), the situation in Europe can first be illustrated using central concepts of mobility research—starting with the outflow and inflow rates. The *outflow rates* in the columns of Table 9.2 (i.e. the percentages that add up to 100% in the vertical) indicate the extent to which the social origin of the parents (measured here by the level of education) is inherited. Thus, two-thirds of those who had a father with an academic background and 71% of those who had a mother with the same background have themselves attained an academic degree. These values must be weighted with the probability of the children of parents without an academic background obtaining an academic degree (about a quarter) in order to interpret them meaningfully. The relative odds of children of academics to complete higher education are about six times as high as those of children whose parents have a low level of education, since the corresponding value (odds ratio) has to be calculated as the quotient of the two odds in relation to the complementary probability (rounded: 2/3 divided by 1/3 in relation to ¼ divided by ¾). One third (more precisely: 36% and 33%) of the people whose parents have a low level of education have a low level of education themselves. They have a ten times higher likelihood of having a low level

**Table 9.2** Education and family origin (EU-28, Norway, Switzerland; 2005, 2011, 2019)

| Educational level Respondent | Highest educational level of the father | | | | Highest educational level of the mother | | | |
|---|---|---|---|---|---|---|---|---|
| | Low | Medium | High | Total | Low | Medium | High | Total |
| **Low** | 121,990 | 11,589 | 2668 | 136,247 | 127,265 | 7543 | 1439 | 136,247 |
| Inflow % | 90% | 9% | 2% | 100% | 93% | 6% | 1% | 100% |
| Outflow % | 36% | 7% | 3% | 23% | 33% | 5% | 3% | 23% |
| **Medium** | 152,057 | 98,522 | 26,121 | 276,701 | 177,593 | 85,609 | 13,498 | 276,701 |
| Inflow % | 55% | 36% | 9% | 100% | 64% | 31% | 5% | 100% |
| Outflow % | 45% | 57% | 30% | 46% | 46% | 53% | 26% | 46% |
| **High** | 57,196 | 62,772 | 57,719 | 187,686 | 83,080 | 67,750 | 36,857 | 187,686 |
| Inflow % | 36% | 33% | 31% | 100% | 44% | 36% | 20% | 100% |
| Outflow % | 20% | 36% | 67% | 31% | 21% | 42% | 71% | 31% |
| **Total** | 341,242 | 172,883 | 86,509 | 600,634 | 387,938 | 160,902 | 51,794 | 600,634 |
| Inflow % | 57% | 29% | 14% | 100% | 65% | 27% | 9% | 100% |
| Outflow % | 100% | 100% | 100% | 100% | 100% | 100% | 100% | 100% |

Sources: Ad hoc modules of the EU-SILC surveys 2005, 2011, 2019. 2005 excluding Croatia, Malta, Bulgaria and Romania. 2019 without the United Kingdom.
The table above shows the educational level of the respondents and their parents' educational level

of education themselves, since people from more educated families have only about a 5% chance of having a low level of education.

The row percentages in Table 9.2 (i.e. the percentages that add up to 100% on the horizontal line) represent the *inflow rates*, i.e. they show the parental educational background of low, medium and highly educated people. For example, 31% of people with a high level of education had an academic father and 20% had an academic mother. People with a low level of education (ISCED 0–2) often had a father (90%) or a mother (93%) with the same educational background.

However, such tables are too complex for further analyses. Therefore, the results of binary logistic multilevel models are shown below (Table 9.3) in order to determine the significance of social origin for the respondents' own educational attainment controlling for other factors—such as age, gender or migration background. Furthermore, the financial situation of the family of origin is also included as a control variable. The variable to be explained is the probability of the respondent having a high level of education.

In the first model, only the countries in which the survey takes place and the 3 years (as crossed effects) are included. The differences between the countries are considerable, as the chances of academic education are significantly higher in Germany, especially in the Northern and Northwestern European countries, while they are lower in many Central and Eastern European countries. The differences between the survey dates point to the importance of educational expansion: in 2011, the chance of completing higher education (in most cases: a university degree) was 16% higher and in 2019, 34% higher than in 2005. The next model (column 2) examines the individual determinants of the chance of obtaining a higher education. This chance is one third higher for women than for men. People older than 54 had a 15% lower chance—a reflection of educational expansion. People with a migration background have a 10% lower chance than natives. The influence of social origin is also extraordinarily high. If the father or mother have a low level of education, the chance is halved compared to people who have parents with a medium level of education. If, on the other hand, the interviewee has a parent with an academic degree, this chance roughly doubles (+131% and +93% respectively). In addition to the educational level of the parents, which can be seen as an indicator of the *cultural capital* of the family of origin (Bourdieu, 1983), the *economic capital* of the families of origin also has a considerable influence: with every point that the financial situation of the family of origin improves on a five-point scale, the respondent's chance of obtaining an academic degree increases by 21%. Overall, this model explains 16% of the respondents' chances of having a high level of education.

This model can also be used to calculate the country-specific effects if the nationality of the respondents is included as a dummy (not shown here). In 12 countries, the chance of obtaining an academic degree is lower than in Germany: in Austria, Bulgaria, the Czech Republic, Croatia, Hungary, Italy, Lithuania, Latvia, Malta, Poland, Romania and Slovakia. In other countries, especially in the service-centred countries of Continental, Northern and Northwestern Europe, but also in Greece, Portugal and Spain, the chance of graduation is higher.

**Table 9.3** Influence of family of origin on the chance of having a high level of education (2005, 2011, 2019; EU-28, Norway, Switzerland)

| | (1) | (2) | (3) |
|---|---|---|---|
| Women (Ref. men) | | 1.320** | 1.320** |
| | | (0.009) | (0.009) |
| 55 years and older (Ref. 25–54 years) | | 0.849** | 0.852** |
| | | (0.008) | (0.009) |
| Migration background (Ref. natives) | | 0.899** | 0.903** |
| | | (0.011) | (0.011) |
| Educational background of the father (Ref. medium education) | | | |
| - Low | | 0.509** | 0.678** |
| | | (0.005) | (0.011) |
| - High (academic) | | 2.314** | 2.539** |
| | | (0.028) | (0.042) |
| Educational background of the mother (Ref. medium education) | | | |
| - Low | | 0.497** | 0.595** |
| | | (0.005) | (0.008) |
| - High (academic) | | 1.933** | 2.196** |
| | | (0.027) | (0.049) |
| Interaction low (F) * low (M) | | | 0.645** |
| | | | (0.013) |
| Interaction low (F) * high (M) | | | 0.860** |
| | | | (0.036) |
| Interaction high (F) * low (M) | | | 0.890** |
| | | | (0.025) |
| Interaction high (F) * high (M) | | | 0.790** |
| | | | (0.024) |
| Financial situation of the family of origin (when the respondent was 14 years old) | | 1.214** | 1.211** |
| | | (0.004) | (0.004) |
| Constant | 0.422** | 0.634** | 0.593** |
| | (0.040) | (0.060) | (0.056) |
| Respondents | 510,599 | 510,599 | 510,599 |
| Wald Chi$^2$ | | 60,514 | 61,270 |
| McFadden pseudo-R$^2$ | | 0.164 | 0.166 |
| AIC | 576,880 | 503,523 | 502,983 |

Source: EU-SILC (2005, 2011, 2019). Binary logistic regression with crossed random effects (country, year). Dependent variable: Higher education degree of the respondent. The coefficients are odds ratios. In brackets: standard errors. M: mother; F: father. $+ p < 0.10$, $* p < 0.05$, $** p < 0.01$

In the third model (column 3), the interaction effects between parental educational backgrounds are included. This is crucial because the educational levels of the parents are strongly correlated—a phenomenon known as educational homogamy (Blossfeld & Timm, 2003). Due to the increasingly higher education of women, this correlation becomes even stronger. The corresponding correlation coefficients rise from 0.61 (2005) to 0.67 (2019). Knowing the father's educational attainment, one can thus reduce the error in predicting the mother's educational attainment by 45% (2019). The accumulation of social opportunities and risks can be seen very clearly in model (3). If both parents have low education, the children's chances of obtaining an academic degree are reduced by 75% (0.584*0.671*0.664) compared to parents with medium education, while the chances of children with highly educated parents are more than four times higher than those of children of parents with a medium education. A privileged parental home is thus a true opportunity turbo.

In the next step, whether educational expansion actually leads to *social closure,* in the sense of a relative deterioration in educational opportunities for children with a lower social background, will be discussed on the basis of the models in Table 9.4. As indicators for an expansion of the education system, the share of academically qualified persons in the working-age population aged 25–64 and second, the level of public expenditure on education (as a percentage of gross domestic product) were chosen. A counter-thesis to the thesis of social closure would be the assumption that with the progressive modernisation of the economy and society, social origin loses its previous role for children's educational opportunities. The share of employees in the service sector can be taken as an indicator for such a *modernisation.* The corresponding models are shown in columns 4–9 in Table 9.4. If the share of academically qualified persons in the population is chosen as an indicator for educational expansion, then, as expected, respondents have a higher chance of having an academic degree (column 4). Respondents with less qualified fathers benefit significantly more than respondents with medium and highly educated fathers (column 5). In contrast to Shavit and Blossfeld (1993), it can thus be stated that educational expansion improves the educational opportunities of persons with a lower educational background when controlling for other individual factors. The next two models point in a similar direction. The model in column 6 shows that the level of public spending on education has no significant impact on respondents' educational opportunities. However, it does make it easier for respondents from lower social backgrounds—the father has a low educational attainment—to attend university. The advantages of respondents who have an academic father, on the other hand, are significantly lower (column 7). Higher educational expenditure is thus an important factor for a "democratisation" of educational opportunities, as Dahrendorf (1965) had already expected in the early phases of educational expansion. An advanced education system is thus an important prerequisite for better relative educational opportunities and more educational equality, also for respondents from families with a low educational background. The last two columns of Table 9.4 test the modernisation thesis. First, it shows that a higher share of employment in the service sector is associated with a higher chance of academicisation (column 8). Even though the service sector includes both low-skilled and higher-skilled jobs, the demand for high-skilled persons increases in a service society. In the last model in Table 9.4 (column 9), the interaction with the father's educational background is also included. Here, too, a small, albeit significant, relative advantage for children with less educated fathers can be observed when employment in the service sector is higher.

**Table 9.4**  Influence of family of origin and national contexts on the chance of attaining a high level of education (2005, 2011, 2019; EU-28, Switzerland, Norway)

| | (4) | (5) | (6) | (7) | (8) | (9) |
|---|---|---|---|---|---|---|
| Educational background father (Ref. medium) | | | | | | |
| - low | 0.514** | 0.491** | 0.509** | 0.511** | 0.503** | 0.502** |
| | (0.005) | (0.005) | (0.005) | (0.005) | (0.005) | (0.005) |
| - high | 2.285** | 2.426** | 2.314** | 2.298** | 2.378** | 2.393** |
| | (0.027) | (0.030) | (0.028) | (0.028) | (0.028) | (0.029) |
| National graduate rate | 1.033** | 1.025** | | | | |
| | (0.001) | (0.001) | | | | |
| - Academicisation * low education (father) | | 1.018** | | | | |
| | | (0.001) | | | | |
| - Academicisation * high education (father) | | 0.986** | | | | |
| | | (0.001) | | | | |
| Spending on education | | | 1.009 | 0.971 | | |
| | | | (0.049) | (0.048) | | |
| - Education expenditure * low education (father) | | | | 1.127** | | |
| | | | | (0.009) | | |
| - Education expenditure * high education (father) | | | | 0.865** | | |
| Services | | | | | 1.014** | 1.012** |
| | | | | | (0.001) | (0.001) |
| - Services * low education (father) | | | | | | 1.006** |
| | | | | | | (0.001) |
| - Services * high education (father) | | | | | | 0.987** |
| | | | | | | (0.001) |
| Constant | 0.580** | 0.586** | 0.633** | 0.629** | 0.619** | 0.619** |
| | (0.036) | (0.037) | (0.060) | (0.059) | (0.050) | (0.050) |
| Respondents | 510,599 | 510,599 | 510,599 | 527,718 | 510,599 | 510,599 |
| Wald Chi$^2$ | 61,286 | 62,286 | 60,514 | 63,250 | 60,747 | 61,116 |
| McFadden pseudo-R$^2$ | 0.186 | 0.186 | 0.164 | 0.164 | 0.174 | 0.174 |
| AIC | 502,198 | 501,398 | 503,589 | 521,764 | 503,189 | 503,003 |

Source: See Table 9.3. The models control for the individual characteristics previously discussed (Table 9.3), but they are not shown here

How are these results to be interpreted? On the one hand, the effects of individual characteristics confirm the overwhelming influence of social origin on respondents' educational opportunities. However, social origin plays a somewhat smaller role in countries with more highly qualified working-age individuals, higher educational expenditure and a more developed service sector. This refers mostly to the service-centred countries of Northern and Northwestern Europe, such as the United Kingdom, Ireland, the Netherlands, Sweden, Denmark or Finland.

In sum: An extraordinarily high degree of intergenerational social closure can be observed in Europe. Highly educated groups succeed in monopolising better wage, career and life opportunities—also for their children who inherit these advantages.

This social closure of an educated elite is reduced by the expansion of the education system, by higher education spending and by tertiarisation processes. Social closure is therefore lower in the Northern and Northwestern European countries than in the Southern and Central European periphery. The higher income and labour market opportunities in these countries are therefore distributed more fairly; the impact of social origin slightly decreases.

## 9.4   Educational Poverty and Its Structural Determinants[2]

In the previous sections, it has been shown that low education is a central cause of lower labour force participation, higher unemployment risks, low wages and low disposable income. These risks of poverty, exclusion and unemployment are also at the centre of the debate on educational poverty (Quenzel & Hurrelmann, 2019). Two of the most important explanatory factors for educational poverty are—as just shown—social origin and a migration background. In addition to these family-related factors, national contextual conditions also play an important role. In particular, the comparative studies by the OECD on education have highlighted the importance of inclusive school systems (OECD, 2019; Schleicher, 2019).

The discussion now turns to whether the more or less central position of a region in the national and European context as well as the regional economic structure are also important factors for explaining educational poverty. Following the description of the group-specific distribution of educational poverty, the countries where the corresponding educational risks are concentrated will be identified. Subsequently, the regional variation of educational poverty and its structural determinants are discussed.

Educational poverty is—as previously shown—mostly a Southern European phenomenon (Table 9.5). In other regions—also in Central and Eastern Europe— the educational level of the employable population is higher. The age-specific educational poverty rates show that mainly older cohorts are affected—an indication of the educational expansion of recent decades. Young people in Southern Europe are also better educated. However, the expansion of higher education took place later and less intensively in Southern Europe than in other parts of Europe. A similarly large gap between the educational opportunities of young people and older people can also be found on the British Isles—albeit at a much lower level. On the British Isles, the proportion of low-skilled young people is lower than among their peers in all other parts of the EU, but also compared to the older British and Irish. Overall, younger people are better educated than older people. Educational poverty affects men and women equally across Europe. The proportion of educationally poor is slightly higher among Scandinavian, Southern European and Anglo-Saxon men and slightly lower among Continental and Eastern European men than among women.

---

[2]This section is based on Heidenreich (2019).

**Table 9.5** Regime- and group-specific distribution of educational poverty (18–64 years; EU-28, Switzerland, Norway; 2013)

| | Brit. Isles | Continental Europe | Southern Europe | Eastern Europe | Scandinavia | EU-28. CH. NO |
|---|---|---|---|---|---|---|
| Above poverty threshold | 10.3 | 13.6 | 35.0 | 11.5 | 14.8 | 18.0 |
| Poor households | 18.7 | 26.9 | 55.9 | 34.7 | 22.7 | 36.4 |
| Men | 12.2 | 14.3 | 41.1 | 14.3 | 17.2 | 21.0 |
| Women | 10.9 | 16.6 | 37.1 | 16.4 | 14.4 | 20.9 |
| 15–24 years | 6.1 | 21.1 | 26.9 | 22.4 | 26.7 | 20.8 |
| 25–55 years | 9.5 | 11.9 | 36.1 | 11.7 | 11.5 | 17.9 |
| 55–64 years | 23.0 | 23.1 | 56.9 | 21.7 | 21.6 | 30.7 |
| Without migration background | 13.8 | 13.6 | 41.5 | 14.8 | 14.7 | 20.8 |
| European migration background | 4.3 | 23.4 | 26.6 | 16.6 | 10.4 | 18.2 |
| Non-European background | 1.7 | 27.9 | 38.0 | 17.0 | 20.9 | 25.5 |
| Employed | 7.6 | 10.8 | 32.4 | 9.4 | 11.4 | 14.8 |
| Unemployed | 24.2 | 28.4 | 48.8 | 22.1 | 22.3 | 35.1 |
| Routine tasks | 28.1 | 42.2 | 65.1 | 40.0 | 34.0 | 47.0 |
| Operating machinery, repair | 15.1 | 18.6 | 46.7 | 14.7 | 20.1 | 25.0 |
| Complex tasks | 4.7 | 6.7 | 18.3 | 1.3 | 8.1 | 8.0 |
| Problem-solving | 1.7 | 2.5 | 5.6 | 0.4 | 3.4 | 2.6 |
| Upper service class | 2.5 | 4.4 | 10.3 | 1.0 | 4.6 | 4.7 |
| Intermediate employees | 7.4 | 14.0 | 28.8 | 4.2 | 15.8 | 15.5 |
| Small employer, self-employed | 12.4 | 13.3 | 50.7 | 22.4 | 18.8 | 29.1 |
| Lower sales and service tasks | 13.5 | 19.7 | 39.0 | 9.2 | 17.5 | 21.5 |
| Lower technical and routine tasks | 26.4 | 32.4 | 65.0 | 23.2 | 26.6 | 38.1 |
| Single-person household | 17.2 | 14.6 | 31.2 | 15.5 | 18.2 | 18.4 |
| Adults without children | 12.9 | 16.9 | 43,5 | 13,9 | 16,2 | 22.5 |
| Single parent households | 14.4 | 20.2 | 29.4 | 16.9 | 20.9 | 20.4 |
| Adults with children | 8.3 | 14.0 | 37.4 | 16.4 | 13.4 | 20.2 |
| EU-28, CH, NO | 11.6 | 15.5 | 39.1 | 15.4 | 15.8 | 20.9 |

Source: Own calculations based on EU-SILC 2013

The educational level of people with a migration background is particularly low in Continental Europe. In Scandinavia, people from third countries are significantly less educated than the native population. In general, the shares of people with low education is also significantly higher among those with low incomes, the unemployed, people employed in simple and routine jobs, people from third countries and nonskilled and skilled workers, indicating an accumulation of social disadvantages among these groups (Table 9.5).

Educational poverty is often explained by specific features of national school systems. For example, on the basis of the PISA studies, the importance of a more or less selective school system or educational expenditure has been highlighted (Schleicher, 2019). However, Quenzel and Hurrelmann (2010, 18; own translation) point also to the role of economic structures for educational inequalities: "The 'knowledge society' is not only characterised by an increase in professionals or technological changes, but also by a change in the structures and mechanisms of knowledge generation and knowledge articulation (…) and by an increase in complexity (…)." This draws attention to the question of whether, in addition to social origin and institutional factors—the two factors that according to Solga (2017, p. 446) are decisive for the genesis of educational poverty—economic structures might have an influence on the educational level of the population. Given the previously described centre-periphery structures and the regime-specific growth models discussed in Chap. 4, these structures might also explain the different levels of educational poverty in Europe. Such a perspective, which looks at the supply side of the labour market, has so far rarely been use for explaining educational poverty. The following analysis looks at how educational poverty evolves in an innovation-centred, but also increasingly unequal knowledge society.

Shifting the level on which explanations are sought is related to the role of economic structures. International comparative studies focus in general only on the national determinants and effects of educational poverty (OECD, 2019). The regional variation of educational poverty even within the same country has been largely ignored, because comparative studies of education systems assume in general a homogeneity of education systems in the whole national territory. Therefore, regional patterns of educational inequalities are largely ignored. This reflects on the one hand the broadly uniform national regulation of public education, but also the problematic implications of regionally diverging patterns of education, as this might undermine the assumed territorial equality of living conditions. This equality in the whole national territory is constitutive for the cohesion of a modern nation-state; regional disparities in the education system would undermine it. In the following, the regional dimension of educational poverty will be examined in more detail. This dimension is linked to the role of the economic structure, because—despite the predominantly national regulation of the education system—regional variations in these structures may lead to considerable differences in the demand for skilled labour and thus also in the educational requirements, even within the same national context. In the following, thus it will be shown that educational poverty varies considerably not only between, but also within the different European states calling into question the assumption of uniformly regulated and equipped national education systems. Subsequently, the regional determinants of educational poverty are analysed on the basis of European regional data. It can be shown that regional patterns of educational poverty can also be explained by regionally diverging economic and labour market structures.

Three partly complementary processes can be expected: Firstly, on the basis of Quenzel and Hurrelmann (2010) it can be assumed that the share of the educationally poor decreases with the *shift to a knowledge-based society* (H1). Secondly, in a knowledge society, companies are dependent on the broadest possible pool of highly qualified employees. A *high share of knowledge-based industries and services* therefore goes hand in hand with a lower share of the educationally poor (H2). An alternative to such a knowledge-based dynamic is that the *modernisation of classical labour and industrial structures* and not knowledge-based industries contributes to declining shares of low educated people (H3). Industrialised regions with a higher share of the labour force will be characterised by a lower share of low-qualified people, since strong industrial regions—and not only knowledge-based industries—also depend on a more skilled labour force.

In what follows, these three theses will be discussed on the basis of European regional data. First, the extent and development of regional educational poverty and its variations within and between countries will be described. Following these descriptions, the structural determinants of educational poverty will then be analysed in order to determine the influence of industrial and knowledge-based sectors. Whether high employment shares overall, in industry, in retail trade and catering and in knowledge-based services have a positive effect on the educational level of the population, thus reducing the share of educational poverty, will be examined.

Table 9.6 confirms once again (cf. Sect. 9.1) that educational poverty is highest in Southern Europe and lowest in many Eastern and Northern European countries. More than a quarter of the 25–64 year old population (who have usually completed their initial education but are not yet retired) in Portugal, Malta, Spain, Italy, Greece and Belgium have no vocational or intermediate general education. While the educational poverty rate in the EU-28 is 24.8% (2013), it is lower in Central and Eastern European (13.9%), Scandinavian (17.4%), corporatist-conservative (19.4%) and liberal countries (21.8%) and much higher in Southern European countries (43.4%) than the European average.

Regionally disaggregated figures are available for 20 of the 30 countries considered; for the other eight usually small countries (Malta, Estonia, Luxembourg . . .) such values would not be very meaningful. The regional range is highest in the countries with the highest educational poverty. Spain leads the way with a difference of 30.5 percentage points between the region with the highest and lowest proportion of educational poor (Extremadura–Madrid), followed by Portugal (Algarve–Lisbon), Italy (Apulia–Latium) and Greece (Eastern Macedonia and Thrace-Athens). Even in Germany (Bremen–Chemnitz), this difference amounts to 16.6 percentage points—in spite of the federal structure and the constitutionally anchored focus on equivalent living conditions (cf. Table 9.6). The differences between countries (54 percentage points difference between Portugal and Lithuania), however, are considerably higher than the differences within countries.

Educational poverty in Europe has strongly declined over the last 18 years, from 35.1% (2000) to 21.5% (2018) (Eurostat, table [edat_lfse_04]). The first hypothesis

**Table 9.6** Educational poverty in the EU-28, Switzerland and Norway (2013; % of 25–64 year old population). National mean and regional differences

| | National value | Regional minimum | Regional maximum | Range |
|---|---|---|---|---|
| Portugal | 60.2 | 47.8 | 74.9 | 27.1 |
| Malta | 58.8 | | | |
| Spain | 44.5 | 29.5 | 60.0 | 30.5 |
| Italy | 41.8 | 31.7 | 52.7 | 21.0 |
| Greece | 32.8 | 20.8 | 51.3 | 30.5 |
| Belgium | 27.2 | 17.4 | 33.5 | 16.1 |
| France | 25.0 | 17.3 | 36.5 | 19.2 |
| Romania | 24.3 | 11.6 | 29.5 | 17.9 |
| Netherlands | 24.2 | 18.1 | 28.5 | 10.4 |
| Ireland | 22.9 | 20.9 | 26.6 | 5.7 |
| Denmark | 22.1 | 17.7 | 25.6 | 7.9 |
| United Kingdom | 21.7 | 12.0 | 30.0 | 18.0 |
| Cyprus | 21.5 | | | |
| Luxembourg | 19.5 | | | |
| Croatia | 18.7 | 13.1 | 21.4 | 8.3 |
| Bulgaria | 18.2 | 8.6 | 23.7 | 15.1 |
| Norway | 17.6 | 14.5 | 22.5 | 8.0 |
| Hungary | 17.5 | 8.0 | 23.3 | 15.3 |
| Austria | 17.0 | 13.2 | 20.0 | 6.8 |
| Sweden | 16.8 | 12.7 | 19.1 | 6.4 |
| Slovenia | 14.5 | 11.1 | 17.5 | 6.4 |
| Finland | 14.1 | 14.2 | 19.2 | 5.0 |
| Switzerland | 13.6 | 11.3 | 17.4 | 6.1 |
| Germany | 13.3 | 3.3 | 19.9 | 16.6 |
| Latvia | 10.6 | | | |
| Poland | 9.9 | 6.5 | 17.0 | 10.5 |
| Estonia | 9.4 | | | |
| Slovakia | 8.1 | 4.9 | 9.9 | 5.0 |
| Czech Republic | 7.2 | 3.1 | 13.2 | 10.1 |
| Lithuania | 6.6 | 3.8 | 7.6 | 3.8 |
| EU-28, CH, NO | 24.5 | 3.1 | 74.9 | 71.8 |

Source: Eurostat, table [edat_lfse_04]. Data are sorted by the level of national educational poverty rates (ISCED 0–2). Missing regional values mean that regional disaggregation at the level of NUTS2 is not possible

can thus be confirmed. At the same time, the standard deviation of the regional educational poverty rates has also declined. The European regions have thus become more similar in terms of educational poverty. However, the higher European homogeneity is accompanied by an increase in regional differences on a national scale. The attempt to create equal living and schooling opportunities in the national territory seems to be reaching its limits, also due to Europeanisation and globalisation processes. These increasing regional differences in educational participation can

**Table 9.7** The impact of economic structures on low education (EU-28, Switzerland, Norway; NUTS2 regions; 2000–2018)

| | |
|---|---|
| Employees in trade and gastronomy (%) | 0.044 |
| | (0.0313) |
| Employees in the manufacturing sector (%) | 0.010 |
| | (0.0222) |
| High-tech sectors (%) | −0.38*** |
| | (0.110) |
| Knowledge-based services (%) | −0.34*** |
| | (0.0226) |
| Employment rate (%; 15–64 years) | −0.39*** |
| | (0.0162) |
| Constant | 29.6*** |
| | (2.660) |
| Observations (regions * years) | 3534 |
| Intraclass correlation | 0.93 |
| $R^2$ | 0.92 |

Notes: Standard errors in brackets; * $p < 0.05$, ** $p < 0.01$, *** $p < 0.001$
Source: European regional data ([edat_lfse_04], [htec_emp_reg2], [lfst_r_lfe2emprt])

be interpreted as support for the knowledge society spill-over thesis (H2): Regional technological capabilities vary increasingly within the same country (Heidenreich & Baur, 2015). These huge regional differences in technological capabilities are well-known in economic geography (Krugman, 1991). If the most technologically advanced regions are pioneers in reducing educational poverty, this could explain the increasing regional differentiation in educational poverty. Therefore, it is necessary to examine the influence of regional technological capabilities on educational poverty in order to explain the increasing within-country variation.

The impact of the economic structure on educational poverty can be addressed on the basis of a panel regression (cf. Table 9.7). This model shows which facets of the economic and employment structure are correlated with regional educational poverty. Three of the five chosen indicators—the share of employees in high-tech sectors, in knowledge-based services as well as the employment rate—are negatively correlated with educational poverty (Table 9.7). A high share of *knowledge-based services* is thus associated with lower educational poverty thus supporting the second hypothesis. The share of *industrial employees* is not correlated with educational poverty, which contradicts the third hypothesis. Contrary to expectations, a higher regional share of *employees in retail trade, hotels and restaurants* is not associated with a lower share of educational poverty. High regional shares rates of educational poverty thus can be found in regions with *low employment rates and low shares of employment in high-tech sectors and knowledge-intensive services*. This highlights a vicious circle: Educational poverty blocks the development of advanced economic sectors, just as low employment shares in these sectors could also undermine the basis for higher education rates. This might explain the economic stagnation of many Southern European regions.

In sum: Education systems reproduce and also reflect the double dualisation between advantaged and disadvantaged countries, regions and socio-economic groups. On the one hand, Southern European countries and peripheral regions are particularly affected by educational poverty and, on the other hand, unskilled workers with simple and routine jobs are as well. The extent to which people are affected by educational poverty also varies considerably between the regions of one and the same country. On the basis of European regional data, the development and regional variation of educational poverty was described. While educational poverty and also its regional variation in Europe decreased over recent decades, the regional differences within the nation-states increased, indicating a greater homogeneity in Europe as well as an increasing heterogeneity within the European states. This also reflects the increasingly different economic and technological capabilities and trajectories of regional innovation systems. Thus, it was subsequently investigated to what extent the regional variation in educational poverty can also be explained by the regional economic and labour market structures. The negative correlation between educational poverty and the employment share of high-tech sectors suggests that knowledge-based dynamics are an important factor both for reducing educational poverty and increasing intra-national differences. The negative correlations between employment rates and educational poverty suggest that not only more knowledge-based sectors, but also more inclusive labour market structures contribute to lower educational poverty. In sum: in addition to the well-known national and family-based determinants of educational inequality, regional economic structures also play an often-neglected role in explaining educational poverty.

The previous analyses are based on regionally aggregated data. In the following, microdata will be used for analysing the influence of economic and technological developments on educational inequalities and occupational skills.

## 9.5  Polarisation or Upgrading of Occupational Skills?

In the previous section it was shown that a higher share of knowledge-based industries and services is associated with a lower regional rate of low education. This raises the question of how the occupational skills of the workforce are changing as a result of economic and technological change. Two different theses have been proposed to answer this question. First, it can be expected that the demand for higher skills will continue to rise and that simpler jobs in developed countries will disappear either due to automation or to relocation to low-wage countries. This is the *skill-biased technological change (SBTC) thesis* which expects that due to current technological and economic change, the share of manual and cognitive routine tasks will shrink and the importance of non-routinised cognitive tasks will increase (Autor et al., 2003). A prominent example of this thesis is a study by Reich (1992), which distinguishes three broad occupational groups—routinised production tasks, person-related services and symbolic-analytical services. Reich estimates that about 30%, 25% and 20% of the American labour force are employed in these groups respectively. He predicts a rapid growth of the third group, which will become increasingly important as problem-solvers in advanced industries. In recent years, this upgrading thesis has been challenged by the *polarisation thesis*. Goos and Manning (2007) emphasise that many simple jobs cannot be easily relocated or automated. They even expect a growing importance of some manual jobs and jobs with simple cognitive requirements. According to Goos and Manning (2007), the routinability of activities becomes a decisive factor for the possibility to automate or relocate a task. Examples of simple but hardly routinisable tasks are delivery activities, cleaning work, surveillance and security tasks and many personal care and nursing services. On the other hand, there are many highly routinised activities that can be relocated or automated, even in the middle of the organisational hierarchy (for example, at the level of clerks and machine operators). Current mechanisation, digitalisation and automation processes thus also affect qualified administrative and production activities. These either disappear (according to the findings of Kalleberg, 2011, p. 64 for the USA) or change fundamentally (Frey & Osborne, 2017). As a result, a polarisation of occupational skills can be expected: Simple, but non-routine activities are gaining in importance, as are highly qualified problem-solvers, while the employment share of activities in the middle of the occupational hierarchy are decreasing.

This polarisation thesis has also been studied for Europe (Fernández-Macías, 2012; Goos et al., 2009) and other developed countries (OECD, 2017, Chap. 3). Fernández-Macías (2012)—whose study we follow below—was able to reconstruct three different patterns for the years from 1995 to 2007 based on the European Labour Force Study: Polarisation, upgrading and mid-level upgrading. In the first pattern, employment figures increase mainly at the top and bottom of the job hierarchy. This pattern is found in France, Germany, Belgium and the UK. In the second pattern, which corresponds to the predictions of the SBTC approach, employment numbers increase mainly in the upper wage and skill levels. This pattern is found in Finland, Denmark, Sweden and Ireland. In the third pattern, observed in Italy, Spain, Portugal, Greece and Austria, employment increases mainly in the middle wage groups. In contrast to Goos et al. (2009), Fernández-Macías (2012, p. 174) therefore emphasises that the replacement of routine jobs in the middle is not the only or even the dominant pattern. Instead, he distinguishes Continental European ("polarisation"), Scandinavian ("upgrading") and Southern European ("mid-range upgrading") patterns and explains them by the institutional characteristics and changes in the respective countries. In Continental Europe and the British Isles, deregulation and de-standardisation of labour relations have led to the expansion of low-paid jobs. In Scandinavia, strong trade unions and egalitarian wage structures have eliminated the basis for low-paid work. And in Southern Europe, the introduction of the euro in the first decade led to very low interest rates and thus to an expansion of employment especially in the middle of the occupational hierarchy (for example in construction or administration).

Goos et al. (2009) and Fernández-Macías (2012) only included the 15 countries that were members of the EU until the beginning of 2004. Furthermore, the European Labour Force Survey was used, which has very accurate employment data, but no robust data on wages. This is an important point, as the wage level is taken as an indicator for the quality of work in many studies and also by Fernández-Macías (2012) himself. Therefore, in the following I will replicate the study by Fernández-Macías (2012) with EU-SILC data for the years 2011–2019. This data set provides very precise information on the level of gross hourly wages. In addition, the new EU member states and also the years during and after the euro crisis can now be included. These years are characterised by an accelerated structural change in which many simple jobs may have been automated or relocated.

Similar to Fernández-Macías (2012), all employees who provided information on their wages are assigned to the group characterised by one of the 46 available occupational groups (ISCO-08) and by one of the 13 industries (NACE Rev. 2). The average gross hourly wage in 2011 is assigned to the respective industry-occupation cluster. This wage level is used by Fernández-Macías (2012), but also Goos and Manning (2007) and Goos et al. (2009) as an indicator of the quality of work. There are good reasons for this assumption, since high or low wages are important, though by no means the only indicators of the quality of work (Kalleberg, 2011). Based on the average wage levels, the sector x occupational groups are assigned to one of five wage quintiles thus ranking them as good or bad jobs. These wage quintiles do not always include exactly 20% of all employees, even in 2011, as larger groups can be assigned only to one of the five wage quintiles. The final step is then to determine how the weighted number of employees in each wage quintile has evolved from 2011–2019 (or 2018 in the case of the UK). For example, the share of employees in the lowest quintile in the Netherlands has decreased from 21.62% (2011) to 16.69% (2019), i.e. by 30%, while the top quintile has expanded from 19.88% to 25.33%, i.e. by 22% (see the seventh row in Table 9.8).

Most national patterns confirm the expectations that can be formulated on the basis of the *thesis of skill-biased technological change:* A growth of more demanding and better-paid jobs and a decrease in less well-paid jobs. Such a pattern can be observed for 17 of the 30 countries considered (Table 9.8), especially in the service-centred countries of Luxembourg, Sweden, Norway, the Netherlands, Denmark and Ireland, but also in Austria and Portugal. Fernández-Macías (2012) had already observed this upgrading in four countries of this group, in Luxembourg, Sweden, Denmark and Ireland. In three other countries that were assigned to this group here, however, he diagnosed mid-upgrading or polarisation tendencies (in the Netherlands, Portugal and France).

In eight countries, a different pattern can be identified that corresponds to the predictions of the *polarisation thesis*—for example in Germany, which is strongly industrialised, but also in Belgium, Italy, Romania, Bulgaria and the United Kingdom. This pattern had also already been observed by Fernández-Macías (2012, p. 171) in the UK, Belgium and Germany, as well as in France and the Netherlands, where now clear upgrading tendencies can be identified.

In four countries, employment shares in the two lower wage quintiles increase so much that this pattern was termed downgrading in Table 9.8. This pattern can be identified in the Eastern and Southern European periphery of the EU, in Greece, Spain, Slovakia and Lithuania. The two Southern European countries rely very

**Table 9.8** Employment change in different wage quintiles (EU-28, Switzerland, Norway; 2011–2019)

| | 1st quintile (%) | 2nd quintile (%) | 3rd quintile (%) | 4th quintile (%) | 5th quintile (%) | Observed Pattern |
|---|---|---|---|---|---|---|
| Norway | −9 | 6 | 1 | −7 | 7 | Upgrading |
| Switzerland | 0 | −9 | −12 | 16 | −2 | Upgrading |
| Malta | −52 | −14 | 10 | 19 | 12 | Upgrading |
| Luxembourg | −25 | −20 | −6 | 16 | 20 | Upgrading |
| Sweden | −32 | −14 | 10 | 10 | 13 | Upgrading |
| Netherlands | −30 | 2 | −18 | 10 | 22 | Upgrading |
| Denmark | −19 | −17 | 8 | 11 | 10 | Upgrading |
| Portugal | −12 | −15 | −4 | 8 | 18 | Upgrading |
| Estonia | −8 | −8 | −8 | 14 | 7 | Upgrading |
| Slovenia | −8 | −5 | −4 | −4 | 21 | Upgrading |
| Latvia | −11 | −6 | 5 | −11 | 18 | Polarisation |
| France | −7 | 2 | −16 | 7 | 11 | Upgrading |
| Austria | −8 | −2 | 1 | −3 | 13 | Upgrading |
| Belgium | −2 | −2 | −16 | 9 | 7 | Polarisation |
| Czech Republic | −1 | −3 | −10 | −1 | 14 | Upgrading |
| Cyprus | 1 | 0 | −18 | 11 | 3 | Upgrading |
| Germany | −8 | 2 | −1 | −4 | 10 | Polarisation |
| Hungary | 2 | −5 | −2 | 3 | 2 | Upgrading |
| Poland | 3 | −8 | 2 | −10 | 13 | Upgrading |
| Bulgaria | −2 | 1 | −6 | 2 | 4 | Polarisation |
| Italy | 3 | −3 | −11 | 4 | 3 | Polarisation |
| United Kingdom | −2 | 2 | −7 | 2 | 4 | Polarisation |
| Croatia | −7 | 13 | −9 | −4 | 12 | Polarisation |
| Finland | −8 | 5 | 9 | 8 | −17 | Mid-Upgrading |
| Ireland | −88 | 48 | −43 | −91 | 33 | Polarisation |
| Greece | 19 | 2 | −31 | −3 | −2 | Downgrading |
| Slovakia | 14 | −2 | 4 | −12 | −10 | Downgrading |
| Lithuania | 12 | 6 | −5 | −14 | −3 | Downgrading |
| Spain | 9 | 16 | −8 | −7 | −15 | Downgrading |
| Romania | 12 | 9 | −3 | −31 | 1 | Polarisation |
| EU-28, CH, NO | −1 | 2 | −7 | −1 | 6 | Upgrading |

Source: EU-SILC (2011, 2019). $N_{2011} = 185,665$; $N_{2019} = 204,356$. For the methodology, see Fernández-Macías (2012). The computation refers to persons aged 25–64 (not in education) for whom the occupational and sectoral affiliation is known. The years considered were 2011 and 2019 (or 2018 in the case of the UK). Changes in Ireland are not plausible. Two-digit ISCO-08 codes (46 categories), except for Germany, Slovenia and Malta (one-digit codes) and NACE Rev. 2 (13 codes). Dependent variable: quintiles of gross hourly wages (2011) of all employed persons in (at most) 46*13 occupation-industry cells

heavily on personal services (especially tourism). The increasing weight of lower-paid activities reflects the peripheral position of the respective country in the European and global division of labour. Another pattern identified by Fernández-Macías (2012) could only be identified in Finland—the upgrading of the middle occupational segment accompanied by the decline of the lower and upper groups. Fernández-Macías (2012) had observed this segment mainly in Southern Europe (Greece, Spain, Italy). It can be assumed that the corresponding jobs in Southern Europe were destroyed with the end of the boom that followed the introduction of the euro and the subsequent financial market and euro crises, so that the Southern European "mid-upgrading" has now turned into a downgrading of the occupational structures.

In sum: The polarisation of the occupational skills diagnosed by Goos et al. (2009) and the OECD (2017) is not the only or even the dominant pattern. In the majority of countries, an upgrading of the occupational structure can be observed, i.e. the number of employed persons in occupation-industry groups with higher wages is clearly increasing, while the number employed in occupations in industries that were at the bottom or in the middle of the wage hierarchy in 2011 is tending to shrink. In 12 EU countries, however, lower-paid occupations are becoming increasingly important. The three[3] patterns and their connections with each country's economic structure suggest that the development of skill-specific employment structures is not only determined—as assumed by Fernández-Macías (2012)—by the regime-specific sets of institution in the European countries, but also by their economic structure. Given the high skill requirements in advanced services, an upgrading can be observed in countries with a strong service sector (Netherlands, Luxembourg, Denmark, Sweden, France . . .), while countries with a technologically advanced industrial sector (Germany, Belgium . . .) may also be characterised by polarised occupational structures if simpler manual jobs can still be retained. Peripheral countries have to concentrate on simpler activities, especially in personal services. In addition to the institutional context that shapes the employment relationship, it is thus useful to also consider the respective national growth models.

The picture is even clearer if the quintiles are not defined by the wage levels but—as also suggested by Fernández-Macías (2012)—by the level of education (Table 9.9). A clear upgrading can be observed for 19 of the 30 countries considered. The occupation-industry groups characterised in 2011 by a lower average educational level of the labour force had fewer employees in 2019, while the volume of employment increases in the occupation-industry groups with a higher educational level. In 10 countries, a polarisation of the employment structure can be observed, i.e. employment in the occupation-industry groups with higher levels of education stagnates or decreases compared to the growth of groups with lower levels of education. In Greece, a clear downgrading of the employment structures can be observed, i.e. the quintiles with lower-educated persons grow much more strongly than the quintiles with higher-educated persons. A comparison of Table 9.8 and

---

[3] Ignoring the mid-upgrading which has been found only in Finland.

**Table 9.9** Employment changes in different educational quintiles (EU-28, Switzerland and Norway; 2011–2019)

| | 1st quintile (%) | 2nd quintile (%) | 3rd quintile (%) | 4th quintile (%) | 5th quintile (%) | Observed pattern |
|---|---|---|---|---|---|---|
| Norway | −12 | 1 | −9 | −3 | 18 | Upgrading |
| Switzerland | −13 | −1 | −20 | 9 | 19 | Upgrading |
| Ireland | −59 | −214 | −95 | −100 | 68 | Upgrading |
| Malta | −56 | −47 | 23 | 13 | 20 | Upgrading |
| Luxembourg | −23 | −31 | −3 | 0 | 31 | Upgrading |
| Netherlands | −24 | −24 | −4 | 18 | 18 | Upgrading |
| Portugal | −25 | −22 | −3 | 9 | 24 | Upgrading |
| Sweden | −12 | −18 | −1 | 14 | 10 | Upgrading |
| Romania | −38 | 1 | 12 | 3 | 12 | Upgrading |
| Denmark | −4 | −18 | −15 | 8 | 20 | Upgrading |
| Latvia | −12 | −14 | 0 | 5 | 16 | Upgrading |
| Cyprus | −16 | −7 | −8 | 5 | 19 | Upgrading |
| Croatia | −5 | −16 | −6 | −6 | 25 | Upgrading |
| Germany | −12 | −3 | −2 | 9 | 10 | Upgrading |
| Estonia | −6 | −13 | 0 | 3 | 13 | Upgrading |
| Poland | −7 | −7 | −6 | 1 | 15 | Upgrading |
| Belgium | −13 | 2 | −12 | −4 | 20 | Upgrading |
| Slovenia | 0 | −8 | −18 | 5 | 14 | Polarisation |
| Austria | 0 | −8 | −23 | −4 | 22 | Polarisation |
| France | −2 | −5 | −12 | −9 | 21 | Polarisation |
| Czech Republic | −2 | −10 | 1 | −12 | 18 | Polarisation |
| Bulgaria | −10 | 2 | 3 | 0 | 5 | Upgrading |
| Spain | 14 | −23 | −2 | −3 | 8 | Polarisation |
| Italy | 2 | −4 | −10 | 2 | 8 | Polarisation |
| United Kingdom | 1 | −2 | −13 | 0 | 11 | Polarisation |
| Hungary | 9 | −4 | −20 | 5 | 7 | Polarisation |
| Slovakia | −3 | −16 | −80 | −69 | 49 | Polarisation |
| Lithuania | 2 | 2 | 8 | −8 | 7 | Polarisation |
| Finland | −1 | −2 | −2 | −33 | 22 | Upgrading |
| Greece | −6 | 18 | −28 | −27 | 19 | Devaluation |
| EU-28, CH, NO | −7 | −7 | −5 | −1 | 16 | Upgrading |

Source and notes: See Table 9.8

Table 9.9 shows partially overlapping features. For nine countries, both indicators show an upgrading (e.g. in the Netherlands, Norway, Switzerland, Poland, Portugal and Sweden), for six countries, Belgium, Bulgaria, Germany, Croatia, Latvia and Romania, an upgrading can be observed on the basis of the educational levels, while a polarisation was found on the basis of the average wage levels. For five countries it is the other way round (Austria, Czech Republic, France, Hungary, Slovenia). This points to a relative decoupling of the education system and the economic structure: a strong expansion of the education system need not be immediately accompanied by an upgrading of the economic structures, while a shift to more value-added industries is not constrained by a stable educational structure of the labour force. The situation in Southern Europe is worrying, where the downgrading of the wage and occupational structure is only partially buffered by the expansion of further education.

In contrast to similar analyses (Goos & Manning, 2007; Goos et al., 2014; OECD, 2017), the previous analyses indicate that the upgrading of education and occupational structures has been the dominant European pattern in the last decade. This is in line with the expectations formulated on the basis of the thesis of skill-biased technological change. Similar to Fernández-Macías (2012), however, a polarisation or even a downgrading of the occupational skills can also be observed in many countries. This can also be explained by the economic structures and growth models of those countries. More industrialised countries and countries that have focused on personal services are more likely to rely on simple support activities than countries that have concentrated on advanced services.

If the assumption is correct that economic structures play an important role in the development of employment structures (and not only the institutional contexts as stressed by Fernández-Macías, 2012), then this should also shape the composition and the evolution of the occupational groups and industries. It can be expected that advanced services are associated with higher wages and education levels, while personal services are characterised by lower wages and skill requirements. Industry, on the other hand, creates both demanding and well-paid tasks, but also simpler manual and routine tasks. To test these assumptions, we first look at the occupational and industry-specific patterns of job quality below (Fig. 9.7). As in Table 9.8, the average wage level in the respective industry-occupation group in 2011 is taken as an indicator for the quality of work. These groups are assigned to five quintiles, just as in the previous analyses, so that the total employment volume in each of these quintiles is about 20%. At first glance, the relative weight of well-paid and low-paid jobs confirms expectations (Fig. 9.7): unskilled workers, farmers, salespersons and other service workers are predominantly (73%, 46% and 67% respectively) employed in industry-occupation clusters with lower wages. Managers, academically qualified professionals and also soldiers, on the other hand, are paid well above average. Machine operators, skilled industrial workers, office workers and technicians are located in the middle. These occupational groups are the backbone of industrial production and administration. At the same time, however, considerable parts of the workforce are situated in wage groups that do not correspond to this pattern: Two-fifths of machine operators and road drivers are paid average or even better wages. On the other hand, supposed top earners such as managers are by no means always paid far above average. One-sixth of managers work in sectors where the average wage for such jobs is below the top two quintiles.

Median wages also vary between sectors (Fig. 9.7). Low-wage earners are clearly concentrated in some sectors (for example in the hotel and restaurant industry, in

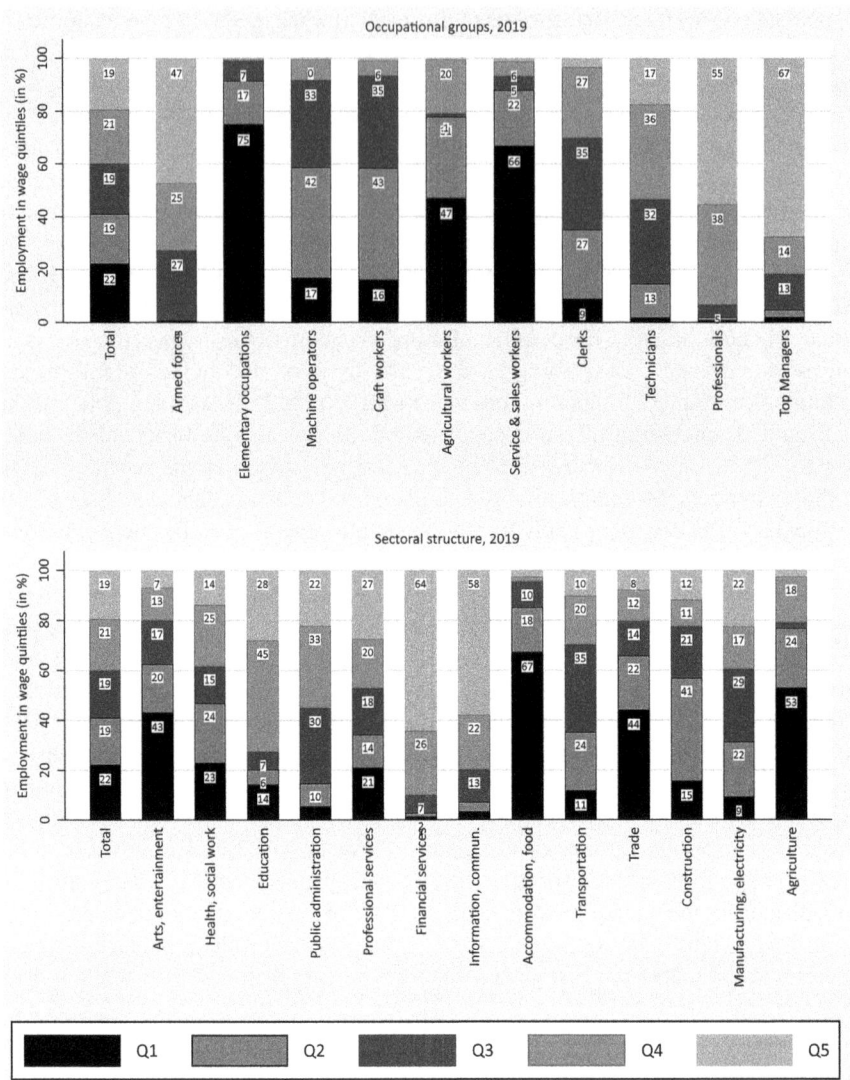

Source: See notes to Table 9.8.

**Fig. 9.7** Occupation- and industry-specific wage levels in the EU-28, Norway and Switzerland (2019)

retail trade, in agriculture or also in the arts, entertainment and recreation sector). An expansion of these industries—for example, through the expansion of tourism—would explain the *downgrading* of the employment structures observed especially in Southern Europe. In knowledge-intensive industries, on the other hand, which are more strongly represented in Northern and Continental Europe and on the British Isles, the share of high-wage earners is particularly high, for example in financial services, in education or in the information and communication industry. A strong position and expansion of these industries would explain the *upgrading* of employment structures. In other sectors, the range of wages in different occupational groups is considerably larger. This applies, for example, to public administration, transport, business services or the social and health sector, where not only well-paid doctors and social workers are employed, but also many low-paid care, cleaning and support workers. In industry, too, employees are almost evenly distributed among the top four of the five wage quintiles. Thus, in countries with a high share of industry a *polarisation of* employment structures can be expected, as the latter sectors are characterised by very heterogeneous wage and also occupational structures. For example, some of the business service providers are certainly top earners (such as IT experts, management consultants or marketing specialists). However, 20% of the employees in business-related services are located in the lowest earnings quintile (such as security, cleaning, warehouse and logistics workers). The occupational and industrial structure thus has a considerable influence on the employment structure as indicated by the respective wage level.

However, the three patterns previously distinguished (upgrading, polarisation and downgrading) do not describe static situations, but developments. This raises the question of how the employment volume is evolving in different industries and occupations: In which industries and occupations in particular are the lower-paid jobs increasing and in which the higher-paid tasks? In order to answer these questions, Fig. 9.8 shows how the number of employees in the five previously distinguished wage and education quintiles for the different occupation-industry groups evolved from 2011–2018/19. Figure 9.8 shows a clear increase in the number of employees in the two lower wage quintiles for office and support workers, technicians, salespersons and other simple services. This is consistent with the expectations of the polarisation thesis. An increase in better-paid tasks can be observed in academic occupations ("professionals"), but not among managers. The middle wage quintile is mainly composed of machine operators, skilled and office workers and technical tasks. Technicians and machine operators in particular are actually gaining in importance—contrary to what has been predicted by the polarisation thesis. A similar pattern emerges in the employment changes in the education quintiles (Fig. 9.8). The industry-specific employment changes (Fig. 9.8a, d) point to a strong expansion in the health and social sectors, in business services and in information and communication technologies. On the one hand, this means an increase in the share of better paid and better educated employees. On the other hand, there are also many low-paid employees in the health and social sectors. Their number is growing, so that the developments in these two sectors point to a clear polarisation. In regard to the education-specific quintiles, this polarisation can also be observed in industry, as both higher- and lower-skilled jobs are gaining in importance. Measured by the average wage level, on the other hand, employment in the upper wage quintiles is mostly increasing—an indication of the good remuneration in the manufacturing industry. The employment changes in the hotel and restaurant sector and in retail trade, on the other hand, support downgrading and polarisation theories, since these two sectors are dominated by lower-paid, but by no

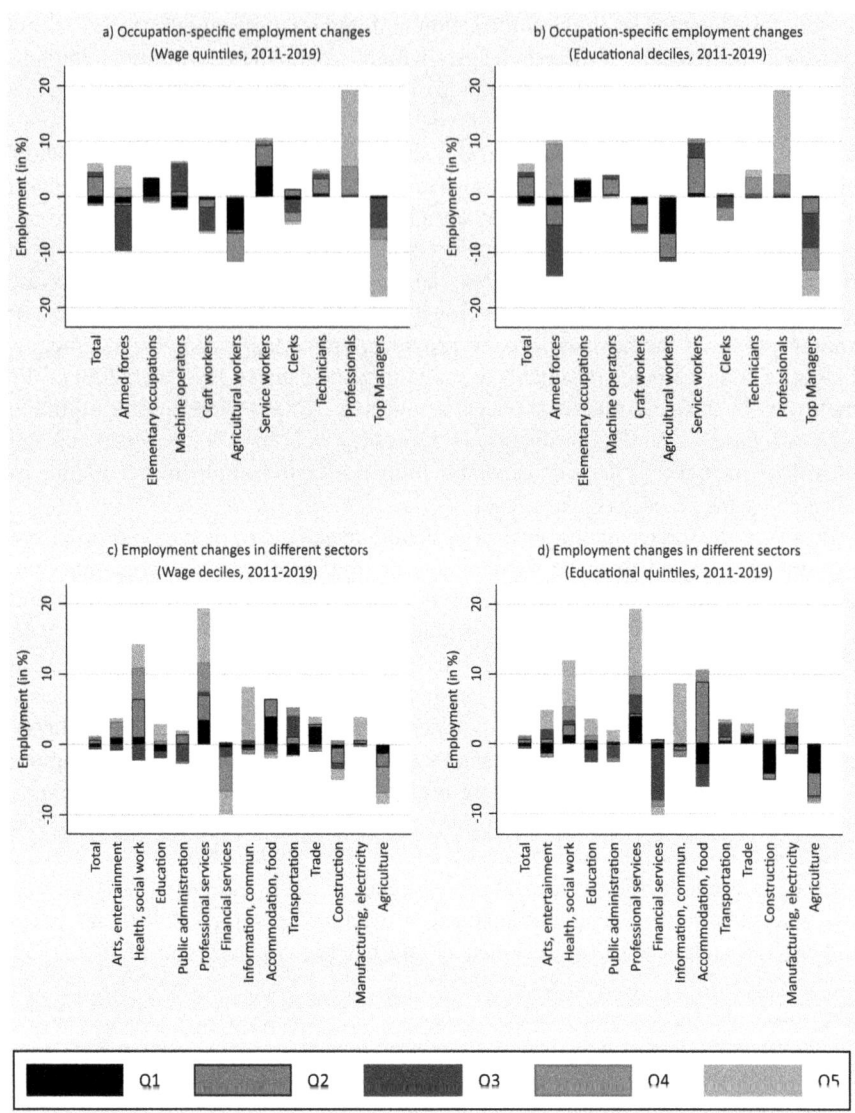

Source: See notes to Table 9.8. The graphs compare employment trends 2011-2019 (or 2018 in the case of the UK) in the industry and activity group clusters that were assigned to one of the respective five quintiles in 2011 based on their median wage level or median education level.

**Fig. 9.8** Employment changes in wage and education quintiles (EU-28, Switzerland and Norway; 2011–2019). (**a**) Occupation-specific employment changes (Wage quintiles, 2011–2019). (**b**) Occupation-specific employment changes (Educational deciles, 2011–2019). (**c**) Employment changes in different sectors (Wage deciles, 2011–2019). (**d**) Employment changes in different sectors (Educational quintiles, 2011–2019)

means lower-skilled employees. This also reflects a gender-specific wage pattern, since in these sectors qualified women also earn less, while in the transport sector and in industry even lower educated men are not necessarily low-paid.

In sum, three patterns of employment changes can thus be distinguished. Especially in the Continental, Northern and Northwestern European countries, an *upgrading* of the employment structure can be observed: Employment quintiles with higher pay and educational competences are gaining in importance, while lower-paid jobs with less qualified employees are losing importance. In Central, Eastern and Southern Europe in particular, but also in some Continental European countries, on the other hand, a *polarisation* or even a *downgrading* of the employment structure can be observed: Either the higher wage and education quintiles grow as strongly as the less demanding and lower-paid jobs or they even lose importance compared to the expanding simple and routine activities in industry and personal services. While these three patterns are usually explained by technological change (Autor et al., 2003) or institutional contexts (Fernández-Macías, 2012), here it has been argued that national economic structures and the related growth models also play a role. A focus on advanced services seems to favour an *upgrading* of the employment structure, while a concentration on manufacturing can be accompanied by a *polarisation* of the employment structure. A focus on simple, personal services, for example in tourism, retail trade and hotels and restaurants, favours a *downgrading* of employment structures.

## 9.6 Conclusion: Between Educational Poverty and Meritocratic Inequalities

In this chapter, it has been shown that the territorial division of Europe is also documented in the educational levels and the occupational skills of the population. Three different patterns of educational and skill inequality have been observed: a low level of education and occupational skills in Southern Europe, a well-developed middle skill segment in Continental, Central and Eastern Europe and a high proportion of academically educated employees with qualified jobs in Scandinavia and on the British Isles. This tripartite division also shapes the occupational and class structures: the upper and lower service classes and qualified service occupations play a crucial role in the Scandinavian and Anglo-Saxon countries, but also in the Continental European countries. In the Southern, Eastern and Central European countries, the proportions of unskilled and skilled workers are higher. The EU is thus territorially divided into countries that rely on a developed education system and entrust more highly educated workers with more demanding tasks, and countries with less developed education systems, where on average lower-skilled workers are employed for simple and routine tasks.

The international differences in educational opportunities, occupational skills and class situations are accompanied by considerable social differences. In the previous chapters, the different employment, wage and income opportunities of higher and lower qualified persons were shown. Section 9.2 showed that disposable income also differs considerably between educational strata, occupational skills and social classes: The household income of the low-skilled and those employed in routine jobs and blue-collar workers is 31%, 19% and 20% lower than that of the high-skilled, problem-solvers and decision-makers and the upper service class, respectively. These meritocratically legitimised differences are at the core of this chapter. However, non-meritocratically legitimised differences are still significant as well. In particular, single parents, young people and those born in or having citizenship of a non-EU country are particularly disadvantaged.

Educational inequalities are inherited to a considerable extent in Europe. The relative chances of children of academics also acquiring an academic degree are about six times higher than the chances of children without highly educated parents. The chances of obtaining a low education if one parent only has a low level of education are ten times as high as for people with highly educated parents. This gap undermines a meritocratic legitimisation of inequalities, since different educational opportunities are inherited in a similar way as wealth. When key socio-demographic characteristics of the respondents are controlled for, children of two academically qualified parents have a 16 times higher chance of acquiring an academic degree compared to children of parents with a low education. Academic parents are thus a real opportunity turbo for their children. In Europe, intergenerational equality of educational opportunities does not exist.

Next, the territorial and social distribution of educational poverty in Europe has been described. On the one hand, the Southern European countries have the highest share of people with a low level of education, on the other hand, the elderly, people from third countries and from poor households, the unemployed and employees with simple and routine jobs are characterised by low education. Educational poverty is a central factor for disadvantage and exclusion in work and life. Due to educational expansion, educational poverty is lower among younger than older people. Within-country differences between "educationally poor" and "educationally rich" regions have been increasing over the last two decades. One reason for this could be the structural change of the economy, as both a high share of knowledge-based services and advanced technologies and a high employment rate are regionally concentrated and contribute to lower regional shares of low-educated persons.

This raises the question of how the occupational skills of the labour force evolve given the current technological and economic transformations. While the thesis of skill-biased technological change predicts an upgrading, other authors expect a polarisation due to the relocation and automation of routinised tasks: Empirically, three patterns have been identified: In 15 of the 30 European countries considered, an *upgrading* of skill levels has taken place—especially in service-centred Scandinavian and Anglo-Saxon countries and in some Continental European countries. In more industrialised countries, on the other hand, a *polarisation* was observed (for example in Germany, Belgium and Italy), while in Southern European countries even an expansion of lower-paid jobs, i.e. a *downgrading,* was observed (for example in Spain and Greece). These different patterns can also be explained by the respective economic structures: While sophisticated, knowledge-based technologies and services require an upgrading of occupational skills, the focus on industrial activities is accompanied by a higher share of manual activities that cannot be routinised without difficulty. A higher share of personal services often implies a higher demand for low-skilled jobs.

This description resembles the situation of Ulysses who on his journeys faced the sea monsters Scylla and Charybdis. These monsters sat on two opposite rocks of a strait and pulled every ship into the abyss that came too close to them. On the one hand, educational expansion and the expansion of knowledge-based technologies and services in Europe are promoting an upgrading of skills structures. As a result, the social gap between higher- and lower-skilled workers, between more demanding and less demanding routine jobs, between service classes and manual and routine jobs is widening. This gap, which has been described for wages, employment opportunities, incomes, economic stress and life satisfaction, is reinforced and delegitimised by inherited cultural and economic capital. Educational opportunities depend to a considerable extent on social origin, so that the gap between the low- and high-educated and qualified cannot be attributed exclusively to the achievements of the highly qualified (Gerhards et al., 2017). These deep and increasing divisions threaten the social cohesion of the European nation-states and Europe as a whole. On the other hand, some European countries and regions do not even have the opportunity to regret the downsides of such a meritocratic division of society. They have concentrated on activities with lower value added and lower education and skill requirements within a European and global division of labour. Southern European regions in particular, with a higher share of personal services, seem to be caught in a vicious circle of low productivity, low education and a devaluation of activity and skill structures. Like Ulysses, Europe must therefore seek its way between the Scylla of the meritocratic fractures of society and the Charybdis of educational poverty and polarised skills structures.

# References

Arntz, M., Gregory, T., & Zierahn, U. (2018). *Digitalisierung und die Zukunft der Arbeit: Makroökonomische Auswirkungen auf Beschäftigung*. Arbeitslosigkeit und Löhne von morgen. ZEW-Gutachten und Forschungsberichte. Zentrum für Europäische Wirtschaftsforschung (ZEW), Mannheim.

Autor, D. H., Levy, F., & Murnane, R. J. (2003). The skill content of recent technological change: An empirical exploration. *Quarterly Journal of Economics, 118*(4), 1279–1333.

Becker, G. S. (1993). *Human capital: A theoretical and empirical analysis, with special reference to education*. University of Chicago Press.

Becker, R., & Lauterbach, W. (2016). Bildung als Privileg: Ursachen, Mechanismen, Prozesse und Wirkungen. In R. Becker & W. Lauterbach (Eds.), *Bildung als Privileg* (pp. 3–53). Springer. https://doi.org/10.1007/978-3-658-11952-2_1

Berger, J. (2019). *Wirtschaftliche Ungleichheit: Zwölf Vorlesungen*. Springer. https://doi.org/10.1007/978-3-658-23682-3

Blossfeld, H.-P., & Timm, A. (2003). *Who marries whom? Educational systems as marriage markets in modern societies. European studies of population: Vol. 12.* Kluwer Academic.

Bourdieu, P. (1983). Ökonomisches Kapital, kulturelles Kapital, soziales Kapital. In R. Kreckel (Ed.), *Soziale Welt Sonderband (Soziale Ungleichheiten)* (Vol. 2, pp. 183–198). Schwartz.

Bourdieu, P. (1984). *Distinction: A social critique of the judgement of taste.* Harvard University Press.

Bourdieu, P. (1991). *Sozialer Raum und "Klassen": Leçon sur la leçon: zwei Vorlesungen. Suhrkamp Taschenbuch Wissenschaft: Vol. 500.* Suhrkamp.

Bourdieu, P. (1996). *The state nobility: Elite schools in the field of power.* Polity.

Dahrendorf, R. (1965). *Bildung ist Bürgerrecht.* Nannen.

DiPrete, T. A. (2007). What has sociology to contribute to the study of inequality trends? A historical and comparative perspective. *American Behavioral Scientist, 50*(5), 603–618. https://doi.org/10.1177/0002764206295009

Drewski, D., Gerhards, J., & Hans, S. (2018). National symbolic capital in a multinational environment: An exploratory study of symbolic boundaries at a European school in Brussels. *Innovation: The European Journal of Social Science Research, 31*(4), 429–448. https://doi.org/10.1080/13511610.2018.1544484

Fernández-Macías, E. (2012). Job polarization in Europe? Changes in the employment structure and job quality, 1995-2007. *Work and Occupations, 39*(2), 157–182. https://doi.org/10.1177/0730888411427078

Frey, C. B., & Osborne, M. A. (2017). The future of employment: how susceptible are jobs to computerisation? *Technological Forecasting and Social Change, 114,* 254–280.

Gengnagel, V., Beyer, S., Baier, C., & Münch, R. (2019). Europeanisation and global academic capitalism: The case of the European Research Council. In M. Heidenreich (Ed.), *Horizontal Europeanisation: The transnationalisation of daily life and social fields in Europe* (pp. 129–151). Routledge.

Gerhards, J., Hans, S., & Carlson, S. (2017). *Social class and transnational human capital: How middle and upper class parents prepare their children for globalization.* Routledge.

Goos, M., & Manning, A. (2007). Lousy and lovely jobs: The rising polarization of work in Britain. *The Review of Economics and Statistics, 89*(1), 118–133.

Goos, M., Manning, A., & Salomons, A. (2009). Job polarization in Europe. *American Economic Review, 99*(2), 58–63. https://doi.org/10.1257/aer.99.2.58

Goos, M., Manning, A., & Salomons, A. (2014). Explaining job polarization: Routine-biased technological change and offshoring. *American Economic Review, 104*(8), 2509–2526. https://doi.org/10.1257/aer.104.8.2509

Heidenreich, M. (2019). Regionale Muster von Bildungsarmut. In G. Quenzel & K. Hurrelmann (Eds.), *Handbuch Bildungsarmut* (pp. 29–38). Springer. https://doi.org/10.1007/978-3-658-19573-1_2

Heidenreich, M., & Baur, N. (2015). Locations of corporate headquarters in Europe. Between inertia and co-evolution. In S. M. Lundan (Ed.), *Transnational corporations and transnational governance* (Vol. 38, pp. 177–208). Palgrave Macmillan. https://doi.org/10.1057/9781137467690_7

ILO. (2012). *International standard classification of occupations // Structure, group definitions and correspondence tables: Structure, group definitions and correspondence tables. ISCO-08: Volume 1 // v. 1.* ILO. Retrieved from https://www.ilo.org/public/english/bureau/stat/isco/index.htm

Jackson, M., Erikson, R., Goldthorpe, J. H., & Yaish, M. (2007). Primary and secondary effects in class differentials in educational attainment: The transition to A-level courses in England and Wales. *Acta Sociologica, 50*(3), 211–229. Retrieved from www.jstor.org/stable/20459999

Kalleberg, A. L. (2011). *Good jobs, bad jobs: The rise of polarized and precarious employment systems in the United States, 1970s to 2000s.* American Sociological Association's Rose series in sociology. Russell Sage Foundation.

Krugman, P. (1991). *Geography and trade. Gaston Eyskens lecture series.* MIT Press.

Lohauß, P., Nauenburg, R., Rehkämper, K., & Rockmann, Ulrike: Wachtendorf, Thomas. (2010). Daten der amtlichen Statistik zur Bildungsarmut. In G. Quenzel & K. Hurrelmann (Eds.), *Bildungsverlierer: Neue Ungleichheiten* (pp. 181–201). VS.

Maassen, P., & Musselin, C. (2009). European integration and the Europeanisation of Higher Education. In A. Amaral, G. Neave, C. Musselin, & P. Maassen (Eds.), *European integration and the governance of higher education and research* (pp. 3–14). Springer. https://doi.org/10.1007/978-1-4020-9505-4_1

Müller, W., Wirth, H., Bauer, G., Pollak, R., & Weiss, F. (2007). Entwicklung einer europäischen sozioökonomischen Klassifikation. *Wirtschaft Und Statistik*. (H. 5), 527–530.

OECD. (2017). *Employment Outlook 2017*. OECD. https://doi.org/10.1787/19991266

OECD. (2019). *What students know and can do: PISA 2018 results* (Volume I). PISA results 2018. OECD. Retrieved from https://www.oecd-ilibrary.org/education/pisa-2018-results-volume-iii_acd78851-en

Parkin, F. (1974). Strategies of social closure in class formation. In F. Parkin (Ed.), *The social analysis of class structure* (pp. 1–18). Tavistock Publications.

Parsons, T. (1970). Equality and inequality in modern society, or social stratification revisited. *Sociological Inquiry, 40*(2), 13–72. https://doi.org/10.1111/j.1475-682X.1970.tb01002.x

Piore, M. J., & Sabel, C. F. (1984). *The second industrial divide: Possibilities for prosperity*. Basic Books.

Powell, J. J. W., & Trampusch, C. (2012). Europeanization and the varying responses in collective skill systems. In M. R. Busemeyer & C. Trampusch (Eds.), *The political economy of collective skill formation* (pp. 284–313). Oxford University Press.

Quenzel, G., & Hurrelmann, K. (2010). Bildungsverlierer: Neue soziale Ungleichheiten in der Wissensgesellschaft. In G. Quenzel & K. Hurrelmann (Eds.), *Bildungsverlierer: Neue Ungleichheiten* (pp. 11–33). VS.

Quenzel, G., & Hurrelmann, K. (Eds.). (2019). *Handbuch Bildungsarmut*. Springer.

Reich, R. B. (1992). *The work of nations: Preparing ourselves for 21st century capitalism*. Vintage.

Rose, D., & Harrison, E. (Eds.). (2010). *Social class in Europe: An introduction to the European socio-economic classification* (Vol. 10). Routledge.

Schleicher, A. (2019). *PISA 2018: Insights and interpretations*. ERIC. Retrieved from OECD Publishing website: https://www.oecd.org/pisa/PISA%202018%20Insights%20and%20Interpretations%20FINAL%20PDF.pdf

Schneider, S. L. (2010). Nominal comparability is not enough: (In-)equivalence of construct validity of cross-national measures of educational attainment in the European Social Survey. *Research in Social Stratification and Mobility, 28*(3), 343–357. https://doi.org/10.1016/j.rssm.2010.03.001

Shavit, Y., & Blossfeld, H.-P. (1993). *Persistent inequality: Changing educational attainment in thirteen countries. Social inequality series: Vol. 214*. Westview Press.

Solga, H. (2017). Bildungsarmut und Ausbildungslosigkeit in der Bildungs- und Wissensgesellschaft. In R. Becker (Ed.), *Lehrbuch der Bildungssoziologie* (pp. 443–485). Springer.

Wacquant, L. J. D., & Bourdieu, P. (1993). From ruling class to field of power: An interview with Pierre Bourdieu on La Noblesse d'Etat. *Theory, Culture & Society, 10*(3), 19–44.

# Chapter 10
# Wealth Inequality and Housing in Europe

**Abstract** This chapter discusses national patterns of wealth inequality and housing in Europe. Wealth inequalities are more than twice the size of income inequalities. This is also a result of the path dependence and heterogeneity of wealth. Apart from the super-rich, who are omitted here, wealth for most households means owning a property. A distinction can be made between, firstly, households with debt-free dwellings, in which the head of the household is usually older, less educated and sicker and has often already retired from working life; secondly, more highly educated, higher-earning, employed owners still paying a mortgage and, thirdly, tenants who are more often at risk of poverty and whose dwellings are more often darker, noisier, and damp. Owning a property is facilitated by a high household income and also by the family of origin and its financial possibilities. Debt-free, inherited properties play a significant role in Central, Eastern and Southern Europe; property purchases in the British Isles and Scandinavia and rented dwellings in Scandinavia and Continental Europe. Housing markets in more developed countries are thus associated with a lower importance of owner-occupied dwellings and a higher importance of property purchases and rentals, and also with greater wealth inequalities.

Previously, the patterns of income inequality in Europe (Chap. 7) and its key determinants, in particular labour force participation (Chap. 5) and wage levels (Chap. 6), have been analysed. Another crucial dimension of economic inequality has so far been excluded, namely wealth inequality.[1] This is not unusual in social science. The decades-long neglect of wealth in the analysis of social inequalities has both systematic and empirical reasons: On the one hand, in modern societies the focus is on income earned through labour or capital—and no longer on ownership of land. This change also determines the class structure. At the centre of bourgeois societies are acquisition classes (*Erwerbsklassen*; in contrast to ownership classes),

---

[1] Assets are all tangible and intangible goods and rights valued in money that a person or a household possesses. Tangible assets include, for example, land, property and companies, while financial assets include cash, stocks, securities or receivables. In contrast to disposable income, wealth refers to stocks and not to flows.

which, according to Max Weber, are determined by "marketability of goods and services" (Weber, 1978, p. 302). This marketability is documented by incomes from labour and capital, i.e. by the inflow of resources and not by their stock, even if some acquisition classes are also property-based if they are defined by the ownership or non-ownership of the means of production. In modern, meritocratic societies, wealth recedes even further into the background, because class position is defined by achievement, education and occupation. Educational classes take centre stage. The shift from a wealth-centred to an occupation- and education-centred inequality structure has been described by Bourdieu (1984, 1996). It is accompanied by the transformation from a family-centred reproduction of social inequalities to a family-based reproduction with a schooling component: the intergenerational reproduction of social inequalities no longer takes place primarily through the transmission of family wealth, but above all through family support in the attainment of educational titles (cf. Sect. 9.3). Thus, theoretical attention focusing on wealth and wealth inequalities clearly declined in the twentieth century.

Empirically as well, incomes and income inequality have become more important in relationship to wealth in the twentieth century. In a large-scale study, the French economist Thomas Piketty (2014) found that the ratio of wealth to disposable income in the twentieth century was significantly lower in France, Germany, the US and other countries than in the previous or the subsequent century. Disposable income was thus the central determinant of living conditions. It enabled the middle classes to make a decent living in the post-war period, while wealth and the income earned through wealth were much less important than at the beginning of the twentieth century. The reasons for this were war-related destruction and a historically exceptional growth of the economy after WWII. Income grew rapidly while accumulated wealth had been destroyed by the two world wars or devalued by technological change (Piketty, 2014). However, the greater importance of income compared to wealth could be a historical exception, as lower growth rates or even a "secular stagnation" (Summers, 2016) in conjunction with zero and negative interest rates from central banks go hand in hand with a relatively greater role of wealth. This raises the question of the level of wealth inequality in Europe, its facets and determining factors and its effects on living conditions. The effects of wealth inequality are manifold. They include the evasion of taxes (Saez & Zucman, 2019), a disproportionate political influence of the super-rich, the decoupling of the interests of the wealthy from those of the rest of the population. Above all, however, wealth inequalities are expressed in the division between property owners and tenants. This is the most concrete form in which most households are confronted with wealth inequality because wealth mostly means property.

In the following sections, we first describe the extent of wealth inequality in Europe and distinguish between four types of households with different relationships to wealth: the super-rich, debt-free property owners, property owners still paying mortgages and tenants (Sect. 10.1). Since wealth inequality for the majority of households means owning their dwelling or not, Sect. 10.2 describes the social situation of owners and tenants, the quality of property and national patterns of property ownership. Subsequently, Sect. 10.3 discusses which individual and national factors influence the ownership or non-ownership of a property and its value, including the economic and cultural capital of the family of origin. The chapter concludes with a brief summary (Sect. 10.4).

## 10.1   Four Worlds of Wealth

In this section, different national patterns of wealth inequality and different types of wealthy and asset-less households will be distinguished. This requires first of all an overview on the very limited availability of data on wealth. Due to considerable underreporting, especially among the super-rich (Bach et al., 2019), and the lack of longer time series (Balestra & Tonkin, 2018), the thesis of a secular increase in wealth inequality can be tested and confirmed only for a very small number of countries (Piketty, 2014). A broad data set such as the *OECD's Wealth Distribution Database* only provides wealth data from 2009 to 2019 for a maximum of 28 countries and for a maximum of 5 years. The *Luxembourg Wealth Study* (LWS) provides wealth data for 18 countries—13 of them European countries—for eight waves starting in 1995 at 5-year intervals. For almost all of the 19 eurozone member states, but also for the non-euro countries Hungary, Croatia and Poland, the OECD data are based on the *Household Finance and Consumption Survey* of the ECB, which were conducted in 2010/1, 2013/4, 2017 and 2020 (European Central Bank, 2021). In Table 10.1, key results of these surveys for 2017—the last year for which sufficient data are available—are shown. For three EU countries (Romania, Bulgaria, Czech Republic) and for Switzerland, none of the above-mentioned sources provide data on wealth inequality. Data for these countries are therefore supplemented by *Credit Suisse data* (Shorrocks et al., 2021) and the *WID* (Alvaredo et al., 2018). In addition to the Gini coefficient, the table also shows the wealth shares of the richest 10% or 5% of households, as such shares are more meaningful than the Gini coefficient in the case of very skewed distributions.

First, it can be seen from Table 10.1 that wealth inequalities are far greater than income inequalities. While the Gini coefficient for income inequality in the eurozone is 0.304 (2017), it is 0.695 for wealth inequality, i.e. it is more than twice as high (all data without between-country inequality). While the 10% of the eurozone population with the highest income accounts for 23% (2017) of total income, the richest decile of the population accounts for 51.9% of all assets, i.e. more than twice as much.

On the basis of the data reported in Table 10.1, three groups of countries can be distinguished: First, wealthier, often Continental and Northern European countries, where the top decile of households owns at least 55% of total wealth and the Gini coefficient of wealth inequality is well above 0.70. This group includes, for example, Denmark, the Netherlands, Austria and Germany, but also Cyprus and Estonia, i.e. countries characterised by relatively egalitarian income structures. The second group includes Southern and Eastern European countries in which the top decile owns less than 48% of total wealth and the Gini coefficient is 0.60 or less. These countries are characterised by relatively egalitarian wealth structures—despite partly

**Table 10.1**  Wealth inequalities in Europe (around 2017)

| | Net wealth means (1000 €) | Net wealth medians (1000 €) | Share of top 5% of wealth | Share of top 10% of wealth | Gini coefficient |
|---|---|---|---|---|---|
| Sweden | | | 59.6 (2020)** | 74.0 (2020)** | 0.872 (2020)** |
| Czech Republic | | | 56.2 (2020)** | 67.3 (2020)** | 0.777 (2020)** |
| Switzerland | | | 51.0 (2020)** | 63.8 (2020)** | 0.781 (2020)* |
| Denmark | | | 45.8 (2019)* | 62.1 (2019)* | 0.736 (2020)** |
| Cyprus | 683.8 | 280.6 | 49.3 | 62.1 | 0.749 |
| Estonia | 133.2 | 66.1 | 45.4 | 58.1 | 0.709 |
| Bulgaria | | | | 57.7*** | 0.701 (2020)** |
| Netherlands | 270.2 | 169.9 | 42 | 56.6 | 0.782 |
| Austria | 476.3 | 278.9 | 43.1 | 56.4 | 0.73 |
| Romania | | | 44.0 (2020)** | 56.0 (2020)** | 0.701 (2020)** |
| Germany | 459.8 | 277 | 40.8 | 55.4 | 0.739 |
| Portugal | 206.7 | 103.1 | 41.6 | 53.9 | 0.679 |
| Norway | | | 40.5 (2018)* | 53.8 (2018)* | 0.785 (2020)* |
| Spain | 320.7 | 167.2 | 39.9 | 52.7 | 0.677 |
| Latvia | 55 | 30.6 | 38.7 | 52.1 | 0.679 |
| Great Britain | | | 39.5* | 52.0* | 0.717 (2020)** |
| Hungary | 84 | 44.8 | 39.2 | 51.3 | 0.649 |
| Ireland | 508.7 | 288.6 | 35.9 | 50.4 | 0.674 |
| Luxembourg | 1219.5 | 732.4 | 38 | 50.2 | 0.652 |
| France | 380.7 | 242.7 | 35.5 | 49.2 | 0.674 |
| Lithuania | 89.1 | 49.2 | 36 | 47.9 | 0.589 |
| Malta | 483.2 | 290.1 | 37 | 47.7 | 0.602 |
| Belgium | 492.5 | 311.3 | 35 | 47.2 | 0.632 |
| Finland | 299.1 | 195.1 | 32.9 | 46.8 | 0.662 |
| Croatia | 122.9 | 75.2 | 35.1 | 46.6 | 0.606 |
| Slovenia | 181.4 | 116.1 | 32.2 | 44 | 0.594 |
| Italy | 298.9 | 201.5 | 30 | 43.4 | 0.606 |
| Poland | 115.7 | 77.5 | 29.6 | 41.3 | 0.567 |
| Greece | 121.6 | 83.9 | 27 | 41.3 | 0.602 |
| Slovakia | 115 | 78.6 | 29.1 | 40.6 | 0.54 |
| Eurozone | 346.1 | 203 | 38.1 | 51.9 | 0.695 |

Source: European Central Bank (2021), OECD Wealth Distribution Database (WDD), Credit Swiss and World Inequality Database (Alvaredo et al., 2018). *: OECD data; **: Shorrocks et al., 2021. ***: WID. The table is sorted by the share of top 10% of wealth. Indicators refer to 2017 unless otherwise stated

high income inequalities. Therefore, in these countries the differences between average and median wealth are smaller than in the first group. The third and intermediary group comprises countries with average wealth inequalities, i.e. a Gini of about 0.66 and a share of the top decile in total wealth of 50–54%. A clear geographical focus cannot be identified for this group; it comprises Southern and Northern European, Eastern and Western European countries.

This tripartite division also sheds light on the relationship between income and wealth inequality, which are hardly correlated at the macrolevel (Fig. 10.1). Semyonov and Lewin-Epstein (2013) as well as Pfeffer and Waitkus (2021, p. 1) emphasise that income and wealth are relatively independent dimensions of national patterns of social inequality. At first sight, this is surprising, since income and wealth are not logically independent of each other as flow and stock variables: High incomes enable the accumulation of wealth *over time (!)*, so that high income inequality could also be associated with higher wealth inequality. Similarly, high wealth also enables high income due to capital income. Empirically, however, high wealth inequality can also be observed in some egalitarian countries such as Denmark, the Netherlands, Austria, Germany, Cyprus and Estonia, while it is much lower in very unequal countries such as Lithuania, Latvia, Italy or Greece (Fig. 10.1).

This raises the question of how wealth inequalities can be explained. A starting point for answering this question is the heterogeneity and path dependency of wealth: At first, wealth is composed of very different types of assets and asset owners (Pfeffer & Waitkus, 2021). Besides property, it consists of financial assets,

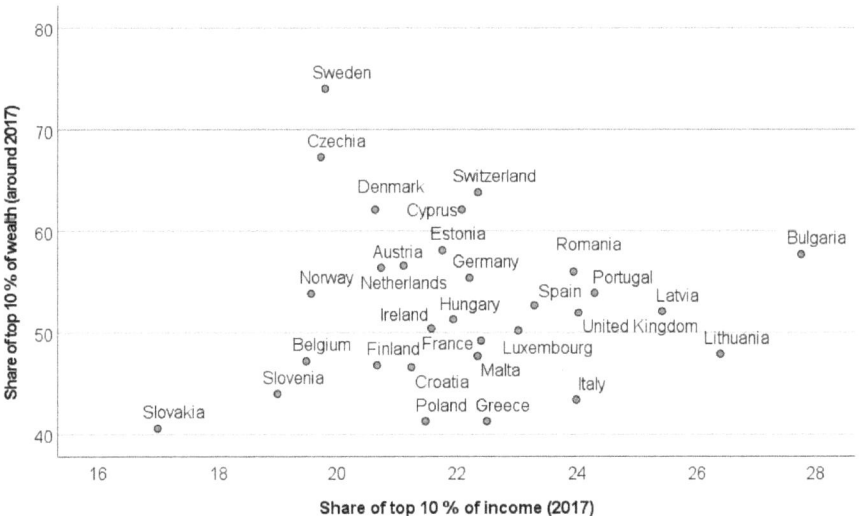

Notes: Income and wealth shares of the highest earning or wealthiest decile of households are shown. 28 EU countries plus Norway and Switzerland. Reference year and sources: See Table 10.1. Own calculations based on EU-SILC 2018.

**Fig. 10.1**   Wealth and income inequalities in 30 European countries (2017)

companies and other valuables. Second, wealth is partly the result of decades- and century-long strategies of wealth accumulation. The decoupling of income and wealth inequality reported in Fig. 10.1 therefore also reflects the fact that wealth is not only the result of current income, but it is also inherited from the family of origin.

In order to deal with the heterogeneity and path dependency of wealth, it is useful to distinguish four "worlds of wealth" (cf. Lauterbach & Kramer, 2009 for another, more fine-grained typology of the wealthy): Firstly, the world of the very and super-rich, i.e. the small share of households that, in addition to their inhabited property, also owns financial assets, business assets or further property and who can often also expect notable inheritances. This group embraces a maximum of 5% of European households, which possess about two-fifths of the total wealth (Table 10.1). This group is often defined by the amount of their disposable net wealth, even though entrepreneurs and their business assets are at the core of this group (cf. three examples in Lauterbach & Tarvenkorn, 2011). As a function of the respective research interests, this group can also be defined as being much smaller: For the USA, Saez and Zucman (2016) reported that only 0.1% of households own 22% (2012) of the total wealth. In the ECB's wealth survey, the impact of this group is documented in an enormous difference between the average and median wealth of the wealthiest tenth of European households, which indicates a very small, very wealthy group of households (1,189,300 € vs. 781,400 €; European Central Bank, 2021, 3 und 5).

For most of the wealthy European households, their major asset is their own dwelling. Across Europe, approximately 55–60% of all households belong to this category (the homeowners minus the first group). According to the European Central Bank (2021), 60.3% of all households in the eurozone owned their main domestic residence in 2017. Eurostat estimates that 66.1% of the eurozone population own their dwelling (table ilc_lvho02). The next section shows that this group can be further divided into debt-free owners and households still paying a mortgage. Owners of debt-free properties—the second group distinguished here—usually acquired or inherited the property some time ago, while owners still paying a mortgage—the third group distinguished here—usually acquired their property only a shorter time ago (Sect. 10.2). The fourth group comprises tenants. In the euro area, 39.7% of all households belonged to this group in 2017. Their median net wealth was 9000 €, compared to 203,000 € in the group of homeowners (European Central Bank, 2021, p. 1). In the 30 countries usually considered in this book (EU-28, Norway, Switzerland), 34.8% of households belong to this group. Their poverty rate is more than twice as high as that of property owners. Even if owning property does not always mean being wealthy, owning a house clearly reduces the risk of poverty.

The heterogeneity of wealth, its sources and the different types of wealthy households also explain why classical multivariate analyses often fail in explaining the distribution of wealth in different countries. For example, Semyonov and Lewin-Epstein (2013) examine numerous national contextual factors that might explain differences in the wealth distribution: Economic output per capita, social protection expenditure, income and wealth taxes, ownership rate, mortgage credit burden . . .

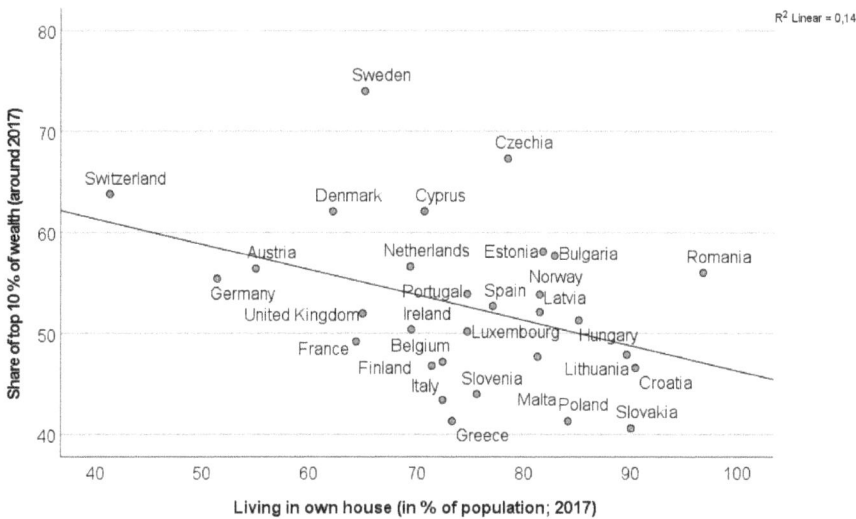

Notes: The figure shows the share of the population living in their own flat or house and the wealth share of the richest decile of households. Sources: See Table 10.1 and Eurostat, Table [ilc_lvho02].

**Fig. 10.2**  Wealth inequality and home ownership in 30 European countries (2017)

However, none of these variables had a significant impact. Therefore, instead of focusing on all types of wealth, we will examine the differences between housing owners and renters, excluding the group of extremely wealthy households. In a similar vein, Pfeffer and Waitkus (2021, p. 7) argue that wealth inequalities should be considered as a population-wide phenomenon and focus on inequalities among the 99% of the (non-super-rich) population. This decision also has methodological implications, as different methods are useful for an investigation of the super-rich and other wealthy households—on the one hand case studies and complete surveys for the small number of super-rich, on the other hand predominantly representative studies for the rest of the population. The latter is the strategy pursued here: The following section focuses on the social differences between homeowners and tenants and between the owners themselves. The question is which factors are decisive for the ownership and value of a dwelling. The group of the super-rich will be excluded (cf. Druyen et al., 2009; Lauterbach et al., 2011).

## 10.2   Living in a Self-Owned Home: An Important Dimension of Social Inequality

In everyday life and for the majority of the population, wealth inequalities are documented by the (lack of) opportunity for home ownership. Property and, in particular, a self-owned house or apartment is the most valuable asset for more than half of all households: Four-fifths of wealth in the euro area (2017: 80.9%; cf. European Central Bank, 2021, p. 21) are real and not financial assets. And 60.2% of these real assets consist of the property used by the household itself, to 23.4% of other property, to 10.6% of the value of self-owned businesses and to 5.8% of the value of household's vehicles and other valuables. Two-thirds of total wealth thus consists of property, while the self-owned dwelling accounts for half of Europe-wide wealth. The self-owned dwelling is therefore a key dimension of wealth inequality (Pfeffer & Waitkus, 2021). A starting point for the analysis of wealth inequality is the question of how high the proportion of households is that live in their own property or rent their dwelling. In this respect, the differences in Europe are considerable (Eurostat, table [ilc_lvho02]): while 96.8% of Romanians, 90.5% of Croats and 90.1% of Slovaks lived in their own property in 2017, in Switzerland this is only the case for 41.3% of the population, in Germany for 51.4%, in Austria for 55%. This suggests that people in wealthier countries in particular are more likely to rent and that this is associated with greater wealth inequality. At the macrolevel, this assumption can be confirmed (Fig. 10.2): One seventh of the wealth inequalities can be explained by the national differences in home ownership or renting rates.

If the super-rich are left out, the explanation of wealth inequalities and its levels thus can be translated into the question of which households own their dwelling and how these households and their homes differ from tenants and their accommodation. In the following, the poverty, exclusion, education and deprivation risks of tenant and homeowner households and the type and quality of their housing are described, thus contributing to the study of the concrete expressions of wealth inequalities. The extensive literature on the national regulation of the housing market is not discussed (Allen et al., 2004; Balchin, 1996), even though selected results are used to interpret the data.

In the following, three different groups on the housing market will be distinguished: firstly, owners without outstanding mortgages or housing loans; secondly, owners with a mortgage or loan (a distinction that has only been possible in EU-SILC since 2010), and thirdly, tenants. In 2019, 45.2% of households in the 30 countries previously mentioned belonged to the first group, 19.9% to the second and 34.9% to the third.

Figure 10.3 shows the risks of poverty, exclusion and deprivation for tenant and homeowner households (a relationship that cannot be interpreted causally, since a higher income makes it easier to buy a house, just as owning a flat reduces the risk of poverty since housing costs are much lower). The poverty risks of tenants are significantly higher than the risks of debt-free and indebted property owners from 2007 to 2019 (Fig. 10.3a). While the poverty risk of debt-free households was 14.9% in 2019, it was 26.8% for tenants in the same year and 6.4% for homeowners who are still paying off their mortgages. Thus, only well-off households can afford to buy a property. The gap to the other household types has widened significantly since 2010. At that time, the poverty rate was still 8.1% for indebted households, 14.1% for debt-free owners and 26% for tenants. Remarkably, the poverty risk is higher for debt-free than for indebted households. The subjective assessment of their own financial situation (Fig. 10.3c) reflects the excellent financial situation of indebted owners: Only 11.3% (2019) of them state that they have difficulties in making ends meet.

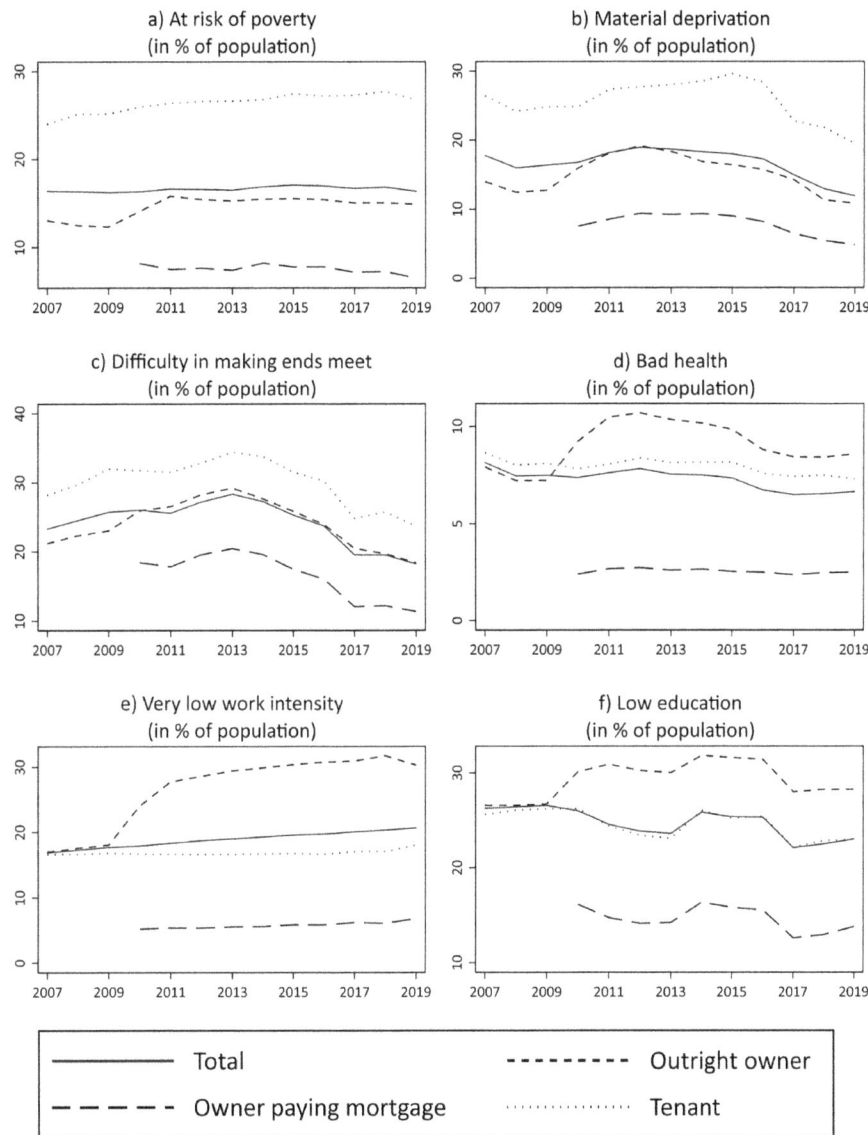

Source: Own calculations based on EU-SILC 2007-2019. The indicators used were defined in section 8.3 (Table 8.3).

**Fig. 10.3** Social risks of tenants and owners in 30 European countries (2007–2019). (**a**) At risk of poverty (in % of population). (**b**) Material deprivation (in % of population). (**c**) Difficulty in making ends meet (in % of population). (**d**) Bad health (in % of population). (**e**) Very low work intensity (in % of population). (**f**) Low education (in % of population)

This proportion is considerably lower than for debt-free owners (18.4%) and renters (23.7%), showing once again that homeowners paying their mortgage are in a comparatively good financial situation. Also the extent of material deprivation (Fig. 10.3b) reflects the economic hardships of tenants (19.5% in 2019) and the good financial position of households paying a mortgage (4.8%). Not surprisingly, only a very small proportion of indebted owners live in a household with a low work intensity (2019: 6.8%; Fig. 10.3e). The adults in these households are still in the middle of their working lives and have to pay off their property—often a decades-long challenge. Many of the older, debt-free owners, on the other hand, are already retired: 30.3% of them report a low work intensity. For tenants, this rate is 18%. The low rate of indebted owners with a low education (2019: 13.8%; Fig. 10.3f) shows that mainly well-off, qualified, employed persons in good health can afford to buy a property. Among older owners, the share of the educationally poor is considerably higher (2019: 28.2%). Not surprisingly, 8.6% (2019) of the significantly older debt-free owners complain of bad health, the figure is only 2.5% for indebted owners and 7.3% for tenants.

In the next step, reported problems with the dwelling and the living environment will be discussed as indicators of the quality of the property (Fig. 10.4). One twentieth of the surveyed households report significant *problems with repaying debts* (such as mortgages) (2019: 4.9%; cf. Figure 10.4a). These problems are higher among tenant and indebted homeowner households. 5.1% (2019) of the households report that their accommodation has *too little daylight or is too dark* (Fig. 10.4b). These problems are particularly high in rented housing (7.4%). Other problems are much more widespread: one fifth of households report *noise pollution*, for example from neighbours, traffic, shops or industry (2019: 18.4%; cf. Figure 10.4c). This mainly affects renters (26.2%), while owners live in quieter areas (13.5% and 15.7% respectively). One seventh report pollution, soot or other *environmental problems* (2019: 15.6%; Fig. 10.4d). Again, this affects significantly more renters (20.5%) than owners (12.7% and 13.6%). One in nine households report *crime*, violence or vandalism in the residential environment (2019: 11.2%; Fig. 10.4e)—especially tenants (15.2%). One-eighth of respondents complain of a *leaking roof, damp walls, floors or foundations, rot* in window frames or floors (2019: 12.6%; Fig. 10.4f). Again, this mainly affects tenants (16.5%). The slightly higher scores for debt-free compared to indebted homeowners show that although the debt-free properties are situated in quieter locations with no environmental issues, they are in a worse condition (10.7% compared to 10%)—presumably because they were bought or inherited a longer time ago. It is noteworthy that most of these problems (too little daylight, crime, leaking roofs, noise pollution) are becoming significantly less severe throughout Europe, while pollution and environmental pollution are stagnating at a high level.

Overall Fig. 10.4 shows that especially tenants suffer from the housing problems mentioned: Surprisingly, repaying loans is as large a burden and at times an even greater one for them as for property owners who still have to service a mortgage loan. Rented dwellings have less daylight, noise and soot pollution is higher, they are more often located in violent neighbourhoods and the roof leaks more often. The figure thus points to a clearly owner-dominated market: tenants do not always have the opportunity to escape massive housing problems by renting another flat, while owners can reduce many of the problems mentioned by repairing their houses—if

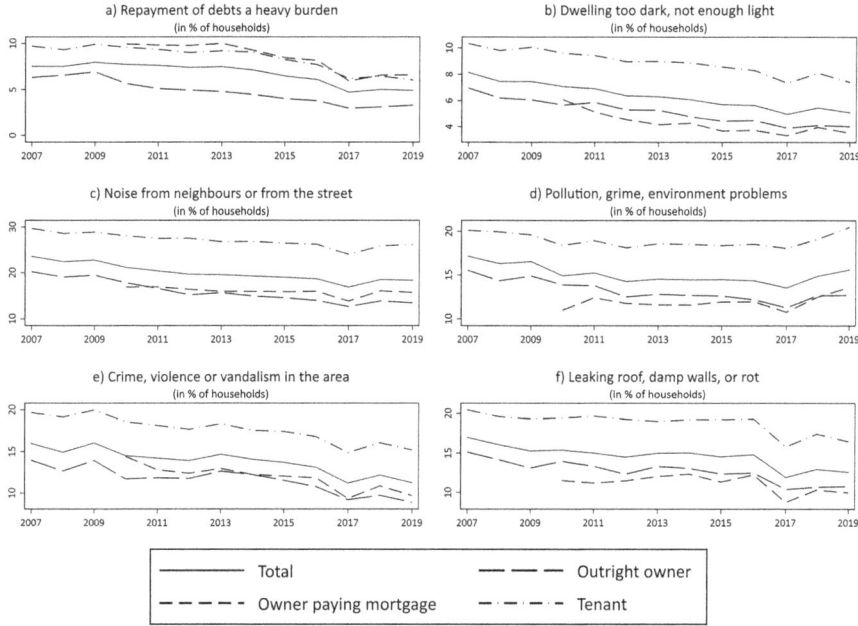

**Fig. 10.4** Housing problems of owners and tenants (2007–2019). (**a**) Repayment of debts a heavy burden (in % of households). (**b**) Dwelling too dark, not enough light (in % of households). (**c**) Noise from neighbours or from the street (in % of households). (**d**) Pollution, grime, environment problems (in % of households). (**e**) Crime, violence or vendalism in the area (in % of households). (**f**) Leaking roof, damp walls, or rot (in % of households)

their properties are not in a better condition anyway. The reported differences in housing quality can thus be understood as the most concrete expression of wealth inequalities.

In Fig. 10.5, the extent of property ownership and the housing and housing environment problems just discussed are shown for five European country groups. With an average ownership rate of 65% (2019), the proportion of households owning their accommodation is highest in Central and Eastern Europe (85.3%) and Southern Europe (73.2%) and lowest in Nordic (62.3%) and Continental European countries (71.7%; Fig. 10.5a). This once again confirms that the ownership rate is negatively correlated with national wealth inequalities (Balchin, 1996, p. 11). On average, about 30% of homeowner households still have loans to service. This proportion is considerably higher in the Scandinavian (62.8%) and Continental European countries (46.8%) and much lower in the Central and Eastern European (10.8%) and Southern European countries (23.4%). The country groups with the highest ownership rates thus also have the lowest shares of indebted households. At the same time, the country groups with the highest ownership rates also have the greatest problems with housing and ancillary housing costs (Central and Eastern Europe: 35.7%; Southern Europe: 39.6% of households), while households in the country groups with the highest renter rates have the least problems (2019: 9.8% in

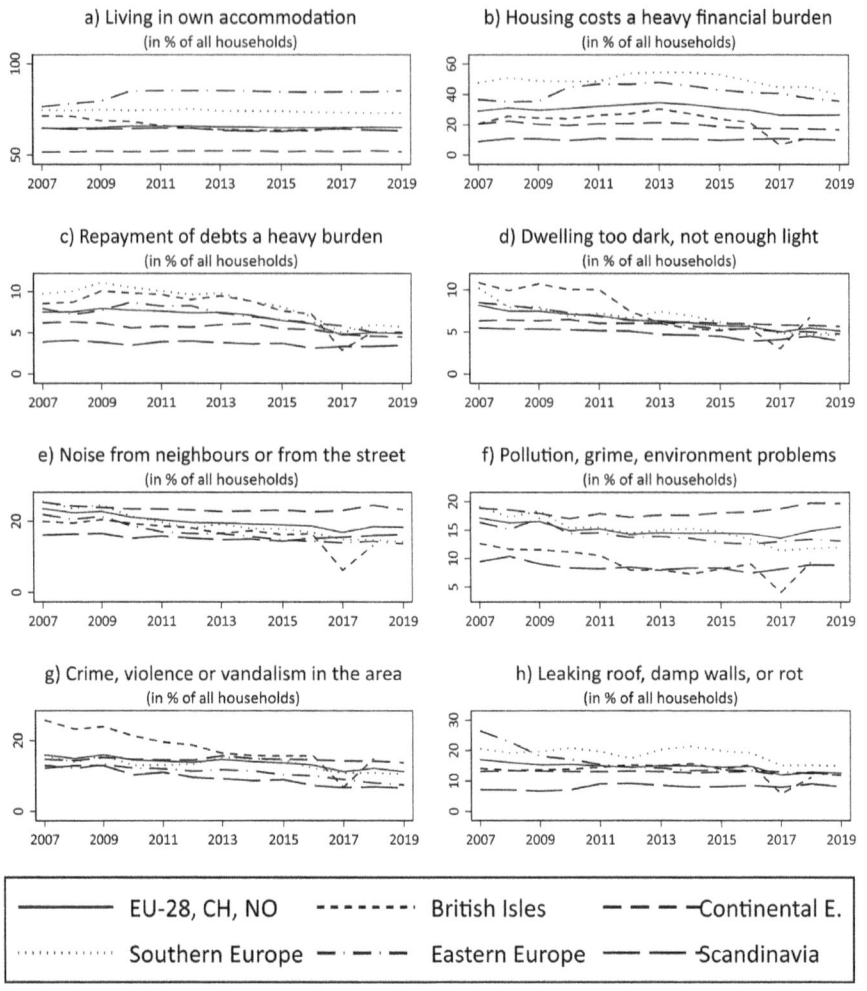

**Fig. 10.5** Housing problems in five European country groups (2007-2019). (**a**) Living in own accommodation (in % of all households). (**b**) Housing costs a heavy financial burden (in % of all households). (**c**) Repayment of debts a heavy burden (in % of all households). (**d**) Dwelling too dark, not enough light (in % of all households). (**e**) Noise from neighbours or from the street (in % of all households). (**f**) Pollution, grime, environment problems (in % of all households). (**g**) Crime, violence or vandalism in the area (in % of all households). (**h**) Leaking roof, damp walls, or rot (in % of all households)

Source: Own calculation based on EU-SILC 2017-2019. Variables hs140-hs190, hh040 were evaluated for 28 EU member states and Norway and Switzerland (until 2000 excluding Croatia, 2019 excluding the UK).

Scandinavia; 16.6% in Continental Europe; Fig. 10.5b). This points to a fundamentally different organisation of housing markets in the five different European country groups distinguished here: Properties in Southern and Eastern Europe are often inherited, which explains the lower debts. Allen et al. (2004) have pointed out the importance of the extended family for Southern European housing markets. In the case of Central and Eastern Europe, a similar pattern has emerged after the privatisation of social housing formerly owned by the state and sold to tenants as a result of right-to-buy policies of post-socialist governments (Lowe & Tsenkova, 2017). In both cases, this means lower mortgage ratios, but not necessarily lower financial burdens, since inherited properties also have to be kept in good condition and often have to be renovated at great expense. In the wealthier countries, on the other hand, more or less strongly regulated housing markets play a more important role than the allocation of dwellings by the family or the state. Families therefore buy a flat or—much more often than in Southern and Eastern Europe—live in rented accommodation. In Scandinavia in particular, this seems to be the more cost-effective option as indicated by the low financial burden from housing—also thanks to social housing or the public regulation of the rental housing market which Balchin (1996, p. 14) describes as a unitarist system not characterised by a separate social housing system.

*Problems in servicing loans* (such as mortgages) are greatest in Southern Europe (paradoxically despite the high ownership rates) and on the British Isles, and by far the least in the Scandinavian countries (Fig. 10.5c). Too little daylight and fear of crime and violence seem to be a particular problem on the British Isles (6.7% and 15% in 2018), while noise nuisance and pollution are high in Continental Europe (23.3% and 19.7% in 2019). Respondents complained about leaking roofs mainly in Central and Eastern Europe and in Southern Europe (2007: 26.4% and 20.6%). In recent years, however, the situation has improved significantly (2019: 11.9% and 14.9%). This list shows that some problems are lower in wealthier countries (leaking roofs, financial burdens), but also that many perceived problems in the living environment (crime, noise, pollution ...) are not related to the wealth of a society.

In sum: the poverty, exclusion and deprivation risks of tenants are significantly higher than those of homeowner households. Three groups can be distinguished on the housing market. At the top are the homeowners still paying mortgage who, thanks to their higher income and education, have taken the risk of buying a property. They are firmly anchored in the labour force, earn well, are healthy, but feel financially challenged due to the burdens of housing and credit costs. Their properties are in better state than debt-free properties. The noise and environmental burdens of their properties are higher than those of debt-free properties. The proportions of households with properties that are not yet fully paid off are highest in the British Isles (2018: 31%) and in Scandinavia (40%). Here, households have also been living in their current accommodation for the shortest period of time (2018: on average since 2005), while the Southern and Eastern European households have been living in their accommodation on average already since 1998 and 1994.

The heads of household with debt-free properties are significantly older; their average age is 63. Either they have inherited the property (sometimes also at a young age) or they have worked all their life for a property and were already able to pay back the last instalment (sometimes shortly before retirement). They are less educated, poorer and sicker than the property owners who are still paying mortgage. The work intensity of households with debt-free properties is significantly lower than that of other households, as many household members are already in retirement age. Their properties are in poorer condition. This also points to the fact that owners of debt-free properties have lived in their homes much longer (in 2018, on average since 1990) than owners who still have mortgages to service who have been in their homes since 2006 and tenants (since 2007). They are located in better, less noisy and less polluted neighbourhoods. The shares of households with debt-free properties are highest in Central, Eastern and Southern Europe (2019: 76% and 56% respectively) highlighting the role of right-to-buy policies, inherited dwellings and the extended family.

Tenants are at a higher risk of poverty and deprivation. In terms of health, educational attainment and work intensity, they are close to the average. They are not a marginalised group—especially in wealthier countries. However, they have to make considerable concessions concerning the cost and quality of accommodation: Their dwellings have less daylight and are darker than others, noise pollution is higher, as is pollution and environmental impact and the risks of crime and vandalism. Roofs are also more likely to leak and walls to be damp. The shares of tenants are highest in Continental Europe (2019: 48%) and in Scandinavia (2019: 37%).

The three "worlds of wealth" discussed in this section also have a geographical component: Property purchases dominate on the British Isles and in Scandinavia; debt-free, often inherited residential property in Central, Eastern and Southern Europe, and rented property in Scandinavia and Continental Europe. The role of property thus differs considerably within Europe. In the less affluent countries of Southern, Central and Eastern Europe, poorer, disadvantaged, health-impaired, unemployed and less educated people also live with their families in their own homes. In these countries, owning a home is, to a certain extent, part of the basic provision for the majority of the population. To a large extent, housing is removed from the market and is part of a subsistence production in which essential goods are provided by traditional, family-centred structures. In the richer, more mobile, more urbanised countries in Europe, this function is taken over to a considerable extent by the housing and rental market and by social housing. A broad, family-centred basic supply of property is being replaced by a publicly regulated and subsidised housing market. Property is often bought or rented also as a result of individualised life courses, living conditions and disposable income. Housing in the wealthier European countries is thus more individualised, privatised, emotionalised, professionalised and decoupled from the family of origin (cf. on the ideal type of modern housing Häußermann & Siebel, 2020, 268). Through this differentiation and individualisation of housing, the ownership or non-ownership of property could become an expression of the considerable wealth inequalities in richer countries.

## 10.3  Determinants of Housing Ownership and Value

This section discusses which individual and household-related factors explain the ownership or non-ownership of the dwelling in which a household lives. Secondly, it analyses which socio-demographic characteristics are correlated with the net worth of the self-owned dwelling. Finally, the importance of the family of origin for owning property is discussed. As in the previous section, only heads of household are included, as these questions can only be discussed meaningfully at the household level.

First, the question of owning or not owning the household's main residence is discussed on the basis of a binary logistic multilevel regression (Fig. 10.6). The desirable distinction between three groups (indebted and debt-free owners, tenants) would require a multinomial logistic multilevel regression. Due to the complexity of the model, however, no convergence could be achieved, so that the distinction between indebted and debt-free property owners has to be omitted. In Fig. 10.6, the relative chances of owning a property are shown, controlling for all other factors

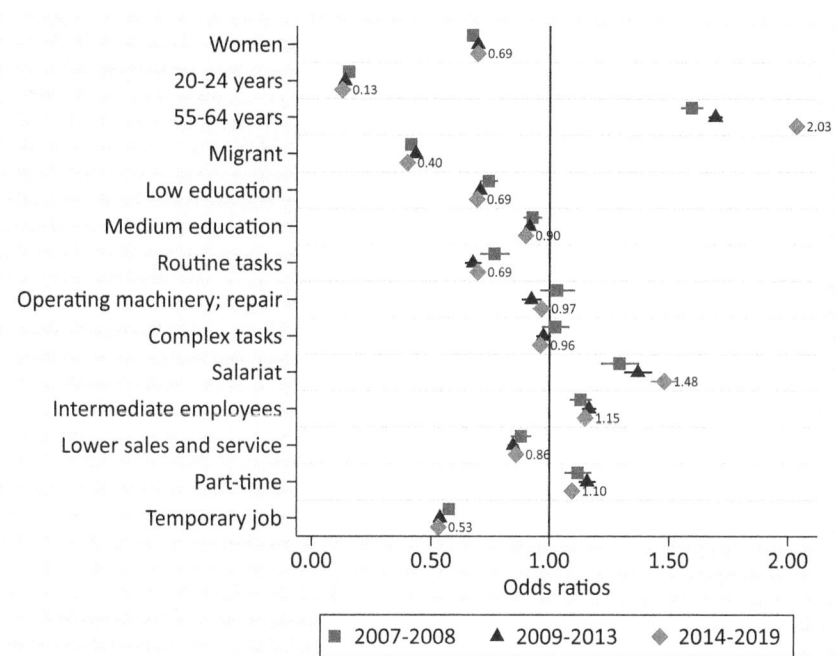

Source: Own calculations based on EU-SILC 2007-2019. The results of three binary logistic regressions are shown. The group-specific odds ratios of household heads living in their own property and not renting are given for the years 2007-2019 for 28 EU countries, Switzerland and Norway (Croatia from 2010, 2019 without the UK). The reference groups are highly qualified, native, male heads of household aged 25-54 with very demanding tasks ("problem solving, decision making, creativity").

**Fig. 10.6** Determinants of housing ownership in 30 European countries (2007–2019)

shown. By far the most important factor in explaining property ownership is *age,* as older heads of household are more likely to have inherited or bought a property. The average age of household heads living in their own debt-free dwelling is 63 years. In a self-owned property that is not yet debt-free, the average age of household heads is 50 years, and for tenant households it is 52 years. This shows that buying a property is a decades-long project for the majority of households—if it is not facilitated by inheritances: After completing education and starting gainful employment, the savings phase begins, followed by the purchase and decades of paying off loans until retirement. Older household heads therefore have significantly higher chances than younger ones to own their dwelling. The value of 2.03 (2014–2019) in Fig. 10.6 means that older heads of household have twice the chance of living in their own property as people aged 25–54. It is noteworthy that this probability has increased significantly compared to the period before the Great Recession. In the wake of the low, zero and negative interest rate policies of the ECB and other central banks, property values have risen so much that households with younger heads have fewer and fewer chances of buying a property. The property ratio in the eurozone has declined significantly from 2007 (71.4%) to 2019 (65.8%) (Eurostat, table ilc_lvho02). This also explains why the opportunities of the *upper service class (salariat)* have increased to 148% compared to manual workers: Buying one's own property is increasingly becoming a privilege of upper social classes due to the considerable and long-term financial burden implied. *Younger people, people with a migration background, temporary employees, employees with routine tasks and the low educated* have a much lower chance of owning their accommodation, even before the financial market and euro crises. In particular, the chances of people with a low educational background have worsened significantly since then. In 2014–2019, they have a 31% lower chance of owning their accommodation in comparison to academics (Fig. 10.6). At the microlevel, this reflects the return of wealth inequality stated by Piketty.

The next step is to look at the financial requirements of property ownership (Table 10.2). As expected, the probability of living in a self-owned house or flat increases with disposable income (column 1). Median national income, on the other hand, is negatively correlated with the probability of living in a self-owned property (model 1). At first sight, this is surprising, since a higher national income could improve the chances of building or buying property. However, it was already shown in Fig. 10.5a that property ownership rates in Central, Eastern and Southern European countries are significantly higher than in Northern, Northwestern and Continental Europe. The negative effect of average disposable income thus points to the described detachment from the family of origin and the search for a home of one's own—even beyond the family of origin. This also explains why wealth inequality tends to be higher in wealthier countries—unlike income inequality (Fig. 10.1).

The positive interaction between national and household income (Table 10.2, model 2) indicates that high-income households in wealthier societies have relatively better chances of owning their dwellings than those in poorer countries. While households with a better income in poorer countries often own the inherited

**Table 10.2** Property ownership as a function of income level and national policies in 30 European countries (2007–2019)

|                                 | (1)       | se        | (2)       | se        |
| ------------------------------- | --------- | --------- | --------- | --------- |
| Disposable income (log.)        | 1.486**   | (0.005)   | 1.517**   | (0.005)   |
| National average income (log.)  | 0.496**   | (0.030)   | 0.722**   | (0.048)   |
| Household x national income     |           |           | 1.669**   | (0.014)   |
| Constant                        | 4.936**   | (12.400)  | 0.570**   | (0.570)   |
| Households                      | 1,499,506 |           | 1,499,506 |           |
| Wald Chi$^2$                    | 98,205    |           | 99,565    |           |
| Intraclass correlation          | 0.136     |           | 0.151     |           |
| McFadden pseudo-R$^2$           | 0.097     |           | 0.084     |           |
| AIC                             | 1,449,834 |           | 1,445,429 |           |

Source: EU-SILC 2007–2019, own calculations; 50% sample of heads of households. Dependent variable: "Living in own property". Binary logistic regressions for 28 EU countries, Switzerland and Norway. Control variables: Gender, age, education, migration status, activity level and social class of head of household. Coefficients are odds ratios. Standard errors in brackets. $+ \, p < 0.10$, * $p < 0.05$, ** $p < 0.01$

homes of their parents and grandparents, higher earning households in richer countries are more likely to have better opportunities than lower-income households to move and buy property in their new place of study, work and residence.

Similar to Semyonov and Lewin-Epstein (2013) I tried to identify, in addition to the average national income, other, "more policy-related" variables that are significantly correlated with property ownership and would allow conclusions to be drawn about national institutions, market structures and policy decisions. Child benefits as a share of gross domestic product, the national employment rate, the social protection rate and the Gini coefficient of national income inequality were included. Child-related financial benefits were expected to have a positive effect, as child benefits could also support property acquisition. Furthermore, a high employment rate was expected to be associated with a lower home ownership rate due to higher mobility requirements. Due to the functional equivalence of property ownership and social protection, a negative effect of expenditures on social protection was hypothesised. A positive effect of high income inequality was assumed, as higher earners would be more likely to be able to afford a property in the face of high inequalities (Dewilde & Lancee, 2013). None of these assumptions could be confirmed. One reason could be that the variable "living in one's own property" is far too unspecific, as it treats almost condemned houses in the remote countryside on an equal footing with million-euro properties in the centre of European capitals. Especially in the question of wealth inequality, for which property ownership was taken as an indicator, it therefore makes sense to take the value of a property into account.

This is possible on the basis of EU-SILC for the year 2020. An ad hoc module asked about the value of the respondent's property and their remaining debts. 165,000 household heads from 16 countries (Austria, Belgium, Bulgaria, Denmark, Estonia, Greece, Spain, Finland, Croatia, Luxembourg, Latvia, Netherlands, Malta, Portugal, Romania and Slovakia) estimated the value of their owner-occupied property and their remaining debts in this survey. Seven-tenths of the properties considered are debt-free. On average, the properties that are not yet debt-free have a remaining debt of 125,000 €. The debt-equity ratio measured against the gross value of the properties not yet paid off is thus 22%. The average property value in the countries (without deduction of debts) ranges between 25,600 € (Bulgaria) and 800,000 € (Luxembourg) per household. On average, the value of owner-occupied property is estimated at 473,000 € (for debt-free property) or 589,000 € (for property not yet debt-free). The fact that properties with outstanding debt are significantly more expensive could either mean that property buyers—in particular in richer countries—buy more expensive, better located properties compared to old owners, that they estimate the value of their property more realistically—and that means mostly: higher—or that the property purchase was more recent and prices have risen in the meantime. The results in Sect. 10.2 support the first assumption.

In Table 10.3, two multilevel regressions are shown which describe the impact of socio-demographic characteristics on the net worth of the household's main residence (after deducting mortgages). The gender of the household head does not play a significant role, but age, migration background, level of education and income are positively correlated with a higher value: Older, native-born, more educated household heads with higher disposable income in richer countries own significantly more valuable properties. The property values of younger owners (up to 24 years) are

**Table 10.3** Value of self-owned dwelling as a function of socio-demographic characteristics in 16 European countries (2020)

|  | (1) | (se) | (2) | (se) |
|---|---|---|---|---|
| Women (Ref. Men) | −0.007 | (0.004) | 0.002 | (0.004) |
| Age (Ref. 25–54 years) |  |  |  |  |
| 20–24 years | 0.059** | (0.013) | 0.076** | (0.012) |
| 55–64 years | 0.238** | (0.005) | 0.240** | (0.005) |
| Migration background (Ref. Native) | −0.143** | (0.009) | −0.119** | (0.009) |
| Education (Ref. Higher education) |  |  |  |  |
| Low education | −0.499** | (0.006) | −0.365** | (0.006) |
| Medium education | −0.225** | (0.005) | −0.158** | (0.005) |
| National income level (log.) |  |  | 1.769** | (0.327) |
| Disposable income (log.) |  |  | 0.243** | (0.033) |
| National*individual income |  |  | −0.235** | (0.090) |
| Constant | 11.595** | (0.241) | 11.497** | (0.129) |
| Heads of households | 162,062 |  | 162,062 |  |
| Wald Chi$^2$ | 8025 |  | 5225 |  |
| Intraclass correlation | 0.552 |  | 0.269 |  |
| McFadden pseudo-R$^2$ | 0.464 |  | 0.484 |  |
| AIC | 413,392 |  | 407,023 |  |

Source: EU-SILC Ad hoc Module 2020, own calculations. Dependent variable: Estimated value of owner-occupied property minus remaining debt. Multilevel regressions for 16 EU countries (AT, BE, BG, DK, EE, EL, ES, FI, HR, LU, LV, MT, NL, PT, RO, SK). Model 2: Random slopes included. Standard errors in parentheses. + $p < 0.10$, * $p < 0.05$, ** $p < 0.01$

higher than those of "middle-aged" heads of households—possibly an indication of transfers of wealth to younger people by inheritance. Education is another key determinant in property ownership and value. Higher educated persons are significantly more likely to accumulate significant wealth through the purchase or inheritance of a property than lower educated household heads. In contrast to Table 10.2, the interaction between national and household income is negative. This might indicate a ceiling effect: in richer countries, the value of housing owned by wealthier households does not increase in proportion to their income. In model 2, random slopes were also included (Heisig & Schaeffer, 2019). These are significantly different from zero. The relationships between national average income and household disposable income thus differ from country to country, highlighting the role of national housing policies and markets. Overall, the relationship between disposable income and property wealth is very high: 47% of the logarithmic property value alone can be explained at the microlevel by the level of national and household income. This points to the influence of national contextual factors. However, these national factors could not be identified: neither the national share of social protection expenditures—which can also be interpreted as an indicator for cushioning social risks and protection against income loss—nor the level of child benefit—which also facilitates the financing of a property—nor the extent of income inequality have an influence on property values.

In sum: The wealth of property owners is strongly correlated with their income, age, migration background and education. Unlike in Fig. 10.1, which refers to all wealthy people and shows a decoupling of wealth and income inequalities, the value of an owner-occupied property is strongly correlated with the household's financial resources. This result also reflects the exclusion of tenant households and the assets mostly held by the super-rich. Apart from the average disposable income of a country, no national factor could be identified that influences the value of a property. This can be interpreted as a strong indicator that high national and individual incomes are the most important factors influencing the value of a property.

Another factor that influences property ownership is *social origin*. A household may own a property either through purchase or inheritance. In both cases, the economic and cultural capital of the family of origin might contribute to it (Bourdieu, 1984). Not only do the income and savings of a household play a decisive role in property ownership, but also the inherited capital of the family of origin. Even if inheritance of wealth is not considered a legitimate source of wealth in a meritocracy, inheritance nevertheless plays an important role (Beckert, 2013). The modernisation of a society does not imply a decreasing importance of inherited capital, as might be expected following Parsons (1970) and other modernisation theorists. Alvaredo et al. (2017) estimate that inherited wealth accounted for 45–60% of total wealth in four European countries (France, the United Kingdom, Germany and Sweden) in 2010. Well-off parents will support their children's wealth accumulation through gifts and inheritances. Even beyond the actual inheritance of wealth, the family of origin could facilitate the wealth of a household by bequeathing their cultural capital or by financially supporting their offspring (Pfeffer & Waitkus, 2021). It was already shown in Chap. 9 that the parents' educational background has a considerable influence on the educational level of their offspring. Therefore, it can be assumed that parental educational capital has both a direct and an indirect influence on wealth accumulation and property ownership: Households with a higher level of education will have better chances of accumulating wealth. This inheritance of favourable or unfavourable conditions for property ownership will be considered in the following. It can be expected that people with more highly educated and better-off parents will have considerable advantages in wealth accumulation and housing ownership in particular.

Even though no direct information is available in EU-SILC on whether a property was bought or inherited, Table 10.4 gives an impression of the extent to which the cultural and economic capital of the family of origin facilitate home ownership. It shows the extent to which this is facilitated by a high level of education of the parents or a good financial situation of the family of origin. First of all, the cultural capital, i.e. the educational level of the parents (Table 10.4, model 1): Both lower and higher educated fathers increase the probability of living in self-owned property by about 3% compared to fathers with a medium level of education. This result is significant,

**Table 10.4** Economic and cultural influence of family of origin on the chance of living in a self-owned dwelling (2005, 2011, 2019; EU-28, Norway, Switzerland)

|  | (1) | (se) | (2) | (se) |
|---|---|---|---|---|
| Women (Ref. Men) | 0.982** | (0.007) | 0.982** | (0.007) |
| 55 years and older (Ref. 25–54 years) | 1.602** | (0.016) | 1.604** | (0.016) |
| Migration background (Ref. Natives) | 0.302** | (0.003) | 0.303** | (0.003) |
| Father's educational background (Ref. Middle education) |  |  |  |  |
| - Low | 1.029** | (0.010) | 1.143** | (0.021) |
| - High (academic) | 1.026* | (0.013) | 1.062** | (0.019) |
| Mother's educational background (Ref. Middle education) |  |  |  |  |
| - Low | 1.157** | (0.012) | 1.241** | (0.018) |
| - High (academic) | 0.923** | (0.013) | 0.941* | (0.023) |
| Financial situation of the family of origin (when the respondent was 14 years old) | 1.086** | (0.003) | 1.085** | (0.003) |
| - Father: low education # Mother: low education |  |  | 0.852** | (0.019) |
| - Father: low education # Mother: high education |  |  | 0.976 | (0.045) |
| - Father: high education # Mother: low education |  |  | 0.929* | (0.029) |
| - Father: high education # Mother: high education |  |  | 0.963 | (0.031) |
| Constant | 4.091** | (0.504) | 3.992** | (0.492) |
| Heads of households | 547,991 |  | 547,991 |  |
| Wald Chi$^2$ | 16,558 |  | 16,611 |  |
| McFadden pseudo-R$^2$ | 0.039 |  | 0.039 |  |
| AIC | 529,346 |  | 529,296 |  |

Source: EU-SILC (2005, 2011, 2019). Binary logistic multilevel regression with crossed random effects (country, year). Dependent variable: Living in own property. The coefficients are odds ratios. In brackets: standard error. $+ p < 0.10$, $* p < 0.05$, $** p < 0.01$

but hard to interpret. In any case, it refutes the assumption that only children with academically qualified fathers have a significant advantage in owning a property. When the mother has a low level of education, the probability increases by 16%; when she has a high level of education, it decreases by 8%. This result might indicate that educational expansion started earlier for women in wealthier countries with lower property ownership rates, while the educational level of women was still low for a long time in Southern and Southeastern Europe (i.e. countries with a higher property ownership rate). The interactions between parental education levels suggest that especially having medium and higher educated parents facilitates the opportunity to own a home (model 2). The influence of the financial situation in the parental home when the respondent was 14 years old is clearer: with each step that this situation improves on the six-point scale (1: very poor, 6: very good financial situation), the chance of owning a property increases by about 9%. This is a strong, highly significant and plausible effect. Therefore, it can be stated that the parents' economic capital has a significant effect on the likelihood of their children owning their own home, but not the parents' cultural capital. The inheritance of property or support for its purchase depend to a considerable extent on the economic capital of the family of origin.

## 10.4 Conclusion

This chapter has discussed the individual and country-specific patterns of wealth and housing inequality in Europe. It was argued that wealth inequalities took a back seat to income inequalities in the twentieth century, as income from employment grew in importance relative to capital income in an employment- and education-centred society. In the twenty-first century this is changing again. Lower growth rates contribute to a relative increase in wealth in comparison to incomes and thus to higher levels of wealth inequality—which are more than twice as high as income inequality. In everyday lives, wealth inequality means for most people diverging opportunities to own their dwelling.

Next, the decoupling of income and wealth inequalities was shown: In some egalitarian Northern and Continental European countries, wealth inequalities are very high, while many Southern and Eastern European countries are characterised by relatively egalitarian wealth structures—partly despite high income inequalities. This decoupling points to the path dependency and heterogeneity of wealth. Four different "worlds of wealth" can be distinguished: First, the super-rich, who make up a maximum of 5% of the population and whose assets consist primarily of financial assets, companies and property not used by themselves; second, the debt-free homeowners (about 40% of all households) and third, the households owning their own dwelling but still paying a mortgage (about 20% of all households). For the latter two groups, their central asset is the dwelling they use themselves. The final group are the tenants (about one-third of all households) with generally minimal and often negative wealth.

The differences between households with debt-free or not yet fully paid-off properties and tenants are considerable. The *heads of households with debt-free properties* are significantly older, less educated, poorer and often already retired from working life. They have either inherited the property or worked for it all their lives. The properties are in worse condition than those of other homeowner households. The shares of debt-free property owners are highest in Central, Eastern and Southern Europe. Household heads who have *not yet paid off* their property are firmly anchored in the labour force, they are more educated and earn well. The shares of these property buyers are highest on the British Isles and in Scandinavia. *Rental housing* is darker, noisier, and damper than others. Renters face significantly higher risks of poverty and deprivation than homeowners. The proportions of tenant households are highest in Continental and Northern Europe.

The higher importance of tenant households and property buyers in Northern, Northwestern and Continental Europe can be interpreted as an indication of the stronger decoupling of younger families from their contexts of origin. While younger people in Southern, Central and Eastern Europe still tend to live with their parents and thus in their parental homes, young people in Northern, Northwestern and Continental European countries tend to choose their places of study, residence and work depending on their own biographical and professional plans. In doing so, they also accept that they will have to leave their place of birth and rent or buy their own property. The lower property ownership rate in wealthier countries thus points to societal individualisation and differentiation processes. However, the ownership of property is in any case facilitated by a well-off family of origin—either through inheritance of a property or through support when buying.

The correlations between income, ownership of a property and its value are very strong. Above all, households with older, native-born, more highly educated heads of household and a higher household income own a property. Younger people, people with a migration background, temporary workers, workers with routine tasks and the low educated can hardly afford to buy their own property. The chances of younger and less educated heads of household have even worsened significantly in recent years. The negative correlation between home ownership and the average national income confirms that even when controlling for socio-demographic composition, the share of property owners in the North, Northwest and Continental European countries is significantly lower than in the Central, Eastern and Southern European countries. However, property is more valuable in the wealthier countries, even when debt is considered.

Apart from a country's level of prosperity, no national context factor could be identified that plausibly explains the ownership and value of a property. Only an in-depth examination of national property markets and housing policies, which is beyond the scope of this chapter, could answer the question of which national institutions explain different shares of home ownership. In addition to national policies, EU policies may also have an influence on the purchase and value of property. The zero and negative interest rate policies of the European Central Bank, which led to a considerable increase in property prices in the wake of the financial market and euro crises from 2008 onwards, will certainly have played a role in declining property ownership rates, thus making it more difficult to buy property. Such effects of European policies on property ownership and value require further research.

# References

Allen, J., Barlow, J., Leal, J., Maloutas, T., & Padovani, L. (2004). *Housing and welfare in Southern Europe. Real Estate Issues: Vol. 16*. Wiley. https://doi.org/10.1002/9780470757536.

Alvaredo, F., Chancel, L., Piketty, T., Saez, E., & Zucman, G. (2018). *World inequality report 2018*. Belhaven Press. Retrieved from https://wir2018.wid.world/

Alvaredo, F., Garbinti, B., & Piketty, T. (2017). On the share of inheritance in aggregate wealth: Europe and the USA, 1900–2010. *Economica, 84*(334), 239–260. https://doi.org/10.1111/ecca.12233

Bach, S., Thiemann, A., & Zucco, A. (2019). Looking for the missing rich: Tracing the top tail of the wealth distribution. *International Tax and Public Finance, 26*(6), 1234–1258.

Balchin, P. N. (Ed.). (1996). *Housing policy in Europe*. Routledge.

Balestra, C., & Tonkin, R. (2018). *Inequalities in household wealth across OECD countries: Evidence from the OECD Wealth Distribution Database* (Working Paper No. 88). OECD.

Beckert, J. (2013). *Erben in der Leistungsgesellschaft. Theorie und Gesellschaft: Vol. 76*. Campus.

Bourdieu, P. (1984). *Distinction: A social critique of the judgement of taste*. Harvard University Press.

Bourdieu, P. (1996). *The state nobility: Elite schools in the field of power*. Polity.

Dewilde, C., & Lancee, B. (2013). Income inequality and access to housing in Europe. *European Sociological Review, 29*(6), 1189–1200. https://doi.org/10.1093/esr/jct009

Druyen, T., Lauterbach, W., & Grundmann, M. (Eds.). (2009). *Reichtum und Vermögen: Zur gesellschaftlichen Bedeutung von Reichtums- und Vermögensforschung*. VS. https://doi.org/10.1007/978-3-531-91752-8

European Central Bank. (2021). The household finance and consumption survey: Wave 2017. *Statistical tables*. Retrieved from European Central Bank website: www.ecb.europa.eu/home/pdf/research/hfcn/HFCS_Statistical_Tables_Wave_2017_May2021.pdf

Häußermann, H., & Siebel, W. (2020). Soziologie des Wohnens: Eine Einführung in Wandel und Ausdifferenzierung des Wohnens. In S. Schipper & L. Vollmer (Eds.), *Wohnungsforschung* (pp. 263–302). transcript Verlag. https://doi.org/10.1515/9783839453513-013.

Heisig, J. P., & Schaeffer, M. (2019). Why you should always include a random slope for the lower-level variable involved in a cross-level interaction. *European Sociological Review, 35*(2), 258–279. https://doi.org/10.1093/esr/jcy053

Lauterbach, W., Druyen, T., & Grundmann, M. (Eds.). (2011). *Vermögen in Deutschland: Heterogenität und Verantwortung*. VS Verlag für Sozialwissenschaften.

Lauterbach, W., & Kramer, M. (2009). "Vermögen in Deutschland" (ViD) – eine quantitative Studie. In T. Druyen, W. Lauterbach, & M. Grundmann (Eds.), *Reichtum und Vermögen: Zur gesellschaftlichen Bedeutung von Reichtums- und Vermögensforschung* (pp. 279–294). VS. https://doi.org/10.1007/978-3-531-91752-8_21

Lauterbach, W., & Tarvenkorn, A. (2011). Homogenität und Heterogenität von Reichen im Vergleich zur gesellschaftlichen Mitte. In W. Lauterbach, T. Druyen, & M. Grundmann (Eds.), *Vermögen in Deutschland: Heterogenität und Verantwortung* (pp. 57–94). VS Verlag für Sozialwissenschaften. https://doi.org/10.1007/978-3-531-92702-2_3

Lowe, S., & Tsenkova, S. (Eds.). (2017). *Housing change in East and Central Europe: Integration or fragmentation?* Routledge. https://doi.org/10.4324/9781315253190

Parsons, T. (1970). Equality and inequality in modern society, or social stratification revisited. *Sociological Inquiry, 40*(2), 13–72. https://doi.org/10.1111/j.1475-682X.1970.tb01002.x

Pfeffer, F. T., & Waitkus, N. (2021). *The wealth inequality of nations* (Stone Center on Socio-Economic Inequality No. No. 35). SocArXiv. Retrieved from 10.31235/osf.io/6msuf

Piketty, T. (2014). *Capital in the twenty-first century*. Harvard University Press.

Saez, E., & Zucman, G. (2016). Wealth inequality in the United States since 1913: Evidence from capitalized income tax data. *Quarterly Journal of Economics, 131*(2), 519–578. https://doi.org/10.1093/qje/qjw004

Saez, E., & Zucman, G. (2019). *The triumph of injustice: How the rich dodge taxes and how to make them pay*. W. W. Norton & Company.

Semyonov, M., & Lewin-Epstein, N. (2013). Ways to richness: Determination of household wealth in 16 countries. *European Sociological Review, 29*(6), 1134–1148. https://doi.org/10.1093/esr/jct001

Shorrocks, A., Davies, J., & Lluberas, R. (2021). *Global wealth databook 2021*. Zurich. Retrieved from Credit Suisse website: https://www.credit-suisse.com/about-us/en/reports-research.html

Summers, L. H. (2016). The age of secular stagnation: What it is and what to do about it. *Foreign Affairs, 95*(2), 2–9. Retrieved from https://www.jstor.org/stable/43948172

Weber, M. (1978). *Economy and society: An outline of interpretive sociology*. (edited by Guenther Roth and Claus Wittich). University of California Press.

# Chapter 11
# Social Cohesion in Europe. Between Europe-Wide Convergence and Social and Territorial Inequalities

**Abstract** The final chapter of this study summarises how nationally regulated worlds of social inequality evolve into a transnational space of social inequalities. It describes in detail the cleavages characterising such a space. It is argued that social inequalities in objective and subjective terms are increasingly produced, perceived, regulated and disputed in a European context. International and especially European frames of reference are becoming more important; inequalities are shaped by EU policies, cross-border social practices are crucial for shaping social inequalities. In a territorial dimension, Europe is divided into a Northern and Western European centre and Southern and Eastern European peripheries. Poverty and deprivation risks are concentrated in Eastern Europe and employment risks in Southern Europe. Along the social dimension, Europeans are divided between different social classes, occupations and education groups. The meritocratic inequalities between low-skilled workers with simple tasks and the upper, academically qualified service class are particularly strong. Both the social and territorial inequalities in Europe threaten the social cohesion in Europe and particularly in the European Union.

The central ideas of this book are the assumptions that the supposedly egalitarian Europe is characterised by deep territorial and social cleavages and that social inequalities are increasingly produced, regulated and perceived in a European context. The previous chapters focused on the question of how territorial and social inequalities in Europe have developed after the eastward enlargement of the EU since 2004, the financial and euro crises from 2008 onwards and the subsequent upswing up to the renewed slump in the wake of the coronavirus crisis in 2020/22. Linked to this is the question of how a world of social inequalities regulated by the nation-state develops into a transnational inequality space and which cleavages determine the conflicts in such a space.

In the post-war world shaped and regulated by sovereign nation-states, national institutions were the central pillars of social integration. Democratic co-determination, welfare state protections, bargaining relationships between employers' and employees' associations, employment protection and co-determination, national collective bargaining relations, education systems and regional redistribution were the institutional bases for the egalitarian capitalism of the post-war period. Not only the globalisation of the economy and technological change, but also European integration contributed to the erosion of this form of "societalisation" (*Vergesellschaftung*; cf. Trenz, 2016) based on the nation-state. Greater cross-border mobility of goods, services, capital and people contributed to the erosion and transformation of national forms of collective bargaining, interest representation, social redistribution and taxation. This weakening of previous forms of interest representation and protection against economic and social risks might undermine previous, national patterns of social integration and cohesion.

However, this does not mean the destruction of national forms of economic, technological, educational and social policy. The results in Sect. 7.4 show that national structures and institutions are still crucial for national patterns of inequality. Perhaps even EU-wide institutions have contributed to the protection of national regulatory structures and their adaptation to opening and liberalisation processes (cf. on the European "rescue" of nation-states Milward, 2000). For example, the European-wide coordinated activation of social and labour market policies (cf. Sect. 5.2) has limited the increase in labour market and income inequalities. The EU also shaped and limited global economic challenges through its trade policies. Despite significant technological, financial and global economic upheavals, the "embedded liberalism" (Ruggie, 1982) of European trade policy enabled it to cushion the effects of more integrated global markets (Hays et al., 2005). Thus, the response to increasing protectionism since 2016 (Trump, Brexit ...) has been the conclusion of trade agreements with, for example, China, Canada, Vietnam, Japan, Latin America, New Zealand or Mexico. In these treaties, the EU brought its interests in sustainability and climate-friendly production, in protecting intellectual property, in guaranteeing workers' rights and in protecting designations of origin to the fore. This may explain why economic globalisation processes in Europe have not—as expected by Alderson and Nielsen (2002)—led to a generalised increase in national income inequalities (cf. Fig. 7.5).

Even if such counterfactual conjectures can hardly be verified, the previous chapters have explored the assumption that Europe is becoming a social space characterised by transnational standards of equality and inequality. In Blau's (1977) terminology: the European space is now also structured by social inequalities and not only by disparities. Europe-wide patterns of social inequality are emerging. In territorial terms, this means greater attention to divisions between central and peripheral countries and regions; in social terms, divisions between different social groups might also be framed in a European context. In order to reconstruct these territorial and social cleavages, the within- and between-nation evolution of social inequalities in Europe was reconstructed in different dimensions (economic, labour market, wage and income inequalities, poverty and exclusion, education and occupational skills, wealth and housing), especially from 2007 to 2018 for in general 30 countries. This period includes the boom phase after the eastern enlargement of the EU and the introduction of the euro, the financial market and euro crises from 2008 onwards and the subsequent upswing. The Europeanisation thesis implies the assumption that social inequalities are also generated, perceived and regulated in a European context (even beyond the territory of the EU; cf. Olsen, 2002). Four facets of Europeanisation have been distinguished: an increasing role of the experiences, practices and achievements of other, in general European countries for assessing the domestic situation, the impact of EU policies, the Europeanisation of benchmarks and frames of reference, and the increasing importance of cross-border social practices.

In the following sections, the results of the previous chapters are summarised with regard to the question of which countries and socio-economic groups are on the winning and losing side in terms of the various dimensions of social inequality previously discussed (Sect. 11.1). Subsequently, a summary is offered regarding in which of the four facets the space of social inequalities has become Europeanised: Is the role that Europe plays in the dimensions of social inequality considered here primarily that of an internationally structured or a supranationally regulated space, a space for transnational perceptions and attitudes or a space for transnational practices (Sect. 11.2)? Finally, whether the described territorial and social lines of division are a threat to social cohesion in Europe and to the European integration process is discussed (Sect. 11.3).

## 11.1   European Fractures

Every market opening process and thus also European integration is accompanied by (at least relative) winners and losers. The aim of the previous chapters was to describe and analyse the numerous socio-economic lines of division that run through Europe. The main focus here was on the double division of Europe and in particular the EU, i.e. the territorial and social fractures between winners and losers (Heidenreich, 2016). In the following, these territorial and social cleavages are summarised in the dimensions considered in Chaps. 4–10.

In Chap. 4, the different economic structures, technological capabilities and growth models in Europe were discussed. It was shown that the European space is divided into a Northern and Continental European centre and a Central, Eastern and Southern European periphery. This centre-periphery structure has a centuries-old tradition. The economic core region of Europe, the urban region between Paris, London, Hamburg, Munich and Milan, known as the Pentagon, can be traced back to Roman trade routes and settlements (Braudel; Flora, 2000; Rokkan & Flora, 1999). Braudel (1979) describes how the European core region shifted from Southern to Northern Europe as part of the shift from commercial to industrial capitalism. Chapter 4 describes the reproduction of this centre-periphery structure in the current phases of European integration. While the creation of the single market and the common currency started from the Continental and Western European core countries of the EU and reflected their preferences (Moravcsik, 1998), the eastern enlargements of 2004–2013 enabled eastern and western European reunification and the reorganisation of the Central and Eastern European periphery. The Central and Eastern European countries (including the Ukraine, which became an EU candidate in 2020) specialised primarily in industrial activities in the context of European and global value chains. In Southern Europe, previous paths of industrialisation—such as the labour-intensive, flexibly manufactured, often design-intensive products of the central Italian industrial regions (Piore & Sabel, 1984) as well as mass production in Northern Italy (Fiat, Olivetti ...)—came under pressure from Chinese and Eastern European competition. Therefore, the growth models of the Southern European countries strengthened their focus on internal demand and tourism (Baccaro & Pontusson, 2016; Hall, 2014; Iversen et al., 2016)—partly complementary to a large agricultural sector. The focus on tourism and internal demand implied a higher share of personal services. As a result, the growth models in the European periphery can be characterised by a successful peripheral *industrialisation* in Central and Eastern Europe and a *deindustrialisation and dependent tertiarisation* in Southern Europe.

In Chap. 5, labour market inequalities in Europe were analysed in three steps. First, the labour force participation of the European population was considered, i.e. the division into active and inactive persons, then the labour market risks faced by the active part of the population, i.e. the division of the labour force into insiders and outsiders, and finally the risks of the unemployed to remain in this status, i.e. to become long-term unemployed. This points to a division into temporarily and permanently excluded groups. First, it has been shown that labour force participation and employment rates are good indicators of the division of European labour markets into countries with more inclusive and more exclusive employment regimes (British Isles and Northern and Continental Europe on the one hand, and Southern, Central and Eastern Europe on the other). The division into core and marginal groups on the labour market is related to different intensities of labour force participation. On the one hand, there are university students, young people and permanently employed men with demanding jobs, on the other hand, health-impaired, older, low-skilled and female persons with simple and routine jobs. These divisions are the result of different national institutions and policy choices. In particular, an advanced education and training system, activation policies and childcare facilities are associated with higher activity rates, as expected by the social investment approach (Morel et al., 2012). Secondly, it has been shown that five labour market risks (unemployment, temporary employment, low wages, solo self-employment and involuntary part-time work) are concentrated in Mediterranean countries (especially in Spain and Greece), while the labour market situation has strongly improved in Central and Eastern European countries (especially in Bulgaria, Hungary and Romania). In social terms, young people, workers with routine tasks, the unskilled and people with health problems are particularly affected by the outsider risks considered, while older people, academics and people with demanding jobs are on the winning side. National economic structures (in particular the share of industry) and institutions (trade unions, education systems, employment and activation policies, austerity policies) are decisive for the extent of labour market risks. These structures and institutions are also shaped to a considerable extent by European policies. This is especially true for European employment policies and the rescue measures in the wake of the euro crisis, which were accompanied by austerity policies (Broschinski et al., 2020). Thirdly, the transition into long-term unemployment is essentially determined by the same national and European policies. Especially the unskilled are affected by these risks.

Chapter 6 focused on the Europe-wide development of wage structures and wage developments in different countries and for different social groups. Contrary to expectations, no strong increase in the wage gaps between the countries particularly affected by the financial and euro crises and other European countries could be observed. Rather, total wage inequalities and also their between-country share remained largely stable in the 15 old EU member states. This points to alternative buffers to economic shocks. The high unemployment levels and job losses in Southern Europe described in Chap. 5 are the flip side of the broad stability of wage inequalities in the EU-15. In Norway, Switzerland and the 28 countries that were part of the EU from 2013 to 2020, a rapid decline in wage inequalities can be observed. Europe thus is characterised by a rapid convergence between high- and low-wage countries, as very low wages in Central and Eastern Europe rose rapidly after the reintegration of these countries into European and global value chains (Fig. 6.2). The rapid economic development of Central and Eastern European countries has reduced the share of between-country wage inequality from more than one third to less than one quarter of the total wage inequality. Rapid economic growth contributed to the decline of the previously very high unemployment rates in the post-socialist countries of Central and Eastern Europe.

In the social dimension, the wage differences between men and women, between young and older people, migrants and natives, qualified and unqualified are considerable. These cleavages are shaped to a considerable extent by national structures. Especially in Southern Europe, group-specific wage differentials are shaped by segmented labour markets and by the still more traditional family structures. National institutions and economic structures also play a role: It could be shown that a high share of industrial employees, strong trade unions, industry-wide and regional wage bargaining, a high minimum wage and high social protection expenditures are associated with more egalitarian wage structures, but also with lower wages. A European influence on domestic or group-specific wage differentials could not be identified.

Chapter 7 analysed the country- and group-specific patterns of income inequality. The most remarkable result is the far-reaching stability of national patterns of social inequalities—in spite of considerable social and economic change. On the basis of a decomposition analysis, the pressures for increasing income inequalities and a more intense status competition due to changes in the occupational and class structure, rising educational levels and smaller households was analysed. It could be shown that these challenges were successfully buffered by a higher labour supply from households (i.e. by a higher employment rates of women and older employees and a higher work intensity), but also by institutional support for lower social groups through social policy and collective agreements.

Chapter 8 proposed two multidimensional indices for measuring exclusion and deprivation. Firstly, the deprivation of the population in terms of educational opportunities, health, financial resources, availability of goods and services and participation in the labour force and, secondly, the disadvantageous working and wage conditions of the labour force were measured by two multidimensional indices. Based on these indices, the territorial and social divisions of the European population can be described more comprehensively than solely on the basis of poverty rates. In territorial terms, a similar pattern emerges in both dimensions: In the Northern, Continental and Western European countries exclusion and deprivation was much lower than in the Central, Eastern and Southern European countries. The range, especially among the Central and Eastern European countries is very wide: While the multidimensional deprivation index in Slovenia, the Czech Republic and Slovakia varies between 13 and 16%, it is one third in Bulgaria and Romania (mainly due to the lower median income and the associated higher Europe-wide poverty and deprivation rates). Despite a higher median income, Greece also has an exceptionally high deprivation rate (2013: 29%) due to high unemployment and low education. With this exception, however, poverty and exclusion risks in Southern Europe are lower than in Eastern Europe. The EU is thus clearly divided into a Northern and Western European centre and a Southern and Eastern European periphery, with poverty and exclusion risks concentrated in Eastern Europe and employment risks in Southern Europe.

In social terms, the two indices for multiple exclusion and deprivation point to the split between low-skilled workers with simple and routine tasks (especially manual workers) and academics of the upper service class with problem-solving tasks. The unskilled are particularly affected by multiple disadvantages.

Chapter 9 analysed the national and Europe-wide development of education and occupational skills as a result of educational expansion and technological and economic change. The chapter highlights the skill divides between service-centred Northern and Western European countries and regions and their highly qualified population, the industrialised regions in Continental, Central and Eastern Europe and the mainly Southern European regions, which rely very heavily on personal services and lower skills. In social terms, the expansion of higher education is accompanied by a considerable split between the higher and lower skilled. This is documented in considerable differences in wages, labour market and income opportunities and an increasingly meritocratic legitimation of inequalities.

In Chap. 10, the national inequalities in wealth and housing in Europe were described. In the territorial dimension, the European centre-periphery structure is documented in lower wealth inequalities, higher rates of home ownership and higher financial burdens and often worse housing conditions in Southern, Central and Eastern Europe and higher wealth inequalities, higher tenant and home buyer rates and in many cases better housing quality in Northern, Northwestern and Continental Europe. In the social dimension, housing inequalities are reflected in a privileged situation of highly educated, native, better-earning property buyers, especially in the wealthier countries, in the often problematic living and housing situations of Southern and Eastern European property owners and the considerable financial burdens and below-average housing quality of tenants.

The territorial and social fractures in Europe are summarised in Table 11.1. A clear pattern emerges: in territorial terms, the classic divisions between Northern and Continental Europe on the one hand and Southern, Central and Eastern Europe on

**Table 11.1** Winners and losers. A comparative presentation of selected results

| Dimensions of social inequality | Countries particularly positively affected | Countries particularly negatively affected | Groups particularly positively affected | Groups particularly negatively affected |
|---|---|---|---|---|
| Economic inequalities (Chap. 4) | Scandinavian and Continental European countries | Southern and Eeastern European countries | | |
| Employment and unemployment (Chap. 5) | Scandinavian and Central and Eastern European countries | Southern European countries | Highly qualified employees with permanent contracts | Low-skilled, temporary workers, single parents, migrants, older people, health-impaired people |
| Wage inequalities (Chap. 6) | Scandinavian and Continental European countries | Southern and Northwestern European countries | Men, older, qualified, native and skilled employees | Women, young, unskilled employees with a migration background |
| Income inequalities (Chap. 7) | Lower inequalities in Continental and Northern Europe | Southern Europe | Higher qualified nationals in core age group | Low-skilled, migrants, health-impaired, single parents |
| Income poverty and exclusion (Chap. 8) | Lower poverty and employment risks in Northern, Western and Continental Europe | High employment risks in Southern Europe, poverty and exclusion risks in Eastern Europe | Highly qualified persons and problem-solvers | Low-skilled persons with simple jobs |
| Educational and skill inequalities (Chap. 9) | Upgrading of occupational skills especially in Northern and Western Europe | Educational poverty especially in Southern Europe | Higher qualified younger and local employees | Older low-skilled workers, also from third countries |
| Wealth and housing (Chap. 10) | Better housing quality, but higher inequalities especially in Northern and Western Europe | Poorer housing quality, but higher ownership rates and lower inequalities in Southern and Eastern Europe | Higher educated, older and higher earning property buyers, partly also renters and property owners | Tenants, younger persons, migrants, lower educated and partly also property owners |

the other once again shape the socio-economic geography of Europe. This traditional centre-periphery structure has been overlaid in recent decades first by the economic development of the Southern European countries and, since the 1990s, by the accession of the Central and Eastern European countries to the EU and the related catching-up processes. These catching-up processes were the basis for the narrative of converging living and income conditions due to European integration. While the identity-forming narrative of the original European Economic Community of six was the project for peace in Europe (i.e. the reining in and integration of Germany), economic convergence was the guiding idea of the Western European EU-15 and the enlarged EU-28. This narrative was plausible in the first decades of European integration, when the countries in Southern Europe, which at that time were still heavily agrarian, developed rapidly as a result of European integration and were able to catch up with the Continental European countries. It was also still plausible for the Central and Eastern European countries since the 1990s, as these countries were able to consolidate and reorient themselves after the collapse of the socialist economic and social order by moving closer to the Western European countries and ultimately by joining the EU and integrating themselves into the European and global economy. Since the financial market and euro crises, the brief dream of a convergence between Northern and Southern Europe has ended. On the contrary: the labour markets, but also the income opportunities for the Southern European populations are deteriorating in relative terms. In Central and Eastern Europe, the situation is still different. Also due to the lower starting point, the income differences between Eastern and Western Europe are still narrowing. This convergence still overlays the far-reaching stability and, in some cases, even the divergence of living conditions in Northern and Southern Europe. Even if there can be no talk of an end to convergence for the EU as a whole (Beckfield, 2019), this process of convergence will most likely weaken in the coming decades. This will raise the question in a new and urgent way of how the cohesion of European countries, despite considerable differences in economic performance and living conditions, can be maintained. The numerous attempts to create more equal living conditions in Europe—such as the ECB's policy of easing the financial constraints of heavily indebted countries, the European rescue funds during the euro crisis or the joint reconstruction programme during the Covid-19 pandemic (Next Generation EU) or the European Green Deal—indicate that this challenge has been recognised by the EU and national policies.

However, the stabilisation of social cohesion in Europe is made more difficult not only by between-country but also by within-country differences. Not only the inequalities between genders, age groups or ethnicities, but also and in particular the inequalities between different occupational groups, educational levels and social classes are striking. Especially the inequalities between low-skilled and high-skilled groups are considerable and they are also increasing in many of the dimensions considered here. These inequalities are exacerbated by their meritocratic legitimisation. If the losers in the competition for education and occupational skills are convinced that they live in a meritocratic society, they can only blame themselves for their disadvantaged situation. This is then documented in shame about their own failure (Walker et al., 2013; Walker & Bantebya-Kyomuhendo, 2014) or even in "death by despair" (Case & Deaton, 2020), i.e. death by drugs, alcohol abuse or suicide. And if the causes of one's own failure are not attributed to oneself but to society, then the blame can be placed on others, such as foreigners, EU bureaucrats or politicians, or on the unjust system. This option seems to motivate populist and Eurosceptic currents, which, at the latest with Brexit, during the pandemic and the war between Ukraine and Russia, are also playing an important role in Europe

(Kriesi & Pappas, 2015; Norris & Inglehart, 2019). It can be stated that the future of European integration depends to a considerable extent on how the divisions between centre and periphery and between different classes, educational levels and skill groups are dealt with.

## 11.2   The Europeanisation of Social Inequalities

The second question discussed in the previous chapters was whether and to what extent social inequalities are increasingly shaped by "Europe", i.e. in particular by the EU and its policies, by cross-border mobility and cross-border contacts, by relationships and exchanges between Europeans. An analysis of the Europeanisation of social inequalities as the result of four different, cross-border societalisation processes in Europe was proposed: Are social inequalities in Europe still primarily caused, regulated and perceived in national spaces and at most compared internationally (*international perspective*)? Do EU policies have a direct impact on people's income, living and working conditions (*supranational perspective*)? Do people increasingly perceive their own life situation in a broader, especially European context (*transnational perceptions and attitudes*)? Are European and transnationally structured social spheres and fields of action accompanied by cross-border careers, strategies and everyday practices (*transnational practices*)? To answer these questions, firstly, various aspects of objective life situations in Europe were examined in an international comparative perspective in order to describe the convergence or divergence of life situations in Europe. Secondly, the influence of European policies on individual and household patterns of social inequality was examined. Thirdly, the extent to which the subjective assessment of one's own life situation depends not only on individual life circumstances but also on the national and European context was discussed. Fourthly, the dimensions in which Europe is the relevant social space and where field-specific Europeanisation processes can be observed were analysed. Table 11.2 presents selected results from the previous chapters with reference to these four dimensions of Europeanisation.

In Chap. 4, the European Union was described as a common economic space with a centuries-long tradition of interdependencies, exchange relations and dependencies. The economic dimension of centre-periphery relations is determined firstly by the central status of national economic and innovation policies (*Europe as an internationally structured space*): While the central countries and regions in Northern and Continental Europe have invested strongly in research and development and in the education and training of the population and are characterised by strong patent activities and knowledge- and innovation-centred economic structures, the corresponding expenditure and indicators in Central, Eastern and Southern Europe are much lower (Heidenreich, 2019b). The coexistence of central and peripheral countries, regions and economic trajectories in Europe can be understood as an expression of an intra-European division of labour (*Europe as a socially relevant transnational space*): The central regions include, on the one hand, the industrial

**Table 11.2** The Europeanisation of social inequalities. A comparative presentation of selected results in four dimensions

| Dimensions of social inequality | Europe as a nationally structured space | Europe as a politically shaped space | Europe as a subjectively relevant transnational space | Europe as a socially relevant transnational space |
|---|---|---|---|---|
| Economic inequalities (Chap. 4) | Central importance of national economic structures and innovation policies | Single market, euro and austerity as determinants of economic growth and unemployment | | Cross-border division of labour in an economically integrated European space |
| Employment and unemployment (Chap. 5) | National education systems, care and activation policies | Activation through European employment policy, higher unemployment through European crisis policy | Europeanisation due to the considerable inequalities in unemployment | Low level of intra-European migration |
| Wage inequalities (Chap. 6) | Egalitarian institutions and segmented labour markets | Liberalisation; negative influence of austerity policies on wage levels, but not on wage inequality | Financial deprivation more painful in rich countries than in poorer countries | Convergence through market integration and stable interstate inequalities in monetary union |
| Income inequalities (Chap. 7) | Convergence of Eastern and Western European countries | No significant influence of austerity policies; correlation between unemployment and financial stress | Own financial situation is assessed in a European context | Possibly EU as protection against rising inequalities |
| Income poverty and exclusion (Chap. 8) | Europe-wide soft coordination of national poverty and inclusion policies | Aligning the risks of poverty and exclusion for nationals and EU citizens in the European single market | Assessment of income and deprivation risks also in a Europe-wide perspective | Shift from non-meritocratic forms of discrimination to meritocratically legitimised inequalities |
| Education and occupational skills (Chap. 9) | National skill structures also the result of a Europe-wide division of labour | Limited European harmonisation of national education policies. Europe-wide recognition of occupational skills | No indication that educational poverty is attributed to the EU | Europe-wide recognition of educational capital and intercultural competences as a prerequisite for (limited) Europe-wide mobility |

core regions in Western and Northern Europe, which are characterised by knowledge-based manufacturing and innovation processes embedded in European and global value chains, and, on the other hand, the advanced, mostly urbanised service regions, where knowledge-based services such as finance, marketing, advertising, politics and administration, research and science are concentrated and where the headquarters of multinational companies and international organisations are often located. This European space is also regulated by the EU (*Europe as a politically shaped space*): the single market, the common currency, the EU enlargements from 2004 onwards, but also the austerity policies coordinated across Europe in the wake of the euro crisis, and the financial support in the wake of the Covid-19 pandemic are important determinants of economic growth and unemployment and have a clear effect on national and regional growth and unemployment rates.

In Chap. 5, it has been shown that labour market policies are first of all nationally (and also locally; cf. Fuertes et al., 2021) regulated and organised (*Europe as a nationally structured space*). At the same time, the field of labour market policies is also increasingly shaped across Europe (*Europe as a politically shaped space*). For example, the shift towards more inclusive forms of employment has been steered across Europe by the European Employment Strategy since 1997 and the Open Method of Coordination (Heidenreich & Bischoff, 2008). The creation of the Single Market and with it the free movement of people has also contributed to a Europeanisation of labour markets, even if the mobility of workers across Europe is still much lower than immigration from non-European states. The introduction of a common currency has also led to a Europeanisation of national policies, as devaluations are now no longer possible and eurozone countries have to resort to alternative buffer mechanisms—such as wage cuts or higher unemployment—in the event of economic shocks. Labour market policies have thus been Europeanised to a considerable extent, for example through mutual learning processes under the Open Method of Coordination and through economic and monetary interdependencies, but also through mutual attention to the different labour market situations during the euro crisis (*Europe as a subjectively relevant transnational space*). In view of the small intra-European migration movements, transnational practices in Europe play a minor role (*Europe as a socially relevant transnational space*).

In Chap. 6, national and Europe-wide wage inequalities have been analysed. Wage policies are particularly interesting for the analysis of Europeanisation processes because, on the one hand, collective bargaining is still largely nationally regulated (*Europe as a nationally structured area*). On the other hand, wages and unit labour costs are essential in a monetary union for reacting to economic shocks. In the field of wage bargaining, too, Europe is thus an important point of reference and thus a *socially relevant transnational space* (Pernicka et al., 2019), even if the regulatory structures of the field are largely national. Also, other EU policies, such as the bailout policies during the euro crisis 2010–2013 and the conditions imposed on national budgetary policies, may also directly influence wages, because austerity policies might reduce wage levels—also due to the significant decline in value added as a result of government spending cuts (Blanchard & Leigh, 2013; Górnicka et al., 2018). This can be confirmed. However, the decline in gross wages in the euro area is significantly smaller than in other European countries. Therefore, despite the claimed negative effects of austerity policies, it can be assumed that the bailout programmes and ECB policies have led to a relative stabilisation of wages (for instance compared to the UK, which was never part of the eurozone). *These results indicate that Europe is also a politically shaped space in the area of wage and collective bargaining policies.* The analysis of low-paid jobs showed that people with such jobs are less satisfied with their financial situation. However, the negative impact on perceived economic stress is particularly high in wealthier and more unequal countries. This could indicate that low-wage earners evaluate their financial situation in the context of their national space as well as in the context of a *transnational space.*

In Chap. 7, the structure, development and perception of income inequalities in Europe have been analysed in order to highlight the inter-, supra- and transnational facets of Europeanisation. First of all, disposable incomes in Eastern and Western Europe converged rapidly since 2006, while the income convergence between Southern, Northern and Western Europe came to a halt since the financial market and euro crises (*Europe as a nationally structured space*). Thus, the previous, decades-long convergence of incomes in the older EU member states reached its limits. From a *supranational perspective,* the assumption that austerity policies during the euro crisis had a negative impact on national patterns of income inequality (*Europe as a politically shaped space*) could be rejected. However, this does not mean that the euro crisis—which was primarily a labour market crisis—had no influence on people's subjective perception of their own financial situation. In Table 7.5 a clear correlation could be observed between the risk of unemployment and exclusion on the labour market and financial stress (*Europe as a subjectively relevant transnational space*). Thirdly, in a transnational perspective, it was shown that people's perception of their financial situation depends not only on the absolute income level and the comparison with their compatriots, but also on their position in the European income hierarchy (*Europe as a socially relevant transnational space*).

In Chap. 8, it has been discussed whether poverty and exclusion are also shaped by the European context. Their effects on life satisfaction were analysed in Sect. 8.5. It could be shown that poverty in a European context (and not only in a national context) has a negative influence on life satisfaction. In a *transnational perspective,* thus, living conditions in other European countries influence people's evaluation of their situation. Furthermore, EU policies have a clear influence on people's living conditions and employment risks (*supranational perspective*): The risks of poverty and exclusion in Central and Eastern Europe have become significantly lower in the course of the post-socialist transition and EU enlargement. The successful economic and political integration of these countries into the EU has contributed at least in the medium term to lower risks in the Baltic countries and Romania, but also in the Central European countries. In Southern Europe, on the other hand, risks increased significantly in the course of the financial market and euro crises. Unemployment and atypical employment were particularly high in Spain and Greece.

The fact that citizens from other EU countries have comparable poverty and deprivation risks to natives, while the risks for citizens from third countries are significantly higher, points to the importance of *European regulatory structures* (Table 8.5). The EU and especially the single market rules prevent other Europeans from being disadvantaged, especially in the labour market. It is therefore not surprising that the life satisfaction of third-country nationals is significantly lower than that of natives and European migrants when the effects of employment risks are controlled for (Table 8.7, Model 4). EU citizens can expect similar working conditions in other EU member states. This facilitates migration as an important facet of *transnational social practices* (Faist, 2014). However, this does not eliminate all the problems migrants face in another country: A comparison of life satisfaction of natives with European and non-European migrants shows that the latter two groups are significantly less satisfied than natives when controlling for poverty and exclusion risks (Table 8.7, Model 3). Differences in life satisfaction are minimal between the two groups of migrants. General challenges faced by migrants, such as learning a new language, establishing a new circle of friends and acquaintances and finding their way in a new cultural context, are thus hardly reduced by the single market.

In Chap. 9, the education and skill structures in Europe and their changes have been analysed. The education systems are mostly shaped by national policies. The increasing heterogeneity in the regional share of low education, however, points to the fact that Europe is not only a *nationally but also regionally structured area* of learning and economic specialisation. In addition, the EU has contributed to a limited European harmonisation of the educational field (*Europe as a politically shaped space*), because the EU has facilitated the Europe-wide recognition of educational and vocational qualifications. No indications were found that Europe or the EU are a subjectively relevant transnational space for education and qualification structures. However, *Europe is a socially relevant transnational space* for migrants. The relatively small wage and income differences between natives and EU migrants in contrast to the considerable disadvantages of third-country nationals (Table 9.1) show that the Europe-wide harmonisation of education, and employment and social conditions is an important prerequisite for Europe-wide migration processes.

In Chap. 10, European dimensions of wealth and housing inequalities could not be discovered due to the overwhelming influence of household-related determinants and national inheritance, tax, and housing policies.

It can be stated that the *national level* is still central to economic, labour market, wage, income and wealth inequalities in Europe. National education, national innovation, labour market, social and housing policies and also national institutions such as the minimum wage, trade unions and the collective bargaining system are decisive for labour market, wage and income inequalities. Thus, there are good reasons for the so-called "methodological nationalism" of inequality research (Beck & Grande, 2007). National structures, institutions and policies are still central determinants of social inequalities and their patterns and dynamics.

However, European states are not closed economic spaces. National policies are partly shaped by EU decisions and coordinated across Europe and implemented in a closely intertwined socio-economic space. In particular, the European internal market, i.e. the freedom of movement of goods, services, capital and people, and the monetary union are central to the Europeanisation of the economy and society and the Europe-wide generation and regulation of social inequalities. Since 2004, the accession of 11 Central and Eastern European countries (plus Malta and Cyprus) to the EU and thus to the European Single Market has led to a rapid economic and social convergence of Eastern and Western Europe. The free movement of people and especially of employees has reduced the differences between the employment and wage situations of locals and other EU citizens—even if intra-European mobility is still significantly lower than mobility between the EU and third countries. However, the free movement of people, goods and services also means increased competition across Europe. In spite of this increasing competition and contrary to expectations, however, no increase in national wage and income inequalities could be observed. This might indicate that European policies have also shaped the European-wide and global liberalisation processes, thus preserving to some extent the social cohesion of the nation-states (cf. for example the disputes on the fiercely contested Services Directive Barnard, 2008). Ruggie (1982) describes this balancing act between liberalisation and regulation as embedded liberalism. However, in the case of the Southern European countries, such a (limited) protection against fierce global competition obviously failed, as the deindustrialisation of these countries shows (Fig. 4.6a).

In addition to the internal market, the common currency in 19 of the currently 27 EU member states has also contributed to the Europeanisation of social inequalities. A common currency means on the one hand the abolition of flexible exchange rates, but on the other hand also the Europeanisation of monetary policy and EU-wide constraints on national fiscal policies. Thus, the Southern European countries were no longer able to rely on devaluations during the financial market and euro crises. In combination with the highly segmented labour market structures, this led to exorbitantly high unemployment rates in the South. At the same time, the European Central Bank has significantly lowered interest rates and provided guarantees and financial support—in addition to the guarantees and loans of the European bailout funds (Almunia, 2020). This may explain why the European austerity policies have had no demonstrable impact on income inequality and why wages in the eurozone have developed even more positively compared to non-EU countries.

Other EU policies may also have an impact on social inequalities. For example, EU anti-discrimination policies may have contributed to reducing gender, age or origin-based inequalities. European employment and activation policies have facilitated the shift towards more inclusive labour market policies. In this respect, the Europeanisation of social inequalities is also driven by the policies and structures of the European Union.

Thirdly, the Europeanisation of subjective standards of comparison and evaluation could be shown. Life satisfaction and perceived financial stress also depend on transnational, especially European, frames of reference. The position of one's own household and country in the European context is decisive for life satisfaction. It could be shown that subjective financial stress also depends on the relative income position in the European context. The European frame of reference thus also plays a role in people's perception of their financial situation. On a very broad empirical basis, this confirms the findings of Lahusen and Kiess (2018) and Delhey and Kohler (2006), who also showed a Europeanisation of subjective inequalities. In contrast to Bach (2015, p. 153), perceived inequality is not limited to the national arena and to the national institutionalisation of social rights. Even if social rights are not anchored at the European level in the same way as they are at the national level, Europeans do evaluate their living and income situation in comparison to other EU citizens.

Fourth, Europeanisation of social inequalities can also be the result of cross-border practices (Delhey et al., 2014; Kuhn, 2011, 2015; Recchi et al., 2019). Unfortunately, there are nearly no data on cross-border practices or transnational networks (Delhey et al., 2019) in EU-SILC. However, some data on intra-European migrants are available. On this basis, the living situation of cross-border mobile Europeans was discussed—also in comparison to migrants from non-EU countries. It was shown that living and working conditions have converged with those of the native population in many dimensions. In 2004, for example, the share of low-wage workers from other EU countries was even lower than among natives—and significantly lower than among third-country nationals (Table 6.4). The poverty and exclusion risk of European migrants is also comparable in some facets to that of the native population (Table 8.5): while the poverty risk—measured by the national poverty threshold—is clearly higher, the poverty risk on a European scale and educational poverty are lower (Tables 8.5 and 9.5). The employment and wage risks of EU nationals are slightly higher than those of natives and much lower than those of third-country nationals (Table 8.6). This points to the relatively successful integration of mobile EU citizens into the labour market and social protection systems of other EU member states. Citizens with a European migration background are more successfully integrated in the labour market than migrants from non-EU countries. The Europeanisation of social inequalities thus means in this case the reduction of disadvantages of EU migrants.

In sum: social inequalities in objective and subjective respects are increasingly produced, perceived, regulated and contested in a European space. This was discussed in four dimensions: Firstly, other countries, and in particular other European countries, are becoming an important benchmark in the design and evaluation of national policies and situations: A high number of unemployed or poor people or low economic growth in the European context put national policies under pressure to justify and adapt, even if the EU has hardly any competence in the respective field. Nation-states move in an international space in which their policies and also their results and impact on living conditions are compared and evaluated. Secondly, EU policies have an increasingly direct and comprehensive influence on people's living conditions. This applies, for example, to the common market and trade policy, monetary and fiscal policy, the coordination of national employment and social policies, refugee policy, and recently also to health policy. Thirdly, Europe has also become a transnational space through the close political, economic, and social interdependencies in which people evaluate their living conditions and financial situation across borders. Fourthly, the EU has also facilitated cross-border social mobility and intra-European migration. It has been shown that this has led to a considerable improvement in the income and employment situation for EU citizens in other EU countries compared to nationals of third countries—but not to a significant improvement in life satisfaction.

Europe, and in particular the EU, is thus becoming an increasingly important point of reference for social inequalities. Even if the EU may not be responsible for the respective policy fields at all, or at least not alone, the corresponding decisions and their consequences are attributed to it. This can be illustrated by the example of the pandemic in 2020/2022. If the member states had not been able to agree on a joint recovery programme in 2020, the unevenly distributed social and economic consequences of the crisis might have destroyed the foundations of European integration. And if Germany, like the USA or the UK, would have ensured that its own citizens had priority for the supply of vaccines in this crisis through treaties or export bans, people's anger, fear and despair would have been an ideal breeding ground for populist, nationalist and Eurosceptic currents in other parts of the EU—similar to what could already be observed to some extent in the euro crisis from 2010 and the accompanying exorbitantly high unemployment rates in Southern Europe. Thus, the Europeanisation of social inequalities might contribute to the creation and deepening of Europe-wide forms of cohesion and conflict. Possible forms and strategies for ensuring Europe-wide cohesion are discussed in conclusion.

## 11.3    Challenges for Social Cohesion in Europe

An unintended consequence of the considerable progress of European integration is that Europe, and in particular the EU, is increasingly confronted with the need to ensure social cohesion in Europe. Until the beginning of the new millennium, the crises of European integration were mainly conflicts between countries and between sovereign nation-states and supranational institutions. Given a broad consensus on the benefits of integrated markets as the "output" of this integration, the legitimacy of EU policies could be taken for granted (Scharpf, 1999). In more recent crises such as the failure of the Constitutional Treaty, the euro, Brexit, refugee crises and the Covid-19 pandemic, the relationship between European citizens and national and European elites has come into focus (Vobruba, 2008). The permissive consensus of Europeans that has existed for decades and which has enabled the deepening and enlargement of the European Union (EU) in an expert- and elite-driven manner, is gradually eroding (Hooghe & Marks, 2009; Risse, 2010). The effects of European institutions, processes and decisions on the living conditions of citizens are now being publicly discussed and also criticised to an unprecedented extent (Lahusen, 2021).

The Europeanisation of social inequalities described here thus raises the question of how social cohesion in Europe can be maintained. The fractures described in the previous chapters, for example the divisions between Northern and Southern Europe, between work-intensive and other households, between skilled and less skilled workers, between single parents and other families, are becoming a threat not only to national but also to European cohesion. Unlike in previous phases of European integration, where the perceived impact on people's living conditions was smaller and more mediated through national policies, the different facets of social inequalities now impact more directly on perceptions of the EU and European policies. This is also indicated by the numerous populist and Eurosceptic movements of recent years. The strengthening of these movements in almost all EU member states (Hutter et al., 2016) cannot be interpreted as an indication of an erosion of European integration. Rather, it reflects a broader and more comprehensive type of European integration and thus the *emergence of a transnational social space* (Heidenreich, 2019a), which is characterised by closer interdependencies and conflicts. The Europeanisation of social inequalities is thus also a consequence of deepening European integration and its stronger impact on Europeans' living conditions.

The previous division of labour between the EU, which primarily promoted the opening of markets even at the expense of national forms of social protection (Höpner, 2017, 2021; Scharpf, 1999), and the nation-states, which were responsible for the socio-political cushioning of the related risks, is thus reaching its limits. Contrary to what is sometimes assumed (Bach, 2015), the previously clear separation between socially integrated national societies and a supranational, society-free space is eroding. Europe is becoming a transnational social space. However, this space is not characterised by clear internal and external borders like an (imagined) nation-state of the 1960s (Bartolini, 2005, p. 369; Schimmelfennig, 2021). Europe is not a closed social space, but an open space characterised by transnational societalisation processes.

This raises the question of how the social cohesion between citizens can be ensured in this transnational space. This is a central challenge for EU policy, which has been tackled, for example, in the context of the euro crisis with the establishment of rescue funds and a fundamental reorientation of the European Central Bank ("whatever it takes")—and in the context of the Covid-19 pandemic with the reconstruction programme "Next Generation" to support the Southern European countries in particular. In this respect, the Europeanisation of social inequalities has put the question of *transnational social cohesion* in Europe onto the agenda.

But what exactly is meant by this? In sociology, social cohesion is understood, following Durkheim (2014), as the result of mutual dependencies in a functionally differentiated society. Durkheim termed the cohesion of such a society organic solidarity and argued that people's self-interests are not sufficient for the development of such cohesion. Classically, the nation-state is the arena for ensuring social cohesion, as the nation-state can be understood as an imagined political community with which citizens can identify (Anderson, 2006). Similarly, transnational cohesion in Europe can be defined by the *perceived affiliation of Europeans to a transnational community limited to Europe, based on common interests and rules and on the mutual recognition of obligations towards other Europeans that shape their practical behaviour. This sense of belonging is also the result of shared experiences and interests and institutionally guaranteed entitlements and membership rights.*

The need for such cohesion can be understood on the basis of the compensation approach. In the previous chapters, it has been shown that Europeanisation, like globalisation of the economy, is accompanied by winners and losers: low-skilled workers with routine jobs in labour-intensive sectors lose their jobs in high-wage countries; less productive companies are displaced; peripheral regions lose out; competition between native and immigrant workers and companies intensifies. The compensation approach (Rieger & Leibfried, 2002; Rodrik, 1997, 2018) argues that these divisions between globalisation winners and losers can be dealt with in two ways—through protectionism or through compensation. In the first case, attempts are made to reverse the globalisation of the economy or to export more than is imported—an on-going strategy with huge costs, as the collapse of the first wave of globalisation before the First World War in particular shows (Hirst et al., 2015). In the second case, the gains of economic opening processes are also redistributed to the (relative) losers, thus strengthening social cohesion. This was a central function of welfare states after World War II (Garrett & Mitchell, 2001; Rodrik, 1997): "To the extent that governments effectively secure income through the institutions of a functionally differentiated social policy (. . .), they can also dispense with protectionist intervention in trade and strict regulation of external economic relations." (Rieger & Leibfried, 2000, 14; own translation) Given the limits of national redistribution in peripheral countries in particular, the need for Europe-wide forms of social protection as a means of ensuring social cohesion might increase. Unfortunately, a stronger need for transnational social cohesion does not mean that such a transnational redistribution actually takes place. This is also shown by the efforts for a social Europe (Leibfried & Pierson, 1995): As early as the 1980s, the then Commission President Jacques Delors campaigned for a social Europe complementary to the European Single Market he had promoted—with limited success, such as the largely inconsequential social dialogue. In the discussion about the foundations of transnational social cohesion in Europe, antagonistic interests and institutions must therefore be taken into account—in particular the existence of nation-states, which ensure social cohesion in the national context and which will hardly be replaced or supplemented by European institutions.

Therefore, European forms of securing social cohesion will differ from national forms. This is especially true for individual social rights and the related redistributive institutions. The EU has hardly developed any (Leibfried & Pierson, 1995). The relevant field of social policy had already been occupied by nation-states for a long time when the European institutions emerged. Instead of redistributing financial resources to individual beneficiaries, the EU therefore relied on other instruments and policies to ensure social cohesion. For decades, the focus was on the common agricultural policy and European structural, cohesion and regional policy. These policies aim to support farmers and less developed regions through financial transfers and thus cushion the consequences of economic Europeanisation (Bachtler et al., 2016; Zimmermann, 2016). These policies thus did not target needy individuals and households, but regions, countries and sectors that were particularly affected by economic integration and liberalisation. However, the scale of these two policies, for which most of the EU funds are used, is limited by the size of the EU budget, which for a long time was around 1% of European GDP. Complementary to these policies, the EU has therefore developed other instruments: In employment and social policy, it relies primarily on regulation (Majone, 1996). In the financial market, banking and euro crises, European cohesion was ensured by guarantees, bonds and low interest rates; in the Covid-19 pandemic, cohesion in Europe was to be secured by keeping the internal market open as far as possible, by bonds and grants (within the framework of the Next Generation fund) and by the Europe-wide procurement and approval of medical products and vaccines. The EU thus has a variety of instruments at its disposal, most of them developed ad hoc, to ensure social cohesion in Europe. In doing so, it can certainly build on broad support among the European population (Gerhards et al., 2020).

Given this background, it is possible to conclude by identifying four principles that could be taken into account in a policy to ensure social cohesion in Europe: *Equality of opportunity through social investment, subsidiarity through open coordination procedures, transnational innovation policies and support for new forms of interpersonal solidarity.* These principles mark a clear departure from national social policies that focus more on equality of outcome through welfare state redistribution, on binding regulations, on creating reliable framework conditions for entrepreneurial investment and on non-intervention in family and civil society structures.

A first principle of European employment and social policy is the higher priority given to equal opportunities.

> At the heart of this policy are the prevention of social exclusion, ensuring equal opportunities for participation in working life (for example, by preventing discrimination and improving the employability of disadvantaged groups), enforcing labour markets as the central allocation mechanism of labour and income, and integrating the various national labour markets in Europe (especially by harmonising national social protection systems and defining minimum labour policy standards). (Heidenreich, 2006, 43; own translation).

This principle has been generalised in the social investment concept (Morel et al., 2012). This concept, already referred to in Chap. 5 and Sect. 7.4, has also been taken up by the European Commission (2013). At the core of this concept is the proposal to invest in people's skills and opportunities to enable them to participate fully in the labour market and in society. The social investment concept proposes investing in education and training of the population, in childcare and care, in active labour market policies and in health care of the population in order to improve equal opportunities for all members of society and especially for the employed. It has been shown above that a higher labour force participation at the household level and a lower share of labour market outsiders (Chap. 5) is a promising way to reduce income inequalities. It has also been shown that childcare contributes to higher, mostly female labour market participation. Higher labour force participation of older people is facilitated by further training opportunities and by public health care, while active labour market policies improve the labour force participation of the long-term unemployed and other labour market outsiders.

Secondly, in most policy fields that are important for ensuring social cohesion, the EU is not the only player. Employment and social policies in particular are largely the responsibility of the nation-states. This reflects the principle of *subsidiarity* anchored in the Treaty on European Union. This raises the question of how the coexistence between national and European policies, institutions and structures can be organised. The EU can only try to coordinate national policies in these fields and set incentives for reforms. This is reflected in the "Open Method of Coordination". The EU does not rely on binding legal norms, but on the voluntary participation of the member states and their willingness to learn from each other. Within the framework of the so-called European Semester, the member states agree on common goals, implement these independently at the national level and jointly evaluate the results achieved. This method is used in particular for the coordinated modernisation of European social and employment policies. While respecting the principle of subsidiarity, the aim is to ensure greater coordination between the different national labour market and social systems through cooperation, mutual learning and the participation of regional and non-governmental actors (federal states, welfare associations, trade unions . . .). This will be achieved by aligning the interpretations of the situation, the problem definitions and the required reform projects. However, the extent to which the agreed goals, targets and recommendations are actually implemented by the member states remains open (Heidenreich & Bischoff, 2008).

The EU's social investment policies also rely mainly on soft policy instruments, but they are increasingly supported by financial incentives (for example in the context of the European Social Fund). *Activation policies* mainly aim at offering enabling and demanding measures by job centres and other, mostly local organisations to employable persons in order to facilitate their reintegration into the labour market through job search and placement services, job creation schemes, job subsidies, training measures, psychological counselling, or benefit reductions (Bonoli, 2010, p. 441). Within the framework of the European Employment Strategy, the EU already has the possibility to encourage the member states to intensify their activating labour market policies and also supports this financially. European coordination of national *education policies and systems* has also become the subject of European forms of coordination—albeit under the more innocuous name of "learning" (Alexiadou et al., 2010; Alexiadou & Lange, 2015). This coordination takes place within the "strategic framework for European cooperation in education and training", which defines maximum levels for school and training dropouts, graduation rates (especially from upper secondary education), continuing education rates and proportions of tertiary graduates. These indicators also feed into the "European Semester" (Zeitlin & Vanhercke, 2018), in which the economic, employment and social policy coordination of the EU member states takes place. *Early childhood care* is also regulated within the framework of this strategic cooperation. The aim is for at least 95% of children to participate in early childhood education. Thus, the Open Method of Coordination is an instrument for organising cooperation between national and European actors in preserving social cohesion in Europe.

Thirdly, the EU cannot ignore the considerable economic differences between the member states, as these are a constant challenge for the interaction of currently

27 sovereign member states. In the past, the EU has mainly focused on economic convergence as a result of market opening processes (Chap. 4). This pattern has continued after the last EU enlargements since 2004, in which 13 mostly Central and Eastern European countries acceded to the EU. The convergence of income conditions since the noughties has been driven primarily by the catching-up processes of these countries, by their economic integration and by the associated reduction in between-country economic differences. This economic and social convergence of the EU is now reaching its limits, as the growth rates of the Central and Eastern European countries are gradually converging with the European average. This brings the diverging development paths of the Western and Southern European countries into focus. In particular, the economic and social development in Southern Europe offers considerable cause for concern. Since the financial market and euro crises, the economic differences and between-country income inequalities in the 15 old EU member states have increased again.

Since such economic divergence can also undermine social cohesion in Europe, the EU can rely on financial transfer payments or on a (to some extent functionally equivalent) European monetary policy. In the eurozone and Covid-19 crises, this approach was chosen. Crisis countries were supported through guarantees, loans, subsidies, the purchase of bonds and interest rate cuts—sometimes against considerable resistance from Northern and Continental European countries and population groups. It will hardly be possible to permanently ensure social cohesion in Europe in this way, as the required sums will exceed the donor countries' capacity and willingness to pay (Streeck, 2014). An alternative would be a Europe-wide research and innovation policy (Borras, 2003; Borrás, 2004; Kaiser & Prange, 2005). This could facilitate the pooling of resources for cutting-edge technologies and services, for example also in fighting the climate crisis in the context of the European Green Deal. Another possibility could be the targeted support of regional innovation systems (Heidenreich & Mattes, 2021). At the centre of such innovation systems are regional cooperation networks, which have particular advantages in bundling and transferring context-specific, often tacit knowledge (Mattes, 2012). Regionally embedded communication and cooperation networks facilitate the translation into new processes and products. In a Europe-wide and globally networked economy, spatial and social proximity are important prerequisites for regionally embedded mutual learning processes.

A fourth principle for enhancing social cohesion in Europe could paradoxically be the support for new, often local interpersonal solidarities (Fuertes et al., 2021). If solidarity is defined as the "mutual obligation to aid each other" (Bayertz, 1999, p. 3), then a policy of social cohesion could focus on new forms of solidarity beyond traditional family structures and nationally organised forms of solidarity. While national forms of solidarity are institutionalised in particular in systems of social security, trade unions and national education systems, new solidarities could be based on interpersonal and local networking. Examples for these would be family and kinship ties, neighbourhood networks, friendships, political initiatives or groups with common interests. In the European context, such initiatives are also discussed under the (at least for an innovation researcher misleading) term "social innovations"

(European Commission, 2020; Moulaert, 2013). Such new forms of interpersonal solidarities are by no means natural and self-evident in a pluralised, highly mobile, individualistic society, but have to be constructed and maintained with considerable time, organisational and emotional effort. The decline of traditional values, the disengagement from traditional ties and structures, the increasing employment participation of all social groups, the demand for flexibility and mobility and more biographical options imply that families, partnerships and other private forms of life, friendships, neighbourhoods and political groups can no longer be taken for granted. But the pluralisation of private forms of life and community also opens up opportunities for new solidarities. This was evident in the Covid-19 pandemic, when people formed new bonds of solidarity at the local level to help each other, shop for the neighbours, sing together, support local businesses, provide information about the crisis or vaccination opportunities or continue to demonstrate for a new climate policy. Non-family-based support networks are emerging, some of which drew on existing infrastructures, but some of which also used new infrastructures such as internet-based groups and platforms. These networks were also a crucial prerequisite in 2015 and 2022 in dealing with the influx of millions of migrants from Syria and Ukraine.

This brings into focus the question of whether transnational organisations such as the EU can meaningfully support such familial and non-familial forms of community and what form such support could take. On a general level, a distinction can be made between public attention (European Commission, 2020), special funding programmes, the provision of technical infrastructures, the development and dissemination of suitable concepts, the offer of specialised services or the provision of digitalised platforms. Examples of this are the support for multi-generational shared flats and other alternative forms of housing, new social media that enable communication and self-organisation both in the local context and across large distances, mentoring programmes and self-help groups for different groups, for example local cycling initiatives or projects for the integration of disabled people or migrants. This list already shows how diverse the starting points for reconstituting and maintaining new solidarities can be. In this respect, the conceptualisation of support for new, interpersonal solidarities could well be a social challenge at the European level, since securing social cohesion will hardly be possible without such forms of "micro-societalisation" (which however were also the basis for populist movements as for example the violent and angry anti-vaxxers protests in 2021).

The Europeanisation of social inequalities thus is not only the basis for current crises of European integration, but it can also generate new forms of transnational social cohesion in Europe. It has been suggested that at the heart of such forms of transnational cohesion are social investments, open coordination procedures, cross-border innovation policies and support for new forms of interpersonal solidarity. First, through social investment in education, childcare, care, activation and public health care, forms of social protection could be developed that are oriented towards the primacy of equality of opportunity. Especially through better education, but also through the provision of other collective goods, all members of society could be given equal opportunities in the competition for attractive working and living conditions. Secondly, European strategies to secure social cohesion will certainly rely on intergovernmental learning processes and supranational coordination of national social and employment policies. Financial incentives could increase the chances of national reforms succeeding. Such reforms are crucial, as it has been shown that social inequalities in Europe are not only income inequalities, but also and above all labour market and educational inequalities, as shown by the different unemployment rates in Southern and Continental Europe (especially for young people and the low-skilled). Thirdly, the considerable economic inequalities in Europe are also due to significant inequalities in research, development and innovation efforts (Heidenreich & Baur, 2015). These will hardly be reduced without stronger European coordination of innovation policies. Fourth, the EU could attempt to support new interpersonal solidarities. Only by developing new transnational, national and community-based forms of social cohesion can the previously described territorial and social cleavages in Europe be overcome.

# References

Alderson, A. S., & Nielsen, F. (2002). Globalization and the great U-turn. Income inequality trends in 16 OECD countries. *American Journal of Sociology, 107*(5), 1244–1299.

Alexiadou, N., Fink-Hafner, D., & Lange, B. (2010). Education policy convergence through the open method of coordination: Theoretical reflections and implementation in 'old' and 'new' national contexts. *European Educational Research Journal, 9*(3), 345–358. https://doi.org/10. 2304/eerj.2010.9.3.345

Alexiadou, N., & Lange, B. (2015). Europeanizing the national education space? Adjusting to the open method of coordination (OMC) in the UK. *International Journal of Public Administration, 38*(3), 157–166. https://doi.org/10.1080/01900692.2014.934836

Almunia, J. (2020). *Lessons from Financial Assistance to Greece: Independent Evaluation Report.* Luxembourg. Retrieved from European Stability Mechanism, website: https://www.esm. europa.eu/publications/lessons-financial-assistance-greece. https://doi.org/10.2852/082453

Anderson, B. (2006). *Imagined communities: Reflections on the origin and spread of nationalism* (Rev. ed.). Verso.

Baccaro, L., & Pontusson, J. (2016). Rethinking comparative political economy: The growth model perspective. *Politics and Society, 44*(2), 175–207.

Bach, M. (2015). *Europa ohne Gesellschaft: Politische Soziologie der Europäischen Integration* (2nd Rev. ed.). *Neue Bibliothek der Sozialwissenschaften.* Springer. Retrieved from https://doi. org/10.1007/978-3-531-93430-3

Bachtler, J., Mendez, C., & Wishlade, F. (2016). *EU cohesion policy and European integration: The dynamics of EU budget and regional policy reform.* Taylor & Francis.

Barnard, C. (2008). Unravelling the services directive. *Common Market Law Review, 45*(2), 323–394.

Bartolini, S. (2005). *Restructuring Europe: Centre formation, system building and political structuring between the nation-state and the European Union.* Oxford University Press.

Bayertz, K. (1999). Four uses of "solidarity". In K. Bayertz (Ed.), *Solidarity* (pp. 3–28). Springer.

Beck, U., & Grande, E. (2007). *Cosmopolitan Europe.* Polity.

Beckfield, J. (2019). *Unequal Europe: Regional integration and the rise of European inequality.* Oxford University Press.

Blanchard, O. J., & Leigh, D. (2013). Growth forecast errors and fiscal multipliers. *American Economic Review, 103*(3), 117–120. https://doi.org/10.1257/aer.103.3.117

Blau, P. M. (1977). *Inequality and heterogeneity: A primitive theory of social structure.* Free Press.

Bonoli, G. (2010). The political economy of active labor-market policy. *Politics and Society, 38*(4), 435–457.

Borras, S. (2003). *The innovation policy of the European Union: From government to governance.* Edward Elgar.

Borrás, S. (2004). System of innovation theory and the European Union. *Science and Public Policy, 31*(6), 425–433.

Braudel, F. (1979). *Le temps du monde: Civilisation, économie et capitalisme, XVe-XVIIIe siècle, tome 3.* Colin.

Broschinski, S., Heidenreich, M., & Pohlig, M. (2020). *Polarization and marginalization during the Eurozone crisis: The persistence of Eurosclerosis* (Oldenburger Studien zur Europäisierung und zur transnationalen Regulierung No. 26). Oldenburg. Retrieved from https://uol.de/cetro/publikationen/oldenburger-studien

Case, A., & Deaton, A. (2020). *Deaths of despair and the future of capitalism.* Princeton University Press.

Delhey, J., Deutschmann, E., Graf, T., & Richter, K. (2014). Measuring the Europeanization of everyday life: Three new indices and an empirical application. *European Societies, 16*(3), 355–377.

Delhey, J., & Kohler, U. (2006). From nationally bounded to pan-European inequalities? On the importance of foreign countries as reference groups. *European Sociological Review, 22*(2), 125–140.

Delhey, J., Verbalyte, M., Aplowski, A., & Deutschmann, E. (2019). Free to move: The evolution of the European migration network, 1960-2017. In M. Heidenreich (Ed.), *Horizontal Europeanisation: The transnationalisation of daily life and social fields in Europe* (pp. 63–84). Routledge.

Durkheim, E. (2014). *The division of labor in society.* Free Press.

European Commission. (2013). *Towards Social Investment for Growth and Cohesion – including implementing the European Social Fund 2014–2020* (Communication from the Commission to the European Parliament, the Council, the European Economic and Social Committee and the Committee of the Regions No. COM(2013) 83 final). Brussels. Retrieved from https://eur-lex.europa.eu/legal-content/EN/ALL/?uri=CELEX%3A52013DC0083

European Commission. (2020). *Social innovation: Inspirational practices supporting people throughout their lives.* Retrieved from http://ec.europa.eu/social/e-newsletter

Faist, T. (2014). On the transnational social question: How social inequalities are reproduced in Europe. *Journal of European Social Policy, 24*(3), 207–222.

Flora, P. (2000). Externe Grenzbildung und interne Strukturierung: Europa und seine Nationen. *Berliner Journal für Soziologie, 10*(2), 151–165. https://doi.org/10.1007/BF03204348

Fuertes, V., McQuaid, R. W., & Heidenreich, M. (2021). Institutional logics of service provision: The national and urban governance of activation policies in three European countries. *Journal of European Social Policy, 31*(1), 1–18. https://doi.org/10.1177/0958928720974178

Garrett, G., & Mitchell, D. (2001). Globalization, government spending and taxation in the OECD. *European Journal of Political Research, 39*(2), 145–177.

Gerhards, J., Lengfeld, H., Ignácz, Z., Kley, F. K., & Pfriem, M. (2020). *European solidarity in times of crisis: Insights from a thirteen-country survey. Routledge advances in sociology.* New York.

Górnicka, L., Kamps, C., Koester, G., & Leiner-Killinger, N. (2018). Learning about fiscal multipliers during the European sovereign debt crisis: Evidence from a quasi-natural experiment. *Working paper series / European Central Bank: no 2154 (May 2018).* Frankfurt a.M.: European Central Bank. https://doi.org/10.2866/957767.

Hall, P. A. (2014). Varieties of capitalism and the euro crisis. *West European Politics, 37*(6), 1223–1243.

Hays, J. C., Ehrlich, S. D., & Peinhardt, C. (2005). Government spending and public support for trade in the OECD: An empirical test of the embedded liberalism thesis. *International Organization, 59*(02), 473–494. https://doi.org/10.1017/S0020818305050150

Heidenreich, M. (2006). Die Europäisierung sozialer Ungleichheiten zwischen nationaler Solidarität, europäischer Koordinierung und globalem Wettbewerb. In M. Heidenreich (Ed.), *Die Europäisierung sozialer Ungleichheit: Zur transnationalen Klassen- und Sozialstrukturanalyse* (pp. 17–64). Campus.

Heidenreich, M. (2016). The double dualization of inequality in Europe: Introduction. In M. Heidenreich (Ed.), *Exploring inequality in Europe* (pp. 1–21). Edward Elgar.

Heidenreich, M. (Ed.). (2019a). *Horizontal Europeanisation: The transnationalisation of daily life and social fields in Europe.* Routledge.

Heidenreich, M. (2019b). Wirtschaftliche und soziale Disparitäten in der EU: Zwischen Konvergenz und Agglomeration. *Informationen Zur Raumentwicklung., 3*, 80–89.

Heidenreich, M., & Baur, N. (2015). Locations of corporate headquarters in Europe. Between inertia and co-evolution. In S. M. Lundan (Ed.), *transnational corporations and transnational governance* (Vol. 38, pp. 177–208). Palgrave Macmillan. https://doi.org/10.1057/9781137467690_7.

Heidenreich, M., & Bischoff, G. (2008). The open method of coordination: A way to the Europeanization of social and employment policies? *Journal of Common Market Studies, 46*(3), 497–532.

Heidenreich, M., & Mattes, J. (2021). Regionale Innovationssysteme und Innovationscluster. In B. Blättel-Mink, I. Schulz-Schaeffer, & A. Windeler (Eds.), *Handbuch Innovationsforschung* (pp. 183–199). Springer. https://doi.org/10.1007/978-3-658-17671-6_12-1

Hirst, P., Thompson, G., & Bromley, S. (2015). *Globalization in question* (3rd ed.). Wiley.

Hooghe, L., & Marks, G. (2009). A postfunctionalist theory of European integration: From permissive consensus to constraining dissensus. *British Journal of Political Science, 39*(01), 1–23.

Höpner, M. (2017). *Grundfreiheiten als Liberalisierungsgebote? Reformoptionen im Kontext der EU-Reformdebatte* (No. 17/10). Cologne.

Höpner, M. (2021). *Dürfen europäische Gesetze Grundfreiheiten einschränken?* (MPIfG Discussion Paper No. 21/2). Max-Planck-Institut für Gesellschaftsforschung. Retrieved from https://www.mpifg.de/pu/dp_abstracts/dp21-2.asp

Hutter, S., Grande, E., & Kriesi, H. (Eds.). (2016). *Politicising Europe: Integration and mass politics.* Cambridge University Press. https://doi.org/10.1017/CBO9781316422991

Iversen, T., Soskice, D., & Hope, D. (2016). The Eurozone and political economic institutions. *Annual Review of Political Science, 19*, 163–185.

Kaiser, R., & Prange, H. (2005). Missing the Lisbon target? Multi-level innovation and EU policy coordination. *Journal of Public Policy, 25*(2), 241–263.

Kriesi, H., & Pappas, T. S. (Eds.). (2015). *European populism in the shadow of the great recession.* ECPR Press.

Kuhn, T. (2011). Individual transnationalism, globalisation and euroscepticism: An empirical test of Deutsch's transactionalist theory. *European Journal of Political Research, 50*(6), 811–837.

Kuhn, T. (2015). *Experiencing European integration: Transnational lives and European identity.* Oxford University Press.

Lahusen, C. (2021). *The political attitudes of divided European citizens: Public opinion and social inequalities in comparative and relational perspective.* Routledge. https://doi.org/10.4324/9781003046653

Lahusen, C., & Kiess, J. (2018). 'Subjective Europeanization': Do inner-European comparisons affect life satisfaction? *European Societies, 21*(2), 214–236. https://doi.org/10.1080/14616696.2018.1438638

Leibfried, S., & Pierson, P. (Eds.). (1995). *European social policy: Between fragmentation and integration*. Brookings Institution.

Majone, G. (1996). *Regulating Europe. European public policy series*. Routledge.

Mattes, J. (2012). Dimensions of proximity and knowledge bases: Innovation between spatial and non-spatial factors. *Regional Studies, 46*(8), 1085–1099.

Milward, A. S. (2000). *The European rescue of the nation-state* (2nd ed.). Routledge.

Moravcsik, A. (1998). *The choice for Europe: Social purpose and state power from Messina to Maastricht. Cornell studies in political economy* (Vol. 1). Cornell University Press.

Morel, N., Palier, B., & Palme, J. (Eds.). (2012). *Towards a social investment welfare state? Ideas, policies and challenges*. Policy Press.

Moulaert, F. (2013). *The international handbook on social innovation: Collective action, social learning and transdisciplinary research*. Elgar.

Norris, P., & Inglehart, R. (2019). *Cultural backlash: Trump, Brexit, and authoritarian populism*. Cambridge University Press.

Olsen, J. P. (2002). The many faces of Europeanization. *Journal of Common Market Studies, 40*(5), 921–952.

Pernicka, S., Glassner, V., Dittmar, N., & Neundlinger, K. (2019). The contested Europeanisation of collective bargaining fields. In M. Heidenreich (Ed.), *Horizontal Europeanisation: The transnationalisation of daily life and social fields in Europe* (pp. 109–128). Routledge.

Piore, M. J., & Sabel, C. F. (1984). *The second industrial divide: Possibilities for prosperity*. Basic Books.

Recchi, E., Favell, A., Apaydin, F., Barbulescu, R., Braun, M., Ciornei, I., Valera, A., et al. (2019). *Everyday Europe: Social transnationalism in an unsettled continent*. Policy Press. https://doi.org/10.1332/policypress/9781447334200.001.0001

Rieger, E., & Leibfried, S. (2000). Wohlfahrtsmerkantilismus. *Aus Politik Und Zeitgeschichte, 48*(2000), 12–22.

Rieger, E., & Leibfried, S. (2002). *Grundlagen der Globalisierung: Perspektiven des Wohlfahrtsstaates* (Vol. 2207). Suhrkamp.

Risse, T. (2010). *A community of Europeans*. Cornell University Press.

Rodrik, D. (1997). Has globalization gone too far? *California Management Review, 39*(3), 29–53.

Rodrik, D. (2018). Populism and the economics of globalization. *Journal of International Business Policy, 1*(1–2), 12–33. https://doi.org/10.1057/s42214-018-0001-4

Rokkan, S., & Flora, P. (Eds.). (1999). *Comparative European politics. State formation, nation-building, and mass politics in Europe: The theory of stein Rokkan*; based on his collected works (1. Publ). Oxford University Press.

Ruggie, J. G. (1982). International regimes, transactions, and change: Embedded liberalism in the postwar economic order. *International Organization, 36*(2), 379–415.

Scharpf, F. W. (1999). *Governing in Europe: Effective and democratic?* Oxford University Press.

Schimmelfennig, F. (2021). Rebordering Europe: External boundaries and integration in the European Union. *Journal of European Public Policy, 28*(3), 311–330. https://doi.org/10.1080/13501763.2021.1881589

Streeck, W, (2014). *Buying time: The delayed crisis of democratic capitalism*. Verso.

Trenz, H.-J. (2016). *Narrating European society: Toward a sociology of European integration*. Lexington Books.

Vobruba, G. (2008). Die Entwicklung der Europasoziologie aus der Differenz national/europäisch. *Berliner Journal für Soziologie, 18*(1), 32–51.

Walker, R., & Bantebya-Kyomuhendo, G. (2014). *The shame of poverty* (1st ed.). Oxford University Press. https://doi.org/10.1093/acprof:oso/9780199684823.001.0001

Walker, R., Kyomuhendo, G. B., Chase, E., Choudhry, S., Gubrium, E. K., Nicola, J. Y., Ming, Y., et al. (2013). Poverty in global perspective: Is shame a common denominator? *Journal of Social Policy, 42*(2), 215. https://doi.org/10.1017/S0047279412000979

Zeitlin, J., & Vanhercke, B. (2018). Socializing the European semester: EU social and economic policy co-ordination in crisis and beyond. *Journal of European Public Policy, 25*(2), 149–174. https://doi.org/10.1080/13501763.2017.1363269

Zimmermann, K. (2016). Local responses to the European Social Fund: A cross-city comparison of usage and change. *Journal of Common Market Studies, 54*(6), 1465–1484. https://doi.org/10.1111/jcms.12395

# Appendix 1: The Variables Used, their Operationalisation and their Sources

| Variable | Operationalisation | Data source |
|---|---|---|
| Microlevel | | |
| Activity group (ISCO-88, ISCO-08) | Skill requirements needed for the job in question: (1) Simple and routine physical or manual tasks; (2) Operating machinery and electronic equipment; driving vehicles; maintenance and repair; (3) complex technical and practical tasks; (4) problem-solving, decision-making, creativity (for unemployed: last job held); see ILO (2012). | EU-SILC (pl050; pl051) |
| Activity rate | Share of employed and unemployed persons in the total population aged 20–64. | EU-SILC (pl030, pl031) |
| Age | (1) 15–24 years, (2) 25–54 years, (3) 55 years and older. | EU-SILC (rx020) |
| Disposable income | Net equivalent household income (adjusted for purchasing power, top and bottom coding). | EU-SILC (hx090) |
| Economic activity; sectoral structure | Economic activity: Local establishment in which the respondent's main occupation is (NACE rev. 1.1/2 since 2008). (1) Agriculture, industry, mining and quarrying, manufacturing, utilities, construction (NACE R2 A–F); (2) Wholesale and retail trade; hotels and restaurants (NACE R2 G–H); (3) Transport, storage and communication (NACE R2 I); (4) Financial intermediation; property, renting and business activities (NACE R2 J–K); (5) Public administration, education, health and social work | EU-SILC (pl110, pl111) |

(continued)

(continued)

| Variable | Operationalisation | Data source |
|---|---|---|
| Microlevel | | |
| | (L–N); (6) Arts, entertainment and recreation (NACE R2 O–U). | |
| Educational level | Highest level of education attained according to ISCED (high/3: Tertiary education – Levels 5–6; medium/2: Secondary and post-secondary, non-tertiary education (3–4); low/1: Primary and lower secondary (0–2). The latter category is also designated as low education or educational poverty. | EU-SILC (pe040) |
| Employment contract | (1) Permanent, (2) Temporary. | EU-SILC (pl140) |
| Employment rate | Share of the employed in the total population aged 20–64. | EU-SILC (pl030, pl031) |
| Gender | (1) Male, (2) Female. | EU-SILC (rb090) |
| Health; sick | Subjective assessment of health status (1: "Very good"; 2: "Good"; 3: "Alright"; 4: "Bad"; 5: "Very bad"). Sick: Bad or very bad state of health. | EU-SILC (ph010) |
| Household type | (1) Single-person household; (2) Adults, no children, (3) Single parents, (4) Adults with children. | EU-SILC (hx060) |
| Life satisfaction | Subjective assessment of life satisfaction: "In general terms, how satisfied are you with your life overall?" Answer on a scale from 0 to 10, where "0" stands for "not at all satisfied" and "10" for "completely satisfied". | EU-SILC 2013 and 2018 (pw010) |
| Long-term unemployment | Employed, unemployed or inactive persons who were unemployed the whole year before the survey (1: Long-term unemployed (LTU), 0: Non-LTU). The long-term unemployment risk (LTU) is the risk of all short-term and long-term unemployed persons to be long-term unemployed. | EU-SILC (pl030, pl031, pl080) |
| Low wage workers | Employees (excluding apprentices) aged 20–64 whose gross hourly earnings fall below two-thirds of the national median (1: Low wage; 0: Higher wage). | EU-SILC (py010g, py010n, pl060, pl100, pl030, pl031, pe010) |
| Material deprivation | Material deprivation measures the percentage of the population unable to afford at least three (for severe deprivation: four) of the following nine items: to face unexpected expenses, to pay their rent, mortgage or utility bills, to go on holiday, to eat meat or proteins regularly, | EU-SILC (hs011-hs031, hh050, hs040, hs050, hs060, hs110, hs090) |

(continued)

(continued)

| Variable | Operationalisation | Data source |
|---|---|---|
| Microlevel | | |
| | to keep their home adequately warm, durable consumer goods such as a washing machine, TV, telephone or car, debt. | |
| Migration status | Foreign nationality or born abroad (0: No; 1: Migration background). In some models: 1: Nationality or place of birth in another European country; 2: Nationality or place of birth in a non-European country. | EU-SILC (pb210; pb220a) |
| Part-time work | (1) Full-time job, (2) Part-time job. | EU-SILC (pl030, pl031, pl080, pl090, pl073-pl076) |
| Poverty | Poverty rate (60% of the national or European median disposable income). | EU-SILC (hx090) |
| Risk of being unemployed | Self-defined current socio-economic status: Unemployed (1: Unemployed, 0: Not unemployed). | EU-SILC (pl030, pl031) |
| Short-term unemployed | Employed, unemployed or inactive persons who were unemployed for 1–11 months in the previous year, regardless of their employment situation, plus the currently unemployed who were not unemployed in the previous year. The short-term unemployment risk is operationalised as the risk of all economically active persons (plus the unemployed who left the labour force in the previous year) to be unemployed for a short period of time. | EU-SILC (pl030, pl031, pl080) |
| Social class (ESEC5 or ESEC6) | (1) Upper service class; salariat (ESEC1–2); (2) Intermediate employees (ESEC3&6); (3) Small employers, self-employed (ESEC4&5), (4) Lower sales and service occupations (ESEC7), (5) Lower technical occupations (ESEC8); (6) Routine occupations. The last two categories can be combined into one category 5 (lower technical and routine occupations). See Rose and Harrison (2010). | EU-SILC (pl050; pl051, pl40, pl031, pl130, pl150). |
| Subjective financial stress | "Thinking of your household's total income, is your household able to make ends meet, namely, to pay for its usual necessary expenses?" (recoded: 1: Very easily; 6: With great difficulty). | EU-SILC (hs120) |
| Wages | Gross hourly earnings of employees (excluding apprentices) aged 20–64. | EU-SILC (py010g, py010n, pl060, pl100, pl030, pl031, pe010) |

(continued)

(continued)

| Variable | Operationalisation | Data source |
|---|---|---|
| Microlevel | | |
| Work intensity of a household | Number of months worked by all household members of working age (18–59 years) in relation to the total number of months that could theoretically be worked in the household. Five different categories are distinguished: Jobless households (0%), very low work intensity (0–19%), low work intensity (20–49%), medium work intensity (50–99%), high work intensity (100%). | EU-SILC |
| **Regional (and national) macrolevel** | | |
| Disposable income (PPS) | Average regional disposable income per inhabitant (in purchasing power standards) for the NUTS2 regions of the EU. | Eurostat, table [nama_10r_2hhinc]. |
| Economic growth | Real growth rate of regional or national gross value added at basic prices – change in percent to the previous year. | Eurostat, table [nama_10r_2gvagr]. |
| Educational level employed | Persons with high, medium and low education levels (in % labour force or in % of the population aged 25–64). | Eurostat, table [lfst_r_lfe2eedu]; [edat_lfse_04]. |
| Educational poverty | Proportion of population aged 25–64 having completed lower secondary education or less (ISCED 0–2). | Eurostat, table [edat_lfse_04]. |
| Employment rate | Employed (as % of population aged 15–64; more recently 20–64). | Eurostat, table [lfst_r_lfe2en2]. |
| High technologies | High-tech sectors (high-tech industries) (as % of total employment). | Eurostat, table [lfst_r_lfe2en2]. |
| High-tech sectors | High-tech sectors (high-tech industries and high-tech knowledge-intensive services) (% of total employment). | Eurostat, table [htec_emp_reg2]. |
| Industrial employees | Employees in industry and construction (NACE B–F; in % of all employees aged 15–64). | Eurostat, table [lfst_r_lfe2en2]. |
| Knowledge-intensive services | Knowledge-intensive services (in % of total employment). | Eurostat, table [htec_emp_reg]. |
| Long-term unemployment (national average) | Unemployed for longer than 1 year (as % of all unemployed). | Eurostat, table [lfsa_upgacob]. |
| Market income | Average market income per inhabitant (in purchasing power standards) for the NUTS2 regions of the EU. | Eurostat, table [nama_10r_2gdp]. |
| Participation or activity rate | All labour force (unemployed and employed) (as % of population aged 15–64; more recently 20–64). | Eurostat, table [lfst_r_lfe2en2]. |
| Patents | Patent applications at the European patent office (per million inhabitants). | Eurostat, table [pat_ep_rtot]. |

(continued)

(continued)

| Variable | Operationalisation | Data source |
|---|---|---|
| **Microlevel** | | |
| Research expenditure | Gross domestic expenditure on Research & Development, in % of gross domestic product. | Eurostat, table [rd_e_gerdreg]. |
| Services | Service employment (NACE G–U; in % of all employees aged 15–64). | Eurostat, table [lfst_r_lfe2en2]. |
| Trade | Employees in wholesale and retail trade, maintenance, transport, hotels and restaurants (NACE G–I; in % of all employees aged 15–64). | Eurostat, table [lfst_r_lfe2en2]. |
| Unemployment | Unemployed (as % of the labour force aged 15–74). | Eurostat, table [lfst_r_lfu3rt]. |
| Value added (GDP) | Average regional gross domestic product per inhabitant (in purchasing power standards) for the NUTS0 and NUTS2 regions of the EU. | Eurostat, table [nama_10r_2gdp]. |
| **National macrolevel** | | |
| Active labour market policy | Expenditure on active labour market policies (categories 2–7; in % of GDP; per percentage point of unemployment). | Eurostat (LMP database) |
| Austerity, austerity policies | Change in the primary balance, i.e. new government debt excluding interest payments, compared to the previous year; in % of GDP). | Eurostat, table [gov_10dd_edpt1]. |
| Deficits | New government deficit (in % of GDP). | Eurostat, table [gov_10dd_edpt1]. |
| Degree of coordination of collective bargaining | (5) Binding standards usually as a result of centralised bargaining; (4) Wage standards based on centralised bargaining; (3) Bargaining guidelines based on centralised bargaining; (2) Mixed bargaining at industry and company level; (1) Fragmented wage bargaining largely confined to individual companies or establishments. Intermediary coordination: Categories 2 and 3. | Visser (2019, Variable Coord). |
| Education spending | Public expenditure on education (in % of GDP). | Eurostat (ESSPROS), table [educ_uoe_fine02]. |
| Employment regimes | (1) "Anglo-Saxon" (UK, IE); (2) "Corporatist-conservative" (AT, DE, FR, LU, NL) (reference category), (3) "Southern Europe" (ES, IT, MT, PT, CY, EL); (4) "Eastern Europe" (BG, CZ, EE, HU, LT, LV, PL, RO, SI, SK); (5) "Scandinavia" (DK, FI, NO, SE). | Inspired by Gallie and Paugam (2000). |
| Family benefits in kind | Social protection benefits for children and families (benefits in kind, % of GDP). | Eurostat, table [spr_exp_ffa] |

(continued)

(continued)

| Variable | Operationalisation | Data source |
|---|---|---|
| Microlevel | | |
| Foreign trade EU | Share of imports from EU-28 countries and exports to EU-28 countries of all imports and exports of the respective country. | Eurostat, table [ext_lt_intratrd]. |
| Further education | Participation rate in education and training (last 4 weeks), in % of population from 25 to 64 years. | Eurostat, table [trng_lfse_01], |
| Globalisation | KOF index of economic globalisation (de facto). | Gygli, Haelg, Potrafke, and Sturm (2019). |
| Income inequality | Gini (in per cent); inequality of household net disposable equivalent income (new OECD equivalence scale; top and bottom coding). | Own calculations based on EU-SILC (hx090) |
| Minimum wage | Ratio of national minimum wages of individual countries to median gross earnings. | Eurostat, table [earn_mw_cur]. |
| Programme countries | Spain, Greece, Portugal, Ireland, Cyprus. | |
| Protection against dismissal | Strictness of union density of employment protection rules (0–6: Very strict). | OECD employment protection database |
| Public debt (in % of GDP) | Public debt (in % of GDP). | Eurostat, table [gov_10dd_edpt1]. |
| Single market index | Integration of the EU internal market for goods, services, capital and labour. | König and Ohr (Gygli et al.; 2013). |
| Social protection | Social protection benefits (in % of GDP). | Eurostat (ESSPROS), table [spr_exp_sum]. |
| Tariff coverage | Employees covered by collective agreements as a proportion of all wage and salary earners. | Visser (2019, Variable UD). |
| Tenure status | 0: Tenant/subtenant; 1: Outright owner, 2: Owner paying mortgage. | EU-SILC (hh021) |
| Trade integration | Average of imports and exports of goods from other EU countries (in % of gross value added). | Eurostat, table [ext_lt_intratrd]. |
| Unemployment benefit | Net replacement rate for a married, average-earning couple at the beginning of unemployment. | OECD |
| Union density | Net union membership in relation to employed wage and salary earners. | Visser (2019, Variable UD). |
| Wage spread | Inequality of gross hourly wages for full-time and part-time employees (D9/D1; D5/D1; D9/D5) Broschinski (2020, p. 119). | Own calculations based on EU-SILC (py010g, pl073, pl074, pl060, pl100). |

# References

Broschinski, S. (2020). *Dynamiken von Lohnungleichheiten in Europa: Betriebliche und arbeitsmarktpolitische Anpassungen während der Eurokrise*. VS. Retrieved from https://www.springer.com/de/book/9783658318932.

Gallie, D., & Paugam, S. (2000). *Welfare regimes and the experience of unemployment in Europe*. Oxford University Press.

Gygli, S., Haelg, F., Potrafke, N., & Sturm, J.-E. (2019). The KOF globalisation index – Revisited. *The Review of International Organizations, 18*(2), 266. https://doi.org/10.1007/s11558-019-09344-2

ILO. (2012). *International standard classification of occupations // Structure, group definitions and correspondence tables: Structure, group definitions and correspondence tables. ISCO-08: Volume I // v. 1*. Genf: ILO. Retrieved from https://www.ilo.org/public/english/bureau/stat/isco/index.htm.

König, J., & Ohr, R. (2013). Different efforts in European economic integration: Implications of the EU index. *Journal of Common Market Studies, 51*(6), 1074–1090.

Rose, D., & Harrison, E. (Eds.). (2010). *Social class in Europe: An introduction to the European socio-economic classification (Vol. 10)*. Routledge.

Visser, J. (2019). *ICTWSS data base. version 6.1*. Amsterdam. Retrieved from Amsterdam Institute for Advanced Labour Studies AIAS website: http://uva-aias.net/en/ictwss

Milton Keynes UK
Ingram Content Group UK Ltd.
UKHW022252031123
431807UK00003B/6